Handbook
of
Data
Management
1999

Sanjiv Purba, *Editor*

CRC Press
Taylor & Francis Group
Boca Raton London New York

CRC Press is an imprint of the
Taylor & Francis Group, an **informa** business

First published 1999 by CRC Press
Taylor & Francis Group
6000 Broken Sound Parkway NW, Suite 300
Boca Raton, FL 33487-2742

Reissued 2018 by CRC Press

Library of Congress Cataloging-in-Publication Data

Handbook of data management / Sanjiv Purba, editor. – 1999 ed.
     p. cm.
   Includes bibliographical references and index.
   ISBN 0-8493-9976-9 (alk. paper)
    1. Database management.   I. Purba, Sanjiv.
  QA76.9.D3H3473   1998b
  658.4'038'0285–dc21   98-38833

A Library of Congress record exists under LC control number: 98038833

Publisher's Note
The publisher has gone to great lengths to ensure the quality of this reprint but points out that some imperfections in the original copies may be apparent.

Disclaimer
The publisher has made every effort to trace copyright holders and welcomes correspondence from those they have been unable to contact.

ISBN 13: 978-1-315-89338-9 (hbk)
ISBN 13: 978-1-351-07248-9 (ebk)

Visit the Taylor & Francis Web site at http://www.taylorandfrancis.com and the
CRC Press Web site at http://www.crcpress.com

Contributors

HEDY ALBAN, *Freelance Writer, Cherry Hill, NJ*

MARY AYALA-BUSH, *Principal, Computer Sciences Corporation, Waltham, MA*

CHARLES BANYAY, *Manager, Deloitte & Touche Consulting Group, Toronto, Ontario, Canada*

DAVID BRASSOR, *Technology Architect, Deloitte & Touche Consulting Group, Toronto, Ontario, Canada*

JEFF BULLER, *Consultant, VISUAL Systems Development Group, Toronto, Ontario, Canada*

JAMES CANNADY, *Research Scientist, Georgia Tech Research Institute, Atlanta, GA*

PATRICIA L. CARBONE, *Principal Staff, Mitretek Systems, McLean, VA*

MARION G. CERUTI, *Scientist, Advanced C4I Systems, Engineering and Integration Group, Command and Intelligence Systems Division, Naval Command, Control, and Ocean Surveillance Center, RDT&E Division, San Diego, CA*

HANNAN CHERVINSKY, *Principal and Cofounder, ABS Systems Consultants Ltd., Pickering, Ontario, Canada*

TIM CHRISTMANN, *Senior Consultant, Deloitte & Touche Consulting Group, Toronto, Ontario, Canada*

CARMINE CUTONE, *Senior Manager, Deloitte and Touche Consulting Group, Toronto, Ontario, Canada*

STEPHEN D'SILVA, *Senior Consultant and Technology Leader, Deloitte & Touche Consulting Group, Toronto, Ontario, Canada*

CHARLES DOW, *Practice Leader, Object-Oriented Technologies, Deloitte & Touche Consulting Group, Toronto, Ontario, Canada*

RICHARD T. DUÉ, *President, Thomsen Dué & Associates, Ltd.,, Edmonton, Alberta, Canada*

LEN DVORKIN, *President, Italex Consulting, Inc., Thornhill, Ontario, Canada*

ELIZABETH N. FONG, *Computer Systems Laboratory, National Institute of Standards and Technology, Gaithersburg, MD*

JUDITH N. FROSCHER, *Principal Investigator, SINTRA Project, Naval Research Laboratory, Washington, DC*

YONGJIAN FU, *Professor, Computer Science, University of Missouri, Rolla, MO*

FREDERICK GALLEGOS, *Adjunct Professor and MSBA-Information Systems Audit Advisor, Computer Information Systems Department, California State Polytechnic University, Pomona, CA*

IDO GILEADI, *Manager, Deloitte & Touche Consulting Group, Toronto, Ontario, Canada*

NARASIMHAIAH GORLA, *Associate Professor, Business Administration, Cleveland State University, Cleveland, OH*

FRITZ H. GRUPE, *Associate Professor, Computer Information Systems, University of Nevada, Reno, NV*

VENKAT N. GUDIVADA, *Dow Jones, Jersey City, NJ*

BARBARA J. HALEY, *College of Business, University of Georgia, Athens, GA*

CANDICE G. HARP, *Human Resources Consultant, Atlanta, GA*

KATHRYN A. HARVILL, *Computer Systems Laboratory, National Institute of Standards and Technology, Gaithersburg, MD*

DAVID C. HAY, *President, Essential Strategies, Inc., Houston, TX*

DEBORAH HENDERSON, *Research Information Coordinator, Ontario Hydro, Pickering, Ontario, Canada*

DAVID K. HOLTHAUS, *Software Specialist, Nationwide Insurance Enterprise, Columbus, OH*

ASHVIN IYENGAR, *Consultant, Object Technologies, Deloitte & Touche Consulting Group, DRT Systems, Toronto, Ontario, Canada*

SUSHIL JAJODIA, *Professor, George Mason University, Fairfax, VA*

JOHN JORDAN, *Principal, Consulting & Systems Integration, Computer Sciences Corporation, Waltham, MA*

WOLFGANG KELLER, *Senior Manager, Software Design & Management Ltd., Munich, Germany*

GIGI G. KELLY, *Professor, Management and Information Science, College of William and Mary, Williamsburg, VA*

KARL KELTON, *Senior Manager, Deloitte & Touche Consulting Group, Toronto, Ontario, Canada*

BONN-OH KIM, *Assistant Professor, Information Systems, Department of Management, University of Nebraska, Lincoln, NE*

STEVEN KREHBIEL, *Doctoral Student, Business Administration, Cleveland State University, Cleveland, OH*

WALTER KUKETZ, *Consulting and Systems Integration, Computer Sciences Corporation, Waltham, MA*

CAROL L. LARSON, *Technical Writer and Desktop Publisher, Hillsboro, OR*

JAMES A. LARSON, *Senior Software Engineer, Intel Architecture Laboratory, Hillsboro, OR*

RICHARD LEE, *Senior Consultant, Operations Reengineering, Deloitte & Touche Consulting Group, Toronto, Ontario, Canada*

PIERRE J. LEMAY, *Senior Consultant, Document Management, PJL Information Systems, Orleans, Ontario, Canada*

DAVID S. LINTHICUM, *Technical Manager, EDS, Falls Church, VA*

GARY LORD, *Partner, KPMG Peat Marwick, Palo Alto, CA*

PHILLIP Q. MAIER, *Member, Secure Network Initiative, Lockheed Martin Corporation, Sunnyvale, CA*

DANIEL MANSON, *Associate Professor, Computer Information Systems Department, California State Polytechnic University, Pomona, CA*

JACK McELREATH, *Managing Partner, Consulting and Systems Integration, Computer Sciences Corporation, Waltham, MA*

LYNDA L. McGHIE, *Director, Information Security, Lockheed Martin Corporation, Bethesda, MD*

MICHAEL K. MILLER, *Senior Data Architect, Worldwide Data Planning and Architecture, NCR Corp., Dayton, OH*

STEWART S. MILLER, *President and Owner, Executive Information Services, Carlsbad, CA*

JAGDISH MIRANI, *Senior Product Manager, Data Warehousing, Oracle Corp., Redwood Shores, CA*

MADHAV MOGANTI, *Advanced Technologies, Bell Laboratories, Naperville, IL*

BRETT MOLOTSKY, *Lotus Notes Product Manager, Omicron Consulting, Philadelphia, PA*

ALI H. MURTAZA, *Senior Consultant, Data Warehousing Service Line, Deloitte & Touche Consulting Group, Toronto, Ontario, Canada*

MARGARET T. O'HARA, *Assistant Professor, Computer and Information Science, Central Missouri State University, Warrensburg, MO*

M. MEDHI OWRANG, *Associate Professor, Computer Information Systems, University of Nevada, Reno, NV*

R. MICHAEL PICKERING, *Consultant, Red Brick Systems, Inc., Toronto, Ontario, Canada*

SRIRAM PIDAPARTI, *Cargill Financial Services Corporation, Minnetonka, MN*

SANJIV PURBA, *Senior Manager, Deloitte & Touche Consulting Group, Toronto, Ontario, Canada*

T.M. RAJKUMAR, *Associate Professor, Department of Decision Sciences and MIS, Miami University, Oxford, OH*

NYAPATHI RAMANA, *Department of Computer Science, University of Florida, Gainesville, FL*

LOIS RICHARDS, *Data Warehousing Project Manager, Dynamic Information Systems Corp., Boulder, CO*

RAVI S. SANDHU, *Professor, Software and Systems Engineering, George Mason University, Fairfax, VA*

CHARLES L. SHEPPARD, *Computer Systems Laboratory, National Institute of Standards and Technology, Gaithersburg, MD*

SANDRA SHUFFLER, *Senior Consultant, Deloitte and Touche Consulting Group, Toronto, Ontario, Canada*

ANTONIO SI, *Assistant Professor, Department of Computing, Hong-Kong Polytechnic University, Hong Kong, China*

MICHAEL SIMONYI, *Independent Consultant, Etobicoke, Ontario, Canada*

MARTIN D. SOLOMON, *C.W. Costello, Inc., Middletown, CT*

DANIEL L. SPAR, *Consultant, Transarc Corp., Falls Church, VA*

NANCY STONELAKE, *Senior Consultant, Deloitte & Touche Consulting Group, Toronto, Ontario, Canada*

WINSTON J. SULLIVAN, *President, WJS, Toronto, Ontario, Canada*

MICHAEL J.D. SUTTON, *Rockland, Ontario, Canada*

BHAVANI THURAISINGHAM, *Lead Engineer, Center for Integrated Intelligence Systems, The MITRE Corporation, Bedford, MA*

DAVID WADSWORTH, *Java Evangelist, Sun Microsystems, Toronto, Ontario, Canada*

DAVID C. WALLACE, *Professor, Applied Computer Science Department, Illinois State University, Normal, IL*

HUGH J. WATSON, *Chair, Business Administration, College of Business, University of Georgia, Athens, GA*

JASON WEIR, *Technical Writer, DataMirror Corporation, Markham, Ontario, Canada*

RONALD A. WENCER, *Management Consultant, Toronto, Ontario, Canada*

NANCY M. WILKINSON, *Consultant, Object-Oriented Design and C++, Westfield, NJ*

JAMES WOODS, *Independent Consultant, Lewisville, TX*

MILES AU YEUNG, *Manager, Deloitte & Touche Consulting Group, Toronto, Ontario, Canada*

DAVID A. ZIMMER, *President, American Eagle Group, Warrington, PA*

MICHAEL ZIMMER, *Senior Data Administrator, Ministry of Health, Victoria, British Columbia, Canada*

Contents

SECTION IV
DATA ADMINISTRATION, SECURITY, AND OPERATIONS

SECTION V
DATA MIGRATION, CONVERSION, AND LEGACY APPLICATIONS

SECTION VI
DATABASE SERVERS AND UNIVERSAL SERVERS

SECTION VII
OBJECT TECHNOLOGY, OBJECT MODELING, AND
OBJECT DATABASES

SECTION VIII
DISTRIBUTED DATABASES, PORTABILITY,
AND INTEROPERABILITY

SECTION IX
DATA REPLICATION

SECTION X
DATA AND THE INTERNET, INTRANET, AND THE
WORLD WIDE WEB

Introduction

DATA MANAGEMENT IS A MAJOR DRIVING FORCE in the ongoing computer revolution. Data comes in many formats, it serves many uses, and it passes through many corporate processes. The purpose of this book is to examine the essential art and science of data management. This handbook focuses on commonly asked questions such as the following:

- What is data?
- What is information?
- What is the relationship between data and processes?
- How does one build a data centric organization?
- Who owns the data in an organization?
- How does one connect heterogeneous data sources in distributed organizations?
- How are data models related to object or component models?

The scope of this handbook covers a full breadth of data management categories including strategy, methodologies, standards, techniques, database products, package solutions, data tools (e.g., modeling tools, database servers, conversion tools), data warehousing, data mining, the Internet, the World Wide Web, and future directions.

This handbook is written by experienced and acknowledged experts in the Information Technology (IT) field and in data management, and as such is a powerful tool for organizations of any size and industry.

NOTABLE VICTORIES

Data management has won significant battles over the past few years. Some of these are described here:

- Corporate data is widely perceived and protected as a corporate asset.
- The growth of data specific roles, such as data modeler, data administrator, and data analyst.
- An imminent release of the next generation of the ANSI SQL standard.
- Data source connectivity to the Internet and World Wide Web.
- Relational database servers have not been replaced by object-oriented databases, and in fact, appear to have proven their importance to

the industry, at least into the next century. This has resulted in continued investments in database server technology.

- Large data warehouses and databases once were defined to be in the hundreds of megabytes range, grew to the gigabyte range, and now are characterized as having entered the terrabyte range.
- Dramatic increases in storage capacities.
- Improved system response times due to improved data access methods and tools.
- Investments in data development methodologies, frameworks, and techniques.
- Continued popularity of modeling tools, conversion tools, and other data centric tools.

THE FORCES OF CHANGE

Data management has changed dramatically over the last few decades. There have been significant improvements in data storage, data access options, data protection, data security, data distribution, and data storage. Where data storage was once at a high premium, so much so that saving two bytes of data when storing dates caught on and spawned a billion dollar Year 2000 problem, it is becoming increasingly inexpensive and easily available. The original 5^1/$_4$" floppy disks were replaced by 3.5" floppy disks — first double density, then high density. Hard disks now routinely offer capacities of 3 GB or more. CD-ROMs can store 500 MB of data, and rumor has it that the next generation of CD-ROMs will store at least 10 times that amount.

There have been many challenges in the last few years to the traditional data management philosophies. Object-oriented technology threatened to replace the importance of corporate data with objects that bundled processes and data together. Computer viruses started to become a data epidemic. Application programs became so large that traditional diskettes no longer could store them. At one time, talk of a Windows 95 release threatened to consume all the free diskettes available in the world. This created the demand for CD-ROMs (which also has swept the music industry). For the few readers who may not know this already, computers with sound cards running Windows 95+ can play music CDs right out of the box.

Large data stores have grown from the megabyte range to the terrabyte range. Most organizations are investing in their own data warehouses or data marts to support executive decision making. This has supported the rapid growth of the data-mining industry. Data stores also are connected to the Internet and the World Wide Web. This popularized multidimensional data stores, a new data modeling technique.

STRATEGIC ISSUES AND METHODOLOGIES

Data management is an enterprise-wide concern. Although it is implemented at a technical level, several strategic issues must be resolved before data management initiatives can begin in most organizations. These include data ownership, data tools selection, building centralized data repositories, and defining corporate models. Data continues to be a valuable corporate asset in most organizations.

Data methodologies serve a useful function in many organizations. They are generally a part of a full life-cycle development methodology. Data methodologies are available in a number of delivery channels. They can be purchased from third parties, bought as part of a modeling tool set, or built inhouse, based on best practices. Development initiatives involving data management will benefit from leveraging data methodologies.

n-TIER ARCHITECTURE, CLIENT/SERVER TECHNOLOGY, AND COMPONENTS

What was once strictly called client/server technology has over the last few years been called many other names. Some even describe client/server as an older architecture that is being replaced by newer network architecture. But things are never straightforward in this profession.

Since the late 1980s, client/server technology essentially consisted of two tiers. One tier was a data tier that typically resided on a dedicated platform physically implemented on a database server (e.g., Sybase SQL Server, Microsoft SQL Server, Oracle, Informix). Some business rules could be maintained in this layer. The user interface was the other tier, and it generally ran on a personal computer type of device. Business logic also was bundled with this layer. Fat client/server implementations were those that contained most of the business logic in the user interface tier. The data tier in this server only managed the applications data. Thin client/server implementations were those in which most of the business logic was moved into the data tier.

The two-tier client/server model was popular and relatively straightforward to implement. However, it had several drawbacks: (1) the client and the server tiers were coupled tightly, so they essentially were stuck with each other and difficult to port; (2) the architecture did not scale well in term of users and system response time; and (3) system management, which had been well enabled in the mainframe environment, was problematic in two-tier architecture. Three-tier architecture was a response to some of these limitations.

In three-tier architecture, the business logic is given its own tier that can run optionally on a dedicated platform. This additional tier addresses many of the limitations posed by two-tier architecture. In a three-tier deployment, there is generally a thin client and a thin server (data tier). The business logic is encapsulated in the business logic tier. The Web-browser is arguably one implementation of a three-tier architecture. So, arguably, is network computing. *n*-tier architecture is supported by component-based development, which is expected to become significantly mainstream in the next few years. This is one area to watch closely.

DATA WAREHOUSING AND DATA MINING

Data warehouses have been around for a long time, but it was Inmon who coined the term and made it a popular discipline. The entire purpose of data warehousing and data mining is to provide information, support decision making, and alert the business of patterns that are detected. Data warehousing also is known as information warehousing. Data warehouses, which were once in the 100 of MB range, have grown to terrabytes in size. Data warehouses support OLAP-type processing, which offers decision support and what-if analysis. It also is supported by a variety of tools and new modeling techniques (e.g., multidimensional database, metadata).

Data mining is a discipline that uses the information stored in a data warehouse to uncover important trends and information for the organization. Data mining can retrieve information that otherwise would go unnoticed.

DOCUMENT MANAGEMENT

Document management satisfies an important requirement in data management. Where an organization has a requirement to store and retrieve complex datatypes, rich text, and blobs with a small set of access keys, document management offers advantages over the traditional relational or indexed databases. Document management is effective in storing large volumes of data that only require access in a limited number of access keys. It also can include such tools as electronic forms, Lotus notes, and Internet/intranet solutions.

INDUSTRY SPECIFIC SOLUTIONS

The next few years are going to see the growth of industry-based solutions that package data management and processes together. Package solutions have been available for decades. However, the widespread acceptance of SAP, Peoplesoft, and Baan are likely to accentuate this trend. Organizations that are looking for new solutions should consider purchasing such things as data models from a third party before building them from the ground up. This will result in more industry-specific data solutions, including models, applications, and processes. The growth of objects and components also will create an industry of reusable code.

THE FUTURE

The last few years in this industry have taught a central truth about information technology. The pace of change in this industry is staggering and difficult to predict with any degree of certainty beyond two or three years. However, experience also has shown the continuing importance of data in this industry. No matter where it is, no matter how it is packaged, no matter how it is accessed, data will undoubtedly play a central role in the health and competitiveness of organizations well into the future.

Database management is in the process of radical changes coming from many different sources, including the following: faster data access, data on the Internet, stronger data protection, larger data stores, combinations of complex datatypes and traditional database servers, component-based development, industry-specific data models and solutions, new tools and databases, data mining, data migration, 64-bit processing, new operating systems, and more demanding data conversions.

GETTING THE MOST OUT OF THIS BOOK

Many authors have contributed their experiences, knowledge, and ideas in the chapters of this book. Each of them are strong players in their respective niches. Taken as a whole, this handbook sweeps across many data management categories. It is divided into 15 sections, each focusing on a particularly useful aspect of data management.

Section I, "Data Development Methodologies, Definitions, and Strategy," focuses on the full life cycle and strategies issues relating to data management. The section defines criteria for selecting a data development methodology, defines an interactive database development methodology, defines an enterprise-wide data organization, defines commonly used database terminology, provides a framework for establishing enterprise-wide data standards, and focuses on several strategic issues relating to data management.

Section II, "Data Models and Modeling Techniques," investigates a variety of modeling techniques, including the traditional approaches to data modeling and process modeling that have created online transaction processing applications (OLTP) all over the world. This chapter focuses on data models, component-based modeling, process and data model integration, dimensional data modeling for data warehouses, and object-oriented aspects.

Section III, "Data Integrity and Quality," offers advice on ensuring the integrity of data and its quality. This section describes how to use database constraints, referential integrity, and data quality.

Section IV, "Data Administration, Security, and Operations," examines the operational aspects of administrating a database environment. This section describes data disaster recovery options, NT domains, DBMS recovery procedures, change management strategies, security controls, E-mail security, and other security models.

Section V, "Data Migration, Conversion, and Legacy Applications," covers a topic that is exceedingly important in today's rapidly merging business environment. This section describes a case study for data conversion, legacy database conversion, and migrating files to the relational model.

Section VI, "Database Servers and Universal Servers," provides examples for using Structured Query Language (SQL) Server Transact-SQL. This section also describes universal data servers and complex data types. Performance improvements also are covered through examples of batch-processing improvements and better indexing schemes. This section also examines operating system support for database servers.

Section VII, "Object Technology, Object Modeling, and Object Databases," covers the relationship and coexistence of object technology and data management. This section describes Microsoft Visual Basic's hot new release's of improved data access methods. This chapter also covers component-based development, ActiveX, CORBA, Rational Rose, JavaBeans, Java, component architectures, and object wrapping.

Section VIII, "Distributed Databases, Portability, and Interoperability," examines issues related to distributed databases, portability, and interoperability. This section describes distributed database design, managing multiple distributed databases, mobile databases, and database gateways.

Section IX, "Data Replication," describes data replication through a variety of techniques and tools. The advantages and types of data replication that are available also are described in this section.

Section X, "Data and the Internet, Intranet, and the World Wide Web," describes the relationship of data management to the Internet, intranet, and the World Wide Web. This section also contrasts Lotus Notes and intranets as corporate solutions. Other topics that are covered include publishing database information on the WWW, Web-enabling data warehouses, and connecting data sources to the Web with minimal programming.

Section XI, "Data Warehousing, Decision Support, and OLAP," describes the different elements of this popular trend. This section defines a framework for Enterprise Data Warehouse projects, and describes dimensional data modeling, contrasts relational models to dimensional models, and focuses on different aspects of OLAP.

Section XII, "Data Mining," focuses on several techniques for mining corporate data for valuable information. This section examines techniques, costs, and tools related to data mining initiatives.

Section XIII, "Document Management," describes the terms of reference for a document management project, compares DBMSs to document management applications, and examines the use of Lotus Notes as an executive information systems (EIS) enabler.

Section XIV, "Industry-Specific and Package Solutions," examines techniques for leveraging the increasingly popular trend of using package solutions or industry-specific prints. This section describes how data management technologies can be used to improve several different industries. It also describes how to integrate several different packages, such as SAP, BAAN, and PeopleSoft.

Section XV, "Emerging Practices and Directions," examines such topics as network demand forecasting, electronic commerce, and multimedia.

Sanjiv Purba

Section I
Data Development Methodologies, Definitions, and Strategy

EFFECTIVE DATA SOLUTIONS MUST START AT THE STRATEGIC LEVEL with an organization's executive. From here they must sweep across the organization touching all relevant departments and incorporating diverse processes and tools. This section contains chapters to define how effective data solutions can be formalized and implemented across the organization. The cornerstone of this involves the selection and implementation of data development methodologies. Data development methodologies are powerful tools that define the activities and the deliverables produced in data-related projects. In some cases, data development methodologies are a component of a larger, full-cycle development methodology. This section contains the following seven chapters:

Chapter 1, "Database Development Methodology and Organization," provides a framework for developing databases from the logical to the physical level in enterprises. The discussion in this section is independent of implementation tools. This chapter also discusses roles and responsibilities to support the database development methodology. The methodology is discussed in the context of a full life-cycle development methodology. The chapter also identifies features that should be considered when selecting or building a corporate data development methodology.

Chapter 2, "A Review of Database System Terminology," begins with a definition of data and then goes on to define various terms commonly used in data management, including data element, data item, schema, data administrator, repository, relational database system, attribute, record, federated database system, middleware, client/server, legacy data, migration, and integration.

Chapter 3, "Developing a Global Information Vision," describes how to provide a global perspective to information and data resources in an organization. This chapter defines a methodology, derived from actual success stories, for showing how a global vision can be constructed and implemented across the wider organization.

Chapter 4, "An Approach for Establishing Enterprise Data Standards," provides practical examples and categories for building a set of enterprise data standards. This chapter is assembled from actual project experiences to describe techniques that work and, as importantly, do not work, when trying to build and implement enterprise data standards. Suggestions for avoiding the common pitfalls experienced by organizations during this initiative also are provided in this chapter.

Chapter 5, "Completeness, Context, and Proportion: Shaping Data Design to the Business," focuses on aligning business requirements with data design. The fundamental fact argued by this chapter is that good data design must be rooted by a solid awareness of the business. This chapter describes how this can be achieved. The recommendations in the chapter are drawn from real-world projects.

Chapter 6, "An Enterprise Decision Framework for System Selection," describes how a decision framework provides assistance to organizations in identifying common challenges encountered by project teams when selecting and implementing enterprise information systems. By choosing an appropriate team and the right partners, by choosing the right system and data design, companies can substantially increase the performance of their enterprise system.

Chapter 7, "The Importance of Data Architecture in a Client/Server Environment," focuses on data architecture as one imperative component of the traditional client/server model. Data architecture has an impact on system performance, system security, application portability, and application scalability. Data architecture often is developed in parallel with technical architecture, organization architecture, and application architecture.

Chapter 1

Database Development Methodology and Organization

Sanjiv Purba

DATABASE DEVELOPMENT IS ONE OF THE FUNDAMENTAL OBJECTIVES of the data management function and certainly one of the end products of the process. In recent years, several trends have impacted the way that databases are built and the role they play in the overall organization. Some of these trends include data warehousing, object-oriented technology, e-commerce, and the emergence of very large databases (VLDBs). Other changes to the landscape include the popularity of complex data types (e.g., BLOBs, video), universal databases, and object databases. Despite these changes, the basis of many online transaction processing applications (OLTP) that run the business is still the relational database and the flat files. This fact is not going to change dramatically over the next few years. If anything, the relational database has proven its value as an enterprise enabler and, like the IBM mainframe, is here to stay for the foreseeable future.

This chapter defines a database development methodology and approach that has proven successful on a variety of projects, such as $100,000 to $15,000,000 budgets, mainframe, client/server, three-tier with OO, and package implementations. This approach promotes viewing methodologies as flexible frameworks that are customized for every specific instance. It allows data-oriented teams to use their personal insight and experience alongside the best practices embedded in the methodology. This chapter also defines organizational roles for a data-oriented environment.

0-8493-9976-9/99/$0.00+$.50
© 1999 by CRC Press LLC

BENEFITS

The complexity that is inherent in constructing relational database solutions can be reduced by using proven database development methodologies on projects. Methodologies are an excellent example of best practices and project lessons. Use of methodologies, therefore, reduces risk on development projects. Methodologies define activities and deliverables that are constructed in projects that were successful. Following these successful lessons can reduce project development time while increasing product quality. Furthermore, the use of methodologies simplifies the process of tracking project progress because there are clear benchmarks that can be reviewed by the project manager. Methodologies that offer templates/deliverables also allow a quickstart to the development process.

SELECTING A DATABASE DEVELOPMENT METHODOLOGY

Development methodologies with well-defined database development phases are commonly available in the marketplace. Some are freely available with modeling or project management tools, although others are found on the World Wide Web. Many of the larger consulting firms have developed proprietary methodologies based on their corporate project experiences and proven best practices. These can be purchased separately or they can be bundled with consulting/mentoring services retained from the firm. The following list identifies some of the features that should be included in any database development methodology that is being considered for deployment in an organization.

- *Linkage to a full lifecycle development methodology*: A full life-cycle methodology supports more than database development. The database development methodology chosen should either be a component of a larger full life-cycle methodology, or link seamlessly with one. Failure to do this could result in mismatched techniques or the development of deliverables that are not used.
- *Techniques*: Many popular development methodologies support a combination of techniques to streamline development of deliverables. The traditional waterfall approach involves producing deliverables in a sequential fashion. Deliverable B is not started until Deliverable A is completed and signed off. This approach, however, historically has proven to be slow on many projects of all sizes. As a result of this experience, a rapid application development (RAD) approach has gained popularity in the past 10 years. RAD produces deliverables in a much smaller timeframe than the older waterfall approach. Iteration and prototyping are cornerstones of most RAD approaches, as are teams that combine technical resources and users during the analysis and design phases of the project lifecycle. RAD has proven to be successful on smaller projects, but has been problematic on the larger

ones due to the complexity of the business requirements. A relatively new approach combines the best elements of both the waterfall and RAD approaches and has proven valuable on larger development projects.

- *Support*: A development methodology (or a database development methodology) is a product, whether an organization has paid for it or not. As such, it is important for the methodology to be supported by the vendor into the future. An unsupported methodology becomes obsolete in sort order. Some questions to ask the vendor include: "How much research is being conducted to improve the methodology?" "Is there a hotline for technical support?," and "When is the next release of the methodology being released?"
- *Price*: The price of the methodology should be considered in whole and in parts and assessed against the value that is received. Consider the one-time cost, training costs, upgrade costs, yearly licence fees, costs per user, customization costs, hardware/software support costs, and costs for future releases.
- *Vendor*: Consider the stability and market share of the vendor providing the methodology. The vendor's references also should be checked to ascertain their support for clients. Vendors that are more stable and have more market share are more likely to improve their methodology with new techniques in the future.
- *Proven Success*: One of the surest ways of selecting a suitable methodology is to check the references of similar organizations that have used it successfully on development projects.
- *Electronic Availability*: The methodology should be available electronically through Lotus Notes, the Internet, or CD-ROM. It also should be available on paper. This makes the methodology widely available to those using it across the organization.
- *Templates/Deliverables*: Reusable templates and deliverables are a good source of best practices that provide the means for quick starting development projects. Many methodologies are demonstrated with these, but the templates/deliverables are not provided to customers. In such cases, it is valuable to try to negotiate the inclusion of templates/deliverables as part of the transaction. If the templates/deliverables still are not offered by the vendor, but the rest of the methodology is acceptable, a pilot project should be used to create reusable templates and deliverables for future projects to use. Although this may slow the pilot project down in the short term, subsequent projects will run more efficiently. It is also desirable to select a methodology architecture that allows additional templates and deliverables to be added to the database on an ongoing basis.
- *Linkages to newer architectures*: The methodology also should support linkages with modules that support data warehousing, object technol-

ogy, e-commerce, and Web architectures. Flexibility in expanding the methodology directly or through deliverable linkages is desirable.

- *Ease of Learning and Use*: Methodologies that are easy to learn and use are more likely to be used on projects. Some methodologies are packaged with training courses from the vendor or other third parties.

It is not unusual to add to this list of features or to assign more weight to a handfull of them because of their importance to a specific organization. Experience has shown that complicating the selection process does not necessarily improve the quality of the final selection. In fact, this can lead to wasted time and intense team debates or arguments that end in worthless stalemates. It is preferrable to build a short list of candidate methodologies by disqualifying candidates that are weak on one or two key features (e.g., not available electronically or purchase price is greater than $100,000). The short list then can be compared to maybe five or six of the features that are of key importance to the organization. It also is useful to conduct a limited number of pilot projects that test the value of a methodology before making a final selection. It is also not unusual to pilot two different methodologies in a conference room pilot (CRP) to make a final determination. This process can take between 6 weeks and 6 months.

HIGH-LEVEL DATABASE DEVELOPMENT METHODOLOGY

This section defines a high-level methodology for database development. This methodology provides a good start for small to medium-size projects; however, a formal third-party methodology should be considered for projects that require more than 6 months of development effort. The activities discussed in this section are mapped to the standard project development framework, which consists of the following main phases: requirements, architecture, design, development, testing, implementation, and post-implementation. These phases can be conducted in parallel or sequentially depending on the exact nature of the methodology, and are restricted to database specific activities.

The subprocesses that are described in this section fit into a larger full life-cycle methodology that would address such activities as corporate sponsorship for the project, project plan definition, organization building, team building, user interface development, application design, technology selection, acceptance testing, and deployment. It is assumed that these activities are completed outside the database development methodology phases.

- *Define Business Requirements*: Business requirements are captured for any system development effort. The requirements also should be used to build the logical data model. They will feed such things as the number of entities, attribute names, and types of data stored in each attribute. These often are categorized by subject area.

- *Borrow or Create the Data Model*: With a solid understanding of the business requirements, it is a good idea to search the market for a data model that can be purchased from a third party. This subsequently can be customized for the organization.
- *Build Logical Data Model*: The logical data model is built iteratively. The first view usually is done at a high level, beginning with a subject area or conceptual data model. Subsequent levels contain more detail. The process of normalization also is applied at this stage. There are many good books on normalization, so normal forms will not be covered. Foreign key fields and potential indexes also can be considered here. It is not necessary to build the logical data model for performance at this time, and physical considerations are left until a later process.
- *Verify the Data Model*: The logical data model is validated iteratively with users, the fields of the user interface, and process models. It is not unusual to make changes to the data model during this verification process. New requirements, which need to be fitted into the data model, also may be identified.
- *Build Data Architecture*: The data architecture is defined in the context of the physical data environment. Considerations, such as the database server, distribution, components, and partitioning, are considered in this step.
- *Build the Physical Data Model*: The logical data model is converted to a physical data model based on the specific database that is used. The physical data model will vary with the choice of database products and tools. The physical data model also contains such objects as indexes, foreign keys, triggers, views, and user-defined datatypes. The physical data model is optimized for performance and usually is denormalized for this reason. Denormalization can result in redundancy, but can improve system performance. Building the physical data model is not a one-stop process. Do not expect to build a final version of the physical data model on the first attempt.
- *Refine the Data Model*: The physical data model is refined continuously as more information becomes available, and the results of stress testing and benchmarking become available to the database development team. The logical data model also should be maintained as the physical data model is refined.
- *Complete Transaction Analysis*: Transaction analysis is used to review system transactions so that the physical data model can be refined for optimum system performance. Transaction analysis results are only meaningful after the business requirements and systems design are fairly solid. Transaction analysis produces statistics showing the access frequency for the tables in the database, time estimates, and data volumes.
- *Populate the Data*: After the database structure is established and the database is created, it is necessary to populate the database. This can

be done through data scripts, applications, or data conversions. This can be an extensive set of activities that requires substantial data mapping, testing, and parallel activities. It is expected that the details of this are included in the full life-cycle methodology.

- *Complete Testing*: Testing a database usually is done in the context of applications and is covered in the full life-cycle methodology. Some specific types of testing, such as stress testing, benchmarking, and regression testing, can be used to refine the performance of the physical data model. These require high volumes of data, testing tools, and distribution tools.

DELIVERABLES

Some of the important deliverables that are created from inception to the creation of a physical database are discussed in this section. It is useful to build a reference database that contains samples of each of these deliverables so that project teams know in advance what they are attempting to build.

- *Requirements Document*: This is the statement of the business requirements for the application being developed. This deliverable can contain narrative and any number of models or prototypes to capture and represent the business requirements.
- *Conceptual Model/Subject Areas*: This is a high-level view of the business subject areas that are within the scope of the data model (e.g., accounting, administration, billing, engineering).
- *Logical Data Model*: This contains entities, attributes, and business rules within the subject areas. The model also shows relationships between the entities. Key fields and foreign keys also can be identified in this model.
- *Transaction Analysis*: This is a list of transactions supported by the system, the entities (and possibly the fields) that are accessed by the transactions, and the frequency with which they are accessed. A create, read, update, and delete (CRUD) matrix is a useful input for helping with this analysis.
- *Physical Data Model*: This is a denormalized version of the logical data model that is optimized for performance under a specific technical environment and refined through the transaction analysis results. The physical data model usually is refined throughout a development cycle and is not finished until implementation. The physical data model contains physical objects such as tables, fields, indexes, foreign keys, primary keys, views, user-defined data types, and rules.
- *Object Model*: An object model supports the logical data model. This often serves as an intermediate layer between an object-based user interface and a relational back-end database.

- *Validation Model*: This is a cross-reference of models, such as process models, to the logical data model to prove its validity. It often includes a mapping between the logical data model with a user interface and reports to identify gaps.
- *Conversion Strategy*: This is a statement of the strategy used to convert data into a new application. The level of detail can vary signficantly. This could be anything from high-level principles to detailed conversion scripts.

TOOLS

Modeling tools are critical for the database development process. There are a number of tools with various add-ons that can be used in this process. Modeling tools should offer support for both data models and process models. It also is becoming more useful for modeling tools to support object models or to link to other tools that do. Tools that support reverse-reengineering from physical databases to generate logical data model or scripts are useful for organizations that require extensive changes to data structures (possibly following a corporate merger).

There are many other tools that are useful in the database development process. Some of these include CASE tools, conversion tools, testing tools, and database server tools.

ORGANIZATION

When staffing a project that involves a data initiative, it is necessary to fill specific roles. The roles defined in this section are generally specific to the data initiative. These roles often are complimented by other roles in full implementation projects. Projects that have high object-oriented content skew the organization towards object-modeling skillsets.

- *Project Sponsor*: Projects should not be initiated or conducted without a senior project sponsor who is positioned to remove obstacles and ensure that the project team has the full support they require to be successful.
- *Project Manager*: The project manager is in charge of the entire project, including the data initiative.
- *Business User*: This person provides the business rules for the application, which are used to derive the entities and attributes necessary to save the data.
- *Business Analyst*: The business analyst provides a critical link between the business user and the data architect by understanding the business requirements and translating them into technical words.
- *Data Architect*: This person has the responsibility of defining the data architecture. This could be distributed, central, standalone, or integrated with a sophisticated overall architecture.

- *Data Analyst:* The data analyst works with the business analyst to build a consistent view of each element of the data. This person understands the linkage between the business and the individual items of data.
- *Data Modeler:* This person works with the data architect to build a logical relational data model and also may get involved in transforming the logical data model into a physical data model.
- *Object Modeler:* The object modeller becomes involved in projects to build an object model, including messages and methods. This person also may be responsible for mapping the object model to the corporate data model.
- *Database Administrator:* This person implements the physical database, maintains and optimizes the physical environment, restricts access to the database by controlling privilege levels for users, offers advice to the development team for converting the logical data model to the physical data model, and holds the overall responsibility for running the database environment on a data-to-day basis.
- *Network Administrator:* The network administrator maintains the physical network, has the responsibility for maintaining the integrity of the physical environment that supports the data environment, and operates at the operating system level and the hardware level. For example, this person would add more physical disk to support larger databases.
- *Developer:* This person uses the database(s) for application development.

PITFALLS

Misuse or misinterpretation of how methodologies should be executed can result in signficantly negative impacts to project timelines. It is not unusual for organizations to use methodologies as process charts or recipes without streamlining any of the activities. This can result in a considerable amount of wasted time as deliverables or activities are produced without an understanding of how they are leading toward a solution. Methodologies should be adjusted for specific projects. Activities or deliverables that are not necessary should be dropped from the project plan.

Methodologies that are too complicated or difficult to learn and use frequently are avoided by project teams. There are some methodologies that may contain information for thousands of project contingencies. However, they require thousands of megabytes of storage or dozens of manuals to store. During tight project timeframes, such methodologies are sidelined quickly.

It is important to update methodologies over time. New project experiences and best practices should be included in the methodology at specific intervals.

CONCLUSION

Database development methodologies are a subset of full life-cycle methodologies. Project teams can access a third-party database development methodology or follow the high-level framework described in this chapter for database development. Database development methodologies also should support parallel development, iteration, high-user involvement, and be accompanied by a database of reusable templates or sample deliverables.

References

Deloitte & Touche Consulting Group Framework for Computing Solutions.
Maguire, S., *Writing Solid Code*. Microsoft Press, Redmond, WA, 1993.
Purba, S., *Developing Client/Server Systems Using Sybase SQL Server System 11*. John Wiley & Sons, New York, 1995.
Smith, P. N. *Client/Server Computing. 2nd. ed.,* Sams Publishing, Indianapolis, IN, 1994.
Willian, P., *Effective Methods for Software Testing*. John Wiley & Sons, New York, 1995.

Chapter 2
A Review of Database System Terminology

Marion G. Ceruti

MANY PUBLICATIONS, TECHNICAL MANUALS, AND MARKETING BRO-
CHURES related to databases originated from sources that exhibit a wide
variety of training, background, and experience. Although the result has
been an expanded technical vocabulary, the growth of standards — particularly with regard to a comprehensive, uniformly accepted terminology —
has not kept pace with the growth in the technology itself. Consequently,
the nomenclature used to describe various aspects of database technology
is characterized, in some cases, by confusion and chaos. This is true for
both homogeneous databases and for heterogeneous, distributed database systems.

The state of imprecision in the nomenclature of this field persists across
virtually all data models and their implementations. The purpose of this
chapter is to highlight some areas of conflict and ambiguity and, in some
cases, to suggest a more meaningful use of the terminology.

GENERAL DATABASE TERMS

What Does the Word *Data* Mean?

According to Webster, the word *data* is a noun that refers to things
known or assumed; facts or figures from which conclusions can be inferred; information. Derived from the Latin word *datum*, meaning gift or
present, data can be given, granted, or admitted, premises upon which
something can be argued or inferred. Although the word *data* is most frequently observed, the singular form, *datum*, is also a real or assumed thing
used as the basis for calculations.

The Department of Defense defines data as a representation of facts,
concepts, or instructions in a formalized manner suitable for communication, interpretation, or processing by humans or by automatic means.

The word *data* is also used as an adjective in terms such as *data set, data fill, data resource, data management,* or *data mining.* A data set is an aggregate of data items that are interrelated in some way.

Implicit in both definitions of data is the notion that the user can reasonably expect data to be true and accurate. For example, a data set is assumed to consist of facts given for use in a calculation or an argument, for drawing a conclusion, or as instructions from a superior authority. This also implies that the data management community has a responsibility to ensure the accuracy, consistency, and currency of data.

Data Element vs. Data Item

In an attempt to define database terms with a view toward practical applications, the Department of Defense (DoD) defines a data element as a named identifier of each of the entities and their attributes that are represented in a database. As such, data elements must be designed as follows:

- Representing the attributes (characteristics) of data entities identified in data models.
- According to functional requirements and logical (as opposed to physical) characteristics.
- According to the purpose or function of the data element, rather than how, when, where, and by whom it is used.
- With singularity of purpose, such that it has only one meaning.
- With well-defined, unambiguous, and separate domains.

Other definitions are that a data element is data described at the useful primitive level; a data item is the smallest separable unit recognized by the database representing a real-world entity.

What is clear from all these definitions is that there is considerable ambiguity in what these terms mean. The author proposes the following distinction between data element and data item:

> A *data element* is a variable associated with a domain (in the relational model) or an object class (in the object-oriented model) characterized by the property of atomicity. A data element represents the smallest unit of information at the finest level of granularity present in the database. An instance of this variable is a *data item.* A data element in the relational model is simply an attribute (or column) that is filled by data items commonly called the "data fill."

This distinction clarifies but does not preclude any of the other definitions.

What Is a Database?

The definitions for the term *database* range from the theoretical and general to the implementation specific. For example, K.S. Brathwaite, H. Darwen, and C.J. Date have offered two different, but not necessarily inconsistent, definitions of a database that are specific to the relational model. Darwen and Date build their definition on fundamental constructs of the relational model, and it is very specific to that model. Brathwaite employs a definition that is based on how databases are constructed in a specific database management system (DBMS).

These definitions are discussed in the next section on relational database terms. Actually, the term *database* can have multiple definitions, depending on the level of abstraction under consideration. For example, A.P. Sheth and J.A. Larson define database in terms of a reference architecture, in which a database is a repository of data structured according to a data model. This definition is more general than that of either Brathwaite or Darwen and Date because it is independent of any specific data model or DBMS. It could apply to hierarchical and object- oriented databases as well as to relational databases; however, it is not as rigorous as Darwen and Date's definition of a relational database because the term *repository* is not defined.

Similarly, P.J. Fortier et al., in a set of DoD conference proceedings, define a database to be a collection of data items that have constraints, relationships, and a schema. Of all the definitions for database considered thus far, this one is the one most similar to that of Sheth and Larson, because the term *data model* could imply the existence of constraints, relationships, and a schema. Moreover, Fortier et al. define *schema* as a description of how data, relationships, and constraints are organized for user application program access. A *constraint* is a predicate that defines all correct states of the database. Implicit in the definition of schema is the idea that different schemata could exist for different user applications. This notion is consistent with the concept of multiple schemata in a federated database system (FDBS). (Terms germane to FDBSs are discussed in a subsequent section.)

L.S. Waldron defines *database* as a collection of interrelated files stored together, where specific data items can be retrieved for various applications. A file is defined as a collection of related records. Similarly, L. Wheeler defines a *database* as a collection of data arranged in groups for access and storage; a database consists of data, memo, and index files.

Database System vs. Data Repository

Both of these terms refer to a more comprehensive environment than a database because they are concerned with the tools necessary for the management of data in addition to the data themselves. These terms are not mutually exclusive. A *database system* (DBS) includes both the DBMS software and one or more databases. A *data repository* is the heart of a comprehensive information management system environment. It must include not only data elements, but metadata of interest to the enterprise, data screens, reports, programs, and systems.

A data repository must provide a set of standard entities and allow for the creation of new, unique entities of interest to the organization. A database system can also be a data repository that can include a single database or several databases.

A. King et al. describe characteristics of a data repository as including an internal set of software tools, a DBMS, a metamodel, populated metadata, and loading and retrieval software for accessing repository data.

WHAT IS A DATA WAREHOUSE AND WHAT IS DATA MINING?

B. Thuraisingham and M. Wysong discussed the importance of the data warehouse in a DoD conference proceeding. A *data warehouse* is a database system that is optimized for the storage of aggregated and summarized data across the entire range of operational and tactical enterprise activities. The data warehouse brings together several heterogeneous databases from diverse sources in the same environment. For example, this aggregation could include data from current systems, legacy sources, historical archives, and other external sources.

Unlike databases that are optimized for rapid retrieval of information during real-time transaction processing for tactical purposes, data warehouses are not updated, nor is information deleted. Rather, time-stamped versions of various data sets are stored. Data warehouses also contain information such as summary reports and data aggregates tailored for use by specific applications. Thus, the role of metadata is of critical importance in extracting, mapping, and processing data to be included in the warehouse. All of this serves to simplify queries for the users, who query the data warehouse in a read-only, integrated environment.

The data warehouse is designed to facilitate the strategic, analytical, and decision-support functions within an organization. One such function is *data mining*, which is the search for previously unknown information in a data warehouse or database containing large quantities of data. The data warehouse or database is analogous to a mine, and the information desired is analogous to a mineral or precious metal.

The concept of data mining implies that the data warehouse in which the search takes place contains a large quantity of unrelated data and probably was not designed to store and support efficient access to the information desired. In data mining, it is reasonable to expect that multiple, well-designed queries and a certain amount of data analysis and processing will be necessary to summarize and present the information in an acceptable format.

Data Administrator vs. Database Administrator

The following discussion is not intended to offer an exhaustive list of tasks performed by either the data administrator (DA) or database administrator (DBA), but rather to highlight the similarities and essential distinctions between these two types of database professionals. Both data administrators and database administrators are concerned with the management of data, but at different levels.

The job of a *data administrator* is to set policy about determining the data an organization requires to support the processes of that organization. The data administrator develops or uses a data model and selects the data sets supported in the database. A data administrator collects, stores, and disseminates data as a globally administered and standardized resource. Data standards on all levels that affect the organization fall under the purview of the data administrator, who is truly an administrator in the managerial sense.

By contrast, the technical orientation of the *database administrator* is at a finer level of granularity than that of a data administrator. For this reason, in very large organizations, DBAs focus solely on a subset of the organization's users. Typically, the database administrator is, like a computer systems manager, charged with day-to-day, hands-on use of the DBS and daily interaction with its users. The database administrator is familiar with the details of implementing and tuning a specific DBMS or a group of DBMSs. For example, the database administrator has the task of creating new user accounts, programming the software to implement a set of access controls, and using audit functions.

To illustrate the distinction between a data administrator and a database administrator, the U.S. Navy has a head data administrator whose range of authority extends throughout the entire Navy. It would not be practical or possible for an organization as large as the U.S. Navy to have a database administrator in an analogous role, because of the multiplicity of DBSs and DBMSs in use and the functions that DBAs perform.

These conceptual differences notwithstanding, in smaller organizations a single individual can act as both data administrator and database administrator, thus blurring the distinction between these two roles. Moreover, as data models and standards increase in complexity, data administrators will increasingly rely on new technology to accomplish their tasks, just as database administrators do now.

RELATIONAL DATABASE TERMS

Because relational technology is a mature technology with many practical applications, it is useful to consider some of the important terms that pertain to the relational model. Many of these terms are straightforward and generally unambiguous, whereas some terms have specific definitions that are not always understood.

A data set represented in the form of a table containing columns and rows is called a *relation*. The columns are called *attributes*, and the rows are called *tuples*.

Darwen and Date define a tuple to be a set of ordered triples of the form <A, V, $\underline{v}$> where A is the name of an attribute, V is the name of a unique domain that corresponds to A, and $\underline{v}$ is a value from domain V called the attribute value for attribute A within the tuple. A *domain* is a named set of values.

Darwen and Date also describe a relation as consisting of a heading and a body, where the heading is a set of ordered pairs, <A,V>; and the body consists of tuples, all having the same heading <A,V>. An *attribute value* is a data item or a datum.

In some respects, a relation is analogous to an array of data created outside a relational DBMS, such as in a third-generation language (3GL) program like C, FORTRAN, or Ada, in which the rows are called records and the columns are called fields. Waldron defines a *field* as a set of related letters, numbers, or other special characters, and defines a *record* as a collection of related fields.

The interchangeability of the terms *record* and *row* has been illustrated by some of the major DBMS vendors in the way in which they report the results of a query to the user. Earlier versions of commercial DBMSs indicated at the end of a query return messages such as "12 records selected." Now, it is more common to see messages such as "12 rows selected" or "12 rows affected" instead.

Relation vs. Relation Variable

The correct manner in which the term *relation* should be used is according to the definition given previously, which specifically includes values v, from domain V. However, the term *relation* has not always been used correctly in the industry. Relation frequently is used as though it could mean either a filled table with data present (correct), or an empty table structure containing only data headers (incorrect). The confusion here stems from a failure to distinguish between a *relation*, which is a filled table with tuples containing attribute values, and a *relation variable* (or relvar), which is an empty table structure with only attribute names and domains from which to choose values. The values of a relation variable are the relations per se. This distinction becomes especially important when mapping between the relational and object-oriented data models.

Database vs. Database Variable

In a manner similar to the relation-relvar dichotomy, a *database variable* is different from a database per se. A database variable (or dbvar) is a named set of relvars. The value of a given dbvar is a set of specific, ordered pairs <R,r>, where R is a relvar and r (a relation) is the current value of that relvar, such that one such ordered pair exists for each relvar in the dbvar and that, taken together, all relvar values satisfy the applicable constraints (in particular, integrity constraints). A value of the dbvar that conforms to this definition is called a database. Some call this a *database state*, but this term is not used very often.

Database vs. DBMS

As all the examples discussed thus far indicate, not all database terminology is as unambiguous as "rows" and "columns." Incorrect understanding of the fundamental concepts in database technology can lead to inconsistent terminology, and vice versa.

DBMS Software Does Not Equal a Database. For example, databases frequently are described according to the DBMS that manages them. This is all well and good, as long as one realizes that references to an Oracle database and Sybase database refer to the databases that are managed using Oracle or Sybase software, respectively. Difficulty arises when this nomenclature results in the misconception that DBMS software is actually the database itself. The assumption that Informix, for example, is a database is as illogical as thinking that the glass is the same as the water in it.

Concept vs. Implementation in Relational Databases

Darwen and Date's definition of a database, as well as that of other database researchers (some of whom are mentioned by name in this chapter and others who are not), does not require the presence of a DBMS. Conceptually, it is possible to have a database without a DBMS or a DBMS without a database, although obviously the greatest utility is achieved by combining the two.

In the context of a specific DBMS environment, Brathwaite defines an IBM DB2 database as "a collection of table and index spaces where each table space can contain one or more physical tables." This definition is inconsistent with Date's definition because it allows for the possibility that the table spaces could be empty, in which case no data would be present. It is not clear that even relvars would be present in this case. That notwithstanding, if physical tables are present, Brathwaite's definition becomes an implementation-specific special case of Date's definition. (Substitute the word "must" for "can" to resolve the problem with Brathwaite's definition.)

Except in the case where the vendor has specified default table and index spaces in the DBMS code, the database and index spaces are not actually part of the DBMS per se. The DBA needs to create both the database space and the index space using the DBMS software.

DATABASE NORMALIZATION

The topic of *database normalization*, sometimes called *data normalization*, has received a great deal of attention. As is usually the case, database normalization is discussed in the following section using examples from the relational data model. Here, the terms *relation* and *table* are used interchangeably. However, the design guidelines pertaining to database normalization are useful even if a relational database system is not used. For example, B.S. Lee has discussed the need for normalization in the object-oriented data model. Whereas the intent of this section is to introduce the correct usage of normalization terminology as it applies to database technology, it is not meant to be an exhaustive exposition of all aspects of normalization.

What Is Database Normalization?

Strictly speaking, database normalization is the arrangement of data into tables. P. Winsberg defines normalization as the process of structuring data into a tabular format, with the implicit assumption that the result must be in at least first normal form. Similarly, Brathwaite defines data normalization as a set of rules and techniques concerned with:

- Identifying relationships between attributes
- Combining attributes to form relations (with data fill)
- Combining relations to form a database

The chief advantage of database or data normalization is to avoid modification anomalies that occur when facts about attributes are lost during insert, update, and delete transactions. However, if the normalization process has not progressed beyond first normal form, it is not possible to ensure that these anomalies can be avoided. Therefore, database normalization commonly refers to further non-loss decomposition of the tables into second through fifth normal form. Non-loss decomposition means that information is not lost when a table in lower normal form is divided (according to attributes) into tables that result in the achievement of a higher normal form. This is accomplished by placing primary and foreign keys into the resulting tables so that tables can be joined to retrieve the original information.

What Are Normal Forms?

A normal form of a table or database is an arrangement or grouping of data that meets specific requirements of logical design, key structure, modification integrity, and redundancy avoidance, according to the rigorous definition of the normalization level in question. A table is said to be in "X" normal form if it is already in "X-1" normal form and it meets the additional constraints that pertain to level "X."

In first normal form (1NF), related attributes are organized into separate tables, each with a primary key. A primary key is an attribute or set of attributes that uniquely defines a tuple. Thus, if a table is in 1NF, entities within the data model contain no attributes that repeat as groups. W. Kent has explained that in 1NF, all occurrences of a record must contain the same number of fields. In 1NF, each data cell (defined by a specific tuple and attribute) in the table will contain only atomic values.

Every table that is in second normal form (2NF) also must be in 1NF, and every non-key attribute must depend on the entire primary key. Any attributes that do not depend on the entire key are placed in a separate table to preserve the information they represent. 2NF becomes an issue only for tables with composite keys. A composite key is defined as any key (candidate, primary, alternate, or foreign) that consists of two or more attributes. If only part of the composite key is sufficient to determine the value of a non-key attribute, the table is not in 2NF.

Every relation that is in third normal form (3NF) must also be in 2NF, and every non-key attribute must depend directly on the entire primary key. In 2NF, non-key attributes are allowed to depend on each other. This is not allowed in 3NF. If a non-key attribute does not depend on the key directly, or if it depends on another non-key attribute, it is removed and placed in a new table. It is often stated that in 3NF, every non-key attribute is a function of "the key, the whole key, and nothing but the key." In 3NF, every non-key attribute must contribute to the description of the key. However, 3NF does not prevent part of a composite primary key from depending on a non-key attribute, nor does it address the issue of candidate keys.

Boyce-Codd normal form (BCNF) is a stronger, improved version of 3NF. Every relation that is in BCNF also must be in 3NF and must meet the additional requirement that each determinant must be a candidate key. A determinant is any attribute, A, of a table that contains unique data values, such that the value of another attribute, B, fully functionally depends on the value of A. If a candidate key also is a composite key, each attribute in the composite key must be necessary and sufficient for uniqueness. Winsberg calls this condition "unique and minimal." Primary keys meet these requirements. An alternate key is any candidate key that is not the primary key. In BCNF, no part of the key is allowed to depend on any key attribute. Compliance with the rules of BCNF forces the database designer to store associations between determinants in a separate table, if these determinants do not qualify as candidate keys.

BCNF removes all redundancy due to singular relationships but not redundancy due to many-to-many relationships. To accomplish this, further normalization is required. Fourth and fifth normal forms (4NF and 5NF) involve the notions of multivalued dependence and cyclic dependence, respectively. A table is in 4NF if it also is in BCNF and does not contain any independent many-to-many relationships.

That notwithstanding, a table could be in 4NF and still contain dependent many-to-many relationships. A table is in 5NF if it is also in 4NF and does not contain any cyclic dependence (except for the trivial one between candidate keys.) In theory, 5NF is necessary to preclude certain join anomalies, such as the introduction of a false tuple. However, in practice, the large majority of tables in operational databases do not contain attributes with cyclical dependence.

What Are Over-Normalization and Denormalization?

Over-normalization of a table results in further non-loss decomposition that exceeds the requirements to achieve 5NF. The purpose of this is to improve update performance. However, most operational databases rarely reach a state in which the structure of all tables has been tested according to 5FN criteria, so over-normalization rarely occurs. Over-normalization is the opposite of denormalization, which is the result of intentionally introducing redundancy into a database design to improve retrieval performance. Here, the database design process has progressed to 3NF, BCNF, 4NF, or even to 5NF. However, the database is implemented in a lower normal form to avoid time-consuming joins. Because the efficiency of "select" queries is an issue in operational systems, denormalization is more common than over-normalization.

The first six normal forms (including BCNF) are formal structures of tables that eliminate certain kinds of intra-table redundancy. For example, 5NF eliminates all redundancy that can be removed by dividing tables according to attributes. Higher normal forms exist beyond 5NF. They address theoretical issues that are not considered to be of much practical importance. In fact, Date has noted that it is not often necessary or desirable to carry out the normalization process too far because normalization optimizes update performance at the expense of retrieval performance. Most of the time, 3NF is sufficient. This is because tables that have been designed logically and correctly in 3NF are almost automatically in 4NF. Thus, for most databases that support real-time operations, especially for those that have tables with predominantly single-attribute primary keys, 3NF is the practical limit. Note that a two-attribute relation with a single-attribute key is automatically in the higher normal forms.

DISTRIBUTED, HETEROGENEOUS DATABASE NOMENCLATURE

What Is a Distributed Database?

Date defines a distributed database as a virtual database that has components physically stored in a number of distinct "real" databases at a number of distinct sites.

Federated Database Systems vs. Multidatabase Systems. M. Hammer and D. McLeod coined the term *federated database system* to mean a collection of independent, preexisting databases for which data administrators and database administrators agree to cooperate. Thus, the database administrator for each component database would provide the federation with a schema representing the data from his or her component that can be shared with other members of the federation.

In a landmark paper ("Federated Database Systems for Managing Distributed, Heterogeneous and Autonomous Databases," *ACM Computing Surveys,* Vol. 22, No. 3, September 1990), Sheth and Larson define FDBS in a similar but broader architectural sense to mean a collection of cooperating but autonomous component database systems that are possibly heterogeneous. They also define a *nonfederated database* system as an integration of component DBMSs that is not autonomous with only one level of management, in which local and global users are not distinguished. According to Sheth and Larson's taxonomy, both federated and nonfederated database systems are included in a more general category called *multidatabase systems.* These multidatabase systems support operations on multiple-component DBSs.

Sheth and Larson further divide the subcategory of FDBS into two types: loosely coupled and tightly coupled FDBS, based on who creates and maintains the federation and how the component databases are integrated. If the users themselves manage the federation, they call it a *loosely coupled* FDBS; whereas, if a global database administrator manages the federation and controls access to the component databases, the FDBS is *tightly coupled.* Both loosely coupled and tightly coupled FDBSs can support multiple federated schemata. However, if a tightly coupled FDBS is characterized by the presence of only one federated schema, it has a single federation.

The term *multidatabase* has been used by different authors to refer to different things. For example, W. Litwin et al. have used it to mean what Sheth and Larson call a loosely coupled FDBS. By contrast, Y. Breitbart and A. Silberschatz have defined multidatabase to be the tightly coupled FDBS of Sheth and Larson. Sheth and Larson have described additional, conflicting use of the term *multidatabase.*

The terms *loosely coupled* and *tightly coupled* FDBSs have also been used to distinguish between the degree to which users can perceive heterogeneity in an FDBS, among other factors. In this system of nomenclature (devised by this author and M.N. Kamel), a tightly coupled FDBS is characterized by the presence of a federated or global schema, which is not present in a loosely coupled FDBS. Instead of a global schema, loosely coupled FDBSs are integrated using other software, such as a user interface with a uniform "look and feel" or a standard set of queries used throughout the federation, thus contributing to a common operating environment.

In this case, the autonomous components of a loosely coupled FDBS are still cooperating to share data, but without a global schema. Thus, the users see only one DBS in a tightly coupled FDBS, whereas they are aware of multiple DBSs in the loosely coupled FDBS. Here, the tightly coupled FDBS obeys Date's rule zero, which states that to a user, a distributed system should look exactly like a nondistributed system.

Given this manner in which to characterize an FDBS, a *hybrid FDBS* is possible for which some of the component DBSs have a global schema that describe the data shared among them (tightly coupled), but other components do not participate in the global schema (loosely coupled).

An Expanded Taxonomy. An expanded taxonomy is proposed to provide a more comprehensive system to describe how databases are integrated, and to account for the perspectives of both the data administrator and the users. Essentially, most aspects of Sheth and Larson's taxonomy are logical and should be retained. However, instead of using Sheth and Larson's terms for tightly coupled federated database and loosely coupled federated database, the terms *tightly controlled* federated database and *loosely controlled* federated database, respectively, should be substituted.

This change focuses on the absence or presence of a central, controlling authority as the essential distinction between the two. In this case, the terms *tightly coupled* and *loosely coupled* can then be applied to describe how the user, rather than the data administrator, sees the federation. Given this change, the coupling between components in a federated database will describe how seamless and homogeneous the database looks to the users and applications.

The expanded taxonomy can accommodate federated databases that differ widely in their characteristics. For example, if a tightly controlled federated database is tightly coupled, the global data administrator and the global database administrator have exercised their authority and expertise to provide a seamless, interoperable environment that allows the federation's users to experience the illusion of a single database for their applications and ad-hoc queries.

A tightly controlled federated database can also be loosely coupled, in which case the global data administrator allows the users of the federation to see some heterogeneity with respect to the component databases.

Both conditions are within the realm of possibility. However, a loosely controlled federated database is almost certain to be loosely coupled. This is because a loosely controlled federated database lacks a central authority capable of mediating disputes about data representation in the federated schema and enforcing uniformity in the federation's interfaces to user applications. A loosely controlled federated database is not likely to be tightly coupled.

Local or Localized Schema vs. Component Schema vs. Export Schema. A local or localized database generally starts as a stand-alone, nonintegrated database. When a local, autonomous database is selected for membership in a federation, a local schema is defined as a conceptual schema of the component DBS that is expressed in the native data model of the component DBMS.

When the local database actually becomes a member of a federated database, it is said to be a *component database*. The schema associated with a given database component is called a *component schema*, which is derived by translating a local schema into the common data model of the FDBS. An *export schema* represents the subset of the component schema that can be shared with the federation and its users.

Similarly, Date defines a local schema as the database definition of a component database in a distributed database.

Federated Schema vs. Global Schema vs. Global Data Dictionary. A federated schema is an integration of multiple export schemata. Because the distributed database definition is sometimes called the global schema, federated schema and global schema are used interchangeably.

A global data dictionary is the same as a global schema that includes the data element definitions as they are used in the FDBS. A data dictionary is different from a schema, or database structure specification, because a data dictionary contains the definitions of attributes or objects, not just the configuration of tables, attributes, objects, and entities within that structure.

It is especially important to include the data element definitions with the export schemata when forming a federated database in which multiple data representations are likely. Simply having a collection of database structures is insufficient to complete a useful federated schema. It is necessary to know the meaning of each attribute or object and how it is construed in the component database.

Middleware vs. Midware. In a three-tier client/server architecture designed to connect and manage data exchange between user applications and a variety of data servers, the middle tier that brokers transactions between clients and servers consists of middleware, which is sometimes called midware.

P. Cykana defines middleware as a variety of products and techniques that are used to connect users to data resources. In his view, the middleware solution is usually devoted to locating and finding data rather than to moving data to migration environments.

In addition, Cykana describes two options for middleware, depending on the degree of coupling between the user and the data resource. Loosely coupled middleware products allow flexibility in specifying relationships and mappings between data items, whereas tightly coupled middleware products allocate more authority to standard interfaces and database administrators. Each option has its advantages and disadvantages, as follows:

- *Loosely coupled middleware.* This type of middleware does not require the migration or legacy data structures to be modified, but it allows users to access multiple equivalent migration systems transparently with one standard interface. Its disadvantage is that it does not prevent multiple semantics and nonstandard structures.
- *Tightly coupled middleware.* This option represents a more aggressive strategy that combines applications program interface (API) and graphical user interface (GUI) technologies, data communications, and data dictionary design and development capabilities to provide distributed data access. Data standardization and reengineering are required.

The concept of loose and tight coupling to middleware is somewhat similar to, but also differs slightly from, the loose and tight coupling between data resources as discussed by Sheth and Larson and other researchers. In the case of middleware, the coupling occurs between software at different tiers or layers (between the middle translation layer and the data servers); whereas, in the case of an FDBS, the coupling occurs between data servers that reside at the same tier. (However, this difference does not preclude software that achieves the coupling between data servers from being located in the middle tier.)

G.V. Quigley defines middleware as a software layer between the application logic and the underlying networking, security, and distributed computing technology. Middleware provides all of the critical services for managing the execution of applications in a distributed client/server environment while hiding the details of distributed computing from the application tier. Thus, midware is seen in a critical role for implementing a tightly coupled FDBS.

Similarly, Quigley considers middleware to be the key technology to integrate applications in a heterogeneous network environment.

Database Integration vs. Database Homogenization. Many organizations in both industry and government are interested in integrating autonomous (sometimes called "stovepipe") databases into a single distributed, heterogeneous database system. Many terms describe the various aspects of this integration. The multiplicity of terminology occurs because of the many ways in which databases can be integrated and because of the many simultaneous efforts that are underway to address integration problems.

Because the degree to which database integration takes place depends on the requirements of the organization and its users, the term *integration*, as it is used in various contexts, remains rather vague. For people whose fields of expertise are outside the realm of database technology, it is necessary to hide the specific details of database system implementation behind midware layers and a user interface that together create the illusion of a single, unified database. By contrast, more experienced users with knowledge of multiple DBMS can function efficiently in an environment that preserves some distinctions between the database components.

Within all architectural options, *database integration*, in its broadest sense, refers to the combination and transformation of database components into a database system that is homogeneous on at least one level (e.g., the data level, the schema level, the program interface level, or the user-interface level). Such an integrated database system must satisfy the primary goals of interoperability between database system components, data sharing, consistent data interpretation, and efficient data access for users and applications across multiple platforms.

K. Karlapalem et al. describe the concept of *database homogenization* as the process of transforming a collection of heterogeneous legacy information systems onto a homogeneous environment. Whereas they do not define what they mean by the term *homogeneous environment*, they list three goals of database homogenization:

- To provide the capability to replace legacy component databases efficiently
- To allow new global applications at different levels of abstraction and scale to be developed on top of the homogenized federated database
- To provide interoperability between heterogeneous databases so that previously isolated heterogeneous localized databases can be loosely coupled

This definition of database integration explicitly includes multiple architectures and implementations; by contrast, the description of database homogenization is associated with loose rather than tight coupling of localized databases into a homogeneous environment. Sometimes the term *database normalization* is used incorrectly to mean *database integration*.

Interoperability vs. Interoperation. The conditions necessary for interoperability include:

- Interconnectivity via the necessary networking facilities

- Resolution of system heterogeneity
- Resolution of semantic heterogeneity
- Derivation and integration of schemata and views

There are three levels of heterogeneity, including platform heterogeneity, data model heterogeneity, and semantic heterogeneity. Excluding semantic heterogeneity, the term system heterogeneity is seen to be some combination of platform heterogeneity (e.g., different DBMS software and implementation) and data model heterogeneity (e.g., schemata, query languages, integrity constraints, and nullness requirements). Because Karlapalem et al. have already listed the integration of schemata as an item separate from system heterogeneity, system heterogeneity logically should refer to the differences between DBMS vendors, transaction processing algorithms, query languages, query optimization techniques, integrity constraints, and nullness requirements. If this definition is assumed for system heterogeneity, the necessary conditions for database interoperability listed above become sufficient conditions.

Similarly, computer system heterogeneity and data management system heterogeneity must be resolved as a requirement for interoperability among existing information systems.

The achievement of database interoperability simply supplies users and applications with the ability to interoperate in a common data environment. It does not guarantee that interoperation will occur. Database interoperation results when users and applications take advantage of a common, integrated environment to access, share, and process data across multiple databases.

Legacy Information System vs. Migration Information System. Autonomous systems that become candidates for integration into a more modern, global, and distributed system sometimes have been called migration systems. These systems are supported by migration information systems with migration databases.

The term *migration databases* indicates unambiguously that the database in question has been chosen to be included in some form of a modern database system, especially a distributed system such as an FDBS. By contrast, the term *legacy information system* has been used in two different ways.

At one extreme, some people use legacy information system and legacy database to be synonymous with migration information system and migration database, respectively. Others have referred to a legacy information system as if it were not a migration information system and is therefore deliberately excluded from the final integrated database configuration. This is the opposite extreme.

More commonly than in the extreme cases, a subset of legacy data is deemed important to the users of a shared data resource. This means that some or all of the data in a legacy information system may be migrated during a database integration effort. For example, Cykana describes steps in the data integration process that start with the movement and improvement of data and progress to the shutdown of legacy systems. Karlapalem et al. refer to the difficulty of migrating legacy information systems to a modern computer environment in which some difference is presumed to exist between the legacy system and the modern system.

The author recommends that the following terminology be adopted as standard:

> *Legacy data* and *legacy information system* should refer to the original data and original format, as maintained in the original, autonomous information system before any modification or migration to a new environment has occurred. *Migration data* and *migration information system* should be used to describe the subset of the legacy data and software that has been chosen to be included into a new (and usually distributed) information resource environment. When data and software are modified to accommodate a new environment, they should be called migration instead of legacy.

TERMS ASSOCIATED WITH SEMANTIC HETEROGENEITY

Semantic heterogeneity refers to a disagreement about the meaning, interpretation, or intended use of the same or related data or objects. Semantic heterogeneity can occur either in a single DBS or in a multidatabase system. Its presence in a DBS is also independent of data model or DBMS. Therefore, the terminology associated with this problem is discussed in a separate section.

Semantic Interoperability vs. Database Harmonization

The terms *database integration* and *interoperability* were discussed previously in a general context. For distributed, heterogeneous database systems to be integrated in every respect, semantic heterogeneity must be resolved.

Problems associated with semantic heterogeneity have been difficult to overcome, and the terminology to describe semantic heterogeneity has evolved accordingly. For example, R. Sciore et al. define semantic interoperability as agreement among separately developed systems about the meaning of their exchanged data.

Whereas the exact meaning of the term *database harmonization* is not clear, one can infer that the goal of database harmonization must be related to providing an environment in which conflicts have been resolved between data representations from previously autonomous systems. This definition further implies that the resolution of semantic heterogeneity is a prerequisite for database harmonization.

Although a more precise definition of database harmonization is needed, it appears to be related to the idea of semantic interoperability.

Strong and Weak Synonyms vs. Class One and Class Two Synonyms

A synonym is a word that has the same or nearly the same meaning as another word of the same language. Because a metadata representation will include more attributes (e.g., data element name, type, length, range, and domain) than ordinary nouns, it was necessary to consider various levels of similarity and therefore, levels of synonymy.

M.W. Bright et al. have described the concept of strong and weak synonyms. Strong synonyms are semantically equivalent to each other and can be used interchangeably in all contexts without a change of meaning, whereas weak synonyms are semantically similar and can be substituted for each other in some contexts with only minimal meaning changes. Weak synonyms cannot be used interchangeably in all contexts without a major change in the meaning — a change that could violate the schema specification.

This concept is similar to one (introduced by the author and Kamel) that states that there are two classes of synonym abstraction: Class One and Class Two. Class One synonyms occur when different attribute names represent the same, unique real world entity. The only differences between Class One synonyms are the attribute name and possibly the wording of the definition, but not the meaning. By contrast, Class Two synonyms occur when different attribute names have equivalent definitions but are expressed with different data types and data-element lengths.

Class Two synonyms can share the same domain or they can have related domains with a one-to-one mapping between data elements, provided they both refer to the same unique real-world entity. The concept of a strong synonym is actually the same as that of a Class Two synonym because both strong synonyms and Class Two synonyms are semantically equivalent and they can be used interchangeably because they have the same data element type and length. By contrast, the concept of a Class Two synonym includes (but is not limited to) the concept of a weak synonym because the definition of a weak synonym seems to imply a two-way interchange in some contexts. The main difference is that the interchangeability of Class Two synonyms is determined not only by semantic context, but also by the intersection of their respective domains, as well as their data types and lengths.

Class Two synonyms allow for a one-way, as well as a two-way, interchange in some cases, whereas the "each-other" part in the definition of weak synonyms seems to preclude a one-way interchange. For example, a shorter character string can fit into a longer field, but not vice versa.

SUMMARY

This chapter presents a review of the rapidly growing vocabulary of database system technology, along with its conflicts and ambiguities. The solutions offered address some of the problems encountered in communicating concepts and ideas in this field.

This effort is intended to be a first step toward the development of a more comprehensive, standard set of terms that can be used throughout the industry. More work is needed to identify and resolve the differences in interpretation between the many terms used in data administration, database development, database administration, database research, and marketing as they occur in industry, government, and academia.

ACKNOWLEDGMENTS

This work was created by a U.S. government employee in the course of employment and is therefore in the public domain.

Chapter 3
Developing a Global Information Vision

Tim Christmann

INTRODUCTION

INFORMATION TECHNOLOGY (IT) BUSINESS EXECUTIVES are experiencing increasing professional pressures as their organizations strive to become truly global. In an effort to leverage their resources around the world and serve global customers, companies are turning to information technology as a means of achieving these objectives. IT capabilities have evolved to the point where some would argue that IT can, for the first time, be a strategic enabler in helping a company become truly global. In order for IT to be a strategic enabler for a company on a global basis, all major IT investments must be aligned with the business goals and strategies of the organization. One step toward aligning IT investments with business objectives and strategies is to bring key business and IT leaders to a common understanding or vision of how information will enable the company's strategy and future competitive position in the marketplace.

What Does It Mean To Be "Global"?

In the age of economic globalization, it is not uncommon for companies to expand beyond domestic boundaries into foreign markets in search of new growth opportuntities. If a company has operations around the world, does this make the company a "global business"? In short, the answer to this question is no. Being truly global involves mobilizing company resoures around the world and presenting a common face for the company's key stakeholders — customers, suppliers, shareholders, and employees.

What Is a Global Information Vision?

Let's start with what an information vision is not. It is not a statement conceived in the office of the CIO and posted above the door in the IT department. It is not about having the IT function achieve functional excellency through the use of leading edge technologies.

0-8493-9976-9/99/$0.00+$.50
© 1999 by CRC Press LLC

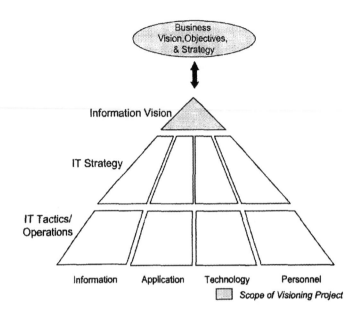

Exhibit 1. Information vision.

An information vision is a clear statement of how an enhanced information base will help the business achieve its strategic objectives. It is stated in business terms and contains a clear link to the competitive positioning of the business. A vision also indicates business outcomes that are recognizable by business and IT leaders alike.

As shown in Exhibit 1, within the IT decision-making hierarchy, the Information Vision provides a link between the business strategy and objectives and the IT strategy. Bringing the key business stakeholders to agreement on the Information Vision provides direction throughout the company on where IT investments should be focused to bring the most value to the company.

OBJECTIVES — "PAY-OFF IDEA"

Why Do You Need an Information Vision in Your Company?

There are a number of objectives that you should achieve as you facilitate the development of your company's information vision:

1. Raise the understanding at all levels in the company of how information and information technology can and will add value for the company.
   - Often executives see the enormous operational and capital expenditures for IT and wonder what value they are getting for their mon-

ey. They fear that deployment of technology solutions may be based on an underlying desire to have the latest technological innovation rather than the pure business value of the investment. Demonstrating the value of IT investments does not stop once an information vision has been established. However, developing an information vision does put into clear business terms how information does and will add value to the business.

- Do your business decision-makers think about information or IT when they are devising their business strategies? Business decision-makers often do not fully understand the capabilities of IT or do not think about how an enhanced information base can enable their business strategies. Engaging key business leaders in the exercise of developing a vision for information in the company will raise their level of awareness.

2. Promote better alignment of IT projects and the business objectives.
- How often do you hear about companies that have sizeable investments in state-of-the-art systems to improve an area or function that is not core to the business? Afterwards they often question how such an enormous investment of capital and human resources has actually changed the company's competitive position? By engaging key business and IT leaders in developing an information vision linked to clear business outcomes, a common understanding is reached with respect to where the value-adding opportunities exist for IT projects. Any project or opportunity not in line with the vision comes immediately under question.

3. Keep IT personnel focused on achieving an enhanced information base for the company rather than implementing new technologies for technology-sake.
- The visioning exercise creates a better focus on the "I" rather than the "T" in Information Technology. By focusing on information, it forces people to question technology investments that do not result in a sufficient improvement to the base of information that will enhance the company's competitive position.

4. Develop an understanding of how a common information vision can benefit the global units and the company as a whole — not just another head-office exercise.
- Often the words of a vision or mission mean little to those not directly involved in composing the statements. Especially if your company operates businesses around the world that have a certain amount of local autonomy, these units may offer some resistance if their interests have not been properly represented in developing the vision or they fail to realize how the vision improves the position of their business. For this reason, it can be beneficial to indicate how enhanced use of information will benefit the local units as well.

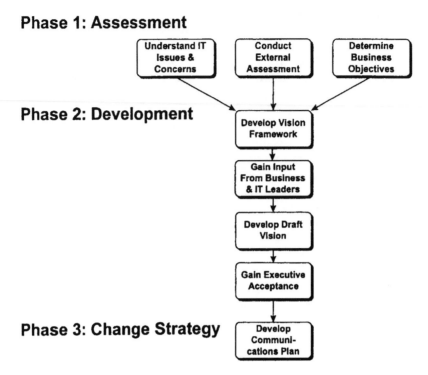

Phase 1: Assessment

Phase 2: Development

Phase 3: Change Strategy

Exhibit 2. The process for developing an information vision.

THE PROCESS

To develop an information vision effectively, it is important to understand that perhaps the greatest value is in the process of developing the Vision rather than in the words of the Vision itself. In order to gain the full value of this exercise, the right level of people in the organization, from both the business and IT community, must be involved in developing the Vision. Having the right people involved, especially from the business community, helps to ensure relevant content, organizational buy-in and business ownership. To ensure relevancy and ownership, the vision must be articulated using words that the business community understands, therefore the words themselves must come from key business leaders. Exhibit 2 outlines the process for developing a Global Information Vision. Exhibit 3 provides the Critical Success Factors for making this a reality.

PHASE 1: ASSESSMENT

If you already have a clear understanding of the current situation of information and information technology in the company then this phase can be condensed. However, it is important to note that there are distinct benefits

Exhibit 3. Critical Success Factors

The following points represent critical success factors in ensuring successful development of an information vision:

- The right level of sponsorship

It is important that this initiative be championed at the highest level in the organization in order to have the desired impact. An information vision should be viewed as an extention of the business strategy by stating how information will help the company achieve its business objectives. Therefore, a successful information visioning initiative will have a sponsor positioned at the same level in the company as the sponsor of a business strategy intiative. These intiatives might even be sponsored by the same individual.

- Involvement from key business leaders

The objectives of the visioning process are aggressive given that they often require the thinking and decision-making of management and staff throughout the company to be changed. One of the best ways to achieve buy-in from these people is to involve them as much as possible in the development process. Executive involvement is key. These people need to be involved to ensure that the vision is clearly aligned with the direction of the business. Also, their involvement lends credibility and importance to the intiative. Senior executives are often somewhat removed from decisions made at lower levels in the company, especially in a global company where decision-making is often decentralized. Therefore, it can be beneficial to have management involvement in the development process from various business areas and geographic regions. Choose representatives from the business areas or regions that are seen as critical to the business and individuals who are viewed as leaders in their respective areas.

- The right language

It is critical for the vision to be perceived as business owned and business led if the stated objectives are to be achieved. Therefore, the vision must be stated in business terms.

- Linked to business outcomes

Linking the vision to specific business outcomes helps people to understand exactly how improving the information base in the company results in business value, especially if they are not involved in developing the vision. It also may help to reveal in which areas IT projects may provide the greatest opportunity in terms of positioning information as a strategic enabler for the business.

---

in conducting a formal assessment to ensure that your understanding is complete.

As part of the assessment, there are three main questions that need to be answered:

1. What is the Current State of the IT?

The assessment phase provides an opportunity to gain a clear understanding of the current situation and bring to the surface any issues or concerns about the current state of information or information technology in the company. These issues or concerns represent not only areas of improvement, they may also represent significant barriers to changing the way people think about the ability of the information and information technology to add value to the business. The business community needs to know that their concerns are being heard. Soliciting input from key business leaders also provides a prime opportunity to begin developing buy-in and ownership for the Vision itself. It is also important to acknowledge past successes or progress that the company has made in IT projects. These successes are often not well known throughout the company and serve to boost the company's collective confidence in its ability to deliver business value through IT.

2. What are the Major External Forces or Pressures Facing IT?

If possible it is beneficial to understand how competitors in the same industry or companies with similar operations are using IT. Presenting this information may serve two purposes. First, if it is determined that competitors are further advanced in the way they are employing IT, it may serve as a strong imperative for change. Exploring how similar companies use IT to gain competitive advantage can also raise the level of education within the company, heightening awareness of what is possible.

In addition, it may be beneficial to articulate what the current possibilities are in IT today. People may ask, 'why does the company need a global vision about information?' It is important for people to understand that for the first time, global communications and real-time information sharing are possible and can deliver significant business value.

3. What are the Business Vision, Objectives, and Strategy?

This third question is perhaps the most important for a number of reasons. First of all, the information vision must be aligned with the vision of the company as a whole. Often the company vision is not explicitly stated or well understood. Therefore, it is important to conduct interviews with key business leaders to gain a clear understanding of where the business leadership intends to take the company in the future and what the critical success factors are for the company as a whole and its core business areas. Secondly, conducting interviews with key business leaders helps build ownership for the vision within the business community. People are more likely to champion the vision when they are part of its development. Finally, it is critical for the vision itself be be stated in business terms. Exhibit 4 provides an example of typical findings that may result from the Assessment Phase.

The Change Imperative

One of the most important outcomes of the Assessment phase is to build a clear understanding of the need for the company to change. The change imperative must be clearly articulated in terms of issues and challenges

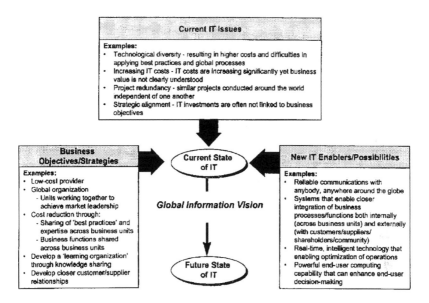

Exhibit 4.   Typical findings from the assessment phase.

facing IT, changing business objectives and strategies, and the new IT capabilities that are available. It is important that the executive group understands the outcomes of the Assessment phase and to agree on the need for change.

PHASE 2: DEVELOPMENT

Different approaches may be used to develop the vision. Perhaps the most effective approach is to facilitate a group of key business leaders, including senior executives and key management personnel through each of the following steps. Although effective, this approach is often very difficult to execute especially if the key business leaders are situated around the world. It important to keep in mind that having active involvement from as many key business leaders as possible is critical to the success of the initiative. Therefore, if it is not possible to conduct steps 1 through 4 as one group, it may be necessary to break the group of targeted participants into smaller focus groups.

Step 1: Develop Vision Framework

Establishing a framework may not be essential but can be beneficial both in developing the vision and communicating it. A framework can provide an effective structure in which to organize ideas regarding how an enhanced information base can enable the business to achieve it's business

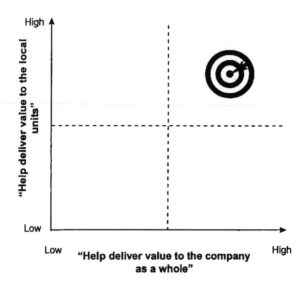

Exhibit 5.   Information vision framework.

objectives. The framework can also prove very useful in communicating how the vision can be linked to specific business outcomes. Exhibit 5 provides an example of a framework that could be used for a global company that is looking for ways to articulate how a common vision for an enhanced information base will not only improve the performance of the company as a whole, but also to improve the performance of the individual business units around the world.

Step 2: Gain Input from Key Stakeholders

Depending on the audience, different techniques can be used to gain input from key stakeholders. Often it is difficult to obtain extensive time with top executives. Therefore it may beneficial to include specific questions during the executive interviews in the Assessment phase that will provide insight into how enhanced information may better enable the business to achieve its objectives.

The following are examples of specific questions that could be used to facilitate input from the key business leaders:

- How can information help the company attain its vision?
- What information would make a difference in the various business units? For customers? For managers?
- What impediments exist today to using information to add value to the organization and to make a difference to the bottom line?

Exhibit 6. Examples of Business Outcomes from Developing an Enhanced Information Base

An enhanced information base will deliver value to the company as a whole by:	An enhanced information base will help to deliver value to the local units by:
• enabling optimization of operations between business units • enabling a learning organization through experience sharing • capturing knowledge about customer needs so that, whenever pertinent, it flows through the company's value chain • allowing the internal organization to be transparent to the customer around the world • enabling people to be more a part of the company as well as their local groups; people will then act in the common interest of global company rather than only in the interest of their own group at the expense of the others • decreasing complexity thereby decreasing costs and improving customer service • facilitating organizational change; reducing organizational boundaries; enabling the creation of virtual teams • increasing decision-making and implementation speed	• enabling optimization of operations within each business unit • capturing and exploiting innovative ideas and opportunities more quickly, more easily • tapping into global expertise for problem solving • tapping into global supplier options to reduce costs • improving operational stability, consistency and reliability • enabling production capacity optimization • increasing decision-making and implementation speed

Using the sample framework presented in Step 1, Exhibit 6 provides some examples of possible ways to add value or enable business strategies. These examples, when linked to the vision, provide clear business outcomes that may result from developing an enhanced information base.

Step 3: Develop Draft Information Vision

This step involves developing a simple statement that combines the strategic objectives and critical success factors of the business with the feedback that has been given regarding how the business could change as a result of having an enhanced information base. An example of this is shown in Exhibit 7.

How the draft Information Vision itself is assembled depends largely on the development approach that has been chosen. If all key business leaders are in one room then the words can be drafted by the group as a whole. If this approach is not possible, or if there is already general concensus among the participants on the business outcomes that can be achieved through an enhanced information base, the vision can be assembled and presented to the key business leaders for review and approval.

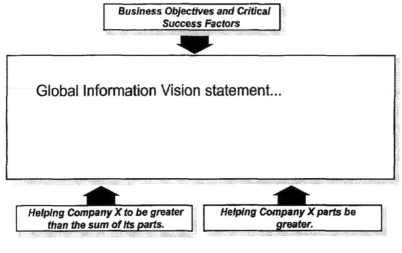

Exhibit 7. Assembling the information vision.

Step 4: Gain Executive Acceptance

It is important that acceptance be given for the vision by the various business leaders involved in developing it. Once again, the vision must be business-owned and business-led. Acceptance will help to ensure that each of the leaders involved will serve as a champion for building an enhanced information base in their respective business areas or regions.

PHASE 3: CHANGE STRATEGY

A successfully executed Information Vision development process will generate a significant amount of awareness among key business leaders of how information can be a strategic enabler for the company. However, it is important to build on the momentum that has been achieved and have a plan for making all company management aware of the vision for how information will be leveraged to create business value. Do not make the mistake of relying on passive or informal communication methods. Instead, a detailed communication plan should be developed to ensure that all key stakeholder groups are aware of the vision. Exhibit 8 highlights a simple approach for developing a communication plan.

Key Messages

First you must identify the key messages that you wish the target audiences to hear and understand. Given the visioning process that has just been completed, typical messages would include:

Exhibit 8.   Approach to developing communication plan.

- Business Vision and Strategy — pick key phrases that link directly to the Information Vision
- Information Vision — emphasize that the statement has been developed and approved by key business leaders
- Business Outcomes — state the business outcomes that can result from developing an enhanced information base are key to making people understand how the vision will change the business

Audiences

Generally, all decision-makers in the company should be made aware of the key messages coming out of the visioning exercise. For the purposes of the communication plan, it is important to specifically identify those audiences that will require targeted communications. Once these audiences have been identified, it is a worthwhile exercise to determine the roles of each group with regard to their use of information and IT and gain an understanding of their specific communication requirements. For example, some groups may simply need to be made aware of the key messages while others may need to incorporate this thinking into their decision-making. The level of communication required for a specific audience will dictate the method used.

Communication Methods

Typically, there are a variety of communication methods available within a company ranging from media tools, such as e-mail or company newsletters, to face-to-face communications, such as executive presentations. It may be necessary to create some specific communication opportunities to match the objectives of the visioning initiative. Compiling a list of the various methods available will help in developing the communication plan.

Developing the Communication Plan

Assembling the communication plan involves determining which methods will be used to communicate the key messages to the target audiences.

Conclusion and Next Steps

Once the Information Vision has been developed and the communication plan has been launched, you may ask yourself, "where to from here?" Once again, given the momentum established during the visioning exercise, it is important to build on this momentum. The following are typical initiatives or deliverables that may provide further value to your company.

Information Strategy. Building on the stated business outcomes from the visioning exercise, an information strategy would provide further detail regarding what the specific information requirements are to achieve these outcomes. The strategy would answer questions such as: What knowledge is critical to the success of the company? How can this knowledge be leveraged further? What are the key strategic and operational decisions in the company? What information would enable these decisions to be made more effectively? An information strategy also provides detail regarding where IT investments should be targeted to deliver the greatest value to the company.

Information Management Plan. Once people acknowledge that information is a valuable resource for the company, they will begin to realize the importance of managing this resource effectively. An information management plan identifies how key information will be defined, managed, delivered, and protected. The plan also identifies who will be responsible for defining, managing, delivering, and protecting key information.

Chapter 4
An Approach for Establishing Enterprise Data Standards

Sanjiv Purba

INTRODUCTION

STANDARDS EXIST IN SOME FORM OR OTHER in most organizations and tend to be wide reaching in establishing how work is performed and delivered within the environment. In the strictest sense, standards should thoroughly describe procedures and outcomes for all the events in an organization. The benefit of this is consistent communication within an organization and reliable deliverables. Implementing standards is a tricky business that can lead to an entirely different set of problems that can also jeopardize the health of the organization. Ideally, it would be best to simply borrow standards that have already been used successfully on similar projects and adapt them with minimal effort. Unfortunately, this is not possible in many real world cases, so another approach is required. As shown in Exhibit 1, simplicity is the key to successfully implementing enterprise data standards in most organizations.

Enterprise data standards are part of the larger, broader "enterprise development standards" category, which includes such topics as development approach, walkthrough procedures, and coding conventions. This paper focuses on establishing enterprise data standards. There are other types of standards in organizations (e.g., development standards), but these are outside the scope of this article. This distinction can sometimes be subjective; for example, consider the case of form naming standards. Is this a data standard or a development standard? For grouping purposes, I prefer to categorize it as a naming convention under data standards. How-

Standards are only useful if they are used;
Standards will only be used if they are understood;
Standards will only be understood if they are simple;
Standards will only be understood if the organization has bought into them;
The organization will buy into standards if they are simple, easily understood, and there is a stake in using them.

Exhibit 1.   Guiding principles.

---

ever, some would prefer to stay pure and categorize it under the more general naming conventions in the development standards.

OBJECTIVES AND BENEFITS OF ENTERPRISE DATA STANDARDS

Data exists within organizations in a variety of formats, some of which include: documents, databases, flat files, paper documents, binary objects, voice, and video. Data is everywhere, and its value is in a constant state of flux, either being modified, deleted, changed, or manipulated in some way. All of this activity is supported by many human resources, both inside and outside the organization. Enterprise data standards support the objectives of bringing consistency and integrity across the organization based on the categories shown in Exhibit 2. This list is not exhaustive, but the categories that are identified are common across many organizations in a variety of industries and provide a good start for beginning this process.

The significant objectives and benefits of each of the categories defined in Exhibit 2 are described in this section, as they pertain to many organizations.

Architecture and Physical Environment Category

Objectives. This includes building a consistent technical data architecture including centralized databases, distributed database servers, and mobile databases. This also includes the physical storage of the data and associated data objects (e.g., indexes) and defines the methods for accessing the data in an n-tier environment from thin or fat clients using embedded SQL or remote procedure calls (RPCs). System management, change management, and version control tools are implemented to meet this objective based on procedures defined in the "Procedures Category."

Benefits. Provides a standard physical environment that is easier to support and enhance. Maintenance and support costs are also reduced. A standard architecture and physical environment also simplify application portability and interoperability.

Procedures Category

Objectives. This includes all the procedures required to support data for operational or development groups. This can include system management,

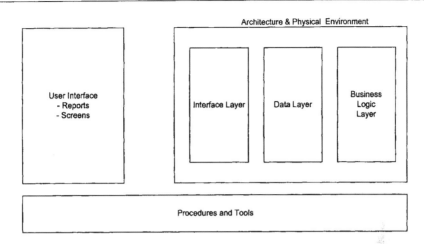

Exhibit 2. Categories of enterprise data standards.

change management, and version control procedures. Included in this group are project naming standards (using tools like Microsoft Source-Save), module check in /check out procedures, support for multiple versions, and delta merging procedures.

Benefits. A significant benefit supported by this category includes the use of proven, consistent procedures for maintaining the integrity of the data environment. It is also becomes easier to measure compliance with the standards processes.

n-tier/Layers Category

Objectives. This category contains anywhere from one to *n* tiers, with three being the most common. The growing popularity of components will continue to increase the number of tiers. The predominant case includes three tiers, namely, user interface tier (or layer), data tier, and the business logic tier. The user interface tier is discussed in the next category. The *n*-tier category includes naming standards in terms of variable names, field names, data object names (e.g., tables, indexes, databases, user-defined datatypes, triggers, stored procedures), forms class libraries, and objects.

Benefits. There are significant benefits derived from standardizing in this category. Application modules are easier to read, build, and maintain. There is increased reuse of code and improved application portability and interoperability. This results in faster development and more accurate debugging. There is a reduced learning curve. The end result is improved product quality.

User Interface Category

Objectives. This category includes all types of user interfaces, including application screens and reports (both online and printed). The objectives in this category are to specifiy placement of data on screens or printed forms. Categories such as screen navigation are outside the scope of this topic.

Benefits. Standards in this category result in consistent look and feel for user screens and printed reports. Users know where to search for specific types of information. An example of this is an error line on a screen or the page number on a report.

CATEGORIES OF ENTERPRISE DATA STANDARDS

Enterprise data standards are required to support both operational and development groups within an organization. Operational groups include those who perform the company's business on a day-to-day basis. These groups require access to information, the ability to manipulate information, procedures, and forms of various kinds. Development groups are more project-focused, in that they are restricted by some sort of timelines and deliverables. These groups require many of the data standards required by the operational groups, but their demands go further. Since development groups get right into the architecture and plumbing of applications, they are dependent on how data is stored, accessed, and manipulated at the code level.

The exhibits that are included in this section provide subcategories for each category defined previously. Each of the subcategories should be considered in your organization and allocated standards. Exhibit 3 shows the subcategories for the Architecture and Physical Environment category.

Exhibit 4 shows the subcategories that are included in the Procedures category. Most of these are focused on protecting data (in databases or files) during the development cycle.

Exhibit 5 shows the subcategories for the *n*-tier/layers category. These are divided between the different tiers in the architecture model. This example covers the business logic tier and the data tier. The user interface layer is covered in Exhibit 6.

Exhibit 6 shows the subcategories for the User interface category. There are two primary subcategories, namely user screens and reports.

PROCESS FOR DEFINING ENTERPRISE DATA STANDARDS

There are many approaches for defining enterprise data standards. Project experience has shown that the best approach for meeting the objectives identified earlier in this article is the early adoption of a simplified set of en-

Exhibit 3.   Architecture and Physical Environment Category

Subcategory	Comments
Data Partitioning	Position nonvolatile data near the client platforms that access it.
Physical Architecture	Data architecture for development, testing, and production.
Data Access	Call stored procedures from client platforms to update database table data.
	Use views to select information from database tables.
	Return minimum number of data rows to the client.
Locking	Assume optimistic locking approach instead of the pessimistic.

Exhibit 4.   Procedures Category

Subcategory	Comments
Change Management Standards	All database objects should be created with SQL Scripts. The scripts should be saved in tools such as Microsoft SourceSave.
System Management Standards	New client platforms will be configured using Microsoft SMS with local data tables for static data values.
Version Control Standards	Check in/Check out, delta management.

terprise data standards that are easily understood and used across the organization. This is best achieved by starting with a set of proven standards from previous projects or from external vendors. For example, companies such as Microsoft, Forte, and Sybase all have publications that define standards to one degree or another. These can be readily found by searching the Websites of the vendors or phoning their marketing or technical departments. Exhibit 7 shows a high level view of a process that should be completed in your organization to define Enterprise Data Standards. This process has been defined through experiences on many small to large projects, and based on observations about what worked well and what did not work so well on the projects.

As shown in Exhibit 7, the "Borrow Approach" is the simplest to define or implement, which involves borrowing data standards from vendors, other successful projects, or organizations such as the American National Standards Institute (ANSI) or International Standards Organization (ISO) that define industry standards. A more complete list of organizations that define standards is provided at the end of this article. Such standards can be used on a small number of sample projects and finetuned into a consistent set of data standards for a wider audience. A review team consisting of a Senior Sponsor (e.g., VP or CIO) and a combination of business analysts, systems analysts, and developers can then finetune the data standards and expand them for the enterprise before deploying them.

Exhibit 5.   *n*-Tier/Layers Category

Subcategory	Comments
General Naming Conventions	All variables names must be in lowercase
	Variables names should be mneumonic and reflect the contents of the variable
	Variable names should not exceed 40 characters in length
	Variable names should start with an alphabetic letter (a–z)
	The remainder of the name can be any combination of letters or digits or the symbol (_). The underscore (_) is used to separate parts of a name
	Variable names cannot contain include embedded spaces
Table Names	Maximum length is 20 characters
	Use the singular form (e.g., customer instead of customers)
	Do not use abbreviations
	Do not use restricted words
Column Names	Preface column name with first two letters of the table name
Index Names	Always contain part of the first 5 letters of the table name
	Number them sequentially starting with '_1'
Rules	Preface rule names with the table name
Views	Do not include more than 4 tables in a view
Stored Procedures	Always comment your Transact-SQL code
	Use the 'SET NOCOUNT ON' option to minimize data traffic
	Avoid the use of NULLS
	Log errors using master error file
	Stored procedure names should not exceed 30 characters in length
Triggers	Delete triggers prefaced with "dl". Insert triggers are prefaced with "in"; update triggers are prefaced with "up"
	Rollback any transactions that result in data integrity errors or which violate referential integrity
Datatypes	All tables must have a timestamp field
	Use ANSI-92 compatible datatypes only
	Minimize the storage required by variables by using the smallest datatype available (e.g., tinyint instead of int)
	Improve performance by using numerics instead of strings
	Avoid variable length strings
	Build joins on columns that share compatible datatypes
	Avoid using NULLS

Exhibit 7 also shows another approach that involves "creating" the data standards because there are no satisfactory ones to be borrowed from another source. The key for making this approach a success is to begin with a framework that is similar to the exhibits shown previously. You will probably want to modify the subcategories in the tables, or even to merge or expand the number of tables that are shown. A champion in the organization, perhaps a business analyst, should then review other projects and define a standard for each subcategory (e.g., all variable names must be prefaced with their datatype, all databases will have project names). It is unlikely

Exhibit 6. User Interface Category

Subcategory	Comments
Screens: Help Screens Menu Screens Drop Down Menus Information Screens Transaction Screens	Include field sizes, field types, field objects
Reports: Project Plans Status Reports Issue Logs	Include page headings, page footers, date, page number, column headings, total columns
Client Requests	Minimize number of SQL requests per transasction

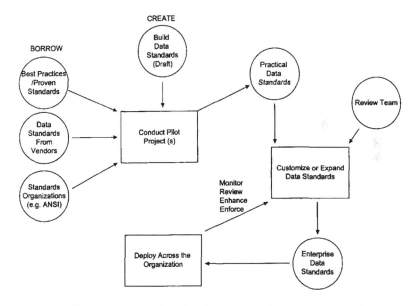

Exhibit 7. Process for defining enterprise data standards.

that this first pass will be complete. The primary challenge is to establish a standards baseline and to begin using them. As in the "borrow" approach, one or more pilot projects are used to validate and enhance the data standards. In the "create" approach, it is likely that several projects will be required to define a satisfactory set of data standards.

There is a third approach that involves combining the "borrow" and "create" approaches. In this instance, standards organizations such as ANSI or ISO can be used to provide a first cut at the data standards. These are then customized as discused in the "create" approach.

Exhibit 7 shows that after the enterprise data standards have been prepared and signed off by the corporate sponsor, the next task is wide deployment. The manner in which this is done is critical for the successful adoption of the enterprise data standards. The first step here is to ensure that the data standards are readily available electronically or on paper. The next step is to communicate the importance, location, and procedures for using the data standards by both the operations and development groups. This message must be communicated to the organization by a senior sponsor, such as a CIO or VP, in order to maximize corporate buy in.

COMMON PITFALLS AND TRAPS

There are several common pitfalls and traps that can befall an organization trying to establish enterprise data standards. One of the obvious problems springs from the "enterprise" term itself. Many organizations view the use of this term to mean "broad consensus required" or "slow adoption". This can lead to several problems, not the least of which is that the standards require too much attention and time to implement, or are too cumbersome to learn, use, or understand. Such standards are usually put aside during tight project timeframes. Too many standards can be as bad as having too few standards. The surest way of ensuring that standards are not used is to spend a lot of time defining them and publishing them in a hundred plus page manual. It is preferable to spend a few days conducting research, and then having a small team publish a single digit page document defining the suggested data standards which are then immediately passed to project teams to test and refine in actual projects.

Another common problem involves the inaccessibility of enterprise standards. To be effective, the standards must be readily accessible to project teams at any time. Furthermore, the standards should also be readily usable. They must also be easy to duplicate. A useful method of achieving these is to use a combination of deployment strategies. A central data repository (e.g., a Website or a Lotus Notes database) can hold the enterprise standards. Project teams throughout the organization should have direct and remote access to the repositories. Reusable templates and deliverables (e.g., screen images) can also be included in the repositories to provide project teams with the ability to get started on their projects quickly. Paper-based, or CD/ROM-based, delivery of the standards and templates should accompany the electronic delivery modes.

MEASURING COMPLIANCE AND ENFORCING STANDARDS

During the pressure of development projects or unexpected operational emergencies, it is not uncommon for all standards, including data standards, to be suspended until the immediate problem is resolved. In some instances, this is acceptable in the short term. However, compliance is important in the long term, and several mechanisms should be used to measure and enforce this, as follows:

- Deliverable walkthroughs. Regular sessions should be scheduled to walkthrough and sign off on project deliverables to ensure that they comply with the published enterprise data standards. DBAs should be involved in this process;
- Audit. Infrequent audits of projects across the enterprise should be used to ensure ongoing compliance with the published standards. Resources on the audit teams can vary over time. A good size for the audit team is about three resources. It is a good idea to rotate resources on and off the teams over a period of time;
- Enforcement. Examples of noncompliance should be documented and the appropriate project manager(s) should be mandated to ensure that the standards are adhered to within a specific timeframe (e.g., one month); and
- Quality plan. Every project plan should be accompanied by a quality plan that includes the activities that will be followed by the project teams to ensure compliance with the standards.

TEN TIPS FOR GETTING STARTED

Many projects have shown that the following tips greatly simplify the process of establishing enterprise-wide data standards:

1. Keep them simple;
2. Borrow, if possible, avoid creating;
3. Use samples from actual projects;
4. Make the standards readily accessible electronically;
5. Do not hesitate to modify enterprise data standards if a good argument is presented;
6. Use standards as reasonable guidelines;
7. Build early successes as showpieces;
8. Build data standard compliance right into the project plan or quality plan;
9. Never create standards in a vacuum;
10. Enforce the use of the data standards.

CONCLUSION

Enterprise data standards should be used by organizations that are building and maintaining nontrivial application systems. The key for establishing enterprise data standards is to keep them as simple as possible and to ensure that they are actually used on projects. It is recommended that standards be borrowed from third parties or vendors. Where this is not possible, it is recommended that a framework, such as the one included in this article, be used to build a first cut of the enterprise standards. These should then be validated in a few pilot projects before rolling them out to the enterprise.

LIST OF ORGANIZATIONS DEFINING STANDARDS

ISO	International Organization for Standardization (Global support)
OSF DCE	Open Software Foundation's (OSF) Distributed Computing Environment (middleware and enterprise standards)
POSIX	applications operating with OS. Deals with system calls, libraries, tools, interfaces, and testing
X/Open	European vendors and manufacturers
COSE	IBM, HP Santa Cruz Operation, Sun Microsystems, UNIX — application/OS implementations
CORBA	Object Management Group's Common Object Request Broker Architecture
IEEE	U.S. Standards body; works to get buy-in from ANSI
SQL Access Group	Call-Level Interface (CLI) and Remote Database Access (RDA)
ISOC	Internet Society. Internet standards and internetworking techniques

Chapter 5

Completeness, Context, and Proportion: Shaping Data Design to the Business

Ronald A. Wencer

THE SYSTEMS DEVELOPMENT CYCLE IS FOUNDED IN THE NOTION OF AB-
STRACTION — the practice of distilling something complex into a simplified
form that establishes better understanding, clarifies direction, and promotes sound decisions. Over the course of time, various tools have been
devised to embody such abstractions including flowcharts, structure diagrams, entity-relation diagrams, data flow diagrams, and object models.
With varying degrees of success, methodologies have devised special processes to orchestrate the proper creation of these tools, constructing over
a project's life an analytical continuum, through which front-end business
abstractions ultimately grow into database tables and objects.

Methodology standards address the integrity of this continuum — if one
follows both the spirit and the form of the rules, the results will be struc-
turally valid. Nevertheless, the end points of the analytical continuum
must be validated against the business environment. Simply stated, requirements either are understood or are not; the delivered system either
works properly or does not. Barring Kismet, information systems can be
only as good as the requirements-gathering exercises from which they flow.

OVERVIEW OF THE PROBLEM

Each of the following recent (and real-world) problems indicates a significant failure of the requirements-gathering process:

1. A retailer tries to link its product and marketing data to a powerful desktop publishing environment, hoping to effect dramatic savings in the preparation of advertising material. After months of effort and significant expenditure, the resulting database and application are rejected by the business area, which deems them fundamentally unworkable.

2. A project manager decides to defer consideration of a relatively unimportant business transaction, for which the project team has been able to garner only a weak, inconsistent understanding from various stakeholders. Subsequently, corporate management decrees that the deferred item must be accommodated. The database structure already established by the project must be revisited, and the partially built applications must be redeveloped.

3. After a brisk prototyping exercise, the pace of requirements gathering seems so slow that management fears a project will stall. To sustain momentum, it directs the project to quickly deliver an incomplete but nominally functional application, speeding delivery by simply not addressing certain requirements. As time passes, the boundaries between the in-scope and the omitted requirements blur; there is a continual retrofitting of changes to the data model (with consequent rewriting of application code). By the time a new application is deployed, it is burdened by many elements of legacy applications: obsolete or absent models, layered amendments to documentation, confused perceptions, and unrecorded changes.

4. A company with a single product line redevelops its data environment to support more flexibility in its product pricing. Two years later, the organization wants to introduce additional product lines, but the recently implemented databases and applications only support billing clients for purchases made against a single product line.

5. After years of preparation, a multimillion dollar development project enters acceptance testing. There is immediate confusion and dismay, as different business areas present vastly different views of the requirements it was to meet. Project documentation is so poor that it offers no useful guidance. The physical data models bear no discernible relationship to the logical models used in earlier project phases. Eventually, the project is reorganized, a new requirements set is gathered and accepted, and the application is retrofitted to meet the changed requirements. Already late, project implementation is delayed by another year.

6. Comparable situations long have been known in the information systems world, but when they occur today, they are subject to more intense scrutiny. As the synergy of technologies yields more automatically generated and more reliable system components, management becomes more aware that any surprises at the end of the day

stem from a flawed understanding of requirements. Those who have identified requirements may be asked the obvious question:

If systems are built by professionals who talk with the people who make the decisions that direct business, why should requirements ever be overlooked or misunderstood? What happened to the value added by data analysis and modeling?

To answer all facets of this question would be difficult. The problems encountered while identifying requirements touch upon the fundamental dynamics of corporate structure. Given that corporations respond to the complexity that permeates their markets and society at large, these dynamics are generally too complex to examine exhaustively. As a matter of practicality, it instead may be sufficient to focus on several key aspects of the requirements-gathering process, beginning with some nuances of the assumptions that underlie the question posed above:

- Systems professionals have skills and experiences that are relevant to gathering complex business requirements in almost any situation.
- Key business stakeholders understand the process of gathering requirements, understand the role and commitments it imposes upon them, and understand the products they are asked to approve.
- As requirements are identified, decision makers and systems professionals exchange information directly and effectively.

Obviously, to the extent that corporate culture tends to conform to these assumptions, fewer obstacles need to be surmounted. No organization would willingly ignore these considerations, although anomalies occasionally do arise. For example, due to an inadequate screening process, poorly qualified resources may be hired, or their expertise may be misunderstood, so that they eventually are placed inappropriately. When such blatant problems exist, however, they tend to cause immediate, visible damage that cannot be ignored, typically prompting management to resolve them quickly.

Of greater concern here are the more subtle difficulties that can occur even in the best corporate environments. These are often pernicious, as they may long go unnoticed — or at least unreported — although they undermine success, as in the cases cited above. It is incumbent upon all concerned to be wary. Although these various difficulties often overlap, for purposes of this chapter they have been grouped into several broad areas of concern.

- Preparedness
- Completeness and proportion
- Context and change
- Anomalies in the continuum
- Prototyping's impacts

The following sections outline the risks inherent in each of these areas and offer suggestions for avoiding or limiting that risk.

PREPAREDNESS

Most business units are not practiced clients of systems development efforts. For many stakeholders, active participation in a significant systems project occurs only once in a career. Even if they have some nominally relevant experience, the novelty introduced by ever-new methodology, tools, and/or technology effectively renders each project a first-time involvement for business participants. Only exceptionally insightful stakeholders can anticipate all the business implications of the difficult systems decisions they must make. Even where the implications are understood, they may be grasped in operational terms that business owners cannot reliably correlate to arcane concepts such as entities, relationships, and keys.

Systems professionals also encounter first-time phenomena in most projects. Today's lean but diversified corporate world seeks to tighten narrowly project scope, targeting quick, focused, and certain payback. On successive projects, an analyst may deal in turn with, for example, Accounts Receivable, Inventory Control, Employee Benefits, and Manufacturing, in each case working with different business policies, different decision makers with different personal styles, different jargon, and different unstated business assumptions.

Thus, in a very real sense every project team begins as an untried novice, much as a new professional sports franchise enters its first season with a mixed team of veterans and rookies who never before have played as a unit. In both cases, early performance is largely unpredictable and the team's eventual success depends upon finding an effective combination of proper management, good training, and coaching principles. For purposes of gathering business requirements, a fundamentally sound combination usually involves the methodical application of standard techniques and steps, which yield prescribed standard deliverables.

Preparation for all team members is a necessity. Although many systems people are trained formally to participate in analytical activities, business people rarely are. Too often they are expected to contribute on demand, without formal preparation. When faced with a data model for the first time, regardless of the notation used, business stakeholders only can believe it means what they are told it means — not a happy situation. Although used only rarely, training and reference materials for preparing business owners for systems-related roles and responsibilities do exist and taking advantage of these resources is an excellent first step.

Once a project is in flight, however, even stakeholders who have received special training will have difficulty simultaneously grappling with abstract concepts (e.g., models) and dealing with the very tactile demands of the business in which they are immersed daily. It is advisable — although rarely feasible — to secure dedicated stakeholder participation throughout the requirements-gathering phase of a project.

It may be possible to mitigate this problem by establishing a special project role, which is intended to lever business stakeholders' input. Essentially, the idea is to prepare a team member, generally someone who already has a solid systems-oriented background in gathering requirements and front-end data analysis, to complement and shepherd the input provided by business-area participants. Note that this person is neither a business advocate nor a surrogate user; rather than adopting either a systems or business unit outlook, the role calls for always maintaining a corporate perspective.

Prior to the start of the formal requirements definition, this person undergoes an intense familiarization with the business area in question. As requirements definition unfolds, the resource's mandate is

- To ensure that all relevant parts of the business receive adequate consideration.
- At appropriate points, to deliberately navigate discussion into, and successfully through, difficult areas that the team might otherwise seek to avoid.
- To probe tactfully the statements of business participants, allowing stakeholders to test their own conclusions.
- To foresee the global implications of local decisions.
- To make sure that stakeholders and systems participants all share a common understanding of the team's work and of the decisions that are reached, especially with respect to data considerations (business area participants often can relate more quickly and effectively to process-oriented notations).
- To feedback to project leadership objective assessments of the quality of the effort, highlighting areas of success and concern, so that techniques can be tailored to the team's constituency.

Candidates for such a role will vary according to organizational setting. Whether they are corporate or consultants, they should be working team members, familiar with an organization's overall direction, and committed to the requirements-gathering process.

It sometimes may be acceptable to merge this role with the traditional role of a facilitator, but doing so is not always advisable. If a culture views them primarily as rules-keepers and pace-setters, there will be little opportunity for facilitators to forge the trust-based alliance with business that makes this role work. Indeed, it may be advantageous to conceal this mandate, so that stakeholders watch the role emerge from the natural dynamics of the team, gradually appreciating this resource's value, and buying into the whole process with greater commitment.

COMPLETENESS AND PROPORTION

Overall, the requirements-gathering process may not seem exciting. Systems professionals may find more appeal in conceptual analysis or in design activities, and business professionals may prefer their respective operational or executive worlds. The prospect of thoroughly defining requirements is even less attractive, as it suggests painfully dull diligence. Unfortunately, there is some accuracy in this perception; the work must be done carefully and completely.

There is, then, always a risk that participants in the process will allocate their time and attention disproportionately:

- They may limit their attention only to things that seem important. This is a serious error, for "important" is a subjective term. As was noted in the Introduction, retrofitting a supposedly inconsequential business requirement into later analysis may be arduous from a database or application perspective.
- Participants may opt to defer real consideration of a poorly-understood area of the business, feeling confident after superficial discussion that details can be resolved later. At a distance, such a decision may seem incomprehensible. If something is too hard to grasp from the high-altitude perspective of requirements investigation, postponing its consideration to more detailed project phases only will introduce artificial constraints; it will not make the investigation any easier. Deciding to ignore it completely is even worse. An elegant study that addresses the simplest 80% of a knotty problem serves little purpose. Remarkably, such decisions seem pragmatic to people struggling under normal project pressures.
- All too often, investigations are influenced by the very human tendency to plunge into great detail where something is labeled "important" or appears to be challenging (or is merely unusual, or at least more interesting than other things), so that teams may find themselves skimming over items that do not seem to warrant immediate attention. When defining requirements, yielding to this temptation leads to a biased view of business, in which the various elements assume disproportionate magnitude and importance. Perhaps this sort of thinking explains one corporate data model, in which employee gender was identified as an entity — one wonders what the attributes might have been.

The concept of treating all requirements objectively, so that a project's documented deliverables reveal a uniform depth of understanding, is a

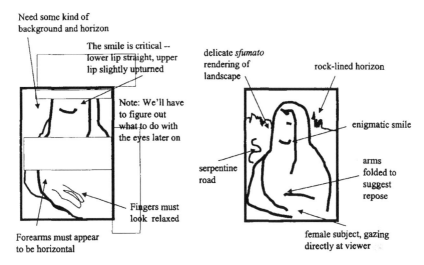

Incomplete, Unbalanced Requirements   **Better Requirements**

Exhibit 1.   Dealing with too much too soon.

guideline common to many well-established methodologies. Despite its value, however, this guideline is respected only infrequently.

Most people intuitively comprehend the risks of gathering and digesting too little information. But there is also a risk in trying to deal with too much too soon, especially if it leads a project to focus only on fragments of the overall problem and to make inadvertent and premature decisions. Exhibit 1 illustrates this risk, in the context of Leonardo da Vinci's well-known *Mona Lisa*. Imagine the artist is concentrating on his subject's smile and on the repose suggested by the positioning of her arms, then going on to paint these in detail, only to discover afterward that he has left no room in the canvas for her forehead. Instead, Leonardo's requirements definition (regardless of whether he documented it or not) must have been closer in concept to the right half of this example.

A close parallel exists in business. Like the artist's canvas, the resources available to a requirements definition effort are finite. Consuming them disproportionately in one or two neighborhoods of concern diminishes the resources that can be devoted to other areas. It also introduces more review cycles and overcomplicates them, and it tends to skew the project's overall findings. Moreover, it does not add true value in the long run; later analysis phases, which are intended to benefit from progressively deeper appreciations of context, will in any event re-examine the same detail.

CONTEXT AND CHANGE

Requirements must be understood as part of a greater whole. Looking some distance beyond a project's nominal boundaries is valuable for several reasons.

- In the long run, most people only understand scope fully when they feel they know both what it includes and what it excludes.
- Boundaries can be contoured properly only if there is a coherent understanding of what lies along both sides of the demarcation.
- The impacts of strategies, markets, and other forces upon specific business areas are localized symptoms of broader conditions, and these factors must be accommodated coherently throughout an organization.
- Provisional local decisions must be tested by seeing what global results they are likely to effect.
- Significant change on the horizon may be detected earlier.
- One reliably cannot evaluate priorities out of context.
- A more generalized awareness makes it easier to free one's understanding from the knowledge of what is, and to instead start conceiving what ought to be.

As noted in Exhibit 2, it is vital for participants to appreciate that the scope of a systems project initially should be fairly broad; it then can be narrowed as work progresses toward implementation. The business stands on safer ground if what ultimately is built fits within a broader valid design, if what is designed fits into a broader valid analytical context, and if what is analyzed fits into a still larger coherent view of business requirements.

Consider some of the cases cited in the Introduction. Clearly, the team charged with enabling greater flexibility in product pricing was at fault — no team member could have looked very far beyond its prescribed scope without discovering the corporate groundwork for creating new product lines. Instead of dealing with this coming change in its data analysis, which would have added no substantial burden to its effort, the team either somehow remained oblivious to what the business was doing or chose to be derelict; whatever the cause, the outcome was unfortunate.

The two teams that were directed first to ignore, but ultimately to address, certain areas of requirements were obviously victims of poor management decisions, most likely decisions made according to incomplete (i.e., excessively localized) reconnaissance. Note that this problem in fact may have originated in the way the team gathered its information, and the sources that it used. To perfectlyaccommodate imprecisely known future

Exhibit 2.   Confirming/Refining Project Scope

Project Phase and Purpose	Risks/Required Action
Initiation	
Scope is set to plan and establish resources for the overall project, based upon project's business objectives.	Scope as set by corporate decision makers may not recognize data or application boundaries properly. Team must map project's objectives to the corporate information context.
	Unexplored relationships with other projects may promote overlaps, inconsistencies, and accidental gaps. Team must inventory the information resources (existing, in-progress, and those still only planned) that touch its objectives in any way.
Requirements Definition	
Scope for analysis phase is confirmed or refined at a data subject level, using the inventory of relevant information resources it has created.	Other projects geared to other objectives may be working with an incompatible understanding of data. Team must review other projects' logical data models at a high level, deriving logical models from physical models if necessary.
Analysis	
Scope for design phase is confirmed or refined at an entity/relationship level, working from internal requirements and external logical models.	Other projects geared to other objectives may work to different business rules, leading to different understandings of entities and relationships. Business constraints may have led other projects to stop short of, or to cross, natural scope boundaries. Team must conduct a detailed review of the boundaries of other relevant projects.
Design	
Scope for build phase is confirmed or refined at a physical model level, working from findings of detailed analysis.	De-normalized physical models used for other projects may not fit the new, expanded corporate context. Team must recognize conflicts, bring them to management attention, and recommend which project(s) can best address them.
	Past reliance on local standards or diverse technologies may not permit graceful integration of other projects with the new data analysis. Team must address any conflicts with existing corporate data and technical architectures.
Build	
Delivery consideration may result in temporal phasing of project; scope for each phase must be defined.	Phasing cannot be arbitrary nor can it generally be determined only with respect to resourcing constraints. Business dependencies and external constraints also must be recognized. Team must devise a viable migration plan that bridges multiple subprojects as necessary.

requirements in a logical data model would be impossible. On the other hand, to exclude them to the extent that the logical data models needed extensive change was probably a situation that could have been avoided readily.

For requirements gathering to begin with a broad investigation, it needs suitable sources of information. If an organization has made a commitment to an overall strategic plan, the context in which to gather requirements is evident, but comprehensively planned business environments are scarce. In many business cultures, formal strategic plans will be incomplete, obsolete, untrusted, or totally lacking. Other sources of strategic direction may be available in the absence of formal plans, such as executive interviews, internal announcements, and marketing communications. If all else fails, one can step back and determine the de facto priorities of various projects and business areas, noting which groups are given the largest budgets, which seem to attract the brightest managers and the most skilled staff, and which teams are the largest.

No matter what sources the team uses to sketch its context, it will be better-equipped for doing so, having learned (or deduced) how other business areas affect its primary area of concern, how that area is likely to be impacted by new corporate initiatives, and how important its internal priorities really are.

One caveat remains: the gathering of requirements may be polluted by political agenda. Managers may compete more than they cooperate; communication to the project team may be withheld, may not be frank, and occasionally may be deliberately inaccurate. Stated corporate policy may be only paid lip-service by local business units, which choose to deviate from overall corporate direction, perhaps actually hindering some aspects of the business' operation in which they have no direct concern.

Ideally, political problems have political solutions. When they are brought to the attention of a project sponsor, some course of action can be found outside the team's activity that either eliminates the difficulty or clarifies the corporation's expectations of the team. In reality, satisfactorily addressing all facets of some political issues may not be always feasible, leaving the team with difficult issues that strain its creativity. If severe problems continue unresolved, the most viable recourse available to the team remains the project sponsor. In some cultures, additional support can be found among the team members' line management, but political sensitivities often make the enlistment of such people difficult.

ANOMALIES IN THE CONTINUUM

When systems and business people discuss requirements, they begin the modeling exercise that ought to forge a continuous chain of understanding that will be extended through later project phases. Despite the rigors of sound practice and the use of standard documentation forms, miscommunication may occur, especially where key participants fail to understand project documents. For example, many systems professionals have seen business owners accept incomprehensible entity-relationship diagrams (even when labels either are so abbreviated or are so small that they are functionally illegible, and when intersecting relationship lines are impossible to trace reliably). Such well-intended but meaningless approval, proffered to allow work to pass officially into a new phase, threatens a project's future by disrupting the continuum of business understanding.

One source of miscommunication is team members' confusing correct form with meaning, most notably with regard to industry-standard modeling forms, some of which may be seen for the first time by a given participant during requirements gathering. Although these forms were developed expressly to establish a standard, unambiguous modeling vocabulary, this vocabulary usually is not mastered quickly by first-time business participants; some systems participants may be no better. Where team resources are not experts, their critical judgment may be impeded by the very formalism that was supposed to assist them. To their eyes, if a diagram contains all the right elements and if it is presented for approval by someone who probably understands it far better than the nominal acceptors, it certainly looks very good — especially if it is printed with a handsome font, using a high-resolution laser printer. If it looks like a data model, it must be one.

A good analogy (Exhibit 3) might be the toy set designed to allow children to construct things from log-shaped blocks — regardless of whether the pieces are assembled to match the proportions of a skyscraper or a shoebox, the child always sees the end-products as log cabins.

One absurd case highlights the risk of such shallow comprehension. When budget cuts sharply reduced funding for systems work, a project director asked his staff to shrink the project's scope with scissors, asking them to cut segments from printouts of different business-area models, which he hoped they would tape together into a coherent new model. (This idea was afterward celebrated as the Frankenstein methodology.)

Such profound lack of understanding on the part of acceptors breeds an overall carelessness in a team's work. Front-end deliverables, including data models, may be assembled only mechanically and without insight, so that models are not underpinned by substantial definitions that ring true to business owners. Basic guidelines, or even integrity rules, may be ignored. A particular area of risk originates with the convenient (but somewhat artificial) division that is made between process and data. Ultimately, neither makes sense without the other, and models should respect their inherent interdependency. In practice, however, some projects exhibit a strong separation between concerns of data and process, attempting to

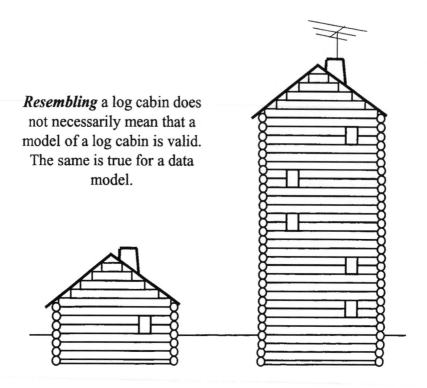

Resembling a log cabin does not necessarily mean that a model of a log cabin is valid. The same is true for a data model.

Exhibit 3. Resemblance vs. actuality.

deal with each in isolation during separate sessions. In the past, at least one corporation adopted a methodology that had rigorous standards for process and data modeling, yet its systems area established two discon-nected, separately managed CASE environments — one for modeling data, the other for modeling process. With such an outlook, the risk of miscom-munication is high.

Communication risks can be minimized through simple diligence. All models should be accompanied by solid definitions (i.e., something of more value than Client: information about the company's clients). The con-sistency of a project's approach to understanding process and data must be validated at designated intervals. Note that some methodologies em-ploy special model forms to depict the manner in which data and process interact.

Evaluating participants' abilities to see past a data model's formalism entails tact and sensitivity (strangely, most dislike being informed publicly of not knowing what one is doing). By and large, modeling failures can be detected by planned off-line quality reviews, devised to target modeling violations and anomalies (e.g., recursive decompositions, inconsistencies between data and process models, etc.). If problems are detected, they can be brought back openly to the project team, which as a body should be prepared to take responsibility for the quality of its work.

PROTOTYPING'S IMPACTS

Many organizations rely on prototyping as part of the discovery process, assembling a combined business/systems team that rapidly evolves a skeletal application. As it provides an excellent forum for creative thinking, a prototyping methodology has undeniable advantages. It moves quickly, and its rapid pace usually motivates the team and promotes management buy-in. It effectively can avoid some problems by concealing abstract data-modeling concerns, letting business people deal directly with screens and tables, setting data issues in a merged process/data context that supports good business validation.

One also must recognize its limitations, however. Limitations are inclined to linger over all possible cases. Seeking to maintain momentum, a prototyping effort may choose to leap over phenomena that cannot be treated effectively in a hands-on-the-keyboard setting. Its emphasis on creativity encourages a freedom from discipline; consequently, discovery prototyping is not concerned inherently with completeness. Although it can be made to work in broad contexts, it is adapted more readily to a scale in which a diverse group quickly can grasp the nature of problems and solutions.

Real-world systems must be defined so that they can deal in an acceptable fashion with the eventualities (data types, transactions, cases, etc.) that are possible within their contexts. If a prototyping exercise does not address all such eventualities, and if it does not define what course of action is acceptable for each, then it must be followed by a more structured (and more laborious) dialogue, which cannot afford to jettison concerns that are difficult to apprehend. The purpose of this dialogue is to test the prototyping results against more formal high-level models and to expand its concepts so that they fill the sphere of concern, encompassing all requirements at a consistent level.

Depending on team dynamics, the models can be drafted as a group by business and systems team members, or they can be prepared offline by specialists and then subjected to careful group review. Again, the prime consideration is one of completeness and balance. It is a mistake to employ prototyping to discover the majority of business requirements, but then merely to trust to the fates that the remainder will be identified without a determined effort.

One also must realize that prototyping demands a specialized skill set, which does not coincide fully with the skill-set that is needed for other methods of requirements gathering. A given team member may not function equally well, or be equally amenable to, all flavors of a requirements dialogue.

Pace is a major consideration. A prototyping team does not grind away tediously; instead, it leaps toward solutions. It needs members who quickly can reach communal decisions that are fundamentally sound. They must be able to voice opinions without fear. They must be objective, dropping yesterday's decisions willingly when superior alternatives are suggested today. Team members must be able to link incompletely articulated concepts to the concrete things that they see, following principles almost intuitively: good prototyping analysts simultaneously think in terms of undefined entities and n-normal forms.

These strengths differ markedly from the contemplative, patient skills of those analysts who sift through business procedures and forms, conduct interviews chiefly by listening critically, and then embody abstracted concepts in the formal models they construct. Such abilities can bring judgement to bear on the outcome of prototyping, validating, and amplifying its results, but they may not be able to add value in the heat of the prototyping process itself. Nonprototyping analysts may need the time to frame definitions and to identify fundamental relationships before they even begin to think of keys. Indeed, subjected to the pressure of a swift pace, their judgement, which normally is based on critical reflection, may so decay as to become a liability.

Not surprisingly, the team dynamics of prototyping are also distinctive. Traditional, nonprototyping settings for gathering requirements are inhibited more easily by cultural divisions (distinctions of rank and differences between the immediate objectives of systems and business units). Such divisions often are rendered meaningless by prototyping's intensity, but analysts who work in traditional settings must deal with them. In contrast, the prototyping dynamic is highly democratic. Ideally, it excludes gurus in favor of peers, who are at ease operating on an even plane.

Thus, placed in a traditional setting (e.g., one in which rank matters), an otherwise experienced prototyping analyst may have difficulty establishing effective give-and-take communication. Conversely, a skilled back-room analyst, who has demonstrated insight in traditional settings, may flounder in prototyping's snap-judgement climate, at a loss without sufficient opportunity to probe more deeply what is being proposed.

Rather than focusing at a true requirements level, a prototyping team's working dialogue is framed in a postanalytical perspective. Once the process is underway, instead of actually defining what is (or is not) needed, people think "We need something like this" or "I don't like the way that works" or "Yes, something like that should handle most of the situations we run into." The intention is primarily to affirm or reject, and only secondarily to state reasons. Reasons are to be digested and evaluated later, at which time one can evaluate the true meaning of the quick decisions reached at the prototyping table.

The basic prototyping dialogue, then, inverts the traditional analytical approach, in which products drafted through off-line analysis are understood, validated, and synthesized by a group. Instead, prototyping first uses group thinking to create products, which subsequently are validated and refined off line.

In the end, with business and systems people alike proposing quasi-system solutions to business problems, prototyping environments may lead to a corporate undervaluing of skills for listening, for reflective synthesis, and for integrating ideas into a larger context — the same skills that are vital to postprototyping information gathering. If a climate relies heavily on prototyping, the in-house experience of its systems professionals may not prepare them adequately to gather and synthesize requirements through nonprototyping activities.

Obviously, when a team is being assembled, the respective experience, abilities, and personal preparation of the candidate members should be reviewed in the context of both prototyping and traditional activities. If adjustments are indicated, they can be achieved through:

- Additional training for individual resources.
- Changes to the team roster.
- Use of consistent methodology from one project to the next.
- Taking the time to properly orient the team as a whole at the project's outset.
- Setting an appropriate project schedule that respects the team's strengths.

CONCLUSION

It is vital that people working together to define business requirements share a clear understanding of the task at hand. Paradoxically, the widespread use of now-standard tools and techniques that address this issue may open a new door to old problems, for businesses may rely on unverified expertise and shallow understanding where there is only the appearance of sound practice. When this occurs, the problems of the past are found reincarnated in today's world, compromising results, undermining the value of data analysis, and perhaps leading to outright failure.

Every project is a new start, and its team is entitled to proper training and management, so that business requirements are collected in context, completely, and with proper regard to coming change.

As in any endeavor, there will be strong business pressures to move too quickly and to stray from the mark. From time to time, projects will be urged to form too narrow a focus, and to heed only the hot buttons of the day. If this happens, the team must still act responsibly, devising a logical data model that later can conform to predictable requirements with minimal business impact.

Regardless of the pressures under which it labors, it is incumbent upon the project team to remain disciplined, to construct a balanced and objective analytical view, and to make itself understood to its management, so that the risk of poor decisions is minimal. The team's sponsor, its fellow employees, the business overall, and the team itself deserve as much.

Chapter 6

An Enterprise Decision Framework for Information System Selection

Richard Lee

THERE HAS BEEN A GREAT DEAL OF TIME AND EFFORT on the part of enterprise resource planning (ERP) package vendors and system integrators (SI) to develop methodologies toward implementation of package solutions. However, there has been little attention to detail prior to implementation of enterprise application packages. There are key considerations that must be resolved prior to implementation to ensure project success.

All business procedures in an enterprise must be viewed from the market perspective and optimized throughout all functional areas. To meet the challenges facing large enterprises in today's constantly changing market, enterprises need an effective system for all lines of business. Seldom does an enterprise have the opportunity to implement a corporate-wide integration strategy; particularly relating competitive systems to corporate systems. Enterprises typically make uniform decisions within a functional area such as corporate financial systems, and migrate to a standard solution for all functional areas, provided that the benefits of dealing with one vendor/one solution outweighs any loss in functionality. In today's market, enterprises tend to have a mixed bag of custom solutions and different application packages.

Package solutions are being chosen in favor of custom development in business areas such as manufacturing, financials, human resources, and customer service. Enterprises are looking for complete and integrated solutions from one vendor. In addition, enterprises have identified that linking business (e.g., financial) systems with an overall organizational system simplifies and accelerates tasks, improves the flow of information, and facilitates scheduling and planning decisions based on consistent data.

Data consistency and quality at the strategic level are increasingly important for enterprises that want to remain flexible to meet the changes in the marketplace. To develop a sound enterprise strategy, the data associated with business processes, customers, competitors, and technologies must be relevant, complete, accurate, and timely. In addition, as an enterprise strategy is rolled out, results are tabulated and modified, when specific plans are initiated. The reported results must be accurate and timely, otherwise, execution of the strategy becomes much more difficult.

Many enterprises are recognizing the importance of developing an effective enterprise data strategy with their enterprise information system strategy. Enterprises are interested in systems that offer more sophisticated capabilities, with tighter integration of key business areas, i.e., supply-chain and sales-force automation. ERP vendors recognize this and now are providing data warehousing capabilities to their software tools. ERP vendors are striving to achieve even tighter integration with data mining and data warehousing capabilities. Enterprises are looking for their new technological solutions to provide them with the ability to stay ahead of their competitors. Vendors have begun offering free extraction and data analysis tools to companies purchasing data warehouses.

Enterprises are setting directional standards for the entire organization that reflects the benefit of dealing with one vendor. With the current functional support offered by many packages, enterprises are adopting one vendor, integrated solutions for corporate systems (e.g., financials, human resources, etc.). For other functional areas, enterprises consider the benefit of dealing with one integrated solution versus the cost of missing functionality.

Application package vendors are expanding and enhancing their solutions to address more functional breadth and depth. As a result, industry vertical solutions are emerging for the large enterprise packages (e.g., SAP, Peoplesoft, Baan and Oracle). In the near future, it will be much easier for enterprises to follow one standard for the entire organization.

DECISION FRAMEWORK

An enterprise-wide strategy provides an organization with a more process-oriented, streamlined information system. Consequently, this allows an enterprise to expand its internal information-processing and communications capabilities. The framework in Exhibit 1 describes the typical decision tree used by management when evaluating large system replacements and deciding on a future direction.

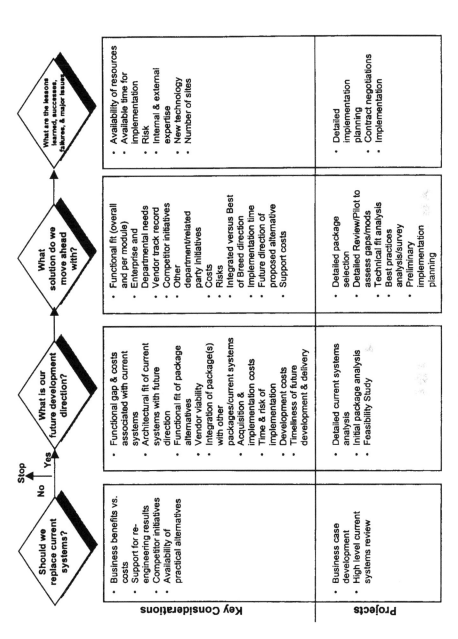

Exhibit 1. Enterprise decision framework.

Should Current Systems be Replaced?

There are a number of key considerations facing enterprises when deciding whether to replace their current systems. Is there a significant business benefit implementing a new system? Is the new system going to support the reengineering projects completed, in-progress, or in the future? Are there significant business and technology issues and problems facing the enterprise today?

Consider the Cost Savings. A typical driving factor behind the selection of an enterprise-wide solution is the cost savings associated with the reduction of redundant manual tasks. Enterprises that utilize integrated, or best-of-breed solutions are reducing manual tasks significantly and reducing the cost of operation and maintenance.

There are a number of other factors that enterprises consider when selecting an enterprise solution. These include resource allocation, resource requirements, application development costs, and payback period. Enterprises have significant reduction in resources when making the transition to the new systems environment. Enterprises that decide to implement a new system require support from cross-functional areas. The number of people required to implement a new application varies widely depending on the organization's needs. The number of full-time equivalents (FTEs) who participate in a migration to the new application can range from as little as six people on a local site basis to over 100 on a worldwide scale. The typical allocation of resources is 25 to 50% information services (IS), 25 to 50% business, 25 to 50% end users.

Furthermore, enterprises that migrate away from their current environment to an integrated environment realize significant reduction in their application development costs. Many enterprises achieve a 25 to 65% reduction in development of software and systems, and end-user computing costs. Regardless of the total cost of the migration, many enterprises achieve a payback period of no more than three years.

Will the New System Support the Re-Engineering Effort. Deciding to replace systems is a major decision in large enterprises. Enterprises spend in the range of $20 to 80 million on the migration project. In almost all cases, enterprises indicate that it is not technology that drives the decision to implement an enterprise-integrated approach. Rather it is the change in which many of the enterprises were conducting the way they did business. In other words, the change is important to support the re-engineered business.

Re-engineering and enterprise application implementation should occur simultaneously for the organization to maximize the value from the implementation. Many enterprises are focused on technology-enabled re-engineering. In these types of projects, re-engineering processes constantly are conformed to how enterprise application packages add value and the ability to be implemented. In most situations, the business case to replace individual lines of business (LOB) systems is a component of an overall business case to re-engineer the organization. Most enterprises transform their existing stove-pipe systems to process-centric organizations.

Other factors that are equally important in the decision to migrate to a new environment include the elimination of redundant tasks, reduction of duplicate information and reconciliation tasks, overall new technology strategy, and removal of departmental functions.

Identifying the Need for Information Access. Another key consideration for many enterprises in deciding whether to replace their current systems is their difficulty in accessing their operational data. Many enterprises never capitalize on the wealth of data amid the maze of multiple legacy systems, due to poor data integrity and quality. Many enterprises replace their existing legacy systems because they do not provide easy access to information. Enterprises are moving away from isolated systems to systems that can share data across different business units and geographic regions.

As the trend toward globalization becomes more important for enterprises, it is imperative that enterprises develop a strong integration between their disparate businesses. Many enterprises have been developing a data warehouse internally or purchasing a third-party data warehouse. Enterprises are aware that it is critical to their global business to develop a sound data warehouse. Everything from sales information to business performance data and manufacturing data can be stored into the data warehouse. Depending on the organization's needs, the data can be accessed and refreshed at any time.

Utilizing the Benefits from Technology. Although technology is not the driving factor in most enterprises' decision to implement a best-of-breed or an integrated solution, it is one of the major considerations. In the past, enterprises had prolonged their existing systems until mature client/server products were available. Only during the past few years has there been any significant consideration by enterprises to utilize client/server technology on a large scale. An increased focus by enterprises during the last few years to purchase off-the shelf client/server packages is a factor in the selection of an enterprise-wide solution.

Many enterprises are interested in taking advantage of the benefits of their client/server architecture. Some of these enterprises are looking to change the way they do business to reap the benefits of client/server applications. An important factor for making the transition to an integrated package is to exploit the client/server capabilities. The graphical user interfaces and distributed computing resources offer benefits and functional capabilities that are not available with the existing legacy systems (e.g., same look and feel across the organization).

Another reason to transition to an integrated package is the potential for tight integration between the vendor's package solution and its data warehouse capabilities. Some enterprises indicate that they would prefer to have a wait-and-see attitude toward standardizing on one vendor's solution.

Another technology consideration for enterprises has been the recent interest in data mining. Data mining has been described as an application that provides sophisticated data search capabilities. Data mining provides the ability for end users to discover trends and correlations in data. Data mining has become very popular in many smaller and medium-sized organizations as the real business value of opening the data warehouse to new users becomes clear, but most projects are fairly modest. The drawback for data mining is that many enterprises do not support the data they need to support data mining or that the enterprises do not clean their legacy data for warehousing.

What Is Our Future Development Direction?

The design of a future development direction can create debates within many enterprises. Enterprises identify the advantages and disadvantages of a packaged solution versus a custom-built solution; and most agree that migration toward a package off-the-shelf solution is essential for their business.

Focus on Core Business Processes. Enterprises realize that developing systems requires valuable time and resources. Antiquated legacy-based systems are not flexible enough to support their business functions. Vendor-bought packages are more than adequate to support their business needs. These enterprises recognize that building applications and systems is not their core business. Purchasing off-the-shelf solutions enables enterprises to focus on their core business processes.

Migrate Toward a Client/Server Based Environment. Enterprises are moving away from legacy-based systems and onto client/server-based architectures. The operational support costs and capital costs are typically two factors that influence an enterprise's future development direction. Enterprises indicate that the operational support costs for the new client/server-based environment are either the same or slightly higher than a legacy-based environment. Operational support costs include ongoing application maintenance and database administration. However, the benefits with using a client/server-based environment far outweigh the costs. Additionally, many enterprises do not monitor closely the capital spent during the migration to a new environment. Of those that do, enterprises estimate their total capital costs for the entire migration project to be from three to ten million dollars.

Alignment with Technology and Data Direction. In many cases, enterprises have implemented or are implementing data warehouses or data marts. The data warehouse strategy must align with the overall data architecture and the ERP package. Enterprises are examining the ERP vendor's competence in the areas of reporting, analysis, and internal data warehousing structure. Enterprises now are asking enterprise application vendors to have a data warehouse integration strategy. To maximize the capabilities of the new environment, a data warehouse must be integrated tightly with an enterprise package. The benefits of this tight integration allow enterprises to pull together information that is isolated on ERP systems at an organization's distant business units.

Enterprise Database Integration. Enterprises support many different database management systems (DBMS), in multiple business areas. Ideally, enterprises are striving to achieve a single enterprise DBMS standard. Realistically, most enterprises are supporting multiple legacy and new databases, due to business requirements. Consequently, enterprises are striving to simplify their DBMS environment by reducing the number of products they support, rather than trying to set a single enterprise DBMS standard.

Before selecting data integration technologies, an organization should map out its current and future data environment/topology. This will provide the enterprise with the location of key corporate data and user performance requirements for each DBMS. As a result of documenting the enterprise data landscape, a sound data integration architecture and data strategy can be completed.

Data Conversion Strategy. Enterprises develop data conversion strategies to understand some of the challenges and differences in technology between legacy systems and integrated enterprise systems when converting data.

Many enterprises have old legacy systems based on a database design and system design that have characteristics including system operations that are primarily hard-coded, data integrity that is difficult to maintain, high data redundancy, and low data integration. As well, legacy data usually does not come from just one system. It can come from many sources not all under one business area's control.

Conversion to the new enterprise application is a very complex activity that requires significant time and resources. The conversion approach is designed to populate the new system with data form the existing system so that there is continuity and accuracy of information between the old and new systems. A successful conversion will address the following aspects: data specification, conversion strategy, data mapping refinement, data purification, historical data strategy, conversion methods and plans, conversion program development, conversion testing, review and refinement, conversion for production, and postconversion data cleanup.

There are a number of factors that impact the conversion effort from a legacy to an integrated enterprise system. These include:

- Technical resources being familiar with the existing system, its database and coding structure.
- Data and code mining to ensure that specific codes and tables can be populated accurately in the new system.
- Data purification to ensure data integrity is maintained.
- Data mapping to identify any gaps between the source systems' data structures and the target system's data structure.

There are many options for data migration. Choosing which options depends on how much effort an enterprise is willing to put into data migration, as well as what type of programming expertise is available in-house. Possible solutions for getting legacy data over to the new system include manual loading of data into the new system; writing programs/codes to extract and load data; utilizing target system vendors' integration solutions for specific application areas (CAD, MRP, data management, etc.); and using computer-aided software engineering (CASE) tools that will handle one or more data source for mapping from legacy systems to current systems.

What Solution Should Be Implemented?

Enterprises cite advantages and disadvantages with choosing an integrated system from one vendor versus best-of-breed. Using a single integrated system from one vendor does provide a common architecture and lower support costs. However, upgrades tend to be more complex because they require everything to be done at once.

Many enterprises implement an integrated solution over a best-of-breed solution for their business systems. Users identify that the only suitable environment that can satisfy all their business requirements is an integrated solution.

Integrated Solution. Only in very rare situations does an enterprise get an opportunity to implement a corporate-wide strategy. In most cases, the strategy to implement a new system is focused on a divisionalized basis. Specific package solutions usually are dictated by the decisions other divisions have made within the enterprise. For example, the financial systems are chosen from the same vendor as a result of the system being utilized in their manufacturing and distribution units.

Enterprises that make the decision to go forward with an integrated approach indicate many reasons for this decision:

- Potential complexities in interfacing the applications for different business groups.
- Achieving substantial cost savings through reduction of redundant efforts and simplification of systems maintenance.
- Avoiding support by multiple vendors.
- Maximizing ability to provide end users with online, and real-time access to data and information.

Another common characteristic among certain world-class enterprises is the development of a new technology strategy. In an integrated business environment, these enterprises identify that functional areas such as general ledger, accounts payable, accounts receivable, and fixed assets, need to share the same relational database, user interface, and reporting tools.

Enterprises identify that a reduction of duplicated information among business units results in overall cost savings to the organization. Enterprises generally agree that an integrated package is better suited to solving this type of situation than a best-of-breed solution.

Prior to migrating to a new environment, it is important for an enterprise to conduct a preliminary analysis of the available packages to support their business needs. For enterprises that undergo these types of activities and projects, the preliminary analysis is not extensive. Enterprises generally identify fairly quickly that an integrated environment is the most appropriate direction for the entire organization.

Best of Breed Solution. Some enterprises initially decide on a best-of-breed environment. But upon a return investigation of their business needs, the solution tends to favor an integrated approach. Many enterprises indicate that the best-of-breed solution does not provide adequate accessibility to common data throughout the entire organization. There are additional interfaces that have to be developed between organizational business units for best-of-breed packages. Additionally, best-of-breed solutions tend to be more expensive than a single vendor integrated solution because they often have higher per seat licenses than that of larger suite vendors, and usually require more than one integrator.

What Are the Lessons Learned, Successes, Failures, and Major Issues?

Lessons Learned. A critical error made by some enterprises is to purchase and install the package solution and expect the organization to re-engineer itself around the new solution. This typically results in chaos as people do not understand the new measurement systems and processes.

Successful organizations initiate re-engineering projects either before or in tandem with the systems project.

Change management often is ignored. There must be a separate and distinct effort to effect change to the target environment. As with all projects, good people make the difference. Successful organizations dedicate their best people to the project. In addition, good people require less management and adapt easier to change.

Large integrated package implementations result in massive change and risk. Successful organizations follow a proven method and proactively manage risk. One area in particular is risk-related to the technology where client/server systems typically are involved. The risk related to failure needs to be managed through techniques such as

- Hiring external experts.
- Installing the environment in advance and testing performance.
- Re-engineering the information systems function.

Most successful installations involve external business experts who can accelerate the project by providing

- Base application knowledge.
- Best practices.
- Practical operational expertise.
- Starter kits.
- A proven method and plan.

Implementing integrated applications is complex and typically years in duration. The project team should deliver quick hits to build commitment.

Many enterprises indicate that one of the biggest hurdles to overcome is the performance and system environment management. It is important for enterprises to have a good understanding of the components that need to be integrated on a large scale. The level of effort varies widely due to the different levels of integration between many enterprises. Depending on the requirements of the organization, the amount of effort required to complete the total migration can range from 18 months to 3 years. Many enterprises complete the migration toward the new environment in different phases, generally categorized by business units or geographic regions. Typically, no more than three phases are required to complete the migration.

The cost of migration can vary depending on the level of integration, the number of sites, the type of applications needed, and the amount of change required for each organization's current environment. The total migration cost can range widely from $800,000 to $80 million. Depending on the enterprise's direction and business needs, the number of sites to which enterprises roll out their business systems varies. The number of sites can range from one to several hundred.

Successes. Some of the success factors include:

- Sizing the project with the appropriate project management skills.
- Obtaining quick hits.
- Utilizing external help appropriately.
- Implementing the correct approach (i.e., big bang, staged).

Many enterprises find that training the users at the outset of the migration and integration is critical to the success of the migration. Every enterprise mentions that obtaining upper management as well as good project management commitment is essential. User satisfaction is a component of the overall successful migration. In general, user satisfaction increases significantly after the new systems migration. Successful change management takes clear management commitment, broadly communicated change imperative and vision, strong education/training, and committed individuals working together to generate an improvement in overall performance.

Major Issues and Failures. Obtaining and coordinating the appropriate resources to carry out the migration to the new system is important in completing the implementation on time and within budget.

Some issues and failures include:

- Using technology over reengineering.
- Ignoring change management.
- Undersizing hardware/response time.
- Underestimating management of IS transformation.

CONCLUSIONS

Enterprises cite several advantages implementing common systems. These include a high degree of process commonality across business units, interchange of personnel, easier reorganizations across business unit lines, and enhanced consistency and comparability of data and information. Several enterprises project large savings in resources and application development costs. Enterprises that implement an integrated system project a payback period of under 3 years. Many enterprises indicate that real-time, enterprise-wide business systems are necessary for global competitiveness. Several enterprises mention that their current systems do not meet the growing requirements of a world-wide operation. A standard system provides more flexibility and adaptability to changes and challenges in business operations. A standard system, with a minimum need for special adaptations, based on open systems with modern technology, is the projected environment for most enterprises. Enterprises value a system that can be expanded by new functions into a larger, totally integrated system.

Many enterprises are migrating away from a mainframe to a client/server environment. Also, enterprises are making the transition from in-house custom-developed applications to off-the-shelf packaged solutions. Enterprises that make this transition indicate that they do not compromise any functionality purchasing off-the-shelf packages compared with custom-developed solutions. There is a significant amount of cost savings in application development costs related to purchased packaged solutions.

Enterprises are implementing integrated solutions over best-of-breed solutions. Cost savings is not the major driver in deciding to choose integrated solutions over best-of-breed solutions. Most enterprises believe there are big business benefits to an integrated solution.

References

Abbott, R., Getting your 'old stuff' into a new PDM system, *Comp.-Aided Eng.,* 16: 3, 56–58, 1997.
Asbrand, D., Is datamining ready for the masses? *Datamation,* 43: 11, 66(5), 1997.
Callaway, E., ERP: test for success, *PCWeek,* 14: 53, 69(2), 1997.
Hoffman, T., Extending ERP's reach, *ComputerWorld,* 11:2, 24(3), 1998.
Linthicum, D. S., Crossing the streams, *DBMS,* 11: 2, 24(3), 1998.
Redman, T. C., The impact of poor data quality on the typical enterprise, *Comm. ACM,* 4: 2, 79–82, 1998.
Stein, T., Not just ERP anymore, *Inform. Week,* 659, 18(4), 1997.
Stein, T., Key word: integration, *Inform. Week,* 649, 223(6), 1997.
Weston, R., Tooling around, *ComputerWorld,* 31: 42, 73(2), 1997.

Chapter 7

The Importance of Data Architecture in a Client/Server Environment

Gary Lord

CLIENT/SERVER TECHNOLOGY CAN BE THOUGHT OF AS A TECHNICAL ARCHITECTURE that is a mix of personal computers and midrange systems with middleware connecting them so that they work together to perform a process. Within this environment, the distribution of data is just as important to a successful implementation as is the distribution of processes.

For the purpose of this chapter, the concepts of data architecture and technical architecture are defined as follows:

- The data architecture depicts the distribution and access mechanisms associated with data for one or more applications. It defines the standards and procedures needed to create consistent, accurate, complete, and timely data. It defines a process for rationalizing data needs across applications and determining its appropriate distribution and placement. It defines the methods for the collection and distribution of all computerized information.
- The technical architecture represents various components and services that make up a suite of applications or a specific application. It describes the classes of technology required to support data storage, application access, processing, and communications and how they fit together. It defines the standards, guidelines, and infrastructure necessary to meet the requirements of the application. The technical architecture encompasses the hardware, operating systems, network facilities, and tools that enable the implementation of systems.

The data and technical architectures are highly integrated in that the technical blueprint includes the classes of technology necessary to support the implementation of the data blueprint.

CREATING A DATA ARCHITECTURE

Significant issues are associated with the creation of a data architecture in a client/server environment. Among these issues are

- Data metrics: Determinants include the size of data, the frequency that data is needed, and the cost associated with getting it, as well as the frequency with which the data changes.
- Data access: Challenges in this area concern whether access is to be ad hoc or controlled and whether it will be for update or read-only purposes.
- Data harvesting: One of the challenges with defining the data architecture is the formulation of appropriate harvesting strategies — that is, how to manage data from transaction systems to data warehouses to departmental servers and, in some cases, to the desktop.
- Data replication: Another challenge is to define under what conditions data should be distributed or replicated.
- Data ownership and security: Issues to resolve include determining who will take responsibility for owning the data and who will have what type of access to what data.

Architecture Definition: High-Level to Lower-Level Design

As with traditional data modeling, the technical architecture and data architecture definition can begin at a high level early in a development effort and progress to more detailed levels throughout the development life cycle. A certain degree of rigor must be applied to develop both the data architecture and the technical architecture concurrently. One approach is to follow the time-tested data modeling concept of conceptual, logical, and physical representations.

The Conceptual Layer. The conceptual layer includes requirements or objectives. This layer describes the "what" in terms of business-linked objectives. The conceptual data architecture is the distribution of conceptual data stores across the technology framework at a very high level. For example, sales data resides in the data warehouse. Edit rules related to sales data reside both in the repository and on the desktop.

The conceptual technical architecture includes application components and services positioned across the various technology platforms. For example, the user interface resides on the desktop. The calculation engine resides on the server. A process resides on the desktop to down-load the edit rules data from the repository when the data changes.

The conceptual layer of the data and technical architectures should be defined during the requirements definition phase of the development project.

The Logical Layer. The logical layer represents design. It describes the engineering specifications and strategies required for implementation at a lower level of detail.

The logical data architecture should include data at the entity and attribute level distributed across the various technology platforms. For example, the sales data that is to reside in the data warehouse includes the sales order master and sales order detail file.

The logical technical architecture should further define the various services and components that make up the application. For example, the graphical user interface (GUI) on the desktop may be made up of seven screens and 12 reports, each referenced by name. The service necessary to propagate the edit rules data from the repository to the desktop actually consists of two services, one on the repository machine and one on the desktop. The service on the repository machine is responsible for processing a request for update. The service on the desktop is responsible for making the request depending on the time of last update.

The logical technical and data architecture should be defined during the high-level design phase of the project. In fact, there may need to be multiple iterations of the logical layer at increasingly more detailed levels of specification.

The Physical Layer. The physical layer describes the products and environments needed for systems implementation. The physical data architecture includes the specific physical environments used to implement the data architecture. For example, the repository may include a relational database; the edit rules data residing on the desktop may be implemented in C tables.

The physical technical architecture would include the specific hardware, software, and middleware needed to implement the technical architecture. For example, the seven user interface screens may be developed in C++ running on a Macintosh. The calculation engine may be developed in VMS C running on a DEC VAX.

The physical layer should be defined at the end of high-level design.

MULTITIER DATA ARCHITECTURES

Data architectures in a client/server environment should be defined according to a four-tier architecture:

- Tier 1: Transaction data: The first tier of the architecture is the transaction data itself. This is the raw data that actually is captured by production systems. An example of production data would be the header and detail accounts receivable transactions captured in a financial system.

- Tier 2: Data warehouse: The data warehouse consists of a subset of data that has been extracted from the transaction systems and placed in the warehouse for use by a variety of information consumers.
- Tier 3: Departmental/functional data extracts: These extracts consist of data sourced from the warehouse but restructured from a relational perspective to meet the needs of a specific information consumer. An example of the data in the departmental extract might consist of a subset of the accounts payable.
- Tier 4: Local data extracts: The local data extracts represent semistatic data that has been downloaded to the desktop. An example of local access data would be lookup data, such as units of measure codes or user interface constraint data.

Separating Users and Providers of Data

A multitier data architecture defines the topology and organization of the data according to the different types of users and providers that access it.

From an access perspective, consumers of the data captured by transaction systems should not be accessing the transaction database directly. From the perspective of consolidation of the data so that it can be harvested, information required by consumers is held in the data warehouse. The information providers thus are separated from the information consumers.

From a concurrency perspective, it makes sense to consolidate and denormalize certain views of the warehouse data into departmental or functional extracts for those consumers with specialized needs.

From a data ownership perspective, again, information consumers are separated from the information providers. Tier 1 databases are owned by the data capture function; tier 2 by the custodians of the warehouse; tier 3 by the groups of consumers; and tier 4 by individual consumers.

Security also is addressed by separating the providers from the consumers. Consumers are only allowed access to the views of the data that are appropriate for their use.

KEY CONCEPTS OF SERVICE-BASED ARCHITECTURES

As the name implies, service-based architectures specify the topology of a system in the form of discrete services and components. They provide a framework for information systems that is user-centric, highly modular, seamlessly integrated, easily shared, platform-independent, and network-oriented.

Apple Computer Inc.'s Virtually Integrated Technical Architecture Lifecycle (VITAL) is an example of a service-based architecture. This environment is discussed to illustrate the concepts of service-based architectures and to show how data and processes can be distributed in a data architecture.

Fundamentals of the VITAL model include desktop integration (i.e., user interface, navigation, information synthesis, training, and consulting); data access (i.e., the information consumption and sharing process); data capture (i.e., the data production/creation process); repository (i.e., definitions of the data, processes, and controls that manage the information as a corporate asset); and infrastructure (i.e., the operating systems software, hardware, and support organization).

Data Capture

The data capture environment supports and promotes the data production functions of the enterprise. Its purpose is to manage the transaction update systems of the business, maintain the accuracy and integrity of business data, manage any direct interfaces required between transaction update systems, and create data snapshots as needed.

The key component of the data capture environment is a suite of modular software services. Taken together, these services handle all of the functions of a major transaction update system. Their modular design and client/server approach increase adaptability while improving performance.

From a multitier data architecture perspective, data capture includes tier 1 (transaction databases).

Data Access

Whereas data capture governs data production functions, the data access environment directly supports information consumers in the organization. The primary duty of data access is to manage the acquisition and distribution of all shareable data throughout the business and to provide access to consistent data that may originate from diverse functions within the organization.

The key component of data access is a shared data warehouse network. The services in this network manage a system of read-only databases that can be distributed globally, regionally, or locally, depending on the needs of the business. Data in the network is replenished regularly from the data capture environment, thus separating information management from transaction update functions, allowing both to be managed optimally.

From a multitier data architecture perspective, data access includes tier 2 (data warehouse) and tier 3 (departmental/functional data extracts).

Repository

The repository contains a uniform set of business rules, data definitions, and system usage rules for the organization. The repository also provides an encyclopedia of metadata or data about all of the software services, data, and other components contained in the enterprise information systems. Repository services manage this metadata, which in turn is used by services in the other environments.

The repository supports the other environments with three classes of services: definition, navigation, and administration. Repository services manage access to metadata. Examples of the types of metadata include standard data definitions, location and routing information, and synchronization management for distributing shared data.

Desktop Integration

The desktop integration environment's purpose is to enhance the role of the desktop in the larger enterprise system. It provides the user interface, personal application support, and interconnection to the enterprise computing network. Essentially, it works as an agent on behalf of knowledge workers, buffering them from the information bureaucracy.

In the VITAL environment, the key component of desktop integration is an integration services manager that coordinates a set of modular software services linking desktop applications to other enterprise tools and software services. The manager works with other VITAL environments to increase the use of desktop computing power. It frees users from the burden of having to remember protocols and log-on strings when accessing data.

From a multitier data architecture perspective, desktop integration includes tier 4 (local data extracts).

Infrastructure

The infrastructure environment is essentially the glue that holds the other environments together. Systems infrastructure is more than just the connectivity required for global enterprise systems. It includes a set of software utility services that support and integrate the other environments so that the services in the other environments do not have to know routing or protocol details.

Systems infrastructure has three main elements: computing resources, network resources, and interface resources. Computing resources include the operating systems and hardware of all devices within the enterprise system. Network resources also include messaging, security, and data transfer services. These and other network services provide the key interfaces between software on separate platforms.

CASE STUDY

To illustrate a data architecture as it relates to technical architecture in a client/server environment, this section examines a specific application. The Insurance Underwriter's Workstation was developed by KPMG Peat Marwick for one of its client companies — a major provider of worker's compensation insurance products. The primary function performed by thr application was to allow underwriters to prepare insurance premiums quotations and produce a report that could be filed with state and federal regulatory agencies.

Problem

The client was using an IBM mainframe-based application for the calculations of insurance premiums. The Rating Plan Quote System (RPQS) performed well and produced rating plan quotes that were acceptable for filing with regulatory agencies. However, the system allowed only a limited number of concurrent users. When the threshold was reached, other users were locked out of the system until someone logged off.

In addition, most of the data reference tables were hard-coded in the program, so when changes needed to be made the programs had to be modified. Finally, users were unable to save quotes. If users needed to re-run a quote because of an error, they had to retype the policy information into the system again.

Opportunity

The client was required by the National Council to support a new calculation for its retrospectively rated policies. This presented an opportunity for the client to evaluate the current application and to decide whether to modify it or create a new application. The client company was committed to using the Macintosh development platform for client/server environment interaction. After evaluating the advantage of the client/server environment, the company opted to discontinue its mainframe stovepipe application and pursue a more strategic alternative for implementing the new calculation for the retrospective rating plan quote system.

In this case, a client/server solution was found using Macintosh as the client interface and the DEC VAX as the host. The approach allowed reference data to be modified without modifying the code. In addition, the user could save the input necessary to calculate a quote, which eliminated the need to retype information, and the user would never be locked out of the system because of concurrent user limitations.

The application also can be examined from a service-based architecture perspective, dividing the application's technical architecture and data architecture into the five environments used in the VITAL architecture. Exhibits 1 through 4 illustrate the distribution of data and processes in this architecture.

Data Capture. The data capture component of new Rate Plan Workstation (RPW) application supports the creation, reading, update, and deletion of the reference-table data. The VAX-based relational database gateway provides the infrastructure for the capturing of reference-table data. The data then was mapped into an operational database.

Referential integrity checks on the data occur based on the metadata associated with the operational database. Once the application is loaded into the operational database, users can run a custom application to propagate their modification to the development database and to the production warehouse immediately or set up a batch job for that night. They also have the option of just propagating the development database so they may test their modifications before putting them into production. When the production propagation occurs, the operational database is copied to the development database and to the production warehouse; then the production warehouse is distributed to the local access databases for users to access through the RPW user interface. Exhibit 1 shows the data capture environment for this application.

Data Access. The data access component (see Exhibit 2) receives the reference table data from the data capture environment and provides the constraint information for data input. The data access component also provides access to the reference-table data for performing the calculation process, passing the completed calculation data to the RPW user interface for storage.

The VAX/relational-based data warehouse provides a central repository from where the local access databases have been populated. The warehouse allows for on-demand update of local access databases. Once the reference-table data is available in the local access databases, a custom application called the calculation manager receives all user requests for system access and calculations. This application handles software validation and, using DecMessage Queue, distributes the calculation requests to a set of VAXs designated to handle parallel calculations.

Desktop Integration. Once the data was available on the local access databases, a MacApp Application was developed to collect valid plan information to perform the calculations for the quote or filing report. Once a plan has been saved, the user can send it to another user through a mail system and they would be able to make modifications, provided their Macintosh was configured so they could run the application.

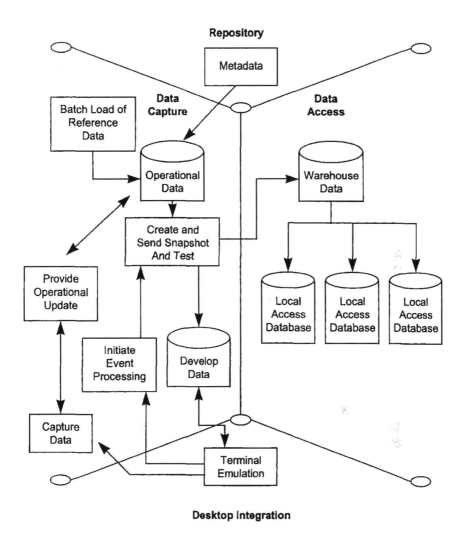

Exhibit 1. Data capture environment for RPW application.

The RPW user interface subsystem is built around a Macintosh front end. The subsystem requests information from the host at different times during user interaction. When a user launches the system, the workstation requests that the host validates the application software version number running on the Mac and validates the versions of the constraint files existing on the Mac. If the user opens a plan that has previously been calculated, the workstation requests that the host verify that the last time reference-table maintenance was performed so that the workstation can in-

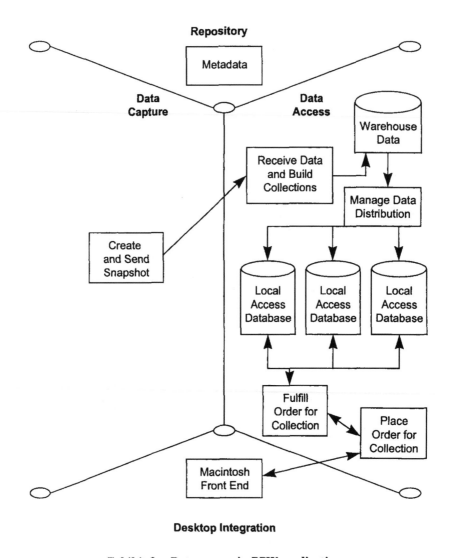

Exhibit 2.   Data access in RPW application.

form the user that the plan may have to be recalculated. The user can request the host to perform the calculation on demand. Local data on the desktop is updated and accessed based on changes to the local access databases and user interaction with the front end. The data integration environment is shown in Exhibit 3.

When new calculation reference tables are issued by the National Council or state change constraint values used in calculations, the production

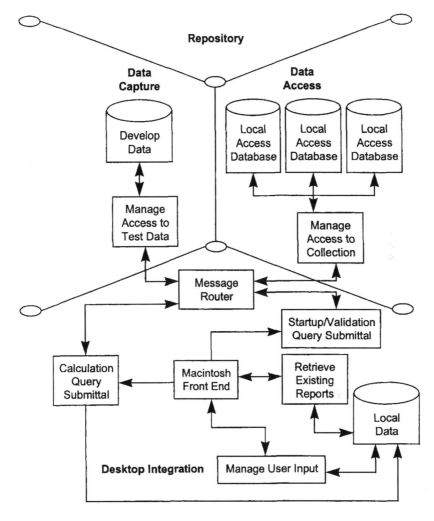

Exhibit 3. Desktop integration in RPW application.

support person has the ability to make such changes without requesting a coding modification. This is accomplished by using the file maintenance user interface.

The file maintenance user interface subsystem was developed on the VAX using an Ingres DBMS to manage the user input screens. A shell was developed around the Ingres application using DCL, which is Digital Equipment Corp.'s connectivity language. This shell creates captive system access when the user logs in, allowing only one user access to table

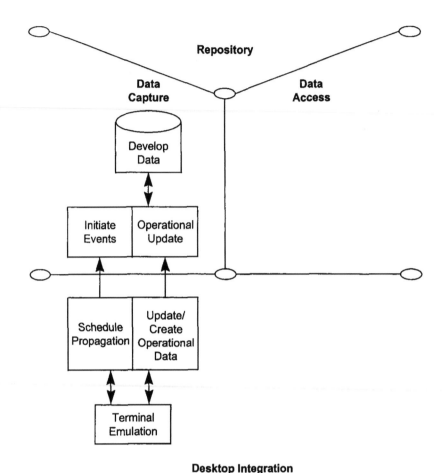

Exhibit 4. File maintenance user interface.

maintenance at a time and providing the user with options for data propagation (Exhibit 4). This desktop component lets the user maintain the reference-table data stored in the operational database and allows the user to control the triggering propagation of the operational database to the development or production environments.

CONCLUSION

This actual case study illustrates how data can be located physically where it is most economically practical in terms of propagation and collection and where it supports an acceptable user response level. One of the best ways to define and validate a data topology that supports this objective is to develop a data architecture using the underlying concepts associated with service-based architectures, a multitier data strategy, and conventional conceptual, logical, and physical data modeling.

Processes, data, and technology can be defined concurrently in a highly integrated development effort. During the requirements definition phase, the relationships between data and the processes it supports should be documented at a very high level. During the high-level design phase, both the data architecture and the technical architecture must be drilled down to lower levels of detail. Finally, during the detail design phase, the data and technical architectures should be defined at the lowest level of detail, including the specific products to be used.

Section II
Data Models and Modeling Techniques

DATA MODELS ARE THE CONCEPTUAL FOUNDATION OF DATA MANAGE-MENT SOLUTIONS. They are used to capture business requirements and to present them in a structured way that ultimately supports the development initiative. They are useful for communicating data design with users and technical resources. They can also be used to sign off on a formal contract with the business. Data models also are useful in object-oriented architecture, and can co-exist and add value to object models. There are many types of data models, modeling techniques, and syntax. There also are an assortment of modeling tools as well as various types of implementation tools. Data models capture one view of an organization, while other types of models, such as process models, can capture different views. Taken together, the different models capture the logical essence of organizations. This section contains six chapters.

Chapter 8, "Making Data Models Readable," provides guidelines for creating accessible data models that are useful for understanding both a business and a database design. The chapter focuses on data model usability.

Chapter 9, "Component Design for Relational Databases," provides a new twist on relational-to-object impedance matching, also referred to as a data-component approach in this chapter. This involves leveraging the advantages of having a component take responsibility for updating data while providing relevant inquiry functions.

Chapter 10, "Practices in Enterprise Data Modeling," describes some of the criticisms of enterprise data modeling and suggests ways of avoiding the potential pitfalls. The chapter stresses how data modeling should be integrated with process specifications. Guidelines for an efficient data model are discussed, and data administration issues are addressed within the context of enterprise data modeling.

Chapter 11, "Integrating Process and Data Models in a Horizontal Organization," describes how process modeling and data modeling can be integrated in a horizontal organization. The chapter discusses the data-focused and process-focused approaches, and offers ways of integrating them into a single method. CASE tools also are reviewed.

Chapter 12, "Object-Oriented Aspects of Windows Component-Based Software," compares the object-oriented nature of two Windows-based, component-based software development languages with a Windows-based, object-oriented language.

Chapter 13, "Data Warehouse Design: Issues in Dimensional Data Modeling," describes the multidimensional modeling concepts and techniques for designing information-rich data warehouses.

Chapter 8
Making Data Models Readable

David C. Hay

Useful systems depend on requirements analysis, of which data modeling is an essential part. Yet data modeling is often abandoned as a cumbersome and ineffective technique that cannot be understood by potential system users. Because the fault lies with the way the models are designed and not with the underlying complexity of what is being represented, guidelines regarding the way the models are constructed and their components named help ensure the creation of accessible models that are useful for both understanding a business and database design.

ENTITY-RELATIONSHIP MODELS (or simply, data models) are powerful tools for analyzing and representing the structure of an organization. Properly used, they can reveal subtle relationships between elements of a business. They can also form the basis for robust and reliable database design.

Data models have gotten a bad reputation in recent years, however, as many people have found them to be more trouble to produce and less beneficial than promised. Discouraged, people have gone on to other approaches for developing systems — often abandoning modeling altogether, in favor of simply starting with system design.

Requirements analysis remains important, however, if systems are ultimately to do something useful for the company. And modeling — especially data modeling — is an essential component of requirements analysis.

It is important, therefore, to try to understand why data models have been getting such a "bad rap." The fault lies in the way most people design the models, not in the underlying complexity of what is being represented.

GOALS OF ENTITY-RELATIONSHIP MODELS

An entity-relationship model has two primary objectives. First, it represents the analyst's public understanding of an enterprise, so that the ultimate consumer of a prospective computer system can be sure that the analyst got it right. Does the analyst really know the business? A properly drawn data model can provide an answer to that question quite vividly. To the user, it addresses the question: "Is this what you want?"

Second, the model represents the fundamental architecture of an enterprise's data, and as such is an ideal starting place for database design. To be sure, the final structure of a database may differ from the data model for good and valid reasons, but the closer it remains to the original structure, the more likely it is to be able to resist requirements for future changes. To the system designer and builder, it sends the message: "This (rigorously described) is what you are to build."

Because data modeling was created within the computer industry, the second objective has often taken priority. As drawn by systems engineers, data models tend to look like electronic schematics — to be read only by other engineers. The morass of boxes and lines makes them quite formidable to all but the most dedicated reader. Many data modeling conventions — and a great many data modeling practitioners — do not put enough weight on the importance of making the model accessible to the outside world.

Indeed, some contend that the models cannot be made accessible to the outside world, so there is no point in even trying.

This article takes the position that not only is it possible to produce model drawings that can be understood by potential systems users, but it is our responsibility to do so. Here follow some guidelines as to how to do this.

There are two major issues in the readability of models. The first, and the one to be discussed most here, is aesthetics. How is the drawing constructed and to what visual effect? The second is the way things in it are named. Are the words on the diagram helpful in divining its meaning?

AESTHETICS

Data modeling was originally an engineering discipline, not an artistic one. For this reason, most modelers pay less attention to aesthetics than they should. Part of the problem is the system of notation they use. Some notations lend themselves to improved aesthetics, while others produce drawings that are nearly impossible to read, regardless of what the modeler does. The rest of the problem is in the way the modeler does his work.

The aesthetic considerations to be discussed here are (1) the ordering or arrangement of symbols on the model, (2) the number of symbols on the model, (3) the number of symbol types there are, and (4) how the various layers of the model interact with each other.

The modeler has control over the arrangement of the drawing, the number of symbols used, and the overall layering of the diagram. The system of notation chosen also affects layering, and determines the number of kinds of symbols that will be present.

Order

How the entities are placed on a page is critical to the viewer's ability to understand a diagram. Typically (especially if the model was produced via an automated tool), there is no rationale to entities relative positions on a diagram. They wind up where ever it is convenient to put them. In some cases, people will rearrange entities to minimize the crossing of lines, but this adds no semantic meaning to the picture.

This has the effect that as one looks at a model drawing, one has no way to get a hold of its overall meaning. A random collection of boxes and lines is seen. There is nothing in its overall shape to tell anything about it.

A very powerful convention for positioning entities is to force all relationships to point in the same direction. The "dead crow" rule — that all crow's feet should have their toes pointing either up or to the left — is followed here. This has the effect of placing the reference entities — the entities describing tangible things in the business — on the lower right, and the transaction entities — those describing what the enterprise does — on the upper left. Others reverse the convention, pointing crow's foot toes south and east. Whichever convention is followed, however, anyone looking at a model following such a convention can now quickly see what it is about (products, laboratory tests, etc.) and what things of interest there are about that.

Too Many Symbols

The simplest thing to be done to improve the appearance of a model is to limit the number of figures on any one drawing. Twenty seems to be about the maximum that is possible without making a drawing completely unreadable, and ten to fifteen is better.

Here, a figure is any two-dimensional graphic object. The number of relationship lines present is less significant, and this will necessarily be a function of the number of things to be connected. The number of line segments can be reduced as well, by eliminating "elbows" in the line. A bent line, after all, is graphically two lines.

Too Many Symbol Types

Clearly, the more different kinds of figures that are on the page, the more confusing the result will be. The question is, how many are needed? Each different kind of symbol is something new for the viewer to learn, and therefore is one more obstacle to understanding. One of the reasons models often become cumbersome is that one tries to do too much with them. There is a limit to the amount of information that can be conveyed on one page.

As a minimum, symbols are needed for:

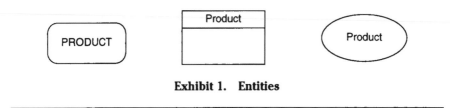

Exhibit 1. Entities

- Entities.
- The existence of relationships between pairs of entities.
- Optionality: Must an occurrence of one entity have a corresponding occurrence of another, or not?
- Cardinality: May an occurrence of one entity have more than one corresponding occurrence of another, or not?

In addition, it is often necessary to represent subtypes of an entity — sets of occurrences that represent subsets of the occurrences of the entity. There is a question, however, as to how elaborate this representation should be. There also is a question of whether to represent attributes of an entity, and how. And finally, many notations — but not all — represent the elements that uniquely identify an occurrence of an entity.

A wide variety of data modeling techniques are being used today. The original notation was invented by Peter Chen. Among those most commonly used since Chen's work are James Martin's Information Engineering and IDEF1X. The latter is the standard for the federal government. Also popular is Oracle's Oracle Method (formerly the CASE*Method), and the Structured Systems Analysis and Design Method (SSADM), which is particularly popular in Europe.

Lately, the object-oriented phenomenon has produced several techniques for drawing "object models" instead of entity-relationship (e-r) models. While object models do include descriptions of the "behavior" of each entity, they otherwise show exactly the same concepts as e-r models. Indeed, James Martin's "object diagrams," for example, are literally his entity-relationship diagrams renamed (although his subtype notation is modified somewhat).[1] Among the most popular object modeling techniques are those published by James Rumbaugh and associates, Sally Shlaer and Stephen Mellor, and the team of David Embley, Barry Kurtz, and Scott Woodfield. Ed Yourdon and Peter Coad have also published a book on object modeling.

A completely different approach to modeling data structure is presented in object-role modeling, formerly known as NIAM.[2]

In this article, examples from many of these techniques will be presented. The principles discussed, however, apply to all of them.

Entities. Representation of the first concept is not controversial. A box, with rounded or square corners (or in some cases, an ellipse) can represent an entity. This is a thing of significance to the organization, about which it wishes to hold information. Entities are the primary objects on an entity-relationship diagram. Exhibit 1 shows some entities.

Be sure, however, to model entities — things of significance to the business — and not just a database design. The concepts and issues that go into database design are by and large not of interest to the general public.

Relationships. At its simplest, a relationship is represented in most techniques by a simple line connecting two entities. Optionality and cardinality are then shown as characteristics of the relationship by additional symbols, as discussed below. In those cases where a relationship itself has attributes and other relationships to it, many techniques endorse simply defining an entity to represent the relationship as itself being a thing of significance to the enterprise. A LINE ITEM, for example, is essentially a relationship between an order and a product, but most approaches treat it as an entity in its own right.

Chen, on the other hand, adds a different symbol (a rhombus) in the middle of the relationship line to depict these entity-like characteristics, without losing the fact that it is something other than an entity that is being represented.

Exhibit 2, for example, shows Chen's example of the three-way relationship PROJ-PART-SUPP, which is the fact that a PART is supplied to a PROJECT by a SUPPLIER. An alternative to this approach would be to replace PROJ-PART-SUPP with an entity of the same name. (Better yet, replace it with an entity that has a meaningful name, such as SUPPLY. See the discussion of names below.) This would mean the same thing, while eliminating the second symbol type. Chen would probably argue that this second approach camouflages the object's role as a relationship. The question to be answered is: How important is that to the viewer's comprehension of the model, and does the distinction have any effect on database design?

Optionality and Cardinality. The most direct way to approach optionality and cardinality is to simply place numbers by the target entity. The Chen, Coad and Yourdon, and several of the object-oriented techniques do this. "Must be at least one but may be any positive number" is shown by "1,m." "Must be exactly one" is shown by "1,1." "May be zero or any number" is shown by "0,m," etc.

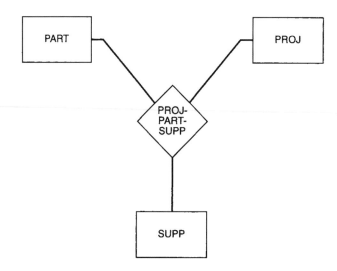

Exhibit 2. Chen's relationship.

This keeps the graphics simple and puts this information on a different graphic "layer" (see below) than the rest of the drawing. It means, for example, that the information must be processed by the left brain as data, rather than the right brain as a graphic experience. This makes the effect less powerful.

A small graphic symbol and its absence can also convey whether or not an occurrence of an entity may have more than one occurrence of a related entity. Another symbol or its absence can convey whether the upper limit of the relationship is 1 or more than 1. As small symbols, these do not compete graphically with the overall presentation of entities and relationships. Typically, a crow's foot or its absence shows cardinality. The Oracle Method uses this convention. James Martin's Information Engineering uses the crow's foot for an upper limit of "many," but instead of just leaving it off for an upper limit of 1, it adds an extra mark across the line.

There is less agreement on the representation of optionality. Martin puts a circle next to the optional entity and a mark across the relationship next to a mandatory entity. ("One and only one" then winds up with two marks next to the entity.) The Oracle Method uses a dashed half-line for an optional relationship and a solid half-line for a mandatory one. SSADM assumes that in most cases the many side is optional and the one side is mandatory, so it only adds a circle in the middle of the line for those cases where the one side is optional. It does not permit the many side to be mandatory.

Exhibit 3 shows Oracle Method's treatment of optionality and cardinality, and Exhibit 4 shows James Martin's symbols. Martin's symbols are a bit more busy, but note how, in both cases, if the symbols for the upper limit

	Upper Limit = 1 (Single line)	Upper Limit = M (Crow's foot)
Lower Limit = 0 (Dashed line)		
Lower Limit = 1 (Solid line)		

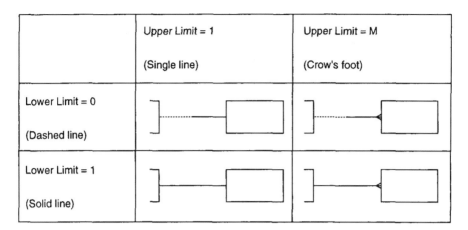

Exhibit 3.   Oracle method cardinality and optionality.

are known, the cardinality is known, regardless of the optionality. Similarly, if the symbols for lower limit are known, then the optionality is known, regardless of cardinality.

Shlaer and Mellor use a different set of graphics (Exhibit 5), but they also show consistency for all combinations of optionality and cardinality.

By far, the most complex system of notation is also one that is widely used — IDEF1X. It is the standard for the U.S. Government and is common elsewhere as well. Unfortunately, it suffers from several problems that make it more complex than necessary for the purposes pursued here.

	Upper Limit = 1 (Single line)	Upper Limit = M (Crow's foot)
Lower Limit = 0 (Circle)		
Lower Limit = 1 (Solid line)		

Exhibit 4.   James Martin cardinality and optionality.

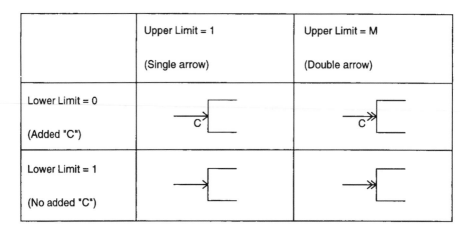

	Upper Limit = 1 (Single arrow)	Upper Limit = M (Double arrow)
Lower Limit = 0 (Added "C")		
Lower Limit = 1 (No added "C")		

Exhibit 5. Shlaer and Mellor cardinality and optionality.

Attributes. There is also a question of whether attributes must be shown, and if so, how.

The tidiest model clearly is one in which attributes are not shown. If the model is being presented to a group for the purpose of communicating the basic nature of the entities and relationships, it is better to omit them. In a presentation of the model, one should describe enough of them to make clear the meaning of each entity, but they do not have to be on the drawing. Adding them as text inside the entity boxes does not have a serious impact on the overall readability of the model, however (as long as there are not too many), so if one wants to include them, go ahead. Exhibit 6 shows this. Note that in this example, the attributes themselves have been flagged as to whether each is mandatory (*) or optional (.). These additional symbols add information without cluttering the overall model.

Some techniques (object-role modeling and Chen) go a step further, however, by showing attributes in additional circles (or ellipses) on the

Exhibit 6. Attributes.

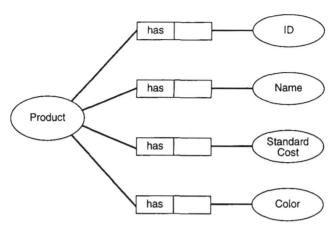

Exhibit 7.   ORM attributes.

drawing. This greatly increases the number of symbols that must be on a page, thus making the model more complex.

Object-role modeling takes the unusual approach of not distinguishing graphically between attributes and entities. This is based on the premise that the relationship between an attribute and an entity is conceptually the same as a relationship between two entities. While this also makes the model more crowded than the notation shown previously, the consolidation of entities and attributes actually reduces the number of kinds of symbols by one. The "not too many objects" rule still applies, though, and this will require the domain of each drawing to be smaller. Exhibit 7 shows our example using object-role modeling, where the relationships between an entity and its attributes have now been made explicit. "ID" and "Name" are shown to be mandatory by the dots on their relationships, next to PRODUCT.

The arrows under has in each relationship simply mean that PRODUCT can have only one value for each attribute — thus requiring the model to be in first normal form. This representation of uniqueness in ORM is difficult to master initially (it is another symbol, after all), but it does allow this technique to represent subtleties not available to conventional e-r modeling. It extends to the relationships between an entity and its attributes the same concepts of optionality and cardinality that have been discussed between entities themselves. The notation is the same whether the ellipses stand for entities or attributes: for cardinality, the presence of a double-headed arrow under the left side of the relationship means that only one occurrence of the object on the right may be applied to an occurrence of the object on the left. Without it, a PRODUCT could have more than one value for "ID." Similarly, the dot or its absence represents optionality for both attributes and entities.

Subtypes and Supertypes. A subtype is an entity that represents a subset of occurrences of another entity — its supertype. An occurrence of the supertype is also an occurrence of one and only one subtype, and an occurrence of a subtype must also be an occurrence of the supertype. Some techniques take the Venn diagram approach of showing the subtypes inside the supertype. Exhibit 8, for example, shows Martin's Information Engineering notation for subtypes and supertypes. This has the advantages of compactness and of emphasizing the fact that an occurrence of the subtype *is* an occurrence of the supertype. The compactness allows the supertype and all its subtypes to count graphically as one object, making it easier to follow the previous "not too many objects" rule.

This has the disadvantage, however, of making it impossible to show the case where a subtype is of more than one supertype ("multiple inheritance" in object-oriented lingo). It is also not possible to show the case where a supertype has more than one set of nonoverlapping subtypes ("orthogonal subtypes").

To represent these situations, it is necessary to show the subtypes outside the supertype entity with a relationship (often called an "isa" relationship) tying them together. While this does provide the added expressiveness, it has the disadvantage of adding objects to the diagram and of reducing the clarity of the subtype concept. Exhibit 9 shows the example from Exhibit 8 in this external version, as specified by the object-modeling technique (described by James Rumbaugh and colleagues). A similar approach is used by other object modeling techinques and IDEF1X.

Multiple inheritance is a bad idea, and every example of it (and its complexity) could be eliminated by doing the model differently. Similarly, subtypes are reserved for the situation where the structure is fundamental, and in these cases it is highly unlikely that there would be more than one set of subtypes for a supertype. The other situations can be handled by defining a ... CATEGORY entity, where each member of the entity may be (or

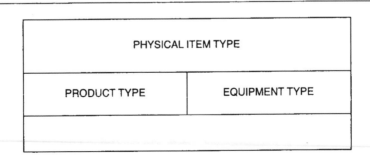

Exhibit 8.   Compact subtypes.

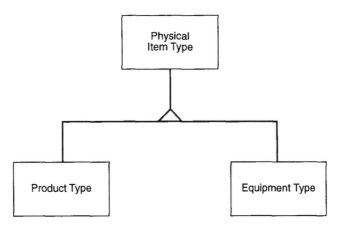

Exhibit 9. "ISA" relationships.

must be) a member of one (or one or more?) ... CATEGORY. For example, Exhibit 10 shows that each PHYSICAL ITEM TYPE must be in one or more PHYSICAL ITEM TYPE categories. Examples of PHYSICAL ITEM TYPE CATEGORY could be "product type" and "equipment type," along with all the other possible subtypes.

Unique Identifiers. An additional concept that can be represented on a model is the set of attributes and relationships that uniquely identify an occurrence of an entity. Many of the notations do not include this information. Some, such as Oracle's Oracle Method, simply add a special symbol

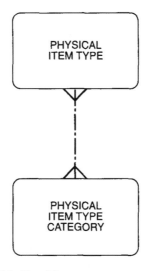

Exhibit 10. The category approach.

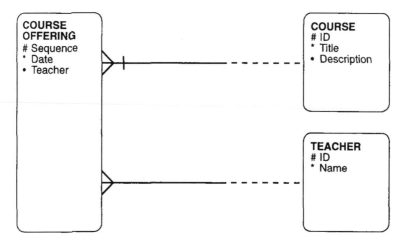

Exhibit 11.   Oracle unique identifiers.

(such as the "#" in Oracle's case) in front of an attribute participating in the unique identifier, and place a symbol (in Oracle's case, an extra mark) across a relationship participating.

In Exhibit 11, COURSE's unique identifier, for example, is simply the attribute "ID." COURSE OFFERING's unique identifier is a combination of the attribute "Sequence" plus the relationship to COURSE. This means that when this model is implemented in tables, the primary key of COURSE ("ID") will become a foreign key in COURSE OFFERING. It and "Sequence" together will form the primary key of that table. Note that COURSE OFFERING is also related to TEACHER, but this is not part of the unique identifier, so it does not have the short line crossing the relationship. Each line is partially solid and partially dashed, according to the rules for optionality described previously. (Each COURSE OFFERING must be related to one COURSE and to one teacher, but each COURSE and TEACHER may or may not be related to a COURSE OFFERING.)

IDEF1X, on the other hand, takes a more dramatic approach. If a relationship participates, the entire line is changed from a dashed line to a solid line, and the entity box so identified is changed from having square corners to having round corners. The identified entity is considered to be conceptually different from those still having the square corners. It is called a "dependent entity." Our example is shown in Exhibit 12. The relationship between COURSE and COURSE OFFERING is solid because it is part of COURSE OFFERING's unique identifier, while the relationship between TEACHER and COURSE OFFERING is dashed. The round corners for dependence happen if any of its relationships are identifying.

In addition, IDEF1X describes the unique identifier yet one more time by using the language of relational database design. Relationships are explic-

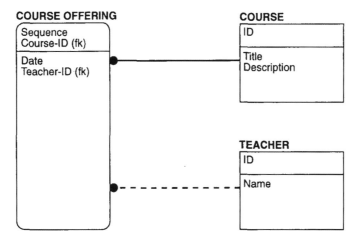

COURSE OFFERING

| Sequence |
| Course-ID (fk) |

| Date |
| Teacher-ID (fk) |

COURSE

| ID |

| Title |
| Description |

TEACHER

| ID |

| Name |

Exhibit 12.   Unique identifiers in IDEF1X.

itly (if redundantly) shown as foreign keys, identified by "(fk)." The unique identifier is referred to as a "primary key" and is shown above the line in the entity box. If the relationship participates in a primary key, the foreign key implied by the relationship is shown accordingly.

This places great emphasis on the concept of dependence, but it is questionable whether this is either meaningful to any users viewing the model, or if it in any way changes the response of system designers, who only really need to know what the unique identifier (to be implemented as a primary key) is.

In summary, the following require additional symbols on the model, and it is not clear whether these are either required to make the model more effective in communicating with users, or useful in providing more information to system developers:

- A distinction between an objectified relationship and an intangible entity
- Multiple inheritance of subtypes
- Orthogonal subtypes
- Attributes as alternatives to entities
- Dependent entities
- Database design references

By not seeking to add these concepts to the model, one can greatly reduce its complexity and make it more accessible to end users.

Bent Lines. Another way extra symbols get added to a diagram is unintentional: elbows in relationship lines. A corner is a shape, one that draws

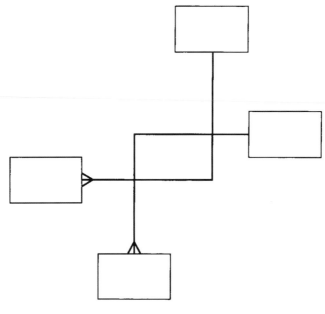

Exhibit 13.   Too many lines.

---

the eye to it as much as any other shape, but one that carries no semantic meaning. Moreover, when the relationship lines become too convoluted, they also create additional graphic figures on the page — figures that add clutter, but do not add information. In Exhibit 13, how many rectangles are observed? How many of them have meaning? The one in the middle is clearly a distraction.

Even if crossing lines are avoided, one does not avoid the problem of ghost shapes. Is there a fifth rectangle in Exhibit 14?

The way to avoid bending lines, of course, is to stretch the entities as necessary. (CASE tools that do not allow this are particularly reprehensible.) Exhibit 15 shows how straighter lines give the entities much greater impact.

Layering. Edward Tufte has said that "among the most powerful devices for reducing noise and enriching the content of displays is the technique of layering and separation, visually stratifying various aspects of data ... the various elements of flatland interact creating non-information patterns and texture, simply through their combined presence."[3]

Tufte's idea of layering is that different kinds of information should be represented in sufficiently different ways so that one can view only part of the picture at once, and easily ignore the rest. When attributes are repre-

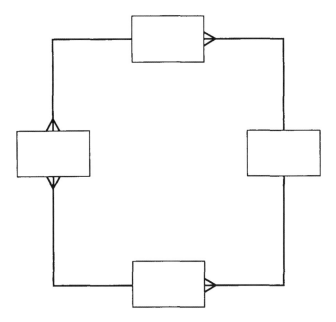

Exhibit 14.   Hidden square?

sented as symbols in their own right, as in Chen's and the ORM technique, they have the same status on the diagram as entities. Similarly, Chen's relationship symbols make the viewer see a relationship as another object on the same level as an entity, even though semantically the author specifically wants it to be considered as different from an entity. That means that the viewer must deal with entities, relationships, and attributes at the same time, with all competing for attention. The graphic distinctions between completely different kinds of information are small.

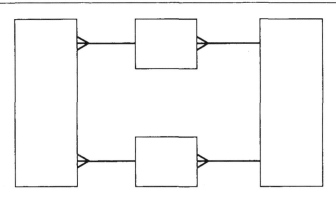

Exhibit 15.   Straighter lines.

There is a natural priority to the concepts discussed here. In working with a user to understand a business, it is most important to know what the entities are and whether the relationships among them are mandatory in either direction. That is, must an occurrence of one entity have an occurrence of another? After that, it is important to ascertain whether an occurrence can have more than one occurrence of the other entity.

Of lesser interest are the specific attributes of each entity.

The lowest priority, and indeed something that probably will not be discussed with the user at all, except in special cases, is whether or not the identity of occurrences of an entity depends on occurrences of another entity. Where this is so, it is usually obvious and not something that requires discussion.

Because of these priorities, graphically, the most dramatic symbols should be the entities and relationships themselves, followed by those used for the cardinality and optionality questions, with perhaps an appended symbol for the unique identifier. In IDEF1X, unfortunately, the most dramatic feature is the least important one — the notation for unique identifier. This involves the relationship line, the shape of the entity box, and the definition of attributes. Among other things, the use of solid and dashed lines means that the unique identifier decision must be made first, in order to draw the model at all.

This issue of convoluted lines also goes to the point of layering as well. As shown in the example above, the use of many lines with elbows can interfere with the viewer's ability to pick out the entities. By restricting oneself to straight lines, even if it means stretching the entities, one focuses the viewer's attention on the entities first. In stretching entities, by the way, there is the opportunity to make the most important entities larger, and the lesser entities smaller, further contributing to effective layering.

POOR NAMING

The most difficult thing for technicians to do is to name things. Many of us became interested in computers, after all, because we did not do all that well in English classes. But names are important. An entity is a thing of significance to the business, about which it wants to hold information. The name of that thing must be meaningful. It cannot be an acronym, or an abbreviation, or a table name. Unfortunately, too many analysts think they are providing table names for a database management system (with their attendant limitations on length), and the readability of the model suffers.

However, one is looking here for the names of things of significance to the business, not tables. In Chen's drawing (Exhibit 2), the entity names PROJ and SUPP are less than fully explanatory. Even worse, PART-PROJ-SUPP is not at all meaningful. Something better would be SUPPLIER, which at least conveys the idea that something is being supplied. Failure to name entities meaningfully makes it virtually impossible to understand what a data model is about.

Relationship names are even harder. Some techniques, such as SSADM and Yourdon's object-modeling technique, do not show relationship names at all. While it is true that this further simplifies the model aesthetically, it deprives the viewer of very important information about the model's meaning. Where they are used, it has become a convention to use verbs as relationship names; but unfortunately, verbs, if not completely meaningless, are often less than expressive of the full implication and meaning of the relationship. "Has" is the most commonly used relationship name, and it tells very little about the true nature of the relationship.

Moreover, when a verb is used, the relationship name often begins to look like a function name — which is the rightful topic of a different kind of model.

It is preferable to use prepositional phrases, since the preposition, after all, is the part of speech that specifically addresses relationships. The Oracle Method has a particularly clever way of doing this: using a normal but highly structured sentence to describe an entire relationship. The relationship names are designed to fit into the following structure, reading the relationship in each direction:

Each
<entity 1>
must be
[or]
may be
<relationship>
one and only one
[or]
one or more
<entity 2>

The sentence neatly captures not only the relationship itself, but also its cardinality and optionality. For example, in Exhibit 16, the relationship shown may be expressed by the two sentences:

1. "Each ORDER may be *composed of* one or more LINE ITEMS."
2. "Each LINE ITEM must be *part of* one and only one ORDER."

As described previously, the presence or absence of crow's feet dictates "one or more" (upper limit many) or "one and only one" (upper limit one). The solid-line half means "must be" (lower limit one), and the dashed-line half means "may be" (lower limit zero).

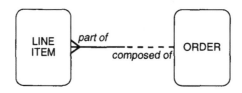

Exhibit 16.   Oracle relationship names

WHAT TO DO?

So, what is a person to do to make a diagram that is attractive and easy to read?

- Limit what one is trying to present to that which is meaningful and important to the audience. While it is desirable to present as much as possible, this exercise rapidly reaches the point of diminishing returns, where the addition of more information to the drawing actually subtracts from its overall effectiveness. Among other things, this means:
    - Using as consistent and spare a notation scheme as possible.
    - Limiting the number of objects appearing on a diagram.
- Arrange the diagram in a rational way.
- Make sure that names are meaningful and clear.
- Use patterns that have been tested.

PRESENTING YOUR MODEL

As important as the construction of a model is, it is equally important to present it in a way that permits the viewer to ease his way into the concepts involved. Models can be presented in an understandable way if a few rules are followed.

First of all, be sure to begin the session with a careful and thorough explanation of just what the objectives are. One cannot build a system without the viewers' assurance of your understanding of their business. This technique is intended to show them your understanding so that corrections can be made if necessary. The presenter is there to be wrong, since it is much cheaper for him/her to be wrong now, than it is to wait and be wrong in the design of a system. Your presentation is in terms of the structure of their data; so by extension, it is really about the structure of their business. Admit that the technique is a bit arcane and point out that it examines business from a perspective that may be unfamiliar to them, so ask their indulgence.

Then, do not begin by presenting a completed model. Even the most artistic model is too frightening to see as a whole. Begin by presenting a slide with one entity. Discuss that entity. What does it mean? What are its attributes? Are there any examples?

Add another one, with a relationship between the two. Discuss the second entity. Then discuss the relationship. Is it true that it must be related to only one? Can a case be imagined where it is related to more than one? One can then add a couple more entities and relationships at a time, discussing each part thoroughly, until the page has been completed. Then build up the next drawing in the same way.

Where there are intersect entities, always present the reference entities first. There may even be a slide showing a many-to-many relationship. Discuss the need for attributes that apply to each occurrence of a pair. Then present the slide with the intersect entity.

In doing the presentation, be sure to have a marking pen handy. It is amazing how quickly the audience becomes so involved that they are able to tell the presenter where he/she has erred. Listen. Where the presenter is wrong (and the presenter *will* be wrong), the slide can be marked to show that the presenter has been listening.

Notes

1. Martin, J. and Odell, J. J., *Object-Oriented Methods*. PTR Prentice-Hall, Englewood Cliffs, NJ, 1995.
2. Halpin, T., *Conceptual Schema & Relational Database Design*. Prentice-Hall, Sydney, Australia, 1995.
3. Tufte, E. R., *Envisioning Information*. Graphic Press, Cheshire, Connecticut, 53, 1990.

Chapter 9

Component Design for Relational Databases

Ashvin Iyengar

INTRODUCTION

COMPONENT-BASED OBJECT-ORIENTED ARCHITECTURES are becoming increasingly popular in building industrial strength applications. However, relational databases are not going to be replaced by object databases in the foreseeable future. This paper explores the ramifications of component-based designs on data management and offers strategies which could be deployed in the use of relational centralized databases with object-oriented component-based application architectures.

WHY RELATIONAL DATABASES ARE HERE TO STAY

From a pure application design perspective, object-oriented databases would be much more suitable for use with object-oriented component-based application architectures. However, the business realities are more complex and include the following considerations:

- Object-oriented databases are not mature enough to be entrusted with the job of managing large corporate data;
- It is more difficult to find professionals with experience in administration as well as the design of object-oriented databases;
- The vast majority of corporations are currently using relational databases to manage business information; and
- Most current live applications have been designed and developed to work with relational databases.

MOVING TOWARDS A COMPONENT-BASED ARCHITECTURE STANDARD

The subject of object-oriented design and programming involving relational databases has been well explored. More often than not, the data

0-8493-9976-9/99/$0.00+$.50
© 1999 by CRC Press LLC

model is constructed using pure relational database modeling techniques with little if any consideration for object-oriented design techniques. This necessitates the use of impedance matching techniques to allow object-oriented applications to interact with relational data models.

Application architectures are becoming increasingly component based to satisfy the need for flexible as well as manageable systems. The effort to move away from large monolithic applications has been underway for a number of years. This has resulted in the adoption of client-server based architecture as the de facto standard in the industry. However, with lack of proper design, client-server architectures became just as monolithic as mainframe applications and thus inherited all the maintenance problems associated with large monolithic applications. Object-oriented design techniques and multi-tiered architectures were adopted in order to solve this problem. Component design is a natural next step in the evolution of application architectures since it combines the principles of object-oriented design with multi-tiered application architecture. In addition, industry-wide acceptance of the incremental and iterative software development methodology over the old waterfall development methodology has provided an additional thrust towards component-based design.

Some of the other factors contributing towards making component-based application design the de facto standard are:

- The maturing of technologies like DCOM (distributed component object model) and CORBA.
- The plethora of new technologies encouraging the design and deployment of components over the Web (e.g., JavaBeans).
- The ability to design, develop, and deploy components using high level, widely used applications like Visual Basic.
- The potential for using third-party components along with in-house applications in order to fulfill specific needs (e.g., a professional third-party charting component).
- The resulting relative ease of component replacement.

BACKGROUND OF MULTI-TIERED ARCHITECTURES

The current thrust is towards the use of distributed, component-based application architectures. The ever-increasing need to deploy applications over the Web and the resulting security considerations have led to a n-tiered architecture, using, at the very least, three distinct tiers.

- Web server
- Application server
- Database server

Whereas, a number of studies have shown that pure object-oriented applications are difficult to design and develop and that the payoffs information technology (IT) executives had hoped for in terms of reuse are seldom realized, multi-tiered architecture is here to stay. Three-tiered architecture is, in fact, the industry standard and a wide variety of application development environments from Smalltalk to Visual Basic support and encourage the use of this standard architecture.

In general, a three-tiered architecture has the following layers:

- Interface layer
- Business layer
- Data layer

The driving force behind three-tiered architecture is the need to support both flexibility and robustness in applications. De-coupling the interface layer from the database offers the advantage of changes in the database that need not affect the interface layer directly, thereby isolating the effects of a change in either layer. The interface layer describes how the application interacts with the outside world. If the outside world is comprised of end users, then the interface layer refers to a user interface. Alternatively, if it is comprised of client applications, it refers to an application interface.

Arguably, the main payoff involved in object-oriented architectures is not reuse but rather change management. Effective change management is also the goal of three-tiered architectures. Since three-tiered architectures are easier to implement with object-based (if not object-oriented) systems, new life has been extended to object-based systems. In this article, a distinction is being made between object-oriented and object-based systems. Object-based systems implement classes and objects, but do not permit other aspects of object-oriented programming like inheritance and polymorphism. So whereas the three pillars of object-oriented programming can be said to be encapsulation, inheritance, and polymorphism, object-based programming concerns itself with mainly encapsulation.

A leading example of an object-based application development is Visual Basic. Visual Basic is to the client-server world what Cobol is to the mainframe world. Since classes in Visual Basic are implemented using DCOM (distributed component object model), it is extremely easy to develop and deploy components using Visual Basic.

An object-based component can be described as a set of objects collaborating to provide a common functionality and implementing a common interface. Thus, an object-based component improves the encapsulation aspect of object-based applications. By virtue of this it also increases the flexibility as well as robustness of an object-based application, since changes to the component are isolated.

It has already been argued that the main thrust towards three-tiered architecture is coming from a need for effective change management. Change management, as used in this paper, encompasses the concepts of flexibility and robustness. It has also been argued that object-based applications by virtue of their support for encapsulation are a natural choice for the implementation of business solutions with underlying multi-tiered architectures. Since a component-based architecture enhances the ability of multi-tiered architectures to deliver on its promise, it would be logical to conclude that component-based multi-tiered architectures are here to stay.

So the prevalent application development environment can be said to have the following features:

- Multi-tiered architecture
- Relational databases
- Object-based applications
- Component-based application architecture

APPLICATION ARCHITECTURE EXAMPLE

Now this article will take an example where a set of three tables provides a certain functionality (e.g., hold information pertaining to interest rates in a portfolio management system) and three discrete applications that interact with these three tables. It will start with a simple two-tiered application architecture example and note the problems in the chosen context.

Then it will move to a more object-oriented version of the same problem and again note the problems with the approach. Finally, it will illustrate a solution to the same problem using a data-component approach.

In Exhibit 1, Application A1 is responsible for displaying and maintaining information in M1 (the set of tables T1, T2, and T3 constituting a sub data model). Applications A2, A3 use the information in M1 to do their processing. Note that Application A1 interacts with all the tables in M1, whereas Applications A2, A3 interact with only T3.

The shortcomings of two-tiered applications have already been noted. In this case, the tight coupling between the applications and the data is obvious, and consequently, flexibility is severely compromised. Also, there are three different applications interacting with the same data and consequently, complexity is increased since a change in data storage/design would necessitate change to all the client applications.

To make this design more object-oriented, now move to Exhibit 2 which illustrates a three-tiered object-oriented architecture. Applications A1, A2, and A3 contain their own relational to object mapping layer (also known as impedance matching layer). Now consider that new business rules necessitate a change to M1. M1 is a sub data model corresponding to functional-

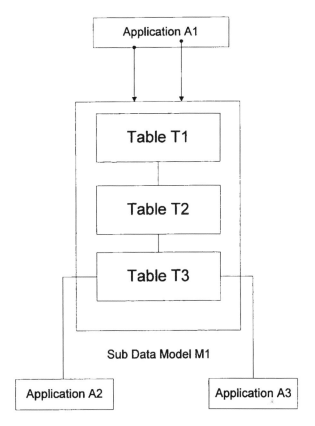

Exhibit 1.   Two-tier application architecture.

---

ity F1 (e.g., performance history of various investment options in a portfolio management system). If the new data model involves changing the way information is represented in T3, then all applications involving T3 (in this case Applications A1, A2, and A3) have to be updated. In addition to requiring duplication of effort this design increases the risk of application malfunction, since it is possible to miss updating an application which needs updating. Also note that even aside from complicating change management, this design involves duplication of effort in terms of data access as well as relational to object mapping.

In order to solve the above-mentioned problems, modify the design to produce a more object-oriented approach by introducing components. Exhibit 3 introduces a component C1 that encapsulates sub data model M1. This makes C1 a data-component. Consequently, to the methodology illustrated in Exhibit 3 is referred to as the data-component approach.

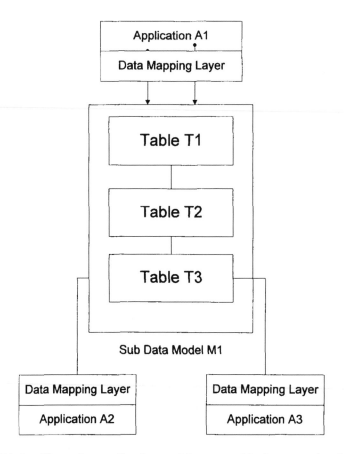

Exhibit 2. Three-tier application architecture with data-mapping layer.

ADVANTAGES/FEATURES OF THE DATA-COMPONENT APPROACH

The data-component approach, as illustrated in Exhibit 3, offers the following features and advantages:

- Applications do not access the tables directly but use the interface functions provided by the interface layer in C1.
- Satisfies an important OOD (object-oriented design) requirement: keep function and data together.
- Eliminates redundant data access as well as data mapping.
- Separates the GUI from the business logic — an important requirement of three-tier client server computing.
- Allows implementation of n-tiered architecture since C1 can be deployed on an application server.
- Provides much better change management (which as elaborated before, is an even greater benefit of object-oriented development than re-

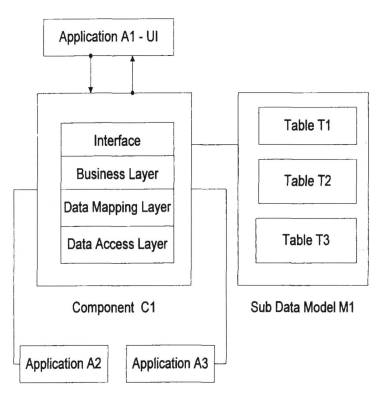

Exhibit 3. Application architecture example using data-component approach.

use), since changes in the data model no longer affect client applications directly. The only time the client applications are affected is when changes to the data model/functionality affect the interface between C1 and the client applications.

- Allows implementation of multiple interface or different views of data thus adding a new twist to the classic MVC (Model View Controller) object-oriented architecture.
- Provides data source independence, since changing the source of the data will affect only the data access and data mapping layers of the component and the client applications will be insulated from any such change.
- Reduces the effort involved in allowing new applications to access the data.

DISADVANTAGES/LIMITATIONS OF THE DATA-COMPONENT APPROACH

The data-component approach as illustrated in Exhibit 3 has the following possible disadvantages or limitations:

- If used indiscriminately, this approach could lead to a proliferation of components thereby increasing the number of applications.
- Large applications using a large number of components could experience performance degradation, especially while loading the application.
- Each component will possibly have registration requirements, so the task of installing and distributing applications will be more complex.
- This approach deals primarily with discrete, non-overlapping use cases. Overlapping use cases will create additional complexities that have not been addressed in this approach.

DATA-COMPONENT GRANULARITY CONSIDERATIONS

To prevent proliferation of components, the granularity of the components can be increased. For example as shown in Exhibit 4, use cases U1 and U2 use sub data models M1 and M2 correspondingly.

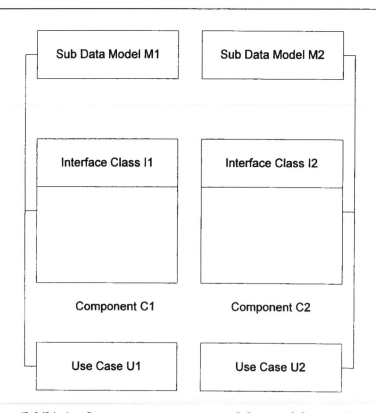

Exhibit 4.   One-to-one component to subdata model example.

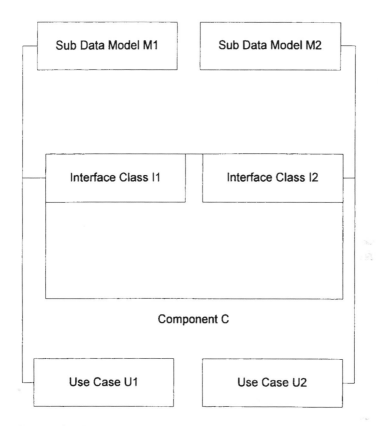

Exhibit 5.   One-to-many component to subdata model example.

Instead of having components C1 and C2 that correspond to use cases U1 and U2, if U1 and U2 are closely related, a single component C (with interfaces I1 and I2) can serve U1 and U2, as illustrated in Exhibit 5.

The same exercise of combining related use cases into components could be carried out through the application design space thereby bringing component proliferation under control.

IMPLEMENTATION OF THE COMPONENT-BASED DESIGN USING MICROSOFT'S ARCHITECTURE

Even though the component technology war between CORBA and DCOM is far from over, the fact remains that DCOM (in some form) has been around longer and is used widely in the industry. It also has, arguably, more opportunities to mature into a stable industrial strength technology. Consequently, Microsoft's DCOM platform is discussed in the implementation of the data-component approach illustrated in Exhibit 3.

In Microsoft's DCOM technology there are two main types of components:

1. ActiveX Exe
2. ActiveX DLL

The difference between the two types of components is that the ActiveX Exe is an out-of-process component while the ActiveX DLL is an in-process component. In-process components usually offer significantly better performance than out-of-process components. However, in-process components and their client applications must reside on the same physical machines. With out-of-process components there is no such restriction, therefore out-of-process components offer greater flexibility in terms of deployment at the cost of application performance.

The choice between in-process and out-of-process components would therefore depend on the physical architecture. Note that three-tier software architectures can be deployed using two-tier physical architectures. In a two-tier implementation, the database runs on a database server and the user interface layer as well as the business layer runs on the client desktops. This kind of implementation is also called fat-client, since most of the applications are deployed on individual workstations. Whereas this might be sufficient for a small shop, for larger shops, distribution as well as maintenance of all the various components on individual workstations can prove to be a daunting as well as error-prone task. For this reason, larger shops may prefer to implement a physical three-tier architecture which would involve client workstations interacting with an application server which in turn would interact with a database server. While this approach alleviates some of the distribution problems inherent in the two-tier architecture, a new problem is created with multiple workstations accessing the same application on the application server concurrently. Clearly, it would be counter-productive to start up a new copy of the application for every workstation that needs it. Therefore, some sort of a queuing solution is inevitable. It is in this respect that the DCOM architecture is yet to mature. Microsoft's solution to the problem involves use of MTS (Microsoft's transaction server), but that may not be a universally viable solution for every situation.

It is also worth noting that even though it is technically easy to convert an ActiveX DLL to an ActiveX Exe, there are other considerations involved which might necessitate knowledge of the physical architecture in advance. The main consideration is network traffic. With out-of-process components, performance requirements usually dictate the use of fewer but longer messages, whereas with in-process components, frequencies of messages do not result in performance penalties.

If the generic architecture example illustrated in Exhibit 3 were to be implemented on a Microsoft platform, the following notes may apply:

- The interface layer of component C1 interfaces with Applications A1, A2, and A3. Since A2 and A3 are inquiry-only applications, they can share a common interface. So, we would have two interface classes, I1 and I2. I1 will implement the interface needed for A1 and I2 would implement the interface needed for applications A2 and A3. In some cases, classes I1 and I2 could be implemented in a separate ActiveX DLL. This has the advantage of providing de-coupling between the client and server applications. In practice, this has to be weighed against the cost of distributing this additional component. There will also be a minor performance penalty involved in separating the interface classes in a separate component, since an additional program will have to be loaded.
- Another factor to be considered while designing the interface layer is the number of parameters needed for the component to query and present the information. Assume for starters a method M1 in component C1, where the number of input parameters is n and the method returns only one value. A change in the input parameters would entail changing method M1 and therefore changing the interface. Therefore, except for trivial methods, it would make sense to encapsulate the data flowing between the component and its client applications, in classes. In this example a class C1M1 would contain all the input parameters as well as result values for method M1 in Component C1. M1 now would be passed a reference to object OC1MI (corresponding to class C1M1). With this approach, if method M1 were to need a new input parameter or need to return an extra result value, the interface would remain unchanged and changes would be restricted to class C1M1 and its usage.
- The business layer of the component should contain most of editing rules and the business logic. Including the editing logic in the business layer of the component goes a long way towards ensuring data integrity since applications that update the data maintained by the component have to use the interface layer of the component. Note that the business layer is not exposed directly to the outside world. External applications can only use the methods exposed by the interface layer, which in turn will interact with the business layer. Also, since the interface layer does not directly interact with the data layer of the component, the business layer has a chance to enforce its business rules and ensure logical integrity.
- The data layer of the component typically consists of two internal layers namely a relational to object mapping layer and a data access layer. The data access layer is responsible for the actual interaction with the database. The data mapping layer is responsible for mapping relational data into objects. Each record in a relational database is essentially an array of values. If a query returns more than one record (a RecordSet in Microsoft-speak), then we are dealing with a two-dimensional array. The data-mapping layer typically converts a single record to an object and a RecordSet to a collection of objects. Also, for per-

sistent data, the object in the data mapping layer must know how to access the objects in the data access layer in order to store updated data. It is also worthwhile noting that the data access layer could be implemented as a separate component in itself. That way multiple applications can use the data access layer to manage their interactions with the physical database.

Following are examples of the architectures discussed in this paper:

1. The business layer has classes B1 and B2 that correspond to the interface layer classes I1 and I2. B1 and B2 interact with classes R1,R2,...., RN which implement various business rules. B1 and B2 also interact with corresponding classes DM1 and DM2, which belong to the data mapping layer of the data layer. DM1 and DM2 in turn interact with classes DA1, DA2, and DA3, which access/update data in Tables T1, T2, and T3.

2. Instead of having separate classes B1 and B2, depending on the application, a single class B may suffice.

3. Again, depending on the application, a single class DA may provide the functionality provided by DA1, DA2, and DA3.

4. Note that DM1 and DM2 provide the business view of the data model and this case is basically driven by the choice of B1 and B2 as the business classes. Depending on the requirements, classes DM1, DM2, and DM3 could correspond to DA1, DA2, and DA3 or any other combination that makes sense.

5. Note that classes DM1 and DM2 could create and return a variety of objects. For example, object O11 might correspond to a specific record in the table T1. Object O12 might correspond to a collection of records. Alternatively, O12 may be implemented as an object containing a collection of O11 objects. Similarly, objects O21 through O2N might correspond to Table T2. Alternatively, O21 through O2N might correspond to data linked between Tables T2 and T3 if appropriate.

The possibilities are endless. The examples listed previously illustrate some of the considerations that might come into play during the design of the component. To reiterate one of the main points in this article, effective change management, assume that a change is to be made to this design. Instead of accessing data in Tables T2 and T3 directly, applications must use a View instead. In this case, only relevant classes in the data access layer and maybe the data mapping layer will need to be changed. All other classes in the business and the interface layer of the component can remain unchanged. Also, the client applications using the component remain unaffected. Thus use of a multi-tiered component-based architecture has provided for flexibility (providing ease of change by restricting the area of change) as well as robustness (limiting the scope of the effect of change).

DATA-COMPONENT MINING

Data-component mining is the process by which an existing data model can be analyzed and broken up into sub data models with associated data-components. One approach to component mining is to study the data model to identify loosely coupled sets of entities. Each such set of entities can be called a sub-data model. Each such sub-data model is a good candidate for a component and more so if the sub-data model is used by more than one application. Use cases have become a standard way of defining requirements/functionality in object-oriented design. A list of existing as well as future use cases can also provide a valuable perspective during data-component mining design. Related use cases can be combined to help identify sub-data models and consequently corresponding data components.

For example, in a portfolio management system, analysis of the ERD (entity relationship diagram) of the data model might suggest that the set of entities containing historical performance data could constitute a sub-data model M1. Similarly, the set of entities pertaining to investment choices in a client's portfolio could constitute another sub-data model M2. There is now a potential use for two data components: C1 corresponding to model M1 (historical performance data) and C2 corresponding to model M2 (client's investment choices). Alternatively, it could start with use cases. For example, consider the following use cases:

- U1 — Provide inquiry of client's investment elections.
- U2 — Provide investment election change update/change.
- U3 — Provide inquiry of investment performance data.
- U4 — Provide update of investment performance data.
- U5 — Calculate portfolio values for a given client.

U1 and U2 deal with the same information (a client's investment choices). Similarly, U3 and U4 deal with the same information (investment performance data). U5 deals with the client's investment choices as well as investment performance data. Since investment performance data is independent of a client's investment choices, the entities in the data model corresponding to investment performance data, can be said to be loosely coupled with the entities pertaining to client investment elections. Therefore, investment performance data as well as client investment choices are both candidates for sub-data models with corresponding data components. The implementation of U5 would then involve use of both data components.

CONCLUSION

The data component approach to data management can be valuable in an environment involving object-oriented applications and relational databases. The primary advantage provided by this approach is ensuring that the application responsible for updating information is responsible for providing inquiry of the same information, thereby providing for superior change management. This approach can be used in any environment that allows development of component-based applications.

Chapter 10

Practices in Enterprise Data Modeling

Wolfgang Keller

ENTERPRISE DATA MODELING has recently been in the crossfire of attacks asserting that it is completely useless. Most critics say that such an inflexible, top-down, and centralist approach is not equipped to deal with problems like changing environments, pressure from global markets, and decentralization. A central data model is said to be a contradiction to a decentralized organization. Critics say that the rapid change will make the data model outdated before the data analysts can bring it to market.

If analyzed, most of the arguments against data modeling have their roots in existing problems and frequent errors in practice. However, this does not mean that enterprise data modeling in general is faulty or useless. Many of the arguments can be attributed to improper use of data modeling equipment.

Data modeling was invented to avoid the problems associated with isolated, nonintegrated systems. This chapter is designed to help users avoid some typical errors by focusing on correct data modeling practices.

ARGUMENTS AGAINST ENTERPRISEWIDE DATA MODELS

The following is a list of common arguments against data modeling. Many financial institutions and other organizations are reconsidering their data modeling practices in light of the bad press they have been receiving. A financial application is used as an example throughout this chapter because information processing is one of the core activities of the banking business.

Critics of data modeling assert that it:

- Is not able to keep pace with new developments. Information processing systems of financial institutions must be adapted rapidly to change because of the globalization of markets and new requirements for customer service.

- Cannot provide a bank with information systems that adapt with the speed of innovation. New financial instruments require fast adaptation of IS capabilities.
- Acts as a brake and not a booster for rapid systems development.
- Promotes structures that should not be changed. Change is the norm in systems development. This adds to the characterization of data modeling as a brake.
- Creates additional complexity in the process of software development. Applications development is impaired by the use of top-down data modeling practices.
- Can lead to the violation of normalization rules, with the consequent need to adapt the integrated systems.
- Has to incorporate all possible future options of a system, which slows operation to a standstill. The level of abstraction tends to increase indefinitely until no one is able to understand the results of the process.
- Is useless, if purchased off the shelf as a prefabricated data model.

STARTING POINTS FOR BETTER DATA MODELING

The following four requirements should be the starting points for data modeling. These goals are essential to a reasonable process of software development. Despite the criticism, these basic requirements are often acknowledged as essentials of any software development process:

- Integrated systems are a prerequisite for the survival of a financial institution, to manage complexity and to master interdependencies. Data modeling was invented to integrate systems and important terminology. The goals of this effort are reuse and data integration.
- The separate systems of an enterprise must use consistent terms to provide a consistent processing of data across the boundaries of several systems.
- Integration of old and new systems is necessary for routine systems development. As system integration is the norm in systems development, bottom-up strategies and reengineering of old systems must be supported. Good data modeling practice will provide support for this process.
- Fundamental structures or invariants of a business are the basis for all systems development.

Is Enterprise Data Modeling Really That Bad?

The rebuttals to the arguments will show that most of the problems with data modeling can be fixed by a data modeling process that is oriented toward goals.

Data Modeling Does Not Accommodate Rapid Change. *Rebuttal:* No attempt should be made to model transitory facts in a data model. Hardwired organization schemes are not subject to data modeling. The core of business activities and business rules is subject, however, to data modeling. A bank account will stay the same for years. Such an object is not subject to rapid change. Data modeling should concentrate on such core entities.

Data Modeling Is Inefficient for Financial Instruments. *Rebuttal:* There are data models for financial instruments that use factorization to describe them. A new instrument is a combination of known elements — a pattern of thinking that is well known from linear or polynomial functions or from industrial part list problems. No developer will try to model each new function or product; instead, it is sufficient to find the set of parameters that fully describe the function. This decomposition is often called a "high level of abstraction." Some argue that it is too high to understand. This depends on the granularity of the basic elements used to describe a product or instrument.

Data Modeling Slows Down Projects. *Rebuttal:* Data modeling can accelerate projects by acting as a service function. Data administration groups can report on entities that already exist and about how other groups solved problems in a reference model. A data administration group that does reviews only after project completion is indeed a slowdown. A data administration group that helps projects by reporting on current problem-solving efforts is a very important step toward reuse and reusable objects.

Data Modeling Promotes Inflexible Structures. *Rebuttal:* The basic structure of a bank account is an entity that does not change.

Applications Development Is Slowed by Top-Down Methods. *Rebuttal:* There is no law that says developers have to work from the top down when practicing data modeling. There should be a framework, called a top-level data model, (e.g., level A or B of an enterprise data model). But no developer will seriously try to go all the way down to level C before starting his or her first project. Instead, most developers recommend a process that creates a top-down frame of about 50 entities on a B level. This frame is then filled from the bottom up by projects with their project data models.

Normal Forms Are Violated. *Rebuttal:* There is also no law saying there must be a fifth normal form. Models, such as reference models, are often highly normalized. This should not lead to the conclusion that denormalization at the logical level is forbidden in every case. In a level C logical data model, there is no need to stick with the highest normal form available on the market at the time of creation.

Data Modeling Is Inflexible for Future Change. *Rebuttal:* The problem of having to model all future options in a certain problem can be discussed using the example of financial instruments. The same approach is valid for the abstraction level of several reference data models — it has to fit the needs of many corporations. To adapt a reference model to individual needs, it should not be made more abstract, but it should be simplified to adapt it to the needs of the organization that uses it.

Reference Data Models Are Useless. *Rebuttal:* Reference data models, also called application platforms, are often mistaken for off-the-shelf, prefabricated data models intended for use in every financial institution. However, they are very useful, and can be tailored to specific organizations.

Alternatives to Data Modeling

The question most of the critics leave unanswered is, what happens if data modeling is not performed? The first alternative is to build island solutions, as in the pioneering days of data processing. These islands are connected via interfaces. The lack of common terminology leads to problems and considerable effort. The negative experiences with these solutions resulted in a data modeling approach to fix those problems.

Another approach is to take business processes as the fixed point of analysis. Processes can be analyzed, and in most cases, elementary processes will be found that will be grouped in entities. This approach is a purely dogmatic, bottom-up, object-oriented approach.

A practical approach is somewhere between bottom-up and top-down. A healthy mixture of a top-down approach, manifested in level A and B enterprise object models and bottom-up methods represented by project-driven level C logical models, should be much better than any pure, dogmatic approach.

ORGANIZATIONAL ASPECTS: DEFINING GOALS

A formal definition of goals and objectives for data modeling may seem bureaucratic. But a short statement defining the goals of data modeling in a company can be helpful for new employees in the data administration department or for the more experienced employees as a reminder of their goals. When looking at an organization's data modeling procedures, quality and technical issues pertaining to the integration of data modeling should be checked in the software development organization.

The following list of questions is derived from the criticisms and rebuttals of data modeling and should help organizations identify weak spots in their data modeling practice:

- Is there a written definition of the objectives for the data administration group?
- Are the goals consistent with goals stated in this chapter?
- What are the project goals of systems development projects in aspects of data modeling?
- Is there a top-level data model that is publicized and available?

Data Administration as a Service Provider

A data administration group can be of enormous use to project teams, or it can be an enormous source of frustration. If a data administration group comes up with some sound solutions or possible designs before a project starts with specification of details, it can be of great assistance. The data administration department is a service and not a control function. Management may want to ask:

- Is the data administration a service provider or only a review institution?
- Do they have a written statement that they are a service provider?
- What do the project managers think about the service provided by data administration?
- What is the ratio between services and control functions in the data administration department?

Integration of Data Modeling Activities into the Process of Specification

Data modeling should be an integral part of the specification process right from the beginning. This practice will promote reuse and avoid revisiting old arguments. To ensure that data modeling is properly integrated, managers should ask themselves:

- When do the project teams usually meet the data administration group — at the start of a project or at the end in the review?
- Are there separated project data models?
- Are there people who do data modeling on a C level for their own sake, without a project needing it?
- Is there a mechanism that allows projects to borrow parts of the data model for rework and new developments?
- How do projects integrate their results into the global master enterprise data model? Is there any assistance or tool for integration?
- Who supervises the process of integration?

Separated Levels of a Data Model

Reference models separate clearly between different levels of abstraction in a data model. This is required because different levels are different blueprints for different groups of people (A, B levels for business administration, C for data systems professionals). The data administration group should ask:

- Do we have level A and B data models that are more than just a pure copy of a reference model?
- What do the users think about data modeling?
- Is there a repository that strictly separates levels of the data model?
- Will users working on projects see at once which level they are currently looking at when dealing with the dictionary?

Quality of Data Model Contents

The quality of the contents of a data model is often intangible. Typical errors can be seen in existing data models; for example, an account number is the number of an account. Definitions such as this often occur when old pools of data have been reengineered in a sloppy manner. Data administration groups should make sure that data models are of high quality, and if not, examine the reasons why. Sometimes, projects lack the budget to do a proper job, or employees may lack the motivation.

Rate of Change

A low rate of change, combined with efficient software development and systems integration, is an indicator for high-quality data modeling. If data modeling describes the core of the business rather than listing simple organizational facts, the indicator will show a decrease in change.

Managers of data administration should ask themselves:

- Does the data administration monitor the change rate? If so, is it an automatic function?
- Is the change rate seen as a problem? If so, why? What are the reasons for frequent change?
- Is the data administration department clogged with change requests?

Is the Data Model Up to Date?

A data model should reflect the current state of the business for which it is designed. The terminology must reflect the corporate facts and the meaning of certain terms. The data administration department should ensure that the data model is fully up to date and carefully monitor the time it takes to process a change request — the shorter the better.

Quality of Upper Model Levels

The upper level (i.e., A and B levels) of a data model should be understood and approved by the users, because they are the people who run the business and generate the profits that pay for data administration. Data administration should make every effort to find out what users think about modeling efforts. It is also wise for data administration to find out how project teams perceive the quality of the data model.

Data Types As Entities

Data administration should know whether:

- There are data types that are being modeled as entities (e.g., records that have no natural key, but a key that consists of all attributes).
- There are enumeration types coded as attributes that occur in several entities.

DATA ADMINISTRATION: QUALITY ASSURANCE AND SELF-CONTROL

Quality cannot be reached simply by defining formal objectives for quality assurance. In some cases, explicit goals for quality assurance will help lead activities down the right path. This is also true for data modeling activities. In the absence of other goals, some data administration departments adhere to normal forms and similar theoretical approaches as indicators of quality — but this is not the essential goal. It is better to use business-driven objectives such as integration, reuse, and modeling of the core business.

Quality Objectives

There should be a documented statement of the data administration department's quality goals. The goals will be either business driven or theory driven — the order of goals will imply which.

Reuse. Reuse is an explicit goal of many IS organizations and should be measured. The reuse quota is an indicator of the quality of data modeling activities.

Typical reuse quotas from projects are about 50%. Some are less and some are more, depending on the project and previous activities. Projects retrieve information about known entities from a variety of sources. For example, information can be retrieved from a host-based repository only (an adequate method) or from discussions with the data administration group during the design process (a better method), as well as from a repository.

Data Integration at the Physical Level. Physical data integration across several applications is an indicator of good data modeling practice. Another good sign is the presence of logical objects that are implemented over and over again.

Reference models are not off-the-shelf production data models. They have to be fitted to fulfill the individual needs of the organization using them. They should be separated physically or logically from the production data model.

The data administration group may want to analyze its data integration attempts by posing the following questions:

- Is there a physical border between logical, physical, and reference data models?
- Is there a clear logical border? Is it possible to see at first glance whether an entity is in production or an entity from a reference model?
- Is the reference model subject to a version concept?
- Is the production model subject to a version concept? If so, is this separated from the versions of the reference model?
- How is the reference model acquired — paper, or files for a computer-aided software engineering (CASE) tool?

Level of Abstraction. Reference models often have a level of abstraction that is too high for the needs of a single company. The other case, a production model with a higher level of abstraction, should occur only as a rare exception. In most cases, it is useless to raise the production data model to an even higher level of abstraction than a reference model. If there are examples of production models having a higher level of abstraction than reference models in an organization, the reasoning for this should be investigated thoroughly.

Transforming the Logical to a Physical Data Model. A one-to-one implementation of a logical data model can be successful, but in many cases it leads to slow implementations. The transformation process from logical to physical data models requires a great deal of knowledge and experience. It is not economical, and also not very probable that every analyst has the know-how required for this delicate task. Before attempting this task, data administration should find out the following:

- Do projects teams document their decisions? Can those decisions be retrieved by data administration or other projects?
- Are there reviews of the physical data model? If so, who does them?
- Is there a set of design rules somewhere in the company? If not, is there capable help for documenting them?

Dialogs and Data Modeling. The acceptance of data modeling — especially of physical data modeling — will rise when data models and check routines are directly coupled. Automation is crucial for the development of large, consistent systems. Before automation is undertaken, the data administration group should ask:

- Is there an automatic link between the data model or another repository, screen elements, and their captions?
- Is there an automatic reference between screen elements, check routines, and data type definitions?
- Are screen element tables in specifications generated automatically?

Database Access Layers. Database access layers for logical views on a physical model should be generated automatically from relation descriptions. Many companies use either no access layers at all or code frames for access layers. The generation of access layers is not possible without a rigid data modeling practice. The effort saved by not performing access layer programming is a very tangible effect of data modeling. It should be determined whether the software development department uses access layers and, if so, whether they are generated or at least standardized.

Data Types. Most COBOL or PL/I shops do not have a concept of data types. This leads to enumeration types being redundantly described in textual attribute descriptions, structures being described as entities, and other design flaws. It is helpful if an organization has a data type concept that is supported by code-generation facilities and a repository that allows a data type concept.

Data Dictionary Product Properties. It is important for data dictionary software to support requirements concerning the separation of model layers, version concepts, and data types. It is a good sign if the software developers and project teams like the look and feel of the data dictionary. A data dictionary should:

- Support data types such as enumeration types, records, range types, and a code generation facility.
- Be adaptable to changes in its metamodel. Improvement of the software development process can be slowed or made impossible by an inflexible dictionary.
- Have a version concept.
- Support integration of project data models. This is best done using check tools that support the data administration group.
- Support separation of levels, documentation of transformations between levels, and separated production and reference models.

SUMMARY

A broad range of criticism has been brought against data modeling. This chapter focused on the criticism to derive several lists of critical questions concerning organizational, technical, and quality success factors for a good data modeling practice. These questions were used to check the data modeling practice of a large financial institution. Exploring the issues covered and considering the questions posed should help data administration groups avoid some of the problems common to data modeling.

Chapter 11
Integrating Process and Data Models in a Horizontal Organization

David C. Wallace

INFORMATION SYSTEMS ARE CREATED TO HELP ACHIEVE THE GOALS AND OBJECTIVES OF THE ORGANIZATION by integrating them with information technology. Information technology is an extensive concept in which all the new technologies from fax machines to multimedia devices to new computer hardware and software are grouped. To be an effective part of an organization, individuals must understand and use information technology within the organization.

Therefore, an organization that wishes to be successful must first develop a strategic plan, which involves a systematic way of integrating information systems and information technology. Currently, the IS field is focusing on developing both new methodologies and criteria for the evaluation and selection of appropriate methodologies. This is often completed without regard to new trends within the business and organization fields. When that happens, the new methodologies may not meet the needs of the business community and might produce systems that are flawed.

IS methodologies have largely ignored the recent trends within the business management area — the gap between research and practice. One of these major trends focuses on aligning organizational resources around essential processes, or *core processes*. This trend has been identified by F. Ostroff and D. Smith of McKinsey & Company as the horizontal corporation. M.A. Burns, Chairman of Ryder System Inc., states that the horizontal corporation concept is the wave of the future. From such large profit-centered organizations as General Electric, AT&T, Ryder, and Xerox to such small nonprofit organizations as the Police Department at Illinois State University, there is a movement toward the horizontal organization. L.A. Bossidy, chairman of Allied Signal Inc., sees a significant increase in productivity as more organizations restructure themselves around this concept.

In this paradigm, the organization restructures its goals and objectives around the essential processes that define the organization's existence and sequential survival. The result is the flattening of the organizational structure into essential processes — eliminating the traditional hierarchy of bureaucratic divisions, departments, or sections. This allows both profit and nonprofit organizations to be more responsive to their clients or customers. The traditional goals of profitability, market share, and shareholders' satisfaction will not be identified as goals, but as natural outcomes resulting from the emphasis on tying goals to an organization's essential processes.

Integrating recent trends in the business organization field with an effective IS methodology is a critical success factor for an organization. For a profit-centered organization, this will often provide the means to achieve competitive advantages in the market by: enhancing existing products and services, developing new products and services, changing the existing industry and its characteristics, and creating new industries and markets.

For a nonprofit organization, the ability to stretch shrinking resources to meet the demands of its constituents is critical to its success. As budget dollars for local, state, and federal agencies are cut, these agencies still find themselves responsible for meeting the requirements of their charters. They will also need to integrate their IS structures around proven trends within the organization field to achieve their maximum productivity. Therefore, it is important to develop IS methodologies that integrate these recent trends.

THE HORIZONTAL CORPORATION

The horizontal corporation is an approach for all types of organizations — public or private, profit or nonprofit, corporate or sole proprietorships, large or small. The prerequisites for this approach are to redefine corporate goals around strategic actions that will improve the organization's competitiveness, efficiency, or other strategic actions defined by the organization. One important goal for any organization is to focus on improvement.

To meet the challenges of competitive domestic and international markets or the demands for shrinking funding dollars, organizations must constantly review and improve their operations. The organization must know its markets and customers thoroughly to know what it will take to satisfy them. For nonprofit organizations, shareholders include the people they serve and the funding sources on which they depend. Once these corporate goals have been clearly identified, the organization should be able to identify key objectives that will help them achieve these goals (e.g., customer and supplier satisfaction). These key objectives are measurable and identifiable for reach process and should contribute to the organization goals.

The next step requires the organization to identify its essential processes. These processes can be characterized by mission-critical applications or core processes. The applications focus on the very purpose or meaning of the organization (e.g., the identification of new markets and new customers, retention of existing customers, and other critical applications). The very purpose or meaning criteria can be answered by focusing on the actions necessary to accomplish the corporate goals. The key objectives identified in the previous step should provide insight into the identification of the essential processes. For example, customer satisfaction can be achieved through customer support, new product development, and sales and fulfillment. The next series of steps involves the actual restructuring of the organization.

Multidisciplinary Efforts

Once the essential processes have been identified, the organization will restructure itself around these processes. Each process will have a manager who helps facilitate the coordination and communication within the process and with other processes. Each process should link related tasks to yield a product or service to a customer or user. Careful attention should be given to the elimination of tasks that do not support, in some way, the related objectives of the process. Such tasks or activities are a waste of time and resources.

Training, evaluating, and paying employees should be linked to the accomplishments of objectives of the essential processes. Each process is responsible for all tasks needed to produce the end-product or service. This requires each process to be multidisciplinary (e.g., finance, marketing, production, accounting, or sales). The intent is to localize the necessary tasks for an essential process to streamline operations so that the organization can react quickly to changing conditions. Ideally, each task should harmoniously fit together with the next to generate the end result, thereby eliminating layers of bureaucracy that tend to increase costs and delay actions. All essential processes should harmoniously fit together to achieve all strategic goals of the organization.

By eliminating layers of administration and bureaucracy, each process can focus on accomplishing its objectives and becoming better able to meet the constant challenges of a changing market. The upper-level support departments provide additional expertise (e.g., legal, technical, and administrative). Core knowledge and expertise will be provided by the essential process. The main purpose of flattening the organization structure into horizontal layers of essential processes is to allow the organization to function more efficiently and quickly.

Traditional organizational structures require much coordination across department boundaries where such functions as sales, marketing, management, and accounting are often housed. The larger, more complex organizations would often experience long delays and information failure (e.g., lost or misdirected paperwork) as information was passed from one functional area or department to another. By localizing the necessary tasks into one process, the organization can provide a seamless effort in which the amount of information interchange is kept to a minimum, thereby reducing delays and information failures. Companies that have moved toward the horizontal corporate approach have been able to reduce response time significantly and improve overall operating performance.

The horizontal concept is illustrated in Exhibit 1. The essential processes operate on a horizontal level using the multidisciplinary efforts within each process to accomplish their objectives. Each process is not a standalone entity, but is integrated into part of an entire picture in which each part communicates and coordinates with each other part. Realistically, special expertise and strategic direction are needed to monitor changing conditions in the markets and environments in which the organization must exist.

These strategic considerations should be accomplished at a higher level. The more operational and managerial considerations would be held at the process level. Downsized support departments (e.g., finance, legal, accounting, and marketing) will exist at the higher level within the organization to provide the expertise needed by the processes. Strategic direction will be provided by a high-level department. The responsibility for this department will be to provide strategic planning and direction for the organization. Exhibit 1 illustrates the relationship between the essential processes and the higher-level support departments. The interactions between the processes, between the support departments, and between the support departments and the processes are shown with double arrows.

Information, and the systems that support its capture, transformation, and dissemination, are strategic to the survival of the organization. To support horizontal organization adequately, IS personnel must incorporate a methodology that supports the horizontal approach. Without recognizing the recent trends in organizational structure and adopting methods to facilitate their integration, information system resources will not gain full management support and may lose their major impact on the organization.

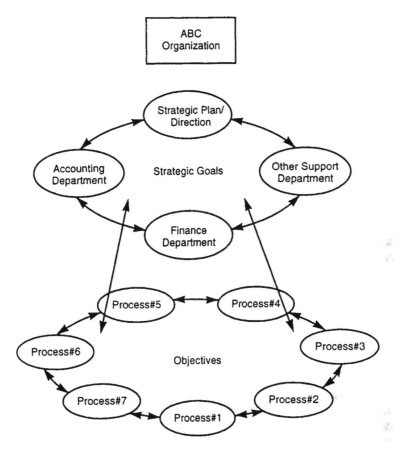

Exhibit 1. Horizontal organization structure.

IS METHODOLOGIES

Integrating IS throughout the organization is a key issue for senior management. Two popular methodologies that can be used to facilitate the integration of information systems within an organization are: a data-focused approach and a process-focused approach.

The Data-Focused Approach

The data-focused approach is currently the more popular methodology. Generally, data models are more stable reflections of how an organization uses data and establishes business rules within its various components. By focusing on the types of data and various attributes and classes they rep-

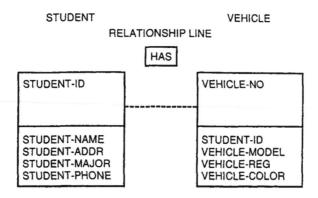

STUDENT   VEHICLE
                    RELATIONSHIP LINE

. DATA MODEL

INCORPORATED BUSINESS RULES, BASED ON THE
DATA STRUCTURE AND RELATIONSHIP LINE:

1. A STUDENT IS UNIQUELY IDENTIFIED THROUGH
   STUDENT ID.

2. A VEHICLE IS UNIQUELY IDENTIFIED THROUGH
   VEHICLE NO.

3. A STUDENT MAY HAVE ZERO OR MANY VEHICLES.

4. A VEHICLE CAN ONLY EXIST IN BUSINESS IF IT IS
   ASSOCIATED WITH ONE STUDENT.

5. A VEHICLE CANNOT BE ADDED UNLESS IT IS
   IMMEDIATELY ASSOCIATED WITH ONE STUDENT.

Exhibit 2.   Data model with associated business rules.

---

resent, a comprehensive, relational, or hierarchical model can be constructed to reflect their relationships within the organization. This model can serve to help simplify and reduce duplication of data, and validate business rules governing relationships and dependencies. Data-focused models are powerful tools for data administrators, but offer little help for senior executives in terms of IS planning unless they are properly presented (see Exhibit 2).

For nontechnical computer personnel, data-focused models are often very difficult to comprehend and implement within an organization. Many experienced IS managers and academics do not fully understand the data modeling process and the related topics of object orientation for developing information systems on the project level as well as on the corporate level.

The Process-Focused Approach

The process-focused methodology looks at IS as a series of related activities that transform data into information. The emphasis is on the processes or activities that comprise a particular information system. A model is generated to reflect the hierarchical relationships of information systems within an organization. Therefore, an information system like accounting can be broken into basic processes (e.g., accounts payable, accounts receivable, payroll, and general ledger).

These processes can be further decomposed into smaller processes. For example, payroll can include the following related processes: generating payroll, generating quarterly payroll reports, generating year-end payroll reports, and updating employee records. Each of these processes can further be decomposed into smaller, related processes. The end result is the hierarchical process structure. Exhibit 3 illustrates this hierarchical relationship between the processes.

Each process has a set of objectives that supports the objectives of the next higher level process that in turn support the overall goals of the organization. Therefore, each activity or process can be justified by the objectives and goals of the organization. An organization model can be created to facilitate the process of evaluating activities within each information system, and to establish an effective decision support system for management. The evaluation process could be used to identify activities that are not contributing to the goals and objectives of the organization, and either eliminate or modify them. A recent study indicates that the process-focused approach remains (or is being reinstated) as the preferred IS planning tool.

The next important step for the process-focused approach is to integrate it into a corporate structure. Recent studies have indicated that se-

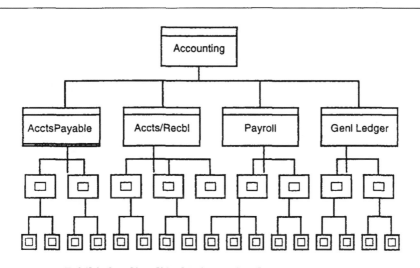

Exhibit 3.   Simplified Information Systems structure.

nior IS managers and senior corporate management are looking for information technology that can be elevated to the organizational level.

Both process-focused and data-focused approaches have made significant effects on the project level where IS personnel have used each technique to develop information systems for specific applications. Yet, neither technique has made any significant effect on the corporate level. A methodology must be developed that can take the strengths of both process- and data-focused approaches and blend them into a corporate model — which can include the recent trends of the horizontal organization. This has been successfully accomplished in industry using the combination of the IDEF0 Activity Modeling and IDEF1X Data Modeling approaches, as well as through the Information Engineering Methodologies of J. Martin and C. Finkelstein.

INTEGRATING INTO THE HORIZONTAL ORGANIZATION

Integrating information systems technology into the corporate organizational structure requires the support of both senior management and lower-level personnel if it is to be successful. It must be a methodology that can be understood and communicated throughout the organization by both computer technical and noncomputer technical personnel to be effective. Since the horizontal organization concept uses multidisciplinary teams within each process, an effective IS methodology must be simple enough to communicate across disciplines and yet be effective in IS planning. Process-focused modeling relies on simple, easy-to-understand symbols that can be used across disciplines. This methodology must be easy and effective enough to be used by all levels within the organization.

Senior executives identified IS planning and information integration as a key issue for competition and survival in today's market. A process-focused methodology is compatible with modeling tasks and activities at the essential process level as well as strategic activities at the higher level. A process-focused approach has been recommended as an appropriate methodology for an organization structure. The data-focused approach is most appropriate for the data administrator. Therefore, an important consideration is to develop a methodology that can integrate the strengths of both process- and data-focused approaches within an organizational model.

With the growth in computer-aided modeling tools (e.g., CASE), the complex task of representing interrelated activities and their associated data components can be accomplished much more easily for both the process- and the data-focused methodologies. Detailed computer specifications can be generated to alleviate the problems of consistency at each level and between levels within each type of model hierarchy. The systems analyst must be very careful in choosing appropriate CASE tools to help facilitate the integration of process- and data-focused models. The CASE tool must be very easy to use and comprehensive enough to allow for easy integration between the two models.

Using Dynamic CASE Tools. The diagrams should have simple, easy-to-follow menus that allow the rapid development of each level of diagram. If the diagraming tool is difficult to use to create and modify different symbols, it becomes a more static tool with which systems analysts will tend to create models that they are reluctant to change. The tool should be aesthetically pleasing to view, and data flows should flow with arcs, straight lines, and right angles. Finally, the tool should be comprehensive enough to allow the systems analyst to move smoothly from the front-end stages (i.e., analysis and design) to the back-end stages (i.e., implementation and installation).

When users and systems analysts work with a CASE tool, the process should be a pleasing experience, thereby allowing the tool to be more dynamic or easily changeable. When the people who work with the model are glad that the model has been created and never have to touch it again, a static model has been created. If the model-creation process was a pleasing experience, they tend not to be bothered by changing it — this is a dynamic model. In the horizontal corporation, information systems change constantly as a result of changes in the competitive environment. Therefore, it is important that the model be a dynamic model capable of changing constantly.

By using simple, easy-to-understand symbols supported by a comprehensive data dictionary, a process model can be generated to represent detailed information processing as well as the more abstract decision-making at the higher level within the organization. The ultimate goal of integrating information systems methodologies into the horizontal organization is to develop a comprehensive organization model using a dynamic CASE tool that can handle constant changes. The major component of this model is a process-focused model supported by a data-focused model representing the higher-level support processes and the essential processes within the organization. This organization model can be used as a blueprint for the restructuring of the traditional hierarchical organization into the newer horizontal organization.

Data Structures. For organizations interested in developing a horizontal structure, the process-focused model can be used to reinforce and enhance communication, information flows, and coordination (i.e., exchanging of information) between the essential processes and the support departments. The data-focused portion of the integrated model supports the processes by ensuring that the data structures used (and perhaps created) by the processes are in their most logical formats. It will remove re-

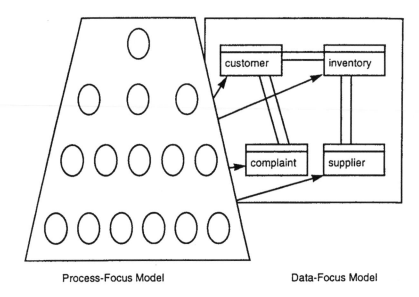

Process-Focus Model   Data-Focus Model

Exhibit 4.   Simplified integration of process and data models.

dundancy and simplify the actual data structures used within the organization.

Exhibit 4 represents the overview of this approach. In addition, more detailed discussions concerning process modeling techniques appear in McLeod's *Systems Analysis and Design: An Organization Approach* (The Dryden Press, 1994) and other comparable process modeling texts.

The arrows in Exhibit 4 illustrate the interaction or connection between the data structures in the process model and the data structure representation in the data model. Each access to a data structure in the process model is represented by either an object (e.g., customer) on the data model, or a relationship between objects (e.g., the connection between customer and inventory, or customer buys inventory). It is beyond the scope of this chapter to provide the detailed process of connecting the process-focused model to the data-focused model.

A possible connection can be established between the process and the data models. Once the process model has been developed, the principles of object orientation can be applied to the construction of a data model that will often provide better insight and use of existing data structures. If a particular data structure on the process model is not in its most logical format (redundancy with other data structures, transitive relationships or other problems associated related with data structures), the data model will show the changes and these changes will eventually be incorporated

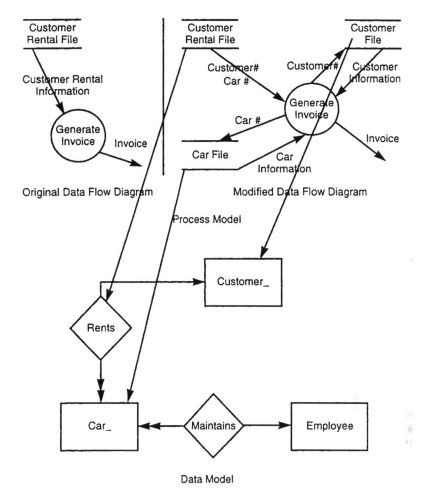

Exhibit 5.   Relationship between data and process models.

into the process model. Exhibit 5 illustrates the creation of a logical data structure model (entity-relationship diagram) and how it influences the changes in the process-focused diagram.

The original diagram accessed a complex data structure identified as a customer rental file. A normalization process generates a data model that in essence created three entities (i.e., customer, employee, and car) with relationships between the objects where customers rent cars and employees maintain cars. The final result is that the process diagram is modified by the data model. The data model is a quality control mechanism that ensures that the data used in the organization are in the most logical format. When that format is assured, data can easily be shared throughout the organization to improve both coordination and communication between the essential processes and the support departments on the higher level.

Data can also be easily maintained, thereby ensuring data integrity. It is the business rules in the activities or processes within the organization that establish the relationships between the various data objects. As the process model is applied to the entire organization, the data model is also extended to the entire organization (generally depicted by Exhibit 2). The end-product is an organization process model supported by an organization data model. The data administrator is responsible for maintaining the data model and coordinating with the various processes and support departments to ensure that changes in the process model are incorporated into the data model, subsequently modifying the process model.

Using the Internet. The Internet has grown at an astonishing rate over the past few years. Companies have been trying to integrate the Internet into their organizations to gain a strategic advantage with customers who now search the Internet for products and services. Developing applications of the Internet is an extension of the electronic data interchange (EDI) between customers and the company — except that the new EDI is open all year with customers all over the world. Now that companies can offer products or services that are bought over the Internet through the use of CGI programming techniques, the amount of overhead needed to maintain a sales operation has been dramatically reduced in may instances.

Understanding the relationship between home page development, CGI programming, network security, and Internet marketing strategies (such as listing the corporate home page on Yahoo, Lycos, WebCrawler, or Infoseek) is critical to the successful integration of Internet strategies into the process and data models of the organization.

CREATING A HORIZONTAL ORGANIZATION

To create a horizontal organization by integrating a process model and a data model, the organization will still have to identify the strategic goals of the organization and key competitive advantages (e.g., customer satisfaction and quality control issues) to achieve these goals.

These key competitive advantages will help the organization identify the core or essential processes necessary to achieve the goals. The next step is the restructuring of the organization. This involves establishing multidisciplinary teams centered around the essential processes. At this point, the teams will identify key objectives that will help them achieve the overall goals of the organization. Once the objectives have been identified, the essential process can be decomposed into several basic subprocesses that will allow the essential process to achieve its objectives. These subprocesses will often be multidisciplinary, involving accounting, finance, marketing, sales, production, and others.

After the essential processes and key subprocesses are identified, the organization should know what support departments are needed to provide more expertise for the essential processes. Of course, the standard support departments (e.g., legal, accounting, and other basic support functions) will probably be identified by both senior-level management and the essential processes. Each subprocess will be decomposed into smaller processes — each with its set of objectives (that support the objectives of its parent subprocess, as was mentioned earlier) — thereby creating a hierarchical information system model.

Again, the process of generating an IS model is not a disguise replacing one hierarchical structure with another. The process modeling concept is the identification of related activities or processes as a means of understanding the various multidisciplinary activities needed for incorporation into an essential process or support department. It shows how the activities within the organization interact, and not necessarily the lines of authority and responsibility often identified in the traditional hierarchical structure. Exhibit 2 shows the hierarchical nature of the process modeling method.

To facilitate the generation of an organization process model, a steering committee should be established at the highest level of the organization, to set such standards and guidelines as naming conventions for data elements and process identification. Each support department and essential process is responsible for developing its portion of the process model. Some overhead training will be needed to provide personnel involved in the development of the process model with basic information about process modeling. Experience has shown that a basic discussion (e.g., type of symbols, use of input data flows, processing, and output data flows) is necessary only to get nontechnical information personnel involved in the development process.

With the advance of group decision support systems (GDSS), a systems analyst can facilitate the decision-making processes used to generate the key objectives and the subprocesses. As each support department and essential process builds its respective model, the steering committee will provide guidance and coordination between all of these components. When each portion of the model (i.e., support departments and the essential processes) is completed, the steering committee will be responsible for bringing each portion together into an overall organization model.

Once the overall process model is created, the data administrator will be responsible for normalizing the data structures and subsequently for generating the data model. The series of steps used to generate the actual data model is beyond the scope of this chapter. But the general concepts of object-oriented analysis and design, along with the normalizing process, are used to generate this data model. Once the data model is completed, the process model must be modified to reflect the more logically created data structures. Exhibit 4 illustrates generally how data models on the project level change the process model. The same approach is used to develop data models on the organizational level and subsequent changes to the organizational level process models.

A CASE tool should be used to expedite the development of the subprocesses for the essential processes and for the support departments. The principles for selecting the appropriate CASE tool were discussed previously. In short, the CASE tool should be process oriented, with the ability to generate data models in support of the process models. The CASE tool should be powerful enough to handle complex organizations involving many levels. It should also be flexible enough to handle the dynamics of change. This decision must not be a trivial decision.

Building a dynamic process and data model is the salient consideration when deciding on an appropriate CASE tool. The methodology that supports the CASE tool is also important. The main point of this chapter is that the horizontal organization can be depicted by a process-focused model supported by a data model. Therefore, the use of a few simple, easy-to-understand symbols is necessary so that both technical and nontechnical IS personnel can use them appropriately.

Getting senior management to commit to a CASE tool and methodology is the underlying foundation of this approach. The use of the CASE tool must be a total effort by all personnel. The maintenance of the process model is the responsibility of each essential process and support department. With the help of the systems analyst component of each process, changes will be the constant force that drives the continual development of the process model. By incorporating users and IS personnel into the process model methodology, a common communication tool (e.g., CASE tool) can be used to help facilitate changes within the organization. Each person within the organization should be able to visualize his or her contribution to the organization and its goals by locating his or her process and its objectives in the process model.

SUMMARY

Incorporating the horizontal concept into today's organization is an important trend that will allow the organization to be more competitive in domestic and international markets for profit organizations and funding sources for nonprofit organizations. The horizontal organization will reduce the amount of bureaucracy that often generates information delays and failures. Organizations will need to be able to change quickly to meet the challenges of a volatile, competitive environment. IS methodologies should integrate recent trends to be successful and accepted by organizations. An effective approach would be to integrate the horizontal organization into an organizational process model supported by a data model. The process model should focus on the essential processes and the support departments in building its information system model.

The process model will help organizations move logically toward the horizontal organization by ensuring that the activities within each essential process and support department support overall the goals of the organization. The process model will also provide better coordination and communication throughout the organization by integrating the information used within it. The data model that supports the process model will ensure that the information is in its most logical format, thereby allowing the various components of the organization that need information to have it in a timely fashion. With the help of an effective, user-friendly CASE tool used as the common communication tool throughout the organization, the process model will become a dynamic tool for change.

Chapter 12
Object-Oriented Aspects of Windows Component-Based Software

Steve Krehbiel
Narasimhaiah Gorla

OBJECT-ORIENTED COMPUTING "FAILED TO DELIVER ON THE PROMISE OF REUSE," whereas reusable component-based software has provided for easy, rapid applications development. Based on the technology trend, only two types of programmers may prevail in the future: those who develop components using C, C++, and assembly language, and those who use component-based development systems to glue the components together into the applications.

This chapter compares the development features of component-based software and object-oriented software and evaluates the object-oriented features of component-based software and object-oriented software. Several concepts usually are associated with component-based languages. In general, components

- Are discrete, distinguishable objects that encapsulate data and properties within the component.
- Respond to and initiate events and actions within the system.
- Usually are provided in the software development package or supplied by third-party suppliers in binary form only with no opportunity for the software programmer to modify or extend the components' underlying source code.

As a means of comparison, objects in object-oriented languages generally may be defined as having four features:

0-8493-9976-9/99/$0.00+$.50
© 1999 by CRC Press LLC

- Identity. Objects are discrete, distinguishable entities.
- Encapsulation. Objects hide internal structure, functions, and operations from external objects.
- Inheritance. Objects share attributes and operations among classes based on hierarchical relationships.
- Polymorphism. Operations behave differently on different object classes.

In particular, this chapter examines two of the most popular component-based software programs, Visual Basic 3.0 and Powerbuilder 3.0, with the most popular object-oriented software, Visual C++ 1.0.

This chapter examines the object-oriented features of these two component-oriented development systems. As a base of comparison, Microsoft's Visual C++ was selected as the object-oriented system's development language.

SYSTEM DEVELOPMENT ENVIRONMENTS

Introduced in 1991 by Microsoft, Visual Basic simplified Windows-based software development for programmers, especially when compared to the original method of writing Windows programs using the C programming language and the Windows' Software Development Kit (SDK) libraries. This section details the development environment and discusses such relevant object-oriented features as class definition, objects, encapsulation, inheritence, and polymorphism.

Visual Basic 3.0

Visual Basic 3.0 is visually oriented, and its development environment allows the programmer to use the mouse to select and move components along with their properties. The developer points at icons on the screen and then, using drag-and-drop techniques, positions these pseudo-objects, or components, on the screen. To change the properties for the object on the screen, the user points at the object with the mouse, brings up the properties of the object using a function key, and changes the properties in a subwindow. Visual Basic's development environment consists of the following elements:

- Projects: A project consists of a definition file that contains all the names of the forms and controls used by the program.
- Forms: Forms are the windows upon which all controls are placed. A form has its own properties, events, and methods.
- Standard and Custom Controls: Controls are the objects, or components of Visual Basic's system development. The custom controls, like forms, have properties, events, and methods. Controls provide the prime functionality for the Visual Basic development system.

- Toolbars: The toolbar holds an icon for each of the controls available to the developer in the system.
- Modules: Modules are separate entities, which consist of Visual Basic code to implement various functions using a highly structured form of BASIC.
- Subroutines: Subroutines, which consist of Visual Basic code modules, are attached to forms and controls.
- Editor: The Visual Basic editor supports most standard text editing features.

Powerbuilder 3.0

Powerbuilder is also visual in the development process. The developer usually selects the objects from menus and uses drag-and-drop techniques to position these pseudo-objects or components on the screen. As with Visual Basic, the system developer changes the properties for the object on the screen using point-and-click technology. Powerbuilder's development environment consists of the following elements:

- Painters: Work in Powerbuilder is done in one of several painters. A painter is the developer's environment for creating the higher-level objects in the system. For example, application painters are for creating the main application object, Window painters for creating forms and their controls, Menu painters for creating menus objects, Database painters for creating databases with their tables, and DataWindow painters to make DataWindows, which are Windows tied directly to the database in use.
- Application: This corresponds loosely to Visual Basic's projects. Application defines the global properties, the icon for the application, and the startup code.
- Windows: These correspond to Visual Basic forms and represent the windows that make up the application, along with the buttons, combo boxes, and other controls in the system. Six types of windows exist: Main, child, pop-up, response, MDI Frame, and MDI Frame with Microhelp. Child windows always are associated with the parent and exist completely within the parent.
- Libraries: These contain the code for objects and events in the system.
- Controls: The programmer creates controls by selecting an icon and then choosing menu options to define it.
- PowerBar: This feature shows icons of the various windows and controls available in the system. The user may not create new PowerBar icons without the use of C++.
- Scripts: PowerScript code modules (scripts) are attached to windows and controls to implement various functions in response to events and methods.

- Editor: Similar to Visual Basic's editor, Powerbuilder's editor has de-sign-time editing and syntax checking, wrapping, and other word-pro-cessor features.

Visual C++ 1.0

Visual C++ 1.0 provides a visually oriented C++ systems development environment, which is focused around the Visual Workbench. The system does not require predefined, binary-coded objects for system development, as does Visual Basic and Powerbuilder; however, the language provides for several functions to make the C++ development process easier. It provides Wizards, which greatly reduce the effort required to make classes and let the developers make their own tools. These tools can be installed on the tools menu within its environment. Visual C++'s development environment consists of the following elements:

- Visual Workbench: The Workbench acts as the central point from which the developer makes the applications programs. It consists of a text editor, project manager, browser, and debugger in a single, integrated development environment.
- Projects: Projects are the main definition file for Visual C++'s Workbench. The project describes the source files and libraries that make up a program, as well as the compiler and linker commands to build the program. The project file consists of a make file and a status file.
- Microsoft Foundation Class Library: This is an extensive library that offers wealth of functionality and features.
- App Studio: This feature provides the tools to create and edit applications resources, including the dialog boxes menus, icons, bitmaps, and cursors.
- App Wizards: These must be used first during the development of a Visual C++ application. Selecting options in AppWizard creates skeleton C++ source files with various levels of functionality.
- Class Wizards: These provide the tools to create new classes, map messages to class-member functions, and map controls to class-member variables.

Each of the three products offers a fully integrated Windows-based development environment. Visual Basic and Powerbuilder offer simpler, quicker development environments based on drag-and-drop and components, as compared to Visual C++, which requires much more code to develop the user interface and screen elements. Visual Basic and Powerbuilder offer less flexibility than Visual C++ in their ability to create new classes and to control the overall operating environment. General usage of Visual C++ requires more systems knowledge of memory usage, stacks, and internal system functions than general usage of Visual Basic and Powerbuilder. Visual C++ requires much more understanding of the

Windows Application Program Interface (API) than the component languages require, though the component languages can use the Windows API through system calls.

CLASS DEFINITION

Visual Basic and Powerbuilder do not have class definitions available to the developer. The standard custom controls that each offers act as a type of class in that objects are the instantiation of these classes. To create new classes or types of components requires the use of a C compiler for these two languages. This is one of the primary weaknesses of these component-based systems.

The classes available to the Visual Basic and Powersoft programmer include such items as labels, text boxes, lines, and literally hundreds of other types of objects, which the user places on the screen for the development of the system. The underlying code for the components is not generally available to the developer, and thus no opportunity exists for having public and private functions. The components do offer the developer, however, some flexibility in how the component is presented to the user. For example, the developer can make the component invisible, change its color, or prevent the end user from having access to the object. No dynamic allocation or de-allocation of class objects from memory is provided.

Visual C++'s classes form the foundation for developing C++ applications. The classes truly are object-oriented in design, with inheritance, encapsulation, and polymorphism capabilities. Objects must be instantiated from classes within the Visual C++ code. Classes can be developed from scratch, or the user may make use of the utility provided in the software called ClassWizard, which walks the user through the development of a new class.

ClassWizard's tools simplify the class creation process. ClassWizard steps the user through the class development process, maps messages to class-member functions, and maps controls to class-member variables. To make a new class with the ClassWizard, the user selects a base class from a listing of available base classes. The system creates the necessary source files, declarations, and implementation code to derive the new class.

OBJECTS

Visual Basic primary objects are forms, which are the window areas that hold the other Visual Basic objects, called controls. The primary form is opened automatically for the developer when he or she starts the Visual Basic development program. No Visual Basic program can be written without including this startup form. Some of the predefined objects include

• Forms, the primary area on which other objects are positioned.

- Labels, which display message labels on the screen.
- Text Boxes, which display program text output/messages.
- List Boxes, which display lists of items.
- Combo Boxes, which display pop-up lists of items.

Visual Basic objects include some system objects, such as Printer, Debug, Clipboard, Screen, and App, which are available in most cases to other Windows programs. New Visual Basic objects can be created only by using C++,which may be added to projects in the form of a VBX. In the marketplace, hundreds of VBX objects perform such tasks as barcode printing, full-featured word processing, database management, spreadsheets, picture and video image manipulation, tab control, and elastic control.

Powerbuilder and Visual C++ Features

Some of the objects that Powerbuilder puts in the development package include

- Windows, the primary area on which other objects are positioned.
- Command, which is pushed/clicked to begin, interrupt, or end process.
- Picture Box, which is similar to command button, yet displays picture on face.
- StaticLine Edit, for entering label text.
- SingleLine Edit, for entering single line of text.
- MultiLine Edit, for entering large blocks of text.
- GroupBox, which divides other controls into groups, like Visual Basic's frames.
- RadioButton, option buttons for individual options.

The object types within the Powerbuilder development world must be developed outside the Powerbuilder environment. Objects are instantiated through menus and point-and-click methods. Placing the object on the window gives the system programmer full functionality of the object.

Visual C++ provides for complete object-derivation from its classes. This is a full C++ implementation of object instantiation, with provisions for such object-oriented techniques as base and derived classes, virtual functions and labels, abstract classes, encapsulation, multiple-inheritance, and polymorphism.

Visual C++ includes the Microsoft Foundation Class Library, which gives the developer classes that allow for printing, toolbars, scrolling, splitter windows, print preview, context-sensitive help, and many reusable components of the class library.

Comparison of Objects

Because the underlying code is not available to the developer in the component-based languages, their flexibility is minimal in comparison to Visual

C++'s. However, the components often meet specific application uses and generally have been well-tested and well-debugged before reaching market. Good component manufacturers must provide solid, bug-free products to stay in business. Even shareware controls may offer solid, well-tested performance for very low costs. Thus, the tradeoff for flexibility and extensibility of Visual C++ objects is the quick and well-tested functionality of components that can be added quickly to the system under development.

ENCAPSULATION

Visual Basic objects include both the data and its behavior properties within the object itself. These data properties can be set at design time and changed by code. Example properties include the name of the control object, screen location coordinates, user visibility, foreground and background color, border style, fonts and size, and caption. Objects also respond to events and methods. Events are fairly standard for most objects: Click, Double Click, MouseMove, LostFocus, and GotFocus.

Similar to Visual Basic, each object has properties, which are called attributes, methods, and events. Attributes are set in the Window Style dialog box and include such characteristics as object position, visibility to user, control access (enabled or disabled), color of foreground and background, three-dimensional look, image (for picture boxes), border style, font and size, and caption. Methods are specific to an object and define how the system reacts to inputs.

Visual C++ provides for data and functions to be encapsulated within its classes and objects. The standard C++ functionality that Visual C++ offers enforces encapsulations so that data is surrounded, or hidden by its functions using public and private functions. The encapsulation is implemented through the class and object code.

Comparison of Encapsulation

The implementation of the concept of encapsulation in Visual Basic and Powerbuilder is much different from the Visual C++ approach. The Visual Basic and Powerbuilder approach is to enforce encapsulation through the use of components, their properties, and their methods and events. The component code is not available to the developer, and thus the manufacturers of the components build in the encapsulation when they develop the component. The Visual C++ requires the programmer to enforce the encapsulation through their code.

INHERITANCE

Visual Basic has some inheritance characteristics, but these are very limited in scope. Visual Basic has no child objects. Control arrays provide the most explicit example of inheritance characteristics, as they provide for code reuse among the objects. Specifically, a control array is an array of objects, in which each member of the array is instantiated in the program. All members of the control array share the same properties, events, and methods and therefore share data and code. For example, several text boxes respond to the same event when clicked, and each of the six objects inherits the code for the click event. The code reuse is a weak form of inheritance displayed by Visual Basic.

POWERBUILDER

Powerbuilder supports inheritance to the extent that parent windows and objects can be used to define child objects. The child object inherits all properties, controls, and scripts of the parent. The child object can be modified by adding, modifying, or deleting controls or by modifying scripts and properties.

PowerBuilder inheritance functionality is supported only for windows, menus, and user objects. To create the child window, menu, or user object, select the inherit button on the painter screen. This launches another painter, which looks just like the painter of the parent, though the caption of the painter mentions that "[the painter is] inherited from [painter type name]." Once in the child, the programmer may change anything on the screen, for example, resizing windows and controls, moving controls, and changing properties of the controls and windows.

However, changes to the child prevent future parent changes from rippling down to the child for that specific item changed. The more that is changed, the less is inherited from the parent during future parent changes. For example, the buttons on the child are moved, and no other changes are made. Then, one year later, the parents' controls and properties are changed significantly. The result is that the changes to the controls and properties are inherited by the child, with the exception of the changes to the button that had been changed. The tie to the parent has been lost for all changed properties of the child. Thus, the developer must be careful what is changed. PowerBuilder includes the reset attributes command to reset any inadvertent changes to child properties. The changes that are inherited by the child occur when the child is regenerated by the system.

Scripts must require explicit handling in the inherited child, as the developer may want to create an additional or use a modified script for child's control in addition to the parent's inherited script. This is handled through extending, overriding, explicit calling, or cutting and pasting.

VISUAL C++

Visual C++ provides for class derivation, which provides inheritance directly and allows for code reuse. Base and derived classes (class hierarchy) for code sharing are used widely within the Visual C++ system development environment. Visual C++ provides support for multiple inheritance, where the subclasses may be derived from more than one base super class.

Comparison of Inheritance

PowerBuilder includes inheritance functions to utilize script and property reuse, which simplify and strengthen the development process greatly. Though the developer is bound by the inheritance techniques built into the package, the use of this object-oriented technique makes this much stronger object orientation than Visual Basic. Powerbuilder's inheritance though is limited in comparison to the inheritance in Visual C++, which offers full base and derived class inheritance.

POLYMORPHISM

Neither Visual Basic nor Powerbuilder offers polymorphism for its component objects. The closest conceptual offering to polymorphism is Visual Basic's variant data type, which allows the program to let the requirement of knowing what the data type is (e.g., integer, string, or single precision) go until the program runs. Once the program is running and is presented with the data, Visual Basic can adapt to whatever type of data is presented for the variant type. This is a weak form of polymorphism. Visual C++ offers full object-oriented polymorphism features that allow the programmer to call member functions for an object without specifying its exact type through the use of virtual functions.

SUMMARY

This chapter reviewed two component-based languages, Power Builder and Visual Basic, and one object-oriented language, Visual C++. It compared their object-oriented features and other software engineering features, demonstrating that although component-based software is weak in object-oriented features, it is stronger by virtue of its several other software engineering features, as compared to object-oriented languages.

The three development systems reviewed offer well-integrated system development environment with plenty of tools and options to help the system developer. In the object-oriented evaluation, however, the only area where the component languages, Visual Basic and Powerbuilder, shine is in the encapsulation comparison, in that the data and functions are encapsulated fully in the object or the component. Exhibit 1 lists the summary of object-oriented features included in the three packages.

Each platform offers identity and encapsulation of the objects. Powerbuilder does offer some inheritance features similar to those found in Visual C++, though on a more modest scale, Visual Basics inheritance is very

Exhibit 1. Object-Oriented Features of Three Development Systems

	Visual Basic	Power Builder	Visual C++
Identity (Distinguishable/ Discrete Objects)	Yes	Yes	Yes
Encapsulation/Information Hiding	Yes	Yes	Yes
Single Inheritance	Very Limited (arrays of objects respond to same events)	Yes (limited to four levels of inheritance)	Yes
Multiple Inheritance	No	No	Yes
Polymorphism	No	No	Yes

limited. The component languages generally fall short of true object systems in class definition, class derivation, polymorphism, and other object-oriented techniques, such as operator overloading.

From a software engineering point of view, solid programming practices should result in high-quality software; software quality comprises reliability (i.e., the probability that the software performs its functions without failure and includes completeness, consistency, simplicity, and traceability), usability (i.e., the relative effort required for software training and operation), maintainability (i.e., the effort required to find and fix errors in software), and adaptability (i.e., the ease with which the system can be altered to meet different user needs and different system constraints, including modifiability, expandability, and portability). (See Exhibit 2.)

In general, the component-based software has better software quality attributes as compared with object-oriented software. Recognizing some limitations that component software has in the object-oriented realm, Visual Basic has a new component model based upon Microsoft's OLE (Object Linking and Embedding) model; OLE servers embed themselves in contain-

Exhibit 2. Software Quality Assessment

	Visual Basic	Power Builder	Visual C++
Reliability	High (Uses Well-Tested Components)	High (Uses Well-Tested Components)	Low (Programmer Has to Test the Code)
Usability	High (Most Code Is Predefined)	High (Most Code Is Predefined)	Low (Need to Write More C++ Code)
Maintainability	High (Easy-to-Understand System)	High (Easy-to-Understand System)	Low (Difficult-to-Understand Code)
Adaptability	Low (Impossible to Change Component Code)	Low (Impossible to Change Component Code)	High (Possible to Modify C++)

er documents and export their internal methods to callers by means of the OLE automation interface. In principle, the OLE controls are extendible through interface pointers rather than through inheritance. Similarly, Visual C++ developers can access Visual Basic's VBXs through code rather than drag-and-drop instantiation of the component languages.

Thus in general, the object-oriented technology is lacking in software quality features; it needs demonstrable improvement to make the software more reusable. Similarly, component-oriented technology is lacking in such object-oriented features as inheritance and adaptability; thus, component-based software developers could create additional classes from scratch and provide modifiable components. This will improve the adaptability of component-based software. More software development efforts are needed that combine the benefits of both worlds, which will result in more effective software.

Chapter 13

Data Warehouse Design: Issues in Dimensional Data Modeling

Jack McElreath

BEFORE BEGINNING A DISCUSSION OF THE METHODS OF MODELING INFOR-
MATION IN A DATA WAREHOUSE, it is important to agree on the type of data
to be stored in the warehouse and how the data differs from traditional operational data.

OPERATIONAL VS. DATA WAREHOUSE APPLICATIONS

Operational applications track business events (e.g., orders and payments) and the entities associated with those events (e.g., customers and
products) from creation to completion. The status of each event is constantly updated, and the general objective of OLTP (online transaction
processing) systems is to get the event processed and completed as soon
as practical; processing usually means cost, and completion usually
means revenue. Data is typically accessed at the detail level; individual
records are read, updated, and replaced. Entities associated with the in-
process events are constantly updated to reflect current attributes, and,
generally, no history of an entity's prior status is maintained. Entities are
usually retained while there is an open business event or likelihood of an
incoming event.

Data warehouse applications capture completed business events and all
associated information necessary for strategic analysis. Events are static
(i.e., history cannot be changed) and held as long as they provide some historical significance. Data is typically accessed at aggregate levels; detail
events are summarized across selected entities or categories. In general,
the information retained for the entities related to completed events is lim-

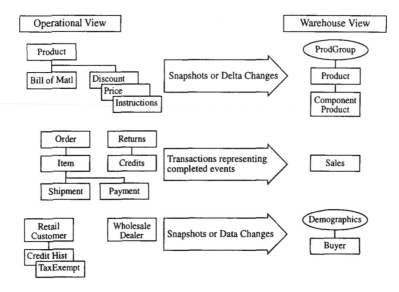

Exhibit 1. Operational and warehouse data models.

ited to that needed for aggregation or filtering of analytical queries; snapshots of entities may be needed to reflect the entity at the time of any associated events.

The operational model is process oriented and, often, application oriented; records and relationships support the flow of data from creation to completion. Warehouse models are analysis oriented and, ideally, subject oriented; records and relationships support the desired query aggregations. Data moves from the operational application to the warehouse but the data view — the model — should be quite different (see Exhibit 1).

Ideally, there should be little redundancy between the operational and warehouse databases. The completed events are purged from the operational database and moved to the warehouse on completion. The entities associated with the events have some necessary redundancy — the same product may be referenced on both active and historical events. However, redundancy should be limited to those entity attributes needed for both processing in the operational system and strategic analysis in the warehouse.

In practice, closed events must often be retained for some period in the operational system and, sometimes, in-process events must be recorded in the warehouse. For example, it may be impractical, inefficient, or undesirable to move the data real-time to the warehouse; it is often more efficient and less intrusive to extract and move the data periodically. It is also common to access recent history in the processing of active events (e.g., prior payment is shown on a new bill) and it may not be practical to cross over to a warehouse on a separate platform to retrieve this data. The goal, however, should be to avoid both of these cases to reduce the data inconsistency problems that accompany redundancy. The fastest way to destroy confidence in systems is to provide different answers to the same data questions because of redundant sources.

EXAMPLE OF EXPENDITURE ANALYSIS

To explore dimensional modeling issues, consider the example of a personal application for strategically analyzing expenditures. Most people certainly have an operational system to buy and pay for items, but many (including me) do not know where their money went, whether outgo matches income, or what their expenses should or will be in the future.

A data warehouse would certainly facilitate analysis. This simple personal application essentially has the same functional issues and analytical challenges as those encountered in any corporate warehouse; it is smaller in volume of data and users but no less complex. The technical issues increase with volume but the business issues and user views are just as difficult as they are in most large corporations.

An example assumes that the individual (me in this case) has an automated system for all cash outlays: purchases, payments, donations, and all other family expenses. This software can be used for all purchases and payments made by check, credit card, or cash to provide a monthly file (more likely a shoe box of illegible receipts) containing completed purchase and payment events. Information about each entity (e.g., stores, people, banks, and credit card issuers) associated with purchases and payments must also be made available to the warehouse. This includes snapshots of the relevant family members, products, and vendors.

Because the transaction volumes or usage patterns to be supported in the warehouse are unclear, I first select my hardware and software platforms. My spouse is currently controlling the operational systems using Quicken Version 1.0 running on a Compaq 286 portable. I think I will probably need a 200-MHz multimedia client hooked to a 64-bit UNIX server with a fiber Internet connection. I will also need software from Cognos, SAS, Oracle, Arbor, and ActiVision, which is easily obtainable from a local retailer. Spending too much time on infrastructure decisions is not worthwhile because the technology becomes obsolete in a few months anyway.

The advantage designers of smaller (in terms of data volume and number of users) warehouses enjoy is that there is probably no need to compromise functional requirements because of technical performance or capacity constraints. The line separating small from large data collections is constantly being raised; 20 years ago, we would become concerned at hundreds of thousands of records; 10 years ago, our concerns started at

1 million records; and today, concern is piqued at tens of millions of records and panic sets in at hundreds of millions. I would have predicted that billions of records would be routinely handled by the year 2000, but the date problems will implode the industry and make all else academic.

ADVANTAGES AND DISADVANTAGES OF DIMENSIONAL MODELING

The general conclusion evolving from the experts and tool vendors of data warehouse solutions is that for the purpose of schematically defining and analyzing historical information, dimensional modeling is preferable to the techniques used to model operational data (usually some form of entity-relationship or network diagram). Dimensional models are, in theory, simpler for users to understand and manipulate. Simplicity is both the benefit and the problem. It is difficult to model complex information with a simple technique. If the model is too complex, it will not serve users' needs; if it is too simple, it cannot answer tough questions.

Dimensional models are logical, not physical constructs; the underlying database for dimensional models is either relational or a multidimensional cube. It may also be necessary, based on the complexity of warehouse data, to employ different modeling techniques in the progression from the user view back to the data source, such as cube for the user, star model for the analyst, and entity relationship for the database administrator (see Exhibit 2). The ideal solution is to have the mapping capability to transparently transform the simpler user view to the complex physical data view,

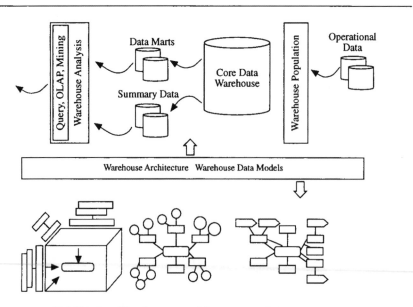

Exhibit 2. Warehouse architecture and data models.

efficiently and correctly. Unfortunately, data warehouse tools have not fully evolved to meet this need.

This shortcoming is the driving force behind the popularity of data marts — a mechanism to create a simple and focused subset of the more complex core warehouse. Their place in the warehouse architecture is also shown in Exhibit 2. If most user access can be satisfied from the custom view, then the complexities of the base warehouse are masked from the user. The problem with this approach is, of course, that as new requirements evolve, the party responsible for creating custom warehouse views (and this is seldom the user) must get involved in fulfilling new queries, potentially delaying information delivery.

Once the data warehouse is populated, the strategic user then forms complex aggregate views of this data to isolate trends and establish profound changes in the management or direction of the enterprise, which, in the case of our example, is the family. Individual events (e.g., a given purchase) are seldom of interest; more often, it is the aggregation of facts across selected dimensions (e.g., total spent on mail-order children's clothing in late summer). In general, individual events are provided only when some highlighted aggregate event must be exploded (i.e., drilled-down) to provide supporting detail. For example, once I have determined that I am spending excessively on sporting equipment, I might drill-down and discover that the purchase of the $500 titanium golf club was the major culprit.

DATA MODELS

In dimensional modeling, the numeric attributes of the event represent facts, such as quantity, cost, discount, and tax. People, places, times, things, and categories associated with the fact are shown as dimensions.

The Star Model

The star model (as shown in Exhibit 3) gets its name from the dimensions that radiate from central facts. An alternative explanation for the name could be that stars shed little light and even that light takes a long time to arrive; actually, stars, like data warehouses, emit a lot of light — it is just that so little ever reaches us.

The Snowflake Model

A snowflake model is an extended star model in which each dimension radiates aggregate categories (see Exhibit 4). These categories (sometimes called outboards) are what provide the richness of analysis within the data model. For example, we might ask how much is being spent by certain family members for clothing products to be used on family pets during the Christmas season. I believe these models are called snowflakes because they crystallize with infinite variety. However, in sufficient quantity, their

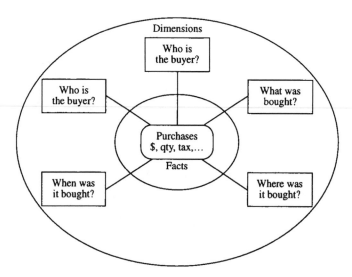

Exhibit 3. The star model.

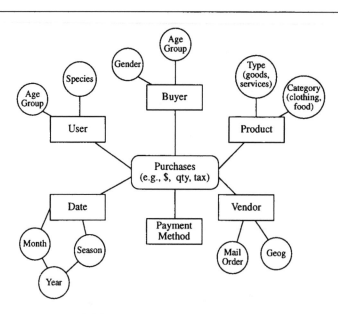

Exhibit 4. The snowflake model.

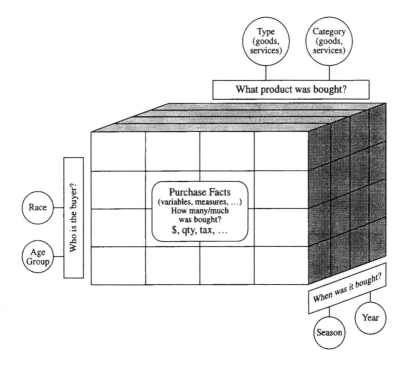

Exhibit 5. The cube model.

---

beauty may be masked by the need to plow through them to make progress.

The Cube Model

Some vendors prefer to visualize the data as a cube — dimensions form the axes of the cube of facts; outboards are shown as hierarchies of each dimension. These multidimensional cube or hypercube models can be effective, but complex aggregations become difficult to envision, draw, or display on a two-dimensional surface. In Exhibit 5, purchases are analyzed at the intersection of three base dimensions (i.e., buyer, month, product); multiple purchases by the same buyer of the same product in the same month are conceptually summarized.

Dimensions may be rotated or eliminated in any requested view, such as drop product from the analysis and show purchases by buyer/month with month on the vertical axis. Hierarchical groupings may be incorporated above each base dimension as outboards or snowflakes. These result in a large number of additional aggregation possibilities, such as age

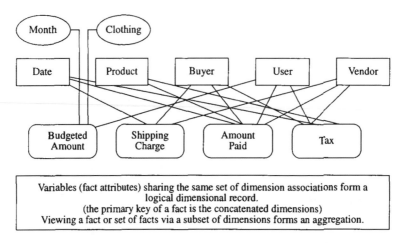

Variables (fact attributes) sharing the same set of dimension associations form a logical dimensional record.
(the primary key of a fact is the concatenated dimensions)
Viewing a fact or set of facts via a subset of dimensions forms an aggregation.

Exhibit 6.   Purist view of dimensional data.

group/month/product and year/product class/gender. It is clear that a relatively small number of dimensions and categories can result in many potential aggregations. The eight types across three dimensions in the exhibit provide more than 100 different permutations (approximately $2^8 - 1$). If we were to construct a 6-dimensional cube with 13 outboards from the snowflake model in Exhibit 4, the possible aggregate permutations would exceed 100,000. Some of these aggregations are surely nonsensical or unnecessary; the trick is to match current and future user requirements to permissible aggregations and further determine which of these aggregations are to materialize statically (i.e., during the data load) versus dynamically (i.e., during the query).

A purist view of dimensional data would define each fact, or variable, separately and associate that variable with 1 to n dimensions (see Exhibit 6). A logical record would then consist of any variables sharing the same set of dimensions (including categories). An aggregated view would occur whenever a variable is viewed through a subset of existing dimensions. For example, tax and amount paid are part of a logical fact record because they have identical dimension associations. Budgeted amount is associated with user, month, and product group. A view of tax and amount paid through month/date, product group/product, and user would be a conceptual aggregation of all facts associated with only those dimensions. Budgeted amount could then be compared to actual expenditures at that level.

Database Management Systems

There is an evolving debate about whether online analytical processing (OLAP) modeling and implementation should be based on relational database management system (DBMS) products, multidimensional DBMSs, or both (e.g., relational for atomic data, multidimensional for aggregations). Although valid arguments can be posed for both, the final outcome is based more on the success of individual DBMS products in providing aggregation capabilities that are flexible (in terms of ease of adding new facts and dimensions), efficient (in terms of acceptable response time), manageable (in terms of data quality), and easy to use (in terms of providing the user with understandable views of complex data).

Another major factor involves the dynamic versus static aggregation decisions and the ability to alter these choices as data usage evolves. Static aggregation would occur as data are loaded; dynamic aggregation would occur as the query is executed. Currently, relational products seem to have the lead in flexibility and efficiency for high volumes and multidimensional products in ease of use.

To meet the needs of complex data warehouses, dimensional models and the associated software tools must evolve to incorporate the following:

- Complex facts where a network of related events can be combined to form a single fact view.
- Complex dimensions containing subsets (including repeating groups) and supersets of data.
- Dimension-to-category associations that include many-to-many relationships (i.e., networks in addition to hierarchies).
- Recursive associations within categories.
- Temporal associations (i.e., point-in-time data).
- Business rules in data derivation.
- Effective aggregate navigation, or the ability to recognize presummarized data.

There are certainly other needs, but these directly affect the modeling of data.

DATA MODELING LEVELS

Data modeling should occur at four levels: conceptual, logical, physical, and technical.

The Conceptual Data Model

The conceptual data model is a high-level definition of the major entities, events, and associations required for the application being defined; it contains few, if any, attributes of the conceptual entities. For a data warehouse, the conceptual model should be subject oriented rather than application oriented, and use dimensions, facts, and categorizations rather than entities, events, and tables. Subject orientation means that data from separate operational applications (e.g., business expenses, donations, rentals, purchases, and budgets) should be consolidated into a single analytical subject (i.e., expenditures).

The Logical Data Model

The logical data model should define all entities/roles, events, categorizations, and relationships necessary to deliver the warehouse user requirements. The model is fully attributed and somewhat normalized. We have been taught that OLTP logical models are defined in third normal form, but the clarity of warehouse data is often improved by denormalizing some information (e.g., derived attributes, business rules, summary data, and data marts). The logical model should not be dictated or affected by the DBMS type (e.g., network, relational, multidimensional, and object) or product (e.g., Oracle, IMS, DB2, and Redbrick) chosen for implementation. In theory, one could convert from any DBMS to any other and use the logical model as a starting point for conversion.

The Physical Data Model

The physical data model is the phase in which the logical model is adapted to the major software and performance constraints of the DBMS, data and usage statistics, and intended processing platform. Physical design decisions are not usually transparent to the applications using the database. Ideally, the physical model mirrors the logical model.

It is more difficult to define the precise line between logical and physical design with warehouse models. Some examples of physical modeling steps include conversion of the dimensional model to a relational or multidimensional structure, data distribution or logical partitioning, entity and referential integrity methods, obvious denormalization needed for performance, and temporal data management options. In many cases, data summarization and creation of distributed custom warehouses are better handled in the logical modeling phase. The major question is whether these decisions involve the clarity of the user view of data (i.e., the realm of the logical model) or are dictated by performance issues or query/DBMS product shortcomings (i.e., the realm of the physical model).

The Technical Data Model

The technical data model incorporates the initial and ongoing tuning of the database, transparent to the applications using it. Indexing, bit maps, physical partitioning, and DASD space management are examples of technical modeling. This is the domain of the database administrator (a complete grasp of the subject usually occurs concurrent with the inability to function as a member of society at large).

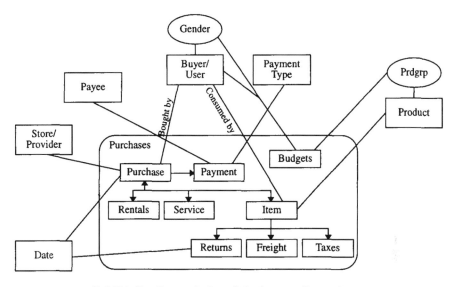

Exhibit 7.   Expanded model of expenditure facts.

Model Expansion

If a dimensional model for the logical model is chosen, it is often necessary to simplify the data (and perhaps the user requirements) or explode complex components to incorporate essential network or hierarchical subsets of information. The warehouse in the family expenditures application is intended to track all expenditures, not just those for real products. What happens when the simple model must be expanded to incorporate payments for such items as services, health care, charity, and tolls? And, if one decides to include budgeted amounts for some dimensions, should returns and reimbursements be included? The model needed to fulfill the user requirements may begin to resemble Exhibit 6's depiction of the explosions of the individual components of the simple dimensional model. Many of these modeling decisions are subjective.

The star model may classify as expenditures a complex collection of components, depending on the type of purchase, method of payment, and the relationships to surrounding dimensions. In defining my family expenditures warehouse, I decided to incorporate all expenditures in a single fact set. I could have created separate fact tables for each class of expenditure — charity contributions, tax payments, highway tolls, and rentals — but any analysis across classes would have become impractical.

The extended model of expenditure facts in Exhibit 7 was created for several reasons, including the following:

- A single purchase can consist of multiple items (e.g., a VCR and a maintenance contract).
- The fact attributes can vary significantly between different expenditures (e.g., goods have quantities, services have hours, not all are taxed, and returns apply only to goods).
- A single purchase could involve multiple payments (e.g., part cash and part credit card, and installment payments).
- Relationships to dimensions may vary based on the type of component (e.g., buyers are associated with all purchases, users are optional and relate to the individual items).
- A single analysis may utilize many of the fact components (e.g., is the rate of returned purchases by female buyers of mail-order goods resulting in increasing freight costs?).
- Budgeted amounts will be created for some dimensions and categories.
- All the preceding are important for strategic analysis.

It may be possible to jam all this information into a single purchase fact by imbedding repeating groups and defining lots of attributes that are exclusive to a subset of records. In fact, this may have to been done during physical modeling if the software constraints or performance constraints leave no option. This model pollution should not be done, however, during logical design. The ideal is to provide software (i.e., query and DBMS) that can deal with complex data and transparently present that data in a simple customized view. Today, one is usually forced to simplify by restricting the core warehouse or by providing customized local repositories (i.e., data marts).

Dimensions can also become complex. Exhibit 8 shows a similar expansion of data for the producer associated with purchases. Provider types have both similarities and differences; stores selling goods may not have the same attributes or higher-level categorizations as other business or private entities providing charity, service, mortgage, or energy. The provider or payee associated with an expenditure could be a person (the plumber), a distributor (Walmart), a manufacturer (Nike), a church or synagogue, a municipal government, and on and on. One could increase the number of dimensions to include all distinct provider types as separate, mutually exclusive, entities, but this usually results in even more complexity and constraints. In general, it is better to consolidate into a single dimension role because it is easier to add a new type to an existing dimension than to add a new dimension to the model.

The following assumptions should be made about our strategic information needs for the provider dimension:

- The base provider describes all attributes common to every provider and serves as the focal point for most fact relationships: the supertypes (i.e., categorizations) above and subtypes (i.e., attributes exclu-

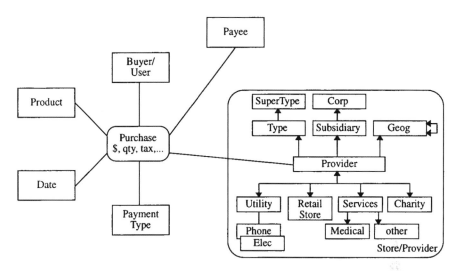

Exhibit 8.   Expansion of data for store/provider associated with purchases.

sive to only some provider types) below. Subtypes may be squashed into the base component during physical design, but it is more informative to segregate them during logical modeling. Repeating groups, or arrays, of subtype data are especially messy and restrictive to imbed in the base entity (i.e., the utility company provides both gas and electricity).

- Some fact relationships may be firmly or optionally to a subtype or supertype rather than the base producer: for example, I donated to United Funds and not to individual member charitable organizations.
- Dimension categorizations must be established, each identifying subjective and objective criteria.
  - Are the categorization levels fixed or recursive? (For example, only permit two levels of corporate affiliations but permit variable levels of geography, such as city, state, country, and planet.)
  - Can a single producer concurrently belong to more than one member of a given category? (For example, producer is both Fortune 500 and pharmaceutical, each subjectively defined as a separate type in my model.)
  - Are the categorizations temporal? (For example, the producer has moved and, therefore, changed geographical affiliations. Do I have to remember the history to analyze older facts?)
  - These dimension categorizations are implemented as metadata in many of the OLAP tools; not only the schema (i.e., type to class), which is truly metadata, but the actual member values (e.g., meat and beverage records aggregate to food).

The ideal model, whether entity-relationship or dimensional, permits a simplistic view of dimensions and facts, transparently consolidating the complex underlying data as needed. For example, if I ask for the total spent on housing last year, it would be most effective if the request could be satisfied from presummarized data marts or from a myriad of detail composing that summary with no effect on the user view. The difficulties, of course, are that the consolidation can result in wrong or misunderstood results, and the DBMS and query software tools are somewhat limited in translating logical models to the supporting physical models.

Section III
Data Integrity and Quality

ENSURING DIRECT DATA INTEGRITY AND REFERENTIAL DATA INTEGRITY is a continuing concern for maintaining the value of application systems. This is true of both OLTP- and OLAP-based applications. Direct data integrity refers to the accuracy of individual items of data (e.g. 'rdd' is an incorrect spelling of 'red'). Referential integrity refers to the integrity of the relationship between items of data (e.g. invoice item records that belong to no invoices have no value). Decisions or activities that are based on corrupted data are pointless and can lead to monetary or material damages. From a quality standpoint, it is necessary to build procedures and processes that ensure data integrity and thus provide confidence about the accuracy of corporate data.

Data integrity and quality are issues any time there is a change to data. They include insert, update, and delete operations against data repositories. In relational database(s), each of these operations must be executed in a specific order to ensure that the data are accurate during and after the operations are complete. For example, a cascading delete begins by removing records belonging to foreign keys. The primary key or parent record should be the last deletion in the operation. An insert of a logical record that consists of multiple physical records begins with an insert of the parent record, followed by inserts of the child records. This is opposite to the delete operation. Transaction processing is also relevant in this example. For example, if a cascading delete operation is interrupted (e.g., due to a power failure or a program failure), none of the records should be deleted. Those that were deleted before the interruption should be rolled back.

This section of the handbook reviews some common approaches for maintaining data and referential integrity in relational databases.

Chapter 14, "Programming Data Constraints Using Microsoft SQL Server," examines some of the commonly available contraints that can be attached to table columns at table creation time. These constraints are saved directly into the SQL Server data dictionary and automatically apply at run time based on the occurrence of specific events. This information also can be applied to some versions of Sybase SQL Server tables because of the historical similarity between the Microsoft and Sybase products.

Chapter 15, "Referential Integrity for Database Design," defines referential integrity, describes its limitations with examples, and then proposes methods of overcoming its limitations. Attribute referential integrity is discussed as it applies to entity relationship and relational data models.

Chapter 16, "Data Quality: An Architectural Solution," discusses the process of integrating data from multiple data sources into a data warehouse while maintaining data quality. This chapter provides advice on resolving problems such as the existence of data from multiple data sources that are inconsistent or from data stores that utilize different data models. Such differences must be resolved when building a data warehouse.

Chapter 14
Programming Data Constraints using Microsoft SQL Server

Sanjiv Purba

MICROSOFT® STRUCTURED QUERY LANGUAGE (SQL) SERVER was one of the first widely released database servers to support the functionality of coding data constraints directly inside the data dictionary itself — as far back as 1987 in colloboration with Sybase. These constraints are attached to tables or table fields with the ANSI '98 Data Definition Language (DDL) commands, "create table" and "alter table." This chapter provides examples of data scripts that will support the following:

- *Identity Constraints*: These constraints can be applied to a single column in a table so that the value in the field is incremented automatically when records are inserted.
- *Key Constraints*: SQL Server supports two types of key constraints, namely "Primary" key and "Foreign" key constraints. Primary key constraints ensure that duplicate records are not inserted into a table. Foreign key constraints ensure that records are not inserted into a table if a foreign key is missing.
- *Default Constraints*: Default contracts are associated with specific columns in tables. If a record is inserted into a table without a data value for a column that has an associated default constraint, the default value is saved in the column with the rest of the record. Default values can be overridden at insert time by a user-supplied data value.

CREATE TABLE CONSTRAINTS

The table creation script developed in the "Database Servers and Universal Servers" section did not take advantage of table constraints or related features. These are used to enforce table data integrity or to provide additional functionality that would otherwise need to be programmed at the client side or within stored procedures. There are several schools of thought regarding the use of these features. From a performance and practicality perspective, these constraints and features are highly useful. From a pure object-oriented perspective, they separate logic from data so that some classes are no longer pure. The author's preference is to make use of the constraints on a case-by-case basis. Constraints use the "sysconstraints" and the "sysreferences" system tables in the Microsoft SQL Server environment.

IDENTITY

A common requirement in transactional systems is to generate a sequential number for each row that is inserted into a table. Common application uses of this include ticket sales, new customers, new employees, and new invoices. Each new record is allocated a code value that is one greater than the previous record. Historically this was done in one of several ways. The first was to maintain an environment variable or a separate table that stored the last code value used. In high load transaction applications this did not work well because of constant locking contention against the table or variable as many users competed to read, lock, and update the value for the next user to retrieve. In such cases, a second method was used that preallocated ranges of numbers to different users or types of users. This reduced contention against single ranges of numbers by distributing users across a range of records. A third method was to use a SELECT command and a built-in function (e.g., MAX) to retrieve the highest number used in a table [e.g., SELECT @code_to_use = (max(code) + 1)]. Each of these offered advantages and disadvantages.

SQL Server's response has been the identity constraint. This feature is identified for a maximum of one column in a table at the time the table is created or altered. This column can be referred to with the logical name: IDENTITYCOL in SQL code that accesses the table. The syntax for allocating an identity constraint to a table column is as follows:

Syntax:

```
CREATE TABLE table_name

    IDENTITY (start, step)
```

Notes:

The "start" value is used for the first row. The "step" is the increment value added for the next insert.

Example:

This example builds a small user table to demonstrate creating a column with an IDENTITY feature. The example also extracts the inserted data from the "city_list" table.

```
USE address

go

DROP TABLE city_list

go

CREATE TABLE city_list

(

    city_code        int  IDENTITY (1000, 1),
    description      char(80)

)

go
```

/* You do not need to specify the IDENTITY column name in an insert command. The city_code will begin with 1000, and be incremented by 1 on every record insert. */

```
insert city_list

    (description) VALUES ("This is a description")

go
```

/* Insert a another record that will have a city_code of 1001 */

```
insert city_list

(description) VALUES ("This is a description")

go
```

/* Display the results */

```
select * from city_list

go
```

/* use the logical name of the IDENTITY column to display the contents of the table */

```
select IDENTITYCOL, description from city_list

go
```

Normally, a value is not specified with the INSERT command for the column that is specified as an IDENTITY column. However, when rows are deleted or not successfully inserted, the number that is automatically generated by SQL Server is not recovered. This means that there can be gaps in the sequencing. In many applications this is not a problem. However, some business processes will use solid sequential series of numbers for auditing purposes. In this case, a gap in the sequential series may cause auditing problems. In such a case it is useful to locate the gaps and fill them in manually. The following sequence of commands does this. Notice the comments explain what is being attempted and what the results actually are

```
INSERT city_list

    (city_code, description)

    VALUES

    (2000, "this should not be accepted without a set
    command")

go
```

This command results in the following error message (unless the SET IDENTITY_INSERT is ON — in which case, add the two lines before the code: [1] SET IDENTITY_INSERT city_list off [2] go): "Attempting to insert explicit value for identify column in table 'city_list'." The following code corrects this error:

```
SET IDENTITY_INSERT city_list on

go

INSERT city_list

    (city_code, description)

    VALUES

    (2001, "this should be successfully inserted into the
    table")

go

SET IDENTITY_INSERT city_list off

go
```

KEY CONSTRAINTS

There are two basic key column constraints that can be applied to table columns with the CREATE TABLE and the ALTER TABLE commands, namely PRIMARY KEY and FOREIGN KEY. There can be no more than one PRIMARY KEY constraint for each table and no more than 31 FOREIGN KEY constraints for each table. The PRIMARY KEY constraint is used to enforce key column uniqueness in a table. When it is specified, two rows are not allowed to exist within the same table with identical primary keys. Once a column is specified as a PRIMARY KEY, it cannot be saved with a NULL value. Key constraints can be created with specific column names or as separate objects.

14-4

PRIMARY KEY Syntax:

```
CREATE TABLE table_name

(

   [column_list  datatype …] [PRIMARY KEY
   [CLUSTERED/NONCLUSTERED]]

)
```

OR

```
CREATE TABLE table_name

(

   [column_list  datatype …],

   CONSTRAINT PK_constraint_name PRIMARY KEY

   [CLUSTERED/NONCLUSTERED] (column1, column2, …)

)
```

Notes:

A clustered index is created by default on the column specified as PRI-MARY KEY. At most, only one "column_name" can be associated with a PRI-MARY KEY in one table.

Examples:

1. This example creates the "city_list" table, specifying the "city_code" field as an IDENTITY column and as a primary key column. This example also indicates that the column should generate a clustered index for the table. The example also extracts the inserted data from the "city_list" table.

```
USE address

go

drop table city_list

go

create table city_list

(

     city_code        int  IDENTITY (1000,1) PRIMARY KEY
                      CLUSTERED,

     description      char(80)

)
```

```
go

create table city_list

(

     city_code          int  IDENTITY (1000,1) PRIMARY KEY
                         CLUSTERED,

     description    char(80)

)

go

/* After parsing the code without errors into the address
database, insert a row into the table */

insert city_list

     (description)

values

     ("this is an example")

go
```

This insert batch can be executed recursively, adding a new record to the "city_list" table each time. Because the PRIMARY KEY field was created with an IDENTITY feature, a new code is generated starting at 1000 with the first insert. This allows each row to be unique. A join against two system tables, sysobjects, and sysindexes can be used to confirm that a clustered index was created in response to the primary key feature. As shown in the following code, an object ID joins the two tables together. In this example, the number of rows in the index is displayed. As an example, the insert code was executed four times, and then the join code was executed. The number of rows retrieved by the join is four. Another insert was then executed to insert a fifth row into the "city_code" table. The join showed that five rows were indexed.

```
select * from city_code

select a.id, b.rows

     from sysobjects a, sysindexes b

          where a.name = "city_list" and a.id = b.id

go
```

As an exercise, it is recommended that the reader adjust the create script for the "city_list" table so that the "city_code" column no longer has an IDENTITY attribute. The insert script also needs to be adjusted as follows: insert "city_list" ("city_code", description) values (2000, "this is a key"). The reader then should try to run the "insert" example twice. Notice that an error message "Violation of PRIMARY KEY constraint 'PK_city_list_5535A961' attempt to insert duplicate key in object 'city_list'. Command has been aborted." The "city_code" (in this case 2000) must be changed on every subsequent insert. As discussed in the application testing chapter, the IDENTITY feature is useful for creating a large number of data rows for stress testing and regression testing.

2. In this example, a PRIMARY KEY constraint is created using two columns as the key:

```
use address

go

drop table address

go

drop table city_state_code

go

create table city_state_code

(

    city            character (20),

    state           character (20),

    CONSTRAINT PK_citystate PRIMARY KEY CLUSTERED (city,
    state)

)   /* the PK represents primary key */

go
```

The FOREIGN KEY constraint is used to ensure referential integrity between related tables. SQL Server accepts up to 31 FOREIGN KEYs per table. A streamlined version of the command syntax for recreating a FOREIGN KEY on a table is as follows:

```
FOREIGN KEY Syntax:

CREATE TABLE table_name

)

    [column_name] FOREIGN KEY [columns] REFERENCES
    [reference_tables]

)
```

OR

```
(

    [column_names    datatypes ....],

    CONSTRAINT contraint_name FOREIGN KEY [(column1,
    column2, ...)]

        REFERENCES [reference_tables(column1, column2,
        ...)]

)
```

Notes:

FOREIGN KEY is validated with the table(s) identified in the REFERENC-ES part of the command.

Examples:

1. This example rebuilds two tables used earlier, customer and member_type, to demonstrate FOREIGN KEY and REFERENCES constraints. The original table generation scripts are modified in this example so that constraints are created with the tables. The "drop table" sequence is important in this example. The customer table, which references the "member_type" table, must be dropped first. Attempting to drop the "member_type" table first displays an error message.

```
USE address

go

drop table customer

go

drop table member_type

go

create table member_type

(

member_type        character(1) PRIMARY KEY,

description        character(30)

)

go

create table customer

(
```

```
customer_no          int  IDENTITY (1000,1) PRIMARY KEY
CLUSTERED,

last_name            char(30),

middle_initial       char(1),

first_name           char(30),

home_phone           char(15),

business_phone       char(15),

fax                  char(15),

email                char(25),

preference           char(80),

member_on            datetime,

member_type          character(1) REFERENCES
                     member_type(member_type)

)
```

/* the member_type table should have a PRIMARY KEY to support the REFERENCES constraint */

go

/* Insert data rows into the two tables. The reference ensures that the member_type value in the customer table occurs in the member_type table. */

insert member_type

    (member_type, description)

    VALUES

    ("O," "Open")

go

insert customer

    (last_name, middle_initial, first_name, home_phone, business_phone,

      fax, email, preference, member_on, member_type)

    VALUES

    ("Okiet," "S," "Joe," "3499999999," "9999999999," "9999999999,"

      "okiet@tobos.com," "not known," "April 25 1997," "O")

go

2. In this example, an attempt is made to enter a customer record with a nonexistent "member_type". The constraint catches this error and does not allow the record to be used in the customer table. The error message: "INSERT statement conflicted with COLUMN FOREIGN KEY constraint 'FK_customer_member_...'. The conflict occurred in database 'address', table 'member_type', column 'member_type'. Command has been aborted." appears in response. Notice that the text of the message is descriptive and highly helpful in identifying the source of the error.

```
INSERT customer

    (last_name, middle_initial, first_name, home_phone,
    business_phone,

     fax, email, preference, member_on, member_type)

    VALUES

    ("Tom," "S," "Joe," "8889999999," "8889999999,"
    "8889999999,"

     "tom@tobos.com," "not known," "April 25 1996," "Z")

go
```

3. In this example, a FOREIGN KEY constraint is created for the address table to ensure that a valid city is being processed. The following example enhances this example to ensure that a valid city and state combination is being processed. This involves several steps. A PRIMARY KEY constraint must be created on the fields that are to be referenced in the "city_state_code" table. A FOREIGN KEY constraint must be created in the address table.

```
use address

go

drop table address

go

drop table city_state_code

go

create table address

(

customer_no          int,

address_code         char(1),
```

```
street1              char(25),

street2              char(25),

city                 char(20),

state_province       char(20),

country              char(15),

zip_pc               char(10),


CONSTRAINT FK_address_city_state FOREIGN KEY (city)

                REFERENCES city_state_code (city)

)

go

create table city_state_code

(

city                 char(20),

state                char(20),

CONSTRAINT PK_citystate PRIMARY KEY CLUSTERED (city)

)

go

/* Test the FOREIGN KEY constraint */


INSERT city_state_code

(city, state)

VALUES

("New York City," "New York")

go

INSERT address

(customer_no, address_code, street1, street2, city,
state_province,

country, zip_pc)

VALUES

(2000, "S," "123 Joe Lane," "street 2," "New York City," "New
York," "USA," "01")

go
```

4. In this example, the FOREIGN KEY constraint is modified to REFER-ENCE two columns in the code table. This also requires a change to the PRIMARY KEY CONSTRAINT to include to matching column fields as well.

```
use address

go

drop table address

go

drop table city_state_code

go

create table address

(

customer_no          int,

address_code         char(1),

street1              char(25),

street2              char(25),

city                 char(20),

state_province       char(20),

country              char(15),

zip_pc               char(10),

CONSTRAINT FK_address_city_state FOREIGN KEY (city,
state_province)

                     REFERENCES city_state_code (city,
                     state)

)

go

create table city_state_code

(

city                 char(20),

state                char(20),

CONSTRAINT PK_citystate PRIMARY KEY CLUSTERED (city, state)

)

go
```

```
/* Test the FOREIGN KEY constraint */

INSERT city_state_code

(city, state)

VALUES

("New York City," "New York")

go

INSERT address

(customer_no, address_code, street1, street2, city,
state_province,

country, zip_pc)

VALUES

(2000, "S," "123 Joe Lane," "street 2," "New York City," "New
York," "USA," "01")

go
```

Note: Testing the Constraints

The reader can test the multicolumn constraints by changing the values in some of the reference columns (e.g., change "New York" to "Texas" in the last example for the address record and attempt to insert the record). The multicolumn constraint traps this because there is no "New York City" and "Dallas" combination in the "city_state_code" table.

Note: Testing the Constraints

It is also possible to use triggers to enforce referential integrity instead of constraints. Constraints are processed before triggers and are conceptually easier to implement because the validation procedure is saved with the table creation code. Constraints, however, are limited to referencing tables in the current database. Triggers do not have this limitation.

DEFAULT CONSTRAINTS

In some of the INSERT scripts that were used earlier, some columns were filled with temporary data (e.g., "not known"). The CREATE/ALTER table commands provide a DEFAULT constraint that inserts a value into a field that is not passed a value.

Syntax:

The syntax for the DEFAULT CONSTRAINT command is as follows:

```
CREATE TABLE table_name
```

```
column1    datatype    DEFAULT (value),

column2    datatype    DEFAULT ('value'),

column3    datatype    DEFAULT value,

column4    datatype    DEFAULT 'value' ...
```

Examples:

1. In this example, defaults are assigned to the optional columns. Several insert commands demonstrate how the defaults are processed.

```
use address

go

drop table address

go

create table address

(

customer_no        int,

address_code       char(1)DEFAULT 'H',

street1            char(25),

street2            char(25) DEFAULT 'Street 2',

city                char(20) DEFAULT 'New York City',

state_province     char(20),

country            char(15) DEFAULT 'USA',

zip_pc             char(10),

CONSTRAINT FK_address_city_state FOREIGN KEY (city,
state_province)

                   REFERENCES city_state_code (city,
                   state)

)

go

/* Enter some records into the address table and take
advantage of the defaults to save time and effort entering
the data */

INSERT address

    (customer_no, street1, state, zip_pc)

    VALUES
```

```
    (2000, "123 Hope Street," "New York," "10002")
go

/* Override the address-code column default within the INSERT
command */

INSERT address

    (customer_no, address_code, street1, state, zip_pc)

    VALUES

    (2000, "S," "123 Hope Street," "New York," "10002")
go
```

2. In this example, defaults are assigned to columns with various datatypes.

```
USE address

go

DROP TABLE deposit

go

CREATE TABLE deposit

(

customer_no          int,

amount               money         DEFAULT 0.00,

deposit_date         datetime      DEFAULT getdate(),

user_id              char (20)     DEFAULT 'Operator'

)

go

INSERT deposit

(customer_no, deposit_date) VALUES (1500, getdate())

go

INSERT deposit (customer_no) VALUES (1600)

go
```

CONCLUSION

This chapter provided scripts to add data constraints to table columns and tables. This included identity constraints, key constraints, and default constraints. The SQL scripts provide a baseline for reestablishing a database environment to the same point. This chapter also provided examples of SQL scripts that test the operation of the data constraints.

Chapter 15
Referential Integrity for Database Design

Bonn-Oh Kim

MAINTAINING THE INTEGRITY OF DATA is one of the most critical issues involved in designing in database systems. In relational database systems, there are four common integrity constraints:

- The key constraint, which states that the values of a primary key must be unique, so there should be no duplicate primary key values.
- Entity integrity, which indicates that a primary key of a relation cannot take null values.
- Referential integrity, which is a constraint to ensure the existence of a tuple of a relation that is referenced by a tuple in another relation.
- Semantic integrity, which states that data in the database systems should be consistent or semantically correct.

A relational database is commonly considered to have referential integrity if there are no unmatched foreign key values. This definition is incomplete because attributes other than a foreign key also require data consistency with other relations. It is also limiting when designing an entity-relationship (E-R) model or relational model because referential integrity is indirectly represented via the foreign key concept.

This chapter discusses attribute referential integrity (ARI), an expanded concept that allows referential integrity to be specified on any attribute of a relation. It also explains the specifications of the new referential integrity constraint on the E-R and relational models. Methods of enforcing the referential integrity constraint are also suggested.

Discussion of the integrity issues is restricted to the relational model, although other data models such as the network or hierarchical model share the same concerns.

THE COMMON DEFINITION OF REFERENTIAL INTEGRITY

Referential integrity in the relational model is defined in various ways. Some definitions assert that to maintain referential integrity, the database must not contain any unmatched foreign key values; others assert that referential integrity is defined only between foreign and primary key relations. However, there is no theoretical reason to specify the referential integrity constraint only on the foreign key. Specifying referential integrity on any attribute of a relation should be possible.

In designing relational database systems, the E-R model can be used as a conceptual tool for specifying data requirements. This practice is widely accepted and supported by various computer-aided software engineering (CASE) tools.

In the E-R model, however, referential integrity is not explicitly represented, although it can be specified on a relationship among entity types. In the E-R model, referential integrity is implicitly represented on a relationship type between the participating entity types. It becomes explicit only after the E-R model is converted into the relational model. That is, referential integrity can be explicitly specified using structured query language (SQL) statements when creating tables.

LIMITS OF THE COMMON DEFINITION OF REFERENTIAL INTEGRITY

The commonly accepted definition of referential integrity is inadequate for representing the referential integrity constraint on attributes that are not a foreign key, as the following example illustrates.

A Sample Case: The Car Rental Company

A small car rental company wants to implement a database system for retaining information on vehicles and rental packages, represented by the objects VEHICLE and RENTAL_PACKAGE, respectively.

For VEHICLE, they would like to retain vehicle identification numbers (VehID#), makes (Make), and vehicle types (VehTypeName). Regarding RENTAL_PACKAGE, the package identification number (PackageID#), rates (Rate), and vehicle types (VehTypeName) need to be retained.

Information on vehicle types in both VEHICLE and RENTAL_PACKAGE should be consistent. RENTAL_PACKAGE is the primary source for information on the vehicle types. In other words, all the vehicle types shown in VEHICLE.VehTypeName should exist in RENTAL_PACKAGE.VehTypeName.

Exhibit 1 shows an E-R model for the above case. In the exhibit, the referential integrity constraint on VehTypeName between RENTAL_PACKAGE and VEHICLE is maintained by creating a new entity type (VEHICLE_TYPE) and two one-to-many relationships between VEHICLE_TYPE and RENTAL_PACKAGE, and VEHICLE_TYPE and VEHICLE.

Exhibit 2 shows a relational model converted from the E-R model in Exhibit 1. In these models, the referential integrity constraint of the vehicle

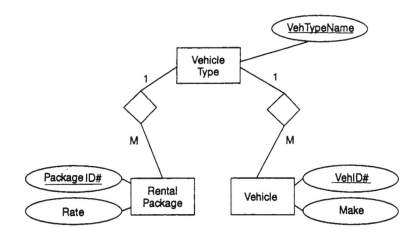

Exhibit 1.   An example of a conventional E-R model.

type information is maintained by specifying a foreign key on VehTypeName on RENTAL_PACKAGE and VEHICLE, respectively.

Even though the models shown in Exhibits 1 and 2 appear to efficiently maintain referential integrity using the foreign keys, they actually incur unnecessary computational costs. That is, an entity type of VEHICLE_TYPE in Exhibit 1 and a relation of VEHICLE_TYPE in Exhibit 2 are created solely for maintaining and enforcing the referential integrity constraint of the vehicle type information.

Unless there is a need to retain more information (i.e., other attributes) in VEHICLE_TYPE, this way of implementing referential integrity is redundant and computationally expensive. Costs for creating and maintaining a unary relation (in the previous example, it is VEHICLE_TYPE) can be eliminated by directly defining the referential integrity between two relations (i.e., VEHICLE and RENTAL_PACKAGE). The following section discusses more direct and explicit representations of referential integrity to remedy this type of anomaly.

ATTRIBUTE REFERENTIAL INTEGRITY (ARI)

Referential integrity is an issue, not only in the context of referencing foreign keys and referenced primary keys. There is also a need to extend and generalize the concept of referential integrity beyond the current definition.

This section defines extended referential integrity and proposes a notation for the E-R model. Unlike the conventional definition of referential integrity, a foreign key is not a part of the definition. This expanded version of referential integrity is referred to as *attribute referential integrity.*

RENTAL_PACKAGE

PK   FK->VEHICLE_TYPE.VehTypeName

PackageID#	Rate	VehTypeName

VEHICLE

PK   FK->VEHICLE_TYPE.VehTypeName

VehID#	Make	VehTypeName

VEHICLE_TYPE

PK

VehTypeName

Exhibit 2. A relational model generated from the E-R model in Exhibit 11-1.

Attribute referential integrity ensures that a value appearing in the referencing attribute of one relation appears in the referenced attribute of the other relation, where these two relations are not necessarily distinct, and referencing or referenced attributes can be a combination of multiple attributes. The following section provides the formal definition.

The Formal Definition of Attribute Referential Integrity

r1 (R1) and r2 (R2) are relations of a schema R1 and R2, respectively. A subset α of R1 is a referencing attribute referring to a referenced attribute β in relation r2 if it is required that for every tuple t1 in r1, there must be a tuple t2 in r2 such that $t1[\alpha] = t2[\beta]$. Requirements of this form are called the *attribute referential integrity constraint.* This can be written as $\prod \alpha_\alpha(r1)\prod_\alpha$

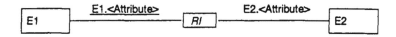

Exhibit 3. Proposed notation for attribute referential integrity.

(r2), where Π is a projection operation in the relational algebra. For an attribute referential integrity constraint to make sense, either $\alpha = \beta$ or α and β must be compatible sets of attributes.

The E-R Model

Exhibit 3 shows a proposed notation for attribute referential integrity on the E-R diagram. RI in the small rectangle indicates that the participating entity types E1 and E2 contain the attributes whose referential integrity should be maintained.

On the line between the RI rectangle and the participating entity types, the referential relationship is represented (i.e., the referencing or referenced attribute is specified), where an underlined attribute represents a referenced attribute. As defined, the referenced attribute contains a superset of all values appearing in the referencing attribute.

Exhibit 4 shows an example of a new E-R model for the previous example. Unlike the first example, there is no need to create a new entity type solely for representing the referential integrity constraint. On the entity types RENTAL_PACKAGE and VEHICLE, the vehicle type attribute (VehTypeName)

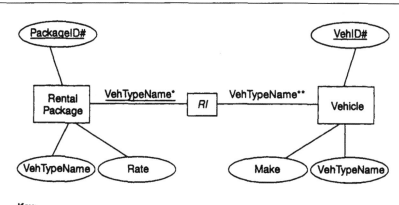

Key:
* Referenced attribute
** Referencing attribute

Exhibit 4. An example of the extended E-R model.

is included instead of separately creating an entity type VEHICLE_TYPE as in Exhibit 1. On the lines emanating from the RI rectangle, a referenced attribute (RENTAL_PACKAGE.VehTypeName), and a referencing attribute (VEHICLE.VehTypeName), are specified explicitly; whereas, in Exhibit 11-1 this referential integrity is implicitly represented via the foreign key concept.

The Relational Model

The ARI constraint can be directly represented on the referencing attribute of a relation by specifying a referenced attribute of the other relation. A notation representing this is:

ARI(<referencing attribute>) → <referenced attribute>

For example, Exhibit 5 shows a set of relations generated from the E-R model shown in Exhibit 4 . By specifying the attribute referential integrity constraint directly on VEHICLE.VehTypeName, there is no need to create a new relation of VEHICLE_TYPE because no foreign keys are involved to specify the referential integrity constraints as in Exhibit 2. Instead, the referential integrity constraint on VehTypeName can be directly and explicitly specified on the referencing attribute, VEHICLE.VehTypeName, referring to the referenced attribute, RENTAL_PACKAGE.VehTypeName.

RENTAL_PACKAGE

PK

TermID#	Rate	VehTypeName

VEHICLE

PK   ARI->RENTAL_PACKAGE.VehTypeName

VehID#	Make	VehTypeName

Exhibit 5.   A relational model generated from the E-R model in Exhibit 11.4.

The conventional referential integrity constraint on the foreign key can be specified using SQL when defining a relation. In this relational model (or SQL based on it), there is no direct way of specifying the attribute referential integrity constraint. However, it can still be specified in the database designer's data dictionary and implemented using a procedural language. Future versions of SQL will include the specifications of the attribute referential integrity constraint on the non-foreign key attributes.

Following is the suggested syntax for specifying the ARI constraint:

```
CREATE TABLE <TableName>

   (<Attribute List> ; This attribute list must include
   the referencing attribute.

   ATTRIBUTE REFERENTIAL INTEGRITY: <Referencing
   Attribute>

REFERENCES <Referenced Attribute>)
```

The relational model shown in Exhibit 5 can be written as follows:

```
CREATE TABLE RENTAL_PACKAGE

   (TermID          #INT,

   RateDECIMAL      (3,1),

   VehTypeName      CHAR(20));

CREATE TABLE VEHICLE

   (VehID#          INT,

   Make             CHAR(20),

   VehTypeName      CHAR(20))

   ATTRIBUTE REFERENTIAL INTEGRITY:

   (VehTypeName) REFERENCES RENTAL_PACKAGE
   (VehTypeName));
```

ENFORCING THE ARI CONSTRAINT

Enforcement of the referential integrity constraint on the foreign key can be conducted in three ways: restriction, cascading, and nullification (i.e., setting to a default value). The attribute referential integrity constraint can be enforced in a similar manner.

First, the delete or update operation on the referenced attribute can be restricted to the case where there are no matching values in the referencing attribute. Second, the delete or update operation on the referenced attribute cascades to delete or update the matching values in the referencing attribute. Finally, the referencing attribute value is set to null or a default value if a matching value in the referenced attribute is deleted or updated.

These three enforcement schemes are not, however, implemented in current database management systems (DBMSs). The attribute referential integrity constraint should be enforced by writing an application program on the database or attaching a procedure (i.e., trigger) to a referenced or referencing attribute.

SUMMARY

Specifying the attribute referential integrity has major advantages in database systems design. An E-R and relational model for a problem domain can be built compactly by dispensing with an entity type and a relation created solely for specifying the referential integrity constraint of a foreign key. Also, the referential integrity constraint of an attribute can be specified directly and explicitly without using foreign keys.

Using the attribute referential integrity concept, a referential semantic constraint can be explicitly represented in the E-R and relational models. In the current DBMS environment, this new integrity constraint can be implemented by writing an attached procedure on a referenced or referencing attribute. In the future, CASE tools and DBMSs will be able to represent the attribute referential integrity constraint.

Chapter 16
Data Quality: An Architectural Solution

Sriram Pidaparti

AS CORPORATIONS EMBARK ON DATA WAREHOUSING EFFORTS, they are unearthing integrity and accuracy problems associated with the operational data. Another major challenge that has emerged is the integration of disparate operational data. This problem is characterized by inconsistent data models, disparate data structures, and poor quality of data that is fundamental to an organization — such as customer data, vendor data, and product data.

It is not uncommon to find a situation in which there are six different descriptions for the same product or four different data structures for customer name and address data. Such situations are common because of:

- Multiple transactional systems that have their own versions of the data stores (both structures and data), for example; different versions of customer data in order processing and billing systems.
- Package installations, business mergers, and acquisitions that incorporate new and different versions of data.
- Multiple instances of the same application used and extended differently in different geographies or departments.
- Different business units that have adopted their own definitions and standards for foundation databased on the belief that their business is different from the other business units.

Addressing these data quality issues at the enterprise architecture level is essential to finding an effective long-term solution. This chapter proposes that the corporate information factory be extended to include a construct called the foundation data store (FDS). The following sections define the foundation data store, describe how it fits into the corporate information factory, and suggest possible implementation approaches.

0-8493-9976-9/99/$0.00+$.50
© 1999 by CRC Press LLC

FDS OVERVIEW AND BENEFITS

Organizations have foundation data whether or not they design and implement it as a separate data store. Some organizations implement reference files/databases (also known in some companies as pillar databases, subject databases, and master databases) for foundation data. The foundation data store is a mechanism to formalize this practice into an architectural construct like the operational data store and data warehouse. The term *foundation data store* is used in this chapter because it appropriately reflects the architectural placement and importance of this data store.

The FDS contains relatively nonvolatile information that is traditionally found in a master file (e.g., customer data, vendor data, organization structures, and product data). This information can be viewed as a centrally maintained or authenticated data store that operational systems would use instead of creating and maintaining their own unique versions of the foundation data.

The information content of the FDS is based on standards for common data definitions, structures, and values. The commonality depends on how diverse an organization is; for example, the more diverse the organization, the less the commonality of data. An example of a high-level, entity-relationship (ER) diagram for a foundation data store is shown in Exhibit 1.

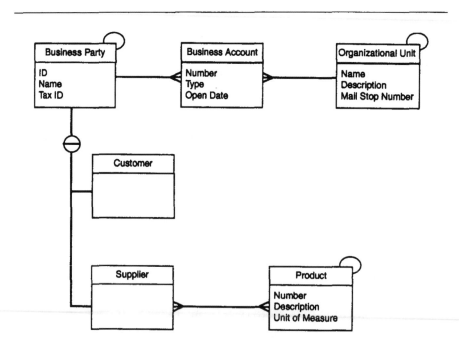

Exhibit 1.   Sample ER diagram for foundation data store.

The FDS data model is only a part of the enterprisewide logical data model; otherwise, it would not contain all the entities and relationships. For example, an enterprise-level data model may have an associative entity called Order that connects the Customer and Product entities, but that entity belongs to the order processing transactional application data model rather than the foundation data model.

It is also possible that only certain attributes of an entity may belong to the FDS data model; for example, a business account balance does not necessarily have to be a foundation data attribute. The major entities of the foundation data store usually translate into dimensions in the informational processing world.

In addition to easier data integration and improved operational data quality, the foundation data store implementation offers the following benefits:

- Reduced effort in developing data warehousing applications because of easier integration of data.
- Better customer service because of data quality improvements.
- Cost savings because of centralized data maintenance and efficient external data vendor management.
- Improved decision-making because of more accurate information.
- More efficient transactional applications development because of reuse and avoidance of duplication of efforts.

FOUNDATION APPLICATION FRAMEWORK

The application or system that updates the foundation data store is primarily a data maintenance application. Therefore, it would not possess the complex processing logic of a transactional application such as an order processing system, production scheduling system, or trading system.

The framework shown in Exhibit 2 is a useful reference for administrators creating a new transactional application or reengineering a legacy ap-

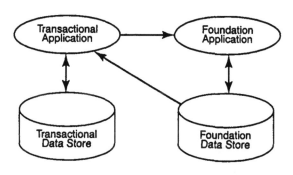

Exhibit 2. Framework for transactional and foundation applications.

	Transactional	Foundation
System Examples	Order processing system Billing system Equities trading system	Customer maintenance Product maintenance Vendor maintenance
Data Entity Examples	Order, invoice, shipment Payment, cash flow	Customer, product, vendor
Volatility	Very volatile	Relatively stable
Volume of Data	Large to very large	Small to large
Key Characteristic	Performance is most critical	Availability is most critical
Application Processing	Process/workflow intensive	Data intensive Mainly limited to table maintenance

Exhibit 3.   Differences between transactional and foundation applications.

plication. Architectural separation of foundation and transactional applications along with their data stores is recommended. The demarcation of update responsibilities is very clear — the transactional application updates its transactional data and the foundation application updates the foundation data store. Access to the foundation data store is critical to the transactional application. Administrators usually need to be able to join data within two data stores. Technology solutions such as gateways make this possible, even across heterogeneous database environments.

The foundation application should be a centrally developed application deployed in a distributed fashion. The purpose of the interaction between foundation and transactional applications, as shown in Exhibit 2, is not only to give the transactional application user access to the foundation application, but to make it appear seamless to the user. For example, to create a new customer entry while taking an order, the customer service representative does not have to log into the foundation application. Exhibit 3 shows the differences between transactional and foundation applications.

FDS AND THE CORPORATE INFORMATION FACTORY

Inmon, Imhoff, and Battas, in their book *Building the Operational Data Store* (New York: John Wiley & Sons, Inc., 1995), proposed a common architecture called the *corporate information factory* that includes the operational data store (ODS), data warehouse, and legacy applications (see Exhibit 4). They describe the flow of data within the corporate information factory as follows:

1. Raw, detailed data is put into the corporate information factory by means of data capture, entry, and transaction interaction with the older legacy applications.

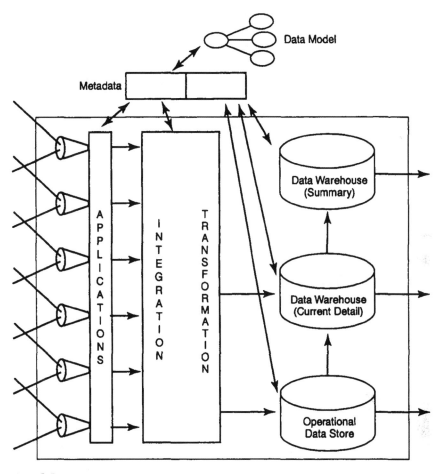

Data Model

Metadata

A
P
P
L
I
C
A
T
I
O
N
S

I
N
T
E
G
R
A
T
I
O
N

T
R
A
N
S
F
O
R
M
A
T
I
O
N

Data Warehouse
(Summary)

Data Warehouse
(Current Detail)

Operational
Data Store

Note: Bulk storage not shown.

Source: Inmon, Imhoff, and Battas, *Building the Operational Data Store* (New York: John Wiley and Sons, Inc., 1995).

Exhibit 4.   Corporate information factory.

2. The raw, detailed data are integrated and transformed and then passed into the operational data store or the current detail level of the data warehouse.
3. As the refined data passes out of the operational data store, this data goes into the current level of the data warehouse.
4. Once the refined data is summarized, the data passes from the current detail level of the warehouse into the summarized level of data in the data warehouse.

The corporate information factory can be extended to include the foundation data store as an integral architectural construct within the framework, as shown in Exhibit 5. The FDS functions as the official source (i.e., system of record) for an organization's foundation data. It maintains and supplies such data to transactional applications, the ODS, and data warehouse. The FDS also collects and conditions external data before that data can be used by an organization. The following sections discuss how the foundation data store relates to the other components of the corporate information factory.

Transactional Applications. Ideally, the transactional applications should not have their own versions of the foundation data, but should access the centrally maintained data store. In another possible configuration, the transactional application could make changes to a local copy of the central store, and the changes would be applied to the central store after authentication.

Integration and Transformation Layer. The implementation of the foundation data store makes the application component more integrated, which leads to a relatively simple and straightforward integration and transformation layer.

Operational Data Store. An ODS application usually uses the current version of the foundation data store. Therefore, ODS applications should be able to directly access the central foundation data store. An alternative is to replicate a subset of the central foundation data store into the ODS environment.

Data Warehouse. The major entities of the foundation data store become dimensions in a data warehouse. The data warehouse contains the historical snapshots of the foundation data store. The detail contained in the warehouse should reference the appropriate snapshot of the foundation data.

While doing comparative and trend analyses, users should be alerted if different summarization algorithms are used for different time periods. For example, if organizational hierarchy is one of the foundation data entities, the results of summarization would depend on the hierarchy that is used in the summarization process. Users should be given an option to view the history based on either the same hierarchy for all time periods or different hierarchies for different time periods.

Data Model. Design and implementation of the foundation data store should be based on a solid logical data model that is an integral part of an enterprise data model. In the case of foundation data, translation from the logical model to the physical design is relatively straightforward, unlike

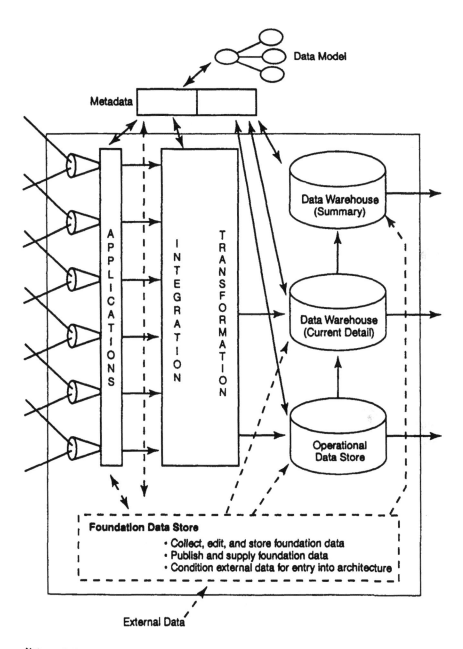

Notes: Bulk storage not shown.

For the sake of clarity, the flows from external data
to the other components of the architecture are not shown.

Exhibit 5. FDS as a component of the corporate information factory.

the design of data warehouse databases or transactional databases that may require a lot of denormalization or summarization.

Metadata. The metadata generated from the data model is used as a basis for the design of the foundation data store. One of the first steps in implementing a foundation data store is documenting the existing foundation data and developing the standards. Metadata is, therefore, a natural by-product of this process. In an organization that has an efficient FDS implementation, the data dictionary of the foundation database supplies a significant portion of the metadata.

External Data. There is a potential need for external data at all levels of the corporate information factory. For example, the data warehouse may contain external information to compare the historical performance of the organization with an external benchmark. Similarly, an order processing system may have electronic data interchange-related external data that is unique to that application.

Some of the external data that an organization uses is foundation information. Typical examples include financial product information from market data providers and name and address lists purchased from vendors. It is essential that the external data be conditioned to adhere to standards before that data is stored in the foundation data store.

External data should also be modeled and documented using the enterprise data model and metadata for it to be appropriately classified and integrated with the internal data in the data warehouse and other data stores.

FDS IMPLEMENTATION STRATEGIES

Implementing the foundation data store requires careful planning and commitment from all levels of an organization, including senior management, business user groups, and IS. The following sections discuss potential architectures for implementing the foundation data store.

Central Data Store with Direct Access. In this strategy, all the applications that require foundation data directly access a central data store. This technically simple solution provides the best data quality. However, it is vulnerable to performance problems and a single point of failure. In addition, this solution does not allow the creation of new foundation data or changes to be made to existing foundation data. Exhibit 6 shows a central data store with direct access.

Central Data Store with Replicated Copies. In this architecture, a subset of the central data store is replicated to allow local applications to access foundation data more rapidly. This solution provides better performance,

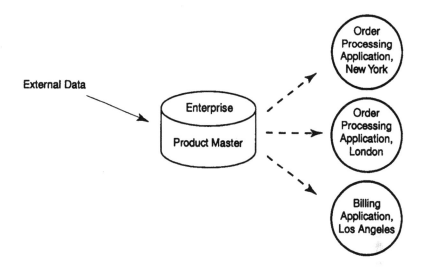

Exhibit 6.   Central data store with direct access.

but is more complex technically and does not allow create and update functions to be performed. Exhibit 7 shows a central data store with replicated copies.

Central Authentication. Central authentication allows individual business units or local offices of an organization to create new foundation data and make changes to existing foundation data. The additions and changes

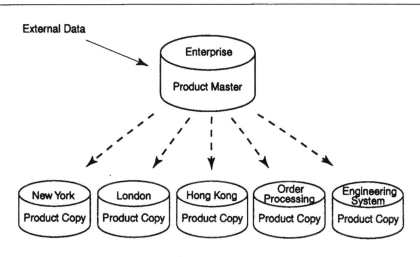

Exhibit 7.   Central data store with replicated copies.

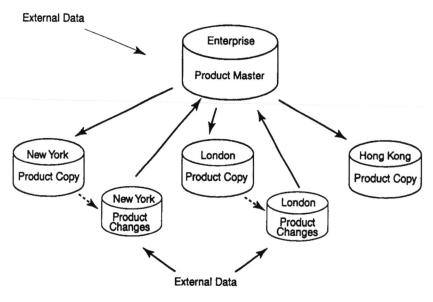

Exhibit 8. Central authentication.

are recorded locally in a database separate from the official replicated copy of the central store. The new and changed data is transferred to a central data store where the additions and changes are authenticated. The authenticated data are transmitted to all the users who requested it. This strategy reduces bottlenecks, but is the most complex technically. Central authentication is illustrated in Exhibit 8.

Consolidated Reference. This strategy is used primarily to implement consolidation standards for reporting and informational processing purposes (see Exhibit 9). Although it is a necessary step for data warehousing initiatives, it does not solve data quality problems in the operational systems.

Consolidated reference is a valid short-term strategy for organizations with urgent data warehousing project commitments and limited resources. A long-term solution to operational data problems, however, would be to implement the central foundation data store, which is the official source for the foundation data. Consolidated reference can be viewed as an intermediate step to implementing the foundation data store.

FDS IMPLEMENTATION FACTORS

An organization must choose the most appropriate implementation strategy based on its own context and situation. Although various factors influence FDS implementation in an organization, the solution depends on

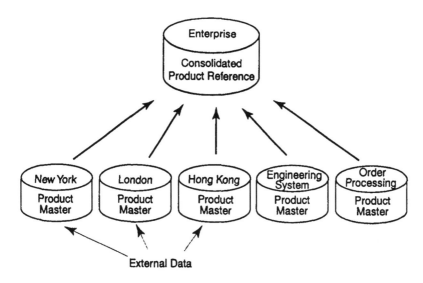

Exhibit 9.   Consolidated reference.

the organizational structure, number of database platforms, number of physical databases, number of geographic locations, and volume of data.

An organization with a decentralized management philosophy may prefer central authentication rather than a central store with direct architecture, as with an organization that does not have a very strong WAN infrastructure. A company that has several transaction systems on various DBMS platforms requires a well-planned technical architecture involving gateways and message queues.

Although it is desirable, it is not necessary to have the same implementation strategy for all of the foundation data. For example, for a particular organization, a central data store with direct access may be more appropriate for vendor data, whereas central authentication may be more appropriate for customer data.

SUMMARY

A foundation data store should be chosen based on organizational structure, number of database platforms, number of physical databases, number of geographic locations, and volume of data. Although it is more manageable, it is not necessary to implement the same strategy for all the foundation data. For example, a central data store with direct access may be more appropriate for vendor data, whereas central authentication may be more appropriate for customer data.

DATA INTEGRITY AND QUALITY

The foundation data store is presented as an architectural component of the corporate information factory. Finding the appropriate implementation strategy and addressing the data quality issues are critical to the long-term success of an organization's data warehousing initiatives.

Section IV
Data Administration, Security, and Operations

MANIPULATING DATA, BE IT AT CREATE TIME, DELETE TIME, OR MODIFI-
CATION TIME, is an important part of the data management challenge. The
other significant challenge is the ongoing maintenance of the physical storage of the data and the operation of the tools that support the data. Data
administration also includes system management, configuration management, and asset management tools and processes. Data also must be secured against viruses, unauthorized access, and corruption. Operations
include the processes and procedures for maintaining data stores, regular
backups, and data recovery procedures. This section contains eight chapters that explore each of these topics.

Chapter 17, "Managing Database Backup and Recovery," discusses how
to invest in a sound database backup and recovery process to protect corporate data. This involves examining the degrees of recoverability required by the business, fault tolerance alternatives, virus infiltration, and
unauthorized tampering through the Internet.

Chapter 18, "Managing NT Domains for Enterprise Architecture," examines the design of the domain model in a Windows NT Server implementation. This has powerful implications on system response time, scalability,
and security.

Chapter 19, "DBMS Recovery Procedures," first explains the need for recovery procedures, and then provides an overview of transaction properties such as atomicity, serialization, and consistency. Reasons for failures
and techniques for recovering from them are discussed and, finally, the issue of data integrity is addressed.

Chapter 20, "Change Management Strategies for Data Administration,"
provides a nontechnical overview of change management at the organizational level. This chapter describes how changes in an organization, such
as downsizing, can affect the data management functions and then discuss-

es strategies for managing the data in the midst of such changes. In particular, data resource management principles are outlined for handling changes. Some of the behavioral as well as cost issues also are discussed.

Chapter 21, "Database Security Controls," describes basic security concepts such as confidentiality, integrity, and availability and provides an overview of various discretionary access control mechanisms. A detailed discussion of multilevel security and mandatory access control mechanisms also is included.

Chapter 22, "E-Mail Security and Privacy," describes some of the problems surrounding e-mail privacy and also proposes a few practical, easy-to-implement solutions within the context of industry standards and guidelines.

Chapter 23, "Security Models for Object-Oriented Databases," describes how database administrators can address the unique security considerations of object-oriented systems. This chapter also focuses on the emerging security model.

Chapter 24, "Security Management for the World Wide Web," provides a solution set to leverage an organization's existing skills, resources, and security implementations in building an underlying baseline security framework for transacting corporate business over the Internet and the World Wide Web.

Chapter 17
Managing Database Backup and Recovery

Michael Simonyi

INTRODUCTION

Management of the corporate database is arguably one of the most mismanaged areas in information technology today. Database technology has evolved from historical glass-house foundations of the past into the point-and-click implementations that come right out of the box today. Where databases and systems were once carefully designed, implemented, and deployed, they are now installed, loaded, and deployed without regard to basic effective design. This article addresses the concepts necessary to formulate a method to protect, back up, and, in the event of failure, recover perhaps the most important aspect of a business — its database. Without proper preparation, planning, and testing, an entire database infrastructure can become the target of lost devices, indexes, degraded backup mechanisms, and corrupted data.

HIGH AVAILABILITY VS. RECOVERABILITY

There are important differences between database availability and recoverability. Database availability can be a driving factor to recoverability, but it does not guarantee recoverability. Database availability is the measurement of production uptime and physical access to production data in a networked environment. In contrast, database recoverability refers to the ability to recover a database successfully in its entirety. Recoverability is a measurement of how accurate and lengthy the process of recovering from partial or total failure can be. The difference lies in the application of backup tools used in conjunction with high-availability tools. The redundancy of high-availability systems in an environment can directly relate to a higher grade of successful backups for the database environment as well as the supporting systems. In this article, a database environment is de-

0-8493-9976-9/99/$0.00+$.50
© 1999 by CRC Press LLC

fined as the database, connecting middleware, and application front-end screens. These technologies are used to complement each other to offer accuracy, reliability, and stability.

METHODS OF DATA PROTECTION

The common methods of data production include the following: (1) tape; (2) mirroring (RAID 0); (3) data guarding (RAID 5); (4) duplexing; (5) partitioning; (6) replication; and (7) clustering. Each of these are explained further in this section.

Before investigating these different methods available for protecting a database environment, this article discusses the business requirements for data recoverability and availability. For example, if a database, in the event of failure, would place individuals in a life-threatening situation or would place the organization into financial chaos and eventual closure, then it is necessary to implement all available methods to become 100% fault tolerant. However, if a failure would be merely an inconvenience, then a simple tape backup procedure may suffice. Most organizations seek the middle ground.

Tape Backup

Tape backup should form the foundation of a corporate backup strategy because of its ease of use and low cost. In order for the tape backup mechanism to be useful it must be well designed and tested regularly. At a minimum, backups should be performed on a daily basis and not less than weekly. If possible, the entire database(s) should be backed up on a daily basis. The database transaction logs should be backed up during and after business hours, or whenever feasible to minimize the risk of lost data.

Mirroring

Mirroring or RAID 0 provides for duplicate sets of data on two separate hard disk drives, a primary and a secondary. This is also known as a master–slave configuration. For each logical write operation there are two physical write operations to the hard disks. This scenario protects against failure of an individual or set of drives. If either the primary or secondary drive fails, the data on the surviving drive allows for system recovery. In most situations, this option is ideal for protection of the database transaction logs. However, it does not offer protection against multiple simultaneous failures.

Data Guarding

Data guarding or RAID 5 has the ability to stripe redundant data across multiple drives (minimum three) in an array. The striping of data protects against a single drive failure in the array. When an array loses a drive, the system still functions by using the redundant data found on the surviving drives. There are two types of RAID 5 available today, namely, software- and hardware-based RAID 5. Hardware RAID is the more desirable implementation method because it was designed with drive failures in mind. Extending the tolerance level of a RAID 5 system can then be achieved by mirroring or duplexing drive arrays. This type of extension allows for whole drive arrays to fail without impacting the system

Duplexing

Duplexing is similar to mirroring except that in a duplexed configuration separate controller cards manage each drive or sets of drives. In essence, duplexing is Raid 0 with an additional layer or redundancy. The second disk controller cards remove a single point of failure that is exhibited in a standard mirroring (Raid 0) configuration.

Partitioning

Partitioning is the ability to deploy a database system across multiple servers where each server houses a different portion of the overall database. Should a server go down, only the component running on that server becomes unavailable. In this scenario the database can continue to function normally, provided applications are written to handle these types of situations. Additional protection can be achieved by employing RAID 0, RAID 5, or duplexing to minimize system downtime further.

Replication

Replication offers the ability to publish the contents (complete or portions thereof) of a database to another or multiple servers in an environment. The technique is similar to partitioning; however, to employ replication requires sophisticated application transaction logic to be used effectively. Replication allows for the mirroring of database transactions to be replicated in a secondary database at the central site or in a distributed location. Ideally, all transactions should be processed at a central database and the transactions should be replaced to the other subscribing sites. This eliminates the difficulty that becomes inherent with transaction logic of the traditional two-phase commit that fails as a result of hardware failures.

Clustering

Clustering is the ability of a group of *n* servers to share or cooperate with each other in utilizing common resources. Clustering allows systems to monitor each other and, in the advent of failure, transfer processing to their counterpart. Clustering is a very reliable method for maintaining a fault tolerant and highly available systems environment; however, vendors approach clustering differently. It is recommended that organizations examine their application architecture and processing requirements prior to selecting a clustering strategy and infrastructure.

Each of these individual methods can be used in tandem with each other to build a graded level of fault tolerance and high availability. Again, as with any other technology, the system requirements dictate the configuration and detail that is ultimately required. In most cases the higher the required tolerance, the more methods that are included in the solution.

Batch Cycles

The size and complexity of the database environment determines the most suitable backup cycle. A small site can afford the luxury of daily full database and transaction log backups. A medium-sized site must perform a mix of backups of full database and transaction log backups on daily and weekly cycles. A large site requires multiple staggered sets of backups and transaction logs on a daily basis with weekly and even monthly cycles backing up segments of the database to achieve a full database backup.

Transaction logs should be backed up at least once during the day. However, this depends on the transaction flow of the database. A low-volume online transaction processing (OLTP) database may only require a single transaction log backup at the end of a business day, before or after any additional processing is enacted on the data. In the case of high-volume OLTP processing environments, the backup of the transaction log may require hourly backups. It will be necessary to gauge the transaction flow of the environment to determine the backup schedule of the transaction logs.

Sample backup schedules for small, medium, and large sites are shown in the tables given in Exhibit 1. With each scenario outlined above, the robustness of the hardware also impacts the backup schedule of an organization. Since most organizations cannot afford to replace hardware on an as-needed basis, different backup schedules may need to be adopted over time, for different pieces of hardware.

ACCURACY OF BACKUPS

Although data backups are important, equally important is the need to determine the accuracy of the data prior to backup and the ability to guarantee the restoration of the contents of the backup into the original database or backup database system. The accuracy or consistency of the backup is paramount for recoverability. Should inconsistent data or data structures be stored onto the backup media, any attempt to restore them will most likely render the database inoperable or, worse, introduce inconsistent data into the production environment that may unknowingly place the organization at risk.

Exhibit 1. Sample Backup Schedules for Small, Medium, and Large Sites

Time	Mon	Tues	Wed	Thurs	Fri	Sat	Sun
Schedule for a Small Site for Database Less Than 10GB							
12am	DB Check	DB Check	DB Check	DB Check	DB Check	DB Check	DB Check
1am		Full DB	Full DB	Full DB	Full DB		
5pm	Tlog	TLog	Tlog	TLog	TLog		
9pm	Purge Log	Purge Log	Purge Log	Purge Log	Purge Log		
Schedule for a Medium Site for Databases Greater Than 10GB but Less Than 100GB							
12am	DB Check	DB Check	DB Check	DB Check	DB Check	DB Check	DB Check
1am						Full DB	
5pm	Tlog	TLog	Tlog	TLog	TLog		
9pm	Purge Log	Purge Log	Purge Log	Purge Log	Purge Log		
Schedule for a Large Site for Databases Greater Than 100 GB							
12am	DB Check	DB Check	DB Check	DB Check	DB Check	DB Check	DB Check
1am	DB Seg 1	DB Seg 2	DB Seg 3	DB Seg 4	DB Seg 5	DB Seg 6	DB Seg 7
5pm	Tlog	TLog	Tlog	TLog	TLog	TLog	TLog
9pm	Purge Log	Purge Log	Purge Log	Purge Log	Purge Log	Purge Log	Purge Log

Times noted are for clarity only.

DB Seg refers to a portion or segment of the database to be backed up. Each segment or portion of the database in conjunction with the transaction logs will provide for a full database backup at any point in time.

Most databases on the market today provide built-in tools that provide some level of data integrity checking that verifies that internal data structures are intact and tables, indexes, and page linkage is consistent. Any warnings or errors reported for these utilities should be acted upon at once. Failure to act on these messages can render a database inoperable and, depending on when the problem surfaced, can cause a loss of data. The following pseudoimplementation provides an approach to handling a database backup.

Generic Backup Stream

Perform a data integrity check on the contents of the database.

1.1. Have inconsistencies been found in the database?
    1.1.1. Send alert to DBA and Operations staff, write events to log file.
    1.1.2. Halt backup stream. (Problem resolution takes place at this point.)
    1.1.3. Reestablish backup stream after problem has been resolved.

1.2. Database is free of defects.
    Begin backup stream.
    Verify completion status.
    Notify operations and DBA of backup completion.

Incremental Backups

Incremental backups are something that should only be performed if it is not possible to complete a full backup during the allotted time frame or backup window. Incremental backups extend the time required for restoring the contents of a database in the event of a failure. Although unavoidable in huge database environments where incremental backups are the mainstay, they should still be staggered in such environments.

Backing Up in a Distributed LAN/WAN Environment

Backing up a distributed database in the LAN/WAN environment can be a nightmarish challenge. Time zones and production uptime in differing geographical areas can affect a reliable and accurate backup. If the data volumes are small and maintainable, it will be possible to coordinate backups and replication over the WAN. Some thought should be given to using redundant WAN links so as not to affect other communications over primary WAN links. If data volumes are extremely high or if the network spans the globe, it may become practical to build a hot site for this type of environment. Whether the site is built and maintained internally or through third-party vendors is purely academic. The rationale is to provide a site for conducting business transactions should the primary production facilities fail. The site should mirror the current production facilities at all times. It can be updated by replication or by use of tape media. Such a site should also be tested on a regular basis to ensure accuracy and guarantee the ability to continue business if failure encroaches upon the production systems (see Exhibit 2).

Administration Tools

As mentioned previously, most products on the market ship together with some sort of administration tool sets to maintain and administer database environments. These tools can be either GUI based or Command line based, and, at a minimum, the following tasks should be included in the process: user management, DDL scripting, data import and export, database consistency, device management, data recovery, and security utilities. Some database vendors also provide additional utilities in the areas of hierarchical storage management (HSM), database cluster management, and online statistics monitoring tools. If a database does not provide for a specific level of administration, there are many third-party products available on the market that can complement most database environments.

Areas to Protect

There are three basic areas of a database that must be protected: the data, of course, being the blood of the system; the catalogs, which are the skeleton of the system; and the transaction logs, which are the heart of a database because they detail all the events that have transpired against the data since the last full backup.

The transaction logs are considered paramount for any database system, especially after a database failure. Without the ability to maintain a readable copy of the transaction logs, any failure in the database places the data at extreme risk. For example, suppose a database is backed up fully once a week on Friday nights. During the week, the transaction logs are written onto the hard disk. If the hard disk that holds the transaction log fails on a Thursday, and no prior backup of the transactions logs has taken place, the database will only be recoverable to the last point of full backup — the preceding Friday.

The database catalogs, as described above, act as the skeleton for the database. They detail the structure of the physical database. The catalogs must be rigorously maintained. Each and every change to the database modifies the catalog. The catalog has two facets to it: the system catalog and the user database catalog. Each has it own specialized backup requirements.

The system catalog defines the database environment, including the disk drives, database devices, configuration, log-on privileges, tuning parameters, and device load points. This catalog must be backed up after every change because it affects the entire database environment. Any changes to the system catalog that are lost will seriously impair the ability

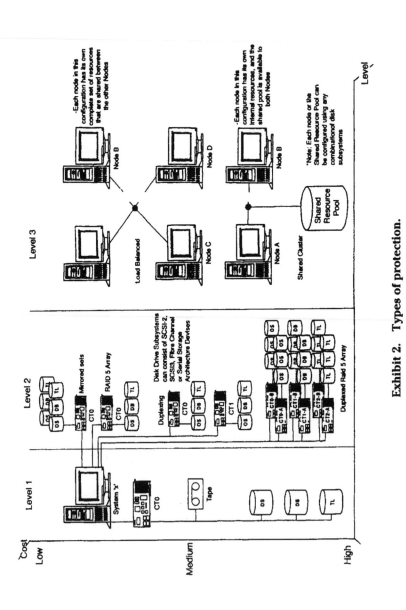

Exhibit 2. Types of protection.

to recover a database. In addition to having a backed-up system catalog, a paper-based reproduction of the system catalog can be beneficial for audit purposes or if the need ever arises to restore an older database backup on a system prior to the installation of a new RAID array. As hardware is added to the system, database load points will vary. This can have undesirable effects when loading an older version of a database back onto the server.

The user database catalog, on the other hand, is the definition of the user database. It contains all the details regarding the tables and indexes used in the physical implementation of the database and must be kept under strict observance. It should follow a strict change control process and must be backed up after each and every change to the database using a version control system. A failure to backup the database catalogs will result in loss of data if the database must ever be reloaded from flat files. The database catalog, sometimes referred to as a schema, is the blueprint of the database, the foundation of the database. It must be kept up to date, and its path of evolution must be able to be retraced.

The data, of course, as the lifeblood of the database and the reason for its existence, must also be safeguarded. The data should be backed up on a daily basis, if time permits, but no less than once a week. Backups should be restored from time to time to verify the validity of the backup and its state. There is no point in performing a backup if it is not tested periodically. What may have been restorable last year may not be restorable now. Also, recoverability from tape backups must be carefully tested.

Levels of Protection

Each of the individual methods provides a level of afforded protection. The base level of protection and last line of defense for a system failure should be a tape backup. This is deemed the last line of defense, as it is the slowest of all methods to get the system back into operation when disaster strikes. The highest level is a hybrid system. Exhibit 3 demonstrates the varying levels of recovery and associated costs.

Exhibit 3. The Varying Levels of Database Recovery and Associated Costs

Method	Level	Cost	Downtime
Tape (mandatory)	Low	Low	Hours
Mirroring	Medium	Low	Minutes to hours
Duplexing	Medium	Low	Minutes to hours
Data Guarding	High	Medium	Minutes
Partitioning	Medium	High	Minutes to hours
Replication	High	High	Minutes
Clustering	Very High	Very High	Seconds to minutes
Hybrid Combinations	Extremely High	Extremely High	Seconds

The application of each method will dictate the level of availability in the system and the degree of time required in recovering from a failure. For example, in a partitioned system the database is distributed between many separate servers. Should one of the servers go down, only a portion of the database becomes unavailable. Its cost is relatively high as there are many servers deployed and it is set up in a modular fashion. Each server then employs its own recovery mechanism.

In defining the level of protection needed to meet particular needs these questions should be asked:

- Can the company run without the database for an extended period of time?
- Are customer relationships risked if the database is unavailable?
- If the system becomes unavailable, is human life at risk?

If the answer is yes to any one of the above questions, some form of high availability solution will be needed to meet the needs. As mentioned previously, a tape backup should form the foundation of any backup strategy. Use the decision tree in Exhibit 4 to help guide the requirements for the backup strategy.

Virus Protection

Although a database system is usually well protected against direct virus attacks, the database should be well secured from the rest of the computing environment. This usually means protecting the database by placing it on a dedicated system, making sure that the only way of reaching the system is via administrative tools, the deployed middleware, or operating system-related administrative tools.

Even with a well-secured database, similar precautions will need to be taken on the front-end systems, as well. Virus-checking utilities should be deployed at the end user client workstations, and at any point in the environment where data will be fed into the database. Of course, this depends on the types of data being stored in the database. If binary large objects (BLOBs) are allowed to be inserted into documents, applications, or images that a virus can attach to, it may be necessary to implement additional levels of virus protection.

Internet and Intranet Firewalls

Database vendors are pursuing the ability to allow corporate data to become extensible to the Web if it is not already there. Most databases provide for this by using extensions to the middleware or database interface, providing extended data types in the database or providing plug-ins to the database. This presents the problem of how to ensure that no one can gain direct access to a corporate database. By implementing hardware/soft-

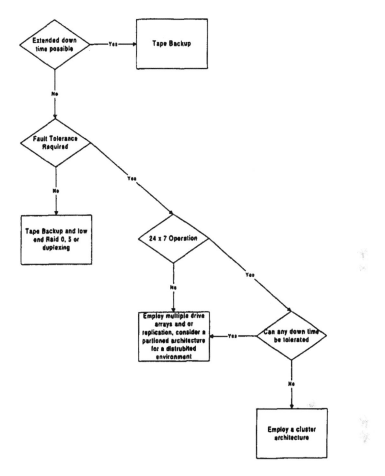

Exhibit 4.   Decision tree for selecting desired level of protection.

---

ware firewall combinations and proxies, it is possible to segregate the database carefully from the publicly exposed portion of a network. This allows construction of unidirectional paths into and out of the database that cannot be easily compromised.

CONCLUSION

In the author's experience, there is never too much protection, only too little. Having a well-thought-out backup-and-recovery procedure in place will save time, money, and embarrassment when things go wrong. All of the topics examined within the body of this article detail methods that can be used to safeguard corporate databases or any other system, for that matter. Readers should pick and choose the pieces that best suit their needs when building a fail-safe environment.

Chapter 18

Managing NT Domains for Enterprise Architecture

David Brassor

ONCE AN APPLICATION HAS BEEN CHOSEN, THE INTERFACES DESIGNED, THE CODE WRITTEN, AND THE APPLICATION TESTED, there is this great new client/server application, and the real fun begins. How does one determine the back-end systems? What database should be used? What operating system? Is it NT™ or UNIX? The focus of this article is to discuss the considerations for a large-scale client/server application under Windows® NT.

Many people question if NT is the right selection for a large-scale client/server application. Being a consultant, the author gives the standard consultant answer, "It depends." What it depends on are many factors such as the size of database, type of application, and the projected growth. Although NT cannot scale to support all client/server applications, NT does hold a viable niche in the market place. The considerations one needs to look at when designing NT architectures are as follows:

- The design of the NT domain structure that defines the layout of the various NT servers across an organization.
- Considerations when managing NT domains.
- Changes to the NT domain model under NT Version 5.0.

DOMAIN DESIGN

NT currently uses a domain model for its logical designs of servers. An NT domain is a logical grouping of network servers and other computers that share common security and user account information. Within do-

0-8493-9976-9/99/$0.00+$.50
© 1999 by CRC Press LLC

mains, administrators create one user account for each user. Users then log on once to the domain, not to the individual servers in the domain.

A domain is simply the administrative unit of Windows NT Server Directory Services. The term domain does not refer to a single location or specific type of network configuration. Computers in a single domain can share physical proximity on a small local area network (LAN) or can be located in different corners of the world, communicating over any number of physical connections, including dial-up lines, ISDN, fiber, Ethernet, Token Ring, frame relay, satellite, and leased lines. Design of the NT domain relies on many components.

Within a domain, domain controllers manage all aspects of user-domain interactions. Domain controllers are computers running Windows NT Server that share one directory database to store security and user account information for the entire domain; they comprise a single administrative unit. Domain controllers use the information in the directory database to authenticate users logging on to domain accounts. There are two types of domain controllers:

1. The primary domain controller (PDC) tracks changes made to domain accounts. Whenever an administrator makes a change to a domain account, the change is recorded in the directory database on the PDC. The PDC is the only domain server that receives these changes directly. A domain has one PDC.
2. A backup domain controller (BDC) maintains a copy of the directory database. This copy is synchronized periodically and automatically with the PDC. BDCs also authenticate user log-ons, and a BDC can be promoted to function as the PDC. Multiple BDCs can exist in a domain.

Windows NT™ Server Directory Services provide security across multiple domains through trust relationships. A trust relationship is a link that combines two domains into one administrative unit that can authorize access to resources on both domains.

There are two types of trust relationships:

1. In a one-way trust relationship, one domain trusts the users in the other domain to use its resources. More specifically, one domain trusts the domain controllers in the other domain to validate user accounts to use its resources. The resources that become available are in the trusting domain, and the accounts that can use them are in the trusted domain. However, if user accounts located in the trusting domain need to use resources located in the trusted domain, that situation requires a two-way trust relationship.
2. A two-way trust relationship really consists of two one-way trusts; each domain trusts user accounts in the other domain. Users can log

on from computers in either domain to the domain that contains their account. Each domain can have both accounts and resources. Global user accounts and global groups can be used from either domain to grant rights and permissions to resources in either domain. In other words, both domains are trusted domains.

Administrators typically group users according to the types and degrees of network access their jobs require. For example, most accountants working at a certain level probably will need access to the same servers, directories, and files. By using group accounts, administrators can grant rights and permissions to multiple users at one time. Other users can be added to an existing group account at any time, instantly gaining the rights and permissions granted to the group account.

There can be two types of group accounts:

1. A *global group* consists of several user accounts from one domain that are grouped together under one group account name. A global group can contain user accounts from only a single domain — the domain where the global group was created. "Global" indicates that the group can be granted rights and permissions to use resources in multiple (global) domains. A global group can contain only user accounts and can be created only on a domain and not on a workstation or member server.
2. A *local group* consists of user accounts and global groups from one or more domains, grouped together under one account name. Users and global groups from outside the local domain can be added to the local group only if they belong to a trusted domain. "Local" indicates that the group can be granted rights and permissions to use resources in only a single (local) domain. A local group can contain users and global groups, but it cannot contain other local groups.

Under NT 4.0 user log-ins may proceed through a pass-through mode. This allows a user at a remote location other than their home domain PDC to log in to their domain server. As long as the server at the current location trusts the users home domain PDC the user can gain access to their home system.

There are many factors involved in designing a domain model to meet each organization's requirements.

- Do I require the ability for users to access their home PDC from any location within the network?
- Do I need to provide access to local resources to users outside of the physical location (items such as drives, printers, CD-ROM etc.)?
- Do I need to provide one-way or two-way trusts among systems within the enterprise?
- Is my MIS support of these systems centralized or de-centralized?

Exhibit 1. Space Requirements for Different Types of Objects

Object	Space Used
User account	1.0K
Computer account	0.5K
Group account	4.0K (average group size = 300 members)

The design of the domain model can make or break an NT Server implementation. It is imperative that all the relevant factors be documented and factored into the design. The limiting factor for the size of a domain is the number of user accounts that can be supported by a single directory database. The maximum recommended size of the directory database file is 40 MB.

A domain consists of user accounts, computer accounts (each computer running Windows NT Workstation or Windows NT Server has a computer account), and group accounts, both built-in and those that users create. Each of these objects occupies space in the directory database file. The practical limit for the size of the directory database file depends on the type of computer processor and amount of memory available in the machine being used as the primary domain controller. Microsoft® successfully has tested directory database files in excess of 40 MB and recommends 40 MB as the upper limit. Different types of objects require different amounts of space in the directory database file, as shown in Exhibit 1.

For a single domain, Exhibit 2 displays some examples of how objects might be distributed.

There are four primary domain models:

1. Single Domain Model
2. Master Domain Model
3. Multiple Master Domain Model
4. Complete Trust Domain Model

Single Domain Model

The single domain model is suited for small organizations with few users and resources. Because there is only one domain in this model there is no trust relationships. Due to the size of this NT implementation this model will not be discussed further.

Master Domain Model

When the network does need to be split into domains for organizational purposes, but the network has a small enough number of users and groups, the master domain model might be the best choice. This model gives one

Exhibit 2. Distribution of Objects for a Single Domain

	User Accounts (1K per account)	Computer Accounts (0.5K per account)	Group Accounts (4K per account)	Total Directory Size
1 workstation per user	2000	2000	30	3.12 MB
2 workstations per user	5000	10,000	100	10.4 MB
2 users per workstation	10,000	5000	150	13.1 MB
1 workstation per user	25,000	25,000	200	38.3 MB
1 workstation per user	26,000	26,000	250	40 MB
1 workstation per user	40,000	0	0	40 MB

both centralized administration and the organizational benefits of multiple domains.

With this model, one domain — the master domain — acts as the central administrative unit for user and group accounts. All other domains on the network trust this domain, which means they recognize the users and global groups defined there. If a company has an MIS department that manages an LAN, it is logical to have the MIS department administer the master domain.

All users log on to their accounts in the master domain. Resources, such as printers and file servers, are located in the other domains. Each resource domain establishes a one-way trust with the master (account) domain, enabling users with accounts in the master domain to use resources in all the other domains. The network administrator can manage the entire multiple-domain network and its users and resources by managing only a single domain.

The benefit of the single master domain model is in its flexibility in administration. For example, in a network requiring four domains, at first it might seem most obvious to create four separate user account databases, one for each domain. However, by putting all user accounts in a single directory database on one of the domains and then implementing one-way trust relationships between these domains, one can consolidate administration of user and computer accounts. One can also administer all resources or delegate these to local administrators. And users need only one log-on name and one password to use resources in any of the domains.

This model balances requirements for account security with the need for readily available resources on the network because users are given permission to access resources based on their master domain log-on identity.

The single master domain model is particularly suited for:

- Centralized account management. User accounts can be managed centrally; add/delete/change user accounts from a single point.
- Decentralized resource management or local system administration capability. Department domains can have their own administrators who manage the resources in the department.
- Grouping resources logically, corresponding to local domains.

Multiple Master Domain Model

In the multiple master domain model, there are two or more single master domains. Like the single master domain model, the master domains serve as account domains, with every user and computer account created and maintained on one of these master domains. A company's MIS groups can manage these master domains centrally. Like the single master domain model, the other domains on the network are called resource domains; they do not store or manage user accounts but do provide resources such as shared file servers and printers to the network.

In this model, every master domain is connected to every other master domain by a two-way trust relationship. Each resource domain trusts every master domain with a one-way trust relationship. The resource domains can trust other resource domains, but are not required to do so. Because every user account exists in one of the master domains, and because each resource domain trusts every master domain, every user account can be used on any of the master domains. Exhibit 3 shows a multiple master domain model. In this example, there is one computer account for each user account; therefore, each master domain can contain as many as 26,000 user accounts.

Users log on to the domain that contains their account. Each master domain contains one PDC and at least one BDC.

The multiple master domain model incorporates all the features of a single master domain and also accommodates:

- Organizations of more than 40,000 users. The multiple master domain model is scaleable to networks with any number of users.
- Mobile users. Users can log on from anywhere in the network, anywhere in the world.
- Centralized or decentralized administration.
- Organizational needs. Domains can be configured to mirror-specific departments or internal company organizations.
- BDCs, which can be distributed between sites to facilitate LAN-WAN interactions.

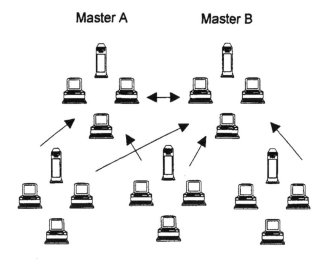

Master A   **Master B**

Exhibit 3.   Multiple master domain model.

Complete Trust Domain Model

The complete trust domain model is suited for companies with major divisions, such as large departments, that need to be split into multiple domains and do not have centralized MIS support. This model offers total decentralized administration through the domains. Exhibit 4 shows an example of a complete trust domain model.

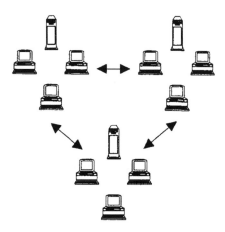

Exhibit 4.   Complete trust domain model.

The complete trust domain distributes administration of users and domains among different departments. Complete trust domains are a good choice for companies that do not require a large amount of domains, as the amount of trust relationships that must be managed becomes an issue. This model is not practical for organizations with centralized MIS departments due to the decentralization of domain administration.

In this model every domain trusts every other domain through two-way trusting relationships. This allows pass-through to occur between any of the domains.

This model requires a high degree of confidence in global groups from other trusted domains.

MANAGING DOMAINS

When one or more domains have been established, use Windows NT Server utilities to perform required domain management tasks:

- Promoting and demoting domain controllers.
- Synchronizing backup domain controllers with the primary domain controller.
- Synchronizing all domain servers.
- Adding, removing, and renaming domain computers.
- Managing domain security, including account policy, audit policy, and trust relationships (with multiple domains).

Promoting and Demoting Domain Controllers

In addition to the primary domain controller (PDC), one should have one or more backup domain controllers (BDCs) per domain.

If the PDC becomes unavailable, a BDC can be promoted to primary domain controller, and the domain continues to function. In such a scenario, the following rules take effect:

- When a BDC is promoted to a PDC, an up-to-date copy of the domain's directory database is replicated from the old PDC to the new one, and the old PDC is demoted to a BDC.
- If a BDC is promoted to PDC while the existing PDC is unavailable (e.g., while it is being repaired), and if the former PDC later returns to service, one must demote the former PDC to BDC. Until it is demoted to a BDC, it will not run the net log-on service, it will not participate in authentication of user log-ons, and its icon in the Server Manager window will be dimmed.

Note: Usually, when a BDC is promoted to a PDC, the system automatically demotes the former PDC to a BDC. However, if Server Manager cannot locate the PDC, the PDC is not demoted, and the user receives a message indicating this condition. The user can choose to proceed without demoting the PDC or wait until the PDC can be demoted.

DIRECTORY DATABASE SYNCHRONIZATION

The directory database is synchronized automatically by Windows NT Server. Based on settings in the registry, the PDC sends timed notices that signal the BDCs to request directory changes from the PDC. The notices are staggered so that all BDCs do not request changes at the same time. When the BDC requests change, it informs the PDC of the last change it received. Thus, the PDC is always aware of which BDC needs changes. If a BDC is up-to-date, the net log-on service on the BDC does not request changes.

Storage of Changes in the Change Log

Changes to the directory database consist of any new or changed passwords, new or changed user and group accounts, and any changes in their associated group memberships and user rights.

Changes to the directory database are recorded in the change log. The size of the change log determines how long changes can be held. The log holds a certain number of changes. As a new change is added, the oldest change is deleted. When a BDC requests changes, those changes that occurred since the last synchronization are copied to the BDC. Because the change log keeps only the most recent changes, if a BDC does not request changes in time, the entire directory database must be copied to that BDC. For example, if a BDC is offline for a time, more changes can occur during that time than can be stored in the change log.

Partial and Full Synchronization

The automatic, timed replication to all domain BDCs of only those directory database changes that have occurred since the last synchronization is called *partial synchronization*. One can use Server Manager to force a partial synchronization of all BDCs in the domain. For example, if a new user is added to the domain and is in great need of certain resources, one can perform a partial synchronization to get the new user's account added to all BDCs as soon as possible.

If needed, one can use Server Manager to force manually a partial synchronization of a particular BDC with the PDC. For example, if access is denied because of a problem with the BDC computer account password (as evidenced by "access denied" messages in the event log), a partial synchronization of the BDC with the PDC fixes the password problem and re-establishes a secure channel.

Sending a copy of the entire directory database to a BDC is called *full synchronization*. Full synchronization is performed automatically when

18-9

changes have been deleted from the change log before replication takes place (as described in the preceding example) and when a new BDC is added to a domain.

The default Net Log-on Service settings for the timing of updates (every 5 minutes) and the size of the change log (holds about 2000 changes) ensure that full synchronization will not be required under most operating conditions.

Note: Full synchronization over a slow WAN link is time-consuming and expensive. To avoid the occurrence of an unplanned full synchronization, increase the size of the change log.

Synchronizing Domain Controllers

In Server Manager, the *Computer* menu command for synchronizing changes, depending on the type of computer that is selected:

- When the primary domain controller is selected, the *Synchronize Entire Domain* command is available on the *Computer* menu. This command copies the latest directory database changes from the PDC to all the BDCs in the domain. *Synchronize Entire Domain* initiates synchronization of all BDCs without waiting for completion of the synchronization in progress.
- When a backup domain controller is selected, the *Synchronize With Primary Domain Controller* command is available on the *Computer* menu. This command copies the latest directory database changes to the selected BDC only.

ADDING, RENAMING, MOVING, AND REMOVING DOMAIN COMPUTERS

Installing Windows NT Server and designating the computer as a domain controller creates a domain. Other computers then can be added to the domain.

Before a computer running Windows NT Workstation or Windows NT Server can be a domain member and participate in domain security, it must be added to the domain. When a computer is added to a domain, Windows NT Server creates an account for the computer. If the added computer is a backup domain controller, it requests a copy of the domain directory database.

When removing a computer running Windows NT Workstation or a computer running Windows NT Server from a domain, the computer's account is removed. To add a computer to another domain, a new computer account must be created and then the computer can join that domain.

Note: To remove a backup domain controller from a domain, one must delete the computer account and reinstall Windows NT Server on that computer, indicating the new domain.

ADDING A DOMAIN WORKSTATION OR SERVER COMPUTER

To add a computer to a domain, one must be logged on to a user account that has the appropriate user rights.

With the appropriate rights, users can add workstations and servers to domains during or after installation:

- Once a domain is created, a member of administrators or account operators local groups can add a backup domain controller to the domain. Primary and backup domain controllers can be added only during installation.

Note: A primary domain controller cannot be added to an existing domain.

- During installation of Windows NT Server, a member of the administrators or account operators group or a user who has the "Add workstation to domain" right can add a computer running Windows NT Server to a domain as a member server.
- During installation of Windows NT Workstation, a member of the administrators or account operators group or a user who has the "Add workstation to domain" right can add a computer running Windows NT Workstation to a domain.
- After installation, a member of the administrators or account operators group or a user who has the "Add workstation to domain" right can add an existing computer running Windows NT Workstation or a member server to a domain using the network option in control panel on the computer being added.
- After installation, a member of the administrators or account operators group, or a user that has the "Add workstation to domain" right can use the *Add To Domain* command in Server Manager to add a computer account to the domain's security database. Then a user at the computer allows the computer to join the domain by typing the domain name in the network option in control panel on the computer being added.

Note: Take care to protect the security of an added computer name. Until the intended computer joins the domain, it is possible for a user to give a different computer that computer name, and then have it join the domain using the computer account just created. If the added computer is a backup domain controller, when it joins it receives a copy of the domain's security database.)

HOW DOES DOMAIN DESIGN CHANGE UNDER NT 5.0

NT 4.0 is designed for small to medium-size networks. The management of the trusts is the first problem. To provide a central server in a domain to manager user log-ons requires a PDC. Domains provide authentication, but must be in constant contact with the PDC. PDCs will disappear in NT 5.0.

Domains are a convenient way to design small networks, but when networks become large organizations must have multiple domains. To provide central log-ons and access to device in other domains one must create trust relationships. For domain A to use domain B devices, domain B must trust domain A. The problem is that this does not mean that domain B can use domain A's devices. To do this, domain A must trust domain B. With large amounts of domains this creates obvious problems. For example if a company has 15 domains and wants to have each domain trust each other, 210 separate trust relationships (15×14) must be created and managed.

The second problem is with the way NT manages users details. The SAM (security accounts manager) manages user, password, and what security groups one has access to. Unfortunately it does not extend itself to manage things such as mail routing, etc.

Microsoft's answer is to create a directory service based on X.500 standards. Active Directory is an extensive database of just about anything attached to a user. The new Active Directory will support managing items such as country, name, department information, etc. This is so the directory structure can be used as a world wide directory structure, managing all users in an enterprise.

Currently to create a share one must define the server name and source (\\server a\data). Under NT 5.0 one can define a share based on the domain name, so if one changes a server name all users of the share do not need to be notified to change the share definition.

CONCLUSION

It is imperative that the time is taken to properly design an NT domain structure. The domain design has so many impacts on a business and IT environments. Use a qualified NT expert when designing a domain structure. Also, keep in mind the changes coming in NT 5.0 when designing a domain. Users will want to move to NT 5.0 once all the bugs are removed. Wait for Service Pack Level 2 at a minimum before making the move to NT 5.0.

Portions of domain design details — © Microsoft Corporation.

Chapter 19
DBMS Recovery Procedures

Frederick Gallegos and Daniel Manson

INTRODUCTION

MANY ORGANIZATIONS, SUCH AS BANKS AND AIRLINES, HAVE ONLINE COMPUTER SYSTEMS that must function at all times. In most online applications, there are many application programs that access data bases concurrently. Therefore, the data bases must be correct and up to date at all times.

Yet technology is imperfect and computer systems and their supporting communications infrastructures are subject to many types of failure. When a system fails, recovery procedures must be in place to restore, validate, and return the system to normal.

Information is an essential tool used by all levels of management in planning and organizing, directing, and controlling an organization. Therefore, the security, availability, and integrity of information are of utmost importance. Technological advances have significantly influenced the way an organization's information is collected, processed, and distributed. Data base management systems (DBMSs) have evolved from some of these technological advances and are of primary concern to auditors and IS managers who are responsible for securing an organization's data while facilitating the efficient dissemination of information. Although DBMSs can organize, process, and generate information designed to meet user needs, the integrity and security of this information are also essential to protect users.

THE IMPORTANCE OF DBMS RECOVERY

Recovery — that is, the return to a fully operational environment after a hardware or software failure — is an important process in today's business world. Moreover, the effects of a system failure on the organization must be curtailed to minimize any substantial financial loss. Actions must be taken to prevent DBMS failures or resolve them quickly if they occur.

0-8493-9976-9/99/$0.00+$.50
© 1999 by CRC Press LLC

It is not always cost effective to implement all possible DBMS controls and use all known review techniques. The choice of whether or not to audit can have a direct impact on the financial consequences caused by these failures. A review of DBMS recovery ensures adherence to appropriate practices and procedures and minimizes business losses. A review further ensures that an organization can recover and return to full operational status following a disaster. For example, the February/March 1997 flooding in the Cincinnati area and the January 1994 earthquake in Los Angeles caused sustained interruption of business in many organizations; those organizations that had established recovery procedures were able to more readily restore operations and minimize losses.

Developing, implementing, maintaining, and auditing the DBMS recover controls and processes involve a considerable amount of money and company resources. Costs and benefits must be considered to ensure that company resources are expended efficiently. Systems managers who are either developing or maintaining a DBMS must understand data base structures and participate in the recovery process. This article explains the process and techniques for reviewing DBMS recovery.

THE RECOVERY PROCESS

The DBMS recovery process is designed to restore data base operations to their prefailure status. Users and IS professionals play a critical role in restoring the DBMS to operation; that is, after the system has been successfully restored, the entire staff must participate to ensure the security, integrity, and validity of the information and its transaction properties.

Transaction Properties

The transaction is the fundamental activity of a DBMS and an area of concern for the reviewer. Transactions maintain consistency constraints or controls determined for an application. This consistency must be maintained at all times, even during a transaction failure. Concurrent processing must also be protected against adverse effects during a transaction failure.

A transaction is a command, message stream, or input display that explicitly or implicitly calls for a processing action (e.g., updating a file). Transaction processing is a sequential process that does not overlap or parallel a single application. It is started with a BEGIN TRANSACTION and ended with an END TRANSACTION identifier. The following typical transaction properties must be reviewed in assessing recovery controls:

- *Atomicity.* During a transaction, either all or none of its operations are performed on the data base; that is, atomicity ensures the preclusion of partially completed transactions.

- *Permanence.* If a transaction completes the END TRANSACTION function, the results of its operation will never subsequently be lost.
- *Serialization of transactions.* If more than one transaction is executed concurrently, the transactions affect the data base as if they were executed in serial order; this ensures that concurrently executing jobs do not use inconsistent data from partially completed transactions.
- *Prevention of cascading aborts.* An incomplete transaction cannot reveal results to other transactions, thereby limiting the effect of a transaction error throughout the entire system.
- *Consistency.* A transaction that reaches its usual end commits its results to memory, thereby preserving the consistency of the data base contents.

Transactions are more effective when written in Sybase, Oracle, Access, Visual Basic, or SQL than in COBOL, FORTRAN, or BASIC. They are well suited to structured programming and can help make systems development a routine process by modularizing the actions being performed in code and simplifying the treatment of failures and concurrency. These transaction properties have specific control functions (that, from a review standpoint, should be organized and verified for DBMS operational validity and reliability).

Causes of DBMS Failure

There are many causes of DBMS failure. When a DBMS fails, it falls into an incorrect state and will likely contain erroneous data. Typical causes of DBMS failures include errors in the application program, an error by the terminal user, an operator error, loss of data validity and consistency, a hardware error, media failures, network transmission error, an error introduced by the environment, and errors caused by mischief or catastrophe.

Typically, the four major types of failure that result from a major hardware or software malfunction are: transaction, system, communications, and media. These failures may be caused by a natural disaster, computer crime, or user, designer, developer, or operator error. Each type of failure is described in the following paragraphs.

Transaction Failure. Transaction failures occur when the transaction is not processed and the processing steps are rolled back to a specific point in the processing cycle. In a distributed data base environment, a single logical data base may be spread across several physical data bases. Transaction failure can occur when some, but not all, physical data bases are updated at the same time.

System Failure. System failure can be caused by bugs in the data base, operating system, or hardware. In each case, the transaction processing is terminated without control of the application. Data in the memory is lost; however, disk storage remains stable. The system must recover in the amount of time it takes to complete all interrupted transactions. At one transaction per second, the system should recover in a few seconds. System failures may occur as often as several times a week.

Communications Failure. With transactional systems now linked globally, the importance of the successful transfer of information to the DBMS is critical in maintaining the currency, reliability, and relevance of financial information. A formidable example is the World Stock Exchanges and their monitoring of the business trading activity worldwide. Transactional activities not recorded or "lost" could mean substantial losses to investors. The ability to recover is critical in this environment.

Media Failure. Disk crashes or controller failures can occur because of disk-write bugs in the operating system release, hardware errors in the channel or controller, head crashes, or media degradation. These failures are rare but costly.

By identifying the type of DBMS failure, an organization can define the state of activity to return to after recovery. To design the data base recovery procedures, the potential failures must be identified and the reliability of the hardware and software must be determined. The following is a summary of four such recovery actions:

- *Transaction undo.* A transaction that aborts itself or must be aborted by the system during routine execution.
- *Global redo.* When recovering from a system failure, the effects of all incomplete transactions must be rolled back. This means the ability of the system to contact all linked DBMSs to retransmit "missing, incomplete, or lost" information across communication networks.
- *Partial undo.* While a system is recovering from failure, the results of completed transactions may not yet be reflected in the data base because execution has been terminated in an uncontrolled manner. Therefore, they must be repeated, if necessary, by the recovery component.
- *Global undo.* If the data base is totally destroyed, a copy of the entire data base must be reloaded from a backup source. A supplemental copy of the transaction is necessary to roll up the state of the data base to the present. This means the ability of the system to contact all linked DBMSs (i.e., client/server) to retransmit "missing, incomplete, or lost" information accross communication networks.

These definitions imply that the transaction is the sole unit of recovery in the data base, which reduces the programmer's required recovery processing inclusions.

Disaster Recovery Tools

There are numerous disaster recovery tools and techniques available that can assist an organization in DBMS recovery. For example, several software programs can scan the network and data bases and record the configuration of the systems. Novell's Netware Management System provides a logical view of the system and network. Other products such as Failover Software by SafePath, LT Auditor, LAN automatic Inventory, Palindrome, IT Service Vision from SAS Institute, and LAN Directory are software support packages that can assist in DBMS documentation and recovery processes and functions.

Several companies use video camera techniques to document equipment, hardware, and software configurations. Others are using CD-ROMs as a technique for saving critical DBMS structures and data. Such applications of media or computer-assisted disaster recovery tools and techniques are providing organizations detailed documentation to aid troubleshooting DBMS problems, identifying weak points in the network or distributed DBMS, and reconstructing destroyed DBMSs.

TECHNIQUES FOR REVIEWING DBMS RECOVERY

The review of a DBMS recovery must ensure that employees with specific responsibilities perform their functions in accordance with operational policy and procedure. There are several useful DBMS recovery review techniques.

There are two ways to make the system operate again. First, all transactions that have occurred since the last backup can be reapplied, which would bring the data base up to date. Second, the current contents of the data base can be taken and all transactions can be backed out until the integrity and validity of the data are restored. Whichever method is selected, it should be documented and a checklist of specific tasks and responsibilities identified.

The DBMS typically provides exhaustive review trails so that the system can know its exact state at any time. These review trails should be complete enough to reconstruct transactions and aid in recovery procedures. A data base administrator should know how to use these review trails in recovery to fully understand the inner workings of the DBMS.

A data base that has been backed up regularly helps the system recover from a failure and begin operating again as soon as possible. Daily backups are sufficient in most organizations. Those organizations that must always have current data must sometimes perform hourly backups. Each backup should be well documented to provide further insight into the review process. This is especially true in data warehousing applications, where the need for a data repository road map is critical. This road map allows anyone who uses the warehouse to track where information originated.

Application Design

It is important to build sound recovery procedures and processes into an application during the design phase. The design of an application should take into consideration the data base control issues that affect backup and recovery processes. These techniques apply to development of data warehousing, data mining, and data mart applications. Possible weaknesses in controls include:

- An inadequate audit trail
- An inadequate service level
- Failure of the DBMS to function as specified
- Inadequate documentation
- Lack of processing continuity
- Lack of management support
- Fraud or embezzlement

The data base administrator should be responsible for examining the backup and recovery controls being considered by the user and developer when reviewing application design. The user and the developer of the application must assess the risks of not having appropriate controls in place to aid in recovery. Some key controls that should be adopted are:

- *Review trails.* A method of chronologically recording system activities that allows the reconstruction, review, and examination of each event in a transaction from inception to the final results.
- *Recovery procedures.* Automated or manual tools and techniques for recovering the integrity of a data base.
- *Application system failure procedures.* Procedures for users to follow in the event that their applications cannot operate.
- *Checkpoint data bases.* Copies of the data base and transaction files that are made at specific points in time for recovery purposes.

At a minimum, these controls should be tested during the module and integration testing phases of development. In terms of a new system review before implementation, these controls are most effective if thoroughly validated and approved by the user and developer before the system is placed into operation. One important issue to be considered in application design is data integrity.

Maintaining Data Integrity. Data integrity concerns the accuracy of the contents of the data base. The integrity of the data can be compromised because of failures (i.e., events at which the system fails to provide normal operation or correct data). Failures are caused primarily by errors, which may originate in programs, interactions between these programs, or the system. With data warehousing, constant oversight by business unit managers as well as DBMS experts is required to maintain the credibility of the data warehouse.

A transaction is a sequence of actions. It should be designed and executed so that it either is successfully completed or has no effect on the data base. A transaction can fail to be completed for the following reasons:

- An action violates a security or integrity constraint.
- The user cancels the transaction.
- An unrecoverable I/O error occurs.
- The system backs out the transaction to resolve a deadlock.
- The application program fails.
- The system crashes.

Semantic Integrity. This refers to the accuracy of the data base despite the fact that users or applications programs try to modify it incorrectly. Assuming that the data base security system prevents unauthorized access, and hence malicious attempts to corrupt data, most potential errors will be caused by incorrect input, incorrect programs, or lack of user understanding.

Traditionally, most integrity checking has been performed by the applications programs and by periodic auditing of the data base. This is essential in data warehousing applications where data-cleansing tools (such as Integrity Toolset by Validity Technology, Inc.) are highly relied on. The following are some problems that occur when relying on application programs for integrity checking:

- Checking is likely to be incomplete because the applications programmer may not be aware of the semantics of the complete data base.
- Each application program relies on other programs that can modify the data base, and a problem in one program could corrupt the whole data base.
- Code that enforces the same integrity constraints occurs in several programs. This leads to unnecessary duplication of the programming effort and exposes the system to potential inconsistencies.
- The criteria for integrity are buried within procedures and are therefore difficult to understand and control.
- Maintenance operations performed by users of high-level query languages cannot be controlled.

Most of these errors could be detected through auditing, although the time lag in detecting errors by auditing can cause problems, such as difficulty in tracing the source of an error and hence correcting it, as well as incorrect data used in various ways, causing errors to propagate through the data base and into the environment. Typically, the most serious errors are spotted by the users, and not the DBMS specialist. Data warehouse and

DBMS builders are very good at identifying technical problems such as erroneous data fields.

The semantics, or meaning, of a data base is partly drawn from a shared understanding among the users, partly implied by the data structures used, and partly expressed as integrity constraints. These constraints are explicitly stated by the individuals responsible for data control. Data bases can also be classified as:

- A single record or set
- Static or transitional
- General or selective
- Immediate or deferred
- Unconditional or conditional

A system of concurrent transactions must be correctly synchronized — that is, the processing of these transactions must reach the same final state and produce the same output. Three forms of inconsistency result from concurrence: lost updates, an incorrect read, and an unrepeatable read. Lost updates can also result from backing up or undoing a transaction.

Correcting Inconsistency Problems. The most commonly used approach to eliminate consistency problems is locking. The DBMS can use the locking facilities that the operating system provides so that multiple processes can synchronize their concurrent access of shared resources. A lock can be granted to multiple processes, but a given object cannot be locked in shared and exclusive mode at the same time. Shared and exclusive modes conflict because they are incompatible. The operating system usually provides lock and unlock commands for requesting and releasing locks. If a lock request cannot be granted, the process is suspended until the request can be granted. If transactions do not follow restrictive locking rules, deadlock can occur. Deadlock can cause the loss of an entire file; therefore, it is critical to have a recovery system in place to alleviate this problem.

The deadlock problem can be solved either by preventing deadlocks, or by detecting them after they occur and taking steps to resolve them. Deadlocks can be prevented by placing restrictions on the way locks are requested. They can be detected by examining the status of locks. After they are detected, the deadlock can be resolved by aborting a transaction and rescheduling it. Methods for selecting the best transaction to abort have also been developed.

A synchronization problem can occur in a distributed data base environment, such as a client/server network. Data bases can become out of sync when data from one data base fails to be updated on other data bases. When updates fail to occur, users at some locations may use data that is not current with data at other locations. Distributed data bases provide different types of updating mechanisms. In a two-phase commit update process, network nodes must be online and receive data simultaneously before updates can occur. A newer update method called *data replication* enables updates to be stored until nodes are online and ready to receive. Update methods must ensure currency in all network data bases.

Security Procedures

A data base usually contains information that is vital to an organization's survival. A secure data base environment, with physical and logical security controls, is essential during recovery procedures.

Physical Security. In some distributed environments, many physical security controls, such as the use of security badges and cipher locks, are not feasible and the organization must rely more heavily on logical security measures. In these cases, many organizational members may have data processing needs that do not involve a data base but require the use of computer peripherals.

Logical Security. Logical security prevents unauthorized users from invoking DBMS functions. The primary means of implementing this type of security is the use of passwords to prevent access to files, records, data elements, and DBMS utilities. Passwords should be checked to ensure that they are designated in an intelligent, logical manner.

Security Logs. Each time an unauthorized user attempts to access the data base, it should be recorded in a security log. Entries in this log should consist of user ID, terminal or port number, time, date, and type of infraction. With this information, it is possible to investigate any serious breaches of security. From the data base administrator's standpoint, evidence that the DBMS is detecting security violations and that a consistent procedure is used to follow them up should be sufficient.

DBMS file mirroring is perhaps the most popular way of backing up critical files. Some products in today's marketplace allow primary production sites to be multilevel mirrored to ensure rapid recovery of critical files in order to keep the business running with minimal service interruption. Other techniques are data libraries designed for enterprisewide backup, high-capacity storage, and data archiving applications

Personnel Control

Data base recovery involves ensuring that only authorized users are allowed access and that no subsequent misuse of information occurs. These controls are usually re-established when a system becomes operational. When operations cease or problems occur, however, controls often become inoperative.

The three primary classes of data base users are data base administrator, applications and systems programmers, and end users — and each has a unique view of the data. The DBMS must be flexible enough to present data appropriately to each class of user and maintain the proper controls to inhibit abuse of the system, especially during recovery, when controls may not be fully operational.

Data Base Administrator. The data base administrator is responsible for ensuring that the data base retains its integrity and is accountable if the data base becomes compromised, no matter what circumstances arise. This individual has ultimate power over the schema that the organization has implemented. Any modifications or additions to this schema must be approved by the data base administrator. Permission to use subschemas (i.e., logical views) is given to end users and programmers only after their intentions are fully known and are consistent with organizational goals.

Because the data base administrator has immediate and unrestricted access to almost every piece of valuable organizational information, an incompetent employee in this position can expose the organization to enormous risk, especially during DBMS recovery. Therefore, an organization should have controls in place to ensure the appointment of a qualified data base administrator.

The data base administrator must ensure that appropriate procedures are followed during DBMS recovery. The data base administrator should also validate and verify the system once it has been recovered before allowing user access so that if controls are not functioning or accessing problem continue, users will not be affected.

Applications and Systems Programmers. After recovery, programmers must access the data base to manipulate and report on data according to some predetermined specification or to access whether data loss has occurred. Each application should have a unique subschema with which to work. After recovery, the data base administrator validates the subschema organization to ensure that it is operating properly and allowing the application to receive only the data necessary to perform its tasks.

Systems programmers must be controlled in a slightly different manner than applications programmers. They must have the freedom to perform their tasks but be constrained from altering production programs or system utility programs in a fraudulent manner.

End Users. End users are defined as all organizational members not included in the previous categories who need to interact with the data base through DBMS utilities or application programs. Data elements of the data base generally originate from end users. As mentioned earlier in a data warehousing application, they are often the ones who recognize data inaccuracies, inconsistencies, and duplication.

Each data element should be assigned to an end user. The end user is then responsible for defining the element's access and security rules. Every other user who wishes to use this data element must confer with the responsible end user. If access is granted, the data base administrator must implement any restrictions placed on the request through the DBMS.

For example, Web site diagnostic tools are available that can detect and report errors and discrepancies such as broken links of an intranet/Internet Web site, missing images, suspect pages, and suspect graphics. Such software even allows a user to access the files containing errors and fix/correct problems with information.

Assigning ownership of specific data elements to end users discourages the corruption of data elements, thereby enhancing data base integrity. Reviewers should ensure that this process exists and is appropriately reinstituted after the recovery process has been completed and operational approval has been provided by the data base administrator.

After recovery, the data base administrator should ensure that all forms of security practices and procedures are reinstated. These processes are a part of data base security.

With data warehousing applications, summary tables are the most powerful performance improvement technique. Summary tables are typically the most frequently used data assembled into tables. Recovery and rebuilding the summary tables are crucial. Data quality must be preserved by running the source data through cleansing tools continuously to ensure accuracy of the warehouse. Personnel responsible for entry and maintenance should be provided with incentives to ensure quality.

CONCLUSION

Review of DBMS recovery is crucial to ensuring the integrity of a corporate information system. To adequately assess this complex issue, a review plan should be developed and procedures should be established for conducting the review. The procedures may involve the use of checklists or automated tools and techniques. The sample review plan and review procedures in Appendix A and the backup and recovery facilities checklist in Appendix B are designed to give guidance in developing these key documents and tailoring them to the organization.

Appendix A

SAMPLE REVIEW PLAN

- Conduct data base survey:
  - Conduct background survey to determine organizational priorities for data bases.
  - Identify data base recovery procedure evidence.
  - Develop a data flow diagram of data base applications scoring high on the organizational priorities. For example, summary tables created by a data warehouse will identify the most frequently used data that can be correlated to organizational priorities.
  - If a data warehouse application, develop a data respository road map to identify origination of information.
  - Identify data base recovery tools and techniques.
  - If a data warehouse application, identify the data cleansing tool set used.
- Identify data base risks:
  - Conduct specific data base risk assessment.
  - Rank data base risks.
  - Develop measurable review objectives for recovery procedures.
  - Develop a review plan.
- Evaluate data base recovery controls:
  - Document data base segregation of authority.
  - Conduct a data base control review.
  - Develop data base control diagrams.
  - Identify and define data base recovery procedure vulnerabilities.
- Perform data base recovery procedure control tests:
  - Create a data base recovery control test plan.
  - Design a data base control test.
  - Conduct the data base recovery control test.
  - Evaluate data base recovery control effectiveness.
  - Evaluate the data base recovery tools and techniques.
- Analyze data base recovery procedure review results:
  - Document findings.
  - Analyze findings.
  - Develop recommendations.
  - Document recommendations.
- Review and report findings:
  - Create a review report.

- Review report reasonableness (i.e., logic).
- Prepare and disseminate report.

REVIEW PROCEDURES

- Equipment configuration:
  - List all the equipment under direct control of the data base.
  - Note any special environmental requirements.
  - Determine the effective throughput.
  - Determine the transaction volume.
  - Estimate the extent of reliance on the data base.
  - Estimate the extent of reliance on data base tools.
  - Estimate the extent of reliance on data cleansing tools.
- Systems maintenance:
  - List and evaluate all data base applications.
  - List and evaluate all data base utilities and support hardware and software used for monitoring and recovery of data bases.
  - List and evaluate all data base documentation, especially data repository road maps, to track orgination of information.
  - Note any backup procedures.
  - Note authority matrices or other authorization procedures.
- System operations:
  - Determine who is responsible for operations.
  - Evaluate effectiveness of existing recovery procedure documentation.
  - Evaluate backup procedures, including backup personnel training, backup schedule, and off-site or distributed storage of backup files.
  - Observe and comment on the level of physical security.
  - Observe and comment on the levels of physical security for hardware and data.
  - Determine whether the automated system bypasses any existing separation of duties.

Appendix B

BACKUP AND FACILITIES CHECKLIST

1. Last date of backup testing and frequency of tests conducted?
2. Does each site maintain backup data in the same format?
3. Are the retention periods for backup data sufficient to ensure the consistency of the data, especially when multilevel mirroring is used?
4. Are there procedures to shut down the fully distributed data base system?
5. Are there procedures to restart and recover one or all stations in the system?
6. Are there procedures to test the restart and recovery procedures?
7. Are all errors discovered by the data base management system (DBMS) logged for follow-up?
8. Are failures in the DBMS documented for supervisory review?
9. Are backup procedures for data base recovery periodically tested at a primary facility? At a backup data center?
10. Are copies of critical files stored at a remote location restricted from unauthorized access?
11. Are duplicate copies of critical documentation kept at a remote location and restricted from unauthorized access?
12. Is at least one file generation kept at a location other than the file storage area?
13. Are there provisions for periodic checkpoints of files (master data base and transactions) to ensure a basis for reconstruction of a damaged or destroyed file?
14. Does management periodically review such instances on which recovery was necessary?
15. Does management follow up preventive or corrective actions taken for data base recovery?

Chapter 20
Change Management Strategies for Data Administration

Michael K. Miller

As companies downsize, rightsize, and become leaner in order to be more competitive, stronger focus must be placed on all staff organizations to determine if they add value. Amid organizational change, a window of opportunity also exists to establish data resource management (DRM) principles within the entire organization. Companies guided by a strong DRM function in establishing an infrastructure to support client/server business systems have the flexibility to respond to rapidly changing business conditions and use all their information resources in the struggle for profitability.

PREPARING THE FOUNDATION FOR RESPONDING TO CHANGE

The data management function may need to answer questions about the value of expending resources on managing the information resource. Many strong forces exert pressure on any organization — technological change, societal change, competition, economic realities, layoffs associated with downsizing and rightsizing, and changing and conflicting management priorities. In combination, these forces create an atmosphere of upheaval. The first thing to determine is which forces are effecting change. Then DRM can determine how it can assist in achieving the change, while at the same time realizing the goals of information sharing.

Depth of Commitment

It is important to plumb the depths of commitment to the data management function and the degree to which the information management mindset has pervaded the corporate psyche. Information about how past DRM initiatives have fared and the degree of difficulty associated with obtaining resources and funding will assist in charting a strategy for increasing and

0-8493-9976-9/99/$0.00+$.50
© 1999 by CRC Press LLC

maintaining the commitment. It is sometimes necessary to reiterate the basic justification for the data management function every time there is a management change.

During downsizing efforts, all business departments are examined to see if they add value. Savvy professionals have an ear to the ground and maintain the right connections to the financial organization in order to recognize potential threats. If an organization, such as DRM, is not prepared to meet the forces of change, it can quickly be swept away with the rising tide of corporate downsizing in order to save money.

Rate of Change

The speed and proportion of changes dictate the urgency of the response. Therefore, the long- or short-term nature of planned changes should be studied. If the organization is strapped financially, it will probably require much more financial justification to get the DRM effort funded. The ability to demonstrate a past record of successes becomes critical for continued existence.

Objectives Setting

Sailors use fixed points from which to chart their course. Data management professionals must also be able to refer to clear landmarks, such as management directives, policies, charters, industry authorities, and common sense.

The guiding light should be the long-term vision of an information utility that allows anyone to have access to the right information at the right time. With this information, DRM sets goals and objectives that are in harmony with the business but that also align with the long-term objectives of information sharing.

Human Nature and the Fear of Change

One of the most intractable problems when trying to change an organization, a direction, or a policy is basic human resistance to change. Many people have difficulty recognizing the value in changing from a comfortable situation to an unsure one. Politics is also ever-present during any human endeavor and must be addressed.

People are often fearful to take steps that are outside the mainstream and thus are afraid to lead. Human nature is an obstacle that must be reckoned with when devising any strategy or program for change.

A conscious effort must be made to understand the pressures that create fear and anxiety among employees during times of change. Usually, people are afraid of losing their livelihood and this reaction creates a defensive mentality that can be counterproductive. People's concerns need to be addressed honestly and forthrightly with the best information available in order to end false rumors. Employees should also be engaged in planning for changes and encouraged to continue with productive activities so they retain a sense of value to the corporation.

Sure Ways to Fail

Lack of Mission or Direction

When there is a lack of direction within an organization, a condition of drift sets in. This leads to busywork and a lack of value being produced. During times of crisis, there is no question as to what department should be eliminated.

No Perceived Value

When business people are looking for ways to trim the budget, they look first at those organizations and people who are not adding value. Even in a case where a data management group is adding value, the group may not have made its contribution apparent to business management. Management's perception is just as important as reality.

Going on the Defensive

When people feel threatened by change, there is a natural defense mechanism that produces a reaction of "circling the wagons" against attackers. This creates hostility and, more importantly, a lack of productivity.

Territorial Issues

Turf wars and a parochial attitude are destructive during times of change. These destructive behaviors divert people's attention away from achieving goals that are valuable to the organization; instead, people focus on nonproductive activities designed to protect their territory.

Inability to Change

When faced with a choice between a status quo situation and total uncertainty, it is only natural that most people will choose the status quo. When, however, the fear of change becomes crippling to the point that the organization cannot move forward, the resultant stagnation and subtle resistance can hamper a successful transition.

Being Self-Centered Instead of Customer-Centric

When humans become fearful, they tend to think about self-preservation and can easily defeat their own best interest. When change is imminent, it is critical to focus on adding value and benefit to the corporation. If the DRM group is crippled by inaction brought on by fear and self-preservation, it will be easy for upper management to trim the group as an unnecessary expense.

Ignoring Human and Culture Issues

Those involved in planning for change must not fail to put human and culture issues at the forefront of consideration. When planning for any kind of technological or organizational change, definite measures must be taken to address the natural human reactions. Plentiful communication, education, and employee participation must be built into the structure of the plan for change.

Failure to Respond to Emerging Technology

In a society where new technology emerges nearly every day, the DRM professional must be responsive. This is another opportunity to ride the wave of change and institutionalize sound information management principles. Business users of information expect to have their information stored in multimedia formats with quick access. DRM must respond with multimedia-capable data bases of information that are Web enabled. Because business users find the World Wide Web easy to access, this becomes an avenue to entrench the data management function as the group that supplies the quality data — when and where it is needed.

Determining the DRM Function's Value

A very important way to counteract the forces of change is to know the value of your function. Throughout the life of the DRM function, ample attention should be paid to the value that the organization adds toward achievement of business objectives. Thus, it is important to establish ways of determining and measuring that added value.

Data management professionals should make every effort to quantify the value of their efforts and document this value. Then, when the latest management fad strikes, DRM will have a solid backlog of documented savings and bottom-line effects to demonstrate to management.

Metrics

Establishing solid metrics for DRM is an elusive goal. Many of the benefits of managing information are intangible and consequently difficult to measure and defend. The effort should be made, however, and the effort should consider the full life cycle of data — not only logical modeling, but also the monetary effects of storing redundant, conflicting data. Cost savings that DRM can contribute, and the relative difficulty in quantifying them, are outlined in Exhibit 1.

IRM Impact	Type of Value Gained	Difficulty to Quantify
Less analyst time in requirements gathering	Cost avoidance	Moderate
Less business analysis time in gathering decision support information from disparate data sources	Cost avoidance	Moderate
Fewer redundant data bases constructed and maintained	Cost reduction	Easy
Fewer human resources needed for accounting and financial analysis	Cost reduction	Easy
More accurate information about customers	Revenue generation	Difficult
Web-enabled access to standard data	Revenue generation	Moderate

Exhibit 1. Ways of quantifying cost savings.

Cost Avoidance

One of the areas that can be quantified is in the area of avoiding costs. Through construction of common data bases within a client/server infrastructure, it is possible to avoid the expense of building redundant data bases. Development costs can be easily quantified based on a company's rich experience; plans to build these data bases can be identified through examination of long-range systems plans.

An example of cost avoidance through reuse of existing standard data definitions is presented in Exhibit 2. When a company wants a new system or data base, analysis time is required of both IT and business people. For an average requirements-gathering workshop, there could be two analysts and seven business people. Empirical evidence within the IT organization should enable DRM analysts to make an approximation of the number of person-hours it takes to define one data entity together with its associated attributes. A conservative figure of 2 hours may, for example, be used for defining business entities. As a repository of existing data definitions grows and is used on successive projects, a greater proportion of the analysis work is already completed when the project starts; therefore, analysis time can be avoided.

Workshop Participant	Person-hours	Comments
Business analyst team	13.0	Includes analyst time before, during, and after the analysis workshop
Data administrator (DA)	3.0	Included DA documentation, consulting, and analysis time
Business expert	7.0	Includes 7 business experts working for one hour in an analysis workshop
Total analysis hours	23.0	
Loaded cost per hour	70.00	Conservative estimate considering all the costs pertaining to a profession
Total cost per entity	1610.00	

Exhibit 2. Cost avoidance through reuse of existing standard data definitions.

True Cost Savings

Another savings classification is actual bottom-line savings that affect the profit-loss statement. Through implementation of common systems with common data bases, it is possible to reduce personnel headcount substantially. Through effective data management, measures of physical data, redundancy, and inaccuracy can be reduced. This results in reduced cycle time, reduced headcount, and greater employee satisfaction.

The spreadsheet shown in Exhibit 3 uses actual cost savings of redundant data base elimination, reduced IS headcount, and reduced staff analysis time for management reporting. It also figures a conservative 1% increase in sales revenue as the result of having integrated, quality customer information.

Defining "Real" Business Contribution

What would be the result if there were no data management organization? How does data management help achieve business objectives? When data management professionals begin to think about their role in hard-dollar terms, it provides a fresh perspective.

Data management professionals can tend to pursue academic questions and theories if they are not tightly focused on helping business achieve solid results. There are many different projects that require attention, but in

Customer Information Environment Actual Cash Flow
USD 000
12-Feb-96

	1996	1997	1998	1999	2000	2001	2002	TOTAL
Capital								
Hardware	(1,800)	(100)	(50)					(1,950)
Software Basic	(70)	(30)	(30)					(130)
TOTAL Capital	(1,870)	(130)	(80)	0	0	0	0	(2,080)
Nonrecurring Expense								
Extracts and Interfaces	(459)	(459)	(75)	(55)	(30)	(30)	(30)	(1,138)
Implementation	(40)	(40)	(40)	0	0	0	0	(120)
Training and Travel	(10)	(10)	(10)	0	0	0	0	(30)
Miscellaneous								0
TOTAL Nonrecurring	(509)	(509)	(125)	(55)	(30)	(30)	(30)	(1,288)
Recurring Expense								
Third-Party Source of Data	(1,075)	(1,075)	(1,075)	(1,075)	(1,075)	(1,075)	(1,075)	(7,525)
IS Administration Headcount	(500)	(500)	(500)	(250)	(250)	(250)	(250)	(2,500)
S/W Maintenance (15% of Software)	0	0	0	0	0	0	0	0
TOTAL Recurring	(1,575)	(1,575)	(1,575)	(1,325)	(1,325)	(1,325)	(1,325)	(10,025)
Incremental Savings								
Redundant Data Base Development	200	600	900	1,200	1,500	1,800	2,100	8,300
Management Reporting-Staff Analysis	2,000	2,000	2,000	2,000	2,000	2,000	2,000	14,000
Manual I/f user/ISS headcount	0	153	1,025	2,100	2,100	2,100	2,100	9,578
Increased Revenues (1% Sales)	10,000	35,000	70,000	70,000	70,000	70,000	70,000	395,000
TOTAL Savings	12,200	37,753	73,925	75,300	75,600	75,900	76,200	426,878
Depreciation								
Hardware	0	(487)	(487)	(487)	(487)	0	0	(1,948)
Software Basic	0	(25)	(25)	(25)	(25)	0	0	(100)
Software Application	0	0	0	0	0	0	0	0
TOTAL Depreciation	0	(512)	(512)	(512)	(512)	0	0	(2,048)
Cash Flow Before Tax	9,821	36,602	73,208	74,733	75,058	75,870	76,170	421,462
Taxes 35% on Non-Cap	(4,092)	(12,856)	(25,651)	(26,157)	(26,270)	(26,555)	(26,660)	(148,240)
Total After Taxes	5,729	23,746	47,557	48,576	48,788	49,316	49,511	273,222
Add Depreciation	0	512	512	512	512	0	0	2,048
TOTAL cash flow after tax	5,729	24,258	48,069	49,088	49,300	49,316	49,511	275,270
NPV 13%	158,979							

Exhibit 3.   Customer Information environment cost savings.

this area, management needs to be ruthless in maintaining focus on those DRM activities that actually have an impact on the business.

The perception of value must reflect how the rest of the company views DRM's efforts. Others may not be aware that the data management group's efforts pay off in terms of dollar savings, greater productivity, increased data integrity, and better decision support. They may only see the data management group as a standards and policy-producing body that has no real value. When DRM management understands how its staff is perceived, then it is possible to craft a response that addresses any deficiencies.

DRM must be tied solidly to achievement of business objectives. No one must be allowed to think of DRM as solely a staff function. To do this, the DRM group should create an objectives chart for themselves and for others to view. All DRM activities should be measured against this chart to determine their true value. If a proposed activity cannot be clearly tied to a corporate objective, then it should be placed at the bottom of the priority list (see the following table).

DRM initiative	Corporate objective
Scalable data warehouse	Know our customers
Metadata standards	Corporate efficiency
Enterprise data bases	Reduce expenses

Sharpening Long- and Short-Term Outlooks

Data management professionals must be a combination of business strategist and data base administrator. They provide the foresight and drive to implement the vision of sharing information throughout the enterprise, whether it is private business or government. They help define the vision for the business person and plot a road map for implementation for the systems developers and network experts.

At all top-flight companies, the business leaders or top executives have a clearly communicated vision. In support of a vision, objectives must also be clearly enunciated by a company's managers. For every company objective, DRM must be able to provide the leadership and direction for attainment of that objective in the information area; DRM does that by establishing principles by which information is managed, processes are reengineered, applications are designed, and by creating an organization that supports the roles and responsibilities of sound information management.

As business leaders outline their business strategies, data management professionals must become a partner with business management in reaching those objectives. All business managers will support the people who help them realize their goals. One of the most effective strategies for assisting managers to meet their objectives is to focus on short-term, incremental deliverables. DRM must be resourceful and flexible enough to adapt its techniques and procedures to reach business goals.

BUILDING STRATEGIC ALLIANCES

Wherever there are people, there are politics. It is important to understand that politics is a fact of life and then determine a constructive approach for dealing with it. Often, any number of people may be attempting to advance their own agendas and goals. Where these goals are constructive for the corporation, DRM can seek to work with people with different agendas and advance the cause of information management.

Building Influence

Within any human organization, there are always individuals who have more influence on the group than do others. The data management group must seek to win the confidence of the rest of the organization by focusing on results, having well-researched solutions to problems, exhibiting a firm grasp of business issues, and by addressing the target group's true concerns. As the DRM solution over time benefits the long-term health of the organization, DRM will become increasingly influential.

Moving with the Movers and Shakers

Movers and shakers are those individuals within an organization who make things happen. People who are placed in responsibility over important projects, managers of successful departments, and others could all be potential allies or champions of DRM efforts. Contacts with these individuals should be cultivated and harnessed.

In addition, informal channels of communication such as the grapevine and rumor mill should be used to advantage, both as a source of information about coming changes and a means of communicating positive information.

Participating in Cross-functional Projects

Data management professionals should seek to be involved in every cross-functional tea   m or special project team that is formed. By knowing what management priorities are, DRM can then focus limited resources on helping those projects succeed.

This will make DRM participation come to be regarded as a critical success factor. Data management professionals are generally well-seasoned business people as well as technology experts. Whenever business people are looking for help, DRM analysts should be presenting themselves as solution providers, offering their services as a fully integrated part of the business.

Being First to Market with the Value

Most organizations are faced with a constantly changing landscape filled with new problems. What was important yesterday is no longer remembered today. DRM groups typically have too few professionals and must therefore allocate their resources to high-visibility projects that provide answers to current problems. For example, to deliver the value in a timely fashion, the scalable data warehouse is a primary vehicle. The DRM group must devote resources to defining and maintaining the metadata so that new information may be made available to business users as soon as possible.

Promoting DRM's Contribution

There is an old saying that a little yeast spreads through the entire loaf of bread dough. The management of information is a critical success factor for a company's success. Only by spreading the DRM gospel before every possible audience will the message begin to sink in and become a way of thinking for the average business person or systems developer.

All leaders face opposition. It can come from old-line programmers, political climbers, budget-conscious managers, or people who simply do not understand the importance of managing the information resource. Opposition sends many people out of meetings muttering under their breath and complaining to their co-workers later. Instead, these events should be viewed as opportunities to make a clearer case to convince opponents and win them over with the quality and thoroughness of your approach.

In every organization, there are many opportunities to promote beneficial programs. Meetings, internal seminars, newsletters, and brochures are just a few. Constant exposure to DRM concepts and principles will eventually result in the program being ingrained in the corporate culture. Why do consumers know certain brands of products more than others? It is because of constant advertising and exposure. DRM can apply the same concepts.

Of course, the first and most important focus of the DRM group should be to drive toward real, measurable, visible results. Often, however, there is a tendency to believe that successes are self-apparent to the rest of the organization when in fact they are not. Successes must be publicized in a method that will ensure that the right people understand the value of data management.

DRM should have its own well-publicized Web site. On this site, there should be quick access to data standards, data warehouse information, data architecture, and other valuable information that is geared to business people's access to information. People will also find the Web site interesting if the DRM professionals each have their own home page with their pictures and personal information.

GAINING AND KEEPING MANAGEMENT COMMITMENT

There is one thing that business management usually understands, and that is the bottom line. It is critical for the DRM group to have prepared its value calculations and to have documented the worth of its contribution.

Quantifying the Costs of Redundant Data and Customer Dissatisfaction

W.E. Demings often asked the question, "How much is a satisfied customer worth?", and the companion question, "How much damage can a dissatisfied customer do?" This point needs to be brought home to managers — that the costs of improper information management are multiplying every hour in terms of lost productivity, dissatisfied customers, and poor decision-making. The costs of maintaining conflicting data on disparate systems and developing multiple interfaces to merge systems, not to mention staff analysis hours to try to make sense of the data, are staggering.

One of the most difficult tasks faced by the data management professional is to put a price tag on the cost of redundant data and processing. The costs of doing business the wrong way must be emphasized when dealing with business management. When a customer gets the runaround from company personnel because they do not have good information, there is a cost associated with that event. It is beneficial to assemble a list of war stories of dissatisfied customers that can be documented. It is then possible to attach a cost to each of these stories, show how better information could have prevented the situation, and come up with a solution. Here, the DRM group can never be seen as an adversary or critic.

With constant exposure to DRM principles of sound information management, business managers will begin to understand that their success is inextricably linked with having quality information at their and every worker's fingertips. For example, increased profitability is often cited as a business objective. DRM has an impact on this objective because managing information has the effects of:

- Reducing IS resources
- Building better information about customer sales
- Reducing cycle time
- Reducing multiple storage, development, and interface costs

A DYNAMIC MIGRATION PLAN

Dynamic means changeable, and that is exactly what DRM plans need to be. One of the main data management functions is to create a plan for migrating to a new information environment and to guide the organization to that goal. During times of change, the plan needs to be altered to meet the altered needs of the corporation. Exhibit 4 displays the goals of the migration to an enterprise data-sharing environment.

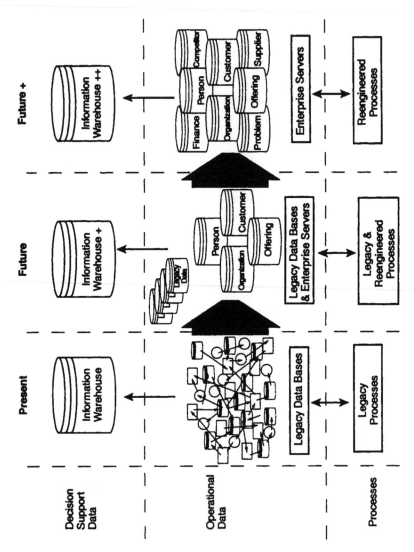

Exhibit 4.   Goals of migrating to a data-sharing environment.

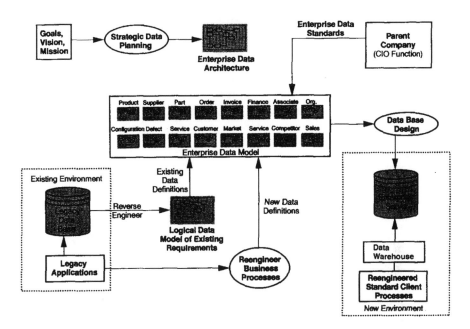

Exhibit 5. Architecture is at the center of data planning.

Organization

There are several organizational models for DRM, most of which can be effective, depending on the people who staff the model. The data management organization needs to be structured so as to support the business in the most effective way. One key aspect is that whatever the scope of information sharing is, it is critical that the data management function is situated in the organization so that it spans that entire scope.

Architecture

A data architecture for the entire company is somewhat less subject to change as organizations shift. Subtle adjustments may be necessary, however, and should be part of the migration plan. Exhibit 5 shows how an architecture is at the center of the data planning environment to support the migration to the vision state.

ARCHITECTURE IS AT THE CENTER OF DATA PLANNING

People and Skills

As organizations change, there is an ebb and flow of personnel requirements. Skills, requirements, and people need to be matched regularly to meet the shifting requirements. It may be beneficial for data management professionals to rotate out into a business function for a couple of years to broaden their experience.

Participation in industry conferences, courses, books, and membership in professional organizations are all means of keeping skill sets at the cutting edge. It is also very important to hone nontechnical skills that are often forgotten — skills such as interpersonal relations, negotiating, and presenting.

Education must be addressed at every level of the DRM organization. Data management professionals need to develop their set of skills to cover a broad range of business and technology issues. Web-enabled access to data standards is now a prerequisite. DRM professionals should develop intranet expertise. The DRM group is also responsible for educating end-users, managers, and systems developers in the importance of sound information management.

Because DRM professionals need to be part visionary, part cheerleader, part technologist, part business person, they must be flexible and adaptable. People who cannot make this transition need to be allowed to find other career opportunities. Pessimists and cynics cannot make a strong contribution in the discipline.

Infrastructure

Data management professionals should participate in infrastructure planning in order to guide a migration to an environment that will support massive decision-support, parallel-processing data base engines, enterprisewide communications capabilities, and easy user access. DRM professionals should be visionaries concerning the future use of data and information. That is why the data warehouse infrastructure should be scalable — able to grow with the need for information without becoming obsolete. It is not only the data warehouse engine that must be sized for future growth, but also the bandwidth and infrastructure for providing Web access to all potential users in the company. There is nothing that turns users off quite like being unable to get rapid response time to critical information.

The focus is on getting quality information to the right person at the right time. The infrastructure should be planned so as to be independent of organizational structures.

DRM Process

Forward-thinking companies are structuring their activities according to a process management scheme instead of a stovepipe functional orientation. The DRM group should be deeply involved in defining the company's process architecture and its own part in that framework. In a process architecture, core processes are defined together with supporting processes. DRM should be a prominently displayed supporting process along with other activities like architecture management, financial management, and technology.

SUMMARY

Several critical success factors are necessary ingredients for success. The DRM program and strategy should be aimed at addressing the four Cs — confidence, competence, commitment, and consistency — and building them into the organization.

Human Issues Are More Important than Technical Ones

In the final analysis, if change is to be instituted in a culture, it will be the human issues that either make or break the effort. Advanced technologies, faster computers, and friendly GUI interfaces are a small piece of the puzzle. The human issues must be studied, understood, and planned for when attempting to change culture, organization, or systems.

At the same time that new responsibilities for DRM employees are defined and new behaviors are expected, the reward and bonus system must be altered to reward the performance that is desired. If people have no incentive to change, it will be next to impossible to effect a true cultural shift. By changing the reward system, however, people will be motivated by their own interests to act in the desired way.

Focus on Results, Not Theories

DRM management must never allow the organization to stray from results-producing activities to academic ones. Analysts have the tendency to gravitate toward theory and abstraction, but this can result in the DRM group being viewed as counterproductive and useless.

Chapter 21

Database Security Controls

Ravi S. Sandhu
Sushil Jajodia

THIS CHAPTER DISCUSSES THE TOPIC OF DATA SECURITY AND CONTROLS, primarily in the context of database management systems (DBMSs), with an emphasis on basic principles and mechanisms that have been successfully used by practitioners in actual products and systems. When appropriate, the limitations of these techniques are noted.

Because discussion focuses on principles and general concepts, it is independent of any particular product (except for a later section that discusses a few specific products). In the more detailed considerations, the discussion is limited specifically to relational DBMSs, which store data in relations that have specific mathematical properties. All examples are given in SQL. It is assumed that readers are familiar with rudimentary concepts of relational databases and SQL.

The chapter begins with a review of basic security concepts, followed by a discussion of access controls in the current generation of commercially available DBMSs. The problem of multilevel security is then introduced, including a review of techniques developed specifically for multilevel security. Next, the various kinds of inference threats that arise in a database system are discussed, along with methods developed for dealing with them. Inference poses a threat to security by allowing higher-classified information to be inferred from lower-classified information. Another section addresses the problem of data integrity, with a discussion of current practice in this area.

BASIC SECURITY CONCEPTS

Data security has three separate, but interrelated objectives:

- *Confidentiality.* This objective concerns the prevention of improper disclosure of information.

0-8493-9976-9/99/$0.00+$.50
© 1999 by CRC Press LLC

- *Integrity.* This objective concerns prevention of improper modification of information or processes.
- *Availability.* This objective concerns improper denial of access to information.

These three objectives arise in practically every information system. There are differences, however, regarding the relative importance of these objectives in a given system. The commercial and military sectors have similar needs for high-integrity systems; however, the confidentiality and availability requirements of the military are often more stringent than those for typical commercial applications.

In addition, the objectives differ with respect to the level of understanding of the objectives themselves and the technology to achieve them. For example, availability is technically the least understood objective, and currently, no products address it directly. Therefore, availability is discussed only in passing in this chapter.

The security policy defines the three security objectives in the context of the organization's needs and requirements system. In general, the policy defines what is improper for a particular system. This may be required by law (e.g., for confidentiality in the classified military and government sectors). However, the security policy is largely determined by the organization rather than by external mandates, particularly in the areas of integrity and availability.

Two distinct, mutually supportive mechanisms are used to meet the security objectives: prevention (i.e., attempts to ensure that security breaches cannot occur) and detection (i.e., provision of an adequate audit trail so that security breaches can be identified after they have occurred). Every system employs a mix of these techniques, though sometimes the distinction between them gets blurred. This chapter focuses on prevention, which is the more fundamental technique: to be effective, a detection mechanism first requires a mechanism for preventing improper modification of the audit trail.

A third technique for meeting security objectives is referred to as *tolerance.* Every practical system tolerates some degree of risk with respect to potential security breaches; however, it is important to understand which risks are being tolerated and which are covered by preventive and detective mechanisms.

Security mechanisms can be implemented with various degrees of assurance, which is directly related to the effort required to subvert the mechanism. Low-assurance mechanisms are easy to implement but relatively easy to subvert. High-assurance mechanisms are notoriously difficult to implement, and they often suffer from degraded performance. Fortunately, rapid advances in hardware performance are alleviating these constraints on performance.

ACCESS CONTROLS IN CURRENT SYSTEMS

This section discusses the access controls provided in the current generation of commercially available database management systems, with a focus on relational systems. The access controls described are often referred to as discretionary access controls as opposed to the mandatory access controls of multilevel security. This distinction is examined in the next section.

The purpose of access controls is to ensure that a user is permitted to perform only those operations on the database for which that user is authorized. Access controls are based on the premise that the user has been correctly identified to the system by some authentication procedure. Authentication typically requires the user to supply his or her claimed identity (e.g.,user name or operator number) along with a password or some other authentication token. Authentication may be performed by the operating system, the database management system, a special authentication server, or some combination thereof.

Granularity and Modes of Access Control

Access controls can be imposed at various degrees of granularity in a system. For example, they can be implemented through the entire database, over one or more data relations, or in columns or rows of relations. Access controls are differentiated with respect to the operation to which they apply. These distinctions are important — for example, each employee may be authorized to read his own salary but not to write it. In relational databases, access control modes are expressed in terms of the basic SQL operations (i.e., SELECT, UPDATE, INSERT, and DELETE), as follows:

- The ability to insert and delete data is specified on a relation-by-relation basis.
- SELECT is usually specified on a relation-by-relation basis. Finer granularity of authorization for SELECT can be provided by views.
- UPDATE can be restricted to certain columns of a relation.

In addition to these access control modes, which apply to individual relations or parts thereof, there are privileges, which confer special authority on users. A common example is the DBA privilege for database administrators.

Data-Dependent Access Controls

Database access controls are often data dependent. For example, some users may be limited to viewing salaries less than $30,000. Similarly, a manager may be restricted to seeing salaries for employees in his or her department. There are two basic techniques for implementing data-dependent access controls in relational databases: view-based access controls and query modification.

View-Based Access Control. A base relation is a relation actually stored in the database. A view is a virtual relation derived from base relations and other views. The database stores the view definitions and materializes the view as needed.

To illustrate the concept of a view and its security application, the following table shows the base relations of EMPLOYEE (the value NULL indicates that Harding has no manager):

NAME	DEPT	SALARY	MANAGER
Smith	Toy	10,000	Jones
Jones	Toy	15,000	Baker
Baker	Admin	40,000	Harding
Adams	Candy	20,000	Harding
Harding	Admin	50,000	NULL

The following SQL statement defines a view of these relations called TOY-DEPT:

```
CREATE   VIEW      TOY-DEPT
AS       SELECT    NAME, SALARY, MANAGER
         FROM      EMPLOYEE
         WHERE     DEPT = 'Toy'
```

This statement generates the view shown in the following table:

NAME	SALARY	MANAGER
Smith	10,000	Jones
Jones	15,000	Baker

To illustrate the dynamic aspects of views, a new employee, Brown, is inserted in base relation EMPLOYEE, as shown in the following table:

NAME	DEPT	SALARY	MANAGER
Smith	Toy	10,000	Jones
Jones	Toy	15,000	Baker
Baker	Admin	40,000	Harding
Adams	Candy	20,000	Harding
Harding	Admin	50,000	NULL
Brown	Toy	22,000	Harding

The view TOY-DEPT is automatically modified to include Brown, as shown in the following table:

NAME	SALARY	MANAGER
Smith	10,000	Jones
Jones	15,000	Baker
Brown	22,000	Harding

Views can be used to provide access to statistical information. For example, the following view gives the average salary for each department:

```
CREATE   VIEW AVSAL   (DEPT,AVG)
AS       SELECT       DEPT,AVG(SALARY)
         FROM         EMPLOYEE
         GROUP BY     DEPT
```

For retrieval purposes, users need not distinguish between views and base relations. A view is simply another relation in the database, which happens to be automatically modified by the DBMS whenever its base relations are modified. Thus, views provide a powerful mechanism for specifying data-dependent authorization for data retrieval. However, there are significant problems if views are modified by users directly (rather than indirectly through modification of base relations). This is a result of the theoretical inability to translate updates of views into updates of base relations (discussed in a later section). This limits the usefulness of views for data-dependent authorization of update operations.

Query Modification. Query modification is another technique for enforcing data-dependent access controls for retrieval. (Query modification is not supported in SQL but is discussed here for the sake of completeness.) In this technique, a query submitted by a user is modified to include further restrictions as determined by the user's authorization.

For example, the database administrator has granted Thomas the ability to query the EMPLOYEE base relation for employees in the toy department as follows:

```
GRANT   SELECT
ON      EMPLOYEE
TO      Thomas
WHERE   DEPT = 'Toy'
```

Thomas then executes the following query:

```
SELECT   NAME, DEPT, SALARY, MANAGER
FROM     EMPLOYEE
```

In the absence of access controls, this query would obtain the entire EM-PLOYEE relation. Because of the GRANT command, however, the DBMS automatically modifies this query to the following:

```
SELECT   NAME, DEPT, SALARY, MANAGER
FROM     EMPLOYEE
WHERE    DEPT = 'Toy'
```

This limits Thomas to retrieving that portion of the EMPLOYEE relation for which he was granted SELECT access.

Granting and Revoking Access

GRANT and REVOKE statements allow users to selectively and dynamically grant privileges to other users and subsequently revoke them if so desired. In SQL, access is granted by means of the GRANT statement, which applies to base relations as well as views. For example, the following GRANT statement allows Chris to execute SELECT queries on the EMPLOYEE relation:

```
GRANT SELECT ON EMPLOYEE TO CHRIS
```

The GRANT statement may also be used to allow a user to act as database administrator, which carries with it many privileges. Because the database administrator DBA privilege confers systemwide authority, no relation need be specified in the command. For example, the following statement allows Pat to act as database administrator, and furthermore, to grant this privilege to others:

```
GRANT DBA TO PAT WITH GRANT OPTION
```

In SQL, it is not possible to give a user the GRANT OPTION on a privilege without further allowing the GRANT OPTION to be given to other users.

Accesses are revoked in SQL by means of the REVOKE statement. The REVOKE statement can remove only those privileges that the user also granted. For example, if Thomas has already granted Chris the SELECT privilege, he may execute the following command to revoke that privilege:

```
REVOKE SELECT ON EMPLOYEE FROM CHRIS
```

However, if Pat had also granted Chris the SELECT privilege, Chris would continue to retain this privilege after Thomas revokes it.

Because the WITH GRANT OPTION statement allows users to grant their privileges to other users, the REVOKE statements can have a cascading effect. For example, if Pat grants Chris the SELECT privilege, and Chris subsequently grants this privilege to Kelly, the privilege would be revoked from both Chris and Kelly if Pat later revokes it from Chris.

These access controls are said to be discretionary because the granting of access is at the user's discretion — that is, users who possess a privilege with the GRANT OPTION are free to grant that privilege to whomever they choose. This approach has serious limitations with respect to confidentiality requirements, as discussed in the following section.

Limitations of Discretionary Access Controls

If a privilege is granted without the GRANT OPTION, that user should not be able to grant the privilege to other users. However, this intention can be subverted by simply making a copy of the relation. For example, the first example of a GRANT statement allows Chris to execute SELECT queries on the EMPLOYEE relation, but it does not allow Chris to grant this privilege to others. Chris can get around this limitation by creating a copy of the EMPLOYEE relation, into which all the rows of EMPLOYEE are copies.

As the creator of COPY-OF-EMPLOYEE, Chris has the authority to grant any privileges for it to any user. For example, with the following statement, Chris could grant Pat the ability to execute SELECT queries on the COPY-OF-EMPLOYEE relation:

```
GRANT SELECT ON COPY-OF-EMPLOYEE TO PAT
```

In essence, this gives Pat access to all the information in the original EMPLOYEE relation, as long as Chris keeps COPY-OF-EMPLOYEE reasonably up-to-date with respect to EMPLOYEE .

Even if users are trusted not to deliberately violate security in this way, Trojan horses can be programmed to do so. The solution is to impose mandatory access controls that cannot be violated, even by Trojan horses. Mandatory access controls are discussed in the following section.

MULTILEVEL SECURITY

This selection introduces the issue of multilevel security, which focuses on confidentiality. Discretionary access controls pose a serious threat to confidentiality; mandatory access controls help eliminate these problems. Multilevel secure database systems enforce mandatory access controls in addition to the discretionary controls commonly found in most current products.

The use of multilevel security, however, can create potential conflicts between data confidentiality and integrity. Specifically, the enforcement of integrity rules can create covert channels for discovering confidential information, which even mandatory access controls cannot prevent.

This section concludes with a brief discussion of the evaluation criteria for secure computer systems developed by the U.S. Department of Defense. It should be noted that although multilevel security systems were developed primarily for the military sector, they are relevant to the commercial sector as well.

Mandatory Access Controls

With mandatory access controls, the granting of access is constrained by the system security policy. These controls are based on security labels associated with each data item and each user. A label on a data item is called a *security classification*, and a label on a user is called a *security clearance*. In a computer system, every program run by a user inherits the user's security clearance — that is, the user's clearance applies not only to the user but to every program executed by that user. Once assigned, the classifications and clearances cannot be changed, except by the security officer.

Security labels in the military and government sectors have two components: a hierarchical component and a set of categories. The hierarchical component consists of the following classes, listed in decreasing order of sensitivity: top secret, secret, confidential, and unclassified. The set of categories may be empty, or it may consist of such items as nuclear, conventional, navy, army, or NATO.

Commercial organizations use similar labels for protecting sensitive information. The main difference is that procedures for assigning clearances to users are much less formal than in the military or government sectors.

It is possible for security labels to dominate each other. For example, label X is said to dominate label Y if the hierarchical component of X is greater than or equal to the hierarchical component of Y and if the categories of X contain all the categories of Y. That is, if label X is (TOP-SECRET, {NUCLEAR, ARMY}) and label Y is (SECRET, {ARMY}), then label X dominates label Y. Likewise, if label X is (SECRET, {NUCLEAR, ARMY}), it would dominate label Y. If two labels are exactly identical, they are said to dominate each other.

If two labels are not comparable, however, neither one dominates the other. For example, if label X is (TOP-SECRET, {NUCLEAR}) and label Y is (SECRET, {ARMY}), they are not comparable.

The following discussion is limited to hierarchical labels without any categories. Although many subtle issues arise as a result of incomparable labels with categories, the basic concepts can be demonstrated with hierarchical labels alone. For simplicity, the labels denoting secret and unclassified classes are primarily used in this discussion.

When a user signs on to the system, that user's security clearance specifies the security level of that session. That is, a particular program (e.g., a text editor) is run as a secret process when executed by a secret user, but is run as an unclassified process when executed by an unclassified user. It is possible for a user to sign on at a security level lower than the one assigned to that user, but not at one higher. For example, a secret user can sign on as an unclassified user, but an unclassified user may not sign on as a secret user. Once a user is signed on at a specific level, all programs executed by that user will be run at that level.

Covert Channels

Although a program running at the secret level is prevented from writing directly to unclassified data items, there are other ways of communicating information to unclassified programs. For example, a program labeled secret can acquire large amounts of memory in the system. This can be detected by an unclassified program that is able to observe how much memory is available. If the unclassified program is prevented from directly observing the amount of free memory, it can do so indirectly by making a request for a large amount of memory itself. Such indirect methods of communication are called *covert channels*. Covert channels present a formidable problem for ensuring multilevel security. They are difficult to detect, and once detected, they are difficult to close without incurring significant performance penalties.

Evaluation Criteria

The *Orange Book* established a metric against which computers systems can be evaluated for security. The metric consists of several levels: A1, B3, B2, B1, C2, C1, and D; listed here in decreasing order of how secure the system is.

For each level, the *Orange Book* lists a set of requirements that a system must have to achieve that level of security. Briefly, the D level consists of all systems that are not secure enough to qualify for any of A, B, or C levels. Systems at levels C1 and C2 provide discretionary protection of data; systems at level B1 provide mandatory access controls, and systems at levels B2 or higher provide increasing assurance, particularly against covert channels. Level A1, which is most rigorous, requires verified protection of data.

In 1991, the U.S. Department of Defense published the "Trusted Database Interpretation of the Trusted Computer System Evaluation Criteria," popularly known as the TDI. The TDI describes how a DBMS and the underlying operating system can be evaluated separately or in conjunction. Several efforts are under way to build secure DBMS products satisfying these criteria.

INFERENCE AND AGGREGATION

Even in multilevel secure DBMSs, it is possible for users to draw inferences from the information they obtain from the database. The inference could be derived purely from the data obtained from the database system, or it could additionally depend on some prior knowledge obtained by users from outside the database system. An inference presents a security breach if higher-classified information can be inferred from lower-classified information.

There is a significant difference between the inference and covert channel problems. Inference is a unilateral activity in which an unclassified user legitimately accesses unclassified information, from which that user is able to deduce secret information. Covert channels, on the other hand, require cooperation of a secret process that deliberately or unwittingly transmits information to an unclassified user by means of indirect communication. The inference problem exists even in an ideal system that is completely free of covert channels.

There are many difficulties associated with determining when more highly classified information can be inferred from lower-classified information. The biggest problem is that it is impossible to determine precisely what a user knows. The inference problem is somewhat manageable if the closed-world assumption is adopted; this is the assumption that if information Y can be derived using information X, both X and Y are contained in the database. In reality, however, the outside knowledge that users bring plays a significant role in inference.

There are two important cases of the inference problem that often arise in database systems. First, an aggregate problem occurs whenever there is a collection of data items that is classified at a higher level than the levels of the individual data items by themselves. A classic example from a military context occurs when the location of individual ships in a fleet is unclassified, but the aggregate information concerning the location of all ships in the fleet is secret. Similarly, in the commercial sector, the individual sales figures for branch offices might be considered less sensitive than the aggregate sales figures for the entire company.

Second, a data association problem occurs whenever two values seen together are classified at a higher level than the classification of either value individually. For example, although the list consisting of the names of all employees and the list containing all employee salaries are unclassified, a combined list giving employee names with their salaries is classified. The data association problem is different from the aggregate problem because what is really sensitive is not the aggregate of the two lists, but the exact association giving an employee name and his salary.

The following sections describe some techniques for solving the inference problem. Although these methods can be extremely useful, a complete and generally applicable solution to the inference problem remains elusive.

Appropriate Labeling

One way to prevent unclassified information X from permitting disclosure of secret information Y is to reclassify all or part of information X such that it is no longer possible to derive Y from the disclosed subset of X. For example, attribute A is unclassified, and attribute B is secret. The database enforces the constraint $A + B \leq 20$, and that constraint is known to unclassified users. The value of B does not affect the value of A directly; however, it does constrain the set of possible values A can take. This is an inference problem, which can be prevented by reclassifying A as secret.

Query Restriction

Many inference violations arise as a result of a query that obtains data at the user's level; evaluation of this query requires accessing data above the user's level. For example, data is classified at the relations level, and there are two relations: (1) an unclassified relation, called EP, with attributes EMPLOYEE-NAME and PROJECT-NAME; and (2) a secret relation called PT, with attributes PROJECT-NAME and PROJECT-TYPE. EMPLOYEE-NAME as the key of the first relation and PROJECT-NAME as the key of the second. (The existence of the relation scheme PT is unclassified.) An unclassified user makes the following SQL query:

```
SELECT   EP. PROJECT-NAME
FROM     EP,PT
WHERE    EP. PROJECT - NAME = PT. PROJECT-NAME AND
         EP.PROJECT - TYPE = 'NUCLEAR'
```

The data obtained by this query (i.e., the project names) is extracted from the unclassified relation EP. As such, the output of this query contains unclassified data, yet it reveals secret information by virtue of being selected on the basis of secret data in the PT relation.

Query restriction ensures that all data used in the process of evaluating the query is dominated by the level of the user and therefore prevents such inferences. To this end, the system can either simply abort the query or modify the user query so that the query involves only the authorized data.

Polyinstantiation

The technique of polyinstantiation is used to prevent inference violations. Essentially it allows different versions of the same information item to exist at different classification levels. For example, an unclassified user wants to enter a row in a relation in which each row is labeled either S (secret) or U (unclassified). If the same key is already occurring in an S row, the unclassified user can insert the U row, gaining access to any information by inference. The classification of the row must therefore be treated as part of the relation key. Thus, U rows and S rows always have different keys because the keys have different security classes.

The following table, which has the key STARSHIP-CLASS, helps illustrate this:

STARSHIP	DESTINATION	CLASS
Enterprise	Jupiter	S
Enterprise	Mars	U

A secret user inserted the first row in this relation. Later, an unclassified user inserted the second row. The second insertion must be allowed because it cannot be rejected without revealing to the unclassified user that a secret row for the enterprise already exists. Unclassified users see only one row for the Enterprise — namely, the U row. Secret users see both rows. These two rows might be interpreted in two ways:

- There are two distinct Starships named Enterprise going to two distinct destinations. Unclassified users know of the existence of only one of them (i.e., the one going to Mars). Secret users know about both of them.
- There is a single Starship named Enterprise. Its real destination is Jupiter, which is known only to secret users. However, unclassified users have been told that the destination is Mars.

Presumably, secret users know which interpretation is intended.

Auditing

Auditing can be used to control inferences. For example, a history can be kept of all queries made by a user. Whenever the user makes a query, the history is analyzed to determine whether the response to this query, when compared with responses to earlier queries, might suggest an inference violation. If so, the system can take appropriate action (i.e., abort the query).

The advantage of this approach is that it may deter many inference attacks by threatening discovery of violations. There are two disadvantages to this approach, however. First, it may be too cumbersome to be useful in practical situations. Second, it can detect only very limited types of inferences — it assumes that a violation can always be detected by analyzing the audit record for abnormal behavior.

Tolerating Limited Inferences

Tolerance methods are useful when the inference bandwidth is so small that these violations do not pose any threat. For example, the data may be classified at the column level, with two relations; one called PD with the unclassified attribute PLANE and the secret attribute DESTINATION, and another called DF with the unclassified attribute DESTINATION and the unclassified attribute FUEL-NEEDED. Although knowledge of the fuel needed for a particular plane can provide clues the destination of the plane, there are too many destinations requiring the same amount of fuel for this to be a serious inference threat. Moreover, it would be too time-consuming to clear everybody responsible for fueling the plane to the secret level. Therefore, it is preferred that the derived relation with attributes PLANE and FUEL-NEEDED be made available to unclassified users.

Although it has been determined that this information does not provide a serious inference threat, unclassified users cannot be allowed to extract the required information from PD and DF, by, for example, executing the following query:

```
SELECT   PLANE,FUEL-NEEDED
FROM     PD,DF
WHERE    PD.DESTINATION = DF.DESTINATION
```

This query would open up a covert channel for leaking secret information to unclassified users.

One solution is to use the snapshot approach, by which a trusted user creates a derived secret relation with attributes PLANE and FUEL-NEEDED and then downgrades it to unclassified. Although this snapshot cannot be updated automatically without opening a covert channel, it can be kept more or less up-to-date by having the trusted user recreate it from time to time. A snapshot or a sanitized file is an important technique for controlling inferences, especially in offline, static databases. It has been used quite effectively by the U.S. Census Bureau.

INTEGRITY PRINCIPLES AND MECHANISMS

Integrity is a much less tangible objective than secrecy. For the purposes of this chapter, integrity is defined as being concerned with the improper modification of information. Modification includes insertion of new information, deletion of existing information, and changes to existing information. Such modifications may be made accidentally or intentionally.

Data may be accidentally modified when users simultaneously update a field or file, get deadlocked, or inadvertently change relationships. Therefore, controls must be in place to prevent such situations. Controls over nonmalicious errors and day-to-day business routines are needed as well as controls to prevent malicious errors.

Some definitions of integrity use the term *unauthorized* instead of *improper.* Integrity breaches can and do occur without authorization violations; however, authorization is only part of the solution. The solution must also account for users who exercise their authority improperly.

The threat posed by a corrupt authorized user is quite different in the context of integrity from what it is in the context of confidentiality. A corrupt user can leak secrets by using the computer to legitimately access confidential information and then passing on this information to an improper destination by another means of communication (e.g., a telephone call). It is impossible for the computer to know whether or not the first step was followed by the second step. Therefore, organizations have no choice but to trust their employees to be honest and alert.

Although the military and government sectors have established elaborate procedures for this purpose, the commercial sector is much more informal in this respect. Security research focusing on confidentiality considers the principal threat to be Trojan horses embedded in programs; that is, the focus is on corrupt programs rather than on corrupt users.

Similarly, a corrupt user can compromise integrity by manipulating stored data or falsifying source or output documents. Integrity must therefore focus on the corrupt user as the principal problem. In fact, the Trojan horse problem can itself be viewed as a problem of corrupt system or application programmers who improperly modify the software under their control. In addition, the problem of the corrupt user remains even if all of the organization's software is free of Trojan horses.

Integrity Principles and Mechanisms

This section identifies basic principles for achieving data integrity. Principles lay down broad goals without specifying how to achieve them. The following section maps these principles to DBMS mechanisms, which establish how the principles are to be achieved.

There are seven integrity principles:

- *Well-formed transactions*. The concept of the well-formed transaction is that users should not manipulate data arbitrarily, only in restricted ways that preserve integrity of the database.
- *Least privilege*. Programs and users should be given the least privilege necessary to accomplish their jobs.
- *Separation of duties*. Separation of duties is a time-honored principle for prevention of fraud and errors by ensuring that no single individual is in a position to misappropriate assets on his own. Operationally, this means that a chain of events that affects the balance of assets must be divided into separate tasks performed by different individuals.
- *Reconstruction of events*. This principle seeks to deter improper behavior by threatening its discovery. The ability to reconstruct what hap-

pened in a system requires that users be accountable for their actions (i.e., that it is possible to determine what they did).

- *Delegation of authority.* This principle concerns the critical issue of how privileges are acquired and distributed in an organization. The procedures to do so must reflect the structure of the organization and allow for effective delegation of authority.
- *Reality checks.* Cross-checks with external reality are an essential part of integrity control. For example, if an internal inventory record does not correctly reflect the number of items in the warehouse, it makes little difference if the internal record is correctly recorded in the balance sheet.
- *Continuity of operation.* This principle states that system operations should be maintained at an appropriate level during potentially devastating events that are beyond the organization's control, including natural disasters, power outages, and disk crashes.

These integrity principles can be divided into two groups, on the basis of how well existing DBMS mechanisms support them. The first group consists of well-formed transactions, continuity of operation, and reality checks. The second group comprises least privilege, separation of duties, reconstruction of events, and delegation of authority. The principles in the first group are adequately supported in existing products (to the extent that a DBMS can address these issues), whereas the principles in the second group are not so well understood and require improvement. The following sections discuss various DBMS mechanisms for facilitating application of these principles.

Well-Formed Transactions. The concept of a well-formed transaction corresponds well to the standard DBMS concept of a transaction. A transaction is defined as a sequence of primitive actions that satisfies the following properties:

- *Correct-state transform.* If run by itself in isolation and given a consistent state to begin with, each transaction will leave the database in a consistent state.
- *Serializability.* The net effect of executing a set of transactions is equivalent to executing them in a sequential order, even though they may actually be executed concurrently (i.e., their actions are interleaved or simultaneous).
- *Failure atomicity.* Either all or none of the updates of a transaction take effect. (In this context, update means modification, including insertion of new data, deletion of existing data, and changes to existing data.)
- *Progress.* Every transaction is eventually completed. That is, there is no indefinite blocking owing to deadlocks and no indefinite restarts owing to live locks (i.e., the process is repeatedly aborted and restarted because of other processes).

21-15

The basic requirement is that the DBMS must ensure that updates are restricted to transactions. If users are allowed to bypass transactions and directly manipulate relations in a database, there is no foundation to build on. In other words, updates should be encapsulated within transactions. This restriction may seem too strong because, in practice, there will always be a need to perform ad hoc updates. However, ad hoc updates can themselves be carried out by means of special transactions. The authorization for these special ad hoc transactions should be carefully controlled and their use properly audited.

DBMS mechanisms can help ensure the correctness of a state by enforcing consistency constraints on the data. (Consistency constraints are also often called integrity constraints or integrity rules.) The relational data model primarily imposes two consistency constraints:

- *Entity integrity* stipulates that attributes in the primary key of a relation cannot have null values. This amounts to requiring that each entity represented in the database must be uniquely identifiable.
- *Referential integrity* is concerned with references from one entity to another. A foreign key is a set of attributes in one relation whose values are required to match those of the primary key of some specific relation. Referential integrity requires that a foreign key either be null or that a matching tuple exist in the relation being referenced. This essentially rules out references to nonexistent entities.

Entity integrity is easily enforced. Referential integrity, on the other hand, requires more effort and has seen limited support in commercial products. In addition, the precise method for achieving it is highly dependent on the semantics of the application, particularly when the referenced tuple is deleted. There are three options: prohibiting the delete operation, deleting the referencing tuple (with a possibility of further cascading deletes), or setting the foreign key attributes in the referencing tuple to NULL.

In addition, the relational model encourages the use of domain constraints that require the values in a particular attribute (column) to come from a given set. These constraints are particularly easy to state and enforce as long as the domains are defined in terms of primitive types (e.g., integers, decimal numbers, and character strings). A variety of dependence constraints, which constrain the tuples in a given relation, have been extensively studied.

A consistency constraint can be viewed as an arbitrary predicate that all correct states of the database must satisfy. The predicate may involve any number of relations. Although this concept is theoretically appealing and flexible in its expressive power, in practice the overhead in checking the predicates for every transaction is prohibitive. As a result, relational

DBMSs typically confine their enforcement of consistency constraints to domain constraints and entity integrity.

Least Privilege. The principle of least privilege translates into a requirement for fine-grained access control. For the purpose of controlling read access, DBMSs have employed mechanisms based on views or query modification. These mechanisms are extremely flexible and can be as fine-grained as desired. However, neither one of the mechanisms provides the same flexibility for highly granular control of updates. The fundamental reason for this is the theoretical inability to translate updates on views into updates of base relations. As a result, authorization to control updates is often less sophisticated than authorization for read access.

Fine-grained control of updates by means of views does not work well in practice. However, views are extremely useful for controlling retrieval. For example, the following table shows two base relations: EMP-DEPT and DEPT-MANAGER:

EMP	DEPT	DEPT	MANAGER
Smith	Toy	Toy	Brown
Jones	Toy	Candy	Baker
Adams	Candy		

The following statement provides the EMP-MANAGER view of the base relations:

```
CREATE   VIEW EMP-MANAGER
AS       SELECT   EMP, MANAGER
         FROM     EMP-DEPT, DEPT-MANAGER
         WHERE    EMP-DEPT.DEPT = DEPT-MANAGER.DEPT
```

This statement results in the following table:

EMP	MANAGER
Smith	Brown
Jones	Brown
Adams	Baker

This view can be updated with the following statement:

```
UPDATE   EMP-MANAGER
SET      MANAGER = 'Green'
WHERE    EMP = 'Smith'
```

If EMP-MANAGER is a base relation, this statement would create the following table:

EMP	MANAGER
Smith	Green
Jones	Brown
Adams	Baker

This effect cannot be attained, however, by updating existing tuples in the two base relations in the first table. For example, the manager of the toy department can be changed as follows:

```
UPDATE   DEPT-MANAGER
SET      MANAGER = 'Green'
WHERE    DEPT = 'Toy'
```

This statement results in the following view:

EMP	MANAGER
Smith	Green
Jones	Green
Adams	Baker

The first updated view of EMP-MANAGER can be realized by modifying the base relations in the first table as follows:

EMP	DEPT	DEPT	MANAGER
Smith	X	X	Green
Jones	Toy	Toy	Brown
Adams	Candy	Candy	Baker

In this case, Smith is assigned to an arbitrary department whose manager is Green. It is difficult, however, to determine whether this is the intended result of the original update. Moreover, the UPDATE statement does not explain what X is.

Separation of Duties. Separation of duties is not well supported in existing products. Although it is possible to use existing mechanisms for separating duties, these mechanisms were not designed for this purpose. As a result, their use is awkward at best.

Separation of duties is inherently concerned with sequences of transactions rather than individual transactions in isolation. For example, payment in the form of a check is prepared and issued by the following sequence of events:

- A clerk prepares a voucher and assigns an account.
- The voucher and account are approved by a supervisor.
- The check is issued by a clerk, who must be different from the clerk in the first item. Issuing the check also debits the assigned account.

This sequence embodies separation of duties because the three steps must be executed by different people. The policy has adynamic flavor in that a particular clerk can prepare vouchers on one occasion and issue checks on another. However, the same clerk cannot prepare a voucher and issue a check for that voucher.

Reconstruction of Events. The ability to reconstruct events in a system serves as a deterrent to improper behavior. In the DBMS context, the mechanism for recording the history of a system is traditionally called an *audit trail*. As with the principle of least privilege, a high-end DBMS should be capable of reconstructing events to the finest detail. In practice, this ability must be tempered with the reality that gathering audit data indiscriminately can generate an overwhelming volume of data. Therefore, a DBMS must also allow fine-grained selectivity regarding what is audited.

In addition, it should structure the audit trail logically so that it is easy to query. For example, logging every keystroke provides the ability to reconstruct the system history accurately. However, with this primitive logical structure, a substantial effort is required to reconstruct a particular transaction. In addition to the actual recording of all events that take place in the database, an audit trail must provide support for true auditing (i.e., an audit trail must have the capability for an auditor to examine it in a systematic manner). In this respect, DBMSs have a significant advantage because their powerful querying abilities can be used for this purpose.

Delegation of Authority. The need to delegate authority and responsibility within an organization is essential to its smooth functioning. This need appears in its most developed form with respect to monetary budgets. However, the concept applies equally well to the control of other assets and resources of the organization.

In most organizations, the ability to grant authorization is never completely unconstrained. For example, a department manager may be able to delegate substantial authority over departmental resources to project managers within his department and yet be prohibited from delegating this authority to project managers outside the department. Traditional delegation mechanisms based on the concept of ownership (e.g., as embodied in the SQL GRANT and REVOKE statements) are not adequate in this context. Further work remains to be done in this area.

Reality Checks. This principle inherently requires activity outside the DBMS. The DBMS has an obligation to provide an internally consistent view of that portion of the database that is being externally verified. This is particularly important if the external inspection is conducted on an ad hoc, on-demand basis.

Continuity of Operation. The basic technique for maintaining continuity of operation in the face of natural disasters, hardware failures, and other disruptive events is redundancy in various forms. Recovery mechanisms in DBMSs must also ensure that the data is left in a consistent state.

SUMMARY

Data security has three objectives: confidentiality, integrity, and availability. A complete solution to the confidentiality problem requires high-assurance, multilevel systems that impose mandatory controls and are known to be free of covert channels. Such systems are currently at the research and development stage and are not available.

Until these products become available, security administrators must be aware of the limitations of discretionary access controls for achieving secrecy. Discretionary access controls cannot cope with Trojan horse attacks. It is therefore important to ensure that only high-quality software of know origin is used in the system. Moreover, database administrators must appreciate that even the mandatory controls of high-assurance, multilevel systems do not directly prevent inference of secret information.

The integrity problem, somewhat paradoxically, is less well understood than confidentiality but is better supported in existing products. The basic foundation of integrity is the assurance that all updates are carried out by well-informed transactions. This is reasonably well supported by currently available DBMS products (e.g., DB2 and Oracle). Other integrity principles — such as least privilege, separation of duties, and delegation of authority — are not well supported. Products that satisfy these requirements are still in development. The availability objective is poorly understood. Therefore, existing products do not address it to any significant degree.

Chapter 22
E-Mail Security and Privacy

Stewart S. Miller

THE MAJORITY OF ELECTRONIC MAIL, OR E-MAIL, is not a private form of communication. E-mail is often less secure than sending personal or business messages on a postcard. Many businesses monitor employee computer files, E-mail, or voice mail. Some corporations monitor E-mail to ensure that trade secrets are not being communicated to the outside world. Because E-mail often travels through many computers, it is easy to intercept messages.

Bulletin board systems, college campus networks, commercial information services, and the Internet are mainly open information systems where hackers can easily tamper with E-mail. Whenever mail is sent over the Internet, the message first arrives at the Internet service provider's (ISP) outgoing mail server. Once there, anyone using that provider can read the mail as it goes out to its destination.

Passwords do not protect E-mail. Most major E-mail and groupware products that combine messaging, file management, and scheduling allow the network administrator to change passwords at any time and read, delete, or alter any messages on the server. Network monitoring programs, including AG Group's LocalPeek, Farallon Computing's Traffic Watch II, and Neon Software's NetMinder, allow network managers to read files sent over the Internet. In fact, these products mimic tools specifically designed for surveillance used primarily on mainframe systems. Encryption is a key element in secure communications over the Internet.

Pretty Good Privacy (PGP) software encrypts E-mail-attached computer files, making them unreadable to most hackers. PGP is a worldwide standard for E-mail security. Anonymous remailers allow users to send E-mail to network newsgroups or directly to recipients so that they cannot tell the sender's real name or E-mail address. For business communications, one of the motivations behind the use of PGP is to prevent the sale of company business plans or customer list information to competitors.

0-8493-9976-9/99/$0.00+$.50
© 1999 by CRC Press LLC

ESTABLISHING SECURE E-MAIL STANDARDS

Secure Multipurpose Internet Mail Extension (SMIME) is a standard for secure E-mail communications that will soon be built into most E-mail products. A secure E-mail standard allows users to communicate safely between separate or unknown mail platforms. SMIME guarantees security end-to-end using digital signature technology. SMIME can be used for applications such as processing business transactions between trading partners over the Internet.

SMIME is one of the only ways to prove a user sent what he or she claims to have sent. The SMIME specification was developed to allow interoperability between various E-mail platforms using Rivest-Shamir-Adleman (RSA) encryption. This standard permits various encryption schemes, various key lengths, and digital signatures. SMIME also supports VeriSign's digital certificates, which is a form of identification used in electronic commerce.

Verification of E-mail services is a key component in preventing fraudulent messages. Netscape Navigator supports VeriSign's Digital IDs and SMIME. Qualcomm, the manufacturer of Eudora, plans to include an application programming interface (API) layer to SMIME in Version 3.0 of its E-mail program. In addition to encryption, SMIME modules link into the Eudora translator and offer PGP. WorldTalk, a manufacturer of gateway mail software, is building SMIME support into its network application router to permit cross-communications throughout disparate E-mail packages in addition to a centralized mail management and Internet access.

When a gateway supports SMIME, businesses can audit files as they enter and leave the company. SMIME can replace software based on PGP code. The difference between the two security technologies is that SMIME uses a structured certificate hierarchy; PGP is more limited because it relies on precertification of clients and servers for authentication.

Businesses are working closely with agencies such as the Internet Engineering Task Force (IETF) to achieve effective security for E-mail on the Internet. The lack of a common E-mail security standard is a hurdle to electronic commerce efforts. The Internet has failed to achieve its full potential because of the lack of secure transmission standards. However, standards are continually being proposed at meetings such as the E-Mail World conference, at which businesses work toward ensuring interoperability between E-mail vendors' implementations.

Secure Directories

Many companies are developing directories of businesses on the Internet. Banyan Systems Inc. has released Switchboard, a highly scalable directory that allows Internet users to locate electronic addresses and other information for businesses worldwide. Switchboard appears to be the biggest Internet address directory in existence. This system also offers safeguards to protect privacy and permit secure communication.

When Internet E-mail users express concerns over privacy, Switchboard implements a feature much like Caller-ID that alerts a listed person whenever anyone asks for the person's address. The recipient, who will be given information about whomever is seeking the address, can then decide whether to allow access.

Privacy Enhanced Mail (PEM)

The IETF is working to establish a standard for encrypting data in E-mail, designed to be a stable specification on which vendors can build products that can work together. Once the specifications have been clarified, the proposed standard is adopted as a final standard. The IETF standard for encryption includes Privacy Enhanced Mail (PEM) technology.

PEM encrypts E-mail into the Multipurpose Internet Mail Extension (MIME), which is the standard for attaching files to an E-mail message. PEM provides a utility called nonrepudiation, in which an E-mail message is automatically signed by the sender. Therefore, privacy is assured so that the author is unable to deny that he or she sent the message at a later point in time. PEM uses the Digital Encryption Standard (DES) and public key encryption technology to ensure that messages are easy for legitimate users to decrypt, yet difficult for hackers to decode.

PGP uses the RSA algorithm along with an enhanced idea encryption algorithm. Although the draft standards for PEM are not yet widely supported, they will probably gain acceptance as the language of the draft is clarified to remove ambiguity regarding the manner in which users are named and certified.

LEADING E-MAIL COALITIONS

Internet Mail Consortium (IMC)

The IMC is a new union of users and vendors interested in developing E-mail standards for the Internet. The group formed because its members feel that present organizations have not acted quickly enough to adopt standards for the Internet. The IMC acts as a link between the E-mail users, vendors, and the IETF.

The IMC plans to build consensus on conflicting Internet mail security protocols by holding informative workshops. This group's goal is to establish one unifying system that will ensure privacy in E-mail communications. The IMC's four founding members are Clorox Co., First Virtual Holdings Inc., Innosoft International Inc., and Qualcomm Inc.

For the IMC to attain its goal, it needs users and vendors to come together and discuss Internet mail issues. The IMC will most likely have even more influence than the Electronic Messaging Association on technical and business issues involving E-mail and the Internet.

Electronic Messaging Association (EMA)

The EMA is one source for users to consult if they have problems with their E-mail. The EMA's primary purpose is assigning standards to E-mail message attachments. In the EMA's efforts to regulate E-mail, security issues have been most prevalent regarding Internet communication. The EMA is making strides toward secure file transfers, thanks to the advent of PGP's success with encryption of E-mail file attachments.

The EMA is composed of corporate users and vendors of E-mail and messaging products. The EMA focuses heavily on the X.400 standard and has recently established a workgroup to research interoperability between Simple Mail Transfer Protocol (SMTP) and X.400 systems.

The EMA formed a Message Attachment Working Group in 1993 whose purpose was to develop a standard for identifying file attachments transmitted from one vendor E-mail system to another. The group was set up to use the IETF's MIME and the X.400 File Transfer Body Part (FTBP) as the method for identifying different attachment types. The FTBP defines an attachment by the application that created it. The EMA formed tests that were considered successful if the attachment was received without experiencing data loss.

Attachment transfers are simple when done from within one vendor's mail system, but difficult when performed across systems. File attachments from Microsoft, Lotus, and WordPerfect were used to make certain that the specification developed was capable of transferring attachments.

The next step is integrating MIME and SMIME support into future E-mail packages. It is typical for X.400 to be used as a backbone system for E-mail connectivity. There is a high degree of interest in developing secure methods of transmitting attachments in SMIME. MIME is the current standard for Internet file attachments, and SMIME is well on its way to becoming the secure standard for E-mail communications.

CORPORATE SECURITY: PROBLEMS AND SOLUTIONS

One of the biggest security problems an organization faces involves how to implement a secure server yet allow access to the applications and resources from the corporate intranet. If an organization's Web or mail server is not protected by a firewall or kept on a secured part of the network, then data is open to hacker attacks. In terms of commercial transactions on the Internet, such a security breach can have lasting repercussions that could make customers lose faith in a company. A hacker could easily alter shipping data, create bogus orders, or simply steal money or products directly from a company's online site.

Security is a full-time job — E-mail is vulnerable to eavesdropping, address spoofing, and wiretapping. A security breach can be anything from unauthorized access by an employee to a hacker break-in. Attacks are not always conducted in a piecemeal fashion. Sometimes they occur on the entire system and focus on stealing or destroying the total assets of a company. Security breaches have resulted in corporate losses ranging from several hundred to several million dollars. Many organizations are not even aware that security breaches occur many times. A hacker can enter and exit a system undetected. Only when data or E-mail becomes lost, stolen, or tampered with do companies start to realize how much money an organization can actually lose in the process.

Internal Precautions

The first step toward preventing data loss is to take internal precautions. Defunct user accounts should be deleted right away, users should not log on at unauthorized or nonbusiness hours, and of course, users should be warned against posting their passwords in easily accessible places. Employees should be up to date concerning corporate security measures. Internal attacks can sometimes be thwarted simply by alerting all users that there are stringent security measures in place. Also, many workers do not realize the value of the data they have access to. Users can be encouraged to be more vigilant if they are made aware of potential losses due to breaches in security.

Firewalls

Firewalls provide an excellent means of keeping data integrity safe. They have the power to block entry points into the system — if an intruder does not have an account name or password, he or she is denied access. When configured correctly, firewalls reduce the number of accounts that are accessible from outside the network, and as a result, make the system much less vulnerable.

Firewalls are an excellent method of keeping attacks from spreading from one point in the network to another. Firewalls restrict users to one controlled location in the network — access is granted (or denied) at one highly guarded point. Firewalls stop hackers from getting close to security defenses and offer the best protection when placed near a point where the internal network or intranet connects to the larger Internet. Any network traffic that comes from or goes out to the Internet must go through the firewall, which then approves each transmission and deems it acceptable or unacceptable.

Preventing E-mail Flooding and Denial of Service

Corporations sometimes fall prey to E-mail "bombs," which essentially flood an E-mail account with several hundred or thousand messages. This overwhelms the entire system and disrupts network services so that other messages cannot get through.

One solution some vendors provide is E-mail filters. If the E-mail bombs are originating from one domain or a few domains, the recipient can simply input those domains into the filter to be screened and deleted before cluttering up an E-mail account.

While an E-mail flood is interrupting service, a hacker can entirely disable or reroute services. These attacks can be combated by programming the system to shut out connections or questionable domains that repeatedly try to log into the system unsuccessfully. Attackers are therefore prevented from inputting multiple passwords in an attempt to gain access and shut down service. However, if repeated attempts on each user account result in shutting the account down, a hacker can effectively deny service to multiple people in an organization by simply trying to access all of the user accounts unsuccessfully. This would effectively deny service to most of the users.

When a security breach is successful, the hacker gains complete access to a user account, and assets are in jeopardy. One effective method of preventing an attack is to run a secure gateway such as Netscape's Commerce Server, which makes it very difficult for hackers to breach Internet security.

Encryption

Most Internet E-mail security measures are accomplished using *encryption* and *authentication* methods. The Internet Privacy Enhanced Mail standard is the method of encrypting E-mail recommended by the IETF.

Another way to secure E-mail contents is the *digital signature* method, which identifies, stores, and verifies hand-written signatures electronically. This process is accomplished when users sign their names using a digitized pen on a computer. The service can record the specific signature metrics, the speed at which the signature is written, and the order of the unique hand-written strokes. The information is used as a basis to match with any computerized document signed by the same individual again. The comparison can determine the identity of the sender for submitting online payments or securing confidential data.

Administrators often encrypt data across wide area networks in addition to using digital signatures in E-mail packages to determine a user's true identity. The combination of encryption and digital signatures helps slow hacker attempts at gaining network access. However, companies still need to guard against the many methods of hacking, including phone tampering and remote access authentication.

The good news is that encryption is becoming universally accepted on the Internet. In some cases, users do not even realize that the latest Netscape Navigator Web browser employs encryption to secure both documents and E-mail messages. It uses the secure socket layer (SSL) protocol, supported by all of the major Web browsers and servers, to accomplish this goal and provide a safer means of communication.

Unlisted Sites

One method of protecting an E-mail site is to take the *unlisted* approach. This is an effective security model that works only if no one knows that a particular site exists. If no one knows the site is there, no one will try to hack it. Unfortunately, this model is only good as long as the site remains a secret; and because the Internet is an open system with multiple search engines, the site will probably not remain secret for long.

An Integrated Strategy

An organization concerned with network security may want to control access at each host and for all network services, which is more effective than the piecemeal approach of securing each service individually. This solution can involve the creation of firewalls for internal systems and the network, as well as incorporating detailed authentication approaches such as a password that expires after each use. Encryption can also be implemented on various levels to protect important data as it travels throughout the network.

SUMMARY

The Internet evolved as an open system; however, it is this very openness that makes this venue of communicating so risky. The expansion of the Internet has promoted the growth of E-mail as a relatively quick, low-cost, easy-to-use method of communication. However, the irrefutable fact is that information is power, which makes this particular form of communicating an attractive target for thieves. This chapter has dealt with the problems surrounding E-mail privacy and proposed a few practical, easy-to-implement solutions.

Chapter 23
Security Models for Object-Oriented Databases

James Cannady

OBJECT-ORIENTED (OO) PROGRAMMING LANGUAGES AND OO ANALYSIS AND DESIGN TECHNIQUES influence database systems design and development. The inevitable result is the object-oriented database management system (OODBMS).

Many of the established database vendors are incorporating object-oriented concepts into their products in an effort to facilitate database design and development in the increasingly object-oriented world of distributed processing. In addition to improving the process of database design and administration, the incorporation of object-oriented principles offers new tools for securing the information stored in the database. This chapter explains the basics of database security, the differences between securing relational and object-oriented systems, and some specific issues related to the security of next-generation OODBMSs.

BASICS OF DATABASE SECURITY

Database security is concerned primarily with the secrecy of data. Secrecy means protecting a database from unauthorized access by users and software applications.

Secrecy, in the context of database security, includes a variety of threats incurred through unauthorized access. These threats range from the intentional theft or destruction of data to the acquisition of information through more subtle measures, such as inference. There are three generally accepted categories of secrecy-related problems in database systems:

- The improper release of information from reading data that intentionally or accidentally was accessed by unauthorized users. Securing da-

0-8493-9976-9/99/$0.00+$.50
© 1999 by CRC Press LLC

tabases from unauthorized access is more difficult than controlling access to files managed by operating systems. This problem arises from the finer granularity that is used by databases when handling files, attributes, and values. This type of problem also includes the violations to secrecy that result from the problem of inference, which is the deduction of unauthorized information from the observation of authorized information. Inference is one of the most difficult factors to control in any attempts to secure data. Because the information in a database is related semantically, it is possible to determine the value of an attribute without accessing it directly. Inference problems are most serious in statistical databases, where users can trace back information on individual entities from the statistical aggregated data.

- The improper modification of data. This threat includes violations of the security of data through mishandling and modifications by unauthorized users. These violations can result from errors, viruses, sabotage, or failures in the data that arise from access by unauthorized users.
- Denial-of-service threats. Actions that could prevent users from using system resources or accessing data are among the most serious. SYN flood attacks against network service providers are an example of denial-of-service threats in which a barrage of messages is sent to the server at a rate faster than the system can deal with them. Such attacks prevent authorized users from using system resources.

Discretionary vs. Mandatory Access Control Policies

Both traditional relational database management system (RDBMS) security models and object-oriented database models make use of two general types of access control policies to protect the information in multilevel systems. The first of these policies is the discretionary policy. In the discretionary access control (DAC) policy, access is restricted based on the authorizations granted to the user.

The mandatory access control (MAC) policy secures information by assigning sensitivity levels or labels to data entities or objects. MAC policies are generally more secure than DAC policies and they are used in systems in which security is critical, such as military applications. However, the price that usually is paid for this tightened security is reduced performance of the database management system. Most MAC policies also incorporate DAC measures as well.

SECURING AN RDBMS VS. OODBMS: KNOW THE DIFFERENCES

The development of secure models for object-oriented DBMSs obviously has followed on the heels of the development of the databases themselves. The theories that currently are being researched and implemented in the security of object-oriented databases also are influenced heavily by the work that has been conducted on secure relational database management systems.

Relational DBMS Security

In traditional RDBMSs, security is achieved principally through the appropriate use and manipulation of views and the SQL GRANT and REVOKE statements. These measures are reasonably effective because of their mathematical foundation in relational algebra and relational calculus.

View-Based Access Control

Views allow the database to be divided conceptually into pieces in ways that allow sensitive data to be hidden from unauthorized users. In the relational model, views provide a powerful mechanism for specifying data-dependent authorizations for data retrieval.

Although the individual user who creates a view is the owner and is entitled to drop the view, he or she may not be authorized to execute all privileges on it. The authorizations that the owner may exercise depend on the view semantics and on the authorizations that the owner is allowed to implement on the tables directly accessed by the view. For the owner to exercise a specific authorization on a view that he or she creates, the owner must possess the same authorization on all tables that the view uses. The privileges the owner possesses on the view are determined at the time of view definition. Each privilege the owner possesses on the tables is defined for the view. If, later on, the owner receives additional privileges on the tables used by the view, these additional privileges will not be passed onto the view. To use the new privileges within a view, the owner will need to create a new view.

The biggest problem with view-based mandatory access controls is that it is impractical to verify that the software performs the view interpretation and processing. If the correct authorizations are to be assured, the system must contain some type of mechanism to verify the classification of the sensitivity of the information in the database. The classification must be done automatically, and the software that handles the classification must be trusted. However, any trusted software for the automatic classification process would be extremely complex. Furthermore, attempting to use a query language such as structured query language (SQL) to specify classifications quickly becomes convoluted and complex. Even when the complexity of the classification scheme is overcome, the view can do nothing more than limit what the user sees — it cannot restrict the operations that may be performed on the views.

GRANT and REVOKE Privileges

Although view mechanisms often are regarded as security freebies because they are included within SQL and most other traditional relational database managers, views are not the sole mechanism for relational database security. GRANT and REVOKE statements allow users to grant privileges selectively and dynamically to other users and subsequently revoke them if necessary. These two statements are considered to be the principal user interfaces in the authorization subsystem.

There is, however, a security-related problem inherent in the use of the GRANT statement. If a user is granted rights without the GRANT option, he or she should not be able to pass GRANT authority on to other users. However, the system can be subverted by a user by simply making a complete copy of the relation. Because the user creating copy is now the owner, he or she can provide GRANT authority to other users. As a result, unauthorized users are able to access the same information that had been contained in the original relation. Although this copy is not updated with the original relation, the user making the copy could continue making similar copies of the relation and providing the same data to other users.

The REVOKE statement functions similarly to the GRANT statement, with the opposite result. One of the characteristics of the use of the REVOKE statement is that it has a cascading effect. When the rights previously granted to a user subsequently are revoked, all similar rights are revoked for all users who may have been provided access by the originator.

Other Relational Security Mechanisms

Although views and GRANT/REVOKE statements are the most frequently used security measures in traditional RDBMSs, they are not the only mechanisms included in most security systems using the relational model. Another security method used with traditional relational database managers, which is similar to GRANT/REVOKE statements, is the use of query modification.

This method involves modifying a user's query before the information is retrieved, based on the authorities granted to the user. Although query modification is not incorporated within SQL, the concept is supported by the Codd-Date relational database model.

Most relational database management systems also rely on the security measures present in the operating system of the host computer. Traditional RDMBSs such as DB2 work closely with the operating system to ensure that the database security system is not circumvented by permitting access to data through the operating system. However, many operating systems provide insufficient security. In addition, because of the portability of many newer database packages, the security of the operating system should not be assumed to be adequate for the protection of the wealth of information in a database.

Object-Oriented DBMS Characteristics

Unlike traditional RDBMSs, secure object-oriented DBMSs (or OODBMSs) have certain characteristics that make them unique. Furthermore, only a limited number of security models have been designed specifically for object-oriented databases. The proposed security models make use of the object-oriented concepts of:

- Encapsulation
- Inheritance
- Information hiding
- Methods (in the OO paradigm, an object contains data and methods; methods are the components that act on the data and provide user access to the data. It helps to think of methods as functions from the structured programming environment.)
- The ability to model real-world entities

The object-oriented database model also permits the classification of an object's sensitivity through the use of class and instance. When an instance of a class is created, the object automatically can inherit the level of sensitivity of the superclass. Although the ability to pass classifications through inheritance is possible in object-oriented databases, class instances usually are classified at a higher level within the object's class hierarchy. This prevents a flow control problem, where information passes from higher to lower classification levels.

Object-oriented DBMSs also use unique characteristics that allow these models to control the access to the data in the database. They incorporate features such as flexible data structure, inheritance, and late binding. Access control models for OODBMSs must be consistent with such features. Users can define methods, some of which are open for other users as public methods. Moreover, the OODBMS may encapsulate a series of basic access commands into a method and make it public for users, while keeping basic commands themselves away from users.

Proposed OODBMS Security Models

Currently only a few models use discretionary access control measures in secure object-oriented database management systems.

Explicit Authorizations

The ORION authorization model is probably the best OODBMS discretional access control security model available today. ORION permits access to data on the basis of explicit authorizations provided to each group

of users. These authorizations are classified as positive authorizations because they specifically allow a user access to an object. Similarly, a negative authorization is used specifically to deny a user access to an object.

The placement of an individual into one or more groups is based on the
role that the individual plays in the organization. In addition to the positive
authorizations that are provided to users within each group, there are a variety of implicit authorizations that may be granted based on the relationships between subjects and access modes.

Data-Hiding Model

A similar discretionary access control secure model is the data-hiding
model proposed by Dr. Elisa Bertino of the Universita' di Genova. This model distinguishes between public methods and private methods.

The data-hiding model is based on authorizations for users to execute
methods on objects. The authorizations specify which methods the user is
authorized to invoke. Authorizations only can be granted to users on public methods. However, the fact that a user can access a method does not
mean automatically that the user can execute all actions associated with
the method. As a result, several access controls may need to be performed
during the execution, and all of the authorizations for the different accesses must exist if the user is to complete the processing.

Similar to the use of GRANT statements in traditional relational database management systems, the creator of an object is able to grant authorizations to the object to different users. The creator also is able to revoke
the authorizations from users in a manner similar to REVOKE statements.
However, unlike traditional RDBMS GRANT statements, the data-hiding
model includes the notion of protection mode. When authorizations are
provided to users in the protection mode, the authorizations actually
checked by the system are those of the creator and not the individual executing the method. As a result, the creator is able to grant a user access to
a method without granting the user the authorizations for the methods
called by the original method. In other words, the creator can provide a
user access to specific data without being forced to give the user complete
access to all related information in the object.

Other DAC Models for OODBMS Security

Rafiul Ahad has proposed a similar model that is based on the control of
function evaluations. Authorizations are provided to groups or individual
users to execute specific methods. The focus in Ahad's model is to protect
the system by restricting access to the methods in the database, not the
objects. The model uses proxy functions, specific functions, and guard
functions to restrict the execution of certain methods by users and to enforce content-dependent authorizations.

Another secure model that uses authorizations to execute methods has been presented by Joel Richardson. This model has some similarity to the data-hiding model's use of GRANT/REVOKE-type statements. The creator of an object can specify which users may execute the methods within the object.

A final authorization-dependent model emerging from OODBMS security research has been proposed by Dr. Eduardo B. Fernandez of Florida Atlantic University. In this model the authorizations are divided into positive and negative authorizations. The Fernandez model also permits the creation of new authorizations from those originally specified by the user through the use of the semantic relationships in the data.

Dr. Naftaly H. Minsky of Rutgers University has developed a model that limits unrestricted access to objects through the use of a view mechanism similar to that used in traditional relational database management systems. Minsky's concept is to provide multiple interfaces to the objects within the database. The model includes a list of laws or rules that govern the access constraints to the objects. The laws within the database specify which actions must be taken by the system when a message is sent from one object to another. The system may allow the message to continue unaltered, block the sending of the message, send the message to another object, or send a different message to the intended object.

Although the discretionary access control models do provide varying levels of security for the information within the database, none of the DAC models effectively addresses the problem of the authorizations provided to users. A higher level of protection within a secure object-oriented database model is provided through the use of mandatory access control.

MAC Methods for OODBMS Security

Dr. Bhavani Thuraisingham of MITRE Corp. proposed in 1989 a mandatory security policy called SORION. This model extends the ORION model to encompass mandatory access control. The model specifies subjects, objects, and access modes within the system, and it assigns security/sensitivity levels to each entity. Certain properties regulate the assignment of the sensitivity levels to each of the subjects, objects, and access modes. To gain access to the instance variables and methods in the objects, certain properties that are based on the various sensitivity levels must be satisfied.

A similar approach has been proposed in the Millen-Lunt model. This model, developed by Jonathan K. Millen of MITRE Corp. and Teresa Lunt of SRI/DARPA (Defense Advanced Research Projects Agency), also uses the assignment of sensitivity levels to the objects, subjects, and access modes within the database. In the Millen-Lunt model, the properties that regulate the access to the information are specified as axioms within the model.

This model further attempts to classify information according to three different cases:

- The data itself is classified.
- The existence of the data is classified.
- The reason for classifying the information also is classified.

These three classifications broadly cover the specifics of the items to be secured within the database; however, the classification method also greatly increases the complexity of the system.

The SODA Model

Dr. Thomas F. Keefe of Penn State University proposes a model called Secure Object-Oriented Data Base (SODA). The SODA model was one of the first models to address the specific concepts in the object-oriented paradigm. It often is used as a standard example of secure object-oriented models from which other models are compared.

The SODA model complies with MAC properties and is executed in a multilevel security system. SODA assigns classification levels to the data through the use of inheritance. However, multiple inheritance is not supported in the SODA model.

Similar to other secure models, SODA assigns security levels to subjects in the system and sensitivity levels to objects. The security classifications of subjects are checked against the sensitivity level of the information before access is allowed.

Polyinstantiation

Unlike many current secure object-oriented models, SODA allows the use of polyinstantiation as a solution to the multiparty update conflict. This problem arises when users with different security levels attempt to use the same information. The variety of clearances and sensitivities in a secure database system result in conflicts between the objects that can be accessed and modified by the users.

Through the use of polyinstantiation, information is located in more than one location, usually with different security levels. Obviously the more sensitive information is omitted from the instances with lower security levels.

Although polyinstantiation solves the multiparty update conflict problem, it raises a potentially greater problem in the form of ensuring the integrity of the data within the database. Without some method of simultaneously updating all occurrences of the data in the database, the integrity of the information quickly disappears. In essence, the system becomes a collection of several distinct database systems, each with its own data.

CONCLUSION

The move to object-oriented DBMSs is likely to continue for the foreseeable future. Because of the increasing need for security in distributed processing environments, the expanded selection of tools available for securing information in this environment should be used fully to ensure that the data is as secure as possible. In addition, with the continuing dependence on distributed data, the security of these systems must be integrated fully into existing and future network security policies and procedures.

The techniques that ultimately are used to secure commercial OODBMS implementations will depend in large part on the approaches promoted by the leading database vendors. However, the applied research that has been conducted to date also is laying the groundwork for the security components that in turn will be incorporated in the commercial OODBMSs.

Chapter 24

Security Management for the World Wide Web

Lynda L. McGhie
Phillip Q. Maier

COMPANIES CONTINUE TO FLOCK TO THE INTERNET in ever-increasing numbers, despite the fact that the overall and underlying environment is not secure. To further complicate the matter, vendors, standards bodies, security organizations, and practitioners cannot agree on a standard, compliant, and technically available approach. As a group of investors concerned with the success of the Internet for business purposes, it is critical that we pull our collective resources and work together to quickly establish and support interoperable security standards; open security interfaces to existing security products and security control mechanisms within other program products; and hardware and software solutions within heterogeneous operating systems which will facilitate smooth transitions.

Interfaces and teaming relationships to further this goal include computer and network security and information security professional associations (CSI, ISSA, NCSA), professional technical and engineering organizations (I/EEE, IETF), vendor and product user groups, government and standards bodies, seminars and conferences, training companies/institutes (MIS), and informal networking among practitioners.

Having the tools and solutions available within the marketplace is a beginning, but we also need strategies and migration paths to accommodate and integrate Internet, intranet, and World Wide Web (WWW) technologies into our existing IT infrastructure. While there are always emerging challenges, introduction of newer technologies, and customers with challenging and perplexing problems to solve, this approach should enable us to maximize the effectiveness of our existing security investments, while bridging the gap to the long awaited and always sought after perfect solution!

0-8493-9976-9/99/$0.00+$.50
© 1999 by CRC Press LLC

Security solutions are slowly emerging, but interoperability, universally accepted security standards, application programming interfaces (APIs) for security, vendor support and cooperation, and multiplatform security products are still problematic. Where there are products and solutions, they tend to have niche applicability, be vendor-centric or only address one of a larger set of security problems and requirements. For the most part, no single vendor or even software/vendor consortium has addressed the overall security problem within open systems and public networks. This indicates that the problem is very large, and that we are years away from solving todays problem, not to mention tomorrows.

By acknowledging todays challenges, bench-marking todays requirements, and understanding our "as is condition" accordingly, we as security practitioners can best plan for security in the twenty-first century. Added benefits adjacent to this strategy will hopefully include a more cost-effective and seamless integration of security policies, security architectures, security control mechanisms, and security management processes to support this environment.

For most companies, the transition to "open" systems technologies is still in progress and most of us are somewhere in the process of converting mainframe applications and systems to distributed network-centric client-server infrastructures. Nevertheless, we are continually challenged to provide a secure environment today, tomorrow, and in the future, including smooth transitions from one generation to another. This article considers a phased integration methodology that initially focuses on the update of corporate policies and procedures, including most security policies and procedures; secondly, enhances existing distributed security architectures to accommodate the use of the Internet, intranet, and WWW technologies; thirdly, devises a security implementation plan that incorporates the use of new and emerging security products and techniques; and finally, addresses security management and infrastructure support requirements to tie it all together.

It is important to keep in mind, as with any new and emerging technology, Internet, intranet, and WWW technologies do not necessarily bring new and unique security concerns, risks, and vulnerabilities, but rather introduce new problems, challenges and approaches within our existing security infrastructure.

Security requirements, goals, and objectives remain the same, while the application of security, control mechanisms, and solution sets are different and require the involvement and cooperation of multidisciplined technical and functional area teams. As in any distributed environment, there are more players, and it is more difficult to find or interpret the overall requirements or even talk to anyone who sees or understands the big picture. More people are involved than ever before, emphasizing the need to communicate both strategic and tactical security plans broadly and effectively throughout the entire enterprise. The security challenges and the resultant problems become larger and more complex in this environment. Management must be kept up-to-date and thoroughly understand overall risk to the corporations information assets with the implementation or decisions to implement new technologies. They must also understand, fund, and support the influx of resources required to manage the security environment.

As with any new and emerging technology, security should be addressed early in terms of understanding the requirements, participating in the evaluation of products and related technologies, and finally in the engineering, design, and implementation of new applications and systems. Security should also be considered during all phases of the systems development life cycle. This is nothing new, and many of us have learned this lesson painfully over the years as we have tried to retrofit security solutions as an adjunct to the implementation of some large and complex system. Another important point to consider throughout the integration of new technologies, is "technology does not drive or dictate security policies, but the existing and established security policies drive the application of new technologies." This point must be made to management, customers, and supporting IT personnel.

For most of us, the WWW will be one of the most universal and influential trends impacting our internal enterprise and its computing and networking support structure. It will widely influence our decisions to extend our internal business processes out to the Internet and beyond. It will enable us to use the same user interface, the same critical systems and applications, work towards one single original source of data, and continue to address the age-old problem: how can I reach the largest number of users at the lowest cost possible?

THE PATH TO INTERNET/BROWSER TECHNOLOGIES

Everyone is aware of the staggering statistics relative to the burgeoning growth of the Internet over the last decade. The use of the WWW can even top that growth, causing the traffic on the Internet to double every six months. With five internal Web servers being deployed for every one external Web server, the rise of the intranet is also more than just hype. Companies are predominately using the web technologies on the intranet to share information and documents. Future application possibilities are basically any enterprise-wide application such as education and training; corporate policies and procedures; human resources applications such as a resume, job posting, etc.; and company information. External Web applications include marketing and sales.

For the purpose of this discussion, we can generally think of the Internet in three evolutionary phases. While each succeeding phase has brought with it more utility and the availability of a wealth of electronic and automated resources, each phase has also exponentially increased the risk to our internal networks and computing environments.

Phase I, the early days, is characterized by a limited use of the Internet, due in the most part to its complexity and universal accessibility. The user interface was anything but user friendly, typically limited to the use of complex UNIX-based commands via line mode. Security by obscurity was definitely a popular and acceptable way of addressing security in those early days, as security organizations and MIS management convinced themselves that the potential risks were confined to small user populations centered around homogeneous computing and networking environments. Most companies were not externally connected in those days, and certainly not to the Internet.

Phase II is characterized by the introduction of the first versions of database search engines, including Gopher and Wide Area Information System (WAIS). These tools were mostly used in the government and university environments and were not well known nor generally proliferated in the commercial sector.

Phase III brings us up to todays environment, where Internet browsers are relatively inexpensive, readily available, easy to install, easy to use through GUI frontends and interfaces, interoperable across heterogeneous platforms, and ubiquitous in terms of information access.

The growing popularity of the Internet and the introduction of the Internet should not come as a surprise to corporate executives who are generally well read on such issues and tied into major information technology (IT) vendors and consultants. However, quite frequently companies continue to select one of two choices when considering the implementation of WWW and Internet technologies. Some companies, who are more technically astute and competitive, have jumped in totally and are exploiting Internet technologies, electronic commerce, and the use of the Web. Others, of a more conservative nature and more technically inexperienced, continue to maintain a hard-line policy on external connectivity, which basically continues to say "NO."

Internet technologies offer great potential for cost savings over existing technologies, representing huge investments over the years in terms of revenue and resources now supporting corporate information infrastructures and contributing to the business imperatives of those enterprises. Internet-based applications provide a standard communications interface and protocol suite ensuring interoperability and access to the organization's heterogeneous data and information resources. Most WWW browsers run on all systems and provide a common user interface and ease of use to a wide range of corporate employees.

Benefits derived from the development of WWW-based applications for internal and external use can be categorized by the cost savings related to deployment, generally requiring very little support or end-user training. The browser software is typically free, bundled in vendor product suites, or very affordable. Access to information, as previously stated, is ubiquitous and fairly straightforward.

Use of internal WWW applications can change the very way organizations interact and share information. When established and maintained properly, an internal WWW application can enable everyone on the internal network to share information resources, update common use applications, receive education and training, and keep in touch with colleagues at their home base, from remote locations, or on the road.

INTERNET/WWW SECURITY OBJECTIVES

As mentioned earlier, security requirements do not change with the introduction and use of these technologies, but the emphasis on where security is placed and how it is implemented does change. The company's Internet, intranet, and WWW security strategies should address the following objectives, in combination or in prioritized sequence, depending on security and access requirements, company philosophy, the relative sensitivity of the companys information resources, and the business imperative for using these technologies.

- Ensure that Internet- and WWW-based application and the resultant access to information resources are protected and that there is a cost-effective and user-friendly way to maintain and manage the underlying security components, over time as new technology evolves and security solutions mature in response.
- Information assets should be protected against unauthorized usage and destruction. Communication paths should be encrypted as well as transmitted information that is broadcast over public networks.
- Receipt of information from external sources should be decrypted and authenticated. Internet- and WWW-based applications, WWW pages, directories, discussion groups, and databases should all be secured using access control mechanisms.
- Security administration and overall support should accommodate a combination of centralized and decentralized management.
- User privileges should be linked to resources, with privileges to those resources managed and distributed through directory services.
- Mail and real-time communications should also be consistently protected. Encryption key management systems should be easy to administer, compliant with existing security architectures, compatible with existing security strategies and tactical plans, and secure to manage and administer.

- New security policies, security architectures, and control mechanisms should evolve to accommodate this new technology; not change in principle or design.

Continue to use risk management methodologies as a baseline for deciding how many of the new Internet, intranet, and WWW technologies to use and how to integrate them into the existing Information Security Distributed Architecture. As always, ensure that the optimum balance between access to information and protection of information is achieved during all phases of the development, integration, implementation, and operational support life cycle.

INTERNET AND WWW SECURITY POLICIES AND PROCEDURES

Having said all of this, it is clear that we need new and different policies, or minimally, an enhancement or refreshing of current policies supporting more traditional means of sharing, accessing, storing, and transmitting information. In general, high-level security philosophies, policies, and procedures should not change. In other words, who is responsible for what (the fundamental purpose of most high-level security policies) does not change. These policies are fundamentally directed at corporate management, process, application and system owners, functional area management, and those tasked with the implementation and support of the overall IT environment. There should be minimal changes to these policies, perhaps only adding the Internet and WWW terminology.

Other high level corporate policies must also be modified, such as the use of corporate assets, responsibility for sharing and protecting corporate information, etc. The second-level corporate policies, usually more procedure oriented typically addressing more of the "how," should be more closely scrutinized and may change the most when addressing the use of the Internet, intranet, and Web technologies for corporate business purposes. New classifications and categories of information may need to be established and new labeling mechanisms denoting a category of information that cannot be displayed on the Internet or new meanings to "all allow" or "public" data. The term "public," for instance, when used internally, usually means anyone authorized to use internal systems. In most companies, access to internal networks, computing systems, and information is severely restricted and "public" would not mean unauthorized users, and certainly not any user on the Internet.

Candidate lower-level policies and procedures for update to accommodate the Internet and WWW include external connectivity, network security, transmission of data, use of electronic commerce, sourcing and procurement, electronic mail, nonemployee use of corporate information and electronic systems, access to information, appropriate use of electronic systems, use of corporate assets, etc.

New policies and procedures (most likely enhancements to existing policies) highlight the new environment and present an opportunity to dust off and update old policies. Involve a broad group of customers and functional support areas in the update to these policies. The benefits are many. It exposes everyone to the issues surrounding the new technologies, the new security issues and challenges, and gains buy-in through the development and approval process from those who will have to comply when the policies are approved. It is also an excellent way to raise the awareness level and get attention to security up front.

The most successful corporate security policies and procedures address security at three levels, at the management level through high-level policies, at the functional level through security procedures and technical guidelines, and at the end-user level through user awareness and training guidelines. Consider the opportunity to create or update all three when implementing Internet, intranet, and WWW technologies.

Since these new technologies increase the level of risk and vulnerability to your corporate computing and network environment, security policies should probably be beefed up in the areas of audit and monitoring. This is particularly important because security and technical control mechanisms are not mature for the Internet and WWW and therefore more manual processes need to be put in place and mandated to ensure the protection of information.

The distributed nature of Internet, intranet, and WWW and their inherent security issues can be addressed at a more detailed level through an integrated set of policies, procedures, and technical guidelines. Because these policies and processes will be implemented by various functional support areas, there is a great need to obtain buy-in from these groups and ensure coordination and integration through all phases of the systems' life cycle. Individual and collective roles and responsibilities should be clearly delineated to include monitoring and enforcement.

Other areas to consider in the policy update include legal liabilities, risk to competition-sensitive information, employees' use of company time while "surfing" the Internet, use of company logos and trade names by employees using the Internet, defamation of character involving company employees, loss of trade secrets, loss of the competitive edge, ethical use of the Internet, etc.

DATA CLASSIFICATION SCHEME

A data classification scheme is important to both reflect existing categories of data and introduce any new categories of data needed to support the business use of the Internet, electronic commerce, and information sharing through new intranet and WWW technologies. The whole area of

Exhibit 1. Sample Data Protection Classification Hierarchy

	Auth.	Trans. Controls	Encryption	Audit	Ownership
External Public Data				(X)	X
Internal Public Data				(X)	X
Internal Cntl. Data	X	X	(X)	X	X
External Cntl. Data	X	X	X	X	X
Update Applications	X	X		X	X

nonemployee access to information changes the approach to categorizing and protecting company information.

The sample chart in Exhibit 1 is an example of how general to specific categories of company information can be listed, with their corresponding security and protection requirements to be used as a checklist by application, process, and data owners to ensure the appropriate level of protection, and also as a communication tool to functional area support personnel tasked with resource and information protection. A supplemental chart could include application and system names familiar to corporate employees, or types of general applications and information such as payroll, HR, marketing, manufacturing, etc.

Note that encryption may not be required for the same level of data classification in the mainframe and proprietary networking environment, but in "open" systems and distributed and global networks transmitted data are much more easily compromised. Security should be applied based on a thorough risk assessment considering the value of the information, the risk introduced by the computing and network environment, the technical control mechanisms feasible or available for implementation, and the ease of administration and management support. Be careful to apply the right "balance" of security. Too much is just as costly and ineffective as too little in most cases.

APPROPRIATE USE POLICY

It is important to communicate management's expectation for employee's use of these new technologies. An effective way to do that is to supplement the corporate policies and procedures with a more user-friendly bulletined list of requirements. The list should be specific, highlight employee expectations and outline what employees can and cannot do on the Internet, intranet, and WWW. The goal is to communicate with each and every employee, leaving little room for doubt or confusion. An Appropriate Use Policy (Exhibit 2) could achieve these goals and reinforce the higher level. Areas to address include the proper use of employee time, corporate computing and networking resources, and acceptable material to be viewed or downloaded to company resources.

Exhibit 2. Appropriate Use Policy

Examples of unacceptable use include but not limited to the following:

1.) Using Co. equipment, functions or services for non-business related activities while on company time; which in effect is mischarging;
2.) Using the equipment or services for financial or commercial gain;
3.) Using the equipment or services for any illegal activity;
4.) Dial-in usage from home for Internet services for personal gain;
5.) Accessing non-business related news groups or BBS;
6.) Willful intent to degrade or disrupt equipment, software or system performance;
7.) Vandalizing the data or information of another user;
8.) Gaining unauthorized access to resources or information;
9.) Invading the privacy of individuals;
10.) Masquerading as or using an account owned by another user;
11.) Posting anonymous messages or mail for malicious intent;
12.) Posting another employee's personal communication or mail without the original author's consent; this excludes normal business E-mail forwarding;
13.) Downloading, storing, printing or displaying files or messages that are profane, obscene, or that use language or graphics which offends or tends to degrade others;
14.) Transmitting company data over the network to non-company employees without following proper release procedures;
15.) Loading software obtained from outside the Corporation's standard company's procurement channels onto a company system without proper testing and approval;
16.) Initiating or forwarding electronic chain mail.

Examples of acceptable use includes but is not limited to the following:

1.) Accessing the Internet, computer resources, fax machines and phones for information directly related to your work assignment;
2.) Off-hour usage of computer systems for degree related school work where allowed by local site practices;
3.) Job related On-Job Training (OJT).

Most companies are concerned with the Telecommunications Act and their liabilities in terms of allowing employees to use the Internet on company time and with company resources. Most find that the trade-off is highly skewed to the benefit of the corporation in support of the utility of the Internet. Guidelines must be carefully spelled out and coordinated with the legal department to ensure that company liabilities are addressed through clear specification of roles and responsibilities. Most companies do not monitor their employee's use of the Internet or the intranet, but find that audit trail information is critical to prosecution and defense for computer crime.

Overall computer security policies and procedures are the baseline for any security architecture and the first thing to do when implementing any new technology. However, you are never really finished as the development and support of security policies is an iterative process and should be revisited on an ongoing basis to ensure that they are up-to-date, accommodate new technologies, address current risk levels, and reflect the company's use of information and network and computing resources.

There are four basic threats to consider when you begin to use Internet, intranet, and Web technologies:

- Unauthorized alteration of data
- Unauthorized access to the underlying operating system
- Eavesdropping on messages passed between a server and a browser
- Impersonation

Your security strategies should address all four. These threats are common to any technology in terms of protecting information. In the remainder of this chapter, we will build upon the "general good security practices and traditional security management" discussed in the first section and apply these lessons to the technical implementation of security and control mechanisms in the Internet, intranet, and Web environments.

The profile of a computer hacker is changing with the exploitation of Internet and Web technologies. Computerized bulletin board services and network chat groups link computer hackers (formerly characterized as loners and misfits) together. Hacker techniques, programs and utilities, and easy-to-follow instructions are readily available on the net. This enables hackers to more quickly assemble the tools to steal information and break into computers and networks, and it also provides the "would-be" hacker a readily available arsenal of tools.

INTERNAL/EXTERNAL APPLICATIONS

Most companies segment their networks and use firewalls to separate the internal and external networks. Most have also chosen to push their marketing, publications, and services to the public side of the firewall using file servers and web servers. There are benefits and challenges to each of these approaches. It is difficult to keep data synchronized when duplicating applications outside the network. It is also difficult to ensure the security of those applications and the integrity of the information. Outside the firewall is simply *outside*, and therefore also outside the protections of the internal security environment. It is possible to protect that information and the underlying system through the use of new security technologies for authentication and authorization. These techniques are not without trade-offs in terms of cost and ongoing administration, management, and support.

Security goals for external applications that bridge the gap between internal and external, and for internal applications using the Internet, intranet, and WWW technologies should all address these traditional security controls:

- Authentication
- Authorization
- Access control
- Audit
- Security administration

Some of what you already used can be ported to the new environment, and some of the techniques and supporting infrastructure already in place supporting mainframe-based applications can be applied to securing the new technologies.

Using the Internet and other public networks is an attractive option, not only for conducting business-related transactions and electronic commerce, but also for providing remote access for employees, sharing information with business partners and customers, and supplying products and services. However, public networks create added security challenges for IS management and security practitioners, who must devise security systems and solutions to protect company computing, networking, and information resources. Security is a CRITICAL component.

Two watchdog groups are trying to protect on-line businesses and consumers from hackers and fraud. The council of Better Business Bureaus has launched BBBOnline, a service that provides a way to evaluate the legitimacy of on-line businesses. In addition, the national computer security association, NCSA, launched a certification program for secure WWW sites. Among the qualities that NCSA looks for in its certification process are extensive logging, the use of encryption including those addressed in this chapter, and authentication services.

There are a variety of protection measures that can be implemented to reduce the threats in the Web/server environment, making it more acceptable for business use. Direct server protection measures include secure Web server products which use differing designs to enhance the security over user access and data transmittal. In addition to enhanced secure Web server products, the Web server network architecture can also be addressed to protect the server and the corporate enterprise which could be placed in a vulnerable position due to served enabled connectivity. Both secure server and secure web server designs will be addressed, including the application and benefits to using each.

WHERE ARE YOUR USERS?

Discuss how the access point where your users reside contributes to the risk and the security solutions set. Discuss the challenge when users are all over the place and you have to rely on remote security services that are only as good as the users' correct usage. Issues of evolving technologies can also be addressed. Concerns for multiple layering of controls and dis-

Where are your Users?

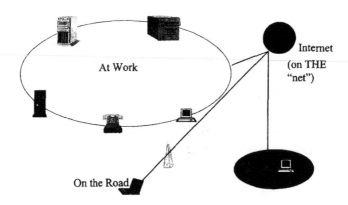

Exhibit 3.   Where are your users?

---

satisfied users with layers of security controls, passwords, hoops, etc. can also be addressed (Exhibit 3).

WEB BROWSER SECURITY STRATEGIES

Ideally, Web browser security strategies should use a network-based security architecture that integrates your company's external Internet and the internal intranet security policies. Ensure that users on any platform, with any browser, can access any system from any location if they are authorized and have a "need-to-know." Be careful not to adopt the latest evolving security product from a new vendor or an old vendor capitalizing on a hot marketplace.

Recognizing that the security environment is changing rapidly, and knowing that we don't want to change our security strategy, architecture, and control mechanisms every time a new product or solution emerges, we need to take time and use precautions when devising browser security solutions. It is sometimes a better strategy to stick with the vendors that you have already invested in and negotiate with them to enhance their existing products, or even contract with them to make product changes specific or tailored to accommodate your individual company requirements. Be careful in these negotiations as it is extremely likely that other companies have the very same requirements. User groups can also form a common position and interface to vendors for added clout and pressure.

You can basically secure your web server as much as or as little as you wish with the current available security products and technologies. The tradeoffs are obvious: cost, management, administrative requirements, and time. Solutions can be hardware, software and personnel intensive.

Enhancing the security of the web server itself has been a paramount concern since the first Web server initially emerged, but progress has been slow in deployment and implementation. As the market has mushroomed for server use, and the diversity of data types that are being placed on the server has grown, the demand has increased for enhanced Web server security. Various approaches have emerged, with no single *de facto* standard yet emerging (though there are some early leaders — among them Secure Sockets Layer [SSL] and Secure Hypertext Transfer Protocol [S-HTTP]). These are two significantly different approaches, but both widely seen in the marketplace.

Secure Socket Layer (SSL) Trust Model

One of the early entrants into the secure Web server and client arena is Netscape's Commerce Server, which utilizes the Secure Sockets Layer (SSL) trust model. This model is built around the RSA Public Key/Private Key architecture. Under this model, the SSL-enabled server is authenticated to SSL-aware clients, proving its identity at each SSL connection. This proof of identity is conducted through the use of a public/private key pair issued to the server validated with x.509 digital certificates. Under the SSL architecture, web server validation can be the only validation performed, which may be all that is needed in some circumstances. This would be applicable for those applications where it is important to the user to be assured of the identity of the target server, such as when placing company orders, or other information submittal where the client is expecting some important action to take place. Exhibit 4 diagrams this process.

Optionally, SSL sessions can be established that also authenticate the client and encrypt the data transmission between the client and the server for multiple I/P services (HTTP, Telnet, FTP). The multiservice encryption capability is available because SSL operates below the application layer and above the TCP/IP connection layer in the protocol stack, and thus other TCP/IP services can operate on top of a SSL-secured session.

Optionally, authentication of a SSL client is available when the client is registered with the SSL server, and occurs after the SSL-aware client connects and authenticates the SSL server. The SSL client then submits its digital certificate to the SSL server, where the SSL server validates the clients certificate and proceeds to exchange a session key to provide encrypted transmissions between the client and the server. Exhibit 5 provides a graphical representation of this process for mutual client and server authentication under the SSL architecture. This type of mutual client/server authentication process should be considered when the data being submitted

Server Authentication

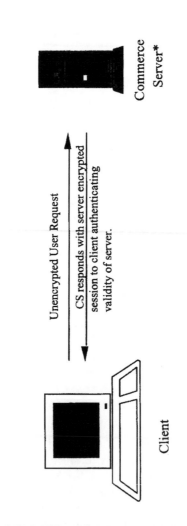

Client

Unencrypted User Request

CS responds with server encrypted session to client authenticating validity of server.

Commerce Server*

*Server may hold its own certificate internally

Exhibit 4. Server authentication.

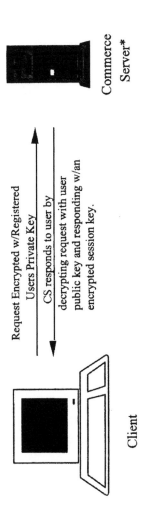

Client & Server Authentication

Request Encrypted w/Registered
Users Private Key

CS responds to user by
decrypting request with user
public key and responding w/an
encrypted session key.

Commerce
Server*

Client

*Assumes CS has access to a key directory
server, most likely LDAP compliant.

Exhibit 5. Client and server authentication.

by the client are sensitive enough to warrant encryption prior to being submitted over a network transmission path.

Though there are some "costs" with implementing this architecture, these cost variables must be considered when proposing a SSL server implementation to enhance your web server security. First of all, the design needs to consider whether to only provide server authentication, or both server and client authentication. The issue when expanding the authentication to include client authentication includes the administrative overhead of managing the user keys, including a key revocation function. This consideration, of course, has to assess the size of the user base, potential for growth of your user base, and stability of your proposed user community. All of these factors will impact the administrative burden of key management, especially if there is the potential for a highly unstable or transient user community.

The positive considerations for implementing a SSL-secured server is the added ability to secure other I/P services for remote or external SSL clients. SSL-registered clients now have the added ability to communicate securely by utilizing Tenet and FTP (or other I/P services) after passing SSL client authentication and receiving their session encryption key. In general the SSL approach has very broad benefits, but these benefits come with the potential added burden of higher administration costs, though if the value of potential data loss is great, then it is easily offset by the administration cost identified above.

Secure Hypertext Transfer Protocol (S-HTTP)

Secure Hypertext Transfer Protocol, (S-HTTP) is emerging as another security tool and incorporates a flexible trust model for providing secure web server and client HTTP communications. It is specifically designed for direct integration into HTTP transactions, with its focus on flexibility for establishing secure communications in a HTTP environment while providing transaction confidentiality, authenticity/integrity, and nonrepudiation. S-HTTP incorporates a great deal of flexibility in its trust model by leaving defined variable fields in the header definition which identifies the trust model or security algorithm to be used to enable a secure transaction. S-HTTP can support symmetric or asymmetric keys, and even a Kerberos-based trust model. The intention of the authors was to build a flexible protocol that supports multiple trusted modes, key management mechanisms, and cryptographic algorithms through clearly defined negotiation between parties for specific transactions.

At a high level the transactions can begin in a untrusted mode (standard HTTP communication), and "setup" of a trust model can be initiated so that the client and the server can negotiate a trust model, such as a symmetric key-based model on a previously agreed-upon symmetric key, to begin encrypted authentication and communication. The advantage of a S-HTTP-enabled server is the high degree of flexibility in securely communicating with web clients. A single server, if appropriately configured and network enabled, can support multiple trust models under the S-HTTP architecture and serve multiple client types. In addition to being able to serve a flexible user base, it can also be used to address multiple data classifications on a single server where some data types require higher-level encryption or protection than other data types on the same server and therefore varying trust models could be utilized.

The S-HTTP model provides flexibility in its secure transaction architecture, but focuses on HTTP transaction vs. SSL which mandates the trust model of a public/private key security model, which can be used to address multiple I/P services. But the S-HTTP mode is limited to only HTTP communications.

INTERNET, INTRANET, AND WORLD WIDE WEB SECURITY ARCHITECTURES

Implementing a secure server architecture, where appropriate, should also take into consideration the existing enterprise network security architecture and incorporate the secure server as part of this overall architecture. In order to discuss this level of integration, we will make an assumption that the secure web server is to provide secure data dissemination for external (outside the enterprise) distribution and/or access. A discussion of such a network security architecture would not be complete without addressing the placement of the Web server in relation to the enterprise firewall (the firewall being the dividing line between the protected internal enterprise environment and the external "public" environment).

Setting the stage for this discussion calls for some identification of the requirements, so the following list outlines some sample requirements for this architectural discussion on integrating a secure HTTP server with an enterprise firewall.

- Remote client is on public network accessing sensitive company data.
- Remote client is required to authenticate prior to receiving data.
- Remote client only accesses data via HTTP.
- Data is only updated periodically.
- Host site maintains firewall.
- Sensitive company data must be encrypted on public networks.
- Company support personnel can load HTTP server from inside the enterprise.

Based on these high-level requirements, an architecture could be set up that would place a S-HTTP server external to the firewall, with one-way communications from inside the enterprise "to" the external server to per-

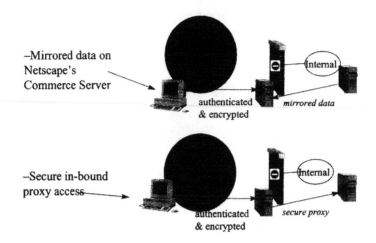

-Mirrored data on
Netscape's
Commerce Server

authenticated
& encrypted

mirrored data

-Secure in-bound
proxy access

authenticated
& encrypted

secure proxy

Exhibit 6. Externally placed server.

form routine administration, and periodic data updates. Remote users would access the S-HTTP server utilizing specified S-HTTP secure transaction modes, and be required to identify themselves to the server prior to being granted access to secure data residing on the server. Exhibit 6 depicts this architecture at a high level. This architecture would support a secure HTTP distribution of sensitive company data, but doesn't provide absolute protection due to the placement of the S-HTTP server entirely external to the protected enterprise. There are some schools of thought that since this server is unprotected by the company-controlled firewall, the S-HTTP server itself is vulnerable, thus risking the very control mechanism itself and the data residing on it. The opposing view on this is that the risk to the overall enterprise is minimized, as only this server is placed at risk and its own protection is the S-HTTP process itself. This process has been a leading method to secure the data, without placing the rest of the enterprise at risk, by placing the S-HTTP server logically and physically outside the enterprise security firewall.

A slightly different architecture has been advertised that would position the S-HTTP server inside the protected domain, as Exhibit 7 indicates. The philosophy behind this architecture is that the controls of the firewall (and inherent audits) are strong enough to control the authorized access to the S-HTTP server, and also thwart any attacks against the server itself. Additionally, the firewall can control external users so that they only have S-HTTP access via a logically dedicated path, and only to the designated S-HTTP server itself, without placing the rest of the internal enterprise at risk. This architecture relies on the absolute ability of the firewall and S-HTTP of always performing their designated security function as defined;

authenticated
& encrypted

Exhibit 7.   Internally placed server.

---

otherwise, the enterprise has been opened for attack through the allowed path from external users to the internal S-HTTP server. Because these conditions are always required to be true and intact, the model with the server external to the firewall has been more readily accepted and implemented.

Both of these architectures can offer a degree of data protection in a S-HTTP architecture when integrated with the existing enterprise firewall architecture. As an aid in determining which architectural approach is right for a given enterprise, a risk assessment can provide great input to the decision. This risk assessment may include decision points such as:

- Available resources to maintain a high degree of firewall audit and S-HTTP server audit.
- Experience in firewall and server administration.
- Strength of their existing firewall architecture.

SECURE WWW CLIENT CONFIGURATION

There is much more reliance on the knowledge and cooperation of the end user and the use of a combination of desktop and workstation software, security control parameters within client software, and security products all working together to mimic the security of the mainframe and distributed application's environments. Consider the areas below during the risk assessment process and the design of WWW security solution sets.

- Ensure that all internal and external company-used workstations have resident and active antivirus software products installed. Preferably use a minimum number of vendor products to reduce security support and vulnerabilities as there are varying vendor schedules for providing virus signature updates.
- Ensure that all workstation and browser client software is preconfigured to return all WWW and other external file transfers to temporary files on the desktop. Under no circumstances should client server applications or process-to-process automated routines download files to system files, preference files, bat files, start-up files, etc.

- Ensure that Java script is turned off in the browser client software desktop configuration.
- Configure browser client software to automatically flush the cache, either upon closing the browser or disconnecting from each Web site.
- When possible or available, implement one of the new security products that scans WWW downloads for viruses.
- Provide user awareness and education to all desktop WWW and Internet users to alert them to the inherent dangers involved in using the Internet and WWW. Include information on detecting problems, their roles and responsibilities, your expectations, security products available, how to set and configure their workstations and program products, etc.
- Suggest or mandate the use of screen savers, security software programs, etc., in conjunction with your security policies and distributed security architectures.

This is a list of current areas of concern from a security perspective. There are options that when combined can tailor the browser to the specifications of individual workgroups or individuals. These options will evolve with the browser technology. The list should continue to be modified as security problems are corrected or as new problems occur.

AUDIT TOOLS AND CAPABILITIES

As we move further and further from the "good old days" when we were readily able to secure the "glass house," we rely more on good and sound auditing practices. As acknowledged throughout this chapter, security control mechanisms are mediocre at best in today's distributed networking and computing environments. Today's auditing strategies must be robust, available across multiple heterogeneous platforms, computing and network based, real-time and automated, and integrated across the enterprise.

Today, information assets are distributed all over the enterprise, and therefore auditing strategies must acknowledge and accept this challenge and accommodate more robust and dicey requirements. As is the case when implementating distributed security control mechanisms, in the audit environment there are also many players and functional support areas involved in collecting, integrating, synthesizing, reporting, and reconciling audit trails and audit information. The list includes applications and applications developers and programs, database management systems and database administrators, operating systems and systems administrators, local area network (LAN) administrators and network operating systems (NOS), security administrators and security software products, problem reporting and tracking systems and helpline administrators, and others unique to the company's environment.

As well as real-time, the audit system should provide for tracking and alarming, both to the systems and network management systems, and via pagers to support personnel. Policies and procedures should be developed for handling alarms and problems, i.e., isolate and monitor, disconnect, etc.

There are many audit facilities available today, including special audit software products for the Internet, distributed client server environments, WWW clients and servers, Internet firewalls, E-mail, News Groups, etc. The application of one or more of these must be consistent with your risk assessment, security requirements, technology availability, etc. The most important point to make here is the fundamental need to centralize distributed systems auditing (not an oxymoron). Centrally collect, sort, delete, process, report, take action and store critical audit information. Automate any and all steps and processes. It is a well-established fact that human beings cannot review large numbers of audit records and logs and reports without error. Today's audit function is an adjunct to the security function, and as such is more important and critical than ever before. It should be part of the overall security strategy and implementation plan.

The overall audit solutions set should incorporate the use of browser access logs, enterprise security server audit logs, network and firewall system authentication server audit logs, application and middle-ware audit logs, URL filters and access information, mainframe system audit information, distributed systems operating system audit logs, database management system audit logs, and other utilities that provide audit trail information such as accounting programs, network management products, etc.

The establishment of auditing capabilities over WWW environments follows closely with the integration of all external WWW servers with the firewall, as previously mentioned. This is important when looking at the various options available to address a comprehensive audit approach.

WWW servers can offer a degree of auditability based on the operating system of the server on which they reside. The more time-tested environments such as UNIX are perceived to be difficult to secure, whereas the emerging NT platform with its enhanced security features supposedly make it a more secure and trusted platform with a wide degree of audit tools and capabilities (though the vote is still out on NT, as some feel it hasn't had the time and exposure to discover all the potential security holes, perceived or real). The point, though, is that in order to provide some auditing the first place to potentially implement the first audit is on the platform where the WWW server resides. Issues here are the use of privileged accounts and file logs and access logs for log-ins to the operating system, which could indicate a backdoor attack on the WWW server itself. If server-based log are utilized, they of course must be file protected and should be off-loaded to a nonserver-based machine to protect against after-the-fact corruption.

Though the server logs aren't the only defensive logs that should be relied upon in a public WWW server environment, the other components in the access architecture should be considered for use as audit log tools. As previously mentioned, the WWW server should be placed in respect to its required controls in relation to the network security firewall. If it is a S-HTTP server that is placed behind (Exhibit 4) the firewall then the firewall of course has the ability to log all access to the S-HTTP server and provide a log separate from the WWW server-based logs, and is potentially more secure should the WWW server somehow become compromised.

The prevalent security architecture places externally accessible WWW servers wholly outside the firewall, thus virtually eliminating the capability of auditing access to the WWW server except from users internal to the enterprise. In this case, the network security audit in the form of the network management tool, which monitors the "health" of enterprise components can be called upon to provide a minimal degree of audit over the status of your external WWW server. This type of audit can be important when protecting data which resides on your external server from being subject to "denial of service" attacks, which are not uncommon for external devices. But by utilizing your network management tool to guard against such attacks, and monitoring log alerts on the status or health of this external server, you can reduce the exposure to this type of attack.

Other outside devices that can be utilized to provide audit include the network router between the external WWW server and the true external environment, though these devices are not normally readily set up for comprehensive audit logs, but in some critical cases they could be reconfigured with added hardware and minimal customized programming. One such example would be the "I/P Accounting" function on a popular router product line, which allows off-loading of addresses and protocols through its external interface. This could be beneficial to analyze traffic, and if an attack alert was generated from one of the other logs mentioned, then these router logs could assist in possibly identifying the origin of the attack.

Another possible source of audit logging could come from "back end" systems that the WWW server is programmed to "mine" data from. Many WWW environments are being established to serve as "front ends" for much larger data repositories, such as Oracle databases, where the WWW server receives user requests for data over HTTP, and the WWW server launches SQL_Net queries to a back end Oracle database. In this type of architecture the more developed logging inherent to the Oracle environment can be called upon to provide audits over the WWW queries. The detailed Oracle logs can specify the quantity, data type, and other activity over all the queries that the WWW server has made, thus providing a comprehensive activity log that can be consolidated and reviewed should any type of WWW server compromise be suspected. A site could potentially discover the degree of data exposure though these logs.

These are some of the major areas where auditing can be put in place to monitor the WWW environment while enhancing its overall security. It is important to note that the potential placement of audits encompasses the entire distributed computing infrastructure environment, not just the new WWW server itself. In fact, there are some schools of thought that consider the more reliable audits to be those that are somewhat distanced from the target server, thus reducing the potential threat of compromise to the audit logs themselves. In general, the important point is to look at the big picture when designing the security controls and a supporting audit solution.

WWW/Internet Audit Considerations

After your distributed Internet, intranet, and WWW security policies are firmly established, distributed security architectures are updated to accommodate this new environment. When planning for audit, and security control mechanisms are designed and implemented, you should plan how you will implement the audit environment — not only which audit facilities to use to collect and centralize the audit function, but how much and what type of information to capture, how to filter and review the audit data and logs, and what actions to take on the violations or anomalies identified. Additional consideration should be given to secure storage and access to the audit data. Other considerations include:

- Timely resolution of violations.
- Disk space storage availability.
- Increased staffing and administration.
- In-house developed programming.
- Ability to alarm and monitor in real time.

WWW SECURITY FLAWS

As with all new and emerging technology, many initial releases come with some deficiency. But this has been of critical importance when that deficiency can impact the access or corruption of a whole corporation or enterprise's display to the world. This can be the case with Web implementations utilizing the most current releases which have been found to contain some impacting code deficiencies, though up to this point most of these deficiencies have been identified before any major damage has been done. This underlines the need to maintain a strong link or connection with industry organizations that announce code shortcomings that impact a sites Web implementation. A couple of the leading organizations are CERT, the Computer Emergency Response Team, and CIAC, Computer Incident Advisory Capability.

Just a few of these types of code or design issues that could impact a sites web security include initial issues with the Sun JAVA language and Netscapes JavaScript (which is an extension library of their HyperText Markup Language, HTML).

The Sun Java language was actually designed with some aspects of security in mind, though upon its initial release there were several functions that were found to be a security risk. One of the most impacting bugs in an early release was the ability to execute arbitrary machine instructions by loading a malicious Java applet. By utilizing Netscape's caching mechanism a malicious machine instruction can be downloaded into a user's machine and Java can be tricked into executing it. This doesn't present a risk to the enterprise server, but the user community within one's enterprise is of course at risk.

Other Sun Java language bugs include the ability to make network connections with arbitrary hosts (though this has since been patched with the following release) and Java's ability to launch denial of service attacks through the use of corrupt applets.

These types of security holes are more prevalent than the security profession would like to believe, as the JavaScript environment also was found to contain capabilities that allowed malicious functions to take place. The following three are among the most current and prevalent risks:

- JavaScripts ability to trick the user into uploading a file on his local hard disk to an arbitrary machine on the Internet.
- The ability to hand out the user's directory listing from the internal hard disk.
- The ability to monitor all pages the user visits during a session.

The following are among the possible protection mechanisms:

- Maintain monitoring through CERT or CIAC, or other industry organizations that highlight such security risks.
- Utilize a strong software distribution and control capability, so that early releases aren't immediately distributed, and that new patched code known to fix a previous bug is released when deemed safe.
- In sensitive environments it may become necessary to disable the browsers capability to even utilize or execute Java or JavaScript — a selectable function now available in many browsers.

In the last point, it can be disturbing to some in the user community to disallow the use of such powerful tools, because they can be utilized against trusted Web pages, or those that require authentication through the use of SSL or S-HTTP. This approach can be coupled with the connection to S-HTTP pages where the target page has to prove its identity to the client user. In this case, enabling Java or JavaScripts to execute on the browser (a user-selectable option) could be done with a degree of confidence.

Other perceived security risks exist in a browser feature referred to as HTTP "Cookies." This is a feature that allows servers to store information on the client machine in order to reduce the store and retrieve requirements of the server. The cookies file can be written to by the server, and that server, in theory, is the only one that can read back their cookies entry. Uses of the cookie file include storing user's preferences or browser history on a particular server or page, which can assist in guiding the user on their next visit to that same page. The entry in the cookies file identifies the information to be stored and the uniform resource locator (URL) or server page that can read back that information, though this address can be masked to some degree so multiple pages can read back the information.

The perceived security concern is that pages impersonating cookies-readable pages could read back a users cookies information without the user knowing it, or discover what information is stored in their cookie file. The threat depends on the nature of the data stored in the cookie file, which is dependent on what the server chooses to write into a user's cookie file. This issue is currently under review, with the intention of adding additional security controls to the cookie file and its function. At this point it is important that users are aware of the existence of this file, which is viewable in the Macintosh environment as a Netscape file and in the Win environment as a cookies.txt file. There are already some inherent protections in the cookie file: one is the fact that the cookie file currently has a maximum of 20 entries, which potentially limits the exposure. Also, these entries can be set up with expiration dates to they don't have an unlimited lifetime.

WWW SECURITY MANAGEMENT

Consider the overall management of the Internet, intranet, and WWW environment. As previously mentioned, there are many players in the support role and for many of them this is not their primary job or priority. Regardless of where the following items fall in the support infrastructure, also consider these points when implementing ongoing operational support:

- Implement WWW browser and server standards.
- Control release and version distribution.
- Implement secure server administration including the use of products and utilities to erase sensitive data cache (NSClean).
- Ensure prompt problem resolution, management, and notification.
- Follow industry and vendor discourse on WWW security flaws and bugs including CERT distribution.
- Stay current on new Internet and WWW security problems, Netscape encryption, JAVA, Cookies, etc.

WWW SUPPORT INFRASTRUCTURE

- WWW servers accessible from external networks should reside outside the firewall and be managed centrally.
- By special approval, decentralized programs can manage external servers, but must do so in accordance with corporate policy and be subjected to rigorous audits.
- Externally published company information must be cleared through legal and public relations departments (i.e., follow company procedures).
- External outbound http access should utilize proxy services for additional controls and audit.
- WWW application updates must be authenticated utilizing standard company security systems (as required).
- Filtering and monitoring software must be incorporated into the firewall.
- The use of discovery crawler programs must be monitored and controlled.
- Virus software must be active on all desktop systems utilizing WWW.
- Externally published information should be routinely updated or verified through integrity checks.

In conclusion, as information security practitioners embracing the technical challenges of the twenty-first century, we are continually challenged to integrate new technology smoothly into our existing and underlying security architectures. Having a firm foundation or set of security principles, frameworks, philosophies and supporting policies, procedures, technical architectures, etc. will assist in the transition and our success.

Approach new technologies by developing processes to manage the integration and update the security framework and supporting infrastructure, as opposed to changing it. The Internet, intranet, and the World Wide Web is exploding around us — what is new today is old technology tomorrow. We should continue to acknowledge this fact while working aggressively with other MIS and customer functional areas to slow down the train to progress, be realistic, disciplined, and plan for new technology deployment.

Section V
Data Migration, Conversion, and Legacy Applications

ALL THE CHAPTERS CONTAINED IN THIS SECTION are of increasing relevance to the information technology (IT) industry due to the globalization of many corporations and the continuing mega-mergers. This results in the need to reengineer business processes, consolidate the organization, and consolidate the data sources. This is done through data migration and conversions and by building bridges to legacy applications.

Data migration refers to the process of migrating or transferring data from one source to another over a project development life cycle. Conversion generally refers to a one-way movement of data. Data conversion involves several steps. Data mapping involves identifying relationships between data items in one system to the data items in another system. The quality of the data being converted always must be determined with extensive user involvement. Data can be corrupt or may require translation to other values. Data scrubbing is a process used to correct the data as or after it is converted. It is imperative to build control reports to keep a running audit trail of any data conversion cycle.

Legacy applications contain most of the data in the world. They involve trillions and trillions of bytes of data. At the first emergence of client/server architecture, projects relied heavily on converting legacy data for the new systems to leverage. The last few years have seen the emergence of data gateways and bridges that accept standard ANSI SQL-type requests to access legacy data in the legacy applications and to return this to other applications.

This section contains four chapters with the following focuses:

Chapter 25, "A Practical Example of Data Conversion," looks at opportunities for categorizing data conversions to remove much of the fear, apprehension, and stagnation that face many data conversion projects. The approach that is defined includes iteration and strong controls. With the number of corporate acquisitions, mergers, and system replacements, it is expected that data conversions are going to become even more common in the industry.

Chapter 26, "Legacy Database Conversion," describes planning activities that the data center manager can undertake to identify and reduce risks associated with converting legacy, nonrelational data to a relational format.

Chapter 27, "Data Conversion: Doing it Right the First Time," describes common problems with data, outlines steps for performing a successful conversion, and suggests methods for correcting errors detected during conversion.

Chapter 28, "Migrating Files to Relational Databases," provides guidelines to determine when and how to migrate files and associated applications to a Relational Database Management System (RDMS).

Chapter 25
A Practical Example of Data Conversion

Charles Banyay

CONVERSION, THE WORD IS ENOUGH TO DIM THE ENTHUSIASM of most systems developers. The word instills fear in some, trepidation and loathing in others. Regardless of the nature of the project with which she/he is involved, if there is any conversion effort involved, the reaction is the same. Exclude it from project scope! Let someone else do it! Although some might suspect that there may be some religious connotation here, and rightly so, the topic of this chapter is not converting from one religion to another. Nor is the topic software conversion, although this would be closer to the mark. This chapter deals with the various forms of the conversion of data.

Even if the project promises to be primarily development and/or implementation, which is usually the dream of most developers. Even if it involves some of the latest state-of-the-art technology, the word conversion immediately throws a pall over all the luster and glitter, and hopes of an interesting endeavor. Most systems implementations involve some form of conversion. When the software changes, the data model or the data itself often changes with it.

For some reason, conversions have come to be associated with the mundane, boring, and tiresome aspects of systems implementation. Most developers would consider conversion efforts as boring, tiresome, and devoid of interesting challenges, when compared to the implementation of state-of-the-art technology.

This is a misconception in many instances. Conversion efforts can be as challenging as any state-of-the-art technology. They can exercise the most creative abilities of technology professionals. An entire chapter probably could be devoted to discussing the possible reasons behind the general lack of enthusiasm for the conversion effort. This chapter, however, will focus on examining the following:

0-8493-9976-9/99/$0.00+$.50
© 1999 by CRC Press LLC

- Different types of conversion efforts that one encounters during systems implementation projects.
- The taxonomy of the conversion effort.
- Common pitfalls that can have rather detrimental effects on the overall effort if one is not aware of them and does not take the necessary precautions before hand.

CLASSIFYING DATA CONVERSIONS

There are a number of different ways to classify a data conversion. One of the most common ways is to classify it by what is involved in the conversion effort. This could be one or more of the following:

- Converting from one hardware platform to another, e.g., a host system upgrade (on PCs this is done on a matter-of-fact basis almost daily).
- Converting from one operating system to another, e.g., UNIX to NT.
- Converting from one file access method to another, e.g., converting from an indexed or flat file structure into a DBMS.
- Converting from one coding structure or format to another, e.g., from EBCDIC to ASCII.
- Converting application software such as upgrading versions of an application or replacing one application with another as in replacing an outmoded payroll application with a state-of-the-art pay benefits system.

One of the most common pitfalls of conversions is to combine into one conversion effort a change of too many variables, e.g., changing hardware, operating system(s), file access method(s), and application software all at once. Sometimes this cannot be avoided. Ideally, however, as few as possible of the variables should be changed at once. With only one variable changing, error detection and correction is the simplest. Any problem can be attributed to the change of the single variable and, thus, can be rectified by analyzing the single variable. With combinations and permutations, the effort increases exponentially.

Unfortunately, as often happens in life, the ideal state is the exception. In general, it is a rare conversion that does not have some combination of the above variables changing at once. The taxonomy of each, however, can be explored individually, as can most of the pitfalls. Some combinations will have unique pitfalls simply due to the combination of changes in variables.

CHANGE IN HARDWARE

In general, the simplest conversion is upgrading hardware, assuming that all of the other variables remain constant, i.e., operating systems, file access method, coding structure and format, and application software. This can be illustrated best in the PC world. PCs have been upgraded with relative ease continuously from one configuration to another for the past 10 years. As long as the operating system does not change the upgrade in hardware usually involves nothing more than copying the files from one hard disk to another. This migration of files usually is accomplished with the assistance of some standard utilities. Using utilities rather than custom-developed software lowers the amount of effort involved in ensuring that the files have migrated successfully. Most utilities provide fairly good audit trails for this purpose. Even files on the same floppies can be used in a 286, 386, 486, or Pentium machine. Data on floppies does not require any conversion.

In environments other than personal computers, the same simplicity of conversion generally holds true. Upgrading from one configuration of mainframe to another is relatively easy. Changing configurations of a minicomputer, such as from one AS/400 to a more powerful configuration of the same or from one HP/3000 to a more powerful HP/3000, generally does not require significant effort. These kinds of conversions generally are imperceptible to the users and are done without much involvement from the user community. There usually is no requirement for any user testing or programmer testing. This cannot be said for the more complex conversions such as changes in the operating system.

MIGRATING FROM ONE OPERATING SYSTEM TO ANOTHER

Changes to the operating system are generally more complicated from a conversion perspective, than changes to hardware. The complexity, however, is usually more pronounced at the application software rather than the data level. There is considerable insulation by the operating system of the application software and associated data from the hardware. In general, there is little to insulate the application software from the operating system. Object-oriented approaches are slowly changing this fact, but for now it is safe to say that a change in operating system requires a more complex conversion effort than a change in hardware.

For individuals who primarily have limited their involvement with technology to the WINTEL world, conversion complexity due to changes in operating system may come as a surprise. In the WINTEL world one generally can change from DOS to Windows 3.x to Windows 95 (or higher) with little or limited problems. In fact, most users do this on a regular basis. This may imply that changes in operating system are as simple as changes in hardware. This is a misconception. The people at Microsoft® and to a limited extent at Intel have spent innumerable hours to ensure that there exists a degree of compatibility between these operating systems that does not exist in any other environment.

Even in the WINTEL world this compatibility is breaking down. As the move to NT accelerates this is becoming evident. Users moving to NT have discovered that many of their favorite software programs are not functioning as they would like them to, or the programs are not functioning at all.

Although some form of conversion effort usually is involved when operating systems are changed, the changes in operating system more definitely impact the application software than the data. The impact on any of the data is usually from indirect sources such as from a change in one of the other variables such as data format or file access method. Different operating systems may support only different data coding structures and/or different file access methods.

CHANGES IN FILE ACCESS METHOD

It is not often that one changes a file access method while leaving the operating system and the application system the same. The general reasons for doing this would be suspect unless the current file access method was being abandoned by whomever was providing support. Another valid reason for changing file access method may be if a packaged application system vendor released a new version of their application. This new version may offer a new data architecture such as an RDBMS. There may be valid reasons, such as better-reporting capability using third-party tools, for upgrading to this new version with the RDBMS. For whatever the reason, a change in file access method usually requires some form of change in data architecture.

A simple illustration of this change in the underlying data architecture would be in converting a flat file sequential access method to an indexed file access method. Some form of indexing would have to be designed into the file structure resulting in a change in the underlying data architecture. A more complex example would be in changing from a sequential access method to a database management system.

This change at the minimum would involve some degree of data normalization and a break up of the single segment or record structure of the file. The resultant change in data architecture would be quite substantive. This type of conversion generally is not simple and requires a comprehensive conversion utility. In the case where it is a packaged application being upgraded, the vendor probably would provide the conversion utility. In the case where a custom-developed application is being converted, the conversion utility probably would have to be custom-developed as well.

In either case, the tasks are straightforward. All of the data must be converted. Every record must have a corresponding entry or entries in some table or tables. Each field in the source file needs to be transferred to the target database. Field conversion is not required. There is only a limited degree of selection involved. The conversion utility is run against the source data to create the target data store. Often there are a number of intermediate steps. Different tables or segments of the database may be created in different steps. The resultant data is verified at each step. Taking a step-by-step approach, one can minimize the number and extent of the reruns of the conversion. This is another example of minimizing the number of variables that can change at once.

There are a number of approaches to ensuring that the resultant data store has the required integrity. These approaches are identical to the ones used to ensure the integrity of data that is converted due to a change in the application software.

The extent of the effort depends on the degree of reliability that is required. The effort has an obvious cost. The lack of data integrity also has a cost. A financial system requires a high degree of data integrity. It can be argued that the data controlling the operation of a nuclear power station requires even a higher degree of integrity.

MIGRATING FROM ONE APPLICATION SYSTEM TO ANOTHER

Changing or upgrading applications always requires converting data from the old to the new application. These conversions are generally the most complex and require the most effort.

One of the first steps in the conversion process is to decide which is the driving application. What is most important in the conversion process? Being exhaustive in converting the data in the old application or ensuring that the new application has the required fields that it needs to operate effectively. This may not be intuitively obvious. This is not to imply that the decision as to which data to convert is at the whim of the person designing the conversion programs.

There is always a base amount of data that must be converted. Many old applications, however, accumulate various codes and indicators over the years that either lose meaning over time or are particular to that application and are not required in a new application. This situation is more particular to operational applications such as payroll, materials management, etc. When converting data in an operational application, the emphasis is on converting the minimum amount of current data for the new application to fulfill its role and be able to operate. The data requirements of the new application drive the conversion design.

Record-keeping applications on the other hand, such as document management systems and pension administration systems need to retain almost all of the information within the current database. These applications generally hold a tremendous amount of history that needs to be retained. Recordkeeping applications as a rule require that the emphasis be on being exhaustive in converting all of the information within the current database. The data requirements of the old application drive the conversion design.

25-5

Generally speaking converting operational applications is considerably easier than converting recordkeeping applications. Populating fields necessary for the operation of a particular piece of software can be done in various ways. New information required for the effective operation of the new application, which is not available from the old application, can be collected from other repositories. This is generally the most time-consuming and complex way of meeting the data requirements of the new application. On the one extreme of the conversion continuum is the possibility of disregarding the old application completely and satisfying the data requirements of the new application by collecting the data from original sources. This approach is particularly useful when the data integrity of the old application is very suspect.

New information also can be provided as defaults based on other data, which are available from the old application. For example, in classifying employees for payroll purposes, give each employee the same classification based on the department where they work. In some instances new information can be fudged if the new data are not critical to the output required. For example, if source medium for an invoice is a required field in a new accounts payable application and it is not a current business requirement to keep source medium, then it could be assumed that all invoices are on paper and the information fudged with that indicator.

Being exhaustive and ensuring that all of the data in an old application are converted to a new application, as a rule, is more complex than meeting the data requirements of a new application. The complexity is not just in the conversion. The old application must be analyzed much more thoroughly to ensure that all of the data are understood and put into proper context. The converted data must be screened much more thoroughly to ensure that everything has been converted appropriately and is in the proper context within the new application. In addition there are still the data requirements of the new application to consider.

Converting historical information often requires shoehorning existing data into fields that were not designed for that data. Very often field conversions are required. For various reasons there may be an array of information in the old application, for which there is only one field in the new application. Pension administration systems are notorious for this. For example, it is not uncommon to have numerous pension enrollment dates depending on the prior plans of which an individual was a member. The new application, especially if it is not sophisticated, may provide only one pension enrollment date.

Acquisitions, mergers, and changes in union agreements and government legislation can cause havoc with historical recordkeeping systems. These then result in a nightmare of a conversion when one of these applications needs to be converted to a new application system. A very common experience is that the conversion routines often approach the complexity of artificial intelligence applications. These are the conversions that tax the abilities of even the most experienced developers. These conversions are also the ones that are potentially the most interesting and challenging to complete.

Once the driving application is determined, the next decision, which is basic to any conversion, is whether an automated conversion is the most effective way of transferring the data to the new application. In certain instances an automated conversion may not be possible. For example, if the source data architecture or the data format is not known and cannot be determined, and there is no export utility provided by the application, then it would be very difficult to develop an automated conversion utility. In certain instances it is simply not cost-effective to develop an automated conversion utility. If the volume of source data is relatively low and the complexity of the data requires conversion routines approaching the complexity of artificial intelligence routines, then a manual conversion effort may be more cost-effective.

The next conversion decision that must be made is how to get the data into the new application. For some reason many application system designers never think of the initial population of their application with the relevant data. It is as if this was supposed to occur by magic. There are four basic ways of populating the new application. In order of relative complexity these are

1. Using a bulk load facility if one is provided by the target application.
2. Generating input transactions into the new application if the application is transaction-based and the format of the transactions is known.
3. Real-time data entry through key stroke emulation.
4. Creating the target database so that it is external to the application.

Bulk load facilities often are provided by most packaged application system vendors. If a bulk load facility is not provided, then the vendor often provides the necessary APIs in order that a bulk load facility can be developed. Bulk load facilities are the most effective tools with which to populate a new application. The bulk load facility generally provides the necessary native edit and validation routines required by the application, while providing the necessary audit capabilities with which to determine the degree of success of the conversion.

If a bulk load facility is not provided and cannot be developed from vendor-provided APIs, then the next best thing is to generate the transactions which ordinarily would be used to enter data into the system. In this way the data is cleansed by the application-provided routines, and one is ensured that the resultant data has the required integrity from the application perspective and is appropriately converted. This approach generally requires multiple conversion routines, possibly one per transaction type and multiple iterations of the conversion as the transactions are loaded.

If neither of the previous methods for converting the data is available, then one can explore using key stroke emulation as a method of entering the data. There are numerous key stroke emulation or screen scraping utilities available that can assist in this endeavor. The trick here is to generate flat files from the source application and then to assemble screens of information that ordinarily are used by the application for data entry. The application is in essence fooled into behaving as if a client was communicating with it for data entry.

There are some technical limitations or challenges with this approach. With large volumes of information, multiple clients with multiple client sessions may have to be established. This is dependent on the efficiency of the client application. The slower the client application and the higher the volume of data, the greater the number of clients who need to operate simultaneously. The more client sessions the higher the risk of malfunction. Auditing this type of conversion effort is usually quite challenging. The audit process needs to be very thorough to ensure that all of the data is converted. As with the previous approaches to conversion, by using this process one is still assured that the data that does make it to the new application have been validated and edited by the application-provided routines.

As a last resort, if it is determined that none of the above alternatives are feasible or available, then one can attempt to use the following approach. The tool of last resort is to convert the data from the source application by constructing the target database from outside the application. In the past, when applications and application data architectures were relatively simple, i.e., a flat file structure, this approach was used quite frequently. The trick here is that the conversion designer must have an intimate knowledge of the application design and underlying data architecture and the context of the data. With a simple application and a simple data architecture, this is not a daunting requirement. With today's complex application packages, however, this approach is almost not supportable. For example, creating the application database for an SAP implementation outside of the application would be out of the question.

Once the decision is made as to which approach to use for the conversion, the actual conversion routines need to be written and tested just like any piece of application code. There usually is no user testing required at this point. When the routines are ready and thoroughly tested the time comes for the actual conversion. This is the trickiest part of the entire effort. It is rare to have the luxury of ample time between running the conversion and certifying the resultant database for live operation. The planning of the actual conversion, checking the resultant database, and certifying the data must be planned with military precision.

Checking the data usually is done using multiple independent audit trails at least providing the count of data records converted and some hash totals on certain fields. The amount of effort expended is usually commensurate with the cost and impact of an error. The users of the data must be involved and have the final sign-off. Whatever audit trails are used, the results and associated statistics must be kept in archives at least for the first few years of operation of the new application. A copy of the source database used for the conversion also should be archived together with some application code that can access the data for reporting purposes. If questions with regard to the conversion process arise at a later date, then one has something to go back to for verification.

After a successful conversion, the last step involves decommissioning the old application. This sounds much simpler than it actually is. It is not unusual; in fact, it is often absolutely mandatory that the old and the new applications be run in parallel for some specified time period. Weaning users from the old application can sometimes be a major challenge. That, however, is not a subject for a chapter on conversions, but is more in the realm of change management.

CONCLUSION

As the preceding discussion illustrates, conversions are not as boring and lacking in challenges as most professionals assume. Neither are conversions as frightening as they are made out to be. Most systems implementations involve some form of data conversion. When the software changes, the data model or the data itself often changes with it. Conversion software design and development can challenge the most creative juices of the most skilled developers. Conversions can be interesting and fun. Keep this in mind the next time you hear the word "conversion."

Chapter 26
Legacy Database Conversion

James Woods

THE MATERIAL PRESENTED IN THIS CHAPTER AIDS THE DATA CENTER MANAGER in planning the move to a relational database system. Encompassing more than the traditional information (e.g., table normalization and project organization), the chapter examines managerial, political, and other considerations and identifies and discusses the more technical considerations.

Before any project is begun, certain questions must be answered. Why is the organization going to a relational database? What are the benefits that managers hope to gain? Now, if the list of benefits comes solely from the vendor's representative, the organization may not get a complete and accurate representation of what is to be gained. Instead, managers need to consider what new capabilities mean specifically to the way the organization does business; for example, how the new system will make it easier or faster to do business, thereby lowering overhead.

One of the things to be considered is the capabilities of the old system as opposed to the capabilities of the new. If the abilities of the new system are drawn as a circle or a set, and the abilities of the old system are likewise drawn, the two should have an area where they overlap, representing the union of the two sets. If project managers target this union to be the result of the conversion, they are losing many of the advantages of the new system. The most desirable objective, therefore, is to gain the whole second set, rather than just the union of those sets. Project managers should not limit the new system by thinking only in terms of the old system.

The legacy system was thought of in terms of applications. The new system should be thought of in terms of models. There is a paradigm shift involved. The most severe shift is to be expected at the technical level. As far as the end user is concerned, there should not be a great difference in the content of the information at the first stage. There certainly may be after the initial conversion because, at that point, it will be possible to implement the wonderful features that have been talked about for years but were never cost-effective to add.

0-8493-9976-9/99/$0.00+$.50
© 1999 by CRC Press LLC

Generally, one of the benefits of moving to a modern database system is the facility of the tools. They are better, faster, and more complete. COBOL, for example, may indeed be the mainstay of business because of the legacy systems, but it is not more powerful than a visually oriented diagramming tool that will automatically set up the users' screens, filter the data, and so forth.

PRECONCEPTIONS AND MISCONCEPTIONS

The announcement of an implementation of a legacy-conversion project gives rise to certain predictable reactions within an organization, and the data center manager needs to be aware of the preconceptions members may hold. Two common expectations are

- There will be no problems with the new system, or at least the new system will present fewer problems than historically encountered with the legacy system. Human nature is such that staff will expect the new system to be without challenges. Everyone hopes to move from the old patched system to the new improved system, one that will not have any problems. This, however, is seldom the case. Whereas the likelihood is that the new system will offer many advantages over the old system, those advantages do not exhibit themselves without effort.
- The new system will be more efficient. On the contrary, database performance very well could be lowered when performing the same tasks using a relational system. A database that must make access path decisions at query time is inherently slower than a system that is preconfigured only to retrieve data in a particular way; such decision-making takes time. However, if a computer hardware upgrade also involved is in the conversion project, the increased demand for central processing unit (CPU) cycles is more than compensated for by the increased power of the new machines. The data center manager should note that if the organization is changing only database systems rather than changing database systems as well as moving to a new, more powerful computer platform, users most likely could suffer a performance hit for at least part of the system, perhaps even a major part. This, of course, depends on the efficiency of the existing system. A broad rule is that generalized solutions cost more CPU cycles than specific solutions do. The system does, however, gain great flexibility in return for the additional CPU cycle cost.

To identify and isolate the potential problem areas, the safest route is to perform benchmarks for both the old and new systems. In fact, many organizations make it a condition of sale. The managers can choose samples of transaction data and run them on both systems. At least one of the sample sets should be large because the response of a database system is seldom linear. Managers also should be sure to include critical applications in the benchmark set. These are the applications that must fly in order for the new system to be a success.

BEYOND NORMALIZATION

Any thorough textbook on relational databases outlines clear instructions on applying standard normalization rules to nonnormalized data. (Normalization refers to a procedure used to ensure that a data model conforms to standards that have been developed to avoid duplication of data and to minimize create, update, and delete anomalies of data. Normalization involves the decomposition of a large relation into smaller relations; this process generally improves data integrity and increases the effectiveness of a database system's long-term maintenance.) Textbook instructions on applying normalization rules generally do not cover some of the difficulties that can be encountered in the conversion of a legacy system. The information content must be reverse-engineered from the legacy database, at which point the actual normalization can begin. The exceptions that almost never are examined within the textbooks fall into two categories:

- The Data-Definition Shift. The definition of the data originated at one point in the system's history in one form and has evolved into another. One reason is that the data usage is subject to change over the course of many years. For example, what used to be a facility location may now be labeled "Material Storage Location." This type of shift has important ramifications when deciding how to represent this data in a relational database.
- Incognito Data. In this situation, the data's name is not necessarily indicative of its function. It is, instead, a statement of the data's original intent. In fact, the name of a data item reflects the understanding of the programmer involved at the time that the first program using that data was written.

DATA REDUNDANCY

On occasion, the conversion process uncovers two or more items of data that conflict. Possibly, they have different names, but they serve similar functions. Under the old system, these two or more items do not come into contact, but they may in the new. The function of each piece of data must be understood clearly before a correct model of that data can be made in the relational database.

Summary Data Redundancy

Many systems store summary data because the cost, in terms of time/CPU cycles, is too high to perform the calculations in real time. However, this stored summary data may not match the actual counts or sums. This causes a difficult and embarrassing situation: The first report on the new system does not balance with the report on the old system. This can be distressing because if the new system is correct the old system has been wrong for an undetermined amount of time. In any case, the summary data should be discarded in favor of direct calculations from the database.

Data Conflicts

It is not unusual to have redundant data conflict. For example, in one system, the vendor record was duplicated for each product line that was supplied by that vendor. There was a bug in the update program that caused the system to update the records of only the active products. During the conversion project, when the data was brought over, sometimes one of the old records was picked up and the demographic data was taken from there. There must be a standard decision reached to apply to all redundant data within the system as to which data will be considered true. The other data must be discarded during the transfer. However, the data center manager should be advised that this could cause the users to see differences between their old reports and new.

HISTORICAL ERROR TRACKS

A scenario common to organizations going through a conversion project is the existence of hidden, damaged data. What very often has happened is that at one time in a company's history an error occurred in an update program; the program was fixed, and the data was corrected. However, some of the damaged data still lingers in the system. It actually may never show up in user reports, but it will stop the new systems' data transfer cold because it violates the very rules that were culled from the program that was supposed to guard that data.

The precaution is simple: Programs must be audited; so must data. For example, a certain field is supposed to contain the groupings of letters INC or SER, which indicate the type of record. Before any transfer attempt is made, a simple program should be written to look at all the records, including historical records if they are to be transferred to the new database, to ascertain that indeed those are the only two codes embedded in the data.

If the database involved employs dictionaries, staff members can use them as a source for the data item name and function, depending on how well the code has been documented. However, if the legacy file or database system does not have a centralized dictionary, then staff members are dependent on the program code to provide the name and function and thereby the implied function of the data item.

AVOIDING HIDDEN PITFALLS

The larger the number of programs and the more extended the lifetime of the system, the more likely it is that the data items involved conflict in intent and purpose and perhaps even form and function. At this point, it might be time to start thinking about the planning of the conversion. Even though the legacy system is presumably well-understood and the relational database is thought to be well-understood, no manager should assume that the translation from the legacy system to the relational database will be the simple matter of applying normalization rules to the legacy system.

The first assumption that leads to numerous problems is that the current staff understands the intricacies of the legacy system. Unless their numbers include at least a few members who originally helped to build the system, the assumption should be otherwise. Each staff member working on the conversion has a specific, applications-oriented view of the data, as opposed to a systemwide view, and the conflicts and the anomalies that staff members in systems development have lived with and accommodated within the application code over the years will not be able to be tolerated easily within the new system. The situation calls for a solution to be found, finally.

The second assumption is that relational databases are well-understood. In academic and theoretical circles, this is a true assumption. It is not, however, necessarily true of the organization's staff, and this staff must be able to support the system. Sending them to the vendor's school is a starting point, but it is not a finish line. They must understand relational databases, but they also must see the need and understand the benefits for the organization.

THE COMPONENTS OF THE CONVERSION PROCESS

The conversion is not a technical process; rather, it is a managerial process with major technical components. The following sections describe two key considerations in the project.

Defining Documentation

Certain preliminary decisions have been made, so the project has been defined loosely. For example, the organization is determined to move to a relational database; managers have chosen which database is to be the replacement system, and a clear picture of the current system has been created. The staff training has been arranged for and the project is set to go in a couple of months. At this point, what is the procedure?

The first step is to document the current legacy system. If the system has inadequate documentation, the project will be besieged by last-minute surprises during the conversion process and while bringing up the new system. If the system is overdocumented (if, indeed, such a thing is possible), the project will be assured of no surprises and a smooth transition. Therefore, logic would dictate that if the staff does err, they should err on the side of too much documentation.

The term documentation requires some definition because what the manager means by documentation and what the programmer means are not necessarily the same thing.

To the programmer, documentation means materials that answer such questions as, "When I get ready to make an application that asks for the insured's middle name, what data item, in what file, will give it to me?" and "Is there an index on that item?"

What managers mean when they ask for documentation is material that answers such questions as, "When I ask you to modify a particular application, is there some documentation that you can use to find out what that application currently does and what the factors are that will be involved in your modification of that process?"

What end users mean when they ask for documentation, of course, is how they "drive" that application. In the context of this chapter, users could include either the end user for terminal systems or the operator for batch systems.

At least three different definitions exist for documentation. For the purposes of the conversion, the term actually refers to a combination of all three, to some degree. Technically, yes, the programmer-level documentation must be complete. The interrelationships that the manager wants must be completely documented. The user information, however, does not need to be complete for the purposes of the conversion, but it still needs to be noted and understood.

One of the determinations to make in the labyrinth of management decisions for a conversion effort of this type is estimating the desired degree of impact on the current organization and end users? Questions to consider are as follows: Will applications look the same? Will they act the same? It may be a highly desirable motive, politically and even sociologically, to keep the impact as small as possible. However, minimizing the effects is not a desirable goal, technically. That would mean the project simply is putting new milk in an old bottle, limiting the benefits of the new system by trying to make the system appear as it always did.

One of the things that users usually insist on, of course, is accurate paper reports. Those reports have, over the years, become a definition of their work. Even though there has been much crowing about the benefits of the paperless office for some time now, it has not materialized yet. This does not mean, however, that the office has to be one or the other, entirely based on paper reports or entirely paperless; it is not an all-or-nothing kind of deal. The new system can reduce the amount of paper and still come out way ahead, and the biggest deterrent to being able to achieve great savings in information acquisition and turnaround is the end user who emotionally may be tied to the reports. It has been their private database; they have been able to mark it up, highlight it, and in general own it. Now, all of a sudden, the new system threatens to take that away from them, and the new database is in a magic box that the end user does not know how to access yet.

Managers must sell the benefits of online information as opposed to printed information. It is to the corporation's benefit to head in this direction, as many of the modern database systems are oriented toward online information retrieval, as opposed to printed information. True, the new system can be created to replicate the old reports, but this approach misses one of the major benefits of an online database.

DATA HISTORY IN THE NEW SYSTEM

Legacy systems typically have a particular way of trapping the data's history. Some remove the record, or a copy of it, to another file. Others record the history within the record itself. A relational database, however, is designed to model the current data flow. It is a model of the current data within the organization. The model reflects the data as it is rather than as it was. Usually, the plan should be to trap the information in a number of historical tables, which must be designed at the outset.

CONCLUSION

In general, time for planning is crucial. Conversions succeed or fail in the planning stage. The management challenge most often is seen as technical, but there are many areas to manage in such an endeavor. The technical planning is a critical activity, but so are managing expectations of the new system, selling the capabilities of the new system, and providing a plan to implement those capabilities into company strategic tools that help put the organization ahead of the competition.

There has never been a conversion that was over planned; however, many have not been planned in sufficient detail to succeed.

Chapter 27

Data Conversion: Doing it Right the First Time

Michael Zimmer

WHEN SYSTEMS DEVELOPERS BUILD INFORMATION SYSTEMS, they usually do not start with a clean slate. Often, they are replacing an existing application. They must always determine if the existing information should be preserved. Usually the older information is transferred to the new system — a process known as data conversion.

Data conversion can involve moving data from flat file systems to relational database management systems (RDBMS). It also can involve changing from systems with loose constraints to new systems with tight constraints.

This chapter focuses on laying the groundwork for successfully executing a data conversion effort the first time around. It is assumed in this chapter that data modeling is being done and that relational database technology is employed. At the logical level, the terms *entity set, entity,* and *attribute* are used in place of the terms *file, record,* and *field.* At the physical level, the terms *table, row,* and *column* are used instead of *file, record,* and *field.* The members of IS engaged in the data conversion effort are referred to as the data conversion team (DCT).

COMMON PROBLEMS WITH DATA

The difficulties of a data conversion effort almost always are underestimated. Usually the conversion costs many times more than originally anticipated. This is invariably the result of an inadequate understanding of the cost and effort required to correct errors in the data. Usually the quality of the existing data is much worse than the users and development team anticipate.

Problems with data can result from missing information and mismatches between the old model (often only implicit) and the new model (usually explicitly documented). Problems also result if the conversion effort is started too late in the project and is under-resourced. The most common sources of problems are data quality and incomplete data.

Costs and Benefits of Data Conversion

Before embarking on data conversion, the data conversion team should decide whether data really needs to be converted and if it is feasible to abandon the noncurrent data. Starting fresh is an option.

The customers may decide that the cost to preserve and correct old information exceeds the benefit expected. Often, they will want to preserve old information, but may not have the resources to correct historical errors. With a data warehouse project, it is given that the data will be converted. Preservation of old information is critical.

The Cost of Not Converting

The DCT first should demonstrate the cost of permitting erroneous information into the new database. It is a decision to be made by user management.

In the long run, permitting erroneous data into the new application usually will be costly. The data conversion team should explain what the risks are to justify the costs for robust programming and data error correction.

Costs of Converting

It is no easier to estimate the cost of a conversion effort than to estimate the cost of any other development effort. The special considerations are that there may be a great deal of manual intervention, and subsequently extra programming, to remedy data errors. A simple copy procedure usually does not serve the organization's needs. If the early exploration of data quality and robust design and programming for the conversion routines is skimped on, IS generally will pay for it.

STEPS IN THE DATA CONVERSION PROCESS

In even the simplest IT systems development projects, the efforts of many players must come together. At the managerial and employee levels, certain users should be involved, in addition to the applications development group, data administration, database administration, computer operations, and quality assurance. The responsibilities of the various groups must be defined clearly.

In the simplest terms, data conversion involves the following steps:

- Determining if conversion is required
- Planning the conversion
- Determining the conversion rules
- Identifying problems
- Writing up the requirements
- Correcting the data
- Programming the conversion
- Running the conversion
- Checking audit reports
- Institutionalizing

Determining If Conversion Is Required

In some cases, data does not need to be converted. IS may find that there is no real need to retain old information. The data could be available elsewhere, such as on microfiche. Another possibility is that the current data is so erroneous, incomplete, or inadequate that there is no reason to keep it. The options must be presented for the clients so that they can decide.

Planning the Conversion and Determining the Conversion Rules

Once the DCT and the client have accepted the need for a conversion, the work can be planned in detail. The planning activities for conversion are standard in most respects and are typical of development projects.

Beyond sound project management, it is helpful for the DCT to keep in mind that error correction activities may be particularly time-consuming. Determination of the conversion rules consists of these steps, usually done in sequence:

- Analyzing the old physical data model
- Conducting a preliminary investigation on data quality
- Analyzing the old logical data model
- Analyzing the new logical data model
- Analyzing the new physical data model
- Determining the data mapping
- Determining how to treat missing information

Analyzing the Old Physical Data Model

Some published development methods imply that development starts with a blank slate. As a result, analysis of the existing system is neglected.

The reverse engineering paradigm asserts that the DCT should start with the existing computer application to discern the business rules. Data conversion requires this approach for data analysis. The DCT can look at old documentation, database definitions, file descriptions, and record layouts to understand the current physical data model.

Conducting a Preliminary Investigation of Data Quality

Without some understanding of data structures for the current application, it is not possible to look at the quality of the data. To examine the quality of the data, the DCT can run existing reports, do online queries and, if possible, quickly write some fourth-generation language programs to examine issues such as referential, primary key, and domain integrity violations that the users might never notice. When the investigation is done, the findings can be documented formally.

Analyzing the Old Logical Data Model

When the physical structure of the data is understood, it can be represented in its normalized logical structure. This step, although seemingly unnecessary, allows the DCT to specify the mapping in a much more reliable fashion. The results should be documented with the aid of an entity-relationship diagram accompanied by dictionary descriptions.

Analyzing the New Physical Data Model

The new logical model should be transformed into a physical representation. If a relational database is being used, this may be a simple step. Once this model is done, the mapping can be specified.

Determining the Data Mapping

This step is often more difficult than it might seem initially. Usually, the exceptions are one old file-to-one new file, and one old field-to-one new field.

Often there are cases where the old domain must be transformed into a new one; an old field is split into two new ones; two old fields become one new one; or multiple records are looked at to derive a new one. There are many ways of reworking the data, and an unlimited number of special cases may exist. Not only are the possibilities for mapping numerous and complex, in some cases it is not possible at all to map to the new model because key information was not collected in the old system.

Determining How to Treat Missing Information

It is common when doing conversion to discover that some of the data to populate the new application is not available, and there is no provision for it in the old database. It may be available elsewhere as manual records, or it may never have been recorded at all.

Sometimes, this is only an inconvenience — dummy values can be put in certain fields to indicate that the value is not known. In the more serious case, the missing information would be required to create a primary key or a foreign key. This can occur when the new model is significantly different from the old. In this case, the dummy value strategy may be appropriate, but it must be explained fully to the client.

Identifying Problems

Data problems only can be detected after the old data structure is fully understood. Once it is determined what the new model will look like, a deeper analysis of the issue can be done.

A full analysis of the issue includes looking for erroneous information, missing information, redundancies, inconsistencies, missing keys, and any other problem that will make the conversion difficult or impossible without a lot of manual intervention. Any findings should be documented and brought to the attention of the client. Information must be documented in a fashion that makes sense to the client.

Once the problems have been identified, the DCT can help the client identify a corrective strategy. The client must understand why errors have been creeping into the systems. The cause is usually a mixture of problems with the old data structure, problems with the existing input system, and data entry problems that have been ongoing. It may be that the existing system does not reflect the business properly. The users may have been working around the system's deficiencies for years in ways that violated its integrity. In any case, the new system should be tighter than the old one at the programming and database level, should reflect the business properly, and the new procedures should not result in problems with usability or data quality.

Documenting the Requirements

After the initial study of the conversion is done, the findings should be documented. Some of this work will have been done as part of the regular system design. There must also be a design for the conversion programs, whether it is a one-time or an ongoing activity. First-time as well as ongoing load requirements must be examined.

Estimates should include the time necessary to extract, edit, correct, and upload data. Costs for disk storage and CPUs also should be projected. In addition, the sizing requirements should be estimated well in advance of hardware purchases.

Correcting the Data

The client may want to correct the data before the conversion effort begins or may be willing to convert the data over time. It is best to make sure that the data that is converted is error-free, at least with respect to the formal integrity constraints defined for the new model.

If erroneous information is permitted into the new system, it probably will be problematic later. The correction process may involve using the existing system to make changes. Often, the types of errors that are encountered may require some extra programming facilities. Not all systems provide all of the data modification capabilities that might be necessary. In any case, this step sometimes can take months of effort and requires a mechanism for evaluating the success of the correction effort.

Programming the Conversion

The conversion programs should be designed, constructed, and tested with the same discipline used for any other software development. Although the number of workable designs is unlimited, there are a few helpful rules of thumb:

- The conversion program should edit for all business rule violations and reject nonconforming information. The erroneous transactions should go to an error file, and a log of the problem should be written. The soundest course is to avoid putting incorrect data into the new system.
- The conversion programs must produce an audit trail of the transactions processes. This includes control totals, checksums, and date and time stamps. This provides a record of how the data was converted after the job is done.
- Tests should be as rigorous as possible. All design documents and code should be tested in a structured fashion. This is less costly than patching up problems caused by a data corruption in a million record file.
- Provisions should be made for restart in case of interruption in the run.
- It should be possible to roll back to some known point if there are errors.
- Special audit reports should be prepared to run against the old and new data to demonstrate that the procedures worked. This reporting can be done in addition to the standard control totals from the programs.

Running the Conversion

It may be desirable to run a test conversion to populate a test database. Once the programs are ready and volume testing has been done, it is time for the first conversion, which may be only one of many.

If this is a data warehouse application, the conversion could be an ongoing effort. It is important to know how long the initial loads will take so that scheduling can be done appropriately. The conversion then can be scheduled for an opportune cutover time. The conversion will go smoothly if contingencies are built-in and sound risk management procedures are followed. There may be a number of static tables, perhaps used for code look-up that can be converted without as much fanfare, but the main conversion will take time.

At the time planned for cutover, the old production system can be frozen from update or run in parallel. The production database then can be initialized and test records removed (if any have been created). The conversion and any verification and validation routines can be run at this point.

Checking Audit Reports

Once the conversion is finished, special audit reports should be run to prove that it worked, to check control totals, and to deal with any problems. It may be necessary to roll back to the old system if problems are excessive. The new application should not be used until it is verified that the conversion was correct, or a lot of work could be lost.

Institutionalizing

In many cases, as in data warehousing, conversion will be a continuous process and must be institutionalized. Procedural controls are necessary to make sure that the conversion runs on schedule, results are checked rigorously, rejected data is dealt with appropriately, and failed runs are handled correctly.

DATA QUALITY

A strategy to identify data problems early in the project should be in place, though details will change according to the project. A preliminary investigation can be done as soon as the old physical data model has been determined. It is important to document the quality of the current data, but this step may require programming resources. Customers at all levels should be notified if there are data-quality issues to be resolved. Knowledge of the extent of data-quality problems may influence the user's decision to convert or abandon the data.

Keeping the Data Clean

If the data is corrected on a one-time basis, it is important to ensure that more erroneous data is not being generated by some faulty process or programming. There may be a considerable time interval between data correction and conversion to the new system.

Types of Data Abnormalities

There may be integrity problems in the old system. For example, there may be no unique primary key for some of the old files, which almost guarantees redundancy in the data. This violation of entity integrity can be quite serious.

To ensure entity integrity in the new system, the DCT will have to choose which of the old records is to be accepted as the correct one to move into the new system. It is helpful for audit routines to report on this fact. In addition, in the new system it will be necessary to devise a primary key, which may not be available in the old data.

Uniqueness

In many cases, there are other fields that also should be unique and serve as an alternate primary key. In some cases, even if there is primary key integrity, there are redundancies in other alternative keys, which again creates a problem for integrity in the new system.

Referential Integrity

The DCT should determine whether the data correctly reflects referential integrity constraints. In a relational system, tables are joined together by primary key/foreign key links. The information to create this link may not be available in the old data. If records from different files are to be matched and joined, it should be determined whether the information exists to do the join correctly (i.e., a unique primary key and a foreign key). Again, this problem needs to be addressed prior to conversion.

Domain Integrity

The domain for a field imposes constraints on the values that should be found there. IS should determine if there are data domains that have been coded into character or numeric fields in an undisciplined and inconsistent fashion. It should further be determined whether there are numeric domains that have been coded into character fields, perhaps with some non-numeric values. There may be date fields that are just text strings, and the dates may be in any order. A common problem is that date or numeric fields stored as text may contain absurd values with the wrong data type entirely.

Another determination that should be made is whether the domain-coding rules have changed over time and whether they have been recoded. It is common for coded fields to contain codes that are no longer in use and often codes that never were in use. Also, numeric fields may contain out-of-range values. Composite domains could cause problems when trying to separate them for storage in multiple fields. The boundaries for each sub-item may not be in fixed columns.

There may be domains that incorrectly model internal hierarchy. This is common in old-style systems and makes data modeling difficult. There could be attributes based on more than one domain. Not all domain problems will create conversion difficulties, but they may be problematic later if it cannot be proven that these were preexisting anomalies and not a result of the conversion efforts.

Wrong Cardinality

The old data could contain cardinality violations. For example, the structure may say that each employee has only one job record, but in fact some may have five or six. These sorts of problems make database design difficult.

Wrong Optionality

Another common problem is the absence of a record when one should be there. It may be a rule that every employee has at least one record of appointment, but for some reason 1% of old records show no job for an employee. This inconsistency must be resolved by the client.

Orphaned Records

In many cases, a record is supposed to refer back to some other record by making reference to the key value for that other record. In many badly designed system, there is no key to refer back to, at least not one that uniquely identifies the record. Technically, there is no primary key. In some cases, there is no field available to make this reference, which means that there is no foreign key. In other cases, the key structure is fine, but the actual record referred back to does not exist. This is a problem with referential integrity. This record without a parent is called an orphan.

Inconsistent Redundancy

If each data item is determined fully by its key, there will be no undesirable redundancy, and the new database will be normalized. If attempts at normalization are made where there is redundant information, the DCT will be unable to make consistent automated choices about which of the redundant values to select for the conversion.

On badly designed systems, there will be a great deal of undesirable redundancy. For example, a given fact may be stored in multiple places. This type of redundancy wastes disk storage, but in some cases may permit faster queries.

The problem is that without concerted programming efforts, this redundant information almost certainly is going to become inconsistent. If the old data has confusing redundancies, it is important to determine whether they are due to historical changes in the business rules or historical changes in the values of fields and records.

The DCT also should determine whether the redundancies are found across files or within individual files across records. There may be no way to determine which data is current, and an arbitrary choice will have to be made. If the DCT chooses to keep all of the information to reflect the changes over time, it cannot be stored correctly because the date information will not be in the system. This is an extremely common problem.

Missing Information

When dealing with missing information, it is helpful to determine whether:

- The old data is complete.
- Mandatory fields are filled in.
- All necessary fields are available in the files.
- All records are present.
- Default or dummy values can be inserted where there is missing information.

Date Inconsistencies

When examining the conversion process, it is helpful to determine whether:

- The time dimension is represented correctly.
- The data spans a long enough time period.
- The data correctly reflects the state of the business for the time at which it was captured.
- All necessary date fields are available to model the time dimension properly.
- Dates are stored with century information.
- Date ranges are in the correct sequence within a given record.
- Dates are correct from record to record.

Miscellaneous Inconsistencies

In some fields, there will be values derived from other fields. A derived field might be computed from other fields in the same record or may be a function of multiple records. The derived fields may be stored in an entirely different file. In any case, the derived values may be incorrect for the existing data. Given this sort of inconsistency, it should be determined which is correct — the detail or the summary information.

Intelligent Keys

An intelligent key results from a fairly subtle data-modeling problem. For example, there are two different independent items from the real world, such as employee and department, where the employee is given a key that consists in part of the department key. The implication is that if a department is deleted, the employee record will be orphaned, and if an employee changes departments, the employee key will have to change. When doing a conversion, it would be desirable to remove the intelligent key structure.

Other Problems

Often other problems with the old data cannot be classified easily. These problems involve errors in the data that cannot be detected except by going back to the source, or violations of various arcane constraints that have not been programmed as edit checks in the existing system. There may be special rules that tie field values to multiple records, multiple fields, or multiple files. Although they may not have a practical implication for the conversion effort, if these problems become obvious, they might falsely be attributed to the conversion routines.

THE ERROR CORRECTION PROCESS

The data correction effort should be run as part of a separate subproject. The DCT should determine whether the resources to correct the data can be made available. A wholesale commitment from the owners of the data will be required, and probably a commitment of programming resources as well. Error correction cannot be done within the context of rapid applications development (RAD).

Resources for the Correction Effort

Concerning resources for the correction effort, the best-case scenario would ensure that:

- Resources are obtained from the client if a major correction effort is required.
- Management pays adequate attention to the issue if a data-quality problem is identified.
- The sources of the problem will be identified in a fair and nonjudgmental manner if a data-quality problem is identified.

Choices for Correction

The effort required to write an edit program to look for errors is considerable, and chances are good that this will be part of the conversion code and not an independent set of audit programs. Some of the errors may be detected before conversion begins, but it is likely that many of the problems will be found during the conversion run.

Once data errors are discovered, data can be copied as is, corrected, or abandoned. The conversion programs should reject erroneous transactions and provide reports that explain why data was rejected. If the decision is made to correct the data, it probably will have to be reentered. Again, in some cases, additional programming can help remedy the problems.

Programming for Data Correction

Some simple automated routines can make the job of data correction much easier. If they require no manual intervention, it could be advantageous to simply put them into the main conversion program. However, the program may require that a user make the decision.

If the existing data entry programs are not adequate for large-scale data correction efforts, some additional programs might have to be written for error repair. For example, the existing system may not allow the display of records with a referential integrity problem, which are probably the very records that need correction. Custom programming will be required to make the change.

SPECIFYING THE MAPPING

Often, crucial information needed for the conversion will be missing. If the old system can accommodate the missing information, it may be a matter of keying it in from original paper records. However, the original information may not be available anymore, or it may never have been collected. In that case, it may be necessary to put in special markers to show that the information is not available.

Model Mismatches

It can be difficult to go from an non-normalized structure to a normalized structure because of the potential for problems in mapping from old to new. Many problems are the result of inconsistent and redundant data, a poor key structure, or missing information. If there is a normalized structure in the old system, there probably will not be as many difficulties. Other problems result from changed assumptions about the cardinality of relationships or actual changes in the business rules.

Discovered Requirements

The requirements of a system almost never are understood fully by the user or the developer prior to construction of the system. Some of the data requirements do not become clear until the test conversions are being run. At that point, it may be necessary to go back and revisit the whole development effort. Standard change and scope control techniques apply.

Existing Documentation

Data requirements are rarely right the first time because the initial documentation is seldom correct. There may be abandoned fields, mystery fields, obscure coding schemes, or undocumented relationships. If the documentation is thorough, many data conversion pitfalls can be avoided.

Possible Mapping Patterns

The mapping of old to new is usually very complex. There seems to be no useful canonical scheme for dealing with this set of problems. Each new conversion seems to consist of myriad special cases. In the general case, a given new field may depend on the values found in multiple fields contained in multiple records of a number of files. This works the other way as well — one field in an old record may be assigned to different fields or even to different tables, depending on the values encountered.

If the conversion also requires intelligent handling of updates and deletes to the old system, the problem is complicated even further. This is true when one source file is split into several destination files and, at the same time, one destination file receives data from several source files. Then, if just one record is deleted in a source file, some fields will have to be set to null in the destination file, but only those coming from the deleted source record. This method, however, may violate some of the integrity rules in the new database.

It may be best to specify the mapping in simple tabular and textual fashion. Each new field will have the corresponding old fields listed, along with any special translation rules required. These rules could be documented as decision tables, decision trees, pseudo code, or action diagrams.

Relational Mathematics

In database theory, it is possible to join together all fields in a database in a systematic manner and to create what is called the "universal relation." Although this technique has little merit as a scheme for designing or implementing a database, it may be a useful device for thinking about the mapping of old to new. It should be possible to specify any complex mapping as a view based on the universal relation. The relational algebra or the relational calculus could be used as the specification medium for detailing the rules of the mapping in a declarative fashion.

DESIGNING THE CONVERSION

Before starting to design a computer program, reentering the data manually from source records should be considered as a possibility.

Special Requirements for Data Warehousing

Data warehousing assumes that the conversion issue arises on a routine, periodic basis. All of the problems that arise in a one-time conversion must be dealt with for an initial load, and then must be dealt with again for the periodic update.

In a data warehouse situation, there most likely will be changes to source records that must be reflected into the data warehouse files. As discussed previously, there may be some complex mapping from old to new, and updates and deletes will increase the complexity greatly. There will have to be a provision for add, change, and delete transactions. A change transaction often can be handled as a paired delete and add, in some cases simplifying the programming.

Extra Space Requirements

In a conversion, it will be necessary to have large temporary files available. These could double the amount of disk space required for the job. If it is not possible to provide this extra storage, it will be necessary to ensure that the design does not demand extra space.

Choice of Language

The criteria for programming languages is not going to be too different from that used in any other application area. The programming language should be chosen according to the skills of the IS team and what will run on the organization's hardware. The most appropriate language will allow error recovery, exception handling, control totals reporting, checkpoint and restart capabilities, full procedural capability, and adequate throughput.

Most third-generation languages are sufficient, if an interface to the source and target databases or file systems is available. Various classes of programs could be used, with different languages for each. For example, the records may be extracted from the old database with one proprietary product, verified and converted to the new layout with C, and input into the new database with a proprietary loader.

SQL as a Design Medium

The SQL language should be powerful enough to handle any data conversion job. The problem with SQL is that it has no error-handling capabilities and cannot produce a satisfactory control totals report as part of the update without going back and requerying the database in various ways.

Despite the deficiencies of SQL as a robust data conversion language, it may be ideal for specifying the conversion rules. Each destination field could have a corresponding SQL fragment that gave the rules for the mapping in a declarative fashion. The use of SQL as a design medium should lead to a very tight specification. The added advantage is that it translates to an SQL program very readily.

Processing Time

IS must have a good estimate for the amount of elapsed time and CPU time required to do the conversion. If there are excessive volumes of data, special efforts will be required to ensure adequate throughput. These efforts could involve making parallel runs, converting overnight and over weekends, buying extra-fast hardware, or fine-tuning programs.

These issues are not unique to conversions, but they must not be neglected to avoid surprises on the day of cutover to the new system. These issues are especially significant when there are large volumes of historical data for an initial conversion, even if ongoing runs will be much smaller.

Interoperability

There is a strong possibility that the old system and the new system will be on different platforms. There should be a mechanism for transferring the data from one to the other. Tape, disk, or a network connection could be used. It is essential to provide some mechanism for interoperability. In addition, it is important to make sure that the media chosen can support the volumes of data and provide the necessary throughput.

Routine Error Handling

The conversion routine must support sufficient edit code to enforce all business rules. When erroneous data is encountered, there might be a policy of setting the field to a default value. At other times, the record may be rejected entirely.

In either case, a meaningful report of the error encountered and the resultant action should be generated. It will be best if the record in error is sent off to an error file. There may be some larger logical unit of work than the record. If so, that larger unit should be sent to the error file and that transaction rolled back.

Control Totals

Every run of the conversion programs should produce control totals. At a minimum, there should be counts for every input record, every rejected record, every accepted record, and every record inserted into each output file or table. Finer breakdowns are desirable for each of these types of inputs and outputs. Every conversion run should be date- and time-stamped with start and end times, and the control report should be filed after inspection.

RECOVERY FROM ERROR

Certain types of errors, such as a power failure, will interrupt the processing. If the system goes out in the middle of a 20-hour run, there will have to be some facility for restarting appropriately. Checkpoint and re-start mechanisms are desirable. The operating system may be able to pro-vide these facilities. If not, there should be an explicit provision in the design and procedures for dealing with this possibility. In some cases, it may be necessary to ensure that files are backed up prior to conversion.

Audit Records

After the data has been converted, there must be an auditable record of the conversion. This is also true if the conversion is an ongoing effort. In general, the audit record depends on the conversion strategy. There may be counts, checksums (i.e., row and column), or even old vs. new compar-isons done with an automated set of routines. These audit procedures are not the same as the test cases run to verify that the conversion programs worked. They are records produced when the conversions are run.

CONCLUSION

Almost all IS development work involves conversion of data from an old system to a new application. This is seldom a trivial exercise, and in many projects it is the biggest single source of customer dissatisfaction. The con-version needs to be given serious attention, and the conversion process needs to be planned as carefully as any other part of the project. Old appli-cations are fraught with problems, and errors in the data will be common. The more tightly programmed the new application, the more problematic the conversion.

It is increasingly common to make the conversion part of an ongoing process, especially when the operational data is in one system, and the management information in another. Any data changes are made on the op-erational system and then, at periodic intervals, copied to the other appli-cation. This is a key feature of the data warehouse approach. All of the same considerations apply.

In addition, it will be important to institutionalize the procedures for dealing with conversion. The conversion programs must be able to deal with changes to the operational system by reflecting them in the data ware-house. Special care will be required to design the programs accordingly.

Chapter 28
Migrating Files to Relational Databases

James A. Larson
Carol L. Larson

RELATIONAL DATABASE MANAGEMENT SYSTEM (RDBMS) FEATURES not generally found in file systems include automatic backup and recovery procedures, transaction processing, business rule enforcement, easy query formulation, and application generation facilities. However, to obtain these benefits, files must be migrated to a relational database. This chapter explains how, when, and why to migrate a file into a relational database, and how to modify an application to a relational database system.

THREE-PHASE MIGRATION STRATEGY

Exhibit 1 illustrates the three phases for migrating files and applications to an RDBMS:

1. Analysis and planning — Before migrating files to a relational database, the costs and benefits should be analyzed, the files and applications should be partitioned into classes to be migrated independently, and a plan for the migration should be developed.
2. Migration — This phase consists of several substeps, which are repeated for each class identified in Phase 1:
   - A relational schema describing the data to be migrated should be designed.
   - Business rules for enforcement by RDBMS should be specified.
   - The database should be populated by migrating data from files into the RDBMS.
   - Applications should be modified to access the RDBMS.
   - The applications and the populated RDBMS should be tested.
   - Production should be switched from the file system to the RDBMS if the tests succeed.
3. Fine-tuning — The database description should be revised to conform to changing application needs. Finally, performance statistics should be analyzed and physical structures, such as the indexes,

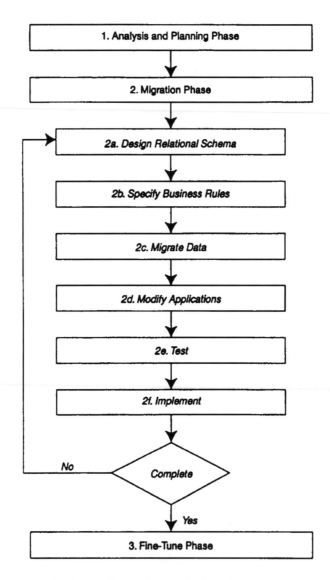

Exhibit 1.   Three phases of migration strategy.

---

should be reimplemented to improve the overall performance of the relational database.

Why Migrate a File into a Relational Database?

File systems are extremely popular among data-processing practitioners. Files store data created by one application and enable other applications to access that data. Files also enable multiple applications to share the same data. As popular as they are, there are some fundamental problems with files.

The Data Dependency Problem. Each application must contain a description of the file's data elements. Whenever a database administrator changes the file's data elements, such as adding a new data element or changing the format of an existing data element, programmers must change the file's description in each application. After the file's description is changed in each application, the programmers must recompile and test the revised applications.

The Business Rule Maintenance Problem. Business rules describe the valid values of each data element and the conditions under which data element values may be changed. Each application that updates data in a file must enforce the business rules. Whenever a business rule changes, programmers must examine each application that updates data and modify those applications to enforce the revised business rule.

The Backup Problem. Data-processing specialists create backup copies of files for use in the event that a file is corrupted or lost. Managing backup copies and file generations is a tedious task that is easy to forget or perform incorrectly.

The Application Queuing Problem. Many files can be accessed by only one application at a time, resulting in lengthy turnaround time and a lot of waiting by users who need to access the files.

RDBMS Benefits

Database management systems and, more recently, relational database management systems, are software systems with facilities to help solve the previously mentioned problems.

Solving the Data Dependency Problem. Database management systems maintain a centralized description of all data elements managed by the DBMS. If a new data element is added to a file, the database administrator only needs to modify this centralized description and those applications affected directly by the change. It is not necessary to recompile and test all applications.

This feature, called data independence, makes it easy for database administrators to change the data structures. Another benefit of centralized data description in database management systems is that users easily can determine the contents of a database and whether it contains the data that will satisfy their needs.

Solving the Business Rule Maintenance Problem. Database management systems contain triggers and stored procedures that enforce business rules. If a business rule changes, the database administrator only needs to update the affected data and to modify the associated triggers and stored procedures, without modifying applications that update the database.

Solving the Backup Problem. Database management systems automatically back up their data and provide utilities so the database administrator can restore the data if the database becomes damaged or lost.

Solving the Application Queuing Problem. Database management systems support concurrency control mechanisms that guarantee that two applications do not try to update the same data element at the same time, but enable multiple applications and users to access the same files at the same time.

PHASE 1: ANALYSIS AND PLANNING

In this phase, the database administrator analyzes the problem and develops plans to migrate files into a relational database system. The first step, designing the relational database, involves:

- Determining which files to include in the relational database.
- Describing each of these files in terms of the relational data model.
- Integrating the descriptions of common data from multiple files.
- Extracting and integrating the business rules from file applications.
- Integrating these business rules into the triggers and stored procedures of the relational database.

Actually migrating data from the files to a relational database involves a separate series of tasks, including:

- Converting file data element formats to database formats.
- Detecting and resolving inconsistencies in data values of common data from multiple files.
- Detecting and resolving incorrect and missing file data.

Migrating existing applications to the database may involve one of the following activities:

- Replacing data I/O commands in the application.
- Restructuring significant portions of the application.
- Rewriting the entire application.

Also, data-processing procedures must be changed to accommodate the database management system. This effort involves changing the way applications are processed. Many applications can be processed in parallel, so explicit backup procedures can be eliminated.

Cost-Benefit Analysis and Other Business Decisions

Several factors affect the decision to stop spending effort and time to maintain an existing file system and begin the conversion to a relational system. Database administrators should consider:

- How frequently data elements are changed and how much effort is necessary to implement the changes.
- How frequently business rules are changed and how much effort is necessary to implement the changes.
- How much effort is expended to create and manage backup file copies.
- The cost of waiting for the results of applications processed sequentially.

Database administrators should perform a cost-benefit analysis by calculating the annual cost of maintaining the existing file system, estimating the total cost of migration to a relational database system, and estimating the annual cost of maintaining a relational database system. From these figures, it is possible to estimate the time required to recoup the cost of migrating to an RDBMS and the expected return on the investment. Other factors that may influence the decision to migrate from a file system to an RDBMS include the availability of trained systems analysts, programmers, and database administrators to carry out the migration, as well as the risk of the project falling behind schedule.

Once these issues are resolved, the users are now ready to enter the second phase of migrating files to a relational database system.

PHASE 2: MIGRATING TO A RELATIONAL DATABASE SYSTEM

Files support three major concepts: record types, fields, and unique identifiers. Each of these three concepts corresponds to similar concepts in the relational data model — a record type corresponds to a relational table, a field corresponds to a relational column, and a unique identifier corresponds to a primary key.

Exhibit 2 illustrates an example file and the corresponding relational table. The four records in the employee file are translated to the four rows of the table with the same name. The three fields of the employee file are mapped to the three columns of the Employee table. Finally, the unique identifier field of the file is mapped to the primary key, EmployeeName, in the relational table. The names of the primary keys are underlined in Exhibit 2. Although the file-to-relational data structure mapping is straightforward for this example, occasionally any one of four problems may arise:

- Some files do not have records with unique identifiers. Exhibit 3 illustrates a file with no unique identifier. One approach for solving this problem is to generate a new column that contains a unique identifier.

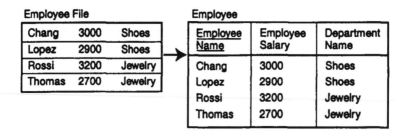

Exhibit 2.   Mapping a file to a table.

In Exhibit 3, the ID column contains generated values that do not exist in the file.

- The order of records in a file implies information not represented by field values. For example, the order of records in the file implies a sequential waiting list or ranking. One approach for solving this problem is to generate a new field containing values that explicitly indicate the ranking among employees. In the corresponding relational table shown in Exhibit 4, this ranking is made explicit by the new column, Rank.
- A single record of a file may contain a repeating group. A repeating group is a set of fields that may occur several times within a record. Exhibit 5 illustrates an example of a file containing three records with some of the records having a group of fields that repeats. This problem could be solved by building a new table for the repeating group. In Exhibit 5, each row of the Child table contains values for fields of the repeating group. The Employee table also contains an Employee column with values that identify the Employee who is the parent or guardian of the child. The Employee column in the Child table sometimes is called a foreign key and is an example of a referential integrity business rule.

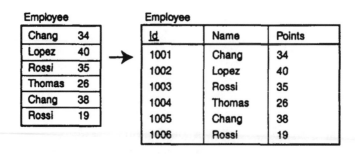

Exhibit 3.   Mapping a file with no unique identifier to a table.

Employee File

Chang	3000	Shoes
Lopez	2900	Shoes
Rossi	3200	Jewelry
Thomas	2700	Jewelry

Employee

Rank	Employee Name	Employee Salary	Department Name
1	Chang	3000	Shoes
2	Lopez	2900	Shoes
3	Rossi	3200	Jewelry
4	Thomas	2700	Jewelry

Exhibit 4. Mapping a file with an implied ranking.

- Some files contain more than one type of record. For example, Exhibit 6 illustrates a file containing two types of records — Department records have a "D" in the first field and Employee records have an "E" in the first field. Records of employees who work for a department follow the record of the department for which they work. The solution to this problem is to split the file into two tables, as shown in Exhibit 6. The Employee table contains the new column, Dept, which relates employees to departments.

Specifying Business Rules

Business rules describe valid data item values and the conditions where they may be changed. Much of the code of traditional file applications is

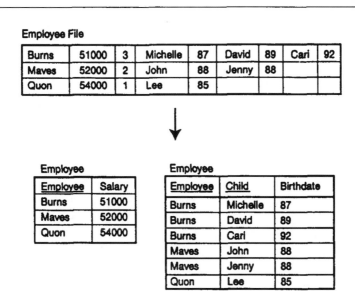

Employee File

Burns	51000	3	Michelle	87	David	89	Cari	92
Maves	52000	2	John	88	Jenny	88		
Quon	54000	1	Lee	85				

Employee

Employee	Salary
Burns	51000
Maves	52000
Quon	54000

Employee

Employee	Child	Birthdate
Burns	Michelle	87
Burns	David	89
Burns	Carl	92
Maves	John	88
Maves	Jenny	88
Quon	Lee	85

Exhibit 5. Mapping a file with a repeating group to two tables.

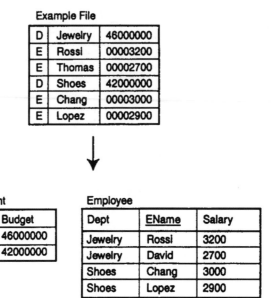

Exhibit 6.   **Mapping a file with multiple record types to two tables.**

devoted to describing business rules and their enforcement. Migrating to an RDBMS provides the database administrator an opportunity to factor application business rules out of the application and centralize them in the database management system. The database administrator must have a good understanding of the data and how it is to be used to specify a complete set of business rules.

Database administrators can specify many business rules nonprocedurally. Nonprocedural business rules include:

- Constraints on a single data item. For example, the values of a person's age must fall into the range 0 to 119. This example illustrates a domain constraint because it restricts values of a data item to take on one of the values within its domain. Database administrators specify a domain constraint for an RDBMS by defining a specific domain of values for a column.
- Constraints among records within a file. For example, no two employee records may have the same value for the employee identifier. This example illustrates an entity integrity constraint. Database administrators specify an entity integrity constraint by declaring that a table has a unique key.
- Constraints between records in two different files. For example, the department number of the department for which an employee works must exist as a value for the primary key of the department file. This

example illustrates a referential integrity constraint. Database administrators specify a referential integrity constraint by declaring that a table have a foreign key.

Stored Procedures

Not all business rules can be specified nonprocedurally. Database administrators use stored procedures to specify nonprocedural business rules.

A stored procedure is a named, compiled procedure that is stored as part of the database. The RDBMS executes a stored procedure whenever a special condition, called a trigger, is executed.

The database administrator defines a trigger by specifying a command (i.e., update, insert, delete), a database object (i.e., a specific table, row, data item), and either a structured query language (SQL) statement or the name of a stored procedure. Whenever the command is executed against the specified object, the SQL statement or stored procedure is executed automatically by the database management system.

Populating the RDBMS

The utilities supplied by the vendor of the RDBMS can be used, or an application can be written to extract, convert, and load files into the RDBMS.

Modifying Applications to Access the RDBMS

Most existing applications are written using procedural file I/O commands where each command accesses a single record of the file. Most RDBMSs also support commands that access a single record in the database management system.

Because of the many messages exchanged between the application and the database management system, it is not recommended that programmers replace procedural file I/O commands with procedural database commands. This may be especially troublesome if the database management system executes on a server and the application executes on a client.

A better approach is to modify the application so it accesses several database records with a single SQL command. An SQL cursor enables procedural application code to sequentially process multiple records returned by a single SQL request. The programmer replaces a loop containing procedural-file I/O commands by an SQL cursor and specifies the appropriate SQL nonprocedural command.

Several other modifications must be made to the application code, including commands to locate and open the database, lock and unlock the portions of the database to be used exclusively by the application, and write the code to examine the various completion codes returned by the

RDBMS. Generally, programmers must make extensive changes to a file application and test it thoroughly.

When modifying a file application to access a relational database, it also is tempting to replace the application user interface with a graphical user interface (GUI). Although transitioning to a GUI adds more risk to the migration effort, it may improve user productivity. Several GUI generators are available to help the programmer and user interface designer specify and implement GUI interfaces.

AVOIDING MIGRATION OF MANY APPLICATIONS AT ONCE

Database administrators can use two approaches — postponing the application modification or postponing the file migration to relational databases — to avoid migrating many applications and files to a relational database system at the same time.

The choice between postponing application modification or file migration is a function of the availability of a gateway, which makes application modification postponement possible and influences the length of the proposed postponement and the relative effort to carry out each type of postponement.

Postponing the Application Modification

Because of the work involved in migrating applications, it is sometimes necessary to postpone modifying some applications. For these applications, it may be possible to quickly generate a utility that extracts data from the database and creates the file structure required by the application. The application then executes against the file structure. Then, any data output by the application must be loaded back into the database. This approach is recommended only when time constraints do not permit immediate application modification.

Postponing the File Migration

Some database management systems support gateways that enable database applications to access nondatabase files. By using gateways, it is possible to modify some applications and keep the remaining applications in production. A file then is migrated to the RDBMS only after all of the applications that access the file have been migrated. This approach is recommended when time constraints do not permit immediate file migration.

Testing the Revised Applications and the Populated DBMS

Database administrators should develop test suites to validate the new relational database and its modified applications. It is recommended that the new database system be run in parallel with the old file system for at least one processing cycle. If something is wrong with the new system, the old system is still available.

Once the new system is in place, the final phase of fine-tuning the database description and the overall performance for efficiency can begin.

PHASE 3: FINE-TUNING

Modern businesses change constantly, and so must the database management systems that support the businesses. As requirements change, the RDBMS must incorporate changes to data items, business rules, and applications that access the relational database.

One of the major reasons for migrating to a relational database is data independence, which is the ability to change the data structure easily with minimal impact to the applications. Database administrators also should refine the physical data organization to provide efficient processing of the current set of applications.

Relational databases also lend themselves to future changes in data-processing strategies. An organization may want to distribute enterprise data across multiple databases on different computers connected by a local area network, control access to a relational database with browsers from anywhere in the world via the Internet, or introduce new data types, especially images, audio, and video.

CONCLUSION

Data should be migrated to an RDBMS only if the savings offered by the DBMS outweigh the expense of the migration. Schemas for the RDBMS should be designed using triggers, SQL statements, and stored procedures to implement business rules.

Finally, an incremental approach should be used to migrate the files and applications to the DBMS with file extractors and by using gateways to postpone file or application migration.

Section VI
Database Servers and Universal Servers

DATABASE SERVERS ARE AN IMPORTANT COMPONENT of the client/server application model. Database servers typically reside on a server platform running on top of a 32+ bit operating system, such as Windows NT, UNIX, AIX, or MVS. They service applications that also run on client platforms running 16 bit or 32 bit operating systems. The client/server model supports a continuum of architectures ranging from thin server–fat client to fat server–thin client, and anywhere in between. The "thin" and "fat" terminology refers to the amount of processing or business logic residing on the client or the server. In a thin client model, the application interface resides on the client platform and captures or displays information to the user. The data is transferred to the fat server where the business processing occurs. In a fat client model, the user interface still captures and presents data to the user; however, the processing also occurs on the client platform. In this model, the thin server acts as a data repository with minimal or no processing. Between these extremes, the business processing can be apportioned between the client and server platforms. The next generation application model extends the basic client/server model by including a web browser on the client platform. Although this model offers many advantages over the strictly thin/fat client/server model, the role of the database server is just as important. It is still the guardian of corporate data.

At a high level, a database server consists of the following components: a data repository, a database engine consisting of a query parser and optimizer, relational database compatibility, SQL (SEQUEL) dialect, database extensions, and a security framework. Distributed database servers allow components to be invoked remotely. One of the major enhancements of database servers over traditional databases is the programmable database engine. This integrates an SQL dialect with database extensions to maintain applications within the database server repository. Applications running on client platforms can invoke applications stored within the database server in this architecture. This provides dramatic improvements to client/server applications by moving processing logic to the database server platform, thus reducing data transfer volumes over local area networks and wide area networks. The database extensions or enhancements provide the capability of writing powerful applications that imbed SQL commands with procedural constructs. In the future, procedural constructs are expected to be supported through standard languages such as JAVA and C++. Microsoft® also is expecting to incorporate Visual Basic script into many of their products, including SQL Server. Such moves will allow components or applets to be distributed and redistributed freely across different technical requirements. Currently, the database extensions are, in essence, proprietary.

Chapter 29, "Creating SQL Server Tables Using DDL Scripts," uses batch scripts to create an example database that is used for testing in later sections of this book. The scripts provided in this chapter can be used by the reader to create personal versions of the test database. This chapter also demonstrates using scripts to repopulate database tables to a consistent baseline everytime they are executed.

Chapter 30, "Microsoft SQL Server: Key Transact-SQL Features," focuses on the common elements of the Transact-SQL dialect that allow SQL Server to be the world's first programmable database server. The constructs in this section provide the reader with the tools to write sophisticated database objects, such as stored procedures, views, and triggers.

Chapter 31, "Selecting Universal Data Server Technology," examines the features offered by universal data servers as compared to database servers. Universal data servers extend relational data servers to support new data types. Database administrators, information processing managers, information technologists, and long-term planners will find this article useful in solving management problems involving new types of data.

Chapter 32, "Middleware, Universal Data Servers, and Object-Oriented Data Servers," examines some of the additional data types that have grown in popularity over the past few years. This section examines four mechanisms, namely, data extraction, middleware, universal data server, and object-oriented data server for supporting complex data types, compound and multimedia. The features, strengths, and weaknesses of each mechanism are summarized. These four mechanisms represent four points of a long-term migration strategy to support the data management of complex data types.

Chapter 33, "Creating Effective Batch SQL Jobs," examines techniques in coding batch SQL routines to build highly reliable and well-performing jobs.

Chapter 34, "The Advancing Art of Indexing," describes the developments and challenges of indexing. The chapter states that efficient retrieval is especially important for decision support applications, which often lack appropriate indexing techniques. Various indexing techniques such as B-Trees, bit-maps, and inverted files are analyzed.

Chapter 35, "Rule Matching and Indexing Techniques," asserts that relational database systems do not meet the needs of many applications and describes rule matching and indexing techniques for rule-based systems. This chapter first describes some rule matching techniques and then covers indexing techniques, with special emphasis on constructing R+ trees.

Chapter 36, "Operating System Support for Database Servers," examines operating system features in UNIX, OS/2, Windows NT, and Netware that allow database servers to perform more efficiently in client/server applications.

Chapter 29

Creating SQL Server Tables Using DDL Scripts

Sanjiv Purba

THE AMERICAN NATIONAL STANDARDS INSTITUTE (ANSI) DATA DEFI-
NITION LANGUAGE (DDL) specifies Structured Query Language (SQL)
commands to define database objects, including tables. The basic command to create tables in SQL Server is the CREATE command. This chapter
defines a script to build a set of tables in a database that will be used in subsequent chapters of this handbook to demonstrate examples of other SQL
commands. This data model is intended to demonstrate one-one, zero-
many, and one-many relationships between table entities.

SQL Server is implemented with a collection of databases, including the
model, tempdb, master, and pubs. The first three databases contain system
information or are used by various SQL commands during normal database
operations. The pubs database, however, contains a sample application
and is intended to facilitate learning of the product. Users can feel free to
modify the information in this database. A pubs baseline always can be re-
installed from the installation CD-ROM. The DDL scripts in this chapter leverage the pubs database to store new tables that are created for the
sample database. The scripts in this chapter were tested under SQL Server
6.5 and SQL Server 7.x Beta on Dell and Tochiba Pentium processors.

DEFINING THE PHYSICAL DATA MODEL

Exhibit 1 shows a simple physical data model that supports a small number of different relationships. The main table is the customer table that
contains information about customers. This table has a one-to-many relationship with the address table. A customer can have many addresses
(e.g., shipping, mailing, and billing). The description for the type of the address is stored in the "address_code" table. The description for the

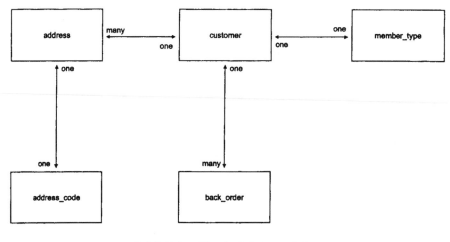

Exhibit 1. Physical data model.

"customer_type" is saved in the "member_type" table. A customer can have many products on back order as indicated in the "back_order" table.

BUILDING THE DDL SCRIPT

The script in this section is constructed to build the tables shown in Exhibit 1. The script can be saved in a text file with any text editor or word processor that can save ASCII text. The name of the text file is *scrcreat.txt*. It is assumed that there is a directory named *test* under the root directory. If this is not the case, one can either create it or use another directory name. Creating this script does not execute its commands. This is done in the next section of this chapter.

A streamlined syntax for creating a table in the SQL Server environment is shown here:

```
create table [database.user.].table_name

(

field_list data_type_list

)

go
```

Note: /* anything between the slashs and stars is considered to be comments by SQL Server.*/

```
/****************************************************/
/* Filename: \test\scrcreat.txt*/
/* Description:        */
/* Change the default database. Run this script*/
/* to create tables.  */
/****************************************************/
use pubs
go


/****************************************************/
/* Drop the tables before recreating them. Ignore*/
/* the information     */
/* message if the tables do not exist.*/
/****************************************************/
drop table customer
go
drop table member_type
go
drop table address
go
drop table back_order
go
drop table address_code
go


/****************************************************/
/* Create the customer table.*/
/****************************************************/
create table customer
(
```

```
        customer_no         int,

        last_name           char(30),

        middle_initial      char(1),

        first_name          char(30),

        home_phone          char(15),

        business_phone      char(15),

        fax                 char(15),

        email               char(25),

        preference          char(80),

        member_on           datetime,

        member_type         character(1)
)


/****************************************************/
/* Create the member_type table.                 */
/****************************************************/
create table member_type
(
    member_type         character(1),
    description         character(30)
)


/****************************************************/
/* Create the address.                            */
/****************************************************/
create table address
(
    customer_no         int,
    address_code        char(1),
    street1             char(25),
    street2             char(25),
    city                char(20),
```

```
        state_province        char(20),

        country               char(15),

        zip_pc                char(10)

)


/*****************************************************/
/* Create the back_order table.                   */
/*****************************************************/
create table back_order
(
        customer_no           int,

        request_date          datetime,

        sequence_no           integer,

        description           char(80),

        required_date         datetime,

        downpayment           money

)


/*****************************************************/
/* Create the address_code table.                 */
/*****************************************************/
create table address_code
(
        address_code          char(1),

        description           char(15)

)
    go
```

RUNNING THE SCRIPT TO CREATE THE TABLES

As shown in Exhibit 2, this Microsoft® SQL Server script can be executed in several ways to generate the tables in the pubs database.

Successful execution of the script generates the database tables directly into the default database, which this script establishes right at the start. If

Exhibit 2. Generating Tables in the "Pubs" Database

Method	Description	Actions
ISQL utility	This is a classic interactive character-based utility that is the underlying engine of the more advanced methods for executing SQL and Transact SQL commands, along with system procedures.	Go to the Operating System Prompt Type: isql /Uuserid /Ppassword /Ifile.txt (e.g., isql /Usa /Ppassword /iscript1.txt)
ISQL with utility	This is an interactive GUI utility that allows execution of SQL and Transact SQL commands and systems procedures. The results appear in a tab within the overall dialogue window. Another tab allows manipulation of query and trace flags.	Select File-Open Select script1.txt Execute the script that loads up
Enterprise Manager	Adminstrative tool that is used to create and manage database objects, generate scripts to manage the objects, and to establish object permissions.	Select database Select database objects Select table

one wants to confirm that the script is executed correctly, sign on to SQL Server and inspect a system table called *sysobjects*, which contains information about each table that exists in the database. This can be done with the following code:

```
isql -Usa -P

use pubs

go

select * from sysobjects

go
```

Conversely, one also can enter the following code into the Microsoft Query Analyzer and select the execute option from the pulldown menu:

```
use pubs

go

select * from sysobjects /* go is not needed in this
case */
```

Note: /* The tables that were created by the script will appear in the scrolling list. If the user was unable to see the tables because the list scrolled too fast, a WHERE clause on the SELECT can be used to reduce the number of rows that are returned by the command. */

```
use pubs

go

select * from sysobjects where <field operator qualifier>

go
```

INSERT DATA INTO THE USER-DEFINED TABLES

The ANSI standard defines a Data Manipulation Language (DML) that is supported by SQL Server to add data to the tables in a database. Specifically, data generally are inserted into user tables that are stored within databases. There are four common methods for adding data to tables:

1. INSERT: The ANSI SQL INSERT command places data into relational tables. It has many formats that are discussed in this chapter.
2. VIEWS: A view combines columns in one or more tables under a single object name. A view first must be created within a database before it can be used. Views are discussed in another section of this handbook.
3. BCP: This is an abbreviation for Batch Copy Procedure. It operates in a normal and a fast copy mode. BCP essentially processes data that is in various formats in input files and adds the data into the relational tables. BCP works faster than the INSERT command and is preferred for manipulating large volumes of data because of its performance improvements. BCP also can be used to extract data from database tables and insert them into ASCII files.
4. Third-Party Tools: Numerous third-party tools are available to insert data into tables using GUI interfaces (e.g., SQL Programmer).

The different forms of the INSERT command are covered in this chapter. The first format of this command has the following syntax:

Format 1:

This format of the INSERT command adds one record or row to the database table identified in "table_name". The table can be in the default database. If it is not, then the "table_name" must be qualified fully as in [[database.user.]tablename]. Specific fields from the table are included within the first parenthesis of the command. There is a one-to-one correspondence to these fields by values contained in the second parenthesis. If fields are identified as NOT NULL in the table creation script, SQL Server will not insert a data row, unless these fields are included in the command

and provided with a NON NULL value. Not all INSERTs are successful, so it is good programming practice to inspect the results of an INSERT attempt and take an appropriate action in the event that the INSERT was unsuccessful. Some reasons for this include a referential integrity violation, insufficient space in the database, and insufficient permissions to write to a table or within a database.

The sequence of the field names must match the order of the values. For example, *value1* will be inserted into *fieldname1*, *value2* will be inserted into *fieldname2*, and *value3* will be inserted into *fieldname3*. SQL Server ensures that the datatypes of the values match the datatypes of the fields. The order of the field names in this command does not have to match the physical order of the table. Values can be literals or functions, such as *convert(parameters)* and *getdate( )*.

SQL Server commands can be entered in upper case (e.g., VALUES), lower case (e.g., values), or mixed case (e.g., VALues). SQL Server displays a message (unless the option NO COUNT DISPLAY) showing the number of rows that are affected by a command. In this case, the message is "(1 row(s) affected)." If the NO COUNT DISPLAY option is selected, SQL Server displays an acknowledgement of success (e.g., "The command(s) completed successfully").

Syntax:

```
INSERT [INTO] table_name
    (fieldname1, fieldname2, ....)
    VALUES
    (value1, value2, ....)
```

Examples:

```
1. INSERT INTO address_code
   (
        address_code,
        description
   )
   VALUES
        ("S," "Summer")
   go
2. INSERT address_code
   (
        address_code,
        description
   )
   VALUES
```

```
       ("2," "Home 2")
    go
```

Format 2:

In this format of the command, a value is provided for every field in the designated table. The order of the values must match the physical order of the fields in the physical table. This command will insert one data row or record to the table.

Syntax:

```
INSERT [INTO] table_name

    VALUES

        (value1, value2, ....)
```

Examples:

```
1. INSERT address_code
       VALUES ("M," "Mailing")
    go
```

The character field lengths that are specified in the table field create statements that are enforced when an attempt is made to insert data into the column fields. For example, the description field in the address was created with a length of 10. An attempt to insert a value that is greater than this length generates the error message: "String/Binary data would be truncated — Command has been aborted."

Format 3:

This format of the command inserts all the matching rows in the select clause associated with "table_name2" into "table_name1". The rows selected from the second table will be inserted/appended into the first table. The number of columns selected from the second table must match the order and the datatypes of the columns in the first table. As shown in examples 3 and 4, it is possible to use placeholders for existing columns. The same INSERT command can be re-executed to insert repeatedly the same set of rows so long as the CREATE TABLE command did not specify constraints to limit duplicate rows or keys. The use of INSERT in this example assumes that "table_name2" already exists.

```
INSERT [INTO] table_name1

    SELECT [column_list] from table_name2

        WHERE clause
```

Examples:

```
1. INSERT newtable
      SELECT address_code, description from address_code
   go
2. INSERT newtable
      SELECT address_code, description from address_code
         WHERE address_code = "R"
   go
3. INSERT newtable
      SELECT address_code, "holder" from address_code
         WHERE address_code = "R"
   go
4. INSERT INTO newtable
      SELECT address_code, NULL from address_code
   go
```

The INSERT command can be initiated from any of the methods that were used to execute the table creation script (e.g., the isql/w command). Many experienced SQL Server professionals prefer using a script to insert data so that they can be rerun whenever the database is reconstructed. Data insert scripts are also useful for establishing stable, consistent environments during application testing phases. The following script inserts sample data records into the tables created by the *scrcreat.txt* script:

```
/*****************************************************/
/* Filename: \test\scrinsert.txt                  */
/* Modification History:                          */
/*                                                */
/* Description:                                   */
/* Insert data rows into the tables in the address
database.                                         */
/*****************************************************/


/* Establish the pubs database as the new default database
*/
use pubs

go


/* Use the truncate command to drop data in the tables before
inserting new data. The truncate command has advantages for
efficiency (e.g. it does not write to the log) over the other
SQL commands that can be used to clear tables.          */
```

```
TRUNCATE TABLE customer

TRUNCATE TABLE member_type

TRUNCATE TABLE address

TRUNCATE TABLE back_order

TRUNCATE TABLE address_code

go


/**********************************************/

/* Insert data rows into the customer table */

/**********************************************/

INSERT INTO customer

(

    customer_no,

    last_name,

    middle_initial,

    first_name,

    home_phone,

    business_phone,

    fax,

    email,

    preference,

    member_on,

    member_type

)

VALUES

(

    1000,

    "Sector,"

    "S,"

    "Vic,"

    "111-222-3333,"
```

```
        "111-333-4444,"
        "111-222-3334,"
        "ssector@asgirus.com,"
        "New Editions,"
        "Jan 01, 1993,"
        "1"
)


/*************************************************/
/* Insert data rows into the member_type table */
/*************************************************/
INSERT INTO member_type
(
    member_type,
    description
)
VALUES
(
    "1,"
    "Coin collector"
)


/*********************************************/
/* Insert data rows into the address table */
/*********************************************/
INSERT INTO address
(
    customer_no,
    address_code,
    street1,
    street2,
    city,
```

```
        state_province,

        country,

        zip_pc

)

VALUES

(

        1000,

        "R,"

        "9999 Asgirus Street,"

        ' ',

        "Mississauga,"

        "Ontario,"

        "Canada,"

        "L5M 3J1"

)


/***********************************************/
/* Insert data rows into the back_order table */
/***********************************************/
INSERT INTO back_order

(

        customer_no,

        request_date,

        sequence_no,

        description,

        required_date,

        downpayment

)

VALUES

(

        1000,

        "Jan 1, 1998,"
```

```
        1,

        "New minted Mexican coins with gold content,"

        "June 1, 1998,"

        100

    )


    /************************************************/
    /* Insert data rows into the address_code table */
    /************************************************/
    INSERT INTO address_code
    (

        address_code,

        description

    )
    VALUES
    (

        "R,"

        "Residence"

    )
    go
```

The previous script adds a single customer to the database with supporting data to complete the table relationships. The script that follows in this section inserts another customer with supporting data to provide for some variation in the results that are selected from the database.

Using batch scripts to insert data into tables requires careful attention to referential integrity (RI) issues. Despite best efforts, mistakes in RI easily can be made while coding the script (e.g., mistyping an "S" for an "R"). Because the data is being inserted directly into the tables, such errors may not be detected. For production data, it is preferable to use validation programs to validate the data before inserting it directly into the table. Another method, which is covered in a different section of this handbook, is to use table constraints for data validation. Batch script data entry is best restricted to test environments.

```
/***************************************************/
/* Filename: \test\scrinser2.txt                   */
/* Modification History:                           */
/*                                                 */
/* Description:                                    */
/* Insert a second customer to the database.       */
/***************************************************/


/* establish the pubs database as the new default database
*/
use pubs
go


/*******************************************/
/* Insert data rows into the customer table */
/*******************************************/
INSERT INTO customer
(
    customer_no,
    last_name,
    middle_initial,
    first_name,
    home_phone,
    business_phone,
    fax,
    email,
    preference,
    member_on,
    member_type
)
VALUES
(
```

```
        2000,

        "Ryder,"

        "R,"

        "Steve,"

        "333-444-4444,"

        "888-888-8888,"

        "999-999-9999,"

        "sryder@tobos.ca,"

        "US,Canadian,"

        "Feb 01, 1997,"

        "2"

    )


/***********************************************/
/* Insert data rows into the member_type table */
/***********************************************/
INSERT INTO member_type

    (

        member_type,
        description

    )

VALUES

    (

        "2,"

        "Stamp Collector"

    )


/*********************************************/
/* Insert data rows into the address table */
/*********************************************/
INSERT INTO address

    (
```

```
    customer_no,
    address_code,
    street1,
    street2,
    city,
    state_province,
    country,
    zip_pc
)
VALUES
(
    2000,
    "S,"
    "8 Juanita Court,"
    " ",
    "New York City,"
    "New York,"
    "U.S.A.,"
    "10007"
)


/**********************************************/
/* Insert data rows into the back_order table */
/**********************************************/
INSERT INTO back_order
(
    customer_no,
    request_date,
    sequence_no,
    description,
    required_date,
    downpayment
```

```
    )

    VALUES

    (

        2000,

        "Jan 1, 1998,"

        1,

        "New US stamp,"

        "April 30, 1998,"

        50

    )


    /**************************************************/
    /* Insert data rows into the address_code table */
    /**************************************************/
    INSERT INTO address_code

    (

        address_code,

        description

    )

    VALUES

    (

        "S,"

        "Summer Cottage"

    )

    go
```

SELECTING DATA

The basic command for retrieving information from tables is the ANSI '92 compliant SELECT command. One use of this statement was demonstrated in conjunction with the INSERT command, where multiple records from one table were inserted into another table. This command has an extensive list of options, some of which are discussed in this section. The SELECT command can be used to retrieve information from user-defined tables and system tables in the database environment. The SELECT command displays information retrieved from relational table(s) in columnar format. The table column names are used as headings for the columns in the output automatically.

Syntax:

```
SELECT ALL/DISTINCT/column_field_names

    FROM table/view hints

        WHERE clause

            ORDER BY clause
```

The "Order By" clause sorts the output by the field(s) that are specified. The default sequence is ascending sequence. The asterick (*) can be used to select all the column fields from a table, as in *SELECT * from table_name*. SQL Server accepts either the double or the single quotes around character values. Consequently, "R" and 'R' would achieve the same result. However, SQL Server is insistent on matching the symbols, so "R' is not syntactically acceptable.

Examples:

1. `SELECT * from address_code`
   `go`
2. `SELECT * from address_code`
       `WHERE address_code = "R"`
   `go`
3. `SELECT description from address_code`
   `go`
4. `SELECT * from customer`
       `ORDER BY last_name`
   `go`
5. `SELECT address_code code, description from address_code`
       `ORDER BY description`

By default, the names of the table fields serve as column headings in the output. The table field name can be overridden by leaving a space and entering another name for the column heading, without surrounding quotes. An example of this is "address_code" code. In this example, "code" will serve as the column heading.

CONCLUSION

Batch scripts offer an effective method for executing DDL and DML SQL code that can be rerun at any time. They also can be put through the rigors of source management, configuration management, and version control to rebuild data environments to specific baselines. This chapter provided examples to create, insert, and retrieve data from a Microsoft SQL Server database.

Chapter 30

Microsoft SQL Server: Key Transact-SQL Features

Sanjiv Purba

THIS CHAPTER EXAMINES SOME OF THE USEFUL TRANSACT-SQL COM-MANDS AND DATABASE OBJECTS that support the development of substantial application modules that are saved inside the Structured Query Language (SQL) Server data dictionary. These include views, stored procedures, triggers, and column constraints (e.g., primary, foreign, and identity). This chapter provides streamlined syntax for creating and manipulating common Transact-SQL database objects to allow the reader the opportunity to learn them in this primer. The list of Transact-SQL features covered in this chapter includes the following:

- *Joins*: This is an ANSI SQL-compliant feature that is used to join multiple SQL Server tables to produce result sets, which are themselves user tables. For example a table of names and addresses can be joined to produce a result set containing name plus addresses. There are several different types of joins, including equi-join and outer join.
- *Subqueries*: Subqueries are similar to joins in terms of their end product. Subqueries are used to produce result sets from a group of SQL Server tables based on variable subqualifiers. For example, "for all employees living in Boston, find the ones that wear red hats."
- *Views*: Views offer a mechanism for accessing multiple physical tables based on a single logical view. Security and permissions can be allocated to the view to control the types of access users of the view have pertaining to the underlying physical tables. Views hide the physical complexity of a database structure from the users accessing the data.

0-8493-9976-9/99/$0.00+$.50
© 1999 by CRC Press LLC

- *Stored Procedures*: Stored procedures were once an extension to the basic SQL Dialect standard. As such, their implementation method varies from database server to database server. For example, both Oracle and Sybase support stored procedures. However, the syntax and implementation of these are not identical — meaning that stored procedures cannot be transferred seamlessly from one tool to the other. This severely restricts their portability and interoperability. However, they offer many advantages that make them highly popular. Microsoft SQL Server and Sybase SQL Server, due to their common ancestry, have similar implementations of stored procedures. Stored procedures support complex programming logic (e.g., if, while, execute commands) that can be leveraged to build sophisticated programs that are invoked from the data server's data dictionary.
- *Triggers*: Triggers are a special kind of stored procedure that automatically are invoked whenever predefined events occur on specific tables. These events can be identified and trapped by the developer. Triggers often are used to maintain referential integrity in a database. For example, selling a product to a customer can fire a trigger to decrement the onhand quantities of that product and perhaps place a new order to the supplier — all from the same trigger.

Note: The SQL Server tables used in this chapter are based on tables that were created in the Chapter 30, "Creating SQL Server Tables Using DDL Scripts."

JOINS

The Relational Data Model is based on mathematical set theory. Each table in a database can be viewed as a mathematical set and, as such, mathematical operations are used to manipulate them. One of the most common operations involves joining two or more tables to create temporary or virtual tables. A join operation across a group of tables relies on foreign key fields in each of the tables involved in the operation and a SELECT command to retrieve the results into the new table. Several types of joins are supported by the ANSI Standard, but this chapter focuses on one of the more commonly used ones, namely the "Equi-Join." In this type of join, a column field in Table A is joined with a field in Table B. The fields are not required to have identical names, but they must have compatible data types. An equi-join operation returns a set that combines rows from Table A and Table B that have matching values in the key/foreign key columns. A join can support more than two tables, however. Due to physical performance reasons the practical guideline is to use between six and eight tables, with a desired limit of four or less. Join operations that involve more than about eight tables become very difficult to maintain from a programming complexity, as well as from a performance perspective. The result set of a join operation can contain all the fields in the matching records or a reduced set of fields, as identified in the JOIN command itself.

An equi-join requires an exact match between columns in separate the tables. The natural join involves two tables in the FROM clause of a SELECT statement without a WHERE clause so that all rows are matched with all other rows in the tables involved in the natural join. The outer join involves the situation where a value in table A does not have a matching key record in the second table. In the equi-join, such a record would be dropped from the result set. In the outer join the result set contains all the records in the equi-join result set plus the records that do not have matches in the remaining tables. There are many practical applications of this. For example, suppose that Table A is a list of depositors and Table B is a list of their deposits. An equi-join selects only depositors who have made deposits. An outer join selects depositors who have made deposits and depositors who have not made deposits yet.

Some other common examples where equi-joins are useful include the following:

- Join two tables, one containing a code for a person's job title as well as the person's name, and the other table being a code table. The resulting set displays the person's name and the actual job description.
- Join three tables, two as in the previous example, and a third one containing all the different addresses corresponding to a person's year-around requirements.

Although equi-joins are a powerful tool for extracting ordered information from relational tables, they have a performance overhead that must be considered and possibly offset through smarter programming techniques. Some methods for doing this include the order of the tables in the join clause, the presence of indexes on the columns specified in the join command, and the number of records in the tables involved in the joins. Badly constructed joins literally can lock up SQL Server and make it virtually inaccessible to production users.

A simplified syntax for performing an Equi-Join on any number of tables is shown in the following:

Syntax:

```
SELECT [alias.]column_list
    FROM table1 alias1, table2 alias2 ....
        WHERE selection_clause
```

Examples:

```
1. SELECT a.first_name, a.last_name, b.description
```

```
    FROM customer a, member_type b
        WHERE a.member_type = b.member_type
    go
 2. SELECT a.first_name, a.last_name, b.description,
        c.address_type, c.street1, c.city
        FROM customer a, member_type b, address c
            WHERE a.member_type = b.member_type AND
                a.customer_no = c.customer_no
    go
```

SUBQUERIES

Subqueries and joins can produce equivalent data result sets in many common cases. Subqueries generally are nested in the WHERE or HAVING clauses of Data Manipulation Language commands, such as SELECT, UPDATE, INSERT, and DELETE. This section provides examples of subqueries that utilize both the EXISTS and the IN keywords. The syntax for a subquery is shown here:

Syntax:

```
  SELECT column_fields FROM table_list

      WHERE [EXISTS/IN] (selection_clause)
```

Examples:

```
 1. /**************************************************/
    In this example, the subquery returns a true/false to the
    WHERE clause when customer_no exists in the address table
    and has an address_type of "R."
    /**************************************************/
    SELECT first_name, last_name, home_phone
        FROM customer
            WHERE EXISTS (SELECT * from address
                WHERE customer_no = customer.customer_no
                AND address_code = "R")
    go


 2. /**************************************************/
    The IN command word can limit the scope of the set.
    /**************************************************/
    SELECT first_name, last_name, home_phone
        FROM customer
            WHERE customer_no IN (SELECT customer_no from ad-
    dress
                WHERE address_code = "R")
    go
```

VIEWS

Views provide a mechanism for accessing one or more tables in a relational database without requiring knowledge of the physical details of how the tables are organized. Views are useful in the following situations:

- Simplifying user access to data by providing non-SQL users with a convenient method of accessing data that they require, however it is organized.
- Combining multiple table under a common object name.
- Implementing a security layer to restrict user access to relevant column names only.

Creating a view is similar to creating a user table in that a view object is created for the default database. This means that the view is actually a physical object. Running views causes a new user table to be built as a result of filtering table columns through the restrictions of the view. Views are identified uniquely with object names within a database. A view must be dropped before a view with the same name can be updated or recreated in that database. Once a view is created, it can be used as a user table name with the SELECT command. Views do not support triggers.

A simplified syntax for the CREAT VIEW command is the following:

Syntax:

```
CREATE VIEW owner.viewname [column_list]

    AS select_clause
```

A simplified syntax for the command to drop a view from a database is as follows:

Syntax:

```
DROP VIEW owner.viewname
```

A simplified syntax to execute a view after it is created is as follows:

Syntax:

```
SELECT [*/column_names] from view_name where search_clause
```

Unlike many other SQL Server commands, view objects are created in the default database only.

Examples:

1. Create a view for a user who only requires a subset of fields in a table. Use a DROP VIEW command to drop the view before trying

to create it to support iterative execution of the CREATE VIEW command. This code can be entered interactively or through an executed script file.

```
DROP VIEW customer_contacts
go


CREATE VIEW customer_contacts
AS
    SELECT   first_name,   last_name,   home_phone,
business_phone
        FROM customer
go


SELECT * FROM customer_contacts
                    /* retrieves all the columns in the view
*/
go


SELECT first_name from customer_contacts
go
```

2. In this example, a view is created to join two tables. This example demonstrates how views can be used to simplify database access by users. Instead of learning to write joins or other complex queries, users use a view name as a virtual table to retrieve their data. However, using views is not free. Someone in the data organization needs to be charged with the responsibility for building and maintaining views for the user community. This often turns into a full-time job. The caretaker of the views must understand the business application.

```
DROP VIEW customer_type
go


CREATE VIEW customer_type
AS
    SELECT a.first_name, a.last_name, b.description
        FROM customer a, member_type b
            WHERE a.member_type = b.member_type
go


SELECT * FROM customer_type
                /* retrieves all the columns in the view */
go
```

STORED PROCEDURES

Stored procedures are an innovation of Sybase SQL Server and Microsoft SQL Server and were an important contribution to the first programmable database server product widely released in 1987. They quickly proved their value in distributed client/server applications and SQL Server (which was essentially the same product in both the Sybase and Microsoft versions until 1995) quickly gained market share. Sales people from the competitor dataserver products found many IS directors asking them a simple question, "Does your product support stored procedures?" For a time, the answer was "no", so SQL Server started to be the product of choice in many industries. Stored procedures are now an integral part of many database servers, including Oracle. Stored procedures also support reuse, security, and software distribution.

Stored procedures can be written inside or outside the SQL Server environment, but they are stored directly in SQL Server system tables, including both sysobjects and sysmessages. Stored procedures themselves are a combination of SQL Data Manipulation Language (DML), Data Definition Langauge (DDL), Data Control Language (DCL), and Transact-SQL. SQL, by itself, does not support repetitive program flows and conditional structures. Transact-SQL provides this enhancement to the basic SQL dialect. The combination of all these command structures enables stored procedures to support programs that are as sophisticated and complex as 3GL and 4GL languages.

Stored procedures are constructed in several steps. A stored procedure can be written using a text editor in the operating system environment, or can be written directly into the SQL Server system tables using the SQL Server Query Analyzer (previously SQL/w) or the SQL Server Enterprise Manager. These are the most common methods of writing and saving stored procedures. Other methods also exist. For example, a stored procedure can be written using a third generation language (e.g., C programming language) with embedded SQL Server. However, this latter method has performance implications that make it less desirable than the other methods in many cases. This method also creates a fat client and a thin server, which creates a high network load for client/server applications. In the case where a stored procedure is written into an operating system file using a text editor, the stored procedure must be parsed into an SQL Server database using ISQL or one of the other methods of invoking SQL commands in the SQL environment. The parse procedure is sometimes called a "compile" procedure, but this is not a true compile in the 3GL sense in that an object module is not created. Rather, the parse procedure interprets the code in the stored procedure and returns error messages if there are syntactical logical errors (e.g., a reference to a database object that does not exist). If the stored procedure commands are interpreted success-fully, the entire code belonging to that stored procedure is saved into the default database system tables.

Because stored procedures are created and stored as database objects, it is necessary to drop them before they are created. The basic syntax for writing a stored procedure is as follows:

Syntax:

```
CREATE PROC[EDURE] proc_name

(

    @parameter          datatype,

    @parameter_list     datatype

)

AS

DECLARE local_variable       datatype,
        local_variable_list  datatype


Transact SQL Statements


RETURN return_code

go
```

A comprehensive list of Transact SQL statements are supported within stored procedures including SQL commands and built-in functions. Stored procedures also can call nested stored procedures or call themselves re-cursively. Stored procedures are dropped from a database using the follow-ing syntax:

Syntax:

```
DROP PROCEDURE proc_name

go
```

Stored procedures that successfully are compiled into the database sys-tem tables can be executed using the following command syntax:

Syntax:

```
EXECUTE proc_name [parameters]

go
```

When working with stored procedures, two names are relevant. The first name is the operating system file name that contains the script for the stored procedure. The second name is the stored procedure name that is saved in the sysobjects table. The operating system file name is *stexple1.sq*l. The stored procedure name is *stexample1*.

Examples:

1. The following example creates a stored procedure in the default database under the object name *stexample1*.

```
/*----------------------------------------------------*/
/*--Code below this line is saved into stexple1.sql--*/
/*----------------------------------------------------*/
/* Filename: stexple1.sql */

/* drop the stored procedure*/
DROP PROC stexample1
go     /* test this procedure without the go. Does it still
work? */

CREATE PROC stexample1
AS
    SELECT 'this is a stored procedure'
    RETURN 0 /* return a 0 code to the calling routine */
go

/*----------------------------------------------------*/
/*--Code above this line is saved into stexple1.sql--*/
/*----------------------------------------------------*/

/* Execute the stored procedure by entering the following
command(s) in the MS SQL Server Query Analyzer, a batch
file, or through an isql session */

stexample1
go
```

Stored procedures (and other objects like views and triggers) are compiled into several system tables within the default database. The text is stored in syscomments under an ID. Several system procedures can retrieve the code for a stored procedure and save it in an ASCII operating system file for modification and recompilation. The sysobjects system table contains header information for all database objects including stored procedures.

2. The following stored procedure inserts one record into the "member_type" code table:

```
/* Filename: stinsert.sql */

/* drop the stored procedure if it exists. */
IF EXISTS (select name from sysboects where name = "insmem-
ber")
BEGIN
    select "stored procedure found"
    DROP PROC insmember
end
go

CREATE PROC insmember
(
    @member_type      char (1),
    @description      char (30)
)
AS
    /**********************************/
    /* Include data validation tests here */
    /**********************************/
    INSERT INTO member_type
    (
        member_type,
        description
    )
    VALUES
    (
        @member_type,
        @description
    )

    /**************************************************/
    /* Test for insert error and take appropriate
    action */
    /**************************************************/
    RETURN 0 /* return a 0 code to the calling routine */
go

/**************************************************/
/* Execute the stored procedure and enter the parameters
in*/
/* the order they are expected by the proc —
member_type                                            */
/* first and description second                          */
/**************************************************/
insmember "B," "Book Collector"
```

```
go

insmember "A," "AAAA" /* insert another member_type */
select * from member_type
              /*display the contents of the member_type ta-
ble*/
go
```

SQL Server displays a success message if the command was successful (e.g., "The command(s) completed successfully"). To review the results of the insert, use the command format: "select * from member_type." Trying to execute the stored procedure without the correct number or data types of the parameters displays appropriate error messages and the insert is not completed. In fact, SQL Server displays meaningful information to identify the missing parameters.

3. The following stored procedure updates the description for an existing "member_type":

```
/* Filename: stupdate.sql */

/* drop the stored procedure if it exists. */
IF EXISTS (select name from sysobjects where name = "upd-
member")
      DROP PROC updmember
go

CREATE PROC updmember
(
    @member_type      char (1),
    @description      char (30)
)
AS
    /*****************************************/
    /* include data validation tests here */
    /*****************************************/
    UPDATE member_type
    SET description = @description
        where member_type = @member_type

    if @@rowcount < 1 /* no rows were affected */
        print "no record found to update" /* raiseerror
        here */
    else
        print "record updated"
    RETURN 0 /* return a 0 code to the calling routine */
        go
```

```
/***************************************************/
/* Execute the stored procedure and enter the
parameters in                                    */
/* the order they are expected by the proc — member_type
first                                            */
/* and description second                        */
/***************************************************/
updmember "B," "Book/Magazines"
go

select * from member_type
go
```

4. The following stored procedure deletes a record from the "member_type" code table based on a "member_type":

```
/* Filename: studelete.sql */

/* Drop the stored procedure if it exists. */
IF EXISTS (select name from sysobjects where name = "delmem-
ber")
DROP PROC delmember
go

CREATE PROC delmember
(
    @member_type      char (1)
)
AS
    DELETE member_type
        WHERE member_type = @member_type

    /***************************************************/
    /* Test for insert error and take appropriate
    action                                         */
    /***************************************************/
    if @@rowcount < 1 /* no rows were affected */
        print "no record found to delete" /*raiseerror
        here*/
    else
        print "record deleted"
    RETURN 0 /* return a 0 code to the calling routine */
go

/***************************************************/
/* Execute the stored procedure and enter the parameters
in                                               */
```

```
/* the order they are expected by the proc — member_type
only                                                      */
/******************************************************/
delmember "A"
go
```

5. The following stored procedure inserts two records into the address
database into the tables: customer and address tables. This example demonstrates issuing a nested procedure call.

```
/* Filename: stins2.sql */

/* Drop the stored procedure if it exists */
IF EXISTS (select name from sysobjects where name = "inscus-
tomer")
    DROP PROC inscustomer
go

/* Drop the stored procedure if it exists */
IF EXISTS (select name from sysobjects where name = "insad-
dress")
    DROP PROC insaddress
go

/*********************************************/
/* Create the inscustomer stored procedure */
/*********************************************/
CREATE PROC inscustomer
(
    @customer_no        int,
    @last_name          char(30),
    @middle_initial     char(1),
    @first_name         char(30),
    @home_phone         char(15),
    @business_phone     char(15),
    @fax                char(15),
    @email              char(25),
    @preference         char(80),
    @member_on          datetime,
    @member_type        character(1),
    @address_code       char(1),
    @street1            char(25),
    @street2            char(25),
    @city               char(20),
    @state_province     char(20),
    @country            char(15),
    @zip_pc             char(10)
```

```
)
AS
DECLARE
@return_code  int /* variable names must begin with @ */

/*************************************/
/* Include data validation tests here */
/*************************************/

INSERT customer
(
    customer_no,
    last_name,
    middle_initial,
    first_name,
    home_phone,
    business_phone,
    fax,
    email,
    preference,
    member_on,
    member_type
)
VALUES
(
    @customer_no,
    @last_name,
    @middle_initial,
    @first_name,
    @home_phone,
    @business_phone,
    @fax,
    @email,
    @preference,
    @member_on,
    @member_type
)

/*********************************************************/
/* Test for insert error and take appropriate action */
/*********************************************************/

/* Call stored procedure to insert address record */
EXECute @return_code = insaddress @customer_no,
@address_code, @street1, @street2, @city, @state_province,
@country, @zip_pc
```

```
/**************************************************/
/* Inspect return_code, test for error and take
appropriate                                       */
/* action                                         */
/**************************************************/

RETURN 0 /* return a 0 code to the calling routine */
go

/******************************************/
/* Create the insaddress stored procedure */
/******************************************/
CREATE PROC insaddress
(
    @customer_no        int,
    @address_code       char(1),
    @street1            char(25),
    @street2            char(25),
    @city               char(20),
    @state_province     char(20),
    @country            char(15),
    @zip_pc             char(10)
)
AS

/***********************************/
/* include data validation tests here */
/***********************************/

INSERT address
(
    customer_no,
    address_code,
    street1,
    street2,
    city,
    state_province,
    country,
    zip_pc
)
VALUES
(
    @customer_no,
    @address_code,
    @street1,
    @street2,
```

```
        @city,
        @state_province,
        @country,
        @zip_pc
    )

    /****************************************************/
    /* Test for insert error and take appropriate action */
    /****************************************************/

    RETURN 0 /* return a 0 code to the calling routine */
    go

    /****************************************************/
    /* Execute the stored procedure and enter the
    parameters in                                      */
    /* the order they are expected by the proc.          */
    /****************************************************/
    inscustomer 3000, "Flanders," "T," "Marsha,"
        "9998888888," "9899899999," "9999998888,"
        "mflanders@tobos.com," "European & Vegetarian Cook
    Books,"
        "Mar 1995," "1,"
        "H," "567 Aeta Rd," " ", "Dallas," "Texas," "USA,"
        "10001"
    go
```

6. The following stored procedure updates two records in the address database inside the tables: customer and address tables. This example demonstrates a nested procedure call.

```
    /* Filename: stupd2.sql */

    /* drop the stored procedure if it exists. */
    IF EXISTS (select name from sysobjects where name = "upd-
    customer")
        DROP PROC updcustomer
    go

    /* drop the stored procedure if it exists. */
    IF EXISTS (select name from sysobjects where name = "updad-
    dress")
        DROP PROC updaddress /* drops all triggers with the ta-
    ble */
    go
```

```
/******************************************/
/* Create the updcustomer stored procedure */
/******************************************/
CREATE PROC updcustomer
(
    @customer_no         int,
    @last_name           char(30),
    @middle_initial      char(1),
    @first_name          char(30),
    @home_phone          char(15),
    @business_phone      char(15),
    @fax                 char(15),
    @email               char(25),
    @preference          char(80),
    @member_on           datetime,
    @member_type         character(1),
    @address_code        char(1),
    @street1             char(25),
    @street2             char(25),
    @city                char(20),
    @state_province      char(20),
    @country             char(15),
    @zip_pc              char(10)
)
AS
    DECLARE
    @return_code int    /* variable names must begin with
    @ */

    /************************************/
    /* Include data validation tests here */
    /************************************/
    UPDATE customer
        SET
            last_name        = @last_name,
            middle_initial   = @middle_name,
            first_name       = @first_name,
            home_phone       = @home_phone,
            business_phone   = @business_phone,
            fax              = @fax,
            email            = @email,
            preference       = @preference,
            member_on        = @member_on,
            member_type      = @member_type
                WHERE
                    customer_no = @customer_no
```

```
/*****************************************************/
/* Test for update error and take appropriate action */
/*****************************************************/

/* Call stored procedure to update address record */
EXECute @return_code = updaddress @customer_no,
address_code, @street1, @street2, @city, @state_province,
@country, @zip_pc

/*****************************************************/
/* Inspect return_code, test for error and take                    */
appropriate                                                        */
/* action                                                          */
/*****************************************************/

     RETURN 0 /* return a 0 code to the calling routine */
go

/*******************************************/
/* Create the updaddress stored procedure */
/*******************************************/

CREATE PROC updaddress
(
      @customer_no        int,
      @address_code       char(1),
      @street1            char(25),
      @street2            char(25),
      @city               char(20),
      @state_province     char(20),
      @country            char(15),
      @zip_pc             char(10)
)
AS
      /***********************************/
      /* include data validation tests here */
      /***********************************/
      UPDATE address
      SET
          address_code    = @address_code,
          street1         = @street1,
          street2         = @street2,
          city            = @city,
          state_province  = @state_province,
          country         = @country,
          zip_pc          = @zip_pc
```

```
        WHERE
            customer_no = @customer_no

/************************************************/
/* test for update error and take appropriate
action                                          */
/************************************************/
    RETURN 0 /* return a 0 code to the calling routine */
go

/****************************************************/
/* execute the stored procedure and enter the
parameters in                                        */
/* the order they are expected by the proc.          */
/****************************************************/
updcustomer 3000, "Flanders," "T," "Marsha,"
    "9998888888," "9899899999," "9999998888,"
    "mflanders@tobos.com," "Asian & Vegetarian Cook
    Books,"
    "Mar 1995," "1,"
    "H," "87 Rhodes Rd," " ", "Dallas," "Texas," "USA,"
    "10001"
go
```

7. The following stored procedure deletes a logical customer record. This requires two tables to be processed for the deletion, namely, customer and address.

```
/* Filename: stdel2.sql */

/* drop the stored procedure if it exists. */
IF EXISTS (select name from sysobjects where name = "del-
customer")
    DROP PROC delcustomer
go

/********************************************/
/* Create the delcustomer stored procedure */
/********************************************/
CREATE PROC delcustomer
(
    @customer_no          int
)
AS
    DECLARE
    @return_code          int /* variable names must begin
                              with @ */
```

```
/**************************************/
/* include data validation tests here */
/**************************************/

DELETE address
    WHERE customer_no = @customer_no

/****************************************************/
/* inspect return_code, test for error and take
appropriate                                         */
/* action                                           */
/****************************************************/
DELETE customer
    WHERE customer_no =@customer_no
    /************************************************/
    /* inspect return_code, test for error and take
    appropriate                                     */
    /* action                                       */
    /************************************************/

    RETURN 0 /* return a 0 code to the calling routine */
go
```

TRIGGERS

Triggers are another SQL Server innovation and a solid feature of the programmable database server. All triggers are stored procedures, but not all stored procedures are triggers. Triggers essentially are stored procedures that are activated by specific events on a table and, hence, use essentially the same system tables as stored procedures. (Triggers use the sysprocedures table.) These events include the following at the table level: *insert a row*, *update a row*, and *delete a row*. Triggers also can be created to fire when specific columns are updated. The guidelines provided for stored procedure creation and maintenance through scripts also apply for triggers. Triggers are created in the current database, but they can access objects in any database within the same SQL Server. There are several reasons to use triggers in an application: (1) referential integrity, (2) cascading operations (inserts/deletes), (3) code reuse, (4) transaction rollbacks, and (5) simplified module development. A trigger is fired by a specified event on a table or a table column. The trigger has access to two trigger tables, namely, *inserted* and *deleted*, before the trigger completes. Insert operations use the inserted trigger table. Delete operations use the deleted trigger table. Update operations use the inserted and deleted trigger tables. These tables are referenced with these specific names, inserted and deleted in the command section of triggers.

It is important to realize that triggers have had a performance overhead since SQL Server first emerged in the marketplace. This overhead performance has been reduced with the release of faster CPU chips and will continue to decline with the release of streamlined SQL Server modules in the future. Before designing a large number of triggers, it is important to benchmark the use of a few triggers to ensure that the application response time is sufficient to meet requirements.

The process for creating and using triggers is similar to that of stored procedures. The difference lies in the execution process. Triggers are not executed explicitly with EXEC command, as stored procedures, but rather they are fired by events occurring against triggers applied to the table. There are some limitations on triggers, including (1) apply to a single table as specified in the syntax; (2) can be nested to 16 levels; (3) cannot contain certain types of commands, such as DROP, ALTER, permissions, update statistics, CREATE, and LOAD. SQL Server has several features to stop trigger infinite loops (e.g., a trigger inserting a record into a table firing an update trigger on the same table firing the update on the same table and so on). The first is the nested level limit and the second is that a trigger does not fire itself. A streamlined syntax for creating triggers is as follows:

Syntax:

```
CREATE TRIGGER owner.trigger_name

    ON owner.table_name

    FOR [INSERT/UPDATE/DELETE]/[INSERT/UPDATE]

    AS

        [IF UPDATE (column_field) [AND/OR column_field(s)]]

        commands
```

The "sp_configure" system procedure can be used to set nested triggers to change the default nested level value. In addition to the limitation that some SQL commands cannot be used inside triggers, environment variable values also are changed during the trigger. When inspecting an environment variable, do so before the variables are changed by commands inside the trigger. The values of the environment variable are local to the trigger.

Examples:

1. Create a trigger to fire when a customer record is deleted as a final warning to the user.

```
use address
go
```

```
drop trigger trdelete_customer
go

CREATE TRIGGER trdelete_customer
ON customer
FOR DELETE
AS
    IF @@rowcount < 1
            /* no records were located by the deletion
            criteria */
        PRINT ("Customer not found. No records deleted")
    ELSE
        PRINT ("Customer Deleted. Save screen image to
        undelete customer.")
go

/* Ensure that the trigger was parsed successfully into the
database */
select * from sysobjects where name = "trdelete_customer"
go
```

Use a join to retrieve the text associated with the trigger from the sys-comments table. Execute the following join using the Microsoft SQL Server Query Analyzer utility.

```
SELECT a.type, b.text
    FROM sysobjects a, syscomments b
        WHERE a.name = "trdelete_customer" AND
            a.id = b.id
go
```

This join displays the following results in the "Results" tab of the Microsoft SQL Server Query Analyzer:

```
type                    text

----                    ---------------------------------

TR                      create trigger trdelete_customer


ON customer

FOR DELETE

AS

    IF @@rowcount < 1
```

```
    PRINT ("Customer not found. No records deleted")

ELSE

    PRINT ("Customer Deleted. Save screen image to
    undelete customer.")
```

The row associated with the table that fires the trigger is updated in the sysobjects table. The following SQL commands display the modified column containing the ID of the delete trigger that was created previously. Notice that the SQL code also displays the columns for other triggers (e.g., insert, update) that could be created for the table as well. Notice that the "deltrig" column in the sysobjects systems table contains the ID of the trigger selected by the join with the syscomments table.

```
select name, id, deltrig, instrig, updtrig, seltrig

    from sysobjects where name = "customer"


select a.type, a.id, b.text

    from sysobjects a, syscomments b

        where a.name = "trdelete_customer" AND a.id =
        b.id
```

Test that the trigger fires when a customer is deleted.

```
delete customer

    where customer_no = 3000

go
```

Note: Table objects within a database are identified within the sysobjects system table. The type column can be used to identify the type of object that a particular row is representing. Some of the common codes are

- S — system procedure
- V — view
- U — user table
- P — stored procedure
- TR — trigger

Using this information, the SELECT command can be used to identify all the objects belonging to a particular type, e.g., SELECT * FROM sysobjects WHERE type = 'P' (to locate all the stored procedures in the default database).

CONCLUSION

This chapter provided the syntax and examples for manipulating some of the commonly used database objects or features offered in SQL Server's Transact SQL dialect. Each of these objects or features form the foundation of modern database servers and three-tier client/server development. It is expected that their value will not diminish in the future, despite the constant changes to technology. Joins and subqueries are used to create virtual tables based on multiple physical tables and user-supplied qualifiers. Views are used to remove the physical complexity of accessing multiple relational tables. Stored procedures are used to build complex modules that are saved in SQL Server's data dictionary and can be executed remotely by clients. This provides a number of advantages: (1) reduced data transferrance on the LAN, (2) simplified change management, (3) modularization of business logic, and (4) module sharing. Triggers, a special type of stored procedure, also were examined in this chapter. Triggers are attached to tables or columns in tables. They automatically are invoked when specific events occur on the tables or columns. Triggers are a tool for enforcing referential integrity on a set of tables.

Chapter 31
Selecting Universal Data Server Technology

James A. Larson
Carol L. Larson

THE PROBLEM

RELATIONAL DATABASE SERVERS are used to store and access the data of an enterprise. This data is highly structured and organized into *relations* consisting of *tuples* and *domains*. In this article, the more familiar terms of *tables* consisting of *rows* and *columns* will be used. The elements of each table column are simple data types such as integers, floating point numbers, short character strings, or dates. However, relational databases store only a fraction of the information important to an enterprise. Much of the information necessary to an enterprise does not lend itself to be represented as simple data types in tables. This information is in the form of:

- Text — Memos, reports, messages, and documents
- Images — Diagrams, illustrations, and pictures
- Audio — Voice messages, audio recordings, and recorded music
- Video — Television commercials and news segments, taped interviews and focus groups, recorded movies, and television programs

Until recently, relational databases could not deal with these data types, leaving enterprises to use manual systems to manage nontabular forms of information.

THE CHALLENGE OF UNIVERSAL DATA SERVERS

Recently, database management system vendors have introduced extensions to relational data servers that store, retrieve, and, in some cases, search nontabular data types. These systems are called object-relational, extended relational, multimedia, and universal data servers. Frequently,

Exhibit 1. Four New Data Types and Their Storage Requirements

New Data Type	Uncompressed Size	Typical Compressed Size	Typical Compression Factor
Text	3.3 KB/page	1.2:1	2.6 KB/page
1280 × 1024 Image with 24 Bits of Color	3.9 MB/image	4:1	1.0 MB/image
High-Quality Audio	176 KB/sec	4:1	44 KB/sec
640 × 480 Video at 30 Frames/Sec	49.1 MB/sec	50:1	1 MB/sec

the term *universal data server* is used to indicate that a relational data server has been extended to support a variety of new data types.

A universal database falls somewhere between a relational database and an object-oriented database. A relational data server contains tables with values (but not pointers) in each column. A universal data server contains tables where some of the columns contain pointers (addresses) to files stored outside of the table. These files contain large or complex data types. An object-oriented data server contains objects consisting of fields, some of which may be large or complex data types. Although an object-oriented data server need not be structured as a table, it may still support SQL requests.

New Data Types

Traditional document management systems manage text and image documents. Usually, text and image documents are augmented by a set of descriptors similar to tables containing fields describing documents. However, most document management systems do support extensible data types. There is little chance that they can be extended to support audio, video, or other new data types such as date and time, unit conversions, and time series.

Exhibit 1 shows four new data types and the storage requirements for information represented using these formats. Even with compression, these data types require significant amounts of disk storage.

Data Storage

How can a relational data server support new data types? One approach is to store each new data type as an element in a relational table. However, these data types are large, may overflow the memory buffers of traditional relational data servers, and are not easily displayed as table elements on the users monitor. Another approach is to divide the data type into smaller chunks and store each chunk as an element in a relational table, and the data server reconstructs the data type from its chunks before presenting the data type to the user. Most relational data server vendors have used yet another approach and have extended their systems by placing physical pointers directly into their relational tables that reference files containing the new data type.

For example, the file names, résumés, and pictures of employees are elements of the relational data table. Users retrieve and update the rows of the table, which includes changing the pointers in the Résumé or Picture column to reference new files. There are, of course, operations to retrieve and present file contents, so users can read résumés and view the pictures of employees.

Searching and Indexing

Relational databases enable users to search on any column of a table. Because it may be expensive to fetch each referenced file into main memory, characteristics about the new data type also are represented in the table. Whenever a table contains a pointer to a new data type, the table also contains attributes about the new data type such as its type, size, date stored, and temporal length (for audio and video data types). These attributes can be searched by using traditional SQL requests. These new data type attributes are derived automatically by the database server. However, none of the attributes describes the information content of the referenced file.

For some data types, information about the content can be extracted automatically. For example, automatic procedures exist for extracting keywords from text. Next, the keywords are placed into the columns of tables. Users may include these keywords as part of their SQL requests. However, extracting keywords is difficult for new data types. Speech recognition algorithms convert spoken audio into text; then, keywords can be extracted from the text. Because of accuracy problems, the algorithm may not be able to extract all significant keywords. In the future, artificial intelligence vision algorithms may be able to examine images and video files and infer attributes about their content. Today, with the exception of text, attributes about the content of a file must be extracted manually.

Most traditional relational data servers use B-trees and/or hashing as indexing mechanisms. New data types often require new data organizational mechanisms. For example, R-trees are useful for organizing the contents of two-dimensional data types. Organizational techniques will emerge for each new data type.

Extensions

It is impossible for data server vendors to anticipate all possible new data types which users might require. Instead, database administrators may extend their universal data servers to support the storage and manipulation of new data types. These extensions enable

Exhibit 2. Examples of New Data Types and Their Extensions

New Data Type	Cross-Industry	Industry-Specific
Multimedia	Text	Medical: MRI, PET, EKG or ECG
	Image	Law Enforcement, Security: Fingerprints
	Audio	Radio: Sound Bites, Preprogrammed Music
	Video	Television: News Tapes, Commercials
Complex	Unit Conversion Date and Time	Medical: Hourly Blood Pressure Readings (Time Series)
		Oil Exploration: Location of Oil Fields (Geo-positioning Data)

- Storage of new data types using an efficient storage organization.
- Indexing techniques to support data access.
- Presentation of the new data type.
- Manipulation of specific data types (for example, graphic images may be rotated, enlarged, or shrunk; audio files may be compressed, decompressed, and converted between .au and .wav formats).
- Query optimization for queries involving new data types.
- Stored procedures for the enforcement of business rules and constraints which affect the new data types (if a new data type is stored as a file in a file system separate from the universal data server, then mechanisms should be installed into the file system to prohibit deleting files without also deleting pointers to the new data type from within the universal database).
- Application programming language extensions for the manipulation of the new data types.

A cottage industry will emerge to provide extensions to popular universal data servers for new data types. Exhibit 2 lists some of the new data types for which extensions have been built.

Although many of the extensions support cross-industry data types, such as text, image, audio, and video, other new data types have been implemented. New data types for date and time and unit conversion (meters from feet, pounds sterling from American dollars) also have been created. A geo-spatial data type pinpoints an object anywhere on Earth's surface. Time series is a new data type consisting of a sequence of values, where each value is associated with a calendar index. Examples of new time series are a sequence of monthly weight measurements or a sequence of monthly expenditures. Other new data types that aggregate tabular data types will certainly be implemented in the future.

JUSTIFYING AND SELECTING A UNIVERSAL DATA SERVER

The two major criteria for switching to a universal data server are

- Requirement 1: The enterprise needs data types not supported by traditional relational data servers.
- Requirement 2: The new data types must be integrated with existing data types.

Requirement 1 recommends that an enterprise truly needs new data types, not that new data types would be nice to have. New data types can be justified by explaining how the enterprise can be more competitive by using the new data types. For example, enterprises producing consumer catalogs may need a database containing text, illustrations, and photographs of products. Extending their product description database to include illustrations and photographs would enhance their catalog usage, especially if the catalog is placed online via the World Wide Web. Other areas benefiting from new data types include the following:

- Office information — Memos, reports, letters, and documents.
- Medical information — X-rays, magnetic resonance imagings (MRIs), positron emission tomographies (PETs), and electrocardiograms (EKGs or ECGs).
- Engineering information — Engineering drawings, blueprints, and load and stress limits.
- Library information — Encyclopedias, histories, dictionaries, biographies, other reference works, archival collections, and literature.
- Geographic information — Satellite images, maps, weather information, geologic data, and census data.
- Training and education — Readings, exercises, workshops, and tests
- Museums — Art, music and recordings, history, science, and sports.

Requirement 2 recommends that new data types be integrated with existing databases. This requirement improves two types of integration — user integration and computational integration. With user integration, users easily access traditional old and new data types together. In the online catalog example, users access pictures of a product and its cost at the same time. With computational integration, old and new data types share the same organizational and indexing mechanisms. Optimization algorithms analyze queries involving both old and new data types. Mechanisms enforcing business rules and constraints apply to both old and new data types.

In addition to supporting the definition and processing of new data types, a universal data server should support all the features and functions of relational data servers. Schema design, data entry, backup and recovery, transaction commit and rollback, security, and the specification and en-

Exhibit 3.   DBMS Vendors and Their Universal Database Servers

DBMS Vendor	Product Name	Web Page
IBM	DB@Universal Database 5.0	www.ibm.com
Informix	Informix-Universal Server	www.informix.com
Microsoft	Microsoft SQL Server 6.5	www.microsoft.com
Oracle	Oracle Universal Server	www.oracle.com
Sybase	Adaptive Server	www.sybase.com
UniSys	Osmos Object-relational Database	www.unisys.com; www.osmos.com
Unidata, Inc.	Universal Object Server	www.unidata.com

forcement of business rules are all features supported by relational data servers and also should be supported by universal data servers. As shown in Exhibit 3, most leading relational data server vendors have announced universal database server products that are upgrades or extensions of their current relational data servers.

Each of the vendors shown in Exhibit 3, along with its partners, continue to enhance its respective universal data servers by implementing additional new data types. If its products do not support the data types currently used by the enterprise, the vendor's partners may provide extension software supporting the needed data types. If not, new data types can be created and installed by designing and implementing the extensions noted above in the Extensions subsection.

Universal data servers may support other new features in addition to extensible data types. Some vendors introduce features in their universal data servers which are available in the products of their competitors. In general, universal data servers support additional transaction and concurrency control capabilities, reporting capabilities, and query features. Database administrators should consider all features of a universal data server to determine if and when a switch should be made to a universal data server. From a pragmatic viewpoint, it is wise to upgrade to a universal data server provided by the vendor of the users current relational database server — the new universal data server from the old vendor will provide more backward compatibility and require less migration effort than would selecting a universal data server from a different vendor.

MIGRATING TO A UNIVERSAL DATA SERVER

Three factors affect the amount of effort required to migrate data to a universal data server:

1. How much analog data is to be migrated and in which digital form should the data be represented?

2. How many values of the required index fields must be extracted manually from the digitized data rather than extracted automatically?
3. How much information about relationships must be generated manually rather than extracted automatically from the data?

Converting from Analog to Digital Form

Most universal data servers manage digitized data only. This enables the data to be stored, retrieved, transferred, and presented to users via common digital hardware and software.

Paper documents must be scanned to digitize their contents. Audio and video analog information must be processed by a digital signal processor (DSP) for conversion to a digital format. Although there may be some manual activities involved with these processes, such as feeding pages into a scanner or inserting cassettes into a tape drive, software and hardware perform the actual conversion automatically.

Some digital forms may be more convenient than others for digital processing. For example, an ASCII representation of text is more convenient than a bitmap of the same text. Optical character recognition converts images of text into ASCII bit strings with accuracy greater than 95%. Speech recognition algorithms convert audio speech into ASCII text provided that the source contains only a single voice at a time with little background noise. Unfortunately, vision algorithms do not exist that can reliably convert images and video captured via a camera into useful ASCII text strings.

Extracting Values for Index Fields

Universal data servers maintain data about data types in such a way that queries about the data types are processed without retrieving and examining the data types. Some values of these fields can be generated automatically. An example is the automatic calculation of the length of an audio clip and the size of a text string. However, values of index fields describing the content of a data type are another matter. If the data type is an image or video, the user must examine the data type and enter the field value. If the data type is text, it may be possible to extract the value from the text using text manipulation routines. As an example, software routines examine the text to extract keywords. By using more-advanced text-processing routines, it may be possible to detect themes by searching for words frequently related to specific themes. For example, Oracles ConText™ is able to examine a text string and extract relevant keywords and themes.

Extracting Relationships between Data Types

Automatically extracting relationships may be possible if the data types have index fields containing values that can be compared with each other.

For example, if both a résumé data type and a picture data type have social security fields, then matching values in the respective social security fields implies that an equivalence relationship exists between the two data types. Such value-based relationships are identified easily. Sometimes relationships can be established by combining two existing relationships. If a savings account and a checking account have the same value for social security number and the checking account and an address file entry have the same name, then the address from the address file is also the address of the owner of the savings account. However, care should be taken to make sure that bogus relationships are not inferred. For example, there is no relationship between a person and a cow if the birth-date field of a person data type and the birth-date field of a cow data type have the same value.

There may exist useful relationships among data types that are not evident by examining the values of their respective index fields. These relationships must be identified and entered manually.

A database administrator may be tempted to minimize the number of index fields and relationships of data types just to make the migration to a universal data server easier. However, queries may be more expensive for the universal data server to process if relevant index fields and relationships are missing. On the other hand, maintaining index fields and relationships between data types that are seldom used in queries is an unnecessary expense. It is the job of the database administrator to design the database carefully to contain the appropriate index fields and relationships.

CONCLUSION

A universal data server should not be used unless an enterprise can truly benefit by using the new data types. Migration to a universal data server should be considered only if it solves a specific enterprise problem, enables users to be more productive, and gives an enterprise a competitive edge over its competitors. In order to minimize conversion costs and efforts, it is wise to purchase a universal data server from the DBMS vendor currently used by the enterprise.

Recommended Reading

Campbell, R., Object-relational databases: the key players, *Databased Web Advisor*, 15(8), 28–35, 1997.
Davis, J. R., Extended relational DBMSs: the technology, Part 1, *DBMS*, 10(7), 42–49, 1997.
Davis, J. R., Universal servers: the players, Part 1, *DBMS*, 10(8), 75–86, 1997.
Stearns, T., Adapting to a new universe, *Information Week*, 652, 73–79, 1997.

Recommended Websites

See the Web pages for the individual universal data server vendors listed in Exhibit 3.

Chapter 32

Middleware, Universal Data Servers, and Object-Oriented Data Servers

James A. Larson
Carol L. Larson

RELATIONAL DATABASE MANAGEMENT SYSTEMS are used widely to store and access an enterprise's data. The data elements managed by relational DBMSs are simple data types such as integers, floating point numbers, short character strings, and dates. However, relational DBMSs do not manage complex data types that may be important to an enterprise. Complex data types include multimedia data types such as text, images, audio, and video, and compound data types such as dates and time series. Until recently, relational DBMSs could not deal with these data types, which left enterprises with file systems or manual systems to manage their nonrelational forms of information.

Different enterprises have different requirements for complex data types. Some enterprises need multimedia data types, some need compound data types, and some need both. Although many enterprises depend heavily upon relational database technology, others rely primarily on file systems, and still others rely on manual procedures to manage noncomputerized multimedia data. It is doubtful that a single mechanism can satisfy these differing requirements.

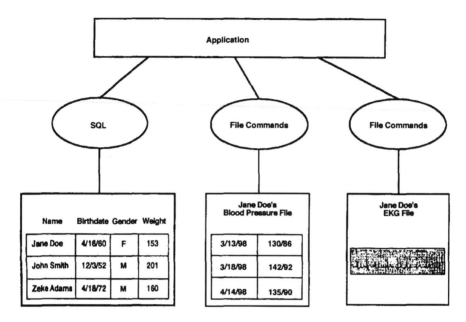

Exhibit 1.   Data extraction mechanism.

THE CHALLENGE OF COMPLEX DATA TYPES

Exhibits 1 through 4 illustrate four different mechanisms for dealing with complex data types. To illustrate the differences among the four approaches, a simple medical information system containing three types of data will be used.

Relational data includes the patient's name, unique identifier, address, date of birth, height, and weight. Typically, this information is stored in a Patient Information table managed by a relational DBMS. In an object-oriented DBMS, the information is contained within the Patient object.

Compound data includes daily blood pressure readings taken over several weeks. For the data extraction and middleware mechanisms, this information may be stored as a file consisting of several records, each containing the <date> and <reading> values. With a universal data server, the information is stored as a single data type called a time series consisting of a sequence of <date, reading> pairs. In an object-oriented data server, the information is represented as a Blood Pressure subobject of the Patient object.

Multimedia data includes the electrocardiogram (EKG) of the patient's heartbeat. With the data extraction, middleware, and universal data server approaches, the EKG is stored as a bit map in a file. In the object-oriented

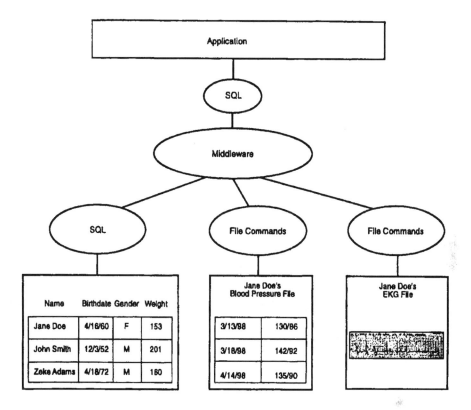

Exhibit 2.   Middleware mechanism.

data server mechanism, the EKG is represented as an electrocardiogram subobject of the Patient object.

Of course, a real medical database would have much more information than illustrated in each exhibit, but the examples will serve to illustrate the differences among the four mechanisms. For this discussion, assume that all data reside on the same computer.

The issues of distributed data are complex and beyond the scope of this article. Please see *Software Architectures for Distributed DBMSs in a Client/Server Environment* by J. A. Larson and C. L. Larson (Auerbach Publication, in press) for more information.

MECHANISMS SUPPORTING COMPLEX DATA TYPES

The first two mechanisms illustrated in Exhibits 1 and 2 enable applications to access existing data structures without migrating data to new types of servers.

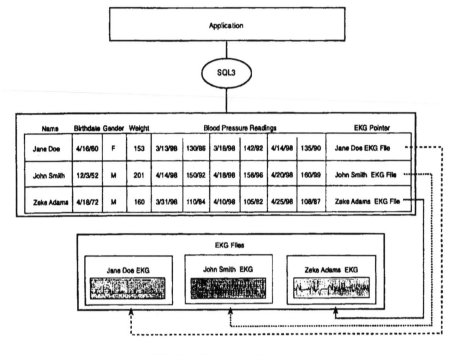

Exhibit 3.   Universal data server.

Data Extraction

In Exhibit 1, applications extract and integrate data from a relational database and a file system. To access relational information about Jane Doe, the application issues an SQL request to the relational DBMS, which returns the Patient Information about Jane Doe by accessing the Jane Doe Blood Pressure and EKG files. The application then merges and formats the information before presenting it to the user.

Middleware

With this approach, commercial middleware acts on behalf of the application to extract multimedia data from files and data from a relational data server. As shown in Exhibit 2, the application first issues an SQL request to the middleware, which passes it on to the relational DBMS, which in turn accesses the database and returns the Patient Information about Jane Doe. Next, the application issues SQL requests to the middleware, which converts the SQL request into file accesses applied to the file system and then returns the Jane Doe Blood Pressure file and the Jane Doe EKG file to the application. The application is responsible for merging the data from the database and the files before presenting it to the user.

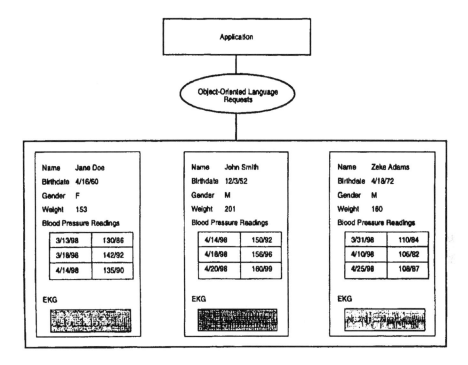

Exhibit 4.   Object-oriented data server.

A special type of middleware, called gateways, enables users to formulate requests in a language that is converted by the middleware to another language for processing. For example, when the application submits a request using SQL, the middleware translates the request to the format required by the underlying data server. Example gateways include the following:

- CrossAccess Data Delivery System from Cross Access Corporation. This system translates DB2 SQL to IMS, IDMS, Model 204, and file systems.
- EDA/SQL from Information Builders Incorporated. This software translates SQL into nonrelational data commands.
- OLE DB and Open Database Connectivity (ODBC) from Microsoft Corporation. These application program interfaces (APIs) and associated implementations enable applications to access many relational data servers, file systems, and other data sources.
- DB2 DataJoiner from IBM. DB2 DataJoiner is a translator that coverts SQL requests into the format required by nonrelational data sources. It also performs other functions, including cross database joins and

data conversions. Unlike most gateways, it has an optimizer to optimize queries involving data from multiple sources.

Gateways enable applications to access existing data sources without migrating the data to a new type of data server.

NEW DATA SERVERS

DBMS venders have introduced two new data servers to manage complex data types.

Universal Data Server. Exhibit 3 illustrates a universal data server, which contains extensions to relational data servers that store, search, and retrieve complex data types. These systems are called object-relational, extended relational, multimedia, and universal data servers. The term universal data server is used frequently to indicate that a relational data server has been extended to support a variety of new data types. The application issues an SQL request to the universal data server, which returns Jane Doe's Patient Information, including the Blood Pressure complex data type, to the application. The universal data server uses pointers in the EKG column to access the bitmap containing Jane's EKG from the file system. Unlike the data extraction and middleware mechanisms, the universal data server integrates data from the file system and the universal database before returning the integrated results to the application, which in turn formats it and presents it to the user.

Object-oriented Data Server. As shown in Exhibit 4, this server stores, retrieves, and searches complex data types. In the object-oriented data server, the complex data types are called objects; they contain data to which the user may apply object-specific functions. Some objects may be similar to tables in relational DBMSs, and other objects may be complex data objects containing multiple nested subobjects. In the medical example, the object-oriented data server retrieves the Patient object for Jane Doe, as well as subobjects EKG and Blood Pressure. The application formats and presents the information to the user.

MECHANISM SELECTION AND EVALUATION CRITERIA

The four mechanisms differ in the features they support and are summarized in Exhibit 5.

Programming Language Support. When using data extraction, middleware, or universal servers, application programs use an Application Program Interface (API) to open a database, submit a request, and retrieve the results. These approaches do not support a programming language that accesses the database directly. However, applications written in an object-oriented language, such as C++ or Java, access objects in an object-orient-

Exhibit 5.   Comparison of Mechanisms

	Mechanism			
Criteria	Data Extraction	Middleware	Universal Data Servers	Object-Oriented Data Servers
Programming language support	No	No	No	Yes
Extensible data type support	No	No	Yes	Yes
User-defined functions	No	No	Yes	Yes
Integrated backup and recovery	No	No	Yes	Yes
Automatic optimizers	No	No	Yes	Yes
SQL access	No	Yes	Yes	Yes
Multimedia access	Yes	Yes	Yes	Yes

ed data server directly. Object-oriented data servers enable programmers to access the database using the programming language without using special I/O commands, such as read and write.

Extensible Data Type Support . With the extracted and middleware approaches, programmers must implement new data types in the application and map the new data types to the data types supported by the underlying data sources. These tasks are taken over by database administrators for the universal and object-oriented data servers. For the universal data servers, database administrators define new data types by defining their representation, storage structure, and access methods using SQL 3. (Although SQL and SQL2 both describe tables, SQL3 describes tables and other complex data types that may be nested.) For object-oriented data servers, database administrators use an object-oriented language to define new data types.

New Functions . Part of defining a new data type is defining new functions involving the new data type. In the extracted and middleware approaches, programmers implement these new functions as part of the application. For universal and object-oriented data servers, database administrators define new functions to operate on the new data types. These functions can enforce business rules on the data, implement new functions required by application programs, and optimize queries.

Integrated Backup and Recovery . With the data extraction and middleware approaches, there is no integrated backup and recovery for both the file system and database. However, both universal and object-oriented data servers provide automatic backup and recovery mechanisms so that the entire database can be backed-up and restored.

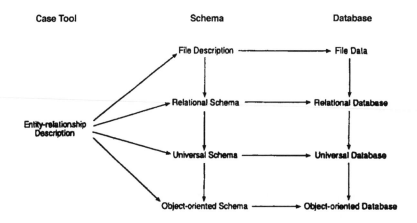

Exhibit 6.   Mappings and conversions among schemas and databases.

Automatic Optimizers . For the data extraction and middleware approaches, the application programmer must code all optimizations directly into the application. Any global query optimization also must be done by the programmer. With the universal and object-oriented data servers, the database administrator specifies optimization procedures for execution by the data server. These optimization procedures are reused by each request submitted to the server.

SQL Access . Although the extraction approach includes a relational DBMS that supports SQL requests, all accesses by applications to the file system must be expressed using traditional file I/O commands. The remaining three mechanisms support SQL requests for accessing all data. With the middleware approach, the middleware translates SQL requests into file I/O commands. The universal data server accepts and executes SQL requests against all data. Objects in most object-oriented data servers can be viewed as tables and, thus, support SQL requests. In addition, object-oriented servers also support requests expressed using an object-oriented language. These requests may include data type-specific functions.

Multimedia Access . All of the mechanisms support access to complex data types.

MIGRATING SCHEMA AND DATA

Exhibit 6 illustrates data models and databases involved in the conversion from files to relational or universal servers and, finally, to object-oriented data servers. Many enterprises use CASE tools to develop conceptual models of the enterprise's data. For example, several CASE tools use the entity-relationship modeling technique to represent the enterprise's data and a database schema for a relational or universal data server. Other CASE tools generate object-oriented syntax for creating object classes for an object-oriented data server.

When migrating from files to relational or universal data servers, file descriptions must be converted into relational schema. Some CASE tools are able to accept file descriptions and generate SQL syntax for creating equivalent relations. However, most database administrators perform this step manually. Chapter 29, "Migrating Files to Relational Databases," gives suggestions for mapping files into relational schema.

When migrating to a universal server, most relational schema do not need to be converted; however, some schema may need to be extended to describe new media and complex data types. CASE tools should be used to modify the enterprise's conceptual schema and, then, to generate a revised relational schema. If the CASE tool does not support media or complex data types, the database administrator may need manually to modify the SQL generated by the CASE tool to incorporate these new data types into the relational schema.

When migrating from relational or universal servers to object-oriented servers, the database administrator must decide whether to model existing data as relations or as more complex objects. To minimize changes to existing applications, most data remain modeled as relations. However, some data should be modeled as objects, especially the new media and compound data types that provide the motivation for switching to an object-oriented data server. Some CASE tools generate either relational or object-oriented schema, which enable the database administrator to avoid manually converting a relational or universal schema into an object-oriented schema. If the enterprise does not have such a CASE tool, then the database administrator must generate object-oriented schema for all new data and existing relational data.

After the schema are in place, the database administrator must populate the new data server with data from the old files and/or databases. This involves writing conversion software that extracts data from the source files or databases, changes the format to conform to the new data schema, and inserts the data into the new data server. Any new data also must be captured and entered into the new data server. This conversion software may be quite complex when migrating from files into relations, especially when integrating data from multiple files. The conversion software is quite simple when converting relations from a relational or universal data server into relations in an object-oriented data server. Capturing and loading new media and compound data into the object-oriented data server may, however, be quite complex. Most database server venders provide conversion software to assist database administrators when migrating data to a new server.

RECOMMENDATIONS

The four mechanisms represent four steps of a migration path from independent relational data servers and file systems (which are integrated by applications that extract data) to integrated object-oriented data servers (which perform the most data management functions). For enterprises requiring complex data types, the long-term goal is clearly to employ an object-oriented data server. The other approaches can be used as intermediate stepping stones before migrating to an object-oriented data server.

If only a handful of applications require complex data types, the data extraction approach is preferred because it provides no disruption for legacy applications.

The middleware approach adds SQL support, which may be desirable for end users who are able to use GUI interfaces to generate SQL requests to all of the data. This positions the data for later upgrade to universal data servers, which support SQL directly.

Universal data servers provide integrated data management support for the new data types, as well as integrating them with the traditional tables of relational data systems. For relational data servers users, this is a reasonable alternative because most major relational data server vendors support universal data servers. The upward migration from relational to universal data servers is straightforward, if the enterprise does not switch vendors.

The object-oriented data server promises to provide the most features and functions. However, some experts feel that object-oriented data servers do not provide performance superior to the relational data servers with their optimizers. In time, the optimizers of object-oriented data servers will improve just as optimizers for relational data servers have improved over the past 10 years. Universal data servers appear to be in a safe holding pattern, providing access to complex data types, until object-oriented data servers provide the features and performance required by users.

Recommended Reading

Barry, D.K., *The Object Database Handbook: How to Select, Implement, and Use Object-Oriented Databases,* John Wiley & Sons, New York, 1996.

Cattell, R. G. G., *Object Data Management: Object-Oriented and Extended Relational Database Systems,* Addison-Wesley, Reading, MA, 1991.

Chamberlin, D., *DB2 Universal Database: IBM's Object-Relational Database Systems,* Morgan Kaufman Publishers, San Francisco, 1988.

Colonna-Romano, J. and Srite, P., *The Middleware Source Book,* Digital Press, Burlington, VT, 1995.

Finn, M., Use OLE DB to Integrate Your Data, *Databased Web Adv.,* Nov. 1997, 64–66.

Francett, B., Middleware on the March, *Software Mag.,* April 1996, 71–76.

Goddard, D., How Middleware Can Help Your Enterprise, *Databased Web Adv.*, May 1996, 100–107.

Larson, J. A. and Larson, C. L., *Designing an Integrated Data Server,* Auerbach Publication No. 22-01-95 (1997).

Larson, J. A. and Larson, C. L., *Migrating Files to Relational Databases,* Auerbach Publication No. 22-01-29 (1996).

Larson, J. A. and Larson, C. L., *Software Architectures for Distributed DBMSs in a Client/Server Environment,* Auerbach Publication (TBA 1998).

Larson, J. A. and Larson, C. L., *Why Universal Data Servers,* Auerbach Publication (TBA 1998).

Loomis, M. E. S. and Chaudhri, A. B., Eds., *Object Databases in Practice,* Prentice-Hall, Upper Saddle River, NJ, 1997.

Making Connections Across the Enterprise: Client-server Middleware, *DBMS,* January 1993, 46–51.

Recommended Websites

For more information about the products mentioned in this chapter, see the following Web pages:

Cross Access Corp. (Cross Access Delivery System), Oakbrook Terrace, IL, http://www.cros-saccess.com/

IBM DB2 DataJoiner: http://www.software.ibm.com/data/datajoiner/

IBM Home Page: http://www.ibm.com/

Information Builders Inc. (EDA/SQL), Two Penn Plaza, New York, NY 10121-2898, 212.736.4433, Fax 212.967.6406, http://www.IBI.com/

Microsoft Corporation, Redmond, Washington, http://www.microsoft.com/

Microsoft Open Database Connectivity (ODBC), http://www.microsoft.com/data/odbc/

Microsoft OLE DB, http://www.microsoft.com/data/oledb/

Chapter 33
Creating Effective Batch SQL Jobs

Len Dvorkin

INTRODUCTION

THE RECENT ARRIVAL OF MATURE RELATIONAL DATABASES, powerful enough to handle mission-critical functions, has provided systems developers with the ability to perform complex processing in a much simpler way than traditional data repositories and languages previously afforded.

This power, however, has represented a double-edged sword when combined with traditional programming approaches and style. When complex business requirements are combined with the power of Structured Query Language (SQL), the result can be code that is syntactically correct, but runs poorly or not at all at production-level data volumes.

This problem commonly occurs during the creation of online transaction processing (OLTP) systems, when a frequently encountered scenario has developers coding and testing an application in a test environment, certifying it as ready for production, and watching it fail with a higher number of users, more data, etc. Fortunately (or unfortunately), this type of failure generally manifests itself directly and clearly, in the form of an online function that stops working, or that only performs slowly.

A more subtle trap relates to batch processing in SQL. Most significant DBMS-based systems have batch components to support them. These components include:

- Internal processing: using data from tables in the system to update other tables within the system.
- Data loading: updating the system's database with data from other systems.
- Data extraction: creation of tables or flat files for use by an outside system.
- Reporting: collection of data from within the system in order to present it for user review.

0-8493-9976-9/99/$0.00+$.50
© 1999 by CRC Press LLC

These components are not as "flashy" as their online cousins; however, they have the potential to seriously impact a system if they are not created and managed correctly. And batch routines are here to stay — the power represented by relational databases does not exempt mature systems from requiring tasks to run automatically and unattended, separately from any online components.

Most of the recurring problems in batch SQL are also frequently encountered when creating SQL for online purposes — after all, the language is the same. However, given the usual purposes of batch SQL, certain traps tend to manifest themselves with annoying frequency, even when coded by experienced developers. This article describes principles and techniques that represent good practice when designing any SQL job, but seem to be forgotten or left out more often when the batch environment is concerned. (See Exhibit 1.)

SQL CODING PRINCIPLES

Joins

A common operation in batch SQL involves combining data coming from multiple tables that have a relationship to each other. These may be a series of transaction tables coming from different sources, or a single transaction table with several foreign keys that need to be referenced.

In these cases, it can be hard to resist the power of SQL's ability to join database lookups across multiple tables. Although careful design of queries can result in a tightly tuned, fast-performing join, most databases use rules coded in an internal optimizer to examine a query and develop the plan that will guide the database engine in processing the query. In complicated joins, it is not uncommon for the database optimizer to make an unexpected decision on the join order and turn what should be a simple query into a large, slow-running database killer.

For example, assume that a report extract is needed for a table with four foreign keys to code tables. As a join, this could be coded as follows:

```
INSERT INTO report_table
SELECT t.column1,
    t.column2,
    a.description,
    b.description,
    c.description,
    d.description,
```

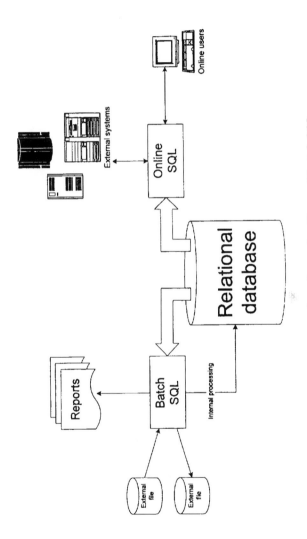

Exhibit 1. Common functions of online and batch SQL.

```
         <other columns>
     FROMtransaction_table t,
         code_table1 a,
         code_table2 b,
         code_table3 c,
         code_table4 d
     WHERE t.code_a = a.code
     AND t.code_b = b.code
     AND t.code_c = c.code
     AND t.code_d = d.code
     AND <other conditions>
```

Under low-volume conditions, or under high-volume conditions when the database statistics are current and the database's query optimizer is working effectively, this query will run well. The first table to be examined will be transaction_table, and code values found there will be used to reference the required code tables.

Sometimes, though, a large number of *where* clauses or a significant change in database volumes can confuse the optimizer, resulting in disastrous query plans (building the result set in the above example from one of the code tables, for instance).

In a batch SQL job, developers are generally not worried about shaving seconds off of transactions. They are much more interested in predictable, arithmetic increases in performance time directly related to database table volumes. (There are exceptions to this statement — some systems have a very restricted batch processing time window within which their processing must be completed. However, the techniques in this article can be used to reduce the server load of a given batch job, or to permit multiple jobs to run concurrently, potentially fixing these "batch window squeeze" situations.) To that end, splitting the single multitable join into separate queries involves a relatively small performance penalty in exchange for a predictable overall runtime. For instance:

```
     loop for each qualified record in transaction_table:
         SELECT :col1 = t.column1,
             :col2 = t.column2,
             :code_a = t.code_a,
             :code_b = t.code_b,
```

```
       :code_c = t.code_c,
       :code_d = t.code_d,
       <other columns>
   FROM transaction_table t
   WHERE <other conditions>
   SELECT :description_a
   FROM code_table1
   WHERE code = :code_a
   SELECT :description_b
   FROM code_table1
   WHERE code = :code_b
   SELECT :description_c
   FROM code_table1
   WHERE code = :code_c
   SELECT :description_d
   FROM code_table1
   WHERE code = :code_d
   INSERT INTO report_table
   VALUES (:col1,
       :col2,
       :description_a,
       :description_b,
       :description_c,
       :description_d,
   <other columns>)
 end loop
```

At the cost of a few extra lines of code, the five-table join in the first example becomes a bulletproof routine with predictable performance under virtually all conditions of data volume or database statistics.

Note that the number of required database lookups in the previous code has not changed from the more complicated example, leaving only a small net extra cost in separate processing of the SQL statements. If these statements are running inside the database engine (in a stored procedure, for instance), the overhead becomes even smaller.

Declarations and Initializations

The top section of any routine should contain declarations of any variables that will be used in the job. If a data value is likely to be changed during testing or after the job is running in production, consider changing it to a "constant" variable. This makes it easier to read and maintain the code. Similarly, table columns containing code values are easier to deal with if their code values are stored in constants. Consider the example below:

```
declare :MIN_DOLLAR_VALUE float = 10.0

declare :SALE char(1) = "S"

declare :RETURN char(1) = "R"


<other processing>


SELECT sum (trans_value)

FROM trans_table

WHERE trans_value > :MIN_DOLLAR_VALUE

AND trans_type = :SALE
```

Read Once, Write Once

Depending on the specific driver program type and database implementation being used, the cost of an SQL table hit is easily 10 times or more expensive than processing a simple logic statement. However, many batch programs are profligate in their use of table access statements. In the following example, a single row in a source table is read once for its index value, a second time for a lookup value, and a third time for other information needed to write to an output table:

```
loop for each qualified record in transaction_table:

    SELECT :index_field = t.index_field

    FROM transaction_table t

    WHERE t.transaction_date = <today>


    < processing of the record >
```

```
SELECT :transaction_type = a.type_description
FROM transaction_table t,
     code_table1 a
WHERE t.index_field = :index_field
AND t.type_code_a = a.type_code_a


< other processing of the record >


INSERT INTO report_table
SELECT t.column1,
       t.column2,
       :transaction_type,
       <other columns>
FROM transaction_table t
WHERE t.index_field = :index_field
end loop
```

When examining this program structure, developers often explain that this is a straightforward approach to satisfying the program's requirements — what is wrong with it? They may be influenced by the method in which a traditional/hierarchical data store is read, where the first access to a record brings all of its data directly into a program cache, and subsequent access to fields on the record are virtually "free" reads of local memory.

However, this is certainly not the case when discussing database access. Each time the (same) row in a table is referenced in a select statement, a nontrivial amount of database work must take place. Most database implementations will cache the affected data row in its local memory pages after the first read, preventing hard disk access in subsequent reads. However, the overhead cost of parsing the statement, determining a query path, supporting a join, identifying the desired row, determining that it is resident in memory, etc., is still significantly higher than that of a simple reference to a local variable in the program's memory space.

This routine can be rewritten with minimum effort to access each table only once, retrieving all columns that will be required in this select statement and saving them locally for use later in the process:

```
loop for each qualified record in transaction_table:
```

```
SELECT :index_field = t.index_field,
    :type_code_a = type_code_a,
    :column1 = column1,
    :column2 = column2,
    <other columns>
FROM transaction_table t
WHERE <conditions>

< other processing of the record >

SELECT :transaction_type = a.type_description
FROM code_table1 a
WHERE a.type_code_a = :type_code_a

< other processing of the record >

INSERT INTO report_table
VALUES (:column1,
    :column2,
    :transaction_type,
    <other columns>
    end loop
```

An analogous situation can occur when writing an output record. Rather than adopting a simple structure that first inserts a skeleton of a new output row, and then updating elements of the same row during processing, the column data to be inserted can be saved in local variables and inserted in a single SQL statement.

Indexes

The optimizers in today's database engines have matured tremendously compared to those of several years ago. For ad hoc, complex queries, it is now often possible to rely on the optimizer to determine the optimum query path that should be taken to minimize a query's runtime.

However, even the best optimizers cannot be used as a safety net for all queries. If a database's internal table statistics are not up to date, for instance, many optimizers will choose poor query plans or even switch to table scans with sometimes disastrous results. This problem can be avoided, to some extent, by regularly running an "update statistics" routine that recreates internal table data volume and distribution statistics. However, in cases where the volume or type of data is changing frequently in a table, even daily or weekly updates of table statistics may not be adequate to guarantee the use of a desired index.

For that reason, good defensive coding practices take the approach that "it's nice to have a database optimizer, but let's not leave anything to chance." Every query on a table of nontrivial size should be examined, with particular attention to ensuring that its where clauses correspond to an existing index. If an appropriate index does not already exist in the database, it should either be added to the table or, if this is not practical, consideration should be given to redesigning the query.

An extremely common development scenario has normally careful developers designing batch jobs without consideration of indexes ("After all, we won't have any users sitting at their desks waiting for this job to finish tonight."), testing the jobs under low-data-volume conditions and verifying their correctness, and then watching in horror as the batch job run time grows steadily under regular data volume conditions.

There may be some exceptions to this principle; for example, when an entire table is being read and processed using a cursor, direct sequential access can be faster than involving any indices. But, in general, every database access in the routine should be explicitly designed to use a predefined index. If this is done, then overall job performance may grow geometrically in proportion to the volume of data being processed, but the time should be manageable and predictable from the start.

Transaction Commitments

One of the common design tradeoffs in batch routines involves decisions concerning committing transactions. As in other aspects of the batch routines, the developer approaches adopted in the construction of online routines do not always correspond well to the design requirements of a batch routine.

Within a transaction block, either all updates are applied to the database, or none of the updates are applied. This makes the approach to determining whether a transaction is required for an online SQL routine (and, if so, what its scope should be) a relatively simple exercise. The programmer simply identifies the logical unit of work, in terms of database changes, which may not be left partially complete in case of data or database problems.

The logical extension of this concept to batch routines would be to place a transaction block around every set of inserts and updates that comprise a single block of work. The problem with this straightforward approach is that the impact of processing individual transactions blocks in a routine reading of an input table of, say, 20,000 rows, can seriously affect the database's performance and logging.

A compromise approach to transaction design in batch routines involves grouping together a larger number of individual input records into a single transaction, and repeatedly beginning and committing transactions when that number of input records has been processed. The following example groups input records into batches of 500 for the purpose of transaction processing:

```
declare :counter int = 0
declare :MAX_RECORDS_IN_COMMIT int = 500


BEGIN TRANSACTION


loop for each qualified record in transaction_table:
    SET :counter = :counter+1
    if :counter = :MAX_RECORDS_IN_COMMIT
        COMMIT TRANSACTION
        BEGIN TRANSACTION
    end if
        <process record>
end loop


COMMIT TRANSACTION
```

Some experience is necessary to determine the best number of rows to include in a single commit block, because this decision depends on the specific database implementation and environment. Establishing this number as a local constant or parameter to the routine (as in the previous example) is an effective way to make it easily tunable based on actual experience.

Note that if the batch routine will be running while online users are working on the system, the MAX_RECORDS_IN_COMMIT value should be kept relatively low to avoid locking an excessive number of rows or pages needed by other processes.

If the input records are not being deleted or flagged in a specific way when they are processed, transaction parameters can be used in conjunction with transaction diagnostic messages to facilitate restartability of the routine. They allow a person responding to a problem encountered when running the routine to determine quickly and accurately how much data had been processed successfully before a problem occurred. In this way, steps can be taken to reset the input source and restart the job without incurring the risk of missing or double-processing input data.

Data All in a Row

Most batch routines, either as part of a recurring loop or as a one-time operation, must read data and conduct processing based on that data. The "read once, write once" approach discussed in this article applies here — the aim is to select data from tables as few times as possible. This may mean storing data in local variables, or organizing the routine in order to defer executing the select statement until all required selection criteria have been established.

If the source data is read in a loop, there are several useful techniques available to "walk through" the qualifying rows.

Cursors. Cursors support a single selection of input data, and one-by-one processing of the results. Depending on the database implementation, it may not be practical to use cursors when the number of input rows is large.

Ascending Key Read. This method stores a starting key position and repeatedly reads additional records with larger key values. This method is most simple when the routine can count on the existence of a sequential key in the source table. If that key is indexed properly, this can also be a very efficient way to read the table rows:

```
declare :current_key int
SET :current_key = <appropriate starting value>


loop:
    SELECT <columns>
    FROM trans_table
```

```
WHERE trans_key = :current_key

if <no rows found>

    exit loop

else

    SET :current_key = :current_key + 1


<process the selected row>

end loop
```

Read and Delete. This is appropriate for cases when the data in the input table does not need to be saved after the routine is complete. This is implemented simply by deleting the rows from the source table as they are processed.

This approach is most suitable for cases where a flat file needs to be processed in a database. The batch jobstream can first transfer the flat file data into a temporary table, and then invoke the batch routine to process the records one by one. If a problem halts the batch routine in midstream, it should be automatically restartable with the (presumably) smaller input table, which would contain all unprocessed rows.

Reading a table using this approach can be highly efficient, especially in database implementations that allow the programmer to specify a row retrieval limit in its syntax (for instance, the "set rowcount 1" statement in SQL Server). With this restriction in place, the read can be a simple, nonindexed select statement that permits the database to retrieve the first physical record encountered with no need to refer to indices or complicated query plans.

The program structure for this approach is somewhat similar to the previous example:

```
loop:
    <restrict selection to 1 row>
    SELECT :key_field = key_field,
        <other columns>
    FROM trans_table
    <remove the single-row restriction>
```

```
if <no rows found>
    exit loop


<process the selected row>


DELETE trans_table
WHERE key_field = :key_field
end loop
```

Read and Flag. This is very similar to read and delete, but is used when the input table must be kept intact after being processed. Rather than deleting each input row as it is processed, a status flag is set in one of its columns indicating that it has been used and should therefore not be picked up on the next loop iteration:

```
declare :PROCESSED char(1) = "P"


loop:
    <restrict selection to 1 row>
    SELECT :key_field = key_field,
        <other columns>
    FROM trans_table
    WHERE processing_status != :PROCESSED
    <remove the single-row restriction>


    if <no rows found>
        exit loop


    <process the selected row>


    UPDATE trans_table
    SET processing_status = :PROCESSED
    WHERE key_field = :key_field
end loop
```

GENERAL PRINCIPLES

Consistency

In many development environments, database routines seem to often suffer from a lack of structure, design, and clean formatting. This is perhaps due to the ease with which they can be coded, and the relatively relaxed formatting restrictions of most SQL implementations. When compared to regular 3GL or 4GL processing code, many database routines are characterized by few (or nonstandard) comments, inconsistent indentation, and capitalization of keywords, resulting in an erratic look and feel. Batch routines, because they tend to be longer and more complex, are particularly impacted by this lack of consistency.

Although there are many standards that could be described as clear, this article does not attempt to define a single "best" one. The important thing is to choose a standard and stick with it for all SQL routines in a system. This coding discipline generally pays for itself many times in reduced overall maintenance time in the long term.

In addition to these cosmetic issues, an objective of clarity can lead a structured development shop to convert complex batch routine syntax into simpler statements, even if this involves a small cost in terms of performance. For example, even if a complex table join has been tested and verified to be correct in all circumstances (including tests under high-volume conditions), it can be worthwhile to review the performance and coding cost involved in splitting it into separate but more simple queries. If this cost is not excessive, it will almost certainly be recovered with interest when the routine needs to be modified because of system problems or new business requirements.

Diagnostics

If a batch routine is running without a user sitting at a screen waiting for its completion, it is very tempting to build it with a minimum of inline diagnostics. Sometimes, a small set of control totals may be generated and saved as part of the job run, but batch routines are commonly built without even that level of output.

Although it is true that there is little need for detailed diagnostics when a job is working correctly, their lack is felt most deeply in the most stressful situations — when problems manifest themselves. In a typical real-life scenario, the complex batch job runs for several months without problems and then, due to some unforeseen data input scenario, starts producing incorrect results. The support staff designated to investigate the problem is faced with a sometimes daunting task of diagnosis and repair, often complicated by less-sophisticated debugging tools for the database environment.

To speed up diagnosis and resolution of these problems, a relatively small amount of developer time and batch job runtime can be applied to producing diagnostic messages directly from the batch routine. A simple but comprehensive approach involves issuing two types of diagnostic messages: control diagnostic messages and transaction diagnostic messages.

Control Diagnostic Messages. These act as milestones along the road of a batch routine. If one section becomes slow or fails to work, then the offending section should be immediately obvious by referencing the control diagnostics. These could read, for instance, as follows:

```
ddMMMyyyy hh:mm:ss ... Routine "process_transactions" started
ddMMMyyyy hh:mm:ss ... Beginning to process input rows from
trans_table
ddMMMyyyy hh:mm:ss ... Processed 1000 input rows
ddMMMyyyy hh:mm:ss ... Processed 2000 input rows
ddMMMyyyy hh:mm:ss ... Processed 3000 input rows
ddMMMyyyy hh:mm:ss ... Processed 4000 input rows
ddMMMyyyy hh:mm:ss ... 4692 input rows processed
ddMMMyyyy hh:mm:ss ... Beginning generation of report_table
ddMMMyyyy hh:mm:ss ... Generation of report_table complete, with
2456 adds and 1205 changes
```

The level of detail and wording can depend entirely on development shop standards, as long as they satisfy their primary purpose — to facilitate quick identification of the likely location of problems.

Transaction Diagnostic Messages. These support a more detailed look at the data being processed by the batch routine. Their existence acts as a record of the data processed, and can be used to quickly answer questions like, "Why didn't product #5682 get reset last night?" or "Why do the sales to customer #7531 appear twice on this morning's reports?"

Transaction diagnostics can represent quite a large quantity of data and, for that reason, they are generally overwritten on a daily or, at least, weekly basis. Using the same example just shown, they could look like this:

```
ddMMMyyyy hh:mm:ss ... Routine "process_transactions" started
ddMMMyyyy hh:mm:ss ... Beginning to process input rows from
trans_table
ddMMMyyyy hh:mm:ss ... Processing product #14, status "A"
ddMMMyyyy hh:mm:ss ... Sales record: Sold 50 units to customer
#5532 at $45
ddMMMyyyy hh:mm:ss ... Sales record: Sold 14 units to customer
#5532 at $48
ddMMMyyyy hh:mm:ss ... Returns record: Returned 12 units from cus-
tomer #5532 at $43
```

```
ddMMMyyyy hh:mm:ss ... Processing product #18, status "A"
ddMMMyyyy hh:mm:ss ... No sales records found
ddMMMyyyy hh:mm:ss ... No returns records found
ddMMMyyyy hh:mm:ss ... Processing product #22, status "D"
ddMMMyyyy hh:mm:ss ... Skipping discontinued product
ddMMMyyyy hh:mm:ss ... Processing product #23, status "A"
```

ddMMMyyyy hh:mm:ss ... Sales record: Sold 10 units to customer #5532 at $2.50

ddMMMyyyy hh:mm:ss ... Sales record: Sold 12 units to customer #18006 at $2.75

ddMMMyyyy hh:mm:ss ... Sales record: Sold 985 units to customer #34925 at $2.60

... and so on

If applicable (or necessary), control diagnostics and transaction diagnostics can be combined into a single output file. The emphasis here is not on a cosmetically fancy report layout — rather, the point should be to produce useful diagnostic information that can be referenced when results of the batch process are in question and details of its processing are needed.

If disk space is not adequate to generate transaction diagnostics on a regular basis, the routine can be coded to issue them only when an input "debug" parameter is set. In normal situations, the debug parameter would be turned off. When specific problems arise and there is a need to trace the routine's running more carefully, the parameter would be turned on. By coding the parameter into the routine from the start, production diagnostics can be turned on and off months or years later without changing a single line of code.

Affecting Other Batch Jobs

In many cases, batch processes will be scheduled for times when there are no online users accessing the database. In these cases, using the power of SQL to access many rows in a single statement can have the dual advantages of simplicity and speed. For example, to copy details from today's transactions to a reporting table, the statement

```
INSERT INTO report_table
SELECT t.column1,
    t.column2,
    <other columns>
FROM transaction_table t,
WHERE t.transaction_date = <today>
```

can certainly be very effective (assuming an appropriate index on the transaction date field).

However, it is very important to realize that in most database implementations, even a single statement like this one places an implicit transaction on all data accessed in its select statement. This lock ensures that either the entire selection is made and inserted into the destination table, or none of it is.

This means that all rows selected by the query are locked for its duration. If the table and/or number of rows being affected is large, this has the potential to freeze any online users or other batch jobs attempting to access the locked records (or pages, depending on the database implementation of locking).

Running this type of query during the day — to create an ad hoc report, for example — is often responsible for frustrating calls to the help desk, where online users report intermittent freezing of their systems in no discernible or reproducible pattern.

The same phenomenon can occur if multiple batch jobs are scheduled concurrently by system administrators. In the worst case, two batch jobs can fall into a deadlock situation where each is holding resources needed by the other.

To avoid this trap, the most important point is to remember that "you are not alone." If query speed and simplicity is paramount, then designers and database/system administrators must be very conscious of the database access contained in these routines and consciously schedule them in such a way to preclude conflicts.

If robustness of the system is important enough to accept a small speed penalty in running the routine, then a walkthrough approach can produce the same ultimate results as the single query, but without locking tables or inflicting performance penalties on other users or processes sharing the database:

```
loop for each qualified record in transaction_table:
    SELECT :col1 = t.column1,
       :col2 = t.column2,
    <other columns>
    FROM transaction_table t
    WHERE t.transaction_date = <today>
    INSERT INTO report_table
```

```
VALUES (:col1,

   :col2,

   <other columns>)

end loop
```

CONCLUSION

Many problems in batch SQL jobs can be avoided by developing and applying a good set of SQL programming instincts. These instincts comprise rules of thumb that sometimes represent simple common sense, but in other cases are not in the natural toolkit of a developer coming from other technology platforms.

However, applying an "ounce" of prevention in the design and construction phases of a project's batch SQL components can easily pay back several "pounds" of savings in future maintenance efforts.

Chapter 34
The Advancing Art of Indexing

Lois Richards

DESPITE THE ENORMOUS SUMS OF MONEY SPENT on client/server, data warehousing, LAN technology, UNIX systems, and PC access tools, the job of delivering information to end-users in an efficient manner remains difficult. With all the new technology and computing power now available, why are IS departments still struggling to answer this fundamental need? More important, is a solution at hand?

IN THE BEGINNING, THERE WAS DATA

In retrospect, it seemed so simple. Of course, data was there to be used. The problem was that traditional systems were designed for record keeping. Data gathering was the priority, not data dissemination. The end-user, however, was unaware of this barrier.

Finance departments were the first to see the benefit of the summary reports and analyses. Marketing departments were not far behind in asking for reports on their customers and prospects. Inventory management, manufacturing, engineering, personnel ... soon all departments could see the need for access to the data in these computerized corporate storehouses.

THEN THERE WERE USERS: THE REIGN OF THE 4GL

What evolved was the decision support system (DSS). DSS applications may access just the back-end or legacy systems, may include data warehousing, or may encompass an enterprisewide client/server information system. Decision support applications all require extensive access to corporate data stowed in the coffers of the computer system. Whether the data base is a relational or other file structure, these decision support inquiries contribute to analyses of the selected data or display of the selected data in reports. In addition, the users submitting these inquiries insist on consistent, immediate response. IS must respond to these demands.

0-8493-9976-9/99/$0.00+$.50
© 1999 by CRC Press LLC

Whenever tackling any daunting task, most practitioners undertake the most obvious issues first. Thus, when it came to providing enterprisewide data access, the most prominent roadblock was getting users onto the system with the appropriate levels of security and programs to access the data they needed.

In the 1980s, such companies as Information Builders, Cognos, and Uniface launched the first revolution in end-user access by selling fourth-generation language (4GL) development tools. Fourth-generation languages made it possible to develop new applications in a fraction of the time required by conventional programming techniques. Meanwhile, PCS were gaining favor in the corporate world. Terminal emulation software sold by the thousands — then millions — as the proliferation of PCS became the new way to get access to the corporate system.

These new applications and terminal emulation techniques allowed a multitude of users to directly access data in corporate systems. The decision support system for the organization's knowledge worker was on its way. Granted, the access was usually reserved for either the data-entry level technician who used the system to enter, update, and delete information, or the hearty few who were confident enough to manipulate the applications. But the revolutionary step of allowing users directly on the system had taken place. The idea of interactive data access had become the norm. Users requested access to data immediately — online!

LET THERE BE UNIVERSAL ACCESS: CLIENT/SERVER AND NETWORKS

Throughout the 1980s and early 1990s, millions of users were brought online. Data bases grew larger while the number of users who accessed them and the frequency of their access continued to expand. Even as users were clamoring for more, organizations were failing to see the return they had expected from their investments in technology.

Even though these new applications allowed access to corporate data, it was in a rigid, predefined manner that protected system resources. Users who were not comfortable with a character environment, or who did not take the time to learn the cryptic commands and data layouts, still needed to depend on the IS department for their data needs. Information could still take weeks to get if it differed from the preestablished reports. Individual access was limited to one system at a time. Access to multiple data sources on various hosts from the same terminal was virtually impossible.

The next step was inevitable. The obvious choice to many was to marry the now-pervasive PC and its user-friendliness with the power of the corporate system. By the early 1990s, most corporations began developing some form of client/server system to increase efficiency and end-user access.

Client/server systems answered, at least temporarily, the next level of end-user access issues. The point-and-click interfaces of Windows and Macintosh systems made interacting with the data far easier. Users no longer had to memorize command sequences to get in and out of applications and data bases. They could perform queries and create reports on the fly, and download data directly into the PC. Advances in network technology made it possible to have access to any number of corporate systems from the same PC or workstation.

With client/server connections, middleware connectivity tools, and networking, IS has solved the second hurdle of providing universal access: users are online and can request information through a relatively intuitive graphical environment. Fast access to information through online inquiry, analysis, and reporting remains a crucial factor if today's knowledge workers are to get their questions answered and work completed. But, as with most elements of progress, this new access has brought with it another dilemma — performance.

THE PERFORMANCE DILEMMA

Unfortunately, there appears to be one indisputable constant: fast is never fast enough.

As users point-and-click their way to the data they need, both users and IS now dread the infamous QFH ("query from hell"). Perfectly reasonable business questions such as "How many customers in the northeast region bought our product last quarter at the promotional price?" can bring even the most powerful server with millions of records to its knees — and all other users along with it. Because of this slow response time, interacting with the data is clumsy at best and impossible at worst.

Without question, CPU-intensive tasks, such as engineering and scientific applications, have seen dramatic increases in speed. In addition, the CPU-intensive tasks required in data base applications, such as sorting, are considerably faster. With CPU speeds increasing and the cost per millions of instructions per second (MIPS) dropping, it might appear that the solution to transaction and analysis bottlenecks experienced in most data base applications has been met. Unfortunately, this is not true.

The reason is that most data base applications benefit only modestly from higher-speed CPUs. Typically, the inability to resolve user queries comes from the application being disk I/O-bound rather than CPU-bound. The CPU is busy reading the data from disk in order to answer, or process, the request. Two basic strategies have emerged in an attempt to solve the performance dilemma:

- Limit the number, type, or timing of the queries that can be done through the client/server system.

- Pull the analytical/historical data into a data warehouse, so that the queries do not affect online production performance.

DSS inquiries and reports require access to large amounts of data, even when only a small subset of records is of interest. Consequently, placing limits on queries is generally unsatisfactory for all involved. The time required to accomplish the DSS request depends on disk throughput rather than CPU speed. While CPU speeds continue to increase and disk capacities see great gains, the transfer speeds (disk I/O) have only made incremental gains. So, users continue to be frustrated about the limits that are set, and IS is again put in the position of "policing" access to data.

Offloading data into a data warehouse only shifts the problem from one data structure to another. The assumption made with moving the data into a query-focused data base is that the data warehouse, unlike a production system, does not require the same response times. Knowledge workers must wait hours, and sometimes days, for information they need.

The solution is to reduce the amount of disk I/O required to get the job done. In data base applications, this means minimizing the amount of I/O needed to select and retrieve a desired subset of records for display or reporting. With this in mind, indexing becomes one of the most important aspects of any decision support system.

INDEXING — THE FUTURE IS NOW

Decision support applications require users to query, analyze, and report data. As data structures increase in size (millions and billions of records of data), the ability to meet the need to query, analyze, and report on data becomes burdensome — even for a super-powered computer. Whether a DSS application is in the conceptual stage or already developed, the issue of making data easily and immediately accessible to users will always be a challenge. Indexing provides a way to realize optimal benefits with minimal investment in new technologies or equipment.

Sophisticated indexing is the most effective way to reduce the disk I/O required to retrieve a subset of data. With advanced indexing techniques, record selections by any criteria are accomplished using few disk reads. As a result, complex selections from large data bases execute in seconds.

Not the New Kid on the Block, But Effective

Data file structures offer several ways to access data. Foremost among them, sequential searches, or table scans, match data to the user's criteria. This technique requires access to every record and, consequently, large disk I/O. If available, an index can expedite this process by decreasing the number of reads.

B-Tree Indexing. The native indexes in relational data bases such as Oracle, Informix, Sybase, and other relational data base management systems (RDBMSs) use a B-tree structure that allows partial key retrievals, sorted retrievals, and concatenation of columns. B-tree indexing has been effectively used for years but has several drawbacks, including:

- *Limited to single attribute.* There is no efficient way to combine multiple criteria to narrow a search through thousands and millions of records.
- *Limited to support of full key values in left-to-right sequence.* Users must enter the search criteria in the same order the data was entered, in order to attain the most efficient search.
- *Limited to exact match of criteria to data stored.* Again, users must be aware of how the data was entered.

Several RDBMSs also have a "hashed" key capability, which is fast but not flexible. Hashed indexes require a full key lookup and a perfect match, including upper or lower case letters, spaces, and punctuation.

Though indexing has been around for as long as the computer file, there have been great advances in indexing technology. Specialized indexes provide new and improved solutions to the high-performance needs of decision support data access. Advanced indexing can deliver true interactive DSS query capabilities to the knowledge worker.

Bit-Map Indexing. One advanced indexing technology is bit-map indexing. Bit-map indexing represents each unique value in the underlying file structure as an array of bits, setting the bits ON or OFF. This indexing structure can provide high-speed index-only processing.

Bit-map indexing has been targeted to be most effective for low cardinality data (i.e., data with few unique values, such as male/female, yes/no, or coded data). Its weakness, however, is in its limitation to high cardinality data (i.e., data with many varying values, such as text data, name fields, and descriptive fields). The more varying the data, the more bit-maps that must be created and maintained.

There is a focus on positioning bit-map indexing as the indexing solution for the data warehouse. This approach often assumes that the data is static (i.e., lower index maintenance) and that the underlying data can be offloaded (i.e., lower online disk utilization).

Inverted File Indexing. Another advanced indexing technology is inverted indexing. Inverted indexes store pointers to the data base as data, and the data from the data base as keys. Inverted file indexing maintains indexes to all values contained in an indexed field.

Inverted indexing delivers the broadest range of function and flexibility for ad hoc data access and analysis. Users can obtain truly interactive access to data across the enterprise.

Inverted indexes expedite fast, ad hoc searches of previously undefined queries. Inverted file indexing allows users to find information based on any combination of qualifying criteria. Regardless of where the criteria occur in a field, query results process in seconds — without serial reads or sequential index.

An Example. For example, a user wants to know, "How many customers in the northeast (NE) region bought a product last quarter at the promotional price?" The traditional index, or B-tree, could quickly identify all the NE region customers, but would be of no use to also select those that bought in the last quarter at a particular price. To find those records, the processor must retrieve the NE region customer records from disk and evaluate each one for the remaining criteria. If the initial selection yields a large result — say, several hundred thousand records — the processor must physically retrieve every record. Next, it must evaluate the transaction date and amount fields for a match to the query criteria. Furthermore, B-tree indexes are required to scan records byte-by-byte. They can be of no use when searching for records where the selection criteria is buried within the record, such as an appended product code or first name in a name field listing lastname-firstname.

In contrast, inverted file indexes sort and store all values in indexed fields. If a table contains sales data with records 1, 5, 13, 22, and 70 representing the NE region, an inverted index would contain NE with pointers to records 1, 5, 13, 22, and 70. They select records almost instantly by simply scanning the index files for the appropriate values and comparing the record IDs for the shared values — the kind of computation a computer excels at doing. This process takes place at the index level. Inverted indexes augment the relational data base to provide the high-performance data access that native B-trees cannot.

RELATIONAL INDEXES VERSUS INVERTED INDEXES

Relational data bases offer great retrieval capabilities and flexibility, allowing users to access the data in whatever way they need — unfortunately, it is often at the cost of performance. Though structured query language (SQL) contains syntax for the addition and deletion of indexes, no syntax is included to refer to an index in a query. Therefore, indexed searches are controlled by the RDBMS and, if available, an optimizer.

When a user submits a query, the RDBMS determines how to resolve the query, choosing an index, if defined, to improve performance. Without an index, a sequential search or table scan will be used. The more complex the query, the greater the likelihood of a table scan, because of the limitation that B-tree indexes provide a single key access. If a query encompasses more than one column, only one B-tree can be used, even if every column in the query is indexed. The optimizer then "weighs" which column of a multicolumn query will generate the smallest result. All other columns in the query are evaluated through a table scan.

Inverted file indexing offers a far more efficient method to access data in an ad hoc decision support environment. Inverted file indexes, in contrast to native B-tree indexes, sort and store all values contained in an indexed field. Since most of the work is being done at the index level, the inverted index will prequalify records before they are actually read. Queries are resolved instantaneously by simply scanning the index files for the appropriate values that meet the selection criteria. In addition, inverted file indexes provide a count of the records that qualify before records are retrieved.

An inverted file structure also provides greater capabilities and flexibility than B-tree indexes. Users can enter queries in any combination to identify records that contain them, without concern for query performance. In multicolumn queries, the index of one column is compared to the index of another column. No data base records are being accessed. The result of a multicolumn query is a list (or address) of the records that qualify — fast and efficiently.

Exhibit 1 compares the functionality of relational access methods and inverted indexing. A subsequent section discusses in more detail the advanced features of inverted indexing.

USING INVERTED FILE INDEXES WITH APPLICATIONS

Only a handful of vendors offer advanced indexing that works on various standard data bases and file structures. A wide variety of applications — online production systems, decision support, data warehousing — can use these indexes to support a variety of data base structures.

Inverted indexes do not change the existing structure in any way, nor do they involve installing some other proprietary database. Consequently, an IS organization can implement one indexing strategy across multiple hardware and data base platforms. As a data base changes, so do the indexes. Therefore, it is possible to synchronize indexes in real time or on a regular schedule (e.g., nightly or weekly).

Inverted file indexing can be integrated into applications in a variety of ways. Application programming interfaces (APIs), Open DataBase Connectivity (ODBC), and callable objects are just a few methods for transparently delivering advanced indexing to business applications.

Search Techniques Access Methods	Sequential Scan	Relational Key	Inverted Index
Keyword Searches	Yes	-	Yes
Partial Key Searches	Yes	Yes[1]	Yes
Progressive Searches (drill-throughs)	-	-	Yes
Multiple Key Combinations	-[3]	Yes[2]	Yes
Automatic Qualifying Count	-	-	Yes
Case Insensitivity	-	-	Yes
Position Insensitivity	-	-	Yes
Pre-Joined Indexes	-	-	Yes
Relational Logic (equal to/greater/less than)	Yes	Yes	Yes
Boolean Logic (and/or/not)	Yes	Yes	Yes
Soundex	-	-	Yes
Excluded Words	-	-	Yes
Concatenated Keys	-[3]	Yes	Yes
Composite Keys	-	-	Yes
Grouping of Columns	-	-	Yes
Batch Indexing	-	-	Yes

[1]Inverted indexing provides partial keyword lookups, whereas partial lookups with a relational index must start with the leftmost byte of the column.
[2]Inverted indexing performs a lookup on each indexed column in combination, whereas only one relational index can be read then the records are scanned for matches on the others.
[3]Inverted indexing and relational indexes can perform lookups on a combination of columns. A sequential scan can obtain the same net effect, with time.

Note: Hashed keys were omitted because of their limited functional capabilities, although they are the optimal when users have a full-key exact match.

Exhibit 1.   Access method comparison.

INVERTED INDEXING

What do users and IS practitioners achieve through inverted indexing? Inverted indexing provides information retrieval capabilities superior to relational indexes. Both users and IS benefit from the added functionality and enhanced performance gained. Users can freely inquire into the corporate data stores while IS need not worry about problematic queries.

Flexible Retrievals

In addition to the tremendous speed advantages that inverted indexing provides, it delivers great flexibility to users in the ways they can search and query data. Users can intuitively search through data, finding records in a way that is obvious and logical. Users are not limited by computer query languages and constructs. Some of these intuitive search capabilities include keyword searches, multiple criteria iterative searches, and qualifying counts.

Keyword Searches. A keyword is any word or value surrounded by spaces or punctuation. Each word or value (keyword) in a column is indexed separately, so that keyword searches perform a fast, efficient lookup on a value that occurs anywhere in a column. Keyword searches are ideal for descriptive data, free-form text, dates, and numeric data, allowing users to find records using words (or strings) that appear anywhere in the indexed column.

In contrast, native relational indexes, B-trees, support searches on full key values in left-to-right sequence. A name field, for example, may contain the last name, followed by the first name (SMITH, JOHN). To efficiently find customer JOHN SMITH, a user must know that SMITH precedes JOHN. A B-tree index on this name field would be useless if users only knew the first name (JOHN) in the record they were searching for. The only alternative is a sequential scan of all the data rows to find an embedded value and do a pattern match.

Progressive Searches and Multiple Key Combinations. Keyword searches can combine multiple keywords against one or more columns. This capability allows users to progressively search, or iteratively "drill through," and refine their queries to contain only that subset of data needed. Users can select and analyze the data in many different ways without incurring the overhead of retrieving the rows.

Relational data bases using SQL do not inherently provide a progressive search capability. Since B-trees are limited to a single attribute, there is no efficient way to combine multiple criteria to narrow your search through thousands or millions of rows of data. The user must enter all the selection criteria up front in one SELECT statement. If the user wants to modify just one component of the selection criteria, or just continue to narrow the search, the user must resubmit the query.

For example, a user submits a query to retrieve on SMITH. If this query qualifies a million records, this may not exactly be the data needed. If the user then needs to either narrow or widen the search, he must submit another retrieval, such as JOHN OR JIM SMITH.

Qualifying Counts. Another feature of keyword searches is the automatic return of qualifying counts. These counts tell users how many rows qualified for the current search criteria. Instant qualification counts provide feedback to the user on how many records fit a given query, before accessing the underlying database. The search can be further qualified, expanded, or discarded if the results are unsatisfactory, without touching the data base itself.

The qualifying count eliminates wasteful sequential reads of massive tables that select no records, or searches that accidentally select almost the whole table. This type of search capability is extremely valuable for applications where minimizing the CPU overhead is important. In a client/server environment, the qualifying count is especially critical in managing network traffic loads. Imagine the impact of an SQL query that inadvertently selects most of a 1-million row table.

B-trees incur additional overhead in order to return a count of qualified records. A qualifying count requires retrieval and tabulation of the underlying data.

Case and Position Insensitivity. Inverted index keyword searches are both case and position insensitive. Users can quickly find the rows that meet their selection criteria wherever the keyword appears and regardless of whether the value is in upper case, lower case, or a combination of both.

B-trees typically require an exact match to the stored data. If a name was entered as SMITH, JOHN, but users searched for Smith, John, they would not find the record. To perform the most efficient index search, the retrieval criteria must exactly match the value in the data base, including upper or lower case letters, spaces and punctuation, and the order entered.

An inverted index lets users index and find records regardless of the data's format. Users can easily find "SMITH," whether it was entered as "Smith," "SMITH," or even "sMith." In addition, because inverted indexing is nonpositional, a retrieval using "JOHN OR JIM AND SMITH" will find any of the following names:

JOHN SMITH   John jim smith   SMITH, JOHN   Smith, Jim JOhn

Multidimensional Capabilities. With inverted indexing, users can enter a combination of keys to invoke a multiple index query. This capability allows users to easily and quickly query any number of criteria across one or more columns, across one or more tables. Thus, true multidimensional function is delivered without the added maintenance and limitations of multidimensional data bases.

For example, consider a SALES-HISTORY data base whose PRODUCT and CUSTOMER tables have inverted indexes on STATE, PRODUCT, DATE, and STATUS. Users can enter any combination of values for a retrieval. A sample retrieval could be: PRODUCT = "ABC OR XYZ," DATE = "95*," STATUS = "Shipped," and STATE = "CA." The inverted indexes on STATE, PRODUCT, DATE, and STATUS invoke a search across multiple indexes, without retrieving the individual data records.

Most RDBMSs can use only one index per SELECT statement. Even if there are indexes on more than one column, the RDBMS uses only index.

An option in relational data bases is to concatenate the columns into one index to provide a keyed retrieval.

Moreover, RDBMSs require a different index definition for each component combination. To retrieve any combination of five columns in a table, a large number of relational indexes (5 factorial, or 120) would be needed. Inverted indexing can provide greater functionality with just five indexes defined. Multidimensional data bases attempt to address multiple column, high-performance querying, but they have met maximum dimension constraints (up to 10 dimensions) and require additional maintenance (both design and star-schema management).

Prejoined Indexes. Inverted indexing allows the indexing of columns from more than one table or file to be combined into a single index. This "prejoining" of the indexes yields fast, optimized cross-table joins for searches that span more than one table.

For example, users could search for all the customers in a particular city and state (from CUSTOMERS table) who ordered a particular product (from PRODUCT table) within a date range (from ORDERS table). The intersection is performed at the index level, rather than incurring the overhead of large table joins and excessive data I/O.

Because each index in an RDBMS is separate and cannot be prejoined, cross-table joins are notoriously slow, especially on large tables. The best the user can do is key the desired columns in both tables and the common column. Even then, the data is intersected by doing a keyed read on one table, joining to the second table, reading all the related rows, and selecting the rows that meet the second criteria. The alternative is to do a parallel sort and merge. The method the optimizer chooses, however, may not be the most efficient.

Some relational data bases try to make retrievals faster by allowing clustered indexes or data clusters, which refers to the physical placement of related rows contiguously on disk. This approach reduces the amount of I/O to read the rows, but the fact remains that more rows are read than meet all the selection criteria. Inverted index retrievals remain the more efficient and flexible option.

Various Search Operations. With inverted file indexing, users can combine various operations to define their search criteria. These operations include relational logic (equal to, less than, greater than), Boolean logic (AND, NOT, OR), and ranges (TO). In addition, a "sounds-like" feature (also known as Soundex) allows phonetic searches on data. Commonly used for name searches, a phonetic search allows users to find, for example, "SMITH" even when spelled "SMYTHE."

Users can easily carry these operations across keyword indexes, in one or more tables, to access data across the enterprise without concern of data navigation or performance constraints.

RDBMSs support most of these operations, except a sounds-like functionality. Still, the more complex the users' criteria, the greater the exposure to poor performance.

Excluded Words. Inverted indexing allows users to designate noise words — words such as "the" or "an" that are typically useless for retrieval — to be excluded from indexing. This feature reduces the amount of time it takes to load indexes and reduces the amount of storage space that indexes require.

RDBMSs are unable to exclude values from indexing.

Composite Keys. A composite key is a virtual key that allows the redefinition of one or more existing columns. Users can easily create indexes from entire fields or parts of fields. For example, a user can break an ACCOUNT-NUMBER column into its components — DIVISION, DEPARTMENT, NATURAL ACCOUNT — without duplicating the data. In addition, composite keys can reorganize the bytes of a column into a new key. An example would be rearranging a MMDDYY date column to YYMMDD.

RDBMSs do not allow composite keys. They require an index to be comprised of an entire column, in its existing order, or a combination of columns.

Grouping of Columns. Grouping is a powerful feature that lets users index several keyword indexes in one index, thus providing the flexibility to query several similar columns at one time. Say, for example, ADDRESS1, ADDRESS2, and ADDRESS3 contained various address information, including city, state, and country. By grouping these three columns, the index treats them as one logical key or retrieval unit. Users can easily retrieve on city, state, or address information, regardless of which column the data was entered into.

RDBMSs do not have a grouping capability.

PERFORMANCE BENCHMARKS

In summary, inverted file indexes allow a variety of sophisticated search techniques: full keyword searches (e.g., find all customers with the word "Mark" somewhere in the company name), multidimensional searches (e.g., find all customers with the word "Mark" somewhere in the company name that has done business with the company in the last 6 months), range searches (e.g., find all records with transactions between June and Decem-

Query Performance Data File Structure	Without Inverted Indexes	With Inverted Indexes
Oracle	33 minutes	1.6 seconds
Sybase	35 minutes	1.9 seconds
Informix	34 minutes	1.8 seconds
Rdb	36 minutes	1.7 seconds
Digital RM	42 minutes	2.5 seconds

Exhibit 2. Performance comparison of a query with and without inverted indexes.

ber), Soundex (e.g., find all records with any word that sounds like Mark [Marc] in the company name), plurality, synonym searches, and searches that ignore differences in capitalization. In addition, inverted file indexes can deliver performance improvements of as much as 1000% on multiple selection searches, allowing retrievals that might otherwise take minutes or even hours to be completed in seconds.

Benchmarks were performed against various data file structures, including relational and flat file. In this case, a query performed on a 1-million record data base needed to find all customers in Texas who ordered in the previous month. This query required a cross-table join, based on a free-format address field in the CUSTOMER file and a date range in the ORDER file. The results are shown in Exhibit 2 and demonstrate that inverted indexing can guarantee consistent performance enhancements for an organization's data access requirements.

SUMMARY

In the rush to serve the constantly expanding demands of knowledge workers, businesses have created a complex environment for IS to develop and maintain enterprisewide data access services. Parallel processing, multidimensional servers, and partitioning are all brute-force methods proposed to address data access performance and query flexibility. Alternatives that minimize I/O and maximize memory processing may deliver the best performance for the price. Inverted file indexing may be a relatively simpler and cost-effective solution for many businesses. These multiple keyword indexes allow users to perform ad hoc queries with minimal impact to online systems. Users are also able to construct complex queries quickly. In addition, by providing feedback to the user on the size of their request before data is retrieved, client/server network traffic is minimized.

Inverted indexing leverages investments in existing hardware and software, allowing for the integration of new technologies while protecting much of the application developed. Inverted indexes provide the broadest range of flexibility for providing true data access across the enterprise. Sometimes, simple is better.

Chapter 35
Rule Matching and Indexing Techniques

Madhav Moganti
Nyapathi Ramana

RULE-BASED SYSTEMS HOLD A PROMINENT POSITION in the field of artificial intelligence (AI). They are used extensively to understand the nature of intelligence in cognitive modeling and in the study of problem-solving and learning systems, which manipulate information that includes thousands of facts and rules. Sophisticated relational data base systems have also become prevalent in the past several years. For a range of problems where data can be represented in a simple, tabular form, these data base systems are an excellent tool.

Relational data base systems do not meet the needs of many applications, including geographical information systems, computer-aided design and manufacturing (CAD/CAM) systems, and expert systems. Rule-based data base systems are a popular solution for these applications. Rule-based systems are also used in document retrieval systems and data base rule systems. Many rule-based system functions — including rule-based inferencing, querying an expert data base system, and retrieving a document using keywords — are computation-intensive functions that run slowly. This slow execution speed precludes the use of these systems in many domains requiring high performance and fast response time. This chapter discusses rule matching and indexing techniques used to significantly speed up the execution of large-scale rule systems.

There is another good reason to speed up the execution of these systems. The cognitive activity of an intelligent agent involves *knowledge search*, which is a search of the knowledge base to find information relevant in solving a given problem. As the intelligence of the agent increases, the size of the knowledge base increases, but the resources needed to perform the knowledge search do not increase. Thus, it is important to speed up the knowledge search as much as possible.

0-8493-9976-9/99/$0.00+$.50
© 1999 by CRC Press LLC

WHY USE MATCHING OR INDEXING TECHNIQUES?

Generally, rule-based systems use large amounts of main and auxiliary memory and are very CPU-intensive. They are far more akin to CPU-bound scientific programs than to I/O-intensive commercial programs. Thus, as a rule-based system expands, it tends to run out of CPU capacity before I/O bandwidth becomes a constraint. In some cases, even before the CPU capacity is filled, the tool itself can impose arbitrary limitations because of certain internal table capacities.

Some of the earliest AI systems had a fixed limit on the maximum number of rules the system could handle. Such a strict limitation was one of the major drawbacks for implementing rule-based system applications on off-the-shelf systems. Rule capacities have expanded greatly since the early systems. The early products often kept all their rules in RAM for fast response time. When an inference engine is not optimized, or is run in an interpretive language, then RAM-based rules are essential. Expanding the rule base onto disk is a common approach to increasing rule capacity.

The most time-consuming step in the execution of rule-based systems is the match step; however, there are algorithms designed to speed up this process. This chapter compares the rule matching algorithms Rete, TREAT, and Gator and presents state-of-the art indexing techniques.

RULE MATCHING TECHNIQUES

The simplest arrangement of rules is to list them in no particular order. With this arrangement, new rules can be tacked on, making it easy to expand the system as more is learned about the problem. With a small number of rules and a high-speed computer, it is practical to search the list of the arbitrarily ordered rules. If there are many rules, they may be partitioned into sublists or contexts on some logical basis. The search strategy uses a metarule based on the logic of the partition to determine which sublist to search first, thus reducing search time.

Another arrangement is to chain the rules into a tree or a graph structure. The search strategy then becomes a matter of searching this structure. Rules in their original form are too wasteful of space and slow down the match time (i.e., time to find all rules that match with assertions) on modest-sized computer systems. The worst case time complexity is $O(n^2)$, where n is the number of rules. In general, the time does not increase proportionally to n^2 and depends on the number of assertions added, which is unpredictable.

To minimize the size of the working knowledge base and to reduce the execution time, the rules are compiled using the graph method, which considers an attribute-value pair as a single instance representing a node in the graph. For example, consider the following two rules:

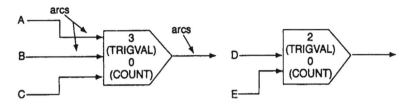

Exhibit 1. Graph representation of rules.

if A .AND. B .AND. C then D.

if D .AND. E then F.

The instances A, B, C, D, and E form the nodes of a graph, as shown in Exhibit 1, making inference execution time proportional to $O(M)$, where M is the total number of assertions. This is because the assertion list is traversed only once and, at each assertion, the emanating arcs are traversed, adding one to the COUNT in the count node. The count node points to the conclusion. When the COUNT in a count node is equal to the TRIGVAL, then the conclusion is added to the end of the assertion list.

RETE, TREAT, AND GATOR IN DATA BASE RULE SYSTEMS

The most popular match algorithms for fast inferencing include Rete, TREAT, and Gator. They transform a set of rules into a network form that is used during inferencing. The match algorithm's performance suffers considerably if all the rules in the rule base cannot be transformed into a network that fits into the main memory.

There are several data base rule systems (DBRSs) that provide rule support for relational DBMSs, including POSTGRES, STARBURST, DIPS, Ariel, and RDL1. In these systems, for any change to the data base, it is necessary to verify whether or not any rules should be fired.

The significant computational requirements of the match step can create bottlenecks in a DBRS. Most of the data base in a DBRS is stored on disk, whereas most rule-based systems are stored in the main memory. Therefore, an efficient match algorithm is even more important to DBRSs than to production systems.

The Rete algorithm is excellent for conducting matching in rule-based systems. A variation of Rete, called TREAT, is even better at matching in main-memory production system applications. These two match algorithms can be used to improve the speed of the match process in DBRSs. But the difficulty with the standard Rete and TREAT algorithms is that they do not provide a way to optimize rule-condition testing based on data base size, predicate selectivity, and update patterns.

The most critical performance factor in implementation of production systems is the rule-condition testing algorithm. The condition testing algorithm is also more important in data base rule systems than it is in main-memory production systems. The design of the Ariel data base rule system involved considerable focus on an efficient rule-condition testing algorithm. Rule conditions in Ariel and other forward-chaining rule systems have essentially the same form as a relational data base query, consisting of a set of selection conditions and joins on one or more relations.

The Rete Match Algorithm

Rete is a match algorithm that compares a large collection of patterns to a large collection of objects without iterating over the sets. An Ariel rule and its associated Rete network are shown in Exhibit 2a and b, respectively. The rule states that the salary of any employee who works for a data base project in New York is to be increased by $1000, and the employee should be moved to project 2. Two types of tokens and six types of nodes are input into the Rete network. The nodes include:

- *Root nodes*. Only one root node exists in a Rete network.
- *t-const nodes*. These nodes test single relation conditions (i.e., selections).
- α *memory nodes*. These nodes keep the temporary results of single-relation selection conditions. Nodes alpha1, alpha2, and alpha3 in Exhibit 22-2b are α memory nodes.
- *andnodes*. An "and" node joins the tokens from left and right input nodes with a join condition.
- β *memory nodes*. These nodes hold the temporary results of joins from the "and" nodes.
- *p nodes*. A "p" node is a special β memory node that holds the conflict set.

An update to the data base is considered a deletion followed by an insertion. The conflict set contains the output of the match process. The rule manager picks one of the rule instantiations in the conflict set and executes the rule, maintaining a binding between the rule and the objects that currently match the rule condition. To generate the best join network for Rete, the arrangement of α memory nodes is very important. Different join structures for Rete networks result in different performance. The three rules for constructing the best Rete network are

- Large α memory nodes should be pushed to the left as far as possible. The intermediate results for this node should be reused as much as possible.
- The α memory nodes with large token generation factors should be pushed to the right as far as possible.

```
DEFINE RULE rule 1
IF       d.No = e.DNo
   AND e.PNo = p.No
   AND d.Loc = "NY"
   AND p.Field = "Database"
FROM   d in department, e in employee, p in project
THEN   replace (e.Sal = e.Sal + 1000, e.PNo = 2)
```

a. An Ariel Rule

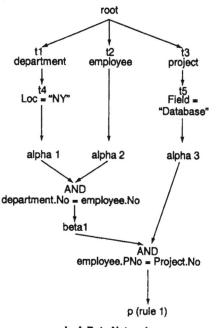

b. A Rete Network

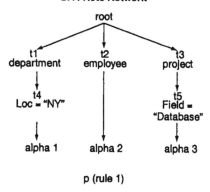

c. A TREAT Network

Exhibit 2.   Rete and TREAT in the data base rule system Ariel.

- Static α memory nodes should be pushed as far to the left as possible. A static memory node is defined as a memory node that is not likely to be changed. Tokens tend to arrive at the right-most α memory nodes. As a result, intermediate results in β memories can be reused in Rete most of the time.

The advantage of Rete is that it can reuse temporary results. The disadvantage is that it needs to maintain β memory nodes. A potential problem with Rete is that the size of β memories may be tremendous in some applications, which may cause excessive paging if stored in virtual memory.

The TREAT Match Algorithm

The TREAT match algorithm was proposed to minimize the time required for maintaining memory nodes. Experiments concluded that if the time required to maintain β memory nodes is less than the time needed to retest join conditions, then it is worthwhile to maintain the β memory nodes. The main performance advantage of TREAT over Rete is that the cost of deleting a fact is often substantially less than the cost of an insertion in TREAT. With Rete, insertion and deletion costs are the same.

TREAT's low delete overhead stems from its not having to maintain β memory nodes. Exhibit 2c shows the TREAT network that corresponds to the Rete network. TREAT only has the root node, t-const nodes and α memory nodes. As a result, the TREAT algorithm requires less memory than Rete and usually executes faster.

In an experiment, Rete and TREAT were compared for five production system applications. TREAT performed better than Rete for all five; in addition, using Rete cost twice as much in some cases. However, the individual factors affecting the performance of Rete and TREAT were not shown. Moreover, only main-memory production system applications were tested, so results may not apply to disk-intensive data base rule systems.

Optimizing TREAT would likely be easier than optimizing Rete, primarily because, for TREAT, it is not necessary to find a static ordering for all join operations in advance. In Rete, join ordering is embedded in the tree of α and β memory nodes for each rule. TREAT is superior to Rete as a rule condition testing algorithm for a data base rule system because it requires less memory and generally performs better. For a given set of rules, there are many possible Rete networks (representing different join trees), but only one TREAT network. For a particular update pattern, some Rete networks may perform very well and others catastrophically poorly. TREAT works well regardless of the update pattern, although it can be outperformed by the right Rete network.

The Gator Network

Because Rete outperforms TREAT in some cases, Gator network — a hybrid version of Rete and TREAT — was developed. The Gator network includes an optimizer that decides which strategy to use based on the rule definition and statistics about the data and update patterns. Gator can be used as a replacement for Rete or TREAT in active data base rule systems and production system interpreters.

Gator networks are general tree structures. Just like Rete and TREAT, the leaf nodes of Gator are α memory nodes that hold data matching, single-relation selection predicates. The β nodes in Gator that hold intermediate join results can have two or more inputs — not just two, as in Rete. The network is suitable for optimization because there are a variety of Gator structures that can be applied to perform pattern matching for a single rule. The algorithm for processing tokens in a Gator network is similar to the algorithms for processing tokens in Rete and TREAT.

Rete, TREAT, and Gator Compared

Rete, TREAT, and Gator are very similar algorithms. The way that Rete and TREAT test selection conditions is identical. The difference lies in how they test joins. A strategy was developed for testing only the selection conditions of data base production rules that can be used to augment Rete and TREAT. Results show that TREAT almost always outperforms Rete in testing join conditions of data base rules. Moreover, TREAT requires less storage than Rete, and is less sensitive to optimization decisions.

TREAT has performed better than Rete in a set of main-memory production system applications. TREAT also outperforms Rete in the context of a data base rule system, which deals with a large amount of persistent data rather than a small set of main-memory data. The comparison does not show, however, how the performance relationship between Rete and TREAT varies for different parameters such as the number of joins in rules or the size of the data base (i.e., working memory). This comparison identified and quantified some performance tradeoffs between Rete and TREAT that have helped subsequent researchers optimize and build new rule matching techniques.

There are a variety of Gator structures that can perform pattern matching for a single rule. In contrast, there is only a single TREAT network for a given rule, and Rete networks are limited to binary-tree structures. Rete networks have a fixed number of β nodes that use up space and take time to maintain. Gator achieves better optimization because the β nodes only materialize when they are beneficial.

In many situations, the optimal discrimination network will have the form of a Gator network, not a Rete or TREAT network. Gator networks are also appropriate when there are storage constraints because the number of internal memory nodes is not fixed, as in Rete. But the challenge is to develop an optimizer with search strategies and heuristics that can find a good Gator network in a reasonable amount of time.

Rete and TREAT in AI Systems

Rete and TREAT network algorithms were compared using the production rule engine in Soar, a main-memory-based tool for building AI programs. For several real and model applications in Soar, Rete always performed better than TREAT. This difference occurs because the testing method counts token generations as the performance metric instead of total time, which is usually I/O time in a data base rule system.

Another difference is that uniform arrival of tokens at different α memory nodes was assumed. Substantial access locality of α memories favors Rete if efficient join plans are used and Rete is able to reuse some intermediate join results. In addition, Soar does not allow deletion of working memory elements, which favors Rete because TREAT is better at deletions. Different comparisons of Rete and TREAT have obtained different results. This indicates that preference of Rete or TREAT depends greatly on the structure of rules, including the number of joins, data update patterns, and the cost of basic operations, such as memory-node access and token generation.

Uni-Rete, a specialization of the Rete match algorithm, is a linear-time match algorithm for rules with unique attributes. In applications implemented in Soar, Uni-Rete performed 10 times better than the Rete algorithm. In a unique-attribute case, Rete creates and stores a token as used and incurs a large memory management overhead. Uni-Rete exploits this bound of a single token per β memory by storing tokens implicitly and reducing the token memory management overhead.

Rete and TREAT in Real-Time Systems

A major obstacle to the use of rule-based systems in embedded control systems is the unpredictability of runtime. Embedded control systems should be responsive to the controlled process. They tend not to employ any complicated predictive mechanisms to avoid computational overhead. The Micro Level Reasoner (MLR) was developed to predict the runtime for Rete and TREAT match algorithms without reducing problem-solving variance.

MRL is based on statistics of token flow ratios at two-input nodes. Although very precise, it cannot guarantee upper bounds for runtime. An upper bound (UB) method that delivers upper bounds for basic match actions was developed to predict the maximum number of comparisons in the network nodes for a basic action.

The UB method classifies the tokens stored in the memories in a way that facilitates the prediction of the number of matches. The UB method works with static interval definitions defined at compile time by the production system implementers.

RULE INDEXING IN ADVANCED DOCUMENT RETRIEVAL SYSTEMS

Although they are not common today, text retrieval systems will become more widely used as paper-intensive organizations such as offices and libraries are automated. One of the striking features of text retrieval systems is the ability to provide highly flexible query mechanisms to satisfy different user requirements. These mechanisms include content-based, keyword-based, and concept-based querying, as well as document ranking and profiling.

Knowledge-based techniques are commonly used to support query processing, text understanding, and classification in document retrieval systems. The purpose is to augment the identification capabilities of information management systems and text processing systems based on semantic contents of texts.

MULTOS. MULTOS is an experimental system for document classification and archiving. The archiving function includes both classification of a document according to given document type and the automatic generation of the conceptual structure of documents, starting from the document text.

RUBRIC. In the RUBRIC system, production rules map semantic concepts into text patterns. By entering a concept, the user initiates a search process on the tree built on all the subconcepts defined in the system as rules. The leaves are elementary notions, which are words used as keys in a document search. Production rules are iteratively applied to prove that if the document contains an expression belonging to the left-hand part of the rule, then the document treats the concept expressed in the right-hand part of the rule.

Although RUBRIC assumes that the knowledge about the application domain is incomplete and incrementally augmentable through user interaction, other approaches assume that a specific application domain can be defined precisely and that the contents of documents in its domain can be represented accordingly. The Kabiria system is based on the premise that a complex document retrieval system is similar to a rule based system, in which document modeling and classification are viewed as tasks of knowledge analysis and representation. Querying a data base for document retrieval is then simply a process of querying a rule-based system.

INDEXING IN RULE BASES

To understand the kinds of extensions that need to be made to rule-based systems, all of the basic issues involved in rule-based programs must be examined systematically. Rete and TREAT match algorithms are implicit indexing techniques. This section discusses indexing techniques developed for rule bases that reside in secondary storage.

A rule-based system is formed from the global data base or the working memory rules and control strategy. The global data base represents the problem states, the transformation rules express how the data base may change to conform to the problem, and the control strategy decides from all the applicable transformations which one should be applied to achieve the solution (i.e., goal state). The interpreter executes a set of rules by repeatedly performing the following functions:

- *Match.* This function determines all rules whose conditions are matched with current contents of the global data base.
- *Conflict-resolution.* This function chooses one of the matching instances of rules using a conflict resolution strategy.
- *Act.* This function executes the actions of the rule.

All the steps constitute one execution cycle of the rule-based system.

Rule Representation

The rules are represented as <attribute, value, operator> tuples. A rule consists of a left-hand side (LHS) part and a right-hand side (RHS) part called condition and action parts, respectively. Both LHS and RHS are the conjunction of condition and action elements. Disjunctions in the condition part are ignored as such a rule can be split into a set of conjunctive rules. The syntax of the rules used is as shown below:

$$\text{if } \langle LHS \rangle \text{ then } \langle RHS \rangle$$

$$\langle LHS \rangle = CL_1 \text{ .AND. } \dots \text{ .AND. } CL_n$$

$$\langle RHS \rangle = CR_1 \text{ .AND. } \dots \text{ .AND. } CR_m$$

Where:

- n is the number of condition elements on the left-hand side.
- m is the number of action elements on the right-hand side.
- CL and CR are represented using a tuple $\langle A_l, V_{Al,j}, O_k \rangle$ where:
  - A_l is the l_{th} attribute name and $1 \le l \le P$.
  - P is the total number of attributes in the rule base.

- $V_{Al,j}$ is the j_{th} value of attribute A_l, and $1 \leq j \leq Q_{Al}$. This value could be an ordinary attribute value or an attribute itself.
- Q_{Al} is the number of different values an attribute A_l can have.
- O_k is an operator, where $1 \leq k \leq R$ and R is the number of different operators in the rule base.

The Basic Approach

A system that stores large amounts of data should provide fast access for retrieval, convenient updates, and economy of storage. In data bases, indexing is an invaluable method of quickly retrieving records from the data base. Similarly, indexing in large rule-based systems mainly aims at fast access for the retrieval of required knowledge from the secondary storage. Following are two levels of indexing:

- Attribute indexing
- Attribute value indexing

The complete indexing mechanism is shown in Exhibit 3, where attribute indexing is represented as level I and attribute value indexing is represented as level II. Clustered attribute sets need not be mutually disjointed.

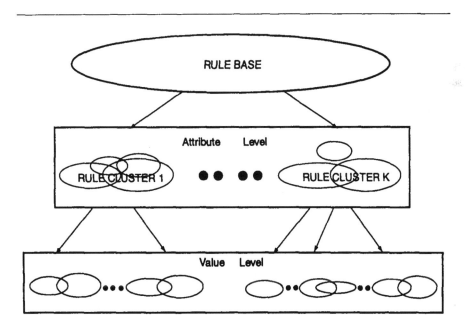

Exhibit 3. Two-level organization of indexing.

DAAG and the R$^+$-Tree

The Directed Acyclic Attribute Graph (DAAG) and R$^+$-tree structures were developed for attribute-level and value-level indexing, respectively. Attribute-level indexing allows all rules that have common attributes to be grouped, increasing the locality of reference, whereas value-level indexing allows rule indexing to be extended to another level using attribute values. Value-level indexing is advantageous when the attribute-level indexing fails to cluster rules into smaller groups.

Consider an example with two range-type attributes, Length and Breadth, where $3 \leq Length \leq 10$ and $50 \leq Breadth \leq 100$. In value-level indexing, the rules containing such types of attributes are represented as points in higher dimensional geometric space, where each attribute is considered a dimension. The problem of searching applicable rules is reduced to a geometric intersection problem that can be efficiently solved using R$^+$-trees. The remainder of this chapter presents a means of maintaining knowledge for large-scale rule bases. The techniques presented are designed to:

- Support large rule bases
- Eliminate unnecessary searches when accessing promising rules for inferencing
- Improve response time
- Improve I/O performance by clustering rules

The DAAG

The main idea behind selecting the DAAG structure for indexing is that in a rule base, the total number of different attributes is considerably less than the total number of condition and action elements. The attributes of condition elements are considered for indexing in the forward-chaining inference mechanism, and attributes of action elements are considered in backward-chaining inferencing. The DAAG structure allows each rule pointer in the rule list to point to either a rule in the secondary storage or to a page number in which the rules reside. It also keeps track of the paths, in a symbol table, of the attributes that contribute to the generation of a rule set/cluster.

```
Input:          Rule base
Output:         DAAG
begin
    root = Create a node with attno = 0
    R = Set of all rules,
    while (R not empty) do {
        L = Get a rule from R
        Remove L from R
        Reorder attributes in L
        Insert attributes in L into the DAAG
```

```
Input:     Rule-Base
Output:    DAAG
begin
      root = Create a node with attno = 0
      R = Set of all rules,
      while (R not empty) do {
            L = Get a rule from R
            Remove L from R
            Reorder attributes in L
            Insert attributes in L into the DAAG
            Update the symbol table
      }
end
```

Exhibit 4. DAAG algorithm.

```
      Update the symbol table
}
end
```

As a DAAG is constructed, the paths in the symbol table are reordered in such a way that the shortest paths of attributes are toward the beginning of the path list. Exhibit 4 shows rule set 1, Exhibit 5 shows the symbol table for rule set 1, and Exhibit 6 shows the DAAG structure for rule set 1.

Reordering of attributes in a rule reduces the complexity of the DAAG structure. This reordering is important because it preserves the relative ordering of conditions among rules (i.e., preserving the priority among attributes). Experimental results show that indexing of the rules with the DAAG structure improves the performance of the large rule bases considerably, and rule identification time depends on the total number of assertions present. Performance increases because the total number of

---

R1 :   if (Position = programmer) .AND. (Age ≥ 35) .AND. (Status = unmarried)
        then (Placement = local)
R2 :   if (Position = programmer) .AND. (Age ≥ 35) .AND. (Status = married)
        then (Placement = local) .AND. (Benefit = yes)
R3 :   if (Placement = local) .AND. (Age ≥ 40) .AND. (Position = programmer)
        .AND. (House = rent)
        then (Loan = approved)
R4 :   if (Placement = local) .AND. (Position = programmer)
        .AND. (Age > 40) .AND. (Age ≤ 50) .AND. (House = own)
        then (Loan = declined)
R5 :   if (Loan = approved) .AND. (Salary ≤ 1500)
        then (Rate = 10)
R6 :   if (Loan = approved) .AND. (Salary > 1500)
        then (Rate = 7)

Exhibit 5.   Example rules (Rule Set 1).

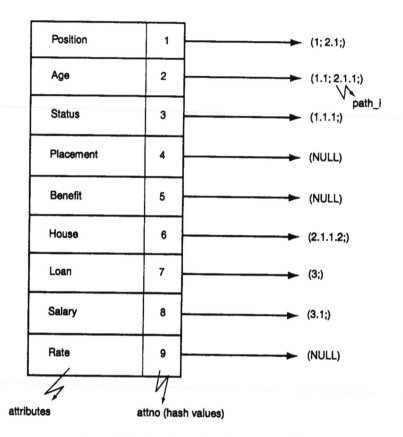

Exhibit 6. Symbol table for Rule Set 1.

---

assertions present are considerably fewer than the number of rules in a rule base. Exhibit 7 shows a graph comparing the execution times of the DAAG indexing with that of a conventional match algorithm that does not use any kind of indexing.

R+-Tree Construction

The R+-tree is constructed for a set of rules that has attributes with range values. For illustration purposes, consider the set of rules given in Exhibit 8. Exhibit 9 shows the R+-tree representation for these rules. A 2-D pictorial representation for the rules in Exhibit 8 is shown in Exhibit 10. An intermediate node in the R+-tree points to a child node in the tree and contains the coordinates of the bounding box that encloses all the bounding boxes of its children. Indexing using R+-trees improves the overall performance of the rule-based system for two reasons: R+-trees eliminate the necessity for searching overlapping hyper-rectangles in the intermediate

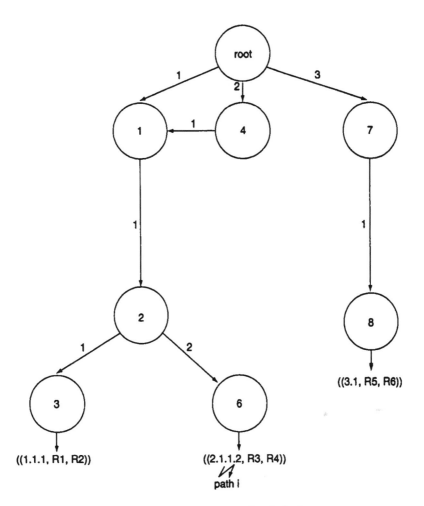

Exhibit 7.   DAAG structure for Rule Set 1.

R1 : if Length ≤ 50 .AND. Length ≥ 25
     .AND. Breadth ≤ 35 .AND. Breadth ≥ 15 .AND. Quality = medium
   then Rank = one
R2 : if Length ≤ 40 .AND. Length ≥ 15
     .AND. Breadth ≤ 55 .AND. Breadth ≥ 25 .AND. Quality = low
   then Rank = two
R3 : if Length ≤ 100 .AND. Length ≥ 75
     .AND. Breadth ≤ 50 .AND. Breadth ≥ 45 .AND. Quality = high then Rank = four
R4 : if Length ≤ 125 .AND. Length ≥ 80
     .AND. Breadth ≤ 65 .AND. Breadth ≥ 40 .AND. Quality = medium
   then Rank = three

Exhibit 8.   Sample rules (Rule Set 2).

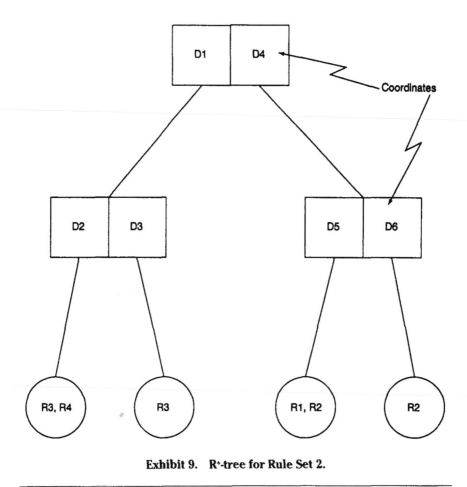

Exhibit 9.   R⁺-tree for Rule Set 2.

nodes of the tree, and the R⁺-tree being searched is always small because of the two-level indexing scheme used.

SUMMARY

This chapter examined several rule matching and indexing techniques, including the match algorithms Rete, TREAT, and Gator. TREAT is superior to Rete as a rule condition testing algorithm for data-based rule systems. For a DBMS, TREAT is a better choice than Rete because it requires less memory and generally performs better. In AI systems, results show that Rete always outperforms TREAT. Rete and TREAT networks can be replaced by Gator networks, which perform well in all cases.

This chapter also discussed the DAAG and R⁺-tree indexing techniques. DAAG and R+-tree structures efficiently cluster the rules in a rule base. The

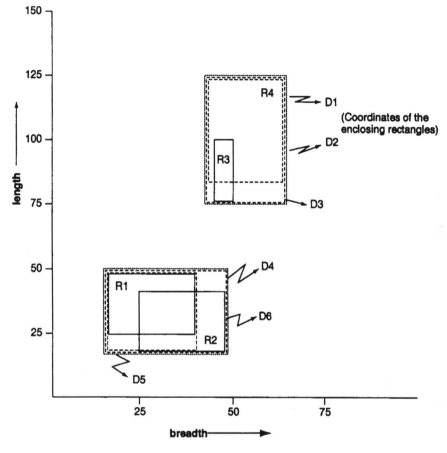

Exhibit 10.   2D pictorial representation of Rule Set 2.

techniques used in these structures improve the runtime response of rule-based systems, eliminate unnecessary searches when accessing rules for inferencing, and improve overall I/O performance.

Chapter 36
Operating System Support for Database Servers

David S. Linthicum

WITH THE EXCITEMENT AND CONFUSION THAT SURROUND PROJECT DOWNSIZING, many organizations fail to factor in operating systems when they design their server systems. This is a big mistake.

Interoperability pitfalls, a scant capacity supply, lack of scalability features, lack of an upgrade path, or the worst server problem of all, poor performance — these are just a few of the client/server problems that arise when organizations fail to account for the operating system that the database server will run under. Lack of attention to the server operating system leads to the failure of downsizing projects. Avoiding these failures is simply a matter of doing some homework.

This chapter explains how to evaluate and select a database server for client/server projects. The discussion is limited to downsizing projects and solutions for UNIX, NetWare, Windows NT, and OS/2. Mainframe and minicomputer operating systems are excluded.

OS SERVICES

Client/server systems differ greatly from older, centralized systems. Client/server systems rely on many components or subsystems to get the job done. These subsystems include the processor, disk drives, network devices, database server software, and user interfaces.

A client/server system is only as effective as its least-effective component. Slow networks, poorly tuned database servers, and lethargic user interfaces all can lead to inefficient processing and user discontent.

The database server is the most critical component of a client/server system, and to a great extent, the operating system determines how fast and reliably the database server will run.

0-8493-9976-9/99/$0.00+$.50
© 1999 by CRC Press LLC

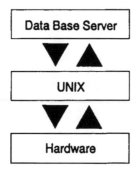

Exhibit 1. The operating system and database server.

The operating system sits between the hardware and the database server software, providing critical services that keep the server up and running (Exhibit 1).The operating system defines how efficiently the database server software can access processor services, memory, disk I/O, and the network.

Beyond the basic operating system (OS) services, certain qualitative aspects of an operating system are important to note. These involve advanced operating system features that include the ability to support multiprocessing computers, such as the new line of multiprocessor servers. Other desirable features protect the data from corruption as well as from unauthorized users.

Most important, the operating system needs to make it possible for servers to run continuously, without interruptions due to crashes or application conflicts.

Is there an operating system that can do all of this and provide the database server with all of the services and amenities it needs to keep itself processing at maximum efficiency? Yes. Solutions do exist.

The remainder of this chapter takes a close look at the operating system components, examining how well each supports a database server. Covered are some of the basic services that an operating system provides and how a database server makes use of them.

Available operating system solutions also are discussed, including UNIX, NetWare, Windows NT, and OS/2, and the features of each. Evaluating and selecting the operating system that best fits for a company's client/server project is covered last.

OPERATING SYSTEMS 101

Database servers place a tremendous processing load on a server and its operating system. Depending on the type of database server employed, a database server launches and communicates with thousands of processes that are running concurrently. These processes share the same processor, memory, disk, network, and other I/O devices.

Each process performs a special activity, such as making database requests, client communications, roll-back/roll-forward recovery operations, security, and execution of stored procedures, to name only a few. To further complicate matters, many database servers manage clients by assigning one or many operating system processes to each client connected to the server.

Using this method, it is not unusual for a database server that supports only 100 clients to have as many as 1,000 processes running under the operating system at any given time. The operating system must handle this type of enormous processing load and manage each process without a complaint.

To evaluate operating systems properly, one must first arm oneself with some basic information. Familiarizing oneself with the base services that operating systems provide to applications that run under them (including database servers) is the first step. These basic services include:

- Task management
- Disk I/O
- Memory management

The number of services offered, and the implementation of each service delivered to the application program varies from operating system to operating system. However, most of the underlying concepts are comparable.

Task Management

Database servers require the operating system to perform several task management operations that administer the process load a database server places on the operating system. To manage these processes effectively, an operating system uses a variety of OS services and concepts that include task preemption, task priority, threads, interprocess communications (IPC), semaphores, and process protection.

Preemptive Multitasking. The task preemption service (also known as preemptive multitasking) allows multitasking operating systems such as NT, UNIX, and OS/2, to allocate processor time effectively for each process, including those launched by the database server.

Task preemption services allow the operating system to tell a particular process to give up the processor for a while, thus giving other processes a chance to execute. If the operating system does not provide task preemptive services, each process must delay execution until another process releases the processor.

An example of a preemptive multitasking operating system is UNIX, where the UNIX kernel allocates processor time among running tasks and never lets one task take complete control of the processor. An example of an operating environment that does not support preemptive multitasking is DOS.

When running under Windows, the process itself (i.e., the Windows Application) must release the processor before others can execute. Windows NT was developed in part to solve this problem by providing task preemptive services to a Windows-like environment. Task preemption is a highly desirable feature, and operating systems that support task preemption provide better environments for database servers.

Process Allocation. Another aspect of process management is process protection and synchronization or the ability to run many processes concurrently without interfering with each other. Operating systems use semaphores to provide these process protection services.

A semaphore, named after a naval flag, is a signal or a flag variable that controls access to a system resource. Semaphores maintain order among all processes going after the data processor, I/O device, or portion of memory. When a resource is busy, the operating system is made aware of this fact and keeps other processes from attempting to use the same resource at the same time. Concurrent access to resources easily could clobber the operating system and the database server.

Task Priority. In addition to controlling processor allocation and process protection, the operating system also should allow execution of processes by priority. This allows the operating system, and therefore the database server, to determine if and which processes should receive additional resources such as processor time, memory, and disk I/O.

This concept of database processing allows certain users to receive a faster repose time, and it is handy if specific users need faster access to the database server to make their workday more productive (i.e., order entry operators and real-time systems).

Multithreading. Most database servers are multithreaded applications. Multithreaded applications can split themselves up into process threads or subtasks. These process threads let the server software take the divide-

and-conquer approach to database processing, allowing applications to multitask within themselves.

Multithreaded processes are ideal for database server applications. Each thread can accept a request from a client as well as respond to the request.

For example, a database server performs operations on the database by opening, reading, and writing to it. All of the database requests could come from different clients, with each incoming request received and processed by a separate server thread. The result is the concurrent processing of all database services, which increases server performance.

Most advanced operating systems such as UNIX and OS/2 support multithreaded applications. DOS does not.

IPC. Another desirable feature of an operating system that supports the database server is the ability for processes to communicate with one another. Interprocess communications (IPC) occur locally within the server or remotely over a network with similar or dissimilar platforms.

Many client/server systems rely on IPC features of an operating system (e.g., Named Pipes) to support communications between the client and the server. However, process-to-process communications within the server are important as well.

Disk I/O

Database servers are well-known disk hogs. It is the job of the operating system to provide punctual information from disk files. Database servers demand that the operating system allows multiprocess file access operations to occur concurrently without delaying I/O requests. In addition, the operating system should provide file- and record-locking services to control concurrent access to database files without file damage.

Some operating systems, such as UNIX and OS/2, provide disk buffering/cache subsystems for temporary storage of information moving to and from the physical disk. This has the effect of increasing I/O performance because the database server, or other applications using disk storage, do not have to wait for the physical disk to complete an operation before reading or writing data.

Moreover, some operating systems use special file systems, such as OS/2's High Performance File System (HPFS). HPFS uses sophisticated data structures and many levels of disk caching to increase disk I/O performance.

Memory Management

Finally, the operating system provides memory management services. The operating system must load large programs such as database servers into memory. Once loaded, the operating system provides other memory management services, such as memory paging operations and protecting reserved portions of memory from other processes.

Virtual Memory. Memory-paging operations allow for a portion of the information stored in memory to move temporarily to disk, thus freeing up memory for other purposes. It is critical that the operating system perform memory-paging activities efficiently, without affecting the performance of the database server.

In operating systems such as Windows NT, virtual memory (VM) is the preferred method of memory management to provide memory protection and memory management features. This technique allows an operating system to simulate more memory than actually exists in the computer.

VM breaks up an application like a database server into smaller chunks that are known as pages. In lieu of loading the entire program into memory, VM only loads as many pages as it can store into memory at any given time. If the running program requires instructions not present in memory, the appropriate pages load into memory (Exhibit 2).

SUPPORTING MULTIPROCESSING SERVERS

In the search to solve performance and scalability problems, many database server vendors are turning toward multiprocessing computers. These

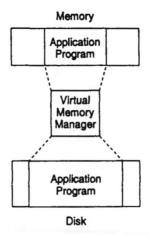

Exhibit 2.   Virtual memory.

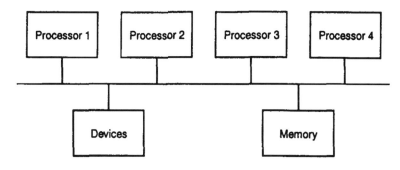

Exhibit 3.   Multiprocessing.

so-called superservers pack quite a punch, considering that some of them can contain more than 1,000 processors. The NCR Model 3700, for example, contains up to 1,024 Intel processors (loosely coupled) running a special version of UNIX.

Using these processor patch systems and the operating systems that support them, database servers can split up queries into several subqueries, processing each concurrently. Most major database server vendors (including Oracle and Sybase) are aligning their servers to make the most of multiprocessing servers. Oracle, for example, boasts a response time of ten seconds where processing once took a minute or more on similar systems using massively parallel processing (MPP) technology and Oracle 7.1's new Parallel Query option.

The idea behind multiprocessing is that by adding additional processors to a server, that server can handle an additional work load (Exhibit 3). This is the ultimate in scalability, considering that to a slow database server, a few more processor cards are just what the doctor ordered. No need to move the database server to larger server systems.

Symmetrical and Asymmetrical Servers

Multiprocessing superservers are either symmetrical or asymmetrical in the manner that they address the processors contained within the server. A symmetrical server allows processors to share access to system resources, including disk, memory, and the network. All processors basically perform the same type of functions and handle any task that comes their way.

In contrast, an asymmetrical server dedicates separate, specialized processors to particular system activities. For example, one processor may handle operating system requests while another runs user processes (Exhibit 4).

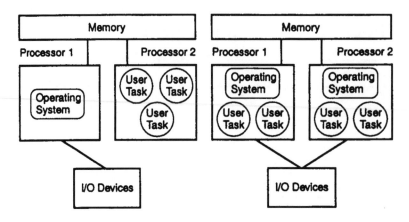

Exhibit 4. Asymmetrical vs. symmetrical.

Sometimes servers come with both symmetrical and asymmetrical characteristics, so the user gets the best of both worlds. Of course, multiprocessing servers rely on the operating system to manage the additional processors.

Multiprocessing operating systems generally are specialized versions of UNIX, although Windows NT is getting into the multiprocessing game as well. UNIX flavors that support multiprocessing include the Santa Cruz Operations' UNIX MPX (multiprocessor extensions) and SunSoft's Solaris (UNIX System V).

Generally, symmetrical operating systems are somewhat more advanced, making better use of system resources that include the multiple processors. They use a process known as scheduler that allocates the process load dynamically to underutilized processors. NCR's multiprocessing version of the UNIX NCR SVR4 operating system is an example of a symmetrical operating system supporting one to legions of Intel processors symmetrically on NCR's 3600 series of superservers.

Loosely vs. Tightly Coupled Methods

There are two distinct methods that make use of multiple processors within a computer system: loosely coupled and tightly coupled.

Loosely coupled refers to a multiprocessing architecture in which each CPU has separate memory and system buses. Generally the CPUs are connected using a network.

In contrast, *tightly coupled* refers to a multiprocessing computer in which each CPU shares the same memory and system bus, as do most multiprocessing servers. Again, one must use an operating system that supports loosely or tightly coupled processors.

A TOUR OF TODAY'S OPERATING SYSTEMS

Now that the basics of operating system services have been addressed, it is time to evaluate the current inventory of operating system solutions that provide a suitable environment for a database server. Remember, all database servers do not run under all operating systems. For example, Oracle 7 runs under all of the operating systems covered in this chapter, whereas Microsoft SQL Server only supports Windows NT and OS/2.

The moral here is to try to find a server vendor that supports the operating system appropriate to a project — or, at the very least, does not allow the database server vendor to dictate the choice of operating system. The customer is the one who has to live with the hardware.

UNIX

UNIX is by far the most versatile operating environment available today. It works well as a database server operating system running on all types of hardware. UNIX runs on most major processors — Intel, RISC, Motorola, the PowerPC, and others.

UNIX has all of the good features that an operating system can have, including reliability, portability, advanced operating system utilities, scalability, and networking features built right into the operating system. Over 20 years old, UNIX is an operating system that has been tested thoroughly. Considering the way UNIX is catching on as a corporate applications development platform, chances are everyone will use UNIX sometime in their career.

One of the major strengths of UNIX is the number of platforms that can run on it. There are versions of UNIX for most computers on the market.

For Intel workstations, one can run Santa Cruz Operation's UNIX, SunSoft's 386/ix or Solaris, Novell's UnixWare, and a few others. On RISC workstations there are Hewlett-Packard's HP/UX, Sun's Solaris, and IBM's AIX. On larger systems one will find DEC's Ultrix running on VAX minicomputers, and even versions of UNIX running on supercomputers. This list increases monthly.

Porting Applications. UNIX sells itself as an open system. Applications are portable from UNIX system to UNIX system. For example, an application created for an Intel version of UNIX is source-code compatible with other versions of UNIX, or at least that is the idea. Database server developers take full advantage of this portability by porting database server software to most versions of UNIX. The concept is, if it runs under one, it should run under them all.

Of course, in practice, this is not as easy as it sounds, but as operating system standards are getting better, so is the ease of porting applications. The IEEE Posix (Portable Operating System Interface for UNIX) standard defines common operating system services. When using a Posix standard operating system, the applications running on that platform are A-to-A source-code compatible with other operating systems supporting the Posix standard.

UNIX has not cornered the market on Posix. Recently Windows NT began supporting Posix standards to become more competitive with UNIX.

The portability of UNIX provides for scalability. Using the portability concept, once one outgrows a server platform and requires more processing power, he or she simply can run a database server and other applications on the newer and faster hardware without completely redoing an application and database. Of course, the server vendor must do the porting.

This scalability concept is easier to implement on multiprocessing computers where increasing the processing power of a database server only entails adding more processors. Servers and applications need not move from server to server. Remember, UNIX is the operating system of choice for multiprocessing computers.

OS/2

IBM Corp.'s OS/2 is a 32-bit operating system for 80386 or greater Intel processors running DOS, Windows, and native 32-bit OS/2 applications. Unlike UNIX, OS/2 only runs on a single processor platform, limiting the options to small Intel-based systems. However, it was the first 32-bit operating system designed specifically for the Intel.

Do not discount OS/2 based on the bad press it has received. This operating system has an underlying operating system layer that is both powerful and reliable. OS/2 currently provides the power for many database servers, including Microsoft SQL Server and Ingres for OS/2, to name just a few. Most of the database servers running under OS/2 are true 32-bit multithreaded applications that take advantage of the complete power of the OS's fully preemptive multitasking environment.

Crash Protection. Despite its unstable history, OS/2 is one of the more reliable operating systems available. OS/2 is almost crash-proof. If a DOS, Windows, or native OS/2 application happens to go haywire, it will not bring down the entire system. Only that particular application will die. Anyone who has experienced a full-server crash (usually due to some small bug) knows the value that full-crash protection offers.

Of course, OS/2 is not the only crash-proof environment. Most versions of UNIX as well as Windows NT demonstrate similar capabilities.

OS/2 can take direct advantage of high-performance devices (e.g., SCSI host adapters) through a tuning facility built into the operating system. Moreover, OS/2 can place files on the physical disk to minimize disk fragmentation, a common problem when using DOS and some versions of UNIX.

OS/2 supports up to 4,096 threads and processes as well as 64,000 semaphores per process, and can address up to 32M bytes of physical memory. The operating system can address 512M bytes of virtual memory.

Windows NT

Microsoft's Windows NT has entered the scene as an advanced operating system for RISC and Intel processors in workstation or server configurations. NT offers some of the best features of OS/2, VMS, and UNIX. It can run 16-bit DOS and Windows applications and 32-bit native NT applications.

NT is packed fully with features, including preemptive multitasking, crash protection, and support for multithreaded applications. Most major database server vendors are planning to support NT, including Microsoft's SQL Server.

Unlike OS/2, Windows NT is finding a home on more than one processor, with support for Intel as well as RISC processors (MIPS and DEC Alpha so far) in single or multiprocessor configurations. Clearly chasing the UNIX market, NT supports the once UNIX-only Posix standard, ensuring application portability with other UNIX environments.

Chasing the server market, NT provides advanced server features, such as built-in disk mirroring, a transaction processing-oriented recoverable file system, and memory-mapped files that allow disk files to link to an array of virtual memory addresses. Like OS/2and UNIX, the process protection feature of NT keeps a server running because processes run in their own virtual machine space under the operating system.

A virtual machine provides an application with a private, simulated computer system. If an application crashes, it only takes down the virtual machine it is running under, leaving the other applications like the database server alive.

NetWare

Novell's NetWare network operating system quickly is becoming a popular platform for many database servers including Oracle and Sybase. Intel-based NetWare allows developers to extend the system services of a NetWare file server using NetWare Loadable Modules (NLMs).

NLMs are program-like files that bind to the NetWare kernel and run with standard network operating system file, print, and communications services. NLM development is open.

Operating system purists do not consider NetWare a true operating system. It does not provide many of the operating system services and protections offered by UNIX, OS/2, and NT. For example, NLMs are not memory-protected and they run at Ring 0, which normally is reserved for the high-priority services of the operating systems. A misbehaved NLM potentially could bring down the entire server. Other disadvantages include the lack of support for preemptive multitasking and threading.

Moreover, NetWare does not provide memory paging services. Once memory is full, the operating environment cannot swap portions of memory to and from disk to allow for additional programs (i.e., NLMs) to load.

Even with these server limitations, NetWare provides a fast and effective environment in which database servers run at light speed. This newfound performance is a function of the advanced optimization features NetWare uses in file server operations. Even with speed as its only real asset, NetWare could prove an inexpensive and available method of entering into client/server computing.

TIPS FOR EVALUATING THE OPTIONS

No single operating system meets all requirements or solves every problem. The operating system that works best for a company largely depends on that company's unique needs. As anyone can see, all operating systems are not created equal. Each provides different functions and facilities. Make sure to take note of them before making any purchasing decisions.

If a server is to support multiple applications, it is important to build firewalls in the operating system to prevent conflicts. For example, if a server runs two independent databases, a failure in one database should not affect the other. Tough, well-tested operating systems such as UNIX and OS/2 that provide process protections make good homes for mission-critical database servers.

Moreover, an operating system should prevent running applications from hogging server-processing time. This makes operating systems such as UNIX, OS/2, and NT-well suited for database servers because they all provide preemptive multitasking services. Operating systems such as MS-DOS and MAC/OS do not.

Another important protection feature is the operating system's ability to protect the memory owned by the database server from those processes that would do that memory harm. For example, NetWare lacks strong memory protection features and makes running a database server a risky proposition. UNIX, OS/2, and NT provide better memory protection features, so a server is less likely to crash.

An additional concern with an operating system is its ability to connect to other operating environments, similar or dissimilar, now and in the near future. In today's corporate networking environment, UNIX, Novell, Windows NT, OS/2, and operating systems for large computers must work and play well with others.

RECOMMENDED COURSE OF ACTION

If an organization is going to depend on its database server, make sure it can depend on the operating system that runs the server. Technical details related to the operating system are just as important as selecting the right user interface or database.

Take time to evaluate your operating system needs and to examine available solutions. With a little planning — and the tips given in this chapter — an operating system could be the most stable segment of a client/server system.

Section VII
Object Technology, Object Modeling, and Object Databases

OBJECT TECHNOLOGY COMBINES PROCESS AND DATA INTO ENCAPSULATED OBJECTS. Object technology leverages data in many formats, from pure object data stores to hybrid databases. Object technology is supported by a suite of object-modeling methodologies, tools, procedures, and databases. This section contains 10 chapters that focus on different aspects of object technology:

Chapter 37, "Data Access Using Microsoft Visual Basic 5.0+," compares and contrasts the different data access methods available in Visual Basic Version 5.0+. This includes RDO, ADO, and DAO. This version of Visual Basic has a strong degree of object orientation. Coupled with Microsoft® Transaction Server (MTS) and ActiveX, Visual Basic is well on the way to becoming a strong component-based tool kit.

Chapter 38, "Component-Based Development," discusses the opportunities available to organizations to leverage component-based development for shorter implementation schedules and code reuse. Component-based development is expected to fuel a strong trade of reusable components from vendors and corporations over the next few years.

Chapter 39, "Developing ActiveX Internet Server Components with Visual Basic and Rational Rose," examines using object-oriented analysis and design techniques with Rational Rose 98 to design robust component-based systems that can be implemented quickly and easily in Visual Basic 5 and deployed in an Internet server-based architecture.

Chapter 40, "A Technical Primer for Getting Started with JavaBeans," provides examples for creating components through JavaBeans. This chapter provides examples for creating and compiling a JavaBean class.

Chapter 41, "JavaBeans and Java Enterprise Server Platform," examines the Java programming language and its interaction with data repositories. JavaBeans are the component object model for the Java platform. Its architecture is explored in this chapter. Enterprise JavaBeans, which offer support for legacy systems and extended enterprise services, also are discussed.

Chapter 42, "Object Technology Essentials," defines what the object paradigm is all about; discusses various concepts, such as abstraction and inheritance; and covers various types of object systems, such as databases, agents, case tools, and brokers.

Chapter 43, "CRC Cards: A Hands-On Approach to Object-Oriented Design," describes the analysis methodology of CRC cards and shows how they can be applied to applications design. The steps in the design process are illustrated with examples. In many cases, using an analysis and design approach is the first step toward information systems design. After the objects and the interactions between them are identified, then the databases and other systems can be designed more efficiently.

Chapter 44, "Component Architectures: COM and CORBA," describes components, classifies them, and focuses on different component standards. This chapter also examines components in the client/server environment and describes the design cycle.

Chapter 45, "Using CORBA to Integrate Database Systems," describes CORBA (common object request broker architecture), a method for addressing interoperability and heterogeneity issues among different database systems.

Chapter 46, "Distributed Objects and Object Wrapping," contrasts current and future trends in distributed object architectures, specifically Open Software Foundation's DCE and the Object Management Group's CORBA.

Chapter 37

Data Access Using Microsoft Visual Basic 5.0+

Stephen D'Silva

THE FUNDAMENTAL AND VITAL PART OF ANY BUSINESS IS DATA both within and without the organization. Data within the organization can provide insights into the performance of the company, and data from outside can enable organizations to be cooperative and competitive. Information technology (IT) plays a very important role in the analysis and presentation of data besides offering other benefits. This is accomplished by computer-based applications, developed and customized using the many development tools available in the market. One of the more popular tools being used to develop business applications is Microsoft₆ Visual Basic.

Data in many organizations resides in databases such as Microsoft Access, Microsoft SQL Server, Sybase SQL Server, Oracle, DB2, Informix, and Ingres. This chapter provides methods and techniques that are available to the Visual Basic developer to access data residing in these databases.

BASIC DATA ACCESS INTERFACES

The following paragraphs describe the basic database interface options available to a developer. These options provide a very low-level interface to the database and, therefore, are not usually the ones that are used by most developers. They compensate, however, for programming difficulty with excellent database access performance. Higher-level interfaces are now available that provide ease of developing data access components with varying levels of performance. These interfaces will be discussed in the next section. Exhibit 1 illustrates the connection between the data access interfaces, the databases, and the client application.

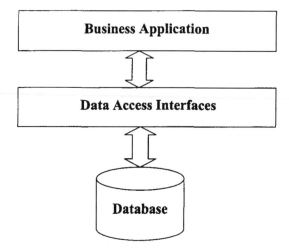

Exhibit 1.   Connection between the data access interfaces, databases, and client application.

NATIVE DATABASE DRIVERS

A few years ago data from database servers could be accessed only by using the native drivers that the database vendors provided for their product. These usually consisted of APIs (Application Programming Interfaces) that included database libraries and, for remote access, network libraries. The developers then would program the database connectivity interface to their applications using these APIs. This method proved to be tedious and time-consuming and had the following disadvantages:

- The database connection interface usually had to be written in the programming language that was used to write the API.
- There was a tight coupling between the APIs and the application program and, therefore, changes in the API could produce errors due to incompatible function calls.
- The application was tied to a database; therefore, if the database were changed, major changes would be required in the application. This resulted in the organization being tied to a single vendor.

The advantage with this approach was performance, as the APIs were fine-tuned to the database.

FILE-BASED AND ISAM DATABASE INTERFACES

Data that has been saved as text or in proprietary data formats in files can be accessed using file input/output (I/O) operations. The Indexed Sequential Access Method (ISAM) is a binary format that was used by the file-based databases to speed up data retrieval. Because most of the ISAM databases used proprietary formats, data access was possible only by using specific data access drivers. The Joint Engine Technology (JET) was developed as an attempt to standardize file and ISAM data access. JET loads ISAM drivers to facilitate communication with ISAM databases in various formats.

MICROSOFT ODBC (OPEN DATABASE CONNECTION)

For the Microsoft Windows platform, Microsoft developed the ODBC standard. This standard was based on the premise that applications needed to be developed using a more general interface to the database and a loose coupling model.

ODBC translates common ODBC SQL and API calls into a format recognizable by an SQL database server. The database connection was established by using a data source specification entry in the ODBC configuration file. The ODBC configuration for the data source included parameters such as database name, database drivers, user ID and password.

The advantage with this method was that it broke down the application-database dependence. This, however, affected the data access performance. ODBC certainly provided a standard and general method to access data residing on SQL databases, thereby reducing the database access task to writing SQL statements.

OLE DB

OLE DB is Microsoft's latest attempt to provide a common interface for all data storage formats such as relational database formats and other unstructured data formats like documents and graphic sources, regardless of location or type. The OLE DB specification is a set of interfaces that expose data from both structured and unstructured data sources using the Microsoft Component Object Model (COM). OLE DB acts as a COM wrapper around the data source, whether the data is in ISAM or SQL format. Clients are not intended to call OLE DB directly because it is a low-level interface to a data source. OLE DB will be the standard to access all types of data formats just as ODBC was for SQL data formats.

OLE DB goes beyond simple data access by partitioning the functionality of a traditional relational database into logical components. There are three main categories of components built on the OLE DB architecture: data consumers, data providers, and service components.

Data consumers are applications that need access to a broad range of data. These include development tools, languages, and personal productivity tools. An application becomes OLE DB-enabled by using the OLE DB API to talk to data.

Data providers make their data available for consuming. They may do this by natively supporting OLE DB or they may rely on additional OLE DB data providers. If a data provider is a native OLE DB provider, an application can talk to it directly, via OLE DB. There is no need for additional drivers or software.

A data provider that natively does not support OLE DB relies on an intermediary in the same way that ODBC data sources rely on ODBC drivers.

The OLE DB Provider for ODBC enables applications to use OLE DB to talk to relational data via ODBC. This means that one can use OLE DB today to get to all of the same data he or she currently uses ODBC to access. ODBC remains the ideal technology for accessing SQL databases, and the OLE DB Provider for ODBC ensures that one can continue writing high-performance database applications.

OLE DB provides a base-level data access functionality: the managing of a tabular rowset.

Service components provide additional functionality such as query processing or cursor engines. A query processor allows SQL queries to be constructed and run against the data source. A cursor engine provides scrolling capabilities for data sources that do not support scrolling.

So for example, if wanting to query Microsoft SQL Server data, one would not need a service component because SQL Server has both a query processor and cursor engine. However, to query a Microsoft Internet Information Server log file one would either build or buy a component that provided querying capabilities for text files.

High-Level Data Access Methods

As mentioned earlier, the high-level data access methods are the ones that developers use to access the database. Though the performance gets reduced, these methods provide the best of both worlds. Exhibit 2 illustrates the different access methods available to the Microsoft Visual Basic developer. These access methods are discussed in detail along with sample code in Visual Basic.

DATA ACCESS OBJECTS (DAO)

DAO is the COM interface to Jet. It is best-suited for use with Microsoft Access, FoxPro, or Dbase files. DAO also will connect ODBC-compliant databases. The current version is Microsoft DAO 3.5 Object Library, which also provides support for remote data sources. Exhibit 3 is the DAO object model. The DAO is the most mature object-based interface for developers and provides optimal performance with ISAM databases; however, it is being de-emphasized and will be replaced by newer access methods.

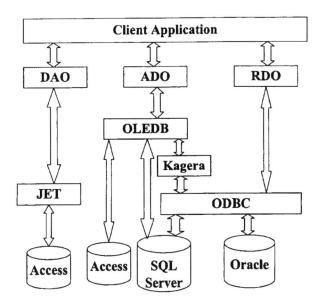

Exhibit 2.   Access methods available to Microsoft Visual Basic Developer.

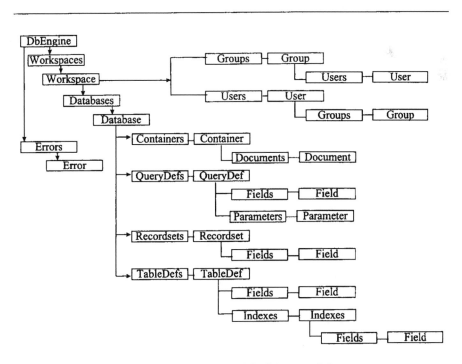

Exhibit 3.   The DAO object model.

ODBCDirect is a feature of DAO that allows for a more direct access to ODBC. When opening ODBC sources through ODBCDirect, the DAO object model separates from the Jet engine. This approach is useful when a combination of ISAM and ODBC data sources are referenced in the same application.

To use DAO in Visual Basic the application first must have a reference to the DAO object library, which currently is Microsoft DAO 3.5 Object Library. Without this an error will be received when an attempt is made to declare the necessary object variables.

The following paragraph describes some of the more useful and commonly used objects within DAO.

Workspace Object

The workspace object is used for setting environment information such as user names and database engines. This object does not have to be created as it automatically is provided. However, it must be created when used with a secured database or when the settings for database are not the same as the default workspace settings.

The Database Object

The database object represents the database that is to be opened and accessed. The database object's methods and properties are used to manipulate data within the open database.

The Recordset Object

A recordset is the data that is returned in response to a query to a database. The recordset object manages the recordsets created with DAO. The recordset object defines a group of records that can be viewed or manipulated. Only one record can be the current record in the recordset containing more than one record.

The example below demonstrates how the DAO objects are used to access data from a database source using both the Jet and the ODBCDirect methods.

```
'Declare as Workspace Object

Dim oWrkSpace As Workspace

'Declare a database object

Dim oMyDatabase as Database

'Declare a recordset object

oRSet as recordset
```

```
'Create workspace object for Jet
Set oWrkSpace = CreateWorkspace("", "admin," "", dbUseJet)
'Open the database
oMyDatabase = oWrkSpace
OpenDatabase("c:\anza\registration.mdb")
'Open a recordset
set oRSet = oMyDatabase.OpenRecordset("Select * from
students," _
    dbOpenDynaset, dbReadOnly)


' Add code to process the data records
'
'Close the objects
oRSet.Close
oMyDatabase.close
```

For ODBCDirect the above code will be as follows:

```
'Declare as Workspace Object
Dim oWrkSpace As Workspace
'Declare a recordset object
oRSet as recordset


'Declare a connection object
Dim oConnect as Connection


'Create workspace object for ODBCDirect
Set oWrkSpace = CreateWorkspace("", "admin," "", dbUseODBC)


'Connect to database using ODBCDirect method
Set oConnect = oWrkSpace.OpenConnection("", , , _
"ODBC;DATABASE = registration; UID=sa, PWD=;DSN=ANZA")
'Open a recordset
```

```
set oRSet = oConnect.OpenRecordset("Select * from students,"
_
    dbOpenDynamic)


    `
    ` Add code to process the data records
    `


    `Close the objects
    oRSet.Close
    oMyDatabase.close
    oWrkSpace.close
```

REMOTE DATA OBJECTS (RDO)

Remote Data Objects (RDO) provides an object layer over the ODBC API. In other words, the RDO provides the performance gains of the ODBC API. RDO allows access to databases from any 32-bit platforms such as Windows 95 and Windows NT using ODBC data sources. RDO provides significant performance and flexibility when accessing remote database engines.

RDO can be used to execute stored procedures and queries that return multiple recordsets. The number of rows that are returned by a query can be limited, and all messages and errors generated by the remote data source can be monitored. Finally RDO supports asynchronous and synchronous operations for data access, and has its own object hierarchy as shown in Exhibit 4.

RDO support is available from the Visual Basic 5.0 Enterprise development version. To use RDO in Visual Basic the application first must have a reference to the RDO object library, which currently is Microsoft Remote Data Object 2.0.

The following paragraphs describe some of the objects within RDO.

The Connection Object

The connection object in RDO represents a connection to the database. It is similar to the database object in DAO. The connection object requires the environment object that automatically is provided by the RDO.

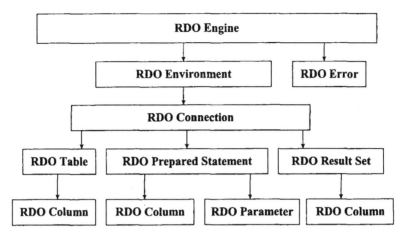

Exhibit 4.   The Remote Data Object (RDO) hierarchy.

The Resultset Object

A resultset object represents the results returned from a query. Result objects are created using the OpenResultSet method of the connection, query, or table objects, namely, rdoConnection, rdoQuery and rdoTable respectively.

The following example demonstrates data access using RDO:

```
'Declare Connection object
Dim oConnect As rdoConnection


'Declare Result set object
Dim oRSet As rdoResultset


'Declare SQL string variable
Dim sAQL As String


'Instantiate a connection object
Set oConnect = New rdoConnection


'Connect to Database
With oConnect
```

```
.Connect = "DSN=ANZA;UID=sa;PWD="

.EstablishConnection

End With


'Format SQL Statement

sSQL = "Select * from students"


'Send query and get result set

Set oRSet = oConnect.OpenResultset(sSQL, rdoOpenKeyset,
rdConcurReadOnly)

'

' Add code to process data

'

' Close Data objects

oRSet.Close

oConnect.Close
```

ACTIVEX DATA OBJECTS (ADO)

ActiveX Data Objects (ADO) represents the future of data access methods and is a fundamental component of Universal Data Access.

ADO is an extensible programming model providing an interface to OLE DB. It is designed to access databases of various types and uses independent data service providers to access specific data.

ADO is COM-based; therefore, any application or language capable of working with COM objects can use it. Active Server Pages for the Internet written using Visual Basic Scripting Language can use ADO. Exhibit 5 shows the ADO object model.

Unlike the situation with DAO or RDO, when using ADO the data access code does not have to work its way through the object hierarchy. Instead of referencing the Workspace object and then a database, ADO can make direct reference to a recordset.

To use ADO in Visual Basic the application first must have a reference to the ADO object library, which currently is Microsoft OLE DB ActiveX Data Objects 2.0 Library.

The following code snippet creates a simple connection to an SQL Server database using ADO:

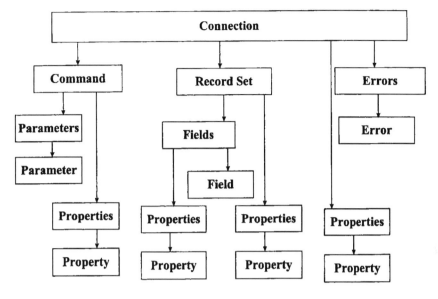

Exhibit 5.   The ActiveX Data Objects model.

```
'Declare and instantiate a recordset object

Dim oRSet As New ADODB.Recordset


'Execute query using open method of recordset object

oRSet.Open "Select * from Students," "DSN=ANZA;UID =
sa;PWD="

'Print Lastname from rows returned by query

Do Until oRSet.EOF

    Print oRSet!LastName

    oRSet.MoveNext

Loop

Close recordset object

oRSet.Close
```

SELECTING WHAT TO USE

This chapter has covered ADO, ODBC, RDO, and DAO with Microsoft Jet. Which should be used today?

Exhibit 6. Suggested Data Access Methods

Data Access Method	Use Case
ADO	• Creating a new application
	• Developing applications using Active Server Pages with IIS
	• Need high performance
DAO	• Data access primarily to Microsoft Jet and ISAM databases
	• Need specific JET database features in application
	• Converting existing application using DAO with JET to use ODBC data
RDO	• Accessing ODBC data and require most functionality
	• Need high performance

Use ADO if ...

Starting an application today. Take a look at using ADO. If it meets one's needs, it makes sense to use it in your Visual Basic, Access, and Office applications. It will be simpler to convert from today's ADO to tomorrow's ADO than to write to RDO/DAO now and convert to tomorrow's ADO. Use ADO if using Active Server Pages with IIS. ADO ships with IIS and was designed to work very well with IIS.

Use DAO if ...

There is a need to access Microsoft Jet or ISAM data or to take advantage of Microsoft Jet features such as compacting and repairing databases, replication, or DDL through the objects. One should use DAO if he or she has an existing application that uses DAO with Microsoft Jet and wants to convert the application to use ODBC data, while achieving better performance.

Use RDO if ...

Accessing ODBC data and desiring the most functionality. ADO today has most of the features of RDO, but not all of them. In the future ADO will be a superset of RDO.

When to Use What

Exhibit 6 provides a description of what access method may be used in a given situation.

Feature Comparison

Exhibit 7 presents a comparison list of major features found in ADO, DAO, and RDO.

Exhibit 7. Major Features of ADO, DAO, and RDO

Feature	ADO 1.5	DAO 3.5	RDO 2.0
Asynchronous connection	Yes	No	Yes
Asynchronous query execution	Yes	Yes	Yes
Batch updates	Yes	Yes	Yes
Error handling	Yes	Yes	Yes
Disconnected recordsets	Yes	No	Yes
Events on column/field	No	No	Yes
Events on connection	No	No	Yes
Events on engine	No	No	Yes
Events on resultset/recordset	No	No	Yes
Events on query	No	No	Yes
Threadsafe	Yes	Yes	Yes
Free-threaded	Yes	No	No
Return value parameters	Yes	Yes	Yes
Independently created objects	Yes	Yes	Yes
MaxRows property on queries	Yes	Yes	Yes
Queries as methods	Yes	No	Yes
Return multiple recordsets	No	Yes	Yes
Efficient Microsoft JET database access	No	Yes	No
Compatibility from Microsoft JET to SQL Server	No	Yes	No

Universal Data Access

Universal Data Access is Microsoft's strategy for providing access to information across the enterprise. Today, companies building database solutions face a number of challenges as they seek to gain maximum business advantage from the data and information distributed throughout their corporations. Universal Data Access provides high-performance access to a variety of information sources, including relational and nonrelational and an easy-to-use programming interface that is tool- and language-independent. These technologies enable corporations to integrate diverse data sources, create easy-to-maintain solutions, and use their choice of best-of-breed tools, applications, and platform services.

Universal Data Access is based on open industry specifications with broad industry support and works with all major established database platforms. Universal Data Access is an evolutionary step from today's standard interfaces, including ODBC, RDO, and DAO, and extends the functionality of these well-known and tested technologies.

The Microsoft Data Access Components enable Universal Data Access. These components include ActiveX Data Objects (ADO), Remote Data Service, (RDS, formerly known as Advanced Database Connector or ADC), OLE DB, and Open Database Connectivity (ODBC).

PROGRAMMING THE DATA SERVICES OBJECTS

With all the data access methods discussed, the common denominator is data access. The differences are many, some of which are the ease or difficulty in programming, object or procedural models, and performance. Other nontechnical but very important factors are when these access methods were introduced and also the time lapsed between the introductions of any two given data access methods. Though these are nontechnical factors, they are very important when it comes to application support within an organization.

Take the case of an organization developing applications using ODBC API to access data. A few months later, with the introduction of RDO offering an easier programming approach and a comparable performance factor, it would be appropriate for developers to move to the newly introduced data access method. This produces a problem to maintain applications depending on different standards. The situation gets worse when the vendor decides to discontinue support for an older data access method. This ordeal is typical and has been faced by many organizations, but the trend to provide newer and better access methods still continues with an increasing frequency.

To take advantage of the newer and better access technologies and still be in a position to effectively manage and maintain applications, there needs to be a fundamental change in the way software is designed and built. The key phrase is independence through loose coupling. What this means is designing and building software that will have no dependence or a very low level of dependence on services or products that have the potential to change or be replaced by newer products.

The answer lies in creating an additional layer, which lies sandwiched between the business application being developed and the vendor-specific data access method. Exhibit 8 illustrates this approach.

This layer will be called "the data services layer" as this is a service that normally is provided in-house as part of the application development infrastructure — similar to a function library for frequently used functions.

In an object-oriented programming environment, this layer could exist as classes with methods that include all the required data access functionality. An example of this class and methods that form the data access services layer is listed in Exhibit 9.

The applications will instantiate objects from this data services class and then invoke methods to get results from a query or insert, delete, and update records. The application will not have any knowledge of or dependence on a vendor-specific data access method. The data access service

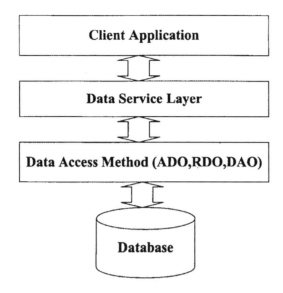

Exhibit 8.   Adding the data service layer.

layer will contain code to access data using a vendor-specific data access method.

The major advantage with this approach is when newer and better data access methods become available; the only part that will require change will be the data access services layer. No change will be required to any application built using this approach.

Exhibit 9.   Classes and Their Methods

Method Name	Description
Class Name: CdataAccess	
OpenRecordSet	Opens a recordset with stored procedure as a parameter
Execute	Executes SQL statements
BeginTrans	Begins a transaction for a batch
CommitTrans	Commits a transaction
RollbackTrans	Rolls back a transaction

Method Name	Description
Class Name: CrecordSet	
MoveNext	Moves pointer to the next record

Properties	Description
Columns	Column Names
EOF	End of File (Record) indicator

OBJECT-ORIENTED DATABASE ACCESS

A lot of data accessed today are stored in flat-file databases navigated with hierarchical pointer-based systems and in tables in relational databases connected by keys. Data are accessed using languages that are usually proprietary. The type of data usually simple and not difficult to manage.

However, this situation is changing rapidly. Some types of data today and in the future will be enormous and complex. We will need to access and organize audio, video, compound documents, geographic information, and other data types. The traditional SQL-based relational database systems are unable to address the type of complex data mentioned previously.

The object-oriented approach has addressed programming issues such as representing business entities as objects. But data still are not stored as objects. Usually there is a data translation layer that converts object data from the application to a relational format and vice versa. This introduces performance problems and data representation issues. Data are represented in the form of complicated relationships using joins. Storing a complex data type in an RDBMS is like disassembling a car before garaging it.

The answer lies in object-oriented database management systems (OODBMS). OODBMS are centered around the concepts of persistence storage meaning that classes, attributes, and instances of objects can be represented within a database in the same way that they are represented in an object-oriented programming language.

This technology is available today vendors such as Object Design Inc., Versant, Gemstone, Objectivity, O2 are marketing OODBMS products.

CONCLUSION

This chapter covered various methods offered by Visual Basic 5.0+ to access data, including ADO, ODBC, RDO, and DAO with Microsoft Jet. Each of these technologies has its place and offers advantages and disadvantages. Microsoft's latest advancement in remote data access is offered in OLE DB, which supports access to a wide variety of data sources, both relational and nonrelational.

Chapter 38
Component-Based Development

Nancy Stonelake

INTRODUCTION

COMPONENT-BASED DEVELOPMENT is being touted as the solution to the latest software crisis. What is it and how true is the hype? The objectives of this article are shown in the following list:

- To define component-based development.
- To describe its benefits and weaknesses.
- To examine the basic architecture and popular component models.
- To examine alternatives and component-based developments in conjunction with current technology and data management.
- To examine some of the challenges facing IT shops that want to move to a component approach.

DEFINITION

Component-based development differs from traditional development in that the application is not developed completely from scratch. A component-based application is assembled from a set of preexisting components. A component is a software bundle that performs a predefined set of functionality with a predefined API. At its simplest level, a component could be a class library or GUI widget; or it may be as complex as a small application, like a text editor; or an application subsystem, like a help system. These components may be developed in house, reused from project to project and passed between departments. They may be purchased from outside vendors who specialize in component development, or bartered between other companies in similar lines of business.

Components can be divided into two broad "types," namely: business components and framework components. Business components encapsulate knowledge of business processes. They may be applied in a vertical industry sector, such as banking, or in a cross-industry standard business function like accounting or e-commerce. Framework components address specific software architecture issues like the user interface, security, or reporting functions.

BENEFITS

How is component-based development better than traditional development practices? If we compare developing enterprise-wide applications to auto manufacturing, current application development is like machining each part from scratch pretty much for every automobile being assembled. This is time consuming and expensive, when most of the parts are the same or similar in configuration. Henry Ford revolutionized manufacturing by standardizing parts and having workers specialize in small aspects of construction. Component-based development works on the same principles and reaps similar benefits.

Due to the similarity between all software applications, using components can reduce design time. Almost all applications have some security system, error handling, and user help functionality. Why are we wasting our time deciding how to provide help to users when the real question is what level of help users need? Components can provide framework solutions that can be tuned to our business requirements. This has the additional benefit of allowing us time to focus on the business logic, which is the key to fulfilling requirements.

Implementation time is reduced because components are already built. Additional coding may be required to integrate the component into the system, but the required functionality is already there.

These two main facts have additional implications. Since components are prebuilt, testing time is reduced. Components are already unit tested; they only require integration testing within the application. Overall, with components we require less design, development, and testing resources. This means we need fewer people with highly specialized and hard-to-find skill sets and we can leverage the people we have to do the things needed in the application.

Additionally, the cost of developing the components can be leveraged over many buyers. Since we acquire components from other departments in the company and pass our components on to them, they share in the costs. Vendors sell to multiple users and they all share in the development and maintenance costs. Component developers can afford to have designer/developers devoted to each component over its life cycle and these resources can become specialists in the component piece.

WEAKNESSES

Component development is an immature industry. This has several effects and implications, primarily: limited vendors, products, and skilled human resources.

At this time there are limited choices in component vendors and company stability may be an issue. While there is a stable set of GUI component vendors, the offerings in true business components are limited. The lack of availability also limits competitive advantage. If all our competitors are using the same business logic, are we doing anything better than they are or are we just matching the pace? Product stability is also an issue. It is important that the API of a component remain constant otherwise we may incur heavy maintenance costs when integrating new product releases.

Component-based development requires a different approach to software development and there are few people who have actually done it. It requires people who can discern what parts of an application may be useful to other applications and what changes may need to be made to support future applications. In other words, you need a good designer/architect with a good crystal ball. To successfully reuse components you must have designers/implementers who are familiar with the component library, so they don't spend all their time looking for components that don't exist. They must also be able to adapt components to fulfill the requirements.

In addition, there must be supporting corporate strategies to promote reuse. No benefit is gained by crafting components that remain unused. Designers and developers need some impetus to change and the resources to support component development must be provided. This means taking the time to develop and locate components and promoting awareness of their availability.

BASIC ARCHITECTURE

Component architecture is based on locating components where they can best serve the needs of the user. This must account for several factors. Speed, processing power, and accessibility. One possible architecture is shown in Exhibit 1.

GUI widget components sit on the client, however business logic may be required locally for complex applications, or on the server for transactional applications. These components can be placed wherever the architect sees fit. Component-based development does not provide an architecture so much as it permits good architectural choices to be implemented.

In distributed environments components can follow the CORBA or DCOM models. Components can be wrapped as CORBA objects or have a CORBA object interface. This makes them accessible through an ORB, permitting ready distribution. Alternatively, components can conform to the COM model and be distributed using the DCOM specifications. While these two distribution models can interwork, that is beyond the scope of this discussion.

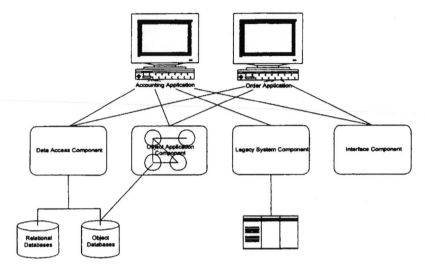

Exhibit 1. Component architecture.

A component architecture can be described as a service-based architecture, like in the SELECT Perspective, where components act as the interface to a "service" which is a black box encapsulation of a collection of related functionality which is accessed through a consistent interface. Services are shared among applications to provide the application functionality. The system is then distributed according to business requirements, rather than software limitations.

COMPONENT TYPES

As mentioned previously, different components address different areas of functionality. These can be divided into framework components and business components. Framework components can be further broken down into data access components, user interface components, and subsystem components. Business components include business logic components and application components. These groupings allow us to place components based on the best configuration for our environment.

Data access components handle database interaction, including creation, deletion, query, and update. While data access components generally access a relational database, components can also access flat files, object databases, or any other persistent storage mechanism. This allows us a mechanism to change the back end data storage without impacting the delivered applications. It also allows us to deliver the same application using different databases with minimal change. The data component is replaced to suit the new environment.

User interface components handle user interaction and define the look and feel of the application. Separation of this component allows us to change the interface so that applications can take on the look and feel of the deployment environment. This helps to reduce training time by offering the user a consistent paradigm across applications.

Subsystem components provide functionality like error handling, security, or user help. They allow for standardization across applications.

Business logic components encapsulate the policies of a business. By separating them from general application or data logic, we can easily change applications to reflect changing business policies, such as offering discounts to large customers, or recommending complementary products.

Application components are small applications that contribute to the functionality of a larger piece, for example text editors. Application components include legacy applications that are wrapped to provide a standard interface for interaction with other components or use within applications.

COMPONENT MODELS

Currently there are two primary component models: JavaBeans and ActiveX. These two models can interact over bridges or by wrapping one as the other.

JavaBeans is the component model for the Java programming language. Because Beans are written in Java they run on any platform. A Bean may implement any functionality but it must support the following features: introspection, customization, events, properties, and persistence. JavaBeans are intended to be integrated with visual development environments and they should have some visually customizable properties, although they may not have a visual representation themselves.

ActiveX is based on the Component Object Model (COM) and was developed by Microsoft. While ActiveX has been a proprietary technology, Microsoft plans to transition it to an industry standards body. ActiveX enables developers to embed event driven controls into Web sites by optimizing the COM model for size and speed. While ActiveX components implemented in different languages can interact, ActiveX components are compiled into platform specific formats. The most common ActiveX implementation is for "Windows-Intel," limiting ActiveX to a Microsoft environment.

The OMG is currently in the process of defining a distributed component model based upon the Object Management Architecture. This will define a CORBA component and make integrating CORBA Components significantly easier.

COMPONENTS, OO, CLIENT SERVER, AND NETWORK COMPUTING

Component-based development has its roots in object-oriented technology and client/server development and can act as an enabler for network computing.

Components extend object technology and object methodologies. Like objects, components should be developed in an iterative, incremental fashion. Components must be identified from existing applications and reworked to apply to new applications. Components and objects incorporate the idea of encapsulation and black box accessibility. With components, as with objects, we are not concerned with how a service is performed internally, only that it is performed correctly. Components are refinements of objects in that the API is defined in a language-independent standard. Components, like objects, communicate through industry standard middleware: CORBA or DCOM. This middleware acts as a layer of abstraction, so that components can be called in the same fashion, regardless of their function. This further hides the component's implementation, whereas direct object communication can rely on implementation specific calls.

Components act as service bundles, relying on tightly coupled object or legacy applications to implement their functionality. Components are then loosely coupled to form applications.

Components can be used to develop stand-alone applications or assembled in a traditional client/server fashion, with components providing server functionality like database access or client functionality on the user interface. Additionally, components allow us to move one step beyond. Components are designed to provide a limited service, and so allow for a true separation of the interface, business logic, and persistence. This allows them to be assembled in a multi-tier relationship and locate the components/tiers in the best place to run them.

Components can also enable network computing. Network computing allows for dynamic deployment, execution, and management of applications. Network computing architectures feature cacheable dynamic propagation, cross-platform capabilities, automatic platform adjustment, and runtime context storage. Since components are small units of work they are easily cacheable. Components written in Java using the JavaBeans specification are cross-platform and ActiveX components can run on any Microsoft friendly platform. Components can be dynamically managed; running on whatever server is appropriate given the current load.

ALTERNATIVES

As shown, component technology can work with client/server and network computing architectures, as well as object-oriented development.

The primary alternatives to component-based development are traditional "from scratch" development and package implementation.

Component-based development is superior to "from scratch" in that we anticipate reduced design, development, and testing time, with a lower bug ratio, since components are prebuilt and pretested. We spend our time developing new components that are missing from our library, and crafting and testing the links between components.

Component-based development is superior to package implementations in its flexibility. We have more control over what features are included based on our needs; additionally we can change those features as our needs change.

CHALLENGES

It looks as if component based development is a good thing. It saves time and money. How can we use components effectively in our own development environments? We will examine several areas: design, component acquisition, implementation, and maintenance.

Remember the idea behind component-based development is to free up our resources to concentrate on finding solutions for business problems. This can take us down several alleys. We may have to make a paradigm choice. If the application needs to be distributed or if the components are developed in multiple languages, we will have to decide whether to use DCOM or CORBA. The environment the application will run in and the available components will influence this choice. When working in an all Microsoft environment DCOM is the obvious choice. Where heterogeneous operating systems are used CORBA is a better choice.

Acquiring components has its own challenges. If they are to be acquired from internal sources, channels for reuse have to be set up. This means components have to be described in a way that other departments can use them easily. There must be a mechanism for publishing their availability; and accounting systems must reflect the costs of component development and recapture on reuse. In short, the whole corporate structure may have to change.

Purchasing components has other problems that may be influenced by corporate culture. While the ideal is that components can be replaced at will, the reality is that an application may become dependent on a component. Corporations may not desire this dependence. When purchasing components the financial stability of the provider company and the product stability must be considered. Will the product be supported in the future, and will its functionality and API remain consistent. Resources must be allocated to identify suitable components, evaluate the risk and future considerations that may impact their use.

Integrating components into an application presents challenges to developers and project managers. If the component is a class library, the object model will be affected. Library considerations can affect the subclass relationship. There may be conflicts between releases if you override methods in a subclass or make extensions to the purchased library.

Components also require good configuration management. You may not just be dealing with your own code releases, but also with the code releases of vendors, and your releases will impact users of your components. Code releases should be scheduled so downstream users can schedule regression testing. Vendor releases should be integrated into the application release and should undergo full regression testing. While there will be a lag time, efforts to keep everyone on the same release should be made, otherwise the releases may diverge into separate products. This will lead to confusion about what the component should do and require additional maintenance resources.

Another issue for project managers is developer resentment. Many developers feel that code that is not developed in-house is not as good as their own code. In addition, there is the old hacker mentality of trying to get into the guts of the component, instead of using the interface. This will make integration of vendor supplied software updates more difficult because the component has lost its "black box" functionality. Staff that can act as advisors on component use are required. The advisors will work with the development teams to recommend components for use on specific projects and harvest new components. Rotating development staff through the advisory positions will build knowledge about the component library and development process and help in identifying functionality that is used across development teams.

Finally, there are long term maintenance considerations. If a component is developed in-house, who is responsible for maintaining it? Is it the developer of the component, or the user who may require modifications to apply it? Organizational change may again be necessary. A software library, with its own dedicated staff, is a good solution to this problem. The library staff is responsible for maintaining the components and managing potential conflict between multiple users. For purchased components, maintenance is also an issue. Vendors may be slow to correct problems, and you may find yourself maintaining the component and feeding the fixes back to the vendor. Even with prompt vendor response, the component must be regression tested and fed into the release schedule.

CONCLUSION

In conclusion, component-based development offers an environment that can facilitate multi-tier architecture and allow a true separation of data, business logic, and user interface. It has the potential to increase developer productivity and lower costs but it is not an approach without risk. The advantages must be weighed against the risks over the entire software life cycle.

References

ActiveX FAQ, Microsoft Corporation, 1996.
Allen, Paul and Frost, Stuart, *Component-Based Development For Enterprise System: Applying the SELECT Perspective,* Cambridge University Press and SIGS Books, 1998.
Austin, T., *Is Network Computing Just a Slogan?* Gartner Group, 1997.
Hamilton, Graham (Ed.), *JavaBeans API specification Version 1.01,* Sun Microsystems, 1997.
Natis, Y., *Component Models Move to the Server,* Gartner Group, 1997.
Smith, D., *Microsoft Bolsters ActiveX: Developers Should Use Caution,* Gartner Group, 1996.

Chapter 39

Developing ActiveX™ Internet Server Components with Visual Basic and Rational Rose

Jeff Buller

THE POPULARITY OF COMPONENT-BASED SOFTWARE has increased steadily over the last few years. Server-side component software is a natural fit for Internet applications because it provides a reliable mechanism for packaging, deploying, and maintaining middle-tier services designed to encapsulate complex business rules. Microsoft's COM/ActiveX™ distributed object technology has emerged as an industry standard for component-based development. With the release of Visual Basic 5, Microsoft® has simplified the task of creating fully functional ActiveX components almost literally to a point-and-click operation.

Visual Basic 5 is an object-based language, which means that ActiveX components can be designed and constructed using object-oriented techniques. With any such object-oriented design process, it is important first to design an object model that will validate the key abstractions and object interfaces necessary to implement components correctly. Rational Rose 98 provides an excellent environment for modeling ActiveX components and is integrated fully with Visual Basic 5 to enable code generation and round-trip engineering.

This chapter discusses the benefits and uses of ActiveX server-based components, component creation with Visual Basic 5, object-oriented modeling techniques that can be used with Rational Rose 98, and finally component deployment considerations.

ActiveX COMPONENTS

Microsoft defines a component as "a discrete unit of code built on ActiveX technologies that delivers a well-specified set of services through well-specified interfaces. Components provide the objects that clients request at run time."

ActiveX is the result of the continuing evolution of Microsoft's distributed object technologies. The component concept was introduced with VBX controls in Visual Basic 3. The next advance came in the form of OLE custom controls (OCX's) with the release of Visual Basic 4. ActiveX components are a more efficient implementation of OLE controls that use resources more efficiently, incorporate more efficient communication protocols, and offer improved compatibility across operating environments. Many of these refinements are the direct result of making ActiveX components more compatible with the Internet environment.

The ActiveX component infrastructure is based on the Microsoft Component Object Model (COM) which Microsoft defines as:

> "an open architecture for cross-platform development of client/server applications based on object oriented technology. Clients have access to an object through interfaces implemented on the object. COM is language neutral, so any language that produces ActiveX™ components can also produce COM applications."

Components based on COM can leverage the benefits of object-oriented technology, including encapsulation and reuse. Components are accessed through well-defined object interfaces, which means that clients need not be concerned with the implementation details of a component to benefit from the services it has to offer. Furthermore, COM interfaces are discovered dynamically by the client, which adds to their flexibility and ease of use. Finally, COM is designed to be language neutral. This is the basis for making COM an industry-wide standard where distributed COM objects can interact, regardless of the language with which they have been developed. This is already largely the case: Visual Basic applications, for example, can interact seamlessly with COM components developed in C++, PowerBuilder, Delphi, and Visual J++, to name a few.

COMPONENTS FOR INTERNET APPLICATIONS

The main prerequisite to using server-based ActiveX components in an Internet application is an application server that supports the COM interface. Examples of COM-compliant server applications include Active Server Pages, Hahtsite, and Jaguar. Many of these Internet application servers provide a programming environment for developing code that will execute in the application server environment in response to an HTTP request.

This server-based code usually is designed to generate HTML dynamically and/or access a database.

Through COM interface support, these server-side programming environments have direct access to instantiate and interface with ActiveX server components. Hahtsite, for example, provides a visual basic programming environment, which supports the CreateObject() function for creating component object instances. Once the component object has been instantiated it can be used in the same manner as a built-in object.

ActiveX server-based components provide an excellent mechanism for encapsulating complex business rules and services on an Internet server. In this configuration, much of the application logic resides on the server, the client/front-end function is reduced mainly to data capture and display. Thin clients are ideal in an Internet environment because they improve browser compatibility and performance. A centralized component-based architecture also results in a client interface that is coupled loosely with the business logic. This loose coupling makes it possible to reuse component functionality in various client implementations, which ultimately increases the flexibility and reusability of the system.

Other benefits of ActiveX components include:

- *Iterative Development*: An iterative development approach focuses on growing a system rather than packing everything into one big release. "Release early, release often" typifies the iterative lifecycle. The key is to focus on architectural concerns during the primary iterations and selectively add functionality during each successive iteration. Component development is a natural fit in the iterative lifecycle because new functionality can be added by creating new components or modifying existing components with minimal impact to the rest of the system.
- *Compatibility*: ActiveX components provide compatibility across all languages that support the COM interface. This includes programming languages such as C++, Visual Basic, Power Builder, Delphi, and Visual J++. (COM is in use on over 150 million systems worldwide.)
- *Productivity*: Products like Visual Basic 5 make it fast and easy to design, test, and deploy Visual Basic applications as ActiveX components. The large number of commercially available components (supported by a U.S. $670 million market — Giga Group) also can provide an alternative to custom development.
- *Maintainable*: Properly designed component systems can be easier to maintain because application logic is packaged into discreet units with well-defined interfaces. This reduces the impact of changes to the system and enables the system to adapt to new requirements. A component architecture also can simplify testing.

- *Reuse*: Properly designed components can be reused by any COM-compatible application or programming environment. Existing custom or commercial components can be extended to add custom behavior and specialized interfaces. This extension is based entirely on the interface of the base component to avoid breaking encapsulation. Components also can collaborate (interface) with other components to form complex application behaviors.
- *Performance*: ActiveX components created with Visual Basic 5 can be compiled to native binary code. In addition, components can be instantiated in-process to run in the application server's memory space. These features both contribute to fast execution, especially when running on a fast server.

Other uses of ActiveX components include the following:

- *Object-Oriented Language Extension*: Many of the application server programming environments do not support custom object creation directly. ActiveX component libraries can be used to extend the capabilities of the programming environment with custom-defined objects that are instantiated through a COM interface.
- *Wrapping*: Specialized components can be developed to wrap existing legacy applications with an object-oriented component interface.

VISUAL BASIC AND OO

Visual Basic 5 is not a true object-oriented language in the strictest sense of the term. Booch (see white paper: "Object-Oriented Development with Visual Basic") refers to the language as object-based because, although it supports the creation of classes and the principle of encapsulation, VB does not support true inheritance and polymorphism. Visual Basic 5 supports a form of inheritance called "interface inheritance," which uses object composition to simulated inheritance. As Gamma states (Design Patterns — Elements of Reusable Object-Oriented Software Page 19, Par 2), "Object composition is an alternative to class inheritance. Here, new functionality is obtained by assembling or composing objects to get more complex functionality. Object composition requires that the objects being composed have well-defined interfaces. This style of reuse is called black-box reuse, because no internal details of objects are visible. Objects appear only as black boxes."

In Visual Basic, object composition refers to the process of declaring or embedding an object in the class definition of another object. In this case, the containing object inherits only the interface of the parent object and does not have direct access to the internals of the parent object. Some would argue that the lack of true inheritance support in Visual Basic (such as one would find in C++) does not make it a viable option for truly leveraging the strengths of object-oriented development. Gamma goes on to say

(Page 25 Par 3) "Object composition in general and delegation in particular provide flexible alternatives to inheritance for combining behavior. New functionality can be added to an application by composing existing objects in new ways rather than by defining new subclasses for existing classes."

In Visual Basic 5, object composition applies both at the class level, when designing and programming the internal workings of a component, and at the component level, when combining components to produce complex system behaviors. In situations when Visual Basic is not sufficient to model complex business rules, components can be created using C++ and accessed via a COM interface.

Is VB the right choice? Ultimately, this will depend on the current development environment and the skills of the development team. It also may depend on the complexity of the business rules that one is trying to model. Is VB a good choice? With good OO development practices and a strong architectural vision, VB will enable one to develop component-based systems quickly and cost-effectively. VB is also an excellent choice for getting started with component-based development.

COMPONENT DESIGN AND DEVELOPMENT

On its own, a component-based development approach does not guarantee a successful system. Component-based systems are equally susceptible to poor analysis and design. Component-based systems also can involve large numbers of interacting objects — a situation that quickly can become unmanageable if not properly documented and understood.

In the Visual Basic environment, a consistent development approach is important on two levels: (1) object-oriented design and development of the internal workings (the guts) of components and (2) defining and scoping the interactions that will occur between components and groups of components that comprise the system as a whole.

Rational Rose is an object-oriented modeling tool from Rational Software corporation that provides the modeling tools necessary to produce high quality, robust component-based systems using Visual Basic 5. Rational Rose for Visual Basic also enables direct generation of Visual Basic code based on a class/component model.

High-Level Features of Rational Rose

Object-Oriented Modeling Features. Rose supports the UML (Unified Modeling Language) notation for creating detailed object models. Object models identify the class abstractions that are used to instantiate objects in the system, relationships between classes, class packaging, and component design. Rose also supports object interaction modeling and object state modeling.

Code Generation. Rose can generate Visual Basic code from a class model directly into a Visual Basic project. The generated project consists, initially, of the class skeleton definitions that contain declarations for all of the classes, class attributes, operations, and relationships that are necessary to implement the desired object behavior. The code generator is customizable.

Round-Trip Engineering. The initially generated Visual Basic skeleton project does not become functional until the developer adds the supporting logic to each of the generated class operations. To synchronize the logical class model with the generated VB project, Rose does two things:

1. The code generator creates protected code regions that separate the generated skeleton from the developer-added logic. This enables Rose to regenerate the project without impacting the custom implementation code.
2. The Rose environment also contains a code analyzer facility that can be used to integrate code level model changes back into the logical class model. Code level model changes can occur when a developer introduces a new class or modifies a class directly in the generated code. The code analyzer also can be used to completely reverse-engineer existing VB projects to create a logical class model.

Component Support. Rose/VB has direct support for component modeling. In Rose, a component in the object model corresponds directly to a VB 5 project (through code generation). The type of component can be any of the VB 5 supported component types including ActiveX DLL, ActiveX EXE, and ActiveX control. Existing ActiveX components (i.e. commercially developed ActiveX controls) also can be represented in the Rose component model. In fact, ActiveX components can be added to a Rose model by simply dragging them from the Windows explorer into the component view of the Rose model.

OOAD IN A NUTSHELL

The process used to discover and build a class model in Rose is entirely up to the user. Using an object-oriented approach, however, enables one to develop loosely coupled (reusable) components that accurately model the functional requirements of the system. Rose modeling techniques are designed to support a scenario-based approach to modeling the desired system/component behavior. Use case analysis provides a systematic approach to deriving objects and object interactions from system usage scenarios. Use case analysis focuses on the external (user) view of the system enabling the modeler to capture the desired system functionality more accurately.

What follows is a very high-level overview of some of the key object-oriented analysis and design (OOAD) techniques that Rational supports for developing object models in Rose.

Modeling System Behavior — Use Cases

Use cases are used to capture the functional requirements of the system. A use case model consists of the use cases that collectively describe the intended functionality of the system. Each use case is a text-based description of the series of events or transactions that a user of the system must complete to perform a particular system function. Users of the system (indeed anything that interacts with the system, including other systems) are referred to as actors. Rose supports the creation of use case model diagrams which represent, on a very high level, the use cases that exist for the system and the actors that initiate the use cases. The bulk of each use case (referred to as the use case report) usually is documented externally using Word or Requisite Pro. Rose allows users to attach use case reports to use cases icons in the use case model diagram. Linkages between Rose and Requisite Pro also are supported.

FINDING OBJECTS AND CLASSES

Objects and classes in the system being modeled are discovered by analyzing use case scenarios. A use case scenario is a particular instance of a use case flow that involves specific object references. For example, part of a use case flow could be an event such as "the user enters his/her PIN number ..." One corresponding scenario might be: "Bob enters his PIN number — 1234 ..." Objects in use case scenarios are identified by repeatedly filtering nouns that appear in the scenario text (e.g., "Bob," "PIN number," "1234"). The filtering process is designed to eliminate nouns that do not correspond to actual objects in the system. Many scenarios must be analyzed in this way to create a comprehensive list of potential system objects.

Once candidate system objects have been identified, classes can be created to represent the common abstractions shared between groups of objects. Classes are named and added to the class model diagram.

OBJECT INTERACTION

Object interaction refers to the interactions that must be supported between objects in the system to produce the functionality described in the use case model. In Rose, object interaction is modeled using a message trace diagram. A message trace diagram shows the sequential series of messages that are exchanged between objects to support the events that occur in a particular use case scenario.

RELATIONSHIPS

Relationships describe the connections or links that must exist between objects to support the message passing that is discovered in the object interaction diagrams. Relationships (also referred to as associations) can be unidirectional, bidirectional, by value (containment), or by reference. Relationships also have multiplicity attributes that indicate the relative number of related objects (e.g., 1 to 1, 1 to many).

OPERATIONS AND ATTRIBUTES

Operations and attributes are assigned on the class level to represent the behavior and state-of-object instances of the class. Class operations ultimately are derived from object interaction modeling and represent the operations that must be available via the object's interface to support interaction with (provide services to) other objects. Attributes are defined to capture the internal state of an object. Attribute values can be modified only through an object's interface (encapsulation).

OBJECT BEHAVIOR

An object's state is represented, at any time, by the combined values of its attributes and the relationships it has to other objects. In Rose, Object behavior is modeled using state diagrams. A state diagram shows the discrete states that an object can be in during its lifetime. It also indicates the transitions that can occur when an object changes from one state to another and the events that cause the transitions to occur. State diagrams are useful for understanding the internal behavior of complex objects. One typically does not need to create a state diagram for each object in the model.

ARCHITECTURAL CONSIDERATIONS

Rose VB directly supports a three-tiered architecture for creating component-based systems. In this architecture, the basic building blocks of the system are components. Components are organized into three distinct service layers:

1. *User services*: User interface-related components that enable the user to interact with the system. Those can include GUI applications, browsers, and ActiveX controls.
2. *Business services*: Commonly referred to as the "middle tier," the business services tier houses components that encapsulate business rules and system functionality. This is the tier in which Internet server-based components are deployed. In many cases, this tier is accessed by the user services tier via an application server of some sort.

3. *Data services*: Components responsible for retrieving and updating persistent data. Persistent data usually is managed by an RDBMS or object-oriented database.

The three-tiered architecture takes full advantage of the reuse benefits of component-based development. It is also a good match for an iterative development approach because system functionality can be added incrementally to each layer as new components are developed.

PERSISTENT COMPONENTS

A use case-driven OOAD approach to modeling components focuses on the external behavior of the system. The emphasis is on designing user-centric component interfaces that accurately implement the behavior described in the use case scenarios. This differs from the typical client/server approach in which a great deal of emphasis is placed on first designing a data model that efficiently will store the data that is manipulated by the system. A client front-end then is created to work with the specific database design. This data-centric approach can result in a system that may not meet the user's needs because it has been adapted (compromised) to work with a specific database design.

In the OOAD process, persistent storage is not considered until the design phase. During that phase, key mechanisms are added to the class model to facilitate the storage and retrieval of entity objects. In a component-based system, persistent components encapsulate business entity objects that can exist independently of the component. This usually is accomplished by storing the attributes of the entity component in a database. When a persistent component is created or destroyed, the associated database attributes are loaded from or saved to the database respectively. During the design activities one must decide where in the component model to place persistence mechanisms. The two main choices are

1. Persistence mechanisms in each persistent component. This approach can simplify the class/component model because very few new classes need to be introduced. Persistence mechanisms become available through the interface of each entity component. The downside is that the persistence logic must be implemented in each persistent component, resulting in redundancy and code bloat. Persistent components also will be coupled very tightly with the storage mechanism resulting in a system that is not easily transportable.
2. Persistence mechanisms in a secondary component that is designed specifically for storing and retrieving one or more entity components. This approach will increase the complexity of the class/component model because new classes/components will be introduced

to encapsulate the persistence mechanisms. However, by placing all persistent storage mechanisms in separate classes/components, the entity components are not coupled directly to the storage mechanism. This increases overall reusability. In some cases, it may be possible to combine persistence mechanisms into a single group (layer) of classes/components that can support persistence for any of the entity classes/components in the system.

ACTIVE DATA OBJECTS

Components developed in Visual Basic 5 can use a number of database access technologies that are supported by Microsoft. These includes the DAO (Data Access Objects) and RDO (Remote Data Objects) programming models, which can support both ODBC and native driver connections.

Active data objects (ADO for short) is Microsoft's latest data access technology, which is based entirely on ActiveX and designed specifically for Internet-based applications. Microsoft describes ADO as a technology that

> "enables you to write an application to access and manipulate data in a database server through an OLE DB provider. ADO's primary benefits are high speed, ease of use, low memory overhead and a small disk footprint."[Source: Microsoft®]

According to Microsoft, OLE DB is "... a specification for a set of data access interfaces designed to enable a multitude of data stores, of all types and sizes, to work seamlessly together... OLE DB goes beyond the simple data access by partitioning the functionality of a traditional relational database into logical components, and the events needed for those components to communicate." [Source: Microsoft®]

ADO provides an excellent key mechanism for persistence in a component object model. Because ADO itself is components-based, it enables the designer to abstract data stores into database components that interact with entity components for storage and retrieval. In addition, OLE DB gives users the flexibility to create data providers for nonrelational data sources such as spreadsheets and flat files.

OTHER BENEFITS OF ADO

- Easy to use. With ADO, Microsoft has encapsulated complex API-based logic into a simplified component object model.
- Consistent Interface. ADO is based on ActiveX and provides a consistent programming interface, regardless of the type or location of the data store being accessed.
- Language neutral. ADO is based on ActiveX enabling it to work with a variety of languages, operating systems, and databases that support the COM interface.

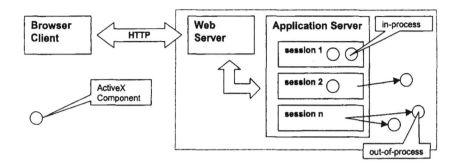

Exhibit 1. Web-based application server architecture.

- Easily integrated. Finally, as with any ActiveX component, ADO components may be integrated easily into the Rose modeling environment. This provides the designer with full access to all the component interfaces and classes that are supported by the ADO object model.

COMPONENT DEPLOYMENT

The task of component deployment is the process of making components available to other components or applications in a controlled, stable, and scalable way. For Internet server-based components this task is simplified somewhat because these components usually are deployed on a single server supporting the data services tier (also referred to as the middle tier). Furthermore, if a COM-compatible application server is used, the creation and management of component object instances can be controlled by application code executed on the application server. Exhibit 1 shows a Web-based application service architecture utilizing components.

REGISTERING ACTIVEX COMPONENTS

ActiveX components must be registered before they can be used by other applications or components. The act of registering an ActiveX component places a server-wide reference to that component in the NT server registry. Component-specific configuration information also can be stored in the registry. When an application attempts to instantiate a component, it uses the registry to locate the required component implementation files (binary files: .dll, .exe, or .ocx) and configuration information. Windows NT provides command line services for registering components with the operating system. VB5 also has a setup wizard that enables one to create a Windows setup program that automatically will install the component support files and register the component on the server.

CHOOSING THE ActiveX COMPONENT TYPE

Choosing the correct component implementation type is critical in determining the run-time characteristics of a component instance such as memory usage, threading, multiuser support, and performance. The recommended component type for server-based components is ActiveX DLL, which provides the following benefits:

- *In process execution*: An ActiveX DLL component executes in the same memory space as the application that instantiates it. This results in better performance because the data exchanged with the component (via the component's interface) does not have to be marshalled across a process boundary.
- *Multithreaded support*: This ensures that multiple instances of the same ActiveX DLL component run in their own memory space (also called thread apartments). This is necessary to avoid contention issues such as blocking in a typical multiuser Internet application environment.
- *Application Server Integration*: ActiveX DLL components integrate seamlessly with application servers that support COM.

MANAGING COMPONENTS ON THE MIDDLE TIER

Component management on the middle tier is required to ensure that the system is scalable and reliable.

Scalability is especially significant in an Internet environment where service requests to the middle tier could be very high. A scalable component architecture should have the ability to dynamically adjust to variations in request loads, manage the creation and destruction of component instances, and optimize available server resources.

Regarding reliability, as the number of components in the system grows so does the complexity of component interaction and collaboration. In many cases, complex business transactions are based on the interaction of groups of middle-tier components. For mission-critical applications it is necessary to guarantee that component collaborations are transaction-based; that is, they either finish completely or roll back completely.

For simpler component systems, a COM-compatible application server usually will provide the basic capabilities necessary to manage components. The Hahtsite application server, for example, manages server resources and allocates memory on a per user-session/request basis. The VB-compatible Hahtsite programming environment can be used to control the creation and collaboration of components available on the server through the development of custom code.

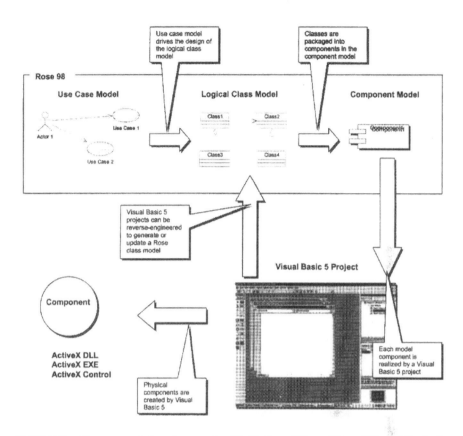

Exhibit 2.   Component development with Rational Rose 98 and Visual Basic 5.

For more complex systems, a transaction monitor such as Microsoft Transaction Server can be used. Microsoft Transaction Server is a comprehensive solution for managing ActiveX component systems on the middle tier. It offers the following features to address directly the problems of scalability and reliability: automatic thread and process management, object (component instance) management, component packaging, database connection pooling, and automatic (component) transaction support.

CONCLUSION

As the popularity and importance of Internet-based applications increases, organizations will be forced to develop robust applications that are usable across many environments and able to adapt to changes quickly. Component-based applications (Exhibit 2) that encapsulate business logic on a centralized server have the potential to deliver on these goals.

Microsoft's distributed object standard, COM, is a proven and widely used technology on which to build a component architecture. Together with systematic object-oriented analysis and design techniques, Rational Rose 98 provides the modeling tools necessary to develop reusable, stable components and component systems designed to meet or exceed user expectations. Visual Basic 5 offers an implementation and programming environment that makes component development fast and easy. Finally, server-based component systems must be scalable and able to handle the potentially high transaction volumes that are typical of the Internet environment. Most COM-compatible application servers will support simple approaches for dealing with these issues, whereas transaction servers such as Microsoft Transaction Server provide the infrastructure and resource control mechanisms that promise to support truly mission critical applications on the Web.

Chapter 40
A Technical Primer for Getting Started with JavaBeans

Charles Dow

SOFTWARE ENGINEERS ALL OVER THE WORLD ARE TIRED OF WRITING THE SAME CODE over and over again. They want to be able to reuse with ease the bulk of the code required to build the plumbing of an application, then be able to concentrate on the business rules and data. To accomplish this, tested and reliable building blocks that can be plugged together using a common protocol are needed.

JavaBeans provides a key piece of the technologies needed for these building blocks. The fact that JavaBeans is simple to develop, uses a modern object-oriented language, and handles the Internet and its associated security issues, makes its appeal unquestionable.

JavaBeans technology is very much like all OO technology; it has rich layers that need to be peeled away like an onion. This chapter is designed to show readers a few of its layers and how easily they can be peeled. Remember, one does not need to know all of the layers to reap the rewards of this remarkable innovation of the recent past. More importantly, by applying a few coding standards, the benefit of using JavaBeans can be obtained without requiring additional effort by developers. JavaBeans are not just for GUI widgets. They can provide far more business value. Components at runtime can be nonvisual (i.e., they do not have a graphical user interface).

SOME HISTORY

JavaBeans 1.0 has been available in JDK 1.1 since February 1997. Apple, Baan, Borland, CI Labs, Corel, Informix, IBM, JUSTSYSTEM, Lotus, Microsoft, Netscape, Novell, Oracle, ParcPlace, Silicon Graphics, SunSoft, Sybase, Symantec, Texas Instruments, Visual Edge, plus many external reviewers, participated in its development. JavaBeans is a Core API, which means one can expect it to be available on all the VMs.

0-8493-9976-9/99/$0.00+$.50
© 1999 by CRC Press LLC

TOOLABILITY

A key design goal for the JavaBeans technology was to provide components that could be manipulated visually by tools. JavaBeans allows developers to create reusable software components that then can be assembled together using visual application builder tools, such as Sybase's PowerJ, Borland's JBuilder, IBM's Visual Age for Java, SunSoft's Java Workshop, Symantec's Visual Cafe, and many, many others. Visit the Website, http://java.sun.com/beans/tools.html for a current listing of tools (available at the time of publication).

SIMPLE BEANS ARE FREE

Wouldn't it be nice to be able to concentrate only on writing the code needed to solve a particular problem and then be able to turn it into a component for others to use? That is possible in Java by following a few simple rules (a.k.a. design patterns) when writing code.

Before learning the name for those rules, follow some steps that will illustrate the process of bean-building.

Step 1. Write a Class

```
// A very simple example
// Time Bean class
// Time.java

import java.text.*;
import java.util.*;
import java.awt.Color;

public class Time {
Date currentDate;
SimpleDateFormat formatter;
String dateString;

public String getDateString () {
currentDate = new Date();
formatter = new SimpleDateFormat ("EEE, MMM d, ''yy");
```

```
dateString = formatter.format(currentDate);

return dateString;

}

public void setDateString (String newString) {

dateString = "No date as yet";

}

}
```

Note: A JavaBean does not have to be an applet or an application. It is a Java class, no more, no less. (Java classes do not have to be simple.)

Step 2. Compile the Class

D:\MyJavaSource\Time javac Time.java — javac is the compiler supplied with the JDK. One can download the JDK from http://java.sun.com/products/jdk/1.1/ (Web address accurate at time of publication). Do not forget to add a source directory to the CLASSPATH before compiling. Once that is done, execute javac from the source directory, as shown above.

Step 3. Create a JAR File for a Bean

A JAR file is the standard archive for Java code. There is one little twist that has to be applied if it is to contain a JavaBean. A manifest should be added. The manifest is a text file that needs to have at a minimum:

```
Name: Time.class

Java-Bean: True
```

Enter a command such as:

```
D:\MyJavaSource\Time jar cfm Time.jar Manifest.txt
Time.class
```

Note: Type jar by itself for a listing of the switches jar will accept. After running the command, you will have Time.jar.[1]

Step 4. Test the Bean

If one does not have the JavaBeans Development Kit (BDK), it can be downloaded from the following site: http://java.sun.com/beans/software/bdk_download.html (Web address accurate at time of publication).

Copy the new *Time.jar* file to the jars sub-directory of the BDK (...\BDK\jars).

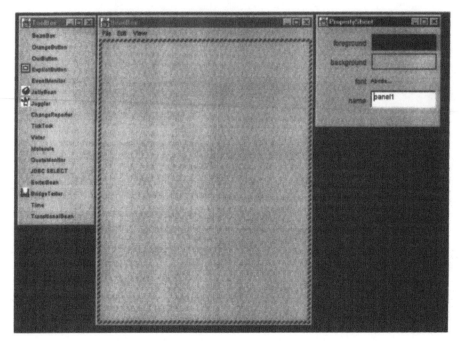

Exhibit 1.   ToolBox, BeanBox, and PropertySheet.

Using the BeanBox[2] supplied for free by JavaSoft (part of the BDK), launch the BeanBox. On Windows NT, use the batch file provided ...\BDK\beanbox run.bat. On other operating systems, please read the documentation that came with the BDK.

The three windows (namely ToolBox, BeanBox, and PropertySheet) shown in Exhibit 1 appear on the screen.

The toolbox contains sample beans provided by JavaSoft. Ignore them at this time. Notice the Time bean is one of the options in the list provided by the Toolbox. This one will be used. Left mouse click on the Time entry in the Toolbox; crosshairs will appear. That signifies that the cursor is loaded. Move the cursor over the BeanBox and Left mouse-click. A button-like shape entitled *Time* will appear. Left mouse click on it to select it. Then choose *Edit, Report* from the menu. A report similar to the one shown in Exhibit 2 will appear.

The *setDateString* is the method to set the DateString property or attribute.

The *get DateString* is the method to get the DateString property. A *get without a set* is a read-only property and vice-versa.

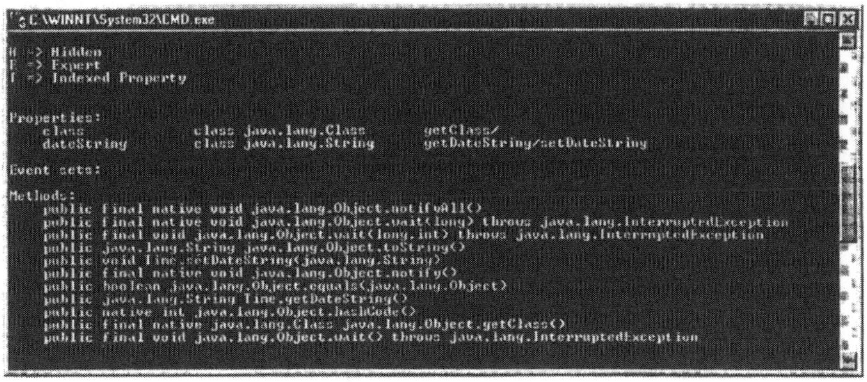

Exhibit 2.   Report 1.

Then a list of Event sets:

```
We have none at this time.
```

Then a list of Methods:

```
Notice, the above will appear for the class and all
```
that it inherits. (This can be turned off.)

HOW DOES THE BEANBOX KNOW?

The BeanBox uses Introspection. Introspection simply put says, "If I know it is a bean (from the Manifest), then I will use the Java Core Reflection API that the JDK provides to allow us to dynamically obtain the fields, methods, and constructors of loaded classes from the class file."

The Introspection process can be assisted better by providing an associated BeanInfo class.

VOILA — OLD CODE INTO BEANS

But what if one did not know the few rules when writing your code? Modify the method names, as shown below (Essentially getting rid of the get and set portions that the Reflection API recommends).

```
// A very simple example

// Time Bean class

// Time.java


import java.text.*;
```

```
import java.util.*;

import java.awt.Color;


public class Time {

    Date currentDate;

    SimpleDateFormat formatter;

    String dateString;


    public String obtainDateString () {

        currentDate = new Date();

        formatter = new SimpleDateFormat ("EEE, MMM d,
``yy");

        dateString = formatter.format(currentDate);

        return dateString;

    }

    public void replaceDateString (String newString) {

        dateString = "No date as yet";

    }

}
```

If the above is compiled, and placed in a Jar with the same manifest file as above the report from the BeanBox that appears is shown in Exhibit 3.

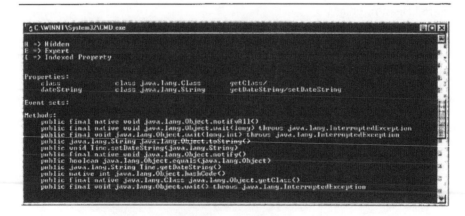

Exhibit 3.   Report 2.

Note: The only property that can be seen by Introspection is the inherited read-only property. All methods are found.

ADDING A BEANINFO CLASS

To make a bean smarter, the BeanInfo[3] class is provided. Developers are encouraged to use this facility. The BeanInfo class will return instances of XxxDescriptor classes to describe the Bean, e.g., BeanDescriptor, EventSetDescriptor, FeatureDescriptor and others when sent the appropriate messages.

To allow one to only provide the information that he or she wants to specify, there is a helper class, SimpleBeanInfo class, that can be inherited from; it will provide appropriate defaults for any method not overridden. The PropertyDescriptor classes should be used so that the BeanBox can see the getter and setter. Following is the BeanInfo class used:

```
// The BeanInfo class that we associate with our Time Bean


import java.beans.*;

public class TimeBeanInfo extends SimpleBeanInfo {


    public PropertyDescriptor[] getPropertyDescriptors() {

        try { PropertyDescriptor aPropertyDescriptor =
        new

        PropertyDescriptor( "dateString," Time.class,

"obtainDateString,""replaceDateString");

        PropertyDescriptor[] anArrayOfPropertyDescriptors =
        {

        aPropertyDescriptor};

        return anArrayOfPropertyDescriptors ;

            } catch (Exception e) {

                System.err.println("Exception occurred "+e);

                return null;

            }

        }

    }
```

Compile as before and use the following command to create the Jar:

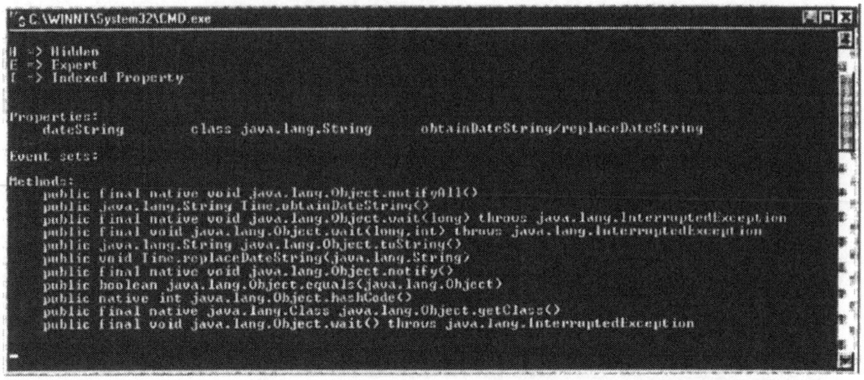

Exhibit 4. Report 3.

```
Jar cfm Time.jar manifest.txt *.class
```

Note: The manifest does not change, because only Time.class is a bean. Run the BeanBox and get the report.

The report from the BeanBox now appears as shown in Exhibit 4.

Note: A more complex bean will have three parts, as follows:

- Properties
- Methods
- Events

There are many other features that Beans could use. After this taste of Beans, readers are encouraged to explore these further. Please note that for illustration purposes the code sample was trivial and broke many of the rules of a well-mannered Bean. The best reference that the author is aware of for JavaBeans Guidelines is a document produced by IBM's WebRunner team http://www.ibm.com/java/education/jb-guidelines.html.

CONCLUSION

JavaBeans is a relatively easy-to-learn tool for building components that provide more functionality than mere widgets. Components provide both functionality and data management in reusable, easy-to-snap together, little pieces that are combined to build sophisticated applications. The World Wide Web can be mined for many of the tools for getting started with JavaBeans.

References

Tremblett, P., Java Reflection, *Dr. Dobb's J.,* Jan. 1998, 36.

Morrison, M., Weems, R., Coffee, P., and Leong, J., How to program JavaBeans, *JavaSoft's Beans Development Kit (BDK),* ZD Press, Indianapolis, IN, May 1977.

Notes

1. For those with Winzip, you can quickly snoop at the jar file and the manifest.mf file contained within.
2. According to the BDK documentation, "the BeanBox is intended as a test container and as a reference base, but it is not intended as a serious application development tool."
3. Look at the documentation for the BeanInfo class.

Chapter 41

JavaBeans™ and Java Enterprise Server™ Platform

David Wadsworth

A MAJORITY OF THE WORLD'S DATA RESIDES ON MAINFRAME SERVERS. This legacy poses many challenges to the information systems (IS) community as it struggles with the demands of business units for new and innovative solutions to business problems. Organizations need to adopt a flexible, secure, and cost-effective architecture that will enable them to remain competitive and enable breakaway business strategies. Adoption of Java™ computing realizes these benefits by providing key technology enablers.

JAVA TECHNOLOGY REVIEW

The Java programming language was introduced to the public in May, 1995. Key features of the language such as platform independence and ease of programming made it an instant success in the software development community. Other features such as safe network delivery and baked-in security have made the language the *de facto* standard for the development and deployment of Web-based applications.

Applications written in the Java programming language are compiled to bytecode that can run wherever the Java platform is present. The Java platform is a software environment composed of the Java Virtual Machine and the Java Core Application Programming Interfaces (API's). Portability of applications is achieved because there is only one virtual machine specification, which provides a standard, uniform programming interface on any hardware architecture. Developers writing to this base set of functionality can be confident that their applications will run anywhere without the need for additional libraries. Core libraries include functional support for GUI development, I/O, database connectivity, networking, math, components (JavaBeans), multithreading, and many others.

Sun's Java computing architecture is an implementation framework that uses standard, currently available network protocols and services to deliver the power of Java applications to the widest possible base of Java platform-enabled devices and users. With this architecture, transactions can be moved transparently to the most cost-effective, appropriate support channel within a network owing to the portable, Write Once, Run Anywhere™ nature of Java applications.

JAVA PLATFORM COMPONENT ARCHITECTURES

Designing and developing applications by means of components has been available for many years. The challenge has been to embrace and extend existing technology with new technology. Until recently, such an approach has been proprietary and difficult to deploy. The Java computing environment with JavaBeans, a component technology and server architecture solution, Java Enterprise Server, enables organizations to simplify greatly access to business systems. What follows is a description of the JavaBeans component model and an overview of the Java Enterprise Server platform.

JAVABEANS

A JavaBean is a reusable Java software component that visually can be manipulated and customized in a builder tool. These application building blocks are constructed so as to communicate easily with each other in a common environment. They also have the ability to store their state on the shelf to be revived at a later date. Because they are written in the Java programming language for deployment on any Java platform, JavaBeans are the platform-independent components for the network.

JavaBean components can range from simple GUI elements, such as buttons and sliders, to more sophisticated visual software components, such as database viewers. Some JavaBeans may have no GUI appearance of their own, but still can be manipulated in an application builder.

The JavaBean API has been designed to be accessible by builder tools as well as manipulated manually by human programmers. The key APIs, such as property control, event handling, and persistence, can be accessed by both hand-crafted applications and builder tools. As well as event handling, property control and persistence, introspection, and customization are distinguishing features of all JavaBeans.

Property Control

Property control facilitates the customizing of the JavaBean at both design and run-time. Both the behavior and appearance of a JavaBean can be modified through the property features. For example, a GUI button might have a property named "ButtonLabel," which represents the text displayed in the button. This property can be accessed through its getter and setter methods. Once properties for a bean are configured, their state will be maintained through the persistence mechanism.

Persistence

The attributes and behavior of a bean are known as the state of the bean. The persistence mechanism within the JavaBean API supports storage of this state once the bean is customized. It is this state that is incorporated into the application and available at run-time. This externalization can be in a custom format or the default. A custom external format allows the bean to be stored as another object type such as an Excel document inside a Word document. The default is reserved for those instances where the bean's state needs to be saved without regard to the external format.

Event Handling

Event handling is a simple mechanism that allows components to be connected based on their production of and/or interest in certain actions. A component or series of components can be sources of events that can be caught and processed by other components or scripting environments. Typical examples of events include mouse movements, field updates, and keyboard actions. Notification of these events generated by a component are delivered to any interested component.

The extensible event-handling mechanism for JavaBeans allows for the easy implementation of the model in application builder tools. Event types and propagation models can be crafted to accommodate a variety of application types.

Customization

Changing the appearance and behavior of a JavaBean is accomplished through the customization features of the JavaBean's API. Each JavaBean contains a list of exported properties, which an application builder can scan and use to create a GUI property editor sheet. The user then can customize the bean using this dynamically created sheet. This is the simplest form of customization.

Another layer of customization is possible by attaching to the bean a customizer class that acts as a properties wizard. This wizard will have a GUI that can be employed to tailor the properties for the related bean in a guided tour fashion. Such wizards are more likely to be found associated with complex beans such as calculator beans or database connection beans. Once customization is completed the properties will be stored using the persistence mechanism.

Introspection

The properties, methods, and events a JavaBean supports are determined at run time and in builder environments by means of introspection. Introspection is a prescribed method of querying the bean to discover its inherent characteristics. Introspection is implemented using the Java programming language rather than a separate specification language. Thus, all of the behavior of the bean is specifiable in the Java programming language.

One introspection model supported by the JavaBeans API provides a default view of the methods, events, and properties. This simple mechanism does not require the programmer to do extra work to support introspection. For more sophisticated components, interfaces are available for the developer of the bean to provide specific and detailed control over which methods, events, and properties are exposed.

Default, low-level reflection of the bean is used to discover the methods supported by the bean. Design patterns then are applied to these methods to determine the properties, events, and public methods supported by the component. For example, if a pair of methods such as setColor and getColor are discovered during the reflection process, the property color is identified by the application of the get/set design pattern for property discovery.

More complex component analysis can be built into the bean by the use of a BeanInfo class. This class would be used by a builder tool to discover programmatically the bean's behavior.

Security

JavaBeans are governed by the same security model as all other Java applets and applications. If a JavaBean is contained in an untrusted applet, then it will be subject to the same restrictions and will not be allowed to read or write files on the local file system or connect to arbitrary network hosts. As a component in a Java application or trusted applet, a JavaBean will be granted the same access to files and hosts as a normal Java application. Developers are encouraged to design their beans so they can be run as part of untrusted applets.

Run-time vs. Design-time JavaBeans

Each JavaBean must be capable of running in a number of different environments. The two most important are the design- and run-time environments. In the design environment a JavaBean must be able to expose its properties and other design-time information to allow for customization in a builder tool. In some cases wizards contained in the bean may be employed to simplify this process.

Once the application is generated the bean must be usable at run time. There is really no need to have the customization or design information available in this environment.

The amount of code required to support the customization and design-time information for a bean could be potentially quite large. For example, a wizard to assist in the modification of bean properties could be considerably larger than the run-time version of the bean. For this reason it is possible to segregate the design-time and run-time aspects of a bean so it can be deployed without the overhead of the design-time features.

JavaBeans Summary

JavaBeans are the component object model for the Java platform. These device-independent components can be customized and assembled quickly and easily to create sophisticated applications.

JAVA ENTERPRISE SERVER PLATFORM

As organizations adopt Internet technologies to enable new business strategies, they are faced with the task of integrating all of their legacy applications, databases, and transaction services with Web-based services. Traditional applications designed in the client/server model do not deploy well in an Internet/extranet environment. Although not new, multi-tier architectures for application development and deployment are best-suited for extending the reach of a company's infrastructure to partners, suppliers, customers, and remote employees. The Java Enterprise server platform provides such an architecture in an open and standards-based environment that it incorporates existing infrastructure while extending their reach to intranets, extranets, and even the Internet. An extensible architecture, the Java Enterprise server platform contains the API's products and tools necessary to construct new enterprise-wide applications and integrate with existing systems.

Traditional mission-critical applications are written to the APIs of the underlying operating system, thereby tying the application to a single operating system. Porting of the application to a new operating system is both difficult and expensive. These same applications may rely on a service, such as a transaction monitor. Access to this service will be through the software vendor's proprietary APIs creating another platform lock and presenting a barrier to moving to a different service provider.

The Java Enterprise server platform is designed to address these platform-lock issues. It extends the notion of "write once, run anywhere" to include "and integrate with everything." Based on a layer and leverage model, the Java Enterprise server platform can be built on top of existing legacy systems such as transaction monitors, database access, system

Platform Neutral Development

Enterprise JavaBeans Components Model

Web Serv.	Nam- ing	Mess.	Dist. Obj.	Secur- ity	Mgt	DB	Trans- action	

Java Virtual Machine

Solaris NT HP-UX AIX MVS IRIX MacOS ... others

Network Serv. TCP/IP SPX/IPX SNA DECnet LanMgr

Physical Network

Exhibit 1. Java Enterprise server platform architecture.

management, naming and directory services and CORBA (Exhibit 1). Interfaces to these services, as well as a component model that provides for application encapsulation and reuse, are integral to the Java Enterprise server platform. The component model includes JavaBeans, components for the client, and Enterprise JavaBeans (EJB's) components for the server.

All of the benefits of rapid application development, scalability, robustness, and security of the JavaBeans component architecture are extended to the Java Enterprise server platform. EJBs also have the ability to provide transactional services. Coupled with these benefits is an open architecture capable of providing ease of development, deployment, and management.

Enterprise JavaBeans, an extension of the JavaBeans architecture, provide a distributed component architecture for developing and deploying component-based, multi-tier applications. Business logic is encapsulated in the Enterprise JavaBeans promoting a high degree of reuse. Access to low-level services such as session management and multithreading is simplified such that developers building applications do not need to deal directly with these functions.

Distributed applications developed with Enterprise JavaBeans can be deployed on any other platform without modifications. Support for transactions and messaging integrate with existing legacy systems and middleware.

The heart of the Enterprise JavaBean platform is the Enterprise Java-Bean executive (Exhibit 2). This run-time executive is used to execute the components that provide the services required by an application. Through

Enterprise JavaBeans

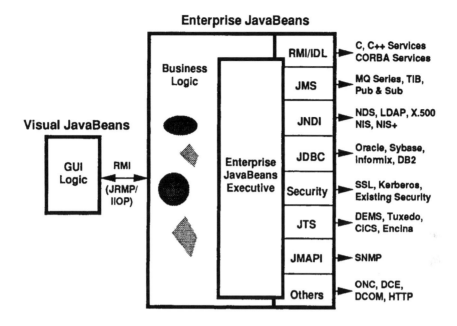

Exhibit 2. Enterprise JavaBeans framework.

its components, the executive manages load balancing and handles multi-threading, transaction management, security, and connection management. This frees programmers to focus on developing the components that contain business logic.

Communication between the client and server in an application does not need to rely on any particular protocol. Both client and server side of the application are coded using the Java programming language. At deployment time the underlying communication stubs are generated automatically. The Java programming language introspection of the application class files is used to generate the communication stubs.

Unlike JavaBeans which use the Java event model, Enterprise JavaBeans use the distributed CORBA event model. The event model supported by the Java programming language is well-suited for local, tightly integrated applications, but does not perform as well in a networked environment where high latency and insecure networks are common. Enterprise Java-Bean events are propagated across the network over CORBA's Internet InterORB Protocol (IIOP) to other components.

Enterprise JavaBeans can be configured automatically as CORBA objects, then accessed through IIOP by clients. These client applications do not have to be written in the Java programming language to access the components. EJB's also can function as COM/DCOM objects for Windows clients.

Access to several key services are offered as part of the Enterprise Java-Bean specification (Exhibit 2). These services are offered through specific Java platform APIs such as JavaIDL/RMI for accessing CORBA, DCE, or ONC services; Java Message Service (JMS) for access to messaging systems such as MQ Series; Java Naming and Directory Interface (JNDI) for accessing multiple naming and directory services such as LDAP and NDS; Java Database Connectivity (JDBC) for connecting to various relational and nonrelational databases; Java security API's providing for encryption and authentication; Java Transaction services (JTS) providing a Java programming language binding to the object transaction services (OTS) of CORBA; Java management API (JMAPI) providing for the management of networked resources such as workstations and routers; and Web services through the Java Server API. Each is detailed below.

JavaIDL

The Java Interface Definition Language (IDL) provides standards-based interoperability and connectivity with CORBA. Through these interfaces, Java applications are able to access existing infrastructure written in other languages. This is one of the key interfaces for legacy system integration. JavaIDL is part of the Java platform core API set and is, therefore, available across multiple platforms.

Java Message Service

Java Message Service (JMS) provides an interface to messaging systems that provide publish/subscribe and message queue services. This platform-independent interface also will support the emerging push/pull technologies.

Java Naming and Directory Interface

Many different kinds of naming and directory services exist in today's enterprises. Directory services such as LDAP, NIS, and NDS provide network-wide sharing of information about the users, systems, applications, and resources that exist on an intranet or the Internet. User information can include log-in IDs, passwords, security access, and electronic mail addresses. System information can include network addresses and machine configurations. The Java Naming and Directory Interface (JNDI) is independent of any specific naming and directory service implementation. Application developers can access multiple namespaces easily through JNDI. A single interface simplifies the access to composite namespaces as well as enabling an application to be portable across different platforms.

Java Database Connectivity

One of the earliest and now core APIs is the Java database connectivity API (JDBC). This is a SQL-based, database-independent API that frees developers from writing database vendor-specific code in their applications. JDBC supports the common database functionality such as remote procedure calls, SQL statements, database connection, and result sets. Because JDBC is implemented via a driver manager, which itself can be implemented in the Java programming language, applets can be delivered to the client with the database connectivity built in. Implementation drivers for all the major RDBMS are already available for JDBC, and a JDBC-to-ODBC bridge is standard in the Java Developer's Kit Version 1.1. JDBC drivers for object-relational DBMSs as well as IBM's IMS are also currently available.

Java Security API

Security is an integral part of the Java Platform and extends to the Java Enterprise Server architecture. There are four key areas that are supported by various security APIs: authentication, authorization, privacy, and integrity.

Authentication is the system's ability to verify or recognize a user. Typically performed at application access or system sign-on, authentication is the first line of defense present in a comprehensive security model. The JavaCard APIs allow smart cards to be employed as secure user authentication devices. These physical cards combined with a secure personal identification number (PIN) enable users to be recognized by the target system. Digital signatures, another authentication method, also are supported through the Java Virtual Machine.

Authorization is the means of determining which data, systems, and services a user can access. The Java Security APIs and access control lists (ACL) are available for managing who can access what. ACLs can be built for each Enterprise JavaBean and consulted whenever the bean is accessed. Based on the user's role some form of access can be given or denied. Transaction servers installed in the application enforce the ACL at run time. Because ACLs are not a static structure they can be moved around the network with an EJB object. These embedded ACLs then can be accessed by the application developer.

Privacy concerns are raised in the context of transmission of sensitive data across public networks. To protect data such as credit card numbers, encryption typically is employed. The Java language cryptography APIs provide application or session-level encryption. This interface can support any encryption implementation including DES.

As data passes through a network, be it private or public, there is a chance for malicious or accidental modification. To prevent such actions it is necessary to be able to guarantee the integrity of the transmission. The same mechanisms for insuring privacy can be used for maintaining integrity of network communications, namely session and application encryption.

Java Transaction Services

Java Transaction Services (JTS) within the Enterprise JavaBean framework are a low-level API not meant as an application programmer interface. JTS programming is targeted to the resource managers and TP monitor programmers. Currently available implementations include BEA Systems Jolt product for Tuxedo access or IBM's JavaCICS for access to mainframe CICS applications.

Java Management API

The Java Management API (JMAPI) is a set of interfaces for the development of distributed network, system, and application management applications. JMAPI is designed to be incorporated into a variety of devices, across diverse network protocols and numerous operating systems. With support for the Simple Network Management Protocol (SNMP), JMAPI can communicate directly with a variety of existing devices. In the future, device manufacturers will incorporate the JMAPI directly in their products. System administrators using applications developed on this foundation are able to easily manage their network, applications, or other systems from any Java platform located anywhere on the network.

Java Server API

The Java Server API is an extensible framework that can be employed to develop network-centric servers quickly. These servers are capable of providing network-based services, such as Web services, file and print services, proxy services, and mail services. To extend the functionality of a Java server a developer can create servlets using the Java Servlet API. Java servlets are programs that can be local to the server or downloaded across the network, then executed on the Java server. These servlets are perfect for processing form data from HTML pages, replacing the platform-dependent CGI-bin scripts in use by many organizations.

SUMMARY

The ability to integrate with legacy systems and extend enterprise services to the network with platform-independent technologies are key benefits of developing a Java Enterprise Server strategy. Enterprise JavaBeans, the component architecture for the Java Enterprise Server, provide a software- and hardware-independent method to access these systems and make them available to business components. These components easily can access services, such as transaction monitors and message systems, DBMSs, and naming services with the assurance of the Java Platforms "write once, run everywhere."

Chapter 42
Object Technology Essentials

Richard T. Dué

OBJECT ORIENTATION IS A FUNDAMENTALLY NEW WAY OF THINKING about information technology. It offers a new approach to reusing information systems plans, requirements, designs, and code. It is ideally suited to the implementation of client/server computing.

Object-oriented (OO) techniques have migrated into mainstream information technology through two paths. The first is the path of incorporation of OO concepts in traditional development and deployment tools and systems. The second is through the acceptance of true OO products. Both benefit from the application of OO techniques.

Object-oriented techniques promise to improve communication among all of the parties involved in the planning, analysis, design, use, and auditing of information systems. The implementation of this new approach involves new languages, new methodologies, new software, and many times, new people. As with any new approach, there are risks as well as rewards along the way.

This chapter gives an overview of object-oriented programming languages (OOPL), object-oriented analysis (OOA), object-oriented design (OOD), and object-oriented enterprise modeling (OOEM) — all of which together are essential for the successful implementation of object technology as part of an IS organization's distributed systems strategy.

SIMULATION METAPHOR

For 25 years, many people from diverse backgrounds have been developing object-oriented approaches, methodologies, techniques, tools, and notations. No one single approach, language, or methodology is accepted by the majority of practitioners. There are many points of view and many different and sometimes conflicting definitions. The most important step in trying to understand this new technology is to clarify which approach and sets of definitions are being used in a particular situation.

0-8493-9976-9/99/$0.00+$.50
© 1999 by CRC Press LLC

The goals of object technology are reuse of system components and improved communications among everyone involved in developing, using, and managing information systems. These goals are pursued by shifting from traditional systems development practices to the assembly of systems from simulation models of real-world objects. These simulations provide formally contracted services that can be reused in a variety of information systems. The assembly of these collaborating sets of simulations depends on the developers:

- Following proven patterns
- Using hierarchical libraries of models
- Employing software brokers

How Object Technology Differs from Traditional Programming

Object orientation, or what is increasingly referred to as object technology, had its origins with the Simula programming language in 1967. Simula was originally developed as a programming language that would develop and use simulation models of things that existed in the real world. These simulation models could be used to help the user understand and control the real-world environment.

The simulation approach is a radical departure from the typical data processing approach of analyzing, designing, and programming the algorithms and data of an information system. Exhibit 1 lists ways in which the object paradigm differs from the traditional information approach.

Traditional data processing is actually carried out on an abstract level from reality. Events, such as business transactions, occur in the real world. Data processing systems, like accounting and management reporting systems, are used to generate, manipulate, and report on data that represent these real-world events. Object technology, by contrast, attempts to create and maintain models of how things behave in the real world and of how real-world events influence this behavior.

Procedural Thinking	Object-Oriented Thinking
What does the system do?	Of what objects is the system comprised?
What is the system's purpose? How does the developer design and code to achieve this functional behavior?	How can the developer model the system dynamically using objects, their behavior, and other objects they use?
Focus on algorithms	Algorithmic functions deferred

Exhibit 1.   A shift of mind-set.

The major benefit of the object-oriented paradigm is that it can facilitate the development and reuse of components in the assembly of new systems. For example, the simulation model of a person can be assembled into systems that describe employees, or customers, or managers. In each case, the person would still have the same name, the same parents, the same spouse and children, would continue to live at the same location, and would continue to grow older. This object-oriented view of the world as tangible objects with behaviors is much easier for most people than trying to cope with a variety of traditional data processing abstractions like files, tuples, and algorithms.

People sometimes mistakenly consider object orientation to be merely a set of techniques, tools, or notations that are used to develop traditional applications programs. By some estimates, more than 80% of programs written in so-called object-oriented programming languages fail to take advantage of the object technology approach that includes object-oriented enterprise modeling and development methodologies as well as applications programming.

ESSENTIAL DEFINITIONS

The lack of generally agreed-upon definitions of object technology terms can be a source of problems. With more than 50 different published methodologies and the lack of any one acknowledged technology leader, even the selection of the basic terms that need to be defined is difficult. The essential terminology includes, at least, the following terms: object, class, contract, encapsulation, identity, inheritance (delegation), messages, and polymorphism.

What Is an Object? The common dictionary definition of an object is something that is perceptible by one or more of the senses, especially vision or touch, or that is intelligible to the mind. The IBM *Dictionary of Computing*, however, has 13 different definitions of object, including "a passive entity that contains or receives data (e.g., bytes, blocks, clocks, fields, files, directories)," and "in SQL, anything that can be created or manipulated with SQL statements, such as databases, tables, views, or indexes." The IBM dictionary defines data objects as "a collection of data referred to by a single name." There is nothing in the IBM definitions that obviously refers to things perceivable to the senses or to simulation models.

These two sets of definitions represent major differences in the interpretation and understanding of the concept of objects. People with a traditional data processing background, especially in relational databases, frequently use the word object in the sense of the IBM dictionary definition, referring to objects as collections of data or as icons that represent collections of data, or programs. In general, the traditional data processing community sees object orientation as an extension to software engineering, with objects replacing modules of code. The traditional data processing approach uses techniques like data flow diagrams, entity-relationship models, and state transition diagrams to separately model the data, the functions, and the behavior of objects.

Most often, those with business or engineering backgrounds define the word object in terms of things in the real world and building models of reality. These people see object orientation as a completely new approach that combines data, process, and behavior into a single, encapsulated entity.

Donald Firesmith, in his review of 16 object-oriented methodologies, found seven basic categories of object definitions:

- An abstraction of a thing.
- A thing.
- An encapsulation of data (or state) and operations on that data.
- An instance (of a class).
- Something with an identity (and an address).
- An abstraction of real-world entities.
- A general term for all object-oriented things.

SELECTING A DEFINITION

It is important that everyone involved in an object-oriented project is using the same philosophical approach and a similar set of definitions. The criteria for making a selection include:

- Whether the philosophical approach is simpler than any other.
- Whether it promotes communication and understanding of the system among all interested parties.
- Whether it promotes reuse of requirements, analysis, design, components, documentation, and testing plans.

The following working definition is recommended:

> An object is something that can be perceived by the mind or the senses. An object can be represented by a uniquely identifiable dynamic simulation model. These simulation models report on the outwardly observable behavior of the object. This behavior can be interpreted simultaneously from a number of different points of view.

Dynamic simulation models of real-world objects can be understood by people with many different backgrounds. Dynamic simulations conform to the original intent of the Simula language. They can be compared to reality. They can easily be shared and reused. Because they provide a single focal point for normalized (i.e., standardized) data and normalized process, they are much simpler to construct and understand than approaches that require multiple models for data, process, and state transitions.

The definitions used in the rest of this chapter are derived from the two major standards groups in the area of object technology: the Object Management Group (OMG), an international software consortium that promotes the practical application of object technology, the ANSI accredited X3H7 Object Management Standards Committee, and the majority consensus of the major object technology methodologists. The rest of the essential definitions are surprisingly in accord.

Class. A class is a template, a "factory" or a "cookie cutter," that can be used to create new objects that share common meaning, structure, or behavior. Every object is a unique instance of a class. Classes contain the definitions of the data structures, methods, and interfaces of software objects. Some classes are only used for conceptual purposes. For example, the class of mammals can be used to group all subclasses of mammals (e.g., tigers, whales). The conceptual class "mammal," however, cannot directly create objects. Instead, the conceptual subclass contains general attributes (e.g., warm-blooded) that are reused or inherited by all of its subclasses.

Encapsulation. Encapsulation is the packaging or hiding of a set of data and procedures into a single structure. Encapsulation provides a clear separation between the external behavior of an object and how that behavior is implemented. For example, one external behavior of a person object is that it grows older. The data and procedures used to implement growing older are hidden from the user.

Identity. Identity means that objects can be uniquely identified. This is a key requirement for the sharing and reuse of objects. Some methodologists are now suggesting that identity may be the key concept of object technology.

Identity requires that something can have recognizable boundaries. By contrast, in the traditional data processing paradigm, the data and the processes that acted on data are stored separately in databases and application programs. The various programs used to process data could contain different definitions of the data elements, and different (possibly conflicting) business rules. The object technology concept of identity means that the same data will always be processed by the same set of procedures.

Inheritance. Inheritance is a relationship among classes that allows classes of objects to have access to the resources of other classes. Inheritance is employed to reuse common resources. Inheritance is expressed in terms of a hierarchy where classes are arranged in terms of "kind of" or "part of" relationships. Another approach to inheritance is called delegation. Delegation is used to break complex systems into simple, cooperating classes that can be called upon to provide services.

Messages. Messages are the primary means by which objects communicate and interact. A message may be an event or it may be a request for a service, or it may be a service provided by an object in response to a request. Objects do not exchange data or processes (which are hidden from view by encapsulation). Instead, they exchange services (i.e., processed data).

Polymorphism. Polymorphism means that different classes of objects may respond to the same message in different ways — that is, although the service requested in a message stays the same (e.g., pay the employees), the data and methods used to provide this service could be changed or updated. Polymorphism allows the underlying classes of objects in a system to be continually improved or updated in a manner that is hidden from the users.

OBJECT-ORIENTED PROGRAMMING

An object-oriented programming language is a language that is capable of implementing the features of object technology.

Selection of an OOPL

Once an organization has decided on its philosophic approach to object technology and has selected a methodology to implement this approach, it can proceed with the selection of an appropriate object-oriented programming language. Exhibit 2 shows the time-line development of languages that can be used for object-oriented programming.

Procedural languages that have been provided with object extensions (e.g., C++, Object-Oriented COBOL) still allow programmers to write code in the traditional, procedure-oriented manner. Organizations should instead investigate those object-oriented programming languages that were designed to support the object paradigm (e.g., Smalltalk, Eiffel, Objective C). Exhibit 3 lists representative object-oriented programming languages.

Object-Oriented CASE Tools. The real advantages of object technology cannot be accessed by writing still more code that has to be debugged and maintained. Ideally, objects should be assembled from existing code.

Visual programming techniques may be employed to assemble existing libraries of classes and objects by manipulating graphical icons instead of writing lines of code. Typical visual programming tools include Window-Builder (Objectshare, Inc.), PARTS (Digitalk), and VisualAge (IBM). Object-oriented CASE tools offer a different, though possibly complementary, approach. These tools (some of which are listed in Exhibit 4) can be used to

Time Frame	Language
1960s	LISP and ALGOL (while not object-oriented, LISP and ALGOL both influenced subsequent object-oriented language development)
	Simula 67
	LOGO 69
1970s	Smalltalk 72
	Mainsail
	Flavors
	C (while not object-oriented, C influenced subsequent object-oriented language development)
1980s	Smalltalk-80
	Softnet 83
	Objective C
	Classical
	C++
	Object Pascal
	Eiffel
1990s	Self
	Emerald/Jade

Exhibit 2. The development of object-oriented programming languages.

translate diagrams developed by the various systems development methodologies into object-oriented code, or even to reengineer existing code into object diagrams.

OBJECT-ORIENTED ANALYSIS AND DESIGN

There are numerous descriptions and comparisons of the nearly 50 published object-oriented analysis and design methodologies. One of the most interesting was prepared by the Object Management Group, which developed a standard questionnaire that was filled out by the methodologists themselves. Exhibit 5 names some of the chief methodologies that IS organizations can choose from.

SELECTION OF AN OBJECT METHODOLOGY

Object methodologies can be generally placed into two categories: evolutionary and revolutionary.

Evolutionary Methodologies. Evolutionary object methodologies are derived from software engineering and information modeling. Evolutionary methodologies (Martin/Odell, Rumbaugh, Yourdon/Coad) break down the

Language	Vendor	Operating System
C++ language systems	AT&T (Greensboro NC)	UNIX
C_Talk	CNS Inc. (Eden Prairie MN)	MS-DOS
C++ and Common View	Computer Associates (Islandia NY)	MS-DOS, UNIX, Windows NT, Windows 95
Classic-ADA with Persistence	Software Productivity Solutions (Melbourne FL)	VMS, UNIX, Aviion
Eiffel	Interactive Software Engineering (Goleta CA)	VMS, UNIX, Macintosh
ENFIN	Easel Corp. (Burlington MA)	MS-DOS, OS/2, Windows
Object Works/Smalltalk	ParcPlace Systems (Sunnyvale CA)	MS-DOS, OS/2, UNIX, VMS, Macintosh
Objective-C	Stepstone Corp. (Sandy Hook CT)	MS-DOS, OS/2, AIX, UX, SunOS, Macintosh
Smalltalk/V	Digitalk, Inc. (Los Angeles CA)	MS-DOS, OS/2, Macintosh
Smalltalk-80	Xerox Corp. (Rochester NY)	Macintosh, Xerox

Exhibit 3.   Representative object-oriented programming languages.

analysis of objects into the separate consideration of an object's data, processes (or methods), and the dynamic modeling of an object's behavior over time. Each perspective is modeled using software engineering and information modeling techniques. Data is modeled with entity-relationship diagrams, process is modeled with data flow diagrams, and behavior is modeled with state transition diagrams.

Revolutionary Methodologies. This approach (favored by Booch, Jacobson, and Wirfs-Brock) models the behaviors of objects (i.e., responsibilities) and the messages (or contracts) that are passed among groups of collaborating objects. Revolutionary methodologies require the user to "think like an object." The CRC (class, responsibilities, and collaborations) technique, developed by Ward Cunningham and Kent Beck, is used to

Product	Vendor	Methodology
Object Maker	Mark V Systems (Encino CA)	*More than 20 object-oriented and software engineering methodologies*
Object Modeler	Iconix Software Engineering (Santa Monica CA)	Rumbaugh, Yourdon/Coad
OMW & Prokappa	Intellicorp (Mountain View CA)	Martin-Odell, Rumbaugh
Ptech	Associate Design Technologies (Westborough MA)	Martin-Odell
Rational Rose	Rational (Santa Clara CA)	Booch
Teamwork/OOA	Cadre Technologies (Providence RI)	Shlaer-Mellor
The Object Engineering Workbench	Innovative Software (Frankfurt am Main, Germany)	Martin-Odell
Systems Architect	Popkin Systems	Various OO methodologies

Exhibit 4. Representative object-oriented CASE tools.

record the classes of objects and their behaviors (responsibilities), and to indicate which objects need to interact (collaborators).

Most of the major methodologists are starting to consolidate the features they have found most useful into their own approaches. Over the next few years, emphasis on the revolutionary methodologies will include some form of Use Case scenarios, CRC modeling, and formal specification and contracting, as well as the use of brokers, layered class libraries, and information system patterns and frameworks consisting of proven collections of objects (these features are described later in this chapter).

ENTERPRISE MODELING

Object-oriented enterprise modeling is the extension of the object approach to building dynamic models of the organization in much the same way that information engineering extended the concepts of software engineering to building static models of the organization. Exhibit 6 compares the development of software engineering over the past 25 years with the work of object practitioners.

- Ada Box Structures Method (Comer 1989)
- ASTS Development Method (Firesmith 1992)
- The Booch Method (Booch 1991)
- Extended Buhr Design Method (Vidale/Hayden 1986)
- Frame-Design Methodology (Andleigh/Gretzinger 1992)
- FUSION (Coleman and Arnold 1992)
- General Object-Oriented Development (Seidewitz/Strak 1986)
- Hierarchical Object-Oriented Design (HOOD Technical Group 1991)
- Layered Virtual Machines/O-O Design (Nielsen/Schumate 1988)
- Method for the O-O Software Engineering of Systems (Henderson-Sellers/Edwards 1993)
- Model-Based O-O Design (Bulman 1987)
- Model-Driven O-O Systems Analysis (Embley et al 1992)
- Multiple-View O-O Design (Kerth 1989)
- Object Behavior Analysis (Gibson 1990)
- Object Behavior Analysis (Rubin/Goldberg)
- Object Modeling Technique (Rumbaugh et al 1991)
- O-O Analysis (Coad/Yourdon 1991)
- O-O Analysis (Martin/Odell 1993)
- O-O Analysis (Stoecklin et al 1988)
- O-O Design (Berard 1993)
- O-O Design (Coad/Yourdon 1991)
- O-O Design (Martin/Odell 1993)
- O-O Domain Analysis (Berard 1993)
- O-O Requirements Analysis and Design (Anderson et al 1989)
- O-O Requirements Analysis (Bailin 1989)
- O-O Requirement Analysis (Berard 1993)
- O-O Role Analysis, Synthesis and Structuring (Reenskaug et al)
- O-O Software Development (Colbert 1989)
- O-O Software Development (Lorenz 1993)
- O-O Software Engineering (Jacobson et al 1991)
- O-O Structured Design (Wasserman et al 1989, 1990)
- O-O Systems Analysis (Seidewitz 1989)
- O-O Systems Analysis (Shlaer/Mellor 1988)
- O-O Systems Development (Henderson-Sellers 1991)
- ObjectOry (Jacobson 1991)
- Responsibility Driven Design (Wirfs-Brock et al 1990)
- Software Construction through O-O Pictures (Cherry 1988)
- Synthesis (Page-Jones, Weiss, and Buhr 1989, 1991)

Exhibit 5.   Object-oriented analysis and design methodologies.

Software/Information Engineering	Object Technology
Structured Programming	*Object-Oriented Programming*
1960s to 1970s Dijkstra, Parnas	1990s Coad, Gamma et al, Beck and Cunningham
Four basic programming structures (Sequence, Do While, Case, If-Then-Else)	Some preliminary work with patterns, idioms
Structured Design	*Object-Oriented Design*
1970s Yourdon, Constintine, et al HIPO, Structure Charts	1980s to 1990s Booch, Wirfs-Brock, et al Use Case, CRC
Structured Analysis	*Object-Oriented Analysis*
1980s Demarco	1990s Numerous notations, but no generally accepted approach
Information Engineering	*Object-Oriented Enterprise Modeling*
1980s Martin, Finkelstein Enterprise modeling	1990s Jacobson, Henderson-Sellers Preliminary work

Exhibit 6. Comparison of software/information engineering and object technology.

The development and implementation of object technology seem to be following the same bottom-up path as the development and implementation of software and information engineering. It has taken 25 years for software engineers to learn that developing quality structured code requires effective structured design methods, including structured analysis that depends on a strategic plan linked to the goals of the organization. If object practitioners apply the lessons of the software and information engineering learning curves, then the time-consuming, resource-intensive, top-down, static enterprise models developed by information engineers can be replaced by dynamic, iterative models of the object that make up the enterprise.

OBJECT-ORIENTED DATABASE MANAGEMENT SYSTEMS

An object-oriented database management system provides persistent storage that supports the object-oriented approach. Certain database transitions become necessary as organizations migrate from the static data models of relational and other traditional database technologies to the dynamic, multimedia models of object technology. For example:

- Computer words, fields, files, and records are replaced by objects and episodic memory.
- Hard data is replaced by soft data (e.g., projections, extrapolations, forecasts, and hypotheses).
- Data is replaced by multimedia information (e.g., text, documents, image, voice, and graphics).
- Preestablished queries are replaced by ad hoc queries.
- Crisp queries are replaced by fuzzy queries.
- Simple retrieval is replaced by complex retrieval from distributed databases.
- Keywords are replaced by memory-based reasoning.
- "As is" presentation is replaced by analytical evaluation.

Over the past 2 years, there has been substantial evolution of the traditional relational database products offered by the largest vendors. Oracle, IBM, Informix, and Sybase have all adopted the phrase "Universal Server" to describe the most current and comprehensive version of their flagship database server product.

Because many organizations have considerable installed bases of the popular RDBMSs, and because those systems have been honed for high transaction volumes, it is unlikely that they will be replaced in the short term. They will, however, continue to evolve to include more object features over time, as evidenced by the universal server architectures. Although object-oriented purists know that the universal server architectures are still fundamentally relational, there are many OO benefits incorporated into the new designs and more are on the way.

Two approaches, specifically, to the development of object-oriented databases are under way. The first approach is to extend the features of existing relational database management systems (RDBMSs) to include object capabilities. Typical products, mostly from large established vendors, include the extensions to Oracle version 8 (Oracle Corp.) and O-OODB (Hewlett-Packard Co.). The second approach is to develop a new database management system based on the object approach. Typical products, mostly from small startup companies, include Gemstone (Servio), Ontos (Ontologic), Versant (Versant), and ObjectStore (Object Design).

NEW APPROACHES REQUIRED FOR OBJECT-ORIENTED SYSTEMS DEVELOPMENT

A new way of thinking requires new methods and techniques of systems development. Among these new approaches are design by contract, hierarchical class libraries, brokers, and agents.

Design by Contract

The design by contract approach requires the development and assignment of multipart contracts to the services provided by each class of objects. These contracts are formal specifications that describe the behavior of each class of objects. Contracts are composed of the following clauses:

- *Preconditions.* The precondition clause specifies all the conditions that must be true before the services of this class of objects can be used. For example, before a paymaster object can pay the employees, there must be money in the bank, there must be employees, there must be an authorization, and it must be payday.
- *Postconditions.* The postcondition clause specifies all of the conditions that will be true after the class of objects provides its services. For example, the paymaster object will pay the employees according to the existing payroll agreements and in conformity with the current taxation requirements.
- *Invariants.* Invariants are those conditions that the class of objects agrees to abide by during its activities. For example, the paymaster object agrees not to overdraw the payroll account without authorization.

Contracts may have other clauses that detail the actions to be taken during error conditions, the methods that the class of objects will actually use to provide its services, and testing procedures. The CRC technique can be used to develop the service contracts. In this case, the class responsibilities are described in terms of the preconditions, postconditions, and invariants of each class of objects involved in the system.

Once the service contracts are developed and tested against predetermined scenarios, the next step is to locate the classes that will supply the required contracted services. Classes may be found directly in class libraries or may be located through the use of software brokers.

Class Libraries

Class libraries are collections of related classes of objects. These collections may be specifically designed for a particular industry (i.e., banking or transportation) or they may be more general collections (i.e., Smalltalk or C++ language libraries). Class libraries may be arranged into layers. The layered approach (shown in Exhibit 7 and discussed next) offers the opportunity to leverage and reuse the work undertaken at the lower levels of the class library. People working at different layers of the class library need not understand the internal workings of the other layers.

Atomic Classes. The layered approach views classes from four levels of abstraction. The first level consists of basic, or atomic, classes. This is the

Layer	Who	What
Layer 1: Atomic or Base Classes	Class Constructors (Software Engineers)	Libraries, software integrated circuits, standard components, reusable functionality, common business objects, standard packaging are available from multiple vendors.
Layer 2: Business Process Models	Model Builders (Business Systems Analysts, Object Modelers)	Comparable to PC boards, these models handle standard business functions (purchasing cycle, customer interactions) and maximize reuse of every atomic class.
Layer 3: Management or Applications	Prototypers (Users)	Solve a business problem by mixing and matching models; independent of model details; produce very little new code; software by assembly, built through rapid prototyping.
Layer 4: Enterprise Engine	Enterprise Modelers, Business Process Engineers	A distributed expert system (inference engine, rule base, data base) for gradual merging of models and applications. Collaborative effort throughout organizations that depends on standard classes and structures, not just a model—an active engine that evolves along with the company.

Source: D. Taylor, "Management Decisions for Object Technology"

Exhibit 7. Layered class libraries.

---

level of object-oriented programmers that develops the lowest-level systems building blocks. This level may be subdivided into further layers or clusters of classes that provide basic services for string handling, graphical user interfaces, mathematical functions, database functions, and communications. This atomic level probably contains 5000 or more members (an estimate based on the size of existing Eiffel, C++, and Smalltalk libraries) that should be developed by object-oriented language or class library vendors. This level provides the essential infrastructure of the object technology approach.

Business Processes. The second layer consists of business process classes, which are the fundamental, stable building blocks of all applications. Data is not necessarily the stable component of the enterprise, especially as enterprises continually reinvent themselves, merge, downsize, and divest. The stable parts of the enterprise are the basic business processes of purchasing, reporting, control, and security. These business process classes will be specified by business systems analysts by combining the basic atomic classes. Little or no code development should be performed at this level.

According to preliminary estimates, this layer should probably only contain from 20 to 30 business process models. These fundamental models include processes such as:

- Mediation (one object requesting a service from another object through a third object).
- Transaction (one object requesting a service directly from another object).
- Transformation (conversion of a service into another form).
- Edit (verification of a service against a standard).

If there is a need for additional atomic classes to specify a business process, the business systems analysts must negotiate with the atomic class developers to provide the new atomic classes. Business systems analysts should not be allowed to program new atomic classes.

Management or Application Classes. The third layer consists of management or application classes. Developed by users, these application classes are assemblies of business processes. Only minimal coding (just that necessary to tie together existing classes) should be undertaken at this level. If the business process classes do not exist in the business process layer for the application modeler to use, the user must negotiate with the business process modeler to provide the required class.

Enterprise Engine. The fourth layer of the model is the enterprise engine level. At this layer, enterprise modelers and business process engineers model the interaction of the application classes to provide a dynamic simulation of the enterprise. These dynamic, real-world simulations will eventually evolve into the accounting, communications, and IS reporting systems of the organization. The model of how the objects that make up the enterprise interact actually becomes the information system.

Design Patterns

Important new work has begun on the identification and development of design patterns. Generative patterns are patterns that have embedded design principles. The user merely follows the guidelines. So far, this work is only preliminary, but considerable resources are now being applied to identify these patterns.

Brokers

Brokers are used to assist in the location of classes or services. Requests for contracted services are sent to the broker (a piece of software in a network). The necessary classes are located. Eventually, networks of brokers will receive "advertisements" from class libraries that will detail available services and their costs.

The Common Object Request Broker Architecture (CORBA) has received a great deal of press over the last 3 years. One reason for this is the Object Management Group's (OMG) excellent promotion of the CORBA benefits of OO functionality as middleware in critical client/server applications.

CORBA is an excellent concept and shows a great deal of promise; however, it has not yet become a fully mature technology. It is primarily used in prototypes and low transaction volume systems. The OMG has specified a complete set of CORBA object request broker (ORB) functions, and no single vendor has implemented full coverage of all ORBs. Additionally, there is a current lack of support in the areas of security and heavy transaction processing. Even with the IIOP inter-ORB protocol, there is no guarantee of vendor-to-vendor ORB compatibility.

To address these issues, the leading CORBA vendor, Iona, has teamed with IBM/Transarc Corporation to link their ORBs to Transarc's Encina product, a Distributed Computing Environment-based transaction processing monitor. The result brings high-level security and transaction-processing capability to the CORBA solution.

Separately from the development of CORBA, Microsoft has pushed their own proprietary object strategy. ActiveX and DCOM (Distributed Component Object Model) are strong object approaches, but are restricted to the growing Microsoft environment. Microsoft has also recognized the importance of middleware and has introduced the Transaction Server to complement their object model for a variety of support functions.

Agents

An agent is an object that is created to do some work on the behalf of another object or person. Agents can be used to help locate design patterns or class libraries across a network. Agents could also be used to interpret object models from various perspectives. For example, an agent viewing the enterprise model from the perspective of the marketing department might interpret the behavior (or the role) of a particular person (e.g., a sales prospect) quite differently than the accounting department (e.g., an employee).

SUMMARY

Object technology is a new way of approaching information technology. The key to understanding this new approach is to understand the particular philosophy of object technology being proposed in a given situation.

Implementation of object technology requires investment in new programming languages and new tools to assemble code. It requires new systems development methods and techniques. New tools, including class libraries, object-oriented database management systems, brokers, and agents need to be installed. The biggest challenge, however, may be getting existing personnel to start to think in terms of the object paradigm.

Because of all the changes that must be made to move to object technology, many traditionally trained personnel may have difficulty in making this transition; evolutionary methodologies may not enforce the movement to the object paradigm. Instead, organizations following the evolutionary approach may only end up with poorly written and inefficient process-driven code that will not yield any of the benefits of the object-oriented approach. Revolutionary methodologies are therefore recommended in many situations.

For organizations with considerable investments in legacy RDBMS environments with high transaction volume, evolution to object orientation will likely take place in stages. The newer design, development, client and server tools/systems are all incorporating more and more OO concepts. The widespread acceptance of Java applets over the Web-browser environment has spurred millions of systems professionals to develop code that is essentially a platform-independent object. As three-tier client/server continues to grow, object orientation will become vital to the proper performance of the middle tier, and will continue its acceptance on the client and server ends as well.

Chapter 43

CRC Cards: A Hands-On Approach to Object-Oriented Design

Nancy M. Wilkinson

PROJECT TEAMS ARE FINDING THAT USING OBJECT-ORIENTED (OO) TECH-
NIQUES helps produce more maintainable and easily extensible programs.
Using OO methodologies and their associated notations and tools formal-
izes the process of software construction and aids communication in large
projects. Project teams wanting to formulate the basis of their object-oriented model may, however, prefer less formal approaches.

Class, responsibility, collaborator (CRC) cards are an informal, hands-on
technique for building object-oriented software. Using CRC cards is an excellent way to introduce database designers and other IS staff to the concept of objects. Shifting from the procedural paradigm to the object-
oriented means moving away from the notions of process, data stores, and
data flows and moving to a world modeled in terms of classes, responsibilities, and collaborators.

THREE ESSENTIAL DIMENSIONS OF AN OO MODEL

CRC concepts are defined as follows:

- Classes are the types of objects in the problem and solution domains.
- Responsibilities of a class define the state and behavior of objects of
  that class.
- Collaborators are other classes whose objects are needed to complete
  a responsibility.

A CRC card is an index card that is annotated and used in group brainstorming sessions. It represents a class of objects and contains informa-

Class name	
responsibilities	*collaborators*

Exhibit 1. Basic format of a CRC card.

tion about its behavior and its interactions with other classes. A complete set of cards describes an object-oriented model for an application. Exhibit 1 illustrates the basic format of a CRC card.

The heart of the technique is the CRC card session, a creative exchange in which classes are discovered, converted into cards, and then assigned responsibilities and collaborators through the physical simulation of the workings of the system. Each participant is responsible for holding, moving, and writing on one or more cards as messages circulate in support of a particular need or activity. Participants create, stack, and sometimes even wave cards as they "become" the objects during the walkthroughs of scenarios that describe the typical use of the application.

CRC cards were introduced in 1989 by Kent Beck and Ward Cunningham to teach object-oriented programming. Although Cunningham originally wrote a computer tool to teach classes, responsibilities, and collaborators (what he believed to be the three essential dimensions of an OO model), it was soon determined that the portability of paper index cards made them more effective for teaching OO programming than a computer-based tool.

THE SCHEDULER APPLICATION

This section introduces a problem that illustrates CRC card syntax and a sample CRC card session. The notion of objects is explained by contrasting a procedural decomposition for the problem with a decomposition from an object-oriented point of view. Neither should be taken as the one

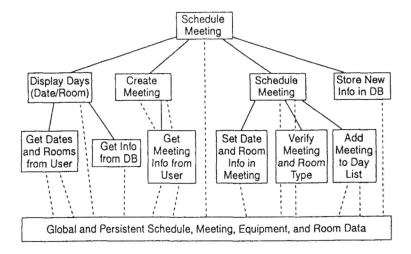

Exhibit 2.   Procedural decomposition of the scheduler application.

true design. They are meant to show how the views differ in their approach and basic building blocks of the design.

Many real-world applications involve the task of scheduling resources in a given domain. Airline reservation systems, operations work management systems, and TV station programming all have a scheduling component. This chapter looks at a small system to schedule meetings and conference rooms for an IS department. This problem, although simple, has many components of larger problems and is based on an actual system.

The scheduler application allows a user to view the availability of conference rooms on particular days, schedule meetings in free slots for a room, and view information about already scheduled meetings. The user can create different types of meetings (i.e., training sessions, demos, or working meetings), providing information such as the number of participants, contacts, and equipment needed. Different types of conference rooms (i.e., classroom, demo room, or project room) may be appropriate for these different types of meetings.

Procedural View

Exhibit 2 looks at the problem of scheduling a meeting from a procedural point of view. The problem is viewed as one controlling process with many smaller subprocesses. Each box or module is a procedure or step in the overall process.

Some data will be local to these processes, but any data that outlasts the invocation of a procedure will be global (i.e., external and potentially accessible, as indicated by the dashed lines) to all the processes. Persistent data that is stored in a database management system (DBMS) is potentially accessed directly by procedures. Here, the global and persistent data includes the information about schedules, meetings, equipment, and rooms. If the structure of this data changes, the entire system must be examined for potential updates.

Object-Oriented View

In contrast, in the OO decomposition of the same problem (as shown in Exhibit 3), classes that correspond closely to things in the problem domain provide the basic building blocks. The task of scheduling a meeting is accomplished by sending the "add meeting" message to a schedule object. The ovals in Exhibit 3 represent classes and the arrows are collaborations, labeled by responsibilities of the pointed-to classes. The bold arrows represent superclass/subclass or "is-kind-of" relationships. For example, subclasses demo room, classroom, and project room "are-kinds-of" conference rooms and inherit the characteristics of their superclass.

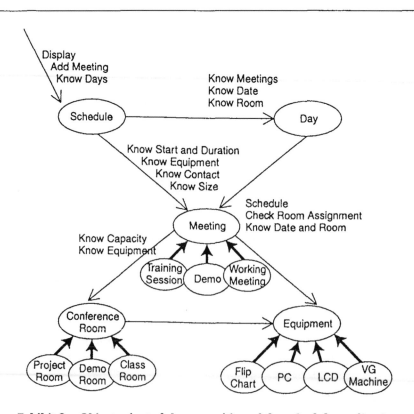

Exhibit 3. Object-oriented decomposition of the schedule application.

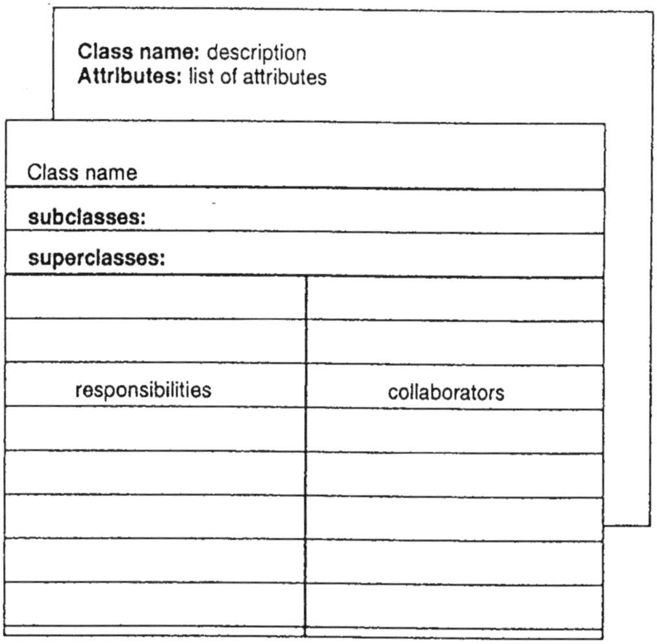

```
Class name: description
Attributes: list of attributes
```

Class name	
subclasses:	
superclasses:	
responsibilities	collaborators

Exhibit 4. Suggested format for a CRC card.

Using the OO approach, classes are assigned parts of the problem and collaborate to perform each task. The data that is global in the procedural view is resident in the state of the objects; therefore, it is accessible only to the object itself. Interaction with a DBMS is likely to be through a well-defined object whose sole job is to interact with the DBMS. If the global or persistent data structure changes, only the behavior of the object responsible for the data needs to be updated. Other objects will continue to interact with that object in the same way.

Elements of a CRC Card

The only essential elements of a CRC card are the class name, a set of responsibilities, and a set of collaborators. However, it is sometimes useful to extend the basic form, and project leaders often customize the card for their own use. The syntax illustrated in Exhibit 4 is most useful in working with projects. It reflects the Wirfs-Brock extensions of the original Beck and Cunningham notion of the cards.

Class Names. A class name is written at the top of each card. Class names represent the entities in the problem and solution domains. Class names form a vocabulary for the CRC card discussion. For example, class names in the scheduling application include meeting, conference room, and equipment, among others. Well-chosen names greatly increase the understandability of the model.

The next two lines of the card are reserved for listing subclasses and superclasses, if they exist. For example, a demo room card in the scheduler application would list conference room on its superclass line (because a demo room "is-a-kind-of" conference room), and conference room would list demo room, classroom, and project room on its subclass lines.

Responsibilities. The rest of the card is divided into two columns. Responsibilities of the class are listed on the left.

Responsibilities include the knowledge that objects of the class maintain and the small tasks they must perform to complete the problem at hand. For example, a meeting would have the responsibilities to "know start time," "know duration," and "know size," as well as a schedule and check room assignment (see Exhibit 5). The object conference room knows which types of equipment can be used.

Responsibility names should be concise but descriptive, and they should always contain an active verb.

Collaborators. The collaborators for the responsibilities are listed on the right of the card. A collaborator is a class whose knowledge or services are needed in order to fulfill a responsibility. For example, meeting objects collaborate with conference room objects to check room assignment. They will use the conference room object's "know equipment" responsibility and its "know capacity" responsibility to determine whether the room can house the equipment needed and the number of people in the meeting.

Collaborators are listed directly across from the responsibilities they help to fulfill. Collaborations exist only to fulfill responsibilities.

Attributes. It is also important to have a succinct description for the abstraction represented by the class. This information can be entered on the back of the card. Formulating this definition may seem the most tedious part of the exercise, but it is also one of the most critical. Agreeing early on about the abstractions helps to avoid problems later.

The back of the card is also used to list attributes. They appear on the back rather than the front because the focus of the CRC card technique is the behavior of the class rather than the structure (it is called a responsibility-driven technique).

Attributes are usually added later to support responsibilities. "Know responsibilities" exist to reflect the information that one class needs from an-

Meeting: The set of objects representing the meetings that have been, or will be, scheduled.

Attributes: size, duration, start time, date, room, equipment, contact

Meeting	
subclasses: Demo, Training Session, Working Meeting	
schedule	
check room assignment	Conference Room
know start time and duration	
know equipment	
know date and room	
know contact	

Exhibit 5.   Meeting CRC card from the scheduler application.

other. However, sometimes participants think about a class in terms of its structure (e.g., a "day" has a list of "meetings") even before they consider what the class does or who might need information about its state. And in design, it may be useful for a database designer to consider attributes of the class as columns for the corresponding relational table. The back of the card is a convenient place to record these attributes.

Exhibits 5 and 6 show the "meeting" and "schedule" CRC cards (front and back) from the scheduler application. Cards such as these reflect the end of the story. The following sections focus on the process of actually creating the cards.

CREATING CRC CARDS

The most important part of the CRC card technique is the session in which they are created. This is where responsibilities are assigned to classes by physically moving and annotating the cards during a simulation of the system. Following is an excerpt of a session.

Schedule: The object representing the entire schedule of meetings and conference rooms.

Attributes: list of days

Schedule	
display	Day, UI
add meeting	Meeting, Day
know days	List

Exhibit 6.   Schedule CRC card from the scheduler application.

Participants and Their Roles

A key activity preceding a CRC card session is the selection of the group of participants. The session should bring together people from all different phases of the project who are responsible for analysis, design, and implementation of the system, as well as the person responsible for database design.

The most important participant in early sessions is the domain expert, but as the sessions shift from analysis to design, the relative makeup of the group will also change. It is also important that someone in the group have expertise in the object-oriented approach to help encourage the best decisions about the choice of classes and distribution of responsibilities. The scheduler application modeling group in this example is made up of:

- A domain expert and user
- The lead designers and implementers
- A database expert
- An OO expert and facilitator

Defining Requirements. Some preparation on the part of the participating group is necessary before embarking on a set of CRC card sessions. The most important input to the process is a notion of the problem, usually in the form of requirements. This notion may be expanded or corrected by domain experts in the session, but the core of this information is necessary to start. Generally, a project that cannot provide this information is not ready to begin modeling.

For example, the scheduler application modeling group has the set of requirements presented earlier as input to their CRC card sessions. The requirements were written by the domain expert and user, Ralph, who admits they are sparse. However, his main purpose in being at the session is to answer any questions and flesh out the requirements.

Identifying Classes. The best way to begin a session is by brainstorming a set of classes. It is not necessary to exhaustively name every class, but it is helpful to have a set to begin creating a scenario. Other classes will be discovered and created later in the session. Once the initial set of classes is agreed upon, the cards are assigned to various participants, often people who have some responsibility for that part of the system.

The scheduler application group brainstorms some classes from the requirements: meeting, conference room, schedule, equipment, contact, day, and user. Examining their list, the group decides that contact is probably an attribute of meeting rather than a class in its own right. They also wonder whether user will really be a class in the final system. Nancy, the OO expert, agrees that user will probably not be part of the software system, but encourages the group to keep it for the execution of scenarios. They can discard it later if it does not acquire any responsibilities.

Ralph, the domain expert, notes that they have not created cards for each of the types of meetings and rooms. The group suspects that the different meeting and room classes will be subclasses of meeting and conference room. Nancy suggests that they should create cards for these classes and use them in the scenarios. Later they can group responsibilities into their superclasses.

Tom, one of the lead designers, takes the classes schedule and equipment; the other designer, Lisa, takes day, conference room, classroom, demo room, and project room. The database designer, Sy, takes all the meeting cards, and Ralph takes user and database.

As they begin to write class names on the index cards, Nancy suggests that each of them write a description of their class on the back as well. Lisa questions the equipment class, wondering if it is really just an attribute of other classes. Sy notes that different types of equipment will need to be stored in different tables in the database, so he would be more comfortable if they were different classes in the model, perhaps a whole hierarchy. Tom, who owns the equipment card, says he will add cards for types of equipment as they do specific scenarios.

Building Scenarios. Next, the team jumps into scenarios. Scenarios illustrate the expected use of the system from a high-level, user point of view. The scenarios drive the use of the cards and the distribution of responsibilities. Scenarios should be specific, and related scenarios should be modeled separately.

For example, the group will do separate scenarios to schedule a training session and a demo, rather than just one scenario to schedule a meeting. Modeling similar scenarios separately may seem tedious; but when a related scenario is executed, many of the necessary responsibilities are already listed.

It is also important to start with best-case scenarios. Worst-case scenarios can be considered when a solid working set of responsibilities is already in place.

The simulation of the scenarios should be dynamic and anthropomorphic. The people who own particular cards should hold the card in the air and "become" the object when a scenario causes control to pass to them. The set of cards on the table provides a static picture of the classes of objects within the system and the relationships among the classes. While executing scenarios, cards are raised to simulate the dynamic behavior of the system where messages are sent to actual objects performing their tasks. Thus, a card is a class when on the table and an object when in the air.

Tom suggests they begin with the scenario, "What happens when a user schedules a meeting?" Nancy tells the group that this scenario needs to be much more specific. Tom changes it to, "What happens when User A schedules a working meeting for 5 to 10 people for the morning of Wednesday, October 9." Nancy volunteers to write down the scenarios as they go along. They may need to redo walkthroughs if significant changes are made to the design. The scenario list will also serve later as input to the documentation and as a set of test cases.

A CRC Card Sample Session

The following dialog is from a CRC card session of the scheduler application modeling group. The participants are Ralph, the domain expert and user representative; Lisa and Tom, the designers; Sy, the database designer; and Nancy, the OO expert and facilitator.

Tom: My responsibility is to add meeting to the schedule card. Whose help do I need? Should I look for available rooms when the user tells me what he/she needs?

The puzzled group looks to Ralph, the domain expert.

Ralph: As a user, I need to see what the whole story is before I can schedule a meeting. What if a room I want is occupied from 9:00 to 10:30? I might shift my meeting. Or if I can see who has the room, I might be able to convince them to switch to another room.

Nancy: It sounds like the scenario, "What happens when User A asks to see the schedule for Wednesday, October 9, for project room B?" actually precedes our first scenario. Should we do this one first?

Tom (holding schedule card):   That is a good idea. Write it down. I guess this is a responsibility to display my schedule card. I will write that down on my card. I need to get the choice of dates from the user. I do not really want to get into UI stuff now. I will just write UI as my collaborator, even though it may turn out that a UI class actually collaborates with me.

Nancy agrees that this is a good idea. It keeps the application concerns separate from the UI. Later, they can design the UI subsystem and decide what view classes are necessary, and the direction of the collaborations.

Ralph: I enter October 9 on the user card.

Tom (holding the schedule card):   How about rooms? Should I ask User A for a list of rooms?

Ralph (holding the user card):   I might be interested in specific rooms, but I might want to enter a room type or some characteristics of rooms for you to show me. Let us say I ask for all conference rooms that can hold 10 people.

Nancy: Just a second. Let us keep the first scenario simple. Did we not say that there was just one room that User A was interested in? Once we have these basic responsibilities in place, we can do a more complicated scenario and specify the additional responsibilities that pertain to that case.

Ralph: Okay. I ask for project room B.

Tom (holding the schedule card):   Once I have that information, I need to go to the database to get the data to create my day objects, one for each date/room combination to display. What kind of a DBMS are we going to use? If it is relational, I will need to make some SQL calls here. But if it is an object-oriented DBMS, I just create the object, correct? So what should I write?

Sy: We are going to begin development with a relational database. I need to understand what tables to build to support the application. I will start by planning to build one table per class. The

43-11

scenarios should help me determine what data is needed in the class interactions and therefore be stored in the tables. But I am beginning to test some products from OODBMS vendors, as well. So, we should not rule out the possibility of changing to an object-oriented DBMS for the next release, depending on how much redesign and re-implementation that would require.

Nancy: If we design things correctly here, the redesign can be minimal. The most important thing is to create a database class that handles all interactions with the DBMS and contains all DBMS-specific code. This will isolate any necessary changes later.

Tom (holding the schedule card): So, I interact with database to get the data. Then I create the day object?

Ralph (holding the database card): Why don't you just ask me for the object you need? This will translate more cleanly to a design for an OO database. I will add this responsibility, "get day" object, to my card. I will check the DBMS to get the data and collaborate with day to create an object from the data.

Lisa (holding the day card): I will write "create" on my card. I need to create my associated room, a project room in this case. I collaborate with database for this.

Ralph: Right, and I get a project room by collaborating with the object project room.

Lisa (holding the project room card): I am using my "create" responsibility.

Ralph: Here you go — day.

Lisa: Next, I create my list of meetings for the day card, with a "know meetings" responsibility. Let us say that two meetings are scheduled for October 9 in this room. I will collaborate with database to get the meeting objects.

Ralph (holding the database card): I will collaborate with meeting here, twice, since the list might hold any kind of meeting.

Sy: Right, I will raise and lower my meeting card twice as I create the two meetings.

Ralph: There you go — day.

Lisa (holds up day card): I will talk to a list class of some sort — we will get one from a standard library that we buy — to add the meetings, with "know meetings" again. Then I am done.

Tom (holding up schedule card):   I will now display this day, collaborating with UI. The group decides to jump back into the original scenario to schedule a working meeting.

Ralph (holding user card):   Then I pick a time slot for my meeting.

Tom (holding schedule card):   I create a new meeting for this time slot, correct? But first, I need to get information from the user about type, size, contact, and equipment for this meeting.

Ralph: I enter 10 for "size" on the user card, "working meeting" as type, "User A" as contact, and "no equipment."

Tom: So I will write "working meeting" as my collaborator on the schedule card.

Sy: I will raise the meeting card while I "create" working meeting. I will use my "know start time," "know duration," "know contact," and "know size" responsibilities to record that information.

Tom (holding schedule card):   I will ask day to add the meeting to its list.

Lisa (holding the day card):   First, I will ask the meeting to schedule itself with my date and room.

Tom: The working meeting object's "schedule" responsibility means that it sets the date and room attributes — "know date and room" should do it. I should also "check room assignment." I will write that on my card. For this I need to collaborate with my conference room to see if it can handle me. Actually, I guess it is a project room in this scenario.

Lisa (holding us the project room card):   I will use my "know equipment" and "know capacity" responsibilities to see if I can handle this meeting. In this case, it is no problem. Any room can handle a working meeting.

Tom: Now that working meeting is scheduled, I can put my card down.

Lisa (holding up the day card):   I now add this meeting to my list and I am done.

Tom (holding up the schedule card):   And I wait to see what the user does next. I guess that is the next scenario.

The group decides to next do a similar scenario for a training session so they can begin to see what all meetings have in common. After that, they schedule a meeting requiring equipment. Eventually, they will model what happens when a user exits and data needs to be stored to the database.

When the scheduler group finishes executing all scenarios — normal and exceptional — and has a grasp on what each class should do, they split up the cards to begin prototyping in an OO programming language. The project is too small to bother with the overhead of a formal methodology, but they may use a commercial CRC card tool to record what they have done. A tool can be useful for documentation and to view collaboration patterns, which help refine the design as they go along. It does not, however, replace the sessions described.

SUMMARY

CRC cards are a useful and popular technique for doing OO design. The methodology is so simple that it does not overwhelm the modeling task, and the group interactions foster a creativeness in the participants that facilitates the brainstorming of good solutions. The sessions get the right people into the room and engage participants in dialog that uncovers the needs of the system.

The cards are also inexpensive, portable, flexible, and readily available. They do not feel as permanent as designs entered into a computer and can be freely added to or ripped up to rapidly revise designs and evaluate different approaches. This supports the iterative nature of object-oriented design and the essential part experimentation plays in all nontrivial software development.

Despite their simplicity, CRC cards actually capture the essential aspects of the design: classes, responsibilities, and the patterns of interactions of the objects of these classes. Because of this, they are not just a simple technique for introducing objects. They can be used effectively for real software development.

Chapter 44

Component Architectures: COM and CORBA

T.M. Rajkumar
David K. Holthaus

DATABASE TECHNOLOGIES HAVE EVOLVED from the hierarchical databases in the 1970s to relational database management systems in the 1980s and object databases and client/server systems in the 1990s. Although the shift from central processing to client/server did not fully leverage object technology, Internet-based technologies promise to provide the infrastructure for objects. Web-based browsers are poised to become the universal clients for all types of applications. These applications increasingly depend on components, automation, and object layers linking systems.

During the same period, it became less and less possible for software developers to quickly, efficiently, and inexpensively develop all of the functions and modules demanded by customers. Therefore, software development methodologies for Internet and Web applications are increasingly focused on component technologies. Component technology breaks the application into intrinsic components and then glues them to create an application. Using components, an application is easier to build, robust, and delivered quickly.

WHAT IS A COMPONENT?

A component is an independently delivered package of software services. A component is language independent and allows reuse in different language settings. Software components can be either bought from outside or developed in-house. Implementation requires that it must be possible to integrate them with other applications using standardized interfaces. They must efficiently implement the functionality specified in the interface. Components may be upgraded with new interfaces.

A component encapsulates methods (i.e., behavior) and data (i.e., attributes). Components must provide encapsulation, but inheritance is not as rigid a requirement. Components may include other components. Components do not necessarily have to be object-oriented, though a large majority of them are because it provides mechanisms to hide the data structure (i.e., encapsulation). Using objects makes components easier to understand and easier to create.

Components may be classified in many different ways. One such classification is based on their function within applications: business or technical components.

Business components usually include the logic that supports a business function or area. These must be developed in-house because it forms part of the core knowledge of an organization. In addition, the business knowledge required to create them generally does not exist outside. They are also difficult to develop because organizations must standardize in some manner. There must be a common vision for the organization, and a common architecture must be present to develop business components.

Technical components are represented by elements that are generic and can be used in a wide variety of business areas. These typically come in the form of GUI components, charting, or interapplication communication components.

A second classification is based on granularity of components. Fine-grained components such as class libraries and encapsulated components are typically small in size and are applicable in a wide range of applications. Although they have large reuse across multiple applications, they are close to code and provide limited productivity to a developer in large-scale applications.

Large-grained components provide broader functionality, but they must be customized for use. A framework is an example of a large-grained component. Frameworks provide two benefits: flow of control and object orientation. A framework is basically groupings of components packages or components that belong to a logically related set and together provide a service. They provide a substrate or lattice for other functional components, and a framework can be composed of other frameworks. They also provide the flow of control within components. This helps in the scale of the solution developed.

Object orientation of frameworks helps with the granularity of the components. Ideally, during the assembly stage, a small number of large components is optimal. However, to increase the generality of the solution created, a large number of small components is the ideal. Large components must be customized prior to delivering needed functionality. Frameworks allow developers to modify and reuse components at various levels of granularity. Frameworks are examples of "white-box" components (i.e., one can look inside the components to reuse them). With inheritance, the internals of parent classes are visible to subclasses in a framework. This provides a developer with flexibility to modify the behavior of a component. Thus, frameworks enable customization, allowing developers to build systems quickly using specialized routines.

Frameworks come in two categories: technical and business. Technical frameworks encapsulate software infrastructure such as the operating system, graphical user interface (GUI), object request broker (ORB), and transaction processing (TP) monitor. Microsoft Foundation Class (MFC) is an example of such a framework. Business frameworks contain the knowledge of the objects in a business model and the relationships between objects. Typically, they are used to build many different components or applications for a single industry. Technically, while not based on components, Enterprise Resource Planning (ERP) and software such as SAP are examples of business frameworks. An application is generally built with both technical and business frameworks (Exhibit 1).

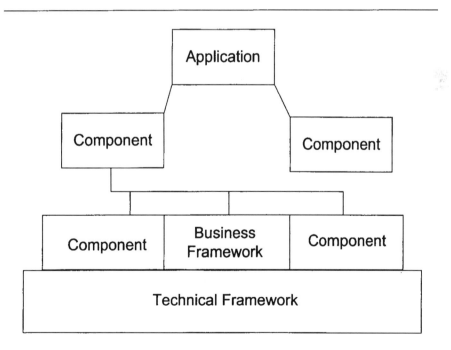

Exhibit 1.   Application integration with components.

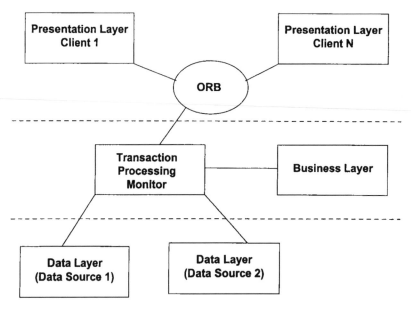

Exhibit 2. Three-layer client/server architecture.

CLIENT/SERVER COMPONENTS

Client/server systems typically use three tiers: presentation layer, business layer, and data or server layer (Exhibit 2). The objective behind the three tiers is to separate the business layer from the presentation and data layers. Changes in one layer are isolated within that layer and do not affect others. Within component technologies, the business layer communicates to the presentation layer and the data layer through an object bus, which is typically an object request broker (ORB). This layering makes the system very scalable.

An ORB is a standard mechanism through which distributed software objects and their clients may interact. Using an ORB, an object and its clients can reside on the same process or in a different process, which they can execute on different hosts connected by a network. The ORB provides the software necessary to convey the requests from clients to objects and responses from object to client. Since the ORB mechanism hides the details of specific locations, hosts, and conversion of data representation, and hides the underlying communication mechanism, objects and clients can interact freely without having to worry about many details. Thus, distributed applications can incorporate components written in different languages and are executable on different host and operating system platforms. This flexibility allows the data layer to be composed of legacy software and relational and object databases.

Business logic may reside on multiple server computers and data may reside on multiple servers. A TP monitor must be used to manage the business logic and to provide centralized control. A TP monitor also manages the logic on the servers by providing an array of mission-critical services such as concurrency, transactions and security, load balancing, transactional queues, and nested transactions. A TP monitor can prestart components, manage their persistent state, and coordinate their interactions across networks. TP monitors thus become the tool to manage smart components in a client/server system with components.

The real benefit of components in client/server applications is the ability to use the divide-and-conquer approach, which enables clients to scale through distribution. In this approach, an application is built as a series of ORBs. Since an ORB is accessible by any application running on a network, logic is centrally located. Developers can change the ORB to change the functionality of the application. If an ORB runs remotely, it can truly reflect a thin client. ORBs are portable and can be moved from platform to platform without adverse side effects to interoperability and provide for load balancing.

COMPONENT STANDARDS

Object models such as ActiveX, which is based on COM, CORBA, and Java Beans, define binary standards so that each individual component can be assembled independently. All component standards share the following common characteristics:

- A component interface publishing and directory system.
- Methods or actions invocable at runtime by a program.
- Events or notifications to a program in response to a change of state in an object.
- Support for object persistence (to store such information as the state of a component).
- Support for linking components into an application.

The following paragraphs describe each standard.

ActiveX, COM, and DCOM

ActiveX is based on COM technology, which formally separates interfaces and implementation. COM clients and objects speak through predefined interfaces. COM interfaces define a contract between a COM and its client. It defines the behavior or capabilities of a software component as a set of methods or properties. Each COM object may contain several different interfaces but must support at least one unknown. COM classes contain the bodies of code that implement interfaces. Each interface and COM class has a unique ID, IID, and CLSID that is used by a client to instantiate an object in a COM server. There are two types of object invocations:

1. In-process memory (DLLs), where a client and object share the same process space.
2. Out-of-process model, where a client and object live in different processes.

Clients can easily call either. A remoting layer makes the actual call invisible to a client. An ActiveX component is typically an in-process server. An actual object is downloaded to a client's machine. DCOM is COM extended for supporting objects across a network. DCOM allows objects to be freely distributed over several machines and allows a client to instantiate objects on remote machines.

CORBA

The Common Object Request Broker Architecture (CORBA) is a set of distributed system standards promoted by the Object Management Group, an industry standards organization. CORBA defines the ORB, a standard mechanism through which distributed software and their clients may interact. It specifies an extensive set of bus-related services for creating and deleting objects, accessing them by name, storing them in a persistent store, externalizing their states, and defining ad hoc relationships between them.

As illustrated in Exhibit 3, the four main elements of CORBA are

1. *ORBs*. This defines the object bus.
2. *Services*. These define the system-level object frameworks that extend the bus. Services include security, transaction management, and data exchange.
3. *Facilities*. These define horizontal and vertical application frameworks that are used directly by business objects.
4. *Application objects*. Also known as business objects or applications, these objects are created by software developers to solve business problems.

A Comparison of CORBA and DCOM

Both CORBA and DCOM use an interface mechanism to expose object functionalities. Interfaces contain methods and attributes as a common means of placing requests to an object. CORBA uses standard models of inheritance from object-oriented languages. DCOM/ActiveX uses the concept of multiple interfaces supported by a single object. DCOM requires that multiple inheritance be emulated through aggregation and containment of interfaces.

Another difference is the notion of object identity. CORBA defines the identity of an object in an object reference, which is unique and persistent. If the object is not in memory, it can be reconstructed based on the reference. DCOM, in contrast, defines the identity in the interface; the reference

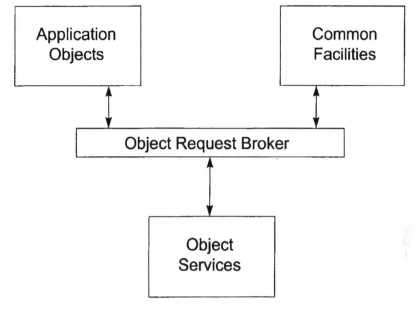

Exhibit 3.   CORBA architecture.

to the object itself is transient. This can lead to problems when reconnecting because the previously used object cannot be directly accessed.

Reference counting is also different in both. A DCOM object maintains a reference count of all connected clients. It uses pinging of clients to ensure that all clients are alive. CORBA does not need to do remote reference because its object reference model allows the recreation of an object if it had been prematurely deleted.

CORBA uses two application program interfaces (APIs) and one protocol for object requests. It provides the generated stubs for both static and dynamic invocation. In addition, a dynamic skeleton interface allows changes during runtime.

DCOM provides two APIs and two protocols. The standard interface is based on a binary interface that uses method pointer tables called *vtables*. The second API, object linking and embedding (OLE) automation, is used to support dynamic requests through scripting languages. OLE automation uses the IDispatch method to call the server.

CORBA is typically viewed as the middleware of choice for encapsulating legacy systems with new object-oriented interfaces, since it provides support for languages such as COBOL and mainframe systems. DCOM has its roots in desktop computing and is well supported there.

Java Beans

Java Beans enables the creation of portable Java objects that can interoperate with non-Java object systems. Unlike ActiveX, which predominately operates in Windows environments, Java Beans is intended to run in diverse environments as long as there exists a Java Virtual Machine that supports the Java Bean API. Java Beans provides the standard mechanisms present in all the component technologies. This standard is still continuing to evolve.

Comparison of Java and ActiveX

Java Beans has all the capabilities of a Java application. However, if one runs a version of Java Beans that has not been signed by a digital source, its capabilities are limited like any other applet. Java also has limited multimedia support. In contrast, ActiveX objects cannot run from the Web unless they are trusted and have access to all of the capabilities of Windows. Hence, ActiveX supports multimedia.

ActiveX and Java both use digitally signed certificates to protect against malicious attacks. In addition, Java Beans is available for a large number of machines and has cross-platform capability. ActiveX is most widely available on the Windows desktop.

Irrespective of the technology standard, bridges, available from different vendors, can translate between standards. Hence, organizations should choose a standard in which they have the greatest expertise for analysis, design, and development.

HOW TO DESIGN AND USE COMPONENTS

As shown in Exhibit 1, applications are built from the composition and aggregation of other simpler components, which may build on frameworks. Application design is broken into component and application development. Component development is divided into component design and implementation. A strong knowledge of an application's domain is necessary to develop frameworks and components. In general, the steps of domain definition, specification, design, verification, implementation, and validation must be done prior to application. The following sections explain these steps.

Domain Definition

This defines the scope, extent, feasibility, and cost justification for a domain. An organization must define the product it plans to build as well as the different business and technical areas that must be satisfied through the use of software.

Domain Specification

This defines the product family (i.e., framework) used for application engineering. It includes a decision model, framework requirements, and a hierarchy of component requirements. The decision model specifies how components will be selected, adapted, and reused to create complete application systems. Product requirements are assessed by analyzing similarities in functions, capabilities, and characteristics, as well as variances among them. The component part of the product family is represented hierarchically. When an organization considers components, it must consider not only what the component can do for the domain now, but also what it will do in the future.

Domain Design

A domain expert must work with the component designer to use a modeling methodology and extract the design patterns that occur in that domain. Design patterns are repeatable designs used in the construction of an application. The architecture, component design, and generation design are specified here. Architecture depicts a set of relationships among the components such as hierarchical, communication, and database. Component design describes the internal logic flow, data flows, and dependencies. Generation design is a procedure that describes how to select, adapt, and compose application systems using the decision model and architecture.

Domain Verification

This process evaluates the consistency of a domain's requirements, specification, and design.

Domain Implementation

During this procedure, components are either developed or acquired off the shelf to fit the architecture. Each component must be tested within the common architecture it supports as well as any potential architecture. Certification of components must be acquired when necessary. Determinations as to how to store it in repositories, the implementation of application generation procedures, and how to transition to an assembly mode must also be made.

Domain validation

This evaluates the quality and effectiveness of the application engineering support. Application engineering consists of the following:

- *Defining requirements.* In this process, an application model that defines a customer's requirements is defined. This model uses the notation specified in the domain engineering steps. Typically, a use-case model can be used to identify requirements. Use cases are behaviorally related sequences of transactions that a user of a system will perform in a dialog.

- *Selecting components and design.* Using rules in the decision model, reusable components are selected based on the component specification (capabilities and interfaces) and design (component logic and parameters).
- *Generating software.* The application is then generated by aggregating components and writing any custom software.
- *Testing.* Testing involves the testing of use cases, components, integration testing, and load testing.
- *Generating documentation.* The application documentation is created.

MANAGING THE COMPONENT LIFE CYCLE PROCESS

Developing with components means an organization must move from doing one-of-a-kind development to a reuse-driven approach. The aim is to reorganize the resources to meet users' needs with greater efficiency. The steps in this process are discussed in the following sections.

Establishing a Sponsor

This involves identifying component reuse opportunities and shows how their exploitation can contribute to an organization's IS goals. Sponsors must be identified and sold on the various ideas.

Developing a Plan

This plan should guide the management of the component development process. The plan includes the following:

1. *Reuse assessment.* This assessment should evaluate the potential opportunity for reuse, identify where the organization stands with respect to reuse, and evaluate the organization's reuse capability. Exhibits 4, 5, and 6 can be used to conduct the assessment.

Exhibit 4.   Assessment of Component Potential for Reuse

Concern	What to Ask
Domain potential	In the given domain, are there applications that could benefit from reuse?
Existing domain components	Are expertise and components available?
Commonalities and variables	Is there a sufficient fit between need and available components? Can they be customized?
Domain stability	Is the technology stable? Do the components meet stable standards? Are the components portable across environments?

Exhibit 5. Assessment of an Organization's Capability to Reuse Components Columns

Application Development	Component Development	Management	Process and Technology
Component identification for use in application	Needs identification, interface, and architecture definition	Organizational commitment, planning	Process definition and integration
Component evaluation and verification	Component needs and solutions	Managing security of components	Measurements and continuous process improvement
Application integrity	Component quality, value, security, and reusability determination	Intergroup (component and application coordination)	Repository tool support and training

2. *Development of alternative strategies.* On the basis of the assessment, an organization can develop a strategy to implement and align the process as well as choose the appropriate methodologies and tools.
3. *Development of metrics.* In the planning stage for implementation, metrics must be used to measure success.

Exhibit 6. Organizational Reuse Capability Model

Stage	Key Characteristics
Opportunistic	• Projects individually develop reuse plan • Existing components are reused • Throughout project life cycle, reuse of components is identified • Components under configuration and repository control
Integrated	• Reuse activities integrated into standard development process • Components are designed for current and anticipated needs • Common architectures and frameworks used for applications • Tools tailored for components and reuse
Leveraged	• An application-line reuse strategy is developed to maximize component reuse over a set of related applications • Components are developed to allow reuse early in the life cycle • Process performance is measured and analyzed • Tools supporting reuse are integrated with the organization's software development efforts
Anticipating	• New opportunities for reuse of components build on the organization's reuse capability • Effectiveness of reuse is measured • Organizations reuse method is flexible and can adapt to new process and product environment

Implementation

The organization finally implements the plan. Incentives can be used to promote reuse by individuals and the organization.

CONCLUSION

Component technology is changing the way client/server applications are being developed. Supporting tools for this software environment are rapidly emerging to make the transition from regular application development to component-based development. With proper training of staff, planning, and implementation, organizations can make a smooth transfer to this new mode of development and rapidly develop and efficiently deliver client/server applications.

Chapter 45

Using CORBA to Integrate Database Systems

Bhavani Thuraisingham
Daniel L. Spar

INTRODUCTION

INFORMATION HAS BECOME THE MOST CRITICAL RESOURCE IN MANY OR-
GANIZATIONS, and the rapid growth of networking and database technologies has had a major impact on information processing requirements.
Efficient access to information, as well as the capacity to share it, have become urgent needs. As a result, an increasing number of databases in different sites are being interconnected. In order to reconcile the contrasting
requirements of the different database management systems (DBMSs),
tools that enable users of one system to use another system's data are being developed. Efficient solutions for interconnecting and administering
different database systems are also being investigated.

There are two aspects to the object-oriented approach to integrating
heterogeneous database systems. In one approach, an object-oriented
data model could be used as a generic representation scheme so that the
schema transformations between the different database systems could be
facilitated. In the other approach, a distributed object management system
could be used to interconnect heterogeneous database systems. This article explores the distributed object management system approach by focusing on a specific distributed object management system: the object
management group's (OMG) CORBA.

INTEROPERABILITY ISSUES

Although research on interconnecting different DBMSs has been under
way for over a decade, only recently have many of the difficult problems
been addressed. Through the evolution of the three-tier approach to cli-

0-8493-9976-9/99/$0.00+$.50
© 1999 by CRC Press LLC

ent/server, the capability of integrating DBMSs has improved significantly. The traditional two-tier client/server approach included the layers of Client and Server.

For small systems, the two-tier approach works reasonably well. For larger systems with greater numbers of connected clients and servers, and greater levels of complexity and requirements for security, there is a substantial need for three-tier architectures. Two-tier systems are notorious for their development of the "fat client," where excessive amounts of code running business logic is required to be loaded on to the client machine.

The three-tier approach breaks client/server components into the layers of:

1. Client (presentation layer)
2. Middleware (business logic)
3. Server (data and resource management)

The result is much more efficient use of resources, and greater plug and play capabilities for both clients and servers. Clients can be super-thin browsers running Java applets, and servers can be efficiently integrated and load-balanced.

With the advent of Web servers, the three tier model becomes "n-tier" since a web server is often placed between the client and middleware layers.

Schema Heterogeneity. Not all of the databases in a heterogeneous architecture are represented by the same schema (data model). Therefore, the different conceptual schemas have to be integrated. In order to do this, translators that transform the constructs of one schema into those of another are being developed. Integration remains most difficult with the older legacy databases that are pre-relational.

Transaction Processing Heterogeneity. Different DBMSs may use different algorithms for transaction processing. Work is being directed toward integrating the various transaction processing mechanisms. Techniques that integrate locking, timestamping, and validation mechanisms are being developed. However, strict serializability may have to be sacrificed in order to create a heterogeneous environment. Independent transaction processing monitor (TP monitor) software is now readily available in the distributed systems marketplace. TP monitor software has been used for years on mainframes, and is now of great assistance in high volume systems such as Internet commerce. Examples include Web-based stock brokerage trading sites.

Query Processing Heterogeneity. Different DBMSs may also use different query processing and optimization strategies. Research is being conducted to develop a global cost model for distributed query optimization.

Query Language Heterogeneity. Query language heterogeneity should also be addressed, even if the DBMSs are based on the relational model. Structured query language (SQL) and relational calculus could be used to achieve heterogeneity. Standardization efforts are underway to develop a uniform interface language.

Constraint Heterogeneity. Different DBMSs enforce different integrity constraints, which are often inconsistent. For example, one DBMS could enforce a constraint that all employees must work at least 40 hours, even though another DBMS may not enforce such a constraint. Moving these business rules over to the application servers on the middle tier and away from the DBMSs on the third tier will also help isolate and correct business rule inconsistencies.

Semantic Heterogeneity. Data may be interpreted differently by different components. For example, the entity address could represent just the country for one component, or it could represent the number, street, city, and country for another component. This problem will be difficult to resolve in older systems that combined multiple domains in a single database field, and often assigned cryptic names to tables and fields that do not reveal their content.

THE COMMON OBJECT REQUEST BROKER ARCHITECTURE (CORBA)

CORBA was created to provide an object-based central layer to enable the objectives of three-tier distributed systems, especially in the area of interoperability.

The three major components of CORBA are the object model, the object request broker (ORB) and object adapters, and the interface definition language (IDL).

The Object Model

The object model describes object semantics and object implementation. Object semantics describe the semantics of an object, type, requests, object creation and destruction, interfaces, operations, and attributes. Object implementation describes the execution model and the construction model. In general, the object model of CORBA has the essential constructs of most object models.

The Object Request Broker (ORB)

The ORB essentially enables communication between a client and a server object. A client invokes an operation on the object, and the object implementation provides the code and data needed to implement the object. The ORB provides the necessary mechanisms to find the object implementation for a particular request and enables the object implementation

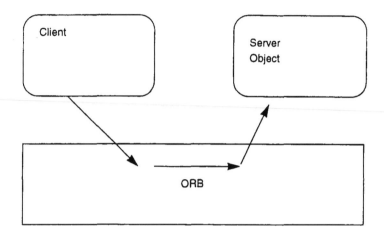

Exhibit 1.   Communication through an Object Request Broker (ORB).

to receive the request. The communication mechanisms necessary to deliver the request are also provided by the ORB.

In addition, the ORB supports the activation and deactivation of objects and their implementations as well as generating and interpreting object references. Although the ORB provides the mechanisms to locate the object and communicate the client's request to the object, the exact location of the object, as well as the details of its implementation, are transparent to the client. Objects use object adapters to access the services provided by the ORB. Communication between a client and a server object using the ORB is illustrated in Exhibit 1.

INTERFACE DEFINITION LANGUAGE (IDL)

IDL is the language used to describe the interfaces that are called by client objects and provided by object implementations. IDL is a declarative language; client and object implementations are not written in IDL. IDL grammar is a subset of ANSI C++ with additional constructs to support the operation invocation mechanism. An IDL binding to the C language has been specified, and other language bindings are being processed. Exhibit 2 illustrates how IDL is used for communication between a client and a server. The client's request is passed to the ORB using an IDL stub. An IDL skeleton delivers the request to the server object.

INTEGRATING HETEROGENEOUS DATABASE SYSTEMS

Migrating legacy databases to new generation architectures is difficult. Although it is desirable to migrate such databases and applications to cli-

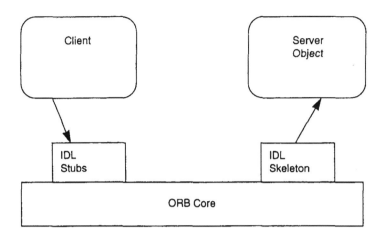

Exhibit 2. **Interface Definition Language (IDL) interface to Object Request Broker (ORB).**

ent/server architectures, the costs involved in many cases are enormous. Therefore, the alternative approach is to keep the legacy databases and applications and develop mechanisms to integrate them with new systems. The distributed object management system approach in general, and the CORBA approach in particular, are examples of such mechanisms.

Although the major advantage of the CORBA approach is the ability to encapsulate legacy database systems and databases as objects without having to make any major modifications (Exhibit 3), techniques for handling the various types of heterogeneity are still necessary. The CORBA approach does not handle problems such as transaction heterogeneity and semantic heterogeneity. However, the procedures used to handle the types of heterogeneity can be encapsulated in the CORBA environment and invoked appropriately.

Handling Client Communications with the Server

A client will need to communicate with the database servers, as shown in Exhibit 4. One method is to encapsulate the database servers as objects. The clients can issue appropriate requests and access the servers through an ORB. If the servers are SQL-based, then the entire SQL query/update request could be embedded in the message. When the method associated with the server object gets the message, it can extract the SQL request and pass it to the server. The results from the server objects are then encoded as a message and passed back to the client through the ORB. This approach is illustrated in Exhibit 5.

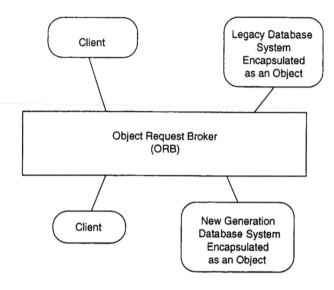

Exhibit 3.   Encapsulating legacy databases.

Handling Heterogeneity

Different types of heterogeneity must be handled in different ways. For example, if the client is SQL-based and the server is a legacy database system based on the network model, then the SQL query by the client must be transformed into a language understood by the server. One representation scheme must be transformed into another. The client's request must first

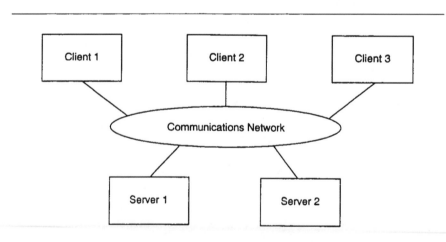

Exhibit 4.   Client/server architecture.

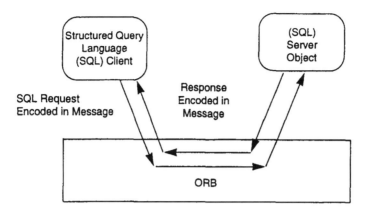

Exhibit 5. **Common Object Request Broker Architecture (CORBA) for interoperability.**

be sent to the module that is responsible for performing the transformations. In this module the transformer could be encapsulated as an object. As illustrated in Exhibit 6, the client's SQL request is sent to the transformer, which transforms the request into a request understood by the server. The transformed request is then sent to the server object. The transformer could directly transform the SQL representation into a network represen-

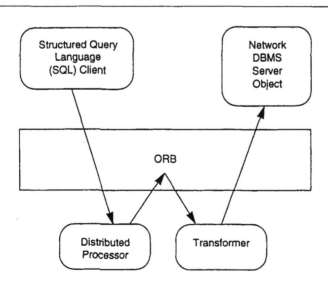

Exhibit 6. **Handling transformations.**

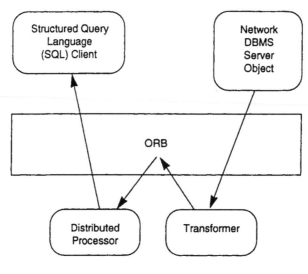

Exhibit 7. Delivering responses.

tation, or it could use an intermediate representation to carry out the transformation.

Handling Transformations

The distributed processor could also be used to perform distributed data management functions. The distributed processor is responsible for handling functions such as global query optimization and global transaction management. This module is also encapsulated as an object and handles the global requests and responses. The response assembled by the server is also sent to the transformer to transform into a representation understood by the client. Response delivery is illustrated in Exhibit 7.

Semantic Heterogeneity. If semantic heterogeneity has to be handled, then a repository should be maintained to store the different names given to a single object or the different objects represented by a single name. The repository could be encapsulated as an object that would resolve semantic heterogeneity. For example, a client could request that an object be retrieved from multiple servers. The request is first sent to the repository, which issues multiple requests to the appropriate servers depending on the names used to denote the object. This approach is illustrated in Exhibit 8. The response may also be sent to the repository so that it can be presented to the client in an appropriate manner. The repository could be an extension of the transformer illustrated in Exhibit 6. All the communications are carried out through the ORB. This example highlights some of the benefits of separating the business logic from the actual data stored in the DBMS servers.

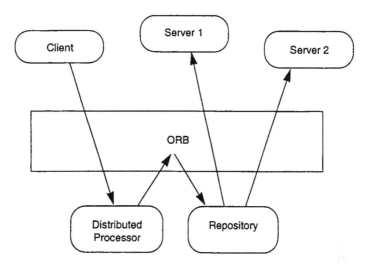

Exhibit 8.   Handling semantic heterogeneity.

CONCLUSION

The rapid growth in distributed systems has placed two key demands on IT managers:

1. How can the most efficient and effective design — the three-tier model — best be implemented to manage a very heterogeneous environment; and
2. How can the semantic meaning of the legacy data elements be best understood so they can be shared across systems.

The CORBA approach is an excellent means of addressing heterogeneity especially with respect to queries, languages, transactions, schemas, constraints, and semantics. However, although CORBA is useful for integrating heterogeneous database systems, there are still several issues that need further consideration. For example, should a server be encapsulated as an object? How can databases be encapsulated? Should an entire database be encapsulated as an object or should it consist of multiple objects? Should stored procedures be encapsulated also?

Although there is still much work to be done, the various approaches proposed to handle these issues show a lot of promise. Furthermore, until efficient approaches are developed to migrate the legacy databases and applications to client/server-based architectures, approaches like CORBA and other distributed object management systems for integrating heterogeneous databases and systems are needed.

Chapter 46
Distributed Objects and Object Wrapping
Hedy Alban

ADVANCES IN SYSTEMS INTEGRATION OVER THE PAST DECADE have resolved connectivity issues at lower layers of the Open Systems Interconnection (OSI) network model. Solutions exist for connecting systems at the hardware level or the transport level. Communications networks, phone lines, cables, and fiber are available to connect systems to local area or wide area networks, hubs, and switches. Connectivity between most operating system platforms is similarly available.

Data sharing among disparate platforms and applications largely is resolved as well. The common architectural features among relational database management systems (DBMSs) enable middleware products to mix and match data from heterogeneous sources, and SQL Access interfaces allow nonrelational data architectures to participate as well.

A variety of replication techniques can enhance access. New and better solutions for data reconciliation among platforms come to market almost daily. A similar variety of approaches is available for preserving transaction integrity in distributed environments.

Although integration solutions are available in the lower layers of the OSI networking model, analogous interoperability at the application level remains elusive. Processing routines are locked into specific applications environments and cannot be invoked except through that specific application. Stored procedures are buried within the proprietary languages of DBMS products, uninvoked during heterogeneous data access, so that they cannot deliver on their promise of universality and consistency. Object-oriented programming fares no better; object systems are not compatible with one another.

As a result, a vast treasure of useful intelligence is trapped within specific contexts. Imagine that the fastest routine for cursor movement was devised for a vertical application that caters to a small number of users. Theoretically, such a function could revolutionize the user interface for other applications that are installed on the same machine or network; however, it may be trapped inside the specific vertical application and remain unavailable for use in other applications. Thus, the customer actually owns an outstanding capability but cannot put it to use except in a very small context.

Sometimes, the dependence of individual processing routines on the proprietary applications that contain them cripples the very mechanisms that have been built up over the years to impose consistency and administrative order at the application level. For example, stored procedures contain processing routines that consistently should be enforced each time a data element is accessed. They are a means for enforcing business rules such as maximum credit limits, ensuring consistent enforcement no matter what application accessed them.

Unfortunately, however, the language of stored procedures is proprietary to each DBMS. When a developer tries to write a multivendor DBMS application or a user tries to access multiple DBMSs through a query tool, the stored procedures fall by the wayside and consistent enforcement disappears.

For these reasons, then, application interoperability is regarded widely as the next step in the evolution toward enterprise-wide networking capability. The requirement is for cooperation among heterogeneous equipment and software applications that are installed currently.

ACHIEVING MULTIPOINT CONNECTIVITY

At present, the remote procedure call (RPC) is the most common technology for application-level interoperability. RPC is the favored technique for implementing cross-platform DBMS stored procedures. It is the mechanism chosen for the Distributed Computing Environment (DCE) architecture promoted by the Open Software Foundation, and the basis for the Sun Solaris network file server (NFS). Currently, there is not a more robust approach than DCE for heavy production environments. It is not the best theoretical answer, but it is the most mature of the developed distributed approaches.

Nevertheless, RPCs are not optimal for many enterprise solutions because they are point-to-point solutions. They are able to connect an individual application with another. As the network becomes more complicated, however, a more comprehensive solution is required.

With a more comprehensive solution and with broad multipoint connectivity throughout the network, it will be possible to enforce business rules consistently, to locate data consistently, to reuse helpful routines in multiple contexts, and to consistently apply application routines to the data.

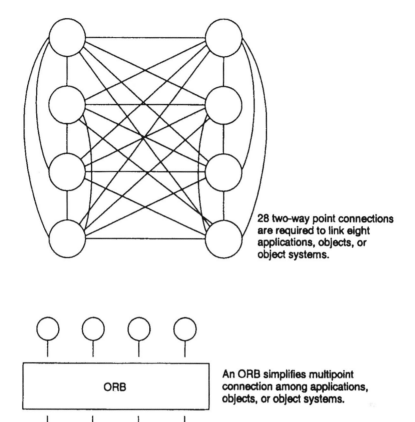

28 two-way point connections are required to link eight applications, objects, or object systems.

An ORB simplifies multipoint connection among applications, objects, or object systems.

Exhibit 1.   Point-to-point vs. multipoint connectivity.

Many theorists and practitioners believe that distributed object technology provides the solution for these problems. Distributed object technology promises to overcome the current obstacles to enterprise-wide client/server implementation. The object request broker (ORB), the engine of a distributed object environment, provides a universal layer for multipoint connectivity (Exhibit 1). The RPC mechanism and the object request broker are explained and contrasted in this chapter and in Exhibit 2.

WHAT ARE DISTRIBUTED OBJECTS?

Distributed objects represent the next generation of client/server facilities. In this context, an object is a chunk of code that represents a business

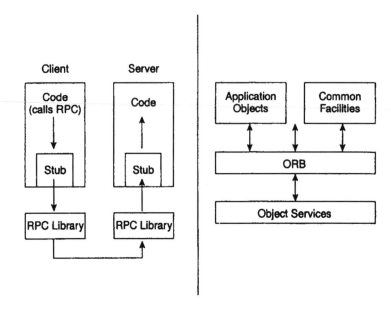

Exhibit 2. RPC vs. ORB

function. A distributed object is an object that can be accessed from anywhere on a network, across platforms, programming languages, and application systems.

Distributed object computing allows developers to build applications as a series of components or services that can be designed and stored across a network and brought together only when needed to perform a specific business function. Developers essentially snap together complex client/server systems simply by assembling and extending reusable distributed objects. A systems builder could select objects from several vendors and connect them as easily as audio components are connected at home today. Individual programming modules (objects) would exist independent of the application for which they were created, free for recombination with other modules in new contexts and for new applications. With distributed object computing, component developers and users can locate code without knowing its location in advance.

Outgrowth of Compound Document Applications

Distributed object technology appeared first in compound document applications. Compound documents contain more than one data format — for example, they may contain a combination of text, charts, and graphical material.

In early practice (which continues, for the most part, even today), each component was created in the tool most appropriate for it (e.g., text in a word processor, charts in a spreadsheet, and graphics in a drawing program) and then assembled into a single whole, usually in a desktop publishing package. To edit the document, users would access the appropriate component via its source application (i.e., the spreadsheet) and then reassemble the edited components into the complete document.

With the advent of distributed object technology, returning to the source application became unnecessary; each component of the document came with its own tools for editing and manipulating it. Thus, for example, the creator could edit a spreadsheet within the same environment that he or she edited the text or drawing. In Microsoft parlance, the compound document is created in a container application that accepts component processing modules from various applications; the function of the component modules appears to the user as selections in a menu bar.

For compound documents, the convenience to the end user of application integration is obvious and important. The significance of application integration goes far beyond this specific application, however. The true significance of application integration comes forth in a networked environment, where it comes into play for the administration and maintainability of the system. It also dovetails with other current practices, like business rules and stored procedures and maintaining consistency across the enterprise.

OBJECT-ORIENTED PROGRAMMING AND DISTRIBUTED OBJECTS

Object orientation is becoming increasingly popular for the benefits of code reuse, adaptability, and the ability to make the computer environment look and feel like the real world as never before. In the context of object-oriented programming, an object generally is defined as a software entity that contains both data and the processing code to manipulate that data.

By definition, classical software objects possess the qualities of inheritance, polymorphism, and encapsulation (although the details of these terms are irrelevant to this discussion). A distributed object, in contrast, is defined and evaluated in terms of its context independence — that is, its ability to function independent of the application (e.g., context) from which it was created.

Therefore, a distributed object need not possess the qualities of the classical software object; instead, it may be a standard sequence of coded statements that are isolated and enveloped in such a way as to become available for interaction with other objects. In modern parlance, a software module can be transformed into a distributed object by encapsulating it in

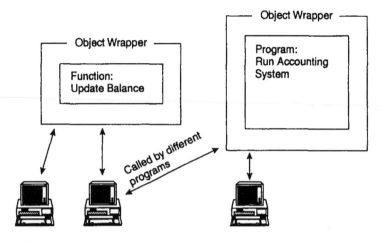

Note:
Large or small objects can be encapsulated in a "wrapper" for modular use.

Exhibit 3.   Object with wrapper.

---

a wrapper (Exhibit 3), thereby exposing it to other distributed objects on the network.

Once a software module is transformed into an object, it can be accessed and executed as if it were a primitive. Object programmers and users no longer view the module or its code. Instead, they view the object as a basic computing element. They manipulate the object itself, not its internals.

Object Wrapping

The chief mechanism for integrating legacy applications into the distributed object environment is wrapping. The simplest form of wrapper, with which most readers are familiar, is the Windows icon. A user can access a DOS application within a Windows environment simply by clicking on its icon. In this situation, the icon is the wrapper for the DOS application, permitting it to be treated like a Windows application; the internals of the application, however, function like a DOS program and not a Windows program.

Technically speaking, it is possible to convert an entire application into a single object by this means. All applications can be converted into distributed objects by this means. Optimally, however, conversion to distributed objects exposes individual application components in a more granular way.

Most applications require a better level of integration, where individual functions of an application are made universally available within the object environment. For example, a programmer might wish to integrate the data access routines of one application into the user interface of another application. The original access routine performs unchanged, but as a whole the routine will be merged into a second application. To accomplish this, the programmer must wrap the required routine and then make it accessible (i.e., expose it) to other objects in the environment.

Wrapping is possible only when clear boundaries exist between objects. In other words, the distributed object must contain all information required for the computer to execute it. In the previous example, if the original application were written in a modular fashion, then it will be easier to isolate the routine for integration into the new application. But even so, the process is not really a clean-cut one.

A typical application, even if it is well-written, modular, and well-organized, will still have dependencies among various portions of the code. At the very least, the definition of variables and working storage areas are defined outside a programming module. The wrapper must accommodate this to operate.

Bridging Legacy and Distributed Object Environments. An object wrapper serves as an interoperability bridge between the legacy system and the object environment. On one side of the bridge, the wrapper links up to legacy system's existing communication facilities. On the other side of the bridge, the wrapper defines the legacy system to the object environment, exposing it within the object environment and bringing specific services, such as security.

During the process of object wrapping, a development team may decide to perform other system enhancements at the same time. For example, an installation may collect metadata at the same time that it performs its analysis for object wrapping, preparing the system for future maintenance projects. Reverse engineering may be in order, or data migration into a more modern DBMS architecture. Sometimes, object wrapping may be used to subdivide a large project into modules with clear boundaries, for future enhancements on a component-by-component basis.

Each legacy system presents a unique integration problem with its own constraints. Some legacy systems may have no API at all, and others may have an extensive proprietary API. Access mechanisms can be sockets, RPCs, or something else. The object wrapper hides these idiosyncracies and presents a consistent and clear interface.

Object wrapping occurs when an organization migrates existing applications into a distributed object environment. During this process, it is wise to seek a path that avoids extensive software rewriting. It is also wise to keep the target environment firmly in mind, to choose wrappers that conform to a set standard so that objects will interoperate once the task is complete.

Wrapping Techniques. Wrapping greatly simplifies and empowers client/server computing. Individual objects within the system are inconsistent internally but, given a uniform interface, can interoperate seamlessly. Some techniques for wrapping include:

- *Layering*: Layering is a basic form of wrapping wherein one form of API is mapped onto another. For example, one can layer a CORBA-based interface over RPC services. This technique is applicable where the existing object already has a clearly defined API and well-defined services.
- *Encapsulation*: Encapsulation is a general form of object wrapping where the original code remains largely intact. An encapsulation is a black box where only the input and the output are revealed externally; underlying implementation is hidden. Encapsulation separates interface from implementation. Encapsulation is a convenient way to wrap legacy systems where source code is inaccessible or nonexistent.
- *Object gateways*: Object gateways implement the most generic form of encapsulation and are used in worst-case situations, where the legacy system provides no API, no access to code, and no scripting interface. With this form of wrapping, all processing occurs within the closed system using that system's menus, user interface, and toolset. The user interacts with the application using the facilities provided by the legacy system. Object gateways can be handy tools for quickly loading multiple legacy applications unchanged into the new object environment.

OBJECT REQUEST BROKERS

The object request broker (ORB) is the engine of the distributed object environment, enabling communication among objects both locally and across the network. ORBs can make requests to other ORBs and can process responses. They hide all differences between programming languages, operating systems, object location, and other physical information that is required for interobject and internetwork communication. All these processes happen behind the scenes, hidden from the user and the client/server application.

Common Object Request Broker Architecture (CORBA)

CORBA is a specification for an object-oriented universal middleware that supports application interoperability in three-tier client/server environments (Exhibit 4). CORBA-compliant tools permit objects to communicate with one another, even if they reside on different platforms and are written in different languages using different data formats. The CORBA

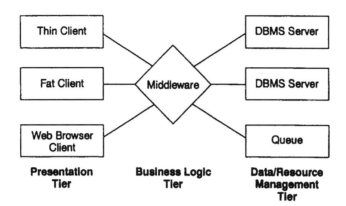

Exhibit 4.   Three-tier client/server architecture.

specification provides a language for multiple object systems to communicate with one another.

CORBA Specifications and Implementation. CORBA-compliant products provide a uniform layer encapsulating other forms of distributed computing and integration mechanisms. CORBA can accept many different implementations.

The RPC, which is the basis for interprocess communication under DCE, is one implementation model. Message-oriented middleware (MOM) is another implementation. Some vendors, like Iona Technologies, are basing CORBA on Open Network Computing (ONC)-compatible RPCs. Other vendors, such as Hewlett-Packard, are using OSF/DCE; some others, like Sun-Soft, are bypassing the RPC layer and implementing CORBA at low layers. CORBA is designed to accept all of these models as well as future solutions that might arise. CORBA-compliant software completes the interoperability task through well-defined interface specifications at the application level.

CORBA defines a high-level facility for distributed computing, the object request broker (ORB). CORBA is a specification for creating ORBs. The ORB functions as a communication infrastructure, transparently relaying object requests across distributed heterogeneous computing environments.

CORBA also defines an Interface Definition Language (IDL), a technology-independent language for encapsulating routines. A universal notation for defining software boundaries, IDL, can be mapped to any programming language. Mappings to C, C++, and Smalltalk, as approved by the Object

Management Group (OMG), are currently available. The mapping is contained within the header files of IDL.

Finally, CORBA includes a set of specifications for common facilities, object services, and application objects. Common facilities define high-level services such as printing and E-mail. Object services define lower-level services such as object creation, event notification, and security. Application objects are all other software, including developer's programs, commercial applications, and legacy systems.

The Object Transaction Service (OTS) subspecification of CORBA is of particular interest to database programmers. OTS defines how atomic transactions can be distributed over multiple objects and multiple ORBs. OTS was designed to interact simultaneously with both ORB-based and traditional TP monitor-based transaction services. OTS can support recoverable nested transactions, even in a heterogeneous environment, that fully support ACID and two-phase commit protocols. OTS is based on technology developed by Transarc Corp., inventors of the Encina transaction processor, which usually functions on top of their DCE product.

Typically, commercial ORB products provide facilities for creating objects and wrappers. The developer first creates an object and defines its boundaries. The developer then submits this IDL code to the ORB product. The compiler in the product translates the IDL code into the target language (e.g., C++). The compiler generates the header files, stubs, and skeleton programs for each interface, exposing the object to other objects within the environment. In an environment where objects use OMG IDL interfaces and are otherwise CORBA-compliant, these objects discover each other at run time and invoke each other's services.

Note that CORBA is a specification, not an actual product. It does not deliver an accompanying reference implementation (i.e., source code) in the way that DCE and UNIX do. Furthermore, CORBA specifies only interfaces among objects; it does not define the object system itself.

Individual vendors build their own products and their own ORBs. CORBA-compliant ORBs interoperate with one another as long as they are referencing version 2 of the CORBA specification. (The various releases of version 1 are too general to guarantee interoperability.) Most object vendors provide developer support for implementing linked library code using OMG IDL interfaces.

Significance of the CORBA Standard. The significance of CORBA will grow as object-oriented systems gather critical mass within the corporate information resource. At present, many corporations already have begun pilot projects and small-scale systems using object technology. They may be working with VBX and OLE 2.0 in the context of their desktop workstations, exploring Internet and intranet applications using Java, and developing some applications with C++ as well. Right now these environments operate as discrete units, but dependencies among them are inevitable. What will bind them together?

Point-to-point solutions provide a quick fix but add complexity to the system. A standard such as CORBA is required if systems builders are to create a flexible, layered structure for connectivity between object systems and avoid point-to-point connectivity. In point-to-point connectivity, one object system requires a specific protocol to connect with, for example, Microsoft's DCOM (Distributed Component Object Model), another to connect with Java, a third to connect with IBM's System Object Model (SOM), and so on. True, it is faster and easier to create point solutions to satisfy immediate requirements, but the market must keep the long view in mind as well.

Fortunately, several of the products just mentioned do indeed comply with CORBA. The only way that a rational format for interoperability will take place is through market pressure. If customers insist on CORBA compliance, then vendors will deliver it; if not, then CORBA will die.

Distributed Computing Environment (DCE)

The Distributed Computing Environment (DCE) provides the means and the tools to transform a group of networked computers into a single coherent computing engine. It is a large and complex middleware product that enables communication among multiple heterogeneous platforms, masking differences among computer platforms. It enables the development of distributed applications that make optimal use of existing computer resources such as storage devices, CPUs, and memory.

DCE enables cooperation among these computer resources and, at the same time, provides tools to deal with such problems as data protection, time and event synchronization, reconciliation of data formats and file-naming schemes among platforms, and so on. An appropriately configured DCE environment allows end users to access multiple computers with a single log-on and to access remote data with the same ease that they access local data.

DCE can be described in terms of its benefits to the end user, the programmer, and the network administrator.

DCE's Benefits for the Network Administrator. DCE provides facilities for organizing an enterprise into administrative units (called cells) and then creating directory services to help programs locate resources within this organization. Following installation, network administrators can move files from one location to another without modifying programs or notifying users.

DCE delivers the following features:

- Multihost replication of files and applications, so that programs can continue to operate even when systems go down and servers are moved around.
- DCE Security Service for cross-system protection by means of authentication.
- DCE Distributed File Server (DFS) for tracking programs and data when they are moved from one computer to another, so that programs need not be recompiled with the new address and users need not be aware of the move.
- DCE Directory Service for look-up capability, so that users and applications can communicate with people and resources anywhere in the network without knowing their physical location.

Although not itself object-oriented, the Distributed Computing Environment can support interoperability among different object strategies. For example, DCE can provide a transport layer above which ORBs communicate with one another. In fact, DCE provides explicit support for ORBs through its DCE Common InterORB protocol.

DCE's Benefits for the Programmer. For applications developers, DCE provides the RPC and threads.

Remote Procedure Calls. The remote procedure call is a mechanism for interprocess communication that ties the client and server application code together. It handles the lower levels of interprocess connectivity, shielding the programmers from the details of that connection. It performs data conversion and manages all lower-level aspects of communication and, when programmed to do so, provides automatic recovery from network or server failure.

The RPC invisibly hides the differences in data formats between heterogeneous computers, reconciling differences in byte ordering, data formats, and padding between data items. It hides these differences by converting data to the appropriate forms needed by the destination system.

To integrate legacy applications into the DCE environment, the programmer can wrap the application with an interface definition. The wrapped application will be available within the DCE environment to all supported systems, but it must be rewritten into a client/server style (i.e., it must be rewritten in modular fashion or given a client/server interface through a DCE-compatible screen scraper or similar tool) to reap the benefits of distributed computing.

Threads. DCE threads enhance performance by allowing the programmer to specify threads for the purposes of task separation and task division. In task separation, the programmer can designate slow-moving tasks (e.g., routines that require user input or retrieval from a slow data storage device) to be performed in a separate thread, so that the flow of the application can continue simultaneously with the slow operation. In task division, a large task can be broken into several smaller tasks and assigned to different processors.

DCE's Benefits for the End User. The end user on a DCE system enjoys the benefits of distributed computing often without being aware of it. In a well-implemented DCE environment, the end user experiences better performance when the workload is better distributed among available resources. The end user also derives benefit from the client/server application that permits a more user-friendly interface and greater end-user autonomy in accessing corporate data. Finally, the end user experiences reduced downtime as a result of DCE's high-availability features. DCE permits access to the entire distributed environment with one log-on.

DCE and CORBA Contrasted

DCE and CORBA share a similar concept of the distributed enterprise, promising a seamless distributed computing environment with transparent interoperability among applications. They share concepts, some facilities, and even terminology. They are so similar, in fact, that many regard CORBA as the next generation of DCE.

In many ways CORBA and DCE are complementary. They are also remarkably similar in the way that they work. Both are developed by a consortium of vendors: DCE is promoted by the Open Software Foundation (OSF); CORBA is endorsed by the Object Management Group (OMG). Both depend on the consensus of their members, and both evaluate technologies that are submitted by their members for adoption. The overlap in membership between the two organizations could explain their remarkable similarity in concept.

Important differences exist as well, as summarized in Exhibit 5.

Exhibit 5. Differences Between CORBA and DCE

CORBA	DCE
Object-based	Nonobject-based
Provides specifications for interfaces only	RPC provides complete specifications and source code for the network computing system
Not yet a fully implemented specification	High level of product maturity and robustness for large-scale, high-security, heavy-transaction systems
Addresses OSI application layer	Addresses OSI presentation and session layers

OSI Model Support. Most important, CORBA and DCE address different layers of the OSI model, and they express the application environment at different levels of abstraction. In fact, CORBA and DCE are considered complementary precisely because they address different layers of the OSI seven-layer mode.

CORBA addresses the application layer of the OSI model, whereas DCE addresses the presentation and session layers. Therefore, DCE contains a lot of the lower-layer information and processing that is necessary for system interoperability to take place.

CORBA, in contrast, does not deal with these low-level details at all. Instead, it specifies a mechanism by which objects can interoperate, even if they are built on disparate low-level processes. CORBA's aim is to provide interfaces between objects so that they can interoperate. CORBA works at the application layer, reconciling incompatibilities between two or more object-oriented systems so that the objects deriving from two or more development systems will interoperate.

A derivative benefit of this application-level interoperability is simplicity or, in analyst jargon, abstraction. CORBA specifications require programmers to examine applications and functions at a higher level of abstraction than any other tool for distributed computing. This high level of abstraction makes it easier for people to grasp the big picture. It insulates the programmer and user from technical details of the computer environment. The resulting applications are flexible, adaptable to change and new technologies, as well as to layering and a divide-and-conquer approach to applications development and reengineering.

Furthermore, CORBA adds a comprehensive layer of support for object-oriented programming. Specifically, it aims to provide interoperability among different object systems. Its primary purpose is to deliver interORB interoperability.

CONCLUSION

Many analysts have jumped on the object bandwagon, proclaiming object-oriented programming to be the breakthrough technology that will enable the industry to upgrade software as quickly as hardware. Like many technologies that are excellent in theory, however, the upfront effort for large-scale conversion is enormous. A golden rule is always to balance theory and practice.

To move from current information structure into the object paradigm requires a enormous rewrite of all code. Although object wrappers could provide a quick fix, wrapped objects do not provide the full benefit of more granular objects.

At the same time, object technology is penetrating every organization, at least to some degree. This is because the technology is infiltrating off-the-shelf applications software, especially at the client level. Similarly, object technology likely will become the norm for developing applications to run on the ubiquitous Internet, where upfront reengineering costs do not come into play and infrastructure issues are predefined largely.

Given the inevitably of object orientation, it is important for object systems work together. A standard for interoperability at the application level, like CORBA, is a necessity.

Nevertheless, CORBA has traveled a rocky road. CORBA had a bad reputation from its initial release. OMG members with different interests slowed down consensus. Because of these delays, many vendors implemented their products ahead of the specification and later were reluctant to retrofit their work for the sake of compliance. In addition, the public was slow to understand the benefits of CORBA beyond DCE. Probably most important, CORBA's viability was shaky because Microsoft products, which account for 80% of the object market, are noncompliant.

Vendors and users seem, at last, to be rallying around CORBA. The growth of the Internet probably has a strong role here — as the market takes off, vendors perceive an opportunity and are more likely to cooperate. They also need the compliance to enhance their own marketability. CORBA has won Microsoft's support for moving its DCOM object infrastructure into compliance with CORBA.

In conclusion, object technology and distributed objects may not be the cure-all for distributed computing issues, but when combined with other integration strategies — most notably the Internet — it can become a practical solution for many specific applications. With a growing market for object technology and Microsoft support in hand, the outlook for CORBA looks better than ever.

Section VIII
Distributed Databases, Portability, and Interoperability

DISTRIBUTED DATABASES ARE FAIRLY COMMON IN CLIENT/SERVER APPLI-
CATIONS. The popularity of the Internet and the World Wide Web make
these even more common. This section looks at various aspects of distributed databases. It also examines system portability and interoperability.

Chapter 47, "Software Architectures for Distributed DBMSs in a Cli-
ent/Server Environment," provides an overview of the capabilities of various software components of distributed DBMSs so that DBAs can select an
architecture to support the features they want.

Chapter 48, "Distributed Database Design," provides an overview of distributed database system concepts, client/server technology, homogeneous distributed database systems, heterogeneity, architectural aspects,
and standards. In addition, the status of commercial products and their
limitations are discussed.

Chapter 49, "Database Gateways and Interoperability," describes issues
on interoperating migrated database systems with the legacy environment.
In the evolutionary migration approach of legacy databases, parts of database are migrated, but access to the legacy environment still is required.
Therefore, gateways are needed for the interoperability between the old
and new systems. Approaches to designing such gateways are detailed.

Chapter 50, "Managing Multiple Databases Across Heterogeneous Hardware and Software Systems," describes various factors that must be taken
into consideration in connecting disparate databases.

Chapter 51, "Mobile and Federated Database Interoperability," describes the architecture and funtionality of interoperating mobile clients
within a federated database system.

Chapter 47

Software Architectures for Distributed DBMSs in a Client/Server Environment

James A. Larson
Carol L. Larson

A CLIENT/SERVER ARCHITECTURE CONSISTS OF SEVERAL COMPUTERS connected by a communications system. Some computers act as servers, and
some act as clients. A user interacts with a client to formulate requests for
information. The requests are transmitted to one or more servers through
a communications system for processing. Each server accesses its local
database or file system to respond to the requests and transmits the results back to the client through the communications system. The cli-
ent/server architecture also allows multiple users to share data by
accessing data on a data server through multiple clients.

Businesses are motivated to use a distributed client/server architecture
because it enables them to:

- Save money by replacing expensive mainframe hardware with less expensive server hardware. A large savings in cost may be realized if
  mainframe computers are phased out and replaced with servers and
  desktop computers.
- Leverage the existing investment in personal computers. Users want
  to access, analyze, and modify data using their PCs.

0-8493-9976-9/99/$0.00+$.50
© 1999 by CRC Press LLC

- Upgrade existing clients and servers or to add additional clients and servers. This gives upgrade flexibility to the system.

A distributed database management system (DBMS) enables users to access multiple servers. The remainder of this article discusses how to choose a distributed DBMS whose software architecture supports the features users need to perform their jobs.

DISTRIBUTED DBMS TECHNOLOGY

Database administrators are responsible for organizing the database so it can be accessed efficiently. The collection of interrelated records in the database is maintained by a data manager, such as a DBMS or a file system. If data managers exist on several computers, they are interconnected with a communications system. If several data managers share a computer, data is transmitted among them by facilities provided by the local operation system. Both cases are examples of distributed databases because different data managers maintain the data.

Access to Multiple Servers. With more and more essential data being collected and stored in desktop computers, users in many organizations are finding they need to access several computers as well as their organization's mainframe system. Distributed DBMSs enable this accessibility.

A data server provides all of the advantages of centralized databases, which allow users to share up-to-date information managed by the server. However, accessing data becomes more difficult for the user when there are multiple data servers. Users must perform the following tasks to access information stored in multiple servers:

- Determine which computers contain the data to be accessed.
- Formulate several queries, which will be executed on a different computer.
- Copy or transfer the results to a single computer for merging.
- Combine and merge the results.
- Extract the answer to the original request from the combined results.

A distributed DBMS helps users to perform these tasks.

DISTRIBUTED DBMS FEATURES

Three important features available in some distributed DBMSs are location and replication transparency, DBMS transparency, and multisite update capability. The availability of these features depends on the software architecture supported by the distributed DBMS. Database administrators choose software to support the desired features.

Location and Replication Transparency. This feature supports a type of data independence, which enables the database administrator to change the physical location and replication of data without modifying existing application programs.

A distributed DBMS supports location transparency if the user is not aware of the location or site of the data being accessed. Replication transparency is supported if the user is not aware that more than one copy of the data exists. Although these features provide increased data independence, they may require the use of sophisticated and expensive software optimizers.

DBMS Transparency. DBMS transparency is the second important feature. A distributed DBMS needs DBMS transparency when it contains multiple types of local database managers. For example, a distributed DBMS that interconnects a file system located at one site, a relational DBMS at a second site, and an IMS DBMS at a third site contains three types of local data managers. When a distributed DBMS supports DBMS transparency, the user formulates requests using structured query language (SQL). A translator, or gateway, transforms each SQL request to the language understood by a participating data manager.

Multisite Update Capability. The third important feature is the ability to update multiple local databases with a single request. Distributed DBMSs require sophisticated distributed concurrency control protocols which guarantee that two or more users do not attempt to update the same data simultaneously. They also require distributed commit protocols that allow distributed DBMSs to determine if and when updates to the database are completed. These protocols add to the complexity of the distributed DBMS, which in turn adds to the communications cost and response time of distributed requests.

DISTRIBUTED DBMS COMPONENTS

Exhibit 1 depicts the major software components of a distributed DBMS in a client/server environment. Distributed DBMS products differ in their components, so the availability of key features also differs.

Distributed DBMSs containing a request optimizer support location and replication transparency, whereas distributed DBMSs containing gateways provide DBMS transparency. Distributed DBMSs containing a sophisticated distributed execution manager enable updates across multiple data managers. The keyword here is sophistication; that is, all distributed DBMSs contain a distributed execution manager to retrieve data from multiple data managers, but not all distributed execution managers are sufficiently powerful to support distributed updates.

Distributed Request Optimizer

The distributed request optimizer hides the existence of multiple databases from the user. The three relational database tables shown in

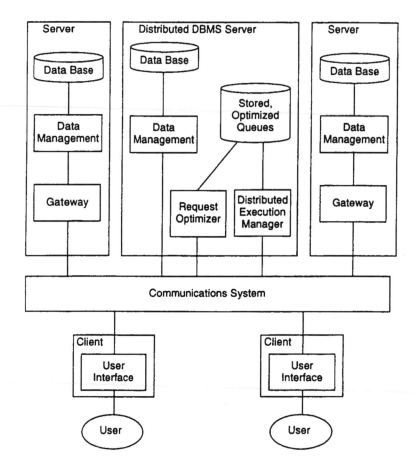

Exhibit 1.   Major components of a distributed DBMS.

Exhibit 2 illustrate this point. Assuming the three tables are visible to a user who wants to retrieve employee Davis' salary, the user needs to retrieve the Davis information from the Employee1 Table at Site1 and Davis information from the Employee2 Table at either Site1 or Site2. The SQL request (query 1) would be written as:

```
select Salary

from Employee1 at Site1

where Name = "Davis"

UNION

select Salary
```

Employee 1 — Site 1

Name	Salary	Department
Ackman	5000	Car
Baker	4500	Car

Employee 2 — Site 2

Name	Salary	Department
Carson	4800	Toy
Davis	5100	Toy

Employee 2 — Site 3

Name	Salary	Department
Carson	4800	Toy
Davis	5100	Toy

Exhibit 2. **Employee database information replicated and distributed to three sites.**

```
from Employee2 at Site2

where Name = "Davis";
```

Alternatively, the user could formulate the request as if all of the data were in a centralized database. The simplified request (query 2) would be:

```
select Salary

from Employee

where Name = "Davis";
```

The distributed request optimizer accesses data location and distribution information maintained by the distributed DBMS and converts query 2 to query 1.

Exhibit 3 illustrates a more compelling example. To change the department number of Smith from 3 to 15, the user or programmer would write query 3:

```
update Employee

set Department = 15

where EmpId = 100;
```

However, if the information in the table in Exhibit 3 is stored in four tables at four different sites (as shown in Exhibit 4), the distributed request optimizer modifies query 3 to the following complex program (query 4):

Employee

Empld	Name	Salary	Tax	ManagerNumber	Department
100	Smith	10000	1000	20	3
200	Jones	1333	122	40	14

Exhibit 3. Centralized employee information.

```
select Name, Sal, Tax, into $Name, $Sal, $Tax

from Employee1

where EmpId = 100;

select ManagerNumber into $ManagerNumber

from Employee2

where EmpId = 100;

insert into Employee3

(EmpId, Name, Department)

(100, $Name, 15);

insert into Employee4

(EmpId, Sal, Tax, ManagerNumber)

(10, $Sal, $Tax, $ManagerNumber);

delete Employee1

where EmpId = 100;

delete Employee2

where EmpId = 100;
```

As this example illustrates, a distributed request optimizer greatly simplifies the task of the user or programmer because the request optimizer hides the four tables in Exhibit 4 from the user. The user or programmer can express the relatively simple request in query 3 terms rather than using the more complicated query 4.

When the database administrator moves a table from one site to another, the users or programmers do not need to modify their requests. Instead, the distributed request optimizer translates the user request with updated information about the table location.

Distributed request optimizers have some disadvantages, but each disadvantage has a counter argument. For example:

Employee 1   (Department <10)

EmpId	Name	Salary	Tax
100	Smith	10000	1000

Employee 2   (Department <10)

EmpId	ManagerNumber	Department
100	20	3

Employee 3   (Department ≥10)

Name	Name	Department
200	Jones	14

Employee 4   (Department ≥10)

EmpId	Salary	Tax	ManagerNumber
200	1333	122	40

Exhibit 4.   Employee information distributed to four sites.

- Distributed request optimizers are expensive to build or purchase. However, the expense should be offset by savings in time necessary for users and programmers to formulate requests.
- Like any general optimizer, it may be possible to program a request that executes faster than the same request generated by the optimizer. However, optimizers take only seconds while programmers may require hours to implement the optimizations.

Gateways

Some distributed DBMSs support multiple types of local data managers. When this occurs, each request or part of a request to be executed by the local data manager must be translated to a format that the local data manager can execute. Gateways perform this type of translation.

If the global request is expressed in SQL and a data manager supports SQL, the transformation may be trivial and only needs to consider different SQL dialects. However, if the global request is expressed in SQL and a database manager does not support SQL, then a much more sophisticated gateway is necessary. The translation problem can be illustrated with some examples.

Example 1. Suppose that a local data manager consists of two files: a Department file containing DepartmentName and Budget and an Employee file containing EmployeeName, Salary, and DepartmentName. The following SQL request must be translated to a program containing file I/O commands:

```
select *

from Employee

where DepartmentName = "Car";
```

Depending on the file structures used by the file system data manager, the resulting program may perform one of the following:

- Search linearly for all records in the Employee file containing the value "Car" in the DepartmentName field.
- Perform a binary search for records in the Employee file ordered by the DepartmentName field.
- Do an index lookup for records in the Employee file indexed by the DepartmentName field.

Example 2. The following SQL request requires that the generated program access and join together records from both the Department and Employee files that have the same value for the DepartmentName field:

```
select *

from Department, Employee

where Department.DepartmentName = Employee.DepartmentName;
```

Depending on the file structures used by the file system data manager, the resulting program may perform one of the following:

- Nested (inner-outer) loop. For each record in Employee, every record in Department is retrieved and tested to determine whether they match.
- Index. For each record in Employee, the index to DepartmentName is used to retrieve matching records in Department.
- Sort-merge join. If both Employee and Department are sorted physically by DepartmentName, then both files should be scanned at the same time to locate matching records.
- Hash join. Records from both Employee and Department files are mapped into the same file using a hashing function applied to DepartmentName. Records with the same value for DepartmentName are placed in the same location within the file.

Gateways have the same disadvantages and advantages as request optimizers:

- Gateways are expensive to build or purchase. However, the expense should be offset with savings in user and programmer time.
- Like any general optimizer, it may be possible to manually translate a request that executes faster than the corresponding request generated by the gateway. However, gateways take only seconds to execute, whereas manual optimization may require hours of programmer time.

Distributed Execution Manager

A distributed execution manager controls and coordinates the execution of requests or pieces of requests by one or more data managers. It also provides distributed concurrency control and commit protocols.

A transaction is a set of reads and writes and ends with a commit (if all operations are successful) or with a rollback (if one or more of the operations is not successful). A distributed DBMS may execute several transactions concurrently as long as one transaction does not try to update data being accessed by another transaction. The execution of several concurrent transactions is said to be serializable if the results are the same as a serial execution of the transactions.

Several approaches are used to guarantee the serializability of concurrently executing transactions, including locking, timestamp ordering, and optimistic approaches. These approaches also are used in centralized databases, but their implementation is much more complicated in distributed systems.

TWO-PHASE COMMIT PROTOCOL

Distributed transactions that update data in several databases need a mechanism to determine whether to commit or rollback changes made in each database. Protocols have been developed to solve these problems; the most popular is the two-phase commit protocol. In the two-phase commit protocol, each local data manager reports its results to the distributed execution manager. When the distributed execution manager determines that all subrequests are completed, it performs the following two-phase commit protocol:

1. It sends a message asking each local data manager if it still can make local changes permanent.
2. After receiving an OK to commit message from each local data manager, it sends a final commit message to each local data manager. If anything goes wrong either before or during the two-phase commit protocol, the distributed execution manager sends rollback messages, which cause all local data managers to undo any changes made to their local databases.

Tool and Replication	Multisite Updates	DBMS Transparency	Location Transparency
MOMS	Somewhat	No	No
TP Monitors	Yes	No	No
DB Middleware	Yes	Yes	No
Distributed DBMSs	Yes	Yes	Yes

Exhibit 5.   Distributed DBMS product classes.

The distributed concurrency control and commit protocol messages add expense and delay to the execution of requests that update data at multiple sites. To avoid these expenses and delays, some distributed database management systems do not permit updates at all, while other only permit updates to a single database. If updates to a single database are permitted, the local data manager performs the concurrency control and may not support the two-phase commit protocol. It is very difficult to modify the local managers to accommodate the distributed concurrency control and commit protocols. This is why most distributed DBMSs that support multisite updates usually support only one type of data manager.

DISTRIBUTED DBMS PRODUCT CLASSES

There are many products that provide various combinations of facilities for managing distributed DBMSs. Exhibit 5 identifies four product classes and three of their features.

Message-oriented middleware (MOM) transfers database requests from the user's site to one or more data servers. While these requests may involve updates, there may be no distributed concurrency control and distributed commitment. Examples of MOM products include MessageQ from Digital Equipment Corp. (DEC), MQSeries from IBM, Pipes from PeerLogic Inc., and MSMQ from Microsoft.

TP monitors process transactions involving data within multiple databases. However, the application must be aware of the command formats in the underlying DBMSs, be aware of the location of each database, and update all copies of any replicated database. Popular TP monitors include BEA Systems' Tuxedo, Transarc's Encina, and Microsoft's Transaction Server.

DB middleware includes Java Database Connectivity (JDBC), Open Database Connectivity (ODBC) and its enhancement, OLE-DB, and IBI's EDA/SQL. All of these middleware toolkits contain facilities that convert user requests into the formats required by the underlying DBMS or file system (DBMS transparency), as well as processing transactions involving multiple databases (multisite updates). However, the application must know the location of each database and update all copies of any replicated database.

Distributed database management systems are marketed by Microsoft, Oracle, IBM, Sybase, and Informix. These systems support transactions involving multiple databases, as well as DBMS transparency and location and replication transparency. For more vendor information, see the recommended Web sites at the end of this paper.

RECOMMENDED COURSE OF ACTION

Database administrators should assess the needs of users and decide if the client/server system is to support one or several data servers. If several data servers are needed, then the database administrator determines which of the following features are needed:

- Location and replication transparency. If this feature is needed, the database administrator should purchase a distributed DBMS that supports a request optimizer.
- DBMS transparency. A requirement for this feature means that the database administrator should build or buy gateways to hide the languages required by heterogeneous data managers.
- Multisite updates. If this feature is needed, it is best to build a sophisticated distributed execution manager that supports concurrency control and commit protocols among the data managers.

After the database administrator has determined which features are necessary, a product should be chosen to meet the user's needs.

Recommended Web Sites

For more information about the products mentioned in this article, see the following Web pages:

- BEA Systems, Inc. (Tuxedo)
  385 Moffett Park Drive
  Sunnyvale, CA 94089-1208
  Telephone: (408) 743-4000
  Fax: (408) 734-9234
  http://www.beasys.com
  http://www.beasys.com/products/tuxedo/index.htm

- Digital Equipment Corp. (DECMessageQ)
  111 Powdermill Road
  Maynard, MA 01754-1418
  Telephone: (978) 493-5111
  http://www.digital.com/decmessageq/

- IBM Home Page
  http://www.ibm.com

- IBM (MQSeries)
  http://www.software.hosting.ibm.com/ts/mqseries/

- Information Builders Inc. (EDA/SQL)
  Two Penn Plaza
  New York, NY 10121-2898
  Telephone: (212) 736-4433
  Fax: (212) 967-6406
  http://www.IBI.com

- Informix Home Page
  http://www.informix.com/

- Java Database Connectivity (JDBC) Home Page
  http://java.sun.com/products/jdbc/index.html

- Microsoft Corporation Home Page
  http://www.microsoft.com/

- Microsoft Message Queue Server (MSMQ)
  http://www.microsoft.com/ntserver/guide/msmq.asp

- Microsoft Open Database Connectivity (ODBC)
  http://www.microsoft.com/data/odbc/

- Microsoft OLE DB
  http://www.microsoft.com/data/oledb/

- Microsoft Transaction Server
  http://www.microsoft.com/ntserver/guide/trans_intro.asp

- Oracle Home Page
  http://www.oracle.com

- PeerLogic, Inc. (Pipes)
  555 De Haro Street
  San Francisco, CA 94107-2348
  Telephone/Fax: (800) 733-7601 or (415) 626-4545
  Fax: (415) 626-4710
  E-mail: info@peerlogic.com
  http://www.peerlogic.com

- Sybase Home Page
  http://www.sybase.com

- Transarc (Encina)
  The Gulf Tower
  707 Grant Street
  Pittsburgh, PA 15219
  Telephone: (412) 338-4400
  Fax: (412) 338-6977
  E-mail: sales@transarc.com
  http://www.transarc.com/afs/transarc.com/public/www/Public/Prod-Serv/Product/Encina/index.html

Chapter 48
Distributed Database Design

Elizabeth N. Fong
Charles L. Sheppard
Kathryn A. Harvill

A DISTRIBUTED DATABASE ENVIRONMENT ENABLES A USER TO ACCESS DATA residing anywhere in a corporation's computer network without regard to differences among computers, operating systems, data manipulation languages, or file structures. Data that are actually distributed among multiple remote computers will appear to the user as if they resided on the user's own computer. This scenario is functionally limited with today's distributed database technology; true distributed database technology is still a research consideration. The functional limitations are generally in the following areas:

- Transaction management
- Standard protocols for establishing a remote connection
- Independence of network technology

Transaction management capabilities are essential to maintaining reliable and accurate databases. In some cases, today's distributed database software places responsibility of managing transactions on the application program. In other cases, transactions are committed or rolled back at each location independently, which means that it is not possible to create a single distributed transaction. For example, multiple-site updates require multiple transactions.

CURRENT DBMS TECHNOLOGY

In today's distributed database technology, different gateway software must be used and installed to connect nodes using different distributed database management system (DBMS) software. Therefore, connectivity among heterogeneous distributed DBMS nodes is not readily available (i.e., available only through selected vendor markets).

0-8493-9976-9/99/$0.00+$.50
© 1999 by CRC Press LLC

In some instances, distributed DBMS software is tied to a single network operating system. This limits the design alternatives for the distributed DBMS environment to the products of a single vendor.

It is advisable to select a product that supports more than one network operating system. This will increase the possibility of successfully integrating the distributed DBMS software into existing computer environments.

In reality, distributed databases encompass a wide spectrum of possibilities, including the following:

- Remote terminal access to centralized DBMS (e.g., an airline reservation system).
- Remote terminal access to different DBMSs, but one at a time (e.g., Prodigy, CompuServe, and Dow Jones).
- Simple pairwise interconnection with data sharing that requires users to know the data location, data access language, and the log-on procedure to the remote DBMS.
- Distributed database management with a generic data definition language and a data manipulation language at all nodes.
- Distribution update and transaction management.
- Distributed databases with replication that support vertical and horizontal fragmentation.
- "True" distributed DBMSs with heterogeneous hardware, software, and communications.

The definition of distributed DBMSs lies anywhere along this spectrum. For the purpose of this chapter, the remote terminal access to data as discussed in the preceding list is not considered a distributed DBMS because a node on the distributed DBMS must have its own hardware, central processor, and software.

Limitations of Commercial Products

Some of the problems that currently frustrate managers and technicians who might otherwise be interested in exploring distributed data solutions include the following:

- A distributed database environment has all the problems associated with the single centralized database environment but at a more complex level.
- There are no basic, step-by-step guidelines covering the analysis, design, and implementation of a distributed database environment.

A distributed DBMS offers many benefits. However, there are also many architectural choices that make the applications design for distributed databases very complex.

To ensure an effective and productive distributed database environment, it is essential that the distributed environment be properly designed to support the expected distributed database applications. In addition, an effective design will depend on the limitations of the distributed DBMS software. Therefore, implementing today's distributed database technology requires identifying the functional limitations of a selected commercial product. Identification of these limitations is critical to the successful operation of an application in a distributed database environment.

DISTRIBUTED DATABASE DEVELOPMENT PHASES

Effective corporationwide distributed database processing is not going to happen overnight. It requires a carefully planned infrastructure within which an orderly evolution can occur. The four major development phases are planning, design, installation and implementation, and support and maintenance.

The Planning Phase. The planning phase consists of high-level management strategy planning. During the planning phase, an organization must consider whether it is advantageous to migrate to a distributed environment. This chapter assumes that migration to a distributed environment is desirable and feasible and that the corporate strategy planning issues and tasks have been identified. The result of this phase is the total management commitment for cost, resources, and a careful migration path toward a distributed database environment.

The Design Phase. The design phase is concerned with the overall design of the distributed database strategy. The overall design task involves the selection of a distributed DBMS environment in terms of the hardware, software, and communications network for each node and how these elements are interconnected. The design of the distributed database environment must incorporate the requirements for the actual distributed database application. The overall design divides into two main tasks: the detailed design of the distributed database environment and the detailed design of the initial distributed database application. In certain cases, the initial application may be a prototype that is intended to pave the way for the full-production distributed database application.

The Installation and Implementation Phase. This phase consists of the installation and implementation of the environment that provides basic software support for the distributed DBMS application. The task of developing the distributed database application could occur in parallel with the installation of the environment.

The Support and Maintenance Phase. The support and maintenance phase consists of support for the distributed DBMS environment and the support and maintenance of the application. Although these support and maintenance tasks can be performed by the same people, the nature of the tasks and responsibilities are quite distinct. For example, the distributed application may require modification of report formats, whereas the distributed environment may require modification to add more memory.

CORPORATION STRATEGY PLANNING

The main task during the strategic planning phase is to obtain the commitment of senior management. The measure of this commitment is the amount of resources — both personnel and equipment — necessary for the development of a distributed DBMS. The factors that must be considered during the strategy planning phase are as follows:

- What are the objectives of the organization's next 5-year plan?
- How will technological changes affect the organization's way of doing business?
- What resources are needed to plan for the development of, and migration to, a distributed DBMS?
- How will outcomes be measured relative to the impact on the organization's competitive position?

The corporate strategy plan must include detailed specifications of the total system life cycle. It must also include a realistic timetable of schedules and milestones. Important consideration must be paid to the allocation of cost for new acquisitions, training personnel, physical space requirements, and other tangible items.

During the strategic planning phase, information must be gathered on the organization's business functions and goals, related constraints and problem areas, and the organization's user groups. Only after the needed information has been gathered is it possible to develop high-level information categories and their interrelationships.

The process of developing the distributed database plan is iterative. The activities involved are performed by IS managers. Although these individuals often have the vision to recognize the long-term benefits of a distributed DBMS environment to an organization, they must rely on the participation and input of those in the organization who are directly involved with the business functions and use information to make decisions and manage operations. There must be considerable interaction among many different people in the organization, each of whom provides feedback to validate and refine the plans.

Strategic planning must first provide a sufficient justification for the expenditure of resources necessary to migrate to a distributed environment. Only after this justification has been accepted and fully approved by senior management can the task of initiating projects to design, develop, and implement a distributed DBMS environment and application start.

OVERALL DESIGN OF DISTRIBUTED DATABASE STRATEGY

A distributed database environment consists of a collection of sites or nodes connected by a communications network. Each node has its own hardware, central processor, and software, which may or may not include a DBMS. The primary objective of a distributed DBMS is to give interactive query and application programs access to remote data as well as local data.

Individual nodes within the distributed environment can have different computing requirements. Accordingly, these nodes may have different hardware and different software, and they may be connected in many different ways. Some of the variations possible in the distributed database environment are discussed in the following sections.

Client/Server Computing

The most basic distributed capability is remote database access from single users at a node. A node may be a mainframe, a minicomputer, or a microcomputer (personal computer). The node that makes the database access request is referred to as a client node, and the node that responds to the request and provides database services is referred to as a service node. The association is limited to the two parties involved — the client and the server. Exhibit 1 represents several different configurations available under a client/server computing environment. The following are descriptions of the different configurations shown in the exhibit.

Client Single-User Node. The operating environment of an individual can be single user or multiuser, depending on the operating system of that node. In a single-user operating environment, a node can be only a client. Such a node may or may not have databases. For non-database client nodes, the software typically consists of front-end application programs used to access remote database server nodes. This front-end software is generally in the form of end-user interface tools (e.g., a query language processor, a form processor, or some other application-specific program written in a third-generation language).

DESIGNING AND MANAGING DATABASES

The front-end software formulates and issues user requests. It processes user requests through its established links with appropriate communications software. The front-end software only captures a user's request and uses communications software to send that request to a remote database node requesting its DBMS to process the request. In addition to the capabilities outlined, single-user nodes with databases allow local data to

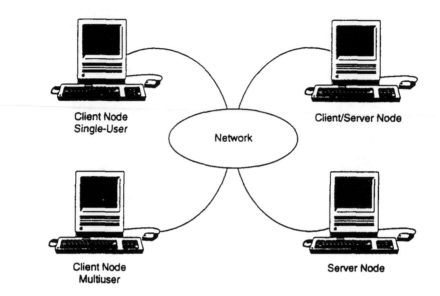

Exhibit 1.   Client/server computing.

be included in the same query operations specified for remote data. Therefore, operationally, the query results will appear as if all data are coming from a central database.

Client Multiuser Node. The functional capabilities outlined for the client single-user node are expanded in the client multiuser node because of the presence of a multiuser operating system at the user node. Such a configuration generally has several user processes running at the same time. At peak use time, the presence of several user processes can cause slower response time than is experienced in a client single-user node. The client multiuser node is more cost-effective, however, because it can allow multiple remote database access at different sites by different users at the same time. This is made possible through an identifiable list of remote server node locations. In addition, as with the client single-user node, the client multiuser node can include local database access in conjunction with access to remote databases.

Server Node. The server node is capable of providing database services to other client requests as well as to itself. It is a special multiuser node that is dedicated to servicing remote database requests and any local processes. This means that incoming requests are serviced, but it does not originate requests to other server nodes. The functional capabilities of a server node are as follows: this node must be included in the server list of some remote client node, there must be an operating DBMS, and there must be a continuously running process that listens for incoming database requests.

Client/Server Node. A node with a database can be a client as well as a server. This means that this node can service remote database requests as well as originate database requests to other server nodes. Therefore, the client/server node can play a dual role.

Homogeneous Distributed DBMS Environment

A completely homogeneous distributed DBMS environment exists when all the nodes in the distributed environment have the same DBMS but not necessarily the same hardware and operating system. However, the communications software for each node must use the same protocol to send or receive requests and data.

Design and implementation of a homogeneous distributed DBMS environment need involve only a single vendor. Any data request issued at a client node does not require translation because the database language and data model are the same across all nodes in the network.

Heterogeneous Distributed DBMS Environment

In a truly heterogeneous distributed DBMS environment, the hardware, operating systems, communications, and DBMSs can all be different. Different DBMSs may mean different data models along with different database languages for definition and manipulation. Any database request issued at a client node would have to be translated so that the server node responding to the request would understand how to execute the request.

Various degrees of heterogeneity can exist. For example, within the distributed environment, different DBMSs can still be compatible if they all support the relational data model and understand SQL, a relational query language that is an ANSI and ISO standard. Presently, however, even among SQL-conforming systems, there is no general communications software that will accept generic SQL statements from any other SQL-conforming DBMS. This is an area in which the pending remote data access standards are needed.

DISTRIBUTED ENVIRONMENT ARCHITECTURE

The design of a distributed database environment can be evolutionary — by incremental interconnection of existing systems, or by developing a totally new distributed DBMS environment using the bottom-up approach. Some of the design issues in adopting either approach are described in the following sections.

Interconnection of Existing Systems

Not all organizations have the luxury of developing the distributed database environment from scratch. Already-existing database management applications are costly investments that are not likely to be replaced all at once by new distributed systems. The existing environment, including hardware, software, and databases, can be preserved by providing a mechanism for producing federated systems (i.e., systems composed of autonomous software components).

The federated approach is a practical, first-step solution toward a distributed database environment. It accommodates a legacy of existing systems while extending to incorporate new nodes. Therefore, it is important to select distributed DBMS software that supports existing computer hardware and allows for expansion. Within a federated system, pairs of nodes can be coupled in ways that range from very loose (i.e., each node is autonomous) to very tight (i.e., each node interacts directly with the other). The various forms of coupling affect the design, execution, and capability of the distributed applications.

The mode of coupling affects the number of translations required to exchange information between each site. Zero translations are needed when both components use the same representations. Some systems may choose to translate the data produced by one site directly to the format required by the other site. A more common method is to translate the data into a neutral format first, and then translate into the target format.

Loose Coupling. Loosely coupled systems are the most modular and in some ways are easier to maintain. This is because changes to the implementation of a site's system characteristics and its DBMS are not as likely to affect other sites. The disadvantage of loosely coupled systems is that users must have some knowledge of each site's characteristics to execute requests. Because very little central authority to control consistency exists, correctness cannot be guaranteed. In addition, loosely coupled systems typically involve more translations that may cause performance problems.

Tight Coupling. Tightly coupled systems behave more like a single, integrated system. Users need not be aware of the characteristics of the sites fulfilling a request. With centralized control, the tightly coupled systems are more consistent in their use of resources and in their management of shared data. The disadvantage of tight coupling is that because sites are independent, changes to one site are likely to affect other sites. Also, users at some sites may object to the loss of freedom to the central control mechanisms necessary to maintain the tight coupling of all the systems.

Cooperation Between Sites

For a truly distributed DBMS environment, a variety of methods are available to specify cooperation between sites. One way of classifying the distributed environment is to define the amount of transparency offered to the users. Another way is to define the amount of site autonomy available to each site, and the way sites interact cooperatively.

Degrees of Transparency. Transparency is the degree to which a service is offered by the distributed DBMS so that the user does not need to be aware of it. One example of transparency is location transparency, which means users can retrieve data from any site without having to know where the data are located.

Types of Site Autonomy. Site autonomy refers to the amount of independence that a site has in making policy decisions. Some examples of policy decisions include ownership of data, policies for accessing the data, policies for hours and days of operation, and human support. In addition, all modifications to the site's data structures must be approved by the cooperating federation of data administrators.

Interconnection of Newly Purchased Systems

An organization will have much more freedom if it decides to establish a distributed database environment from scratch. Currently, vendors are offering homogeneous distributed DBMSs with a compatible family of software. This approach, however, can lock the organization into a single vendor's proprietary products.

Other distributed architecture choices are as follows:

- Identical DBMS products at each node, with possibly different hardware environments but a single proprietary communications network to interconnect all sites.
- Standard conforming DBMS products at each node that rely on standard communications protocols.
- Different DBMSs, using the same data model (e.g., relational), interconnected by a single or standard communications protocol.
- Different DBMSs, using different data models (e.g., relational or object-oriented), interconnected by a single or standard communications protocol.

Some distributed DBMS vendors offer a bridge (gateway) mechanism from their distributed database software to any foreign distributed database software. This bridge (gateway) may be obtained at additional development cost if it has not already been included in the vendor's library of available software.

In the design of a totally new distributed DBMS product, it is advisable to consider a mixture of standard conforming DBMSs and communications protocols. Because the technology and products are changing quickly, the designed architecture must be continuously reviewed to prevent it from being locked into an inflexible mode.

CONSIDERATION FOR STANDARDS

As the trend toward distributed computing accelerates, the need for standards, guidance, and support will increase. Application distribution and use will be chaotic unless there is an architectural vision and some degree of uniformity in information technology platforms. This is particularly true in client/server and workstation environments. To achieve this goal, a systems architecture incorporating standards to meet the users' needs must be established. This architecture must isolate the application software from the lower levels of machine architecture and systems service implementation. The systems architecture serves as the context for user requirements, technology integration, and standards specifications.

The benefits of standardization for both the user and the vendor are many. The number and variety of distributed DBMS products are increasing. By insisting that purchased products conform to standards, users may be able to choose the best product for each function without being locked into a specific vendor. Therefore, small to midsize vendors may effectively compete in the open marketplace. For effective planning and designing of a distributed DBMS environment, it is important for the designers to consider what standards already exist and what standards will be emerging to be able to incorporate standardized products.

There are many areas of distributed DBMS environment in which standards should be applied. Some of the standards relevant to the design of a distributed DBMS include communications protocols, applications programming interfaces, data languages for DBMSs, data representation and interchange formats, and remote data access.

Communications protocol standards are necessary so that systems from different products can connect to a communications network and understand the information being transmitted. An example of a communications protocol standard is the Government Open Systems Interconnection Profile (GOSIP).

The application programming interface (API) standard is directed toward the goal of having portable applications. This enables software applications developed in one computing environment to run almost unchanged in any other environment. An example of an application programming interface standard is the Portable Operating System Interface for Computer Environments (POSIX).

The data languages commonly supported by a DBMS are the data definition language, the data manipulation language, and the data control language. An example of a standard data language for the relational DBMS model is SQL.

To exchange data among open systems, a standard interchange format is necessary. The interchange format consists of a language for defining general data structures and the encoding rules. An example of a standard data interchange language is Abstract Syntax Notation One (ASN. 1).

An important standard for the distributed processing environment is the remote access of data from a client site to a database server site. A specialized remote data access protocol based on the SQL standard is currently under development.

SUMMARY

To start the overall design process, a review of the organization's existing facilities should be conducted. This review is done to determine whether the new distributed database environment can use some or all of the existing facilities. In the decision to move into a distributed environment, requirements for additional functionalities must be identified. Such organizational issues as setting up regional offices may also be involved. The distributed architecture must take into consideration the actual application operating, the characteristics of the user population, and the workloads to be placed on the system. Such an architecture must also incorporate standardized components.

Chapter 49
Database Gateways and Interoperability

Martin D. Solomon

WHENEVER CLIENT/SERVER SYSTEMS ARE DEVELOPED AND INTRODUCED INTO EXISTING LARGE-SIZE INFORMATION SYSTEMS ENVIRONMENTS, the need to have bidirectional access to legacy data is inevitable. Few developers have the luxury of building these systems without first having to inquire against or update to other databases or files somewhere else in the organization's infrastructure.

There are many software options for communicating with the various platforms. Primary choices include masking and screen scraping, advanced program-to-program communications (APPC), database gateway software, messaging software, and file transfer techniques.

This chapter is intended to help database managers understand how database gateways work, whether these products can provide effective solutions for their organizations' business issues, and how to choose and set up the gateway software and support infrastructure.

DATABASE GATEWAY SETUP

All database gateways provide a translation stop or box hop so that the data being shipped can be manipulated for arrival at the destination stop (Exhibit 1). This stop takes the form of a gateway server and provides varying degrees of service, including data translation, resource governing software, and load balancing or connection management tools. This server also manages the communications links and options between the data resources on the host and server platforms. This software is installed and coupled on its host and server counterparts in the enterprise at the location of the user's choice. Frequency and size of the requests coming through this stop determine performance and whether multiple gateway servers are required.

0-8493-9976-9/99/$0.00+$.50
© 1999 by CRC Press LLC

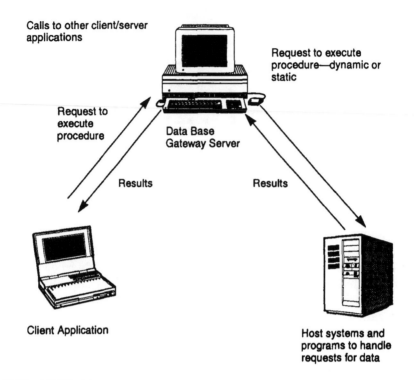

Calls to other client/server applications

Request to execute procedure—dynamic or static

Request to execute procedure

Data Base Gateway Server

Results

Results

Client Application

Host systems and programs to handle requests for data

Exhibit 1.   Client initiated remote procedure call (RPC) to host.

DATABASE GATEWAY CAPACITY PLANNING

Several variables must be considered when choosing database gateway hardware and operating system software. Variables include maximum expected number of concurrent user connections to the gateway server, estimated daily and peak amounts of data to be passed through the gateway server, and the network protocols to be used in gateway access.

Concurrent User Connections

Concurrent user connections are a key determining factor in capacity planning because each user connected to the gateway hardware reserves memory on the server for address space, as much as 256K bytes per user, depending on the gateway software. To determine this parameter, it is important to know what types of applications are traversing the gateway and to gather information pertaining to performance expectations and the types of functions exploited on the gateway.

SQL Access. Many database gateways also support dynamic SQL access for updates to the host data store. Depending on the type of front-end tool used to perform these accesses, data integrity in DB2 for example, may only be assured by carrying a conversational transaction into the transaction processing (TP) monitor (e.g., customer information control system [CICS]). This usually forces the client running the application to remain connected to the gateway and to the TP monitor for extended periods of time to ensure the integrity of the data. Therefore, a moderate-sized departmental application performing data access in this manner could end up maintaining a relatively large number of gateway and TP monitor resources throughout the day if the gateway connections are allocated when the user opens the application.

Static Remote Procedure Calls. In applications performing static remote procedure calls (RPCs) to the host, performance requirements become the key issue. Assuming that the application RPCs are constructed with stable single transaction units of work, the client application has no inherent need to maintain a continuous connection to the gateway server to preserve data integrity once the unit of work or transaction is completed. Each access, however, requires the establishment of a new address space on the gateway and a possible security-check exit routine. This can take anywhere from 50 to 500 milliseconds, depending on the processing speed of the gateway server and network configuration. The additional time spent on reestablishing a connection should be carefully evaluated when designing the application.

Low- and High-Volume OLTP. Low-volume processing, which can be loosely defined as fewer than 2500 online teleprocessing (OLTP) transactions per day, does not usually justify the tradeoff of using more memory and incurring the associated costs for the gain of about 200 milliseconds per transaction. High-volume OLTP-type systems with upwards of 25,000 transactions per day generally require continuous connectivity to provide high-level response times for users.

In both cases — and especially if the expected use of the system cannot be clearly predicted as being at either end of the spectrum — it is worthwhile to invest the short amount of time it takes to code the system for either option. Any number of simple techniques can be used to develop a dynamic switch-type function to toggle the application between a continuous stay-connected mode and that of reestablishing a connection with each cross-platform request. This capability is even more valuable if several applications are expected to share a common database gateway server.

Amount of Data Passing Through the Server

The second determining factor in choosing the gateway hardware and operating system is the amount and frequency of data passed through the gateway server. The limits of technology still dictate that high-volume

OLTP-type applications using the gateway should only send a relatively small amount of data for the average transaction, probably on the order of 1 to 2K bytes to ensure acceptable response time.

Frequently, however, database gateways are shared with other applications and ad hoc query users. With regard to multiple stable applications using static RPC calls, if the hardware requirements have been met for user connections, and the 1 to 2K bytes data-per-request maximum is adhered to, the amount of data being transported can also be managed adequately, provided the transaction workload is evenly distributed throughout the processing time periods.

Planning for ad hoc use and large data transfers (scheduled or otherwise) to and from the host and client/server DBMS poses a larger problem. Some database gateways can transfer large amounts of data across platforms (often to and from the host) using bulk copy functions. Nearly all gateways allow for ad hoc access to the host DBMS through user-friendly query tools. Either of these activities performed during peak processing times could severely impact response times for static applications or even affect host performance in unrelated applications.

For ad hoc query use, user education and tight control through the use of DBMS resource monitors and governors can go a long way in preventing gateway performance problems and maintaining an equally shared resource. If large queries and bulk copy functions must move an excess of about 100K bytes of data more than several times a day, then consideration must be given either to moving these functions to off-hours or acquiring a separate gateway server for those needs.

Network Protocols

Because most database gateway products are available for nearly all protocols, it is logical to remain consistent with the network architecture of the organization. A brief investigation into which protocols are supported by the vendor should be undertaken, but for the most part, performance of database gateway accesses are determined by the application design. If the database gateway applications or users request that large amounts of data be shipped across the network, a brief check should also be made with the network support area to ensure that the infrastructure is in place to support that requirement.

Hardware

Because the hardware choice for a database gateway server is fully dependent on transaction volumes, the amount of data shipped across the gateway, and the number of expected concurrent user connections, the remaining issue will be whether to choose Intel-based or RISC-based processors. In general, the latest Intel processors can comfortably handle at least 1000 moderate-sized (defined as less than 2K bytes each) gateway transactions per hour, with some room to spare for some ad hoc query activity. For higher volumes, or in anticipation of a significant ad hoc query component, it is recommended that a low-end RISC-based unit be acquired so that potential bottlenecks are avoided.

In cases where transaction volumes may be low but a high number of concurrent connections (i.e., more than 300) are expected, the memory needed to support this requirement may tip the scales in favor of the RISC platforms, which can support more memory capacity.

In cases where usage is underestimated, adding additional gateway servers is an option, but load balancing between multiple servers in addition to maintenance and disaster recovery considerations could add substantial "hidden" costs to the effort. Disk space should be of no concern in either case because entire gateway software packages and any logs that are required will not take up more than 200MB. Also, it is recommended that in production, gateway software be installed on dedicated computers.

GATEWAY-TO-HOST SECURITY

Gateway security is often not considered until after the product is in-house and already being used for development. Ideally, the gateway security exits and processing should fit in with the existing security software infrastructure. However, this is almost never the case.

Most standard mainframe-based security packages can interrogate LU6.2-based transaction processing for valid logon IDs and passwords. Delivery of the resulting messages from the attempted logon back to the workstation executing the applications is a much more complicated issue. The application generally requires customized code to decipher the message received from the host security package and the knowledge of how to react to any number of situations, including a combination of incorrect or expired IDs or passwords. In addition, the application is likely to be accessing other systems and software on other platforms that have their own security logic.

For gateway-specific applications, the user may also be accessing other systems and products directly through an unrelated application or tool and traverse the same proprietary security system at the same time. As a result, the user might on occasion log on to the gateway application with a given password, then at some point later, log on to another application system and be informed that his/her password has expired in the interim. If the system includes an E-mail system and an additional RDBMS on different platforms, for example, the potential for frustration is even greater.

Most security packages included with the gateway software are not robust enough to handle even the gateway-to-host security issues involved. A

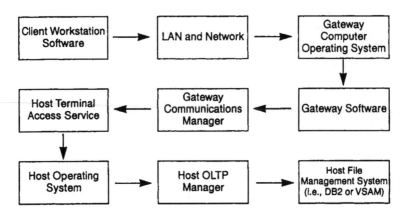

Exhibit 2.   The path of database gateway access requests.

better method, and one that requires the most effort, is to standardize a custom-built front-end security application that automatically reviews and synchronizes user IDs and passwords across all products and platforms when users boot up their workstation. To minimize the inconvenience of this undertaking, the gateway security issues between client and host software could be the first to be addressed in a phased-in approach. Front-end security software could be developed or modified in concert with implementing the test gateway instances and continued through production.

Other alternatives include setting up unsecured gateway access to the host, or having the individual application support personnel code routines. Both of these methods, however, can lead to much larger problems and security risks in the long run.

TECHNICAL SUPPORT

Because they are one of the most complex software products to support, database gateways require coordinated efforts from several system support groups (Exhibit 2). Without the ability to quickly access experts from the database (e.g., mainframe and client/server), OLTP (e.g., CICS), network, workstation, and operating system support areas, resolving gateway problems can prove troublesome.

As with most distributed client/server systems, locating the problem is usually the most time-consuming and difficult part. If the application that uses the gateway solution is not functioning properly, the problem could be purely a workstation health issue or it could indicate network problems to the host processor and related software and hardware experiencing an outage. The potential for loss of valuable time is great if, for example, the problem is a particular mainframe database table being unavailable, yet the individuals who are working to locate the problem are not familiar with or are not in the notification chain for such issues.

The Help Desk. To streamline the process as much as possible, it is recommended that if an information systems help desk is available, the help desk staff should be trained to filter as many gateway-related problems as possible. This means giving help desk personnel documentation that relates how each database gateway instance is connected to each network address, OLTP system, and mainframe database subsystems. Therefore, if DB2 is unavailable, the support staff knows that any gateway traffic using that system is potentially impaired or may not be functioning at all. Because most database gateways rely on the proper functioning of other software products, the alternative to not having a help desk could be longer work interruptions and incorrect support personnel being notified to investigate problems.

Usage Considerations

Most database gateway software is relatively easy to use from a developer and end-user perspective. Nearly all of the complexities of cross-platform and heterogeneous data access are resolved during software installation and setup. Systems programmers handle maintenance and other access requirements behind the scenes. In most cases, the programmer only has to provide a few lines of source code plus minor modifications to a couple of client workstation files to provide access to the desired database or file. Once a few minor modifications are made and the proper drivers are installed, ad hoc users only need to start the desired front-end software program and host access to any number of host databases and files is possible.

The gateway solution may not provide the best fit for every situation, however. One example is an application that provides the client with all of the updates to a particular file unique to that user since the request was last made. Although coding this access using the gateway may be simple, the actual access is relatively time-consuming and resource intensive. A better choice may be a messaging solution where those updates are delivered at regular intervals in the background so that when the request is made, the results are essentially fully in place and quickly available. Similar examples can be found for other types of middleware connectivity choices.

DISASTER RECOVERY

The database gateway server should be placed in a restricted access area, just like any other critical LAN server in the IS shop. The only case to be made against this recommendation is if remote systems management of the gateway software is not possible and maintenance is scheduled frequently. Except for a departmental-type test gateway, this is usually not recommended.

Because the gateway server does not contain any client data, only the customized software to provide a conduit to it, maintaining a hot spare locally or off-site is relatively easy. The cost of the hardware may be a limiting factor for an off-site unit, but local hot or warm spares can be set up on the test servers for emergency use. This can usually be accomplished by setting up and maintaining all of the production software, information, and the required customization on the designated test or development machine. If a major problem arises, the development server can be quickly switched to production mode until the problem is resolved. Depending on the stability of the test environment and the size of the machine, testing may have to be curtailed or discontinued during the outage.

ADD-ON SOFTWARE

Host as Client Processor. In most cases, the database gateway traffic consists of requests from the workstation or client/server database to the host, whether it be to query large mainframe data stores or to perform required updates to those files or databases. In some cases, however, it is necessary for a host-based process to initiate access to server-based data during the course of processing. Some gateway vendors offer additional software that can be installed for this process. Although this type of processing can also be accomplished with native-based code, it may be desirable to have these processes performed through this controlled software with built-in features similar to those used when processing client requests. In either case, it is something that should be considered.

Joins Across Engines and Files. Many database gateway vendors offer products in addition to the core gateway software that allows dynamic joins across platforms and data file systems. This could range from joining host and client/server relational data, as well as host files (e.g., virtual storage access method [VSAM] or sequential). To have such capabilities, a careful watch must be kept on ad hoc queries to prevent CPU resource overuse.

For cases of reasonable ad hoc use where the business requires limited data multisource data access, however, this piece of add-on software could be quite beneficial. As with the core gateway software, these products require complex systems support and maintenance in the background. The relatively steep cost of these products may also play a role in evaluating the need for the additional capabilities provided.

Other Options. Although database gateways provide a great range of functionality for access to disparate data platforms and data stores, the relatively high cost of purchase and deployment may not be justified. This is especially true when just a few small applications require data access across platforms. In these cases, the two primary alternatives are the use of Open Database Connectivity (ODBC) drivers and the TCP/IP File Transfer Program (FTP). Virtually all GUI front-end software is ODBC-compliant. When examining this option, it is important to keep in mind the cost of purchasing an ODBC site license or individual driver for each client. ODBC transactions frequently incur significant overhead, causing them to run slower than those run across gateways.

The FTP process, on the other hand, allows the best performance for data transfer, but requires additional resources to code the data transfers required at each location. Depending on application requirements, this effort can be very complex and require a fairly large commitment of skilled resources to develop.

Web Connectivity

On the tails of the rapidly increasing use of the Internet is the need to integrate HTML and Java Web page scripting languages to back-end databases and files. Because gateway software already provides the analogous access from front-end GUI tools to back-end data stores, this added functionality is the next logical step for this middleware component. Several leading gateway software vendors are beta testing this functionality in terms of gateway add-on components and ODBC drivers to accommodate Web page languages.

At this early stage, issues regarding capacity, performance, and security are similar to those already discussed. Again, extra careful consideration must be given to dynamic calls and front-end application security.

SUMMARY

With a small investment in research and analysis, database gateway software can be quickly implemented and provide relatively straightforward and efficient access to disparate data stores across the enterprise. It is, however, important to carefully consider usage and support requirements before acquisitions begin. Among the key issues to remember:

- The software is best suited for light to moderate OLTP-type processing to and from the host platforms, as well as for enabling controlled ad hoc access to mainframe RDBMSs.
- Although use of the software is simple, background support is complex and usually involves several areas of expertise within the organization. Building and orchestrating an efficient line of support for the gateway product is essential in providing continuous availability through the different platforms.

- Security requirements and routines should be provided concurrently with gateway deployment.
- Because the gateway provides easy access to many environments, it is crucial that the actual use of the tool for specific applications is carefully reviewed to ensure that it is the correct technology for the situation.

Chapter 50

Managing Multiple Databases Across Heterogeneous Hardware and Software Systems

James Woods

A FUNCTIONAL BRIDGE BRINGS TRANSACTIONS FROM ONE DATABASE TO THE OTHERS, so that there is a single update path for all data items. The databases, though physically separated, thus function as one. This chapter reviews, step-by-step, the planning and design decisions related to the communications infrastructure and the designation of the database master. The techniques recommended will work with two or more separate databases.

THE GOAL: A SINGLE FUNCTIONAL DATABASE

Corporate IS management is often challenged when it finds that it must control multiple databases that may reside on separate and disparate systems. However, the cost of not harnessing these multiple databases into a coherent whole is very high.

First, there is the problem of data redundancy. The data that designates a single fact is represented multiple times in the organization. Apart from the obvious storage requirement considerations, there is the problem of inconsistent information. Because the databases each have their own update paths, the data items are likely to have conflicting values. Even if the updates pass along the same value to each data item, it will most likely not be in the same time frame. This leads to information that is out of sync with the other data items. However, more than just one data item is involved in

0-8493-9976-9/99/$0.00+$.50
© 1999 by CRC Press LLC

this problem; the problem is widespread — probably tens or hundreds of data items. Some of those items will be used for critical business decisions.

When the information is summarized and reported to top management, conflicts in the information will become obvious, though it will not be obvious which specific data items differ, only that the information from one department does not square with another. Confidence levels in the integrity of all the databases will drop and the decision support results will be minimized.

Although a single, central database is preferable, the reality is that multiple databases exist. They come into existence for any number of reasons:

- *Independent purchases.* A user department buys and uses a separate system because it believes that is the best answer to its needs or that IS cannot address its informational requirements within an acceptable time frame.
- *Legacy systems.* The system has been in place for some time while IS attended to more urgent matters. Eventually, the need for some form of technical management of the data becomes evident.
- *Acquisitions.* The company has just acquired a new division that has its own database system.

All the problems cited can be avoided if the databases, although physically separate (and possibly residing on different hardware and software platforms), are made to function as a single database. In other words, the update path for one database is the update path for the others. This minimizes all the problems except for data redundancy. Exhibit 1 illustrates, from a user's perspective, how multiple databases can be physically separated yet conceptually linked together.

The remainder of this chapter addresses how to build the bridge from one database to another so that they function as one. Although the scenario described thus far considers two databases, more may be involved. The techniques suggested in this chapter will also work with multiple separate databases.

THE MANAGERIAL CHALLENGE

Although there are substantial technical considerations, the primary challenge is managerial. The reasons are threefold:

- *Departmental and functional areas will cross in the formation of the solution.* Without senior management involvement, turf lines may be drawn and the entire project risks becoming mired in political infighting.
- *The lack of detailed data definitions can cause the cost of the project to go up and the effectiveness of the solution to go down.* This activity is

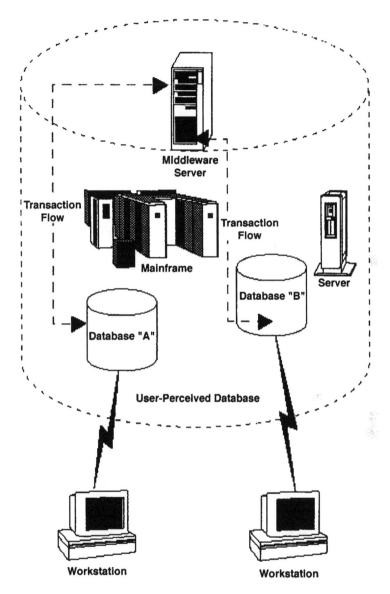

Exhibit 1. **Physically separated but conceptually linked databases (user's perspective).**

not primarily technical but rather managerial. The organization must decide who has what rights to the data and what, exactly, the data represents. As any database administrator can attest, this activity can be hampered by departmental disputes. Senior management support and involvement can help minimize these disputes. An attempt to harness two (or more) databases without a serious data definition effort will produce enough confusion to endanger the entire project.

- *Because the ramifications of project failure can materially affect the organization's bottom line, senior management must be involved.* Management must recognize data as one of the most important assets of the organization.

EVALUATING ALTERNATIVES

Early in the project, alternatives to building a functional bridge might be evaluated. The alternatives fall into two main classes: incorporation versus consolidation of databases.

Incorporation. This technique involves expanding one database to cover the functions of the second. Data items that represent those not currently in the main database are added. New software must be created that provides the functional capabilities of the old system.

Although neither a small nor simple project (depending on the complexity of the replaced system), incorporation of databases does have the advantage that it eliminates the data redundancy problem.

Consolidation of Databases. This alternative involves combining the two databases on the same platform. The databases remain separate but reside on the same hardware and under the same software. A functional bridge must still be built, but the communications aspect is greatly simplified and replaced by internal computer processes. However, as in the incorporation technique, the replaced system's functional capabilities must be replaced with new software.

In each of the alternatives, considerations should be given to the current system load, the number of added users to the primary database, among other factors. Incorporation is technically less ambitious than consolidation and is therefore the preferred of the two methods. However, both of the alternatives are generally more expensive to implement than the functional bridge.

THE FUNCTIONAL BRIDGE SOLUTION: STEP BY STEP

A functional bridge is a method to bring transactions from one database to the other so that there is a single update path for all data items.

Planning the Functional Bridge

The first step, of course, is to plan the bridge. There is a great deal more documentation and planning work required than technical implementation effort in building the bridge. If inadequate planning is performed, it is almost certain that no amount of technical prowess will compensate. There are two main initiatives in the planning phase of the functional database bridge:

- *Evaluations of the existing communications infrastructure, available expertise, and commercial middleware.* These evaluations are primarily technical in nature, although management will have some influence because new capabilities may be indicated. For example, if the current communications infrastructure is deemed inadequate, management must approve the building of the new abilities.
- *Designations of master databases, update frequency, and data ownership.* These designations, although influenced by technical considerations, are primarily management decisions and represent points that could materially alter business practices.

Evaluating the Communications Infrastructure. An evaluation of the existing communications infrastructure should establish the following information:

- *The available communications paths between the databases.* This may be a LAN, WAN, T1 line, batch tape, queuing system, or any other way to move the information between systems.
- *The security of the communications paths.* Because there will now be transaction flow from one database to another, security considerations are important. For example, if the proposed communications channel is a T1 line from another city, it can be considered secure. If, however, the proposed channel is over a UNIX system that is connected to the Internet (without a firewall), then steps should be taken to qualify all incoming transactions before an update (or any other action, for that matter) is applied.
- *The stability of the communications paths.* How reliable is the channel? How often does it go down?
- *The current load on the communications channel.* Is there enough bandwidth to accommodate the new transaction load? This evaluation necessitates an estimate of transactions per unit time.
- *Failure analysis of the communications channel.* What are the ramifications if the communications carrier should fail? And how long can that failure continue before there are serious ramifications?
- *Communications protocols.* Some smaller (or older) systems do not natively possess modern communications protocols. The choices in this case are either to custom-build an interface to the database, perhaps with vendor assistance (though adding a modern communications protocol to a system can be complicated), or to drop back to a less ambitious communications protocol — for example, batch tape transfer instead of TCP/IP transfer.

Designation of the Database Master. With multiple databases, one database must be considered the master database. That is, the values of the data items in the master database are considered to be the final word. This designation as master, however, is on a data basis. For example, the database on the corporate mainframe may be considered the master for customer name and address, whereas the shipping database (which also contains the customer name and address) is considered the master for the shipping date for a customer's order.

In the determination of the master database, the following criteria should be considered:

- *Stability.* How stable is the database? How much maintenance is required?
- *Vendor support.* How effective is the vendor support for this system/database? How promptly does the vendor respond to support calls?
- *In-house expertise.* Who within the organization knows the system/database well enough to answer routine questions and solve performance problems?
- *Available consultant expertise.* If in-house expertise does not exist or should disappear, is there a pool of consultant expertise upon which to draw?
- *Volume of data.* What is the current volume of data on the database? If data fields are added, what are the ramifications?
- *User load on the host system.* How will the transactions affect system performance? Batch updates, for example, can almost negate online response while it is running. Again, an estimate of transaction volume should be made.

Making Critical Design Decisions

Overall Data Architecture. The design phase of the project should not be entirely end-user driven. The end-user maintains a biased view of the data and often requires data items that are actually derived information and not necessarily stored as fields (e.g., average customer order size). A database administrator (DBA) view, in this case, is required.

The DBA should obtain information about the data items in question from the end-users because they know the data. However, the DBA should then take that information and put it into the context of the overall database structure.

For example, the users tell the DBA about a data item called Last_Contact. The DBA is required to find out the context of this field (i.e., contact by whom?). This may be different from the data item in the main database with a similar name.

Database Linkage. A determination should be made of how tightly linked the databases are — that is to say, how often should the cross-communications occur? This factor is, of course, substantially affected by the communications infrastructure available.

Insofar as technically possible, this consideration should be made for business reasons. The update frequency of names and addresses will likely require no more than a batch update, whereas the update frequency of a medical chart location (in a hospital), for example, would require nothing less than a real-time update. The creation of additional communications ability may legitimately be driven by this design decision.

Data Item Map. The organizational aspects of generating the data definitions required for building the functional bridge were mentioned previously. The actual elements of that definition include:

- The name of the data field in both databases.
- The form of the field in both databases.
- The source of the data. It is not unusual for essentially different data to have the same or similar names across databases.
- The update path of the data. Where does the data originate? Is it original data (i.e., someone keys the data) or is it derived from other items in the database? Who audits the data, and who has the authority to change it?

Update Paths. The data definitions now become an essential ingredient to the design of the update paths. Without the documentation of the existing update paths for each data item involved, and the proposed new update paths, it will be impossible to create an effective transaction flow between the databases.

Changes in the update paths will undoubtedly change departmental procedures. This requires the full cooperation of that department's management and, of course, senior management support.

Communications Back-flow. In some cases, it will be necessary to send transactions in more than one direction. Communication in two or more directions is termed back-flow.

For example, names and addresses may originate in the corporate mainframe and it is considered the master. However, there could be a requirement that the data be updated from the satellite database at a customer service center, for example. Transactions must flow from the master to the satellite for a new customer, but also flow from the satellite to the master to ensure quality customer service. Again, these are not technical decisions (although they have technical ramifications). These decisions should be made for business reasons, not solely technical ones.

Ensuring Positive Feedback. No communications path is error free or fully functional 100% of the time. Good communications design requires a positive feedback. The receiving system must tell the sending system that the data it received was acceptable. This requirement is different from the standard acknowledgement/negative acknowledgement (ACK/NAK) code of a communications systems protocol. This feedback is done at the data application level. It must be known not only that all the bits of the address were received (ACK/NAK), but also that the customer number pointed to a real existing customer.

Sometimes, the positive feedback and the back-flow communications can be combined, thus reducing the network traffic. For example, a medical master database that is adding a new patient sends a transaction giving the demographic data. The satellite database reports back the local contract number assigned to the patient, which is added to the master as an alternative key. Thus, both functions are served with a single transaction.

Preventing Feedback Loops. Like a public address system, transaction systems can suffer from feedback. Transactions are usually triggered when a data field is updated. When this transaction arrives at the satellite database, the associated data field is updated as well. If the satellite database also reports changes in the data item, it would, of course, send a transaction to report the change just made. The result is a feedback loop that causes an endless chain of updates.

To avoid feedback loops, the triggering mechanisms must be aware of the source of the update. If the update came from the master database, the satellite database must recognize that fact and prohibit the change from being reported back to the master database.

Split Transactions. Occasionally, more than one satellite database must be updated with the same data from the master. It is good design to split the transaction rather than have the master send two transactions. Middleware software is usually used in this case. The transaction is received by the software and two (or more) transactions are forwarded to the satellite databases. The transactions may not have the same format (or even the same communications protocol), even though they convey the same information.

Recovery. What happens if the satellite system sends a transaction and the communications channel is down? An important feature of the network should be that it is not possible to lose a transaction. Therefore, if the communications channel is down, the software must wait and retry the transaction later. This recovery feature is inherent in some middleware and some gateways. Regardless of where it exists or whether it was bought or built, it must be present in the functional bridge in order to have a reliable communications path.

Common Ground: Constructing the Bridge

Once the above design has been completed, the actual bridge can be constructed. The bridge consists of five parts: transactions, transaction carriers, gateways, middleware, and trigger events.

Transactions. At this stage of design, the data required and the associated update paths should be fully known and documented. Because multiple transaction systems are not unusual, the content of the transactions must be designed so that coherent sets of information are available during update.

Transaction Carriers. This is the protocol of the transactions. There are multiple levels of the communications protocol. The low level is usually handled by the software employed (multiple communications protocols could be involved, however, and ways of translating one protocol to another may be required). On another level, the transaction must have ways of identifying itself to the update software. This requires transaction identification within the transaction itself. Routing information may also be required for complex environments.

Gateways. The software that actually updates the database is typically known as a gateway. In some database systems, the gateway comes as an internal part of the database itself; with others, it must be added.

In extreme cases, it will be necessary to create the gateway. This kind of gateway is likely to be the most difficult to test and debug, since all combinations of data must be tested — a substantial task even for a moderate set of transactions.

Middleware. Early in the project, evaluations of existing commercial middleware should be undertaken. There are several products on the market with a range of capabilities, some better than others. This software can substantially reduce the technical development and support aspect of the project and provide significantly better control than could (or would) be produced in-house.

Middleware is a generic name that refers to software that accepts and sends transactions between disparate clients and servers, usually converting communications protocols along the way. Better commercial versions also offer transaction reformatting and splitting.

Middleware is very effective in larger client/server systems, but requires an initial commitment to infrastructure creation. Middleware capabilities range from basic queuing support to full distributed computing management environments.

The control and statistical aspects of the software are also important because these features give the user the ability to shut down portions of the network and to keep track of the number, size, and status of the transactions.

Trigger Events. These are the events that cause a transaction to be sent or received. The trigger can be as simple as a command at the console (in the case of batch), the act of receiving a TCP/IP transaction, or a relational database stored procedure designed to act as a trigger.

In any case, the trigger event controls the flow of transactions over the bridge. Usually, these triggers must be coded in the database itself because it is at that point that the transaction originates.

SUMMARY

This chapter presents an overall view of the elements required for the successful management of multiple databases. The recommended approach is the construction of a functional bridge that allows the multiple databases to function as a single database.

The construction effort is largely one of management and definition, rather than a challenge of technical implementation. Failure to implement an integration strategy, such as a functional bridge, for databases that contain related data will inevitably result in inaccurate information being supplied to the organization's management.

Chapter 51
Mobile and Federated Database Interoperability

Antonio Si

WIRELESS NETWORKS AND MOBILE COMPUTING HAVE OPENED UP NEW POSSIBILITIES for information access and sharing. The need to interoperate multiple heterogeneous, autonomous databases is no longer confined to a conventional federated environment.

A mobile environment is usually composed of a collection of static servers and a collection of mobile clients. Each server is responsible for disseminating information over one or more wireless channels to a collection of mobile clients. The geographical area within which all mobile clients could be serviced by a particular server is called a cell of that server.

In this mobile environment, databases managed by database servers of different cells might be autonomous. Information maintained in a database will usually be most useful to clients within its geographical cell. In this respect, information maintained by databases of different cells might be disjoint or might be related. A mobile client, when migrating from one wireless cell to another, might want to access information maintained in the database server and relate it to the information maintained in its own database. Such an environment is termed a mobile federation, to distinguish it from a conventional federated environment. The database managed by a mobile client is termed a mobile database, while the database managed by the server is a server database. Using similar terminology, the database system managed by a mobile client is referred to as a mobile component and the database system managed by a server is referred to as a server component.

It is not clear if existing techniques can address interoperability in this newly evolved computing environment. This article presents a reference architecture for a conventional federated environment, proposes a set of

0-8493-9976-9/99/$0.00+$.50
© 1999 by CRC Press LLC

functional requirements that a federated environment should support, and examines existing techniques for a federated environment with respect to each functional requirement in the context of the newly evolved mobile federation.

A WORKING SCENARIO

A tourist would like to discover information about attractions and accommodations within a certain area. With a portable computer equipped with a wireless communication interface, each mobile client (tourist) can receive travel information from the server over a wireless channel. Such an application might be called an Advanced Traveler Information System (ATIS).

In practice, each server database would maintain traveler information restricted to its own cell. For example, a server database serving the city of Los Angeles might provide vacancy information in all hotels within the Los Angeles area, such as the Holiday Inn near the Hollywood freeway. A user might query the server database to obtain all hotels that have vacancies. Information maintained by different server databases might, to a large extent, be disjoint in this application domain, but there might still be some information overlap among different server databases.

For example, a Holiday Inn within the Los Angeles region might decide to maintain partial information on Holiday Inns in other regions, such as Pasadena. It is also important to note that different server databases will, in general, be autonomous, employing different database management tools and even different data models to manage its own information. Exhibit 1 illustrates a snapshot of the information maintained in different server databases and a mobile client who accesses information via a wireless channel.

It would be useful to have a high-level capability that allows structured units of information to be identified from a server database and incorporated into a local database managed by a mobile client. For example, a client might want to maintain information on all hotels in cell 1 and cell 2, since it travels to these two areas the most. A client visiting cell 1 (as shown in Exhibit 1) might issue a query to obtain all hotel information. When the client visits cell 2, the hotel information incorporated into his or her database will have to be interoperated with the existing information that the client previously incorporated from the server database in cell 1. This allows a mobile client to query the information using its own familiar database management tools. These various server databases, together with the local database of the mobile client, form a mobile federation. It is interesting to note that the local database maintained in a mobile client is, in effect, a data warehouse since its data is constructed by integrating data from various data sources.

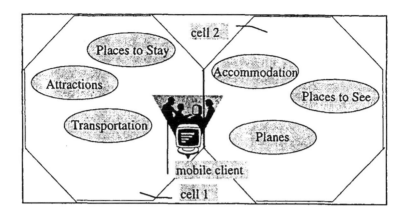

Exhibit 1. Snapshot of ATIS databases.

The objective of a mobile federation is similar to a conventional federated database environment. Both environments are trying to share information among multiple autonomous databases. In a mobile federation, the sharing of information is implicit; the information is shared within the context of a mobile client. In a conventional federated system, the information is shared among the databases themselves. Obviously, the server databases of various cells could also share information among themselves, in which case the server databases form a conventional federated environment as well.

FEDERATED ENVIRONMENT ARCHITECTURE

Exhibit 2 illustrates a typical federated environment. As the exhibit shows, a collection of independent database components is interconnected via a communication network. Each component consists of a database and a schema. A database is a repository of data structured or modeled according to the definition of the schema, which can be regarded as a collection of conceptual entity types. (The implementation of an entity type, of course, depends on the database model employed by the component; it may be a relation in a relational model, or it can be an object class, if an object-oriented model is employed.)

Information Sharing Techniques

Sharing of database information in this federated environment could be achieved at three different levels of granularity and abstraction:

- Entity types belonging to the schema of individual components could be shared such that modeled real-world concepts could be reused.

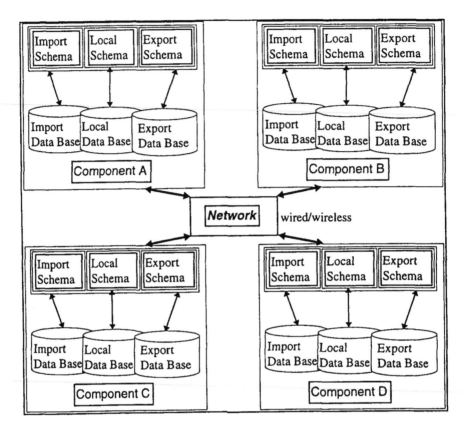

Exhibit 2.   Reference architecture for a federated environment.

- Data instances stored in individual components' databases (the implementation of which also depends on the database model employed) could be shared such that information of modeled real-world entities could be reused.
- Applications developed on a component's database could be shared among any other components. For example, if the server database in cell 1 in Exhibit 1 develops a pathfinder application that allows a mobile client to search for the shortest route to a destination, it could be reused by a mobile client in searching paths within cell 2 as well.

The simplest way to achieve information sharing in a database federation is for a component to simply browse through the content of a nonlocal (i.e., remote) component's database. In this respect, an explorer should be provided. Alternatively, a component could integrate remote information into its local database. The newly integrated information could be reused by the component in the future. To support such reuse of information, the database of a component, say X, is logically partitioned into three different subsets, as shown in Exhibit 2:

- *Local database*. The local database (LD) refers to the set of data instances originally created by X.
- *Import database*. The import database (ID) refers to the set of remote data instances that X retrieves from the export databases of remote components.
- *Export database*. The export database (ED) is a subset of the union of the local database and import database, which represents the set of data instances the component is willing to share with other components. In other words, a component should be able to export its imported data instances if the access privilege constraints specified on the imported instances are not violated.

Similarly, from the reference architecture in Exhibit 1, the schema of a component X is also partitioned into three different subsets. The local schema (LS) refers to the entity types originally created by X and is used to model the local database. The import schema (IS), which refers to the entity types X retrieves from the export schema of remote components, is used to model the import database. Finally, the export schema (ES), which is the subset of the union of LS and IS, is used to model the export database.

Integrating a remote application belonging to a remote component, say Y, into X's local system is difficult because X's local computer system might be different from that of Y. One possibility (proposed by D. Fang, et al.) is to integrate the signature of the remote application into X's local system. To execute the application, X's local data is passed to component Y; the application is run on the remote component using X's data and the results are returned back to X. The Java virtual machine could make application sharing easier.

CHARACTERISTICS OF A FEDERATED DATABASE ENVIRONMENT

Each component within a federation is usually heterogeneous and autonomous in nature. Heterogeneity is a natural consequence of the independent creation and evolution of autonomous databases; it refers to the variations in which information is specified and structured in different components. Autonomy means each component is under separate and independent control.

Heterogeneity

In general, a spectrum of heterogeneities of different levels of abstraction could be classified.

Database model heterogeneity. Each component may use different database models to describe the structure and constraints of its data.

Conceptual schema heterogeneity. Each component may model similar real-world concepts in different ways, such as the different schema used by the different database components of the multiple ATIS databases depicted in Exhibit 1. This is also referred to as semantic heterogeneity. This conceptual schema heterogeneity could be further divided into three discrepancies, each of which can be explained as follows:

- *Naming mismatch.* Two entity types from different components modeling the same real-world concept might use different naming conventions in representing the attributes. In the ATIS database in Exhibit 1, the ranking of a hotel might be modeled by an attribute called "rank" of Places to Stay in component A, while the same information might be modeled by an attribute called "number of stars" of Accommodation in component B.
- *Domain mismatch.* The same attribute of two entity types from different components might be represented in different domains. For example, both Attractions and Places to See of components A and B, respectively, in Exhibit 1 might have an attribute "zip code." However, component A might represent the attribute as an integer, while component B might represent it as a string.
- *Schematic discrepancy.* Data in one database might be represented as entity types in another database. In Exhibit 1, entity type Planes of component B might be represented as an attribute of Attractions in component A.
- *Data specification heterogeneity.* Each component may model similar real-world entities in different units of measure. One component might represent the distance of an attraction in meters, while another component might represent it in miles.
- *Update heterogeneity.* Since each component is under separate and independent control, data instances modeling the same real-world entity in different databases might be updated asynchronously. When the daily rate of a hotel is updated, databases A and B in Exhibit 1 might be updated at different times.
- *Database tools heterogeneity.* Each component may use different tools to manipulate its own database. For example, different components might use different query languages.

Types of Autonomy

Orthogonally, each component can exhibit several different types of autonomy.

Design autonomy. This refers to the ability of a component to choose its own design on the data being managed, the representation of the data instances, the constraints of the data, and the implementation of the component's database system.

Association autonomy. This refers to the ability of a component to decide to what extent the component would like to participate in the interoperability activity. A component is free to share its schema, data, or applications with other components; a component can even decide not to participate in the sharing activity at all.

Control autonomy. This refers to the ability of a component to control the access privileges of any remote component on each of its exported information units (entity types or instances). In general, four types of access control privilege could be granted by a component to a remote component on each of its exported information units:

- Read (R) access to the database instances
- Read definition (RD) access to entity types
- Write (W) access to database instances
- Generate (G) access for creating database instances

These four access privileges form a partial order such that W > G > RD and W > R > RD. Neither G nor R dominates each other. For instance, if component X grants W access privilege to remote component Y on one of its exported entity types, component Y is allowed to read the instances of the entity type as well. By contrast, if X only grants R access privilege to Y on the entity type, Y is not allowed to modify any instances of the entity type.

If an exported unit of a component, say X, is imported from another component, Y, the capability of X to control the access privileges on the exported unit will depend on whether the unit is imported by copy or imported by reference from Y.

Execution autonomy. This refers to the ability of a component to execute local operations without interference from external components. If, for example, component X might run an application on behalf of remote component Y. This autonomy implies that X can run the application as if it is a local execution (i.e., X can schedule, commit, or abort the application freely).

FUNCTIONAL REQUIREMENTS OF A FEDERATED DATABASE ENVIRONMENT

From the perspective of a component, X, several functional capabilities need to be supported in order to be able to participate in the interoperability activity with other components.

Information Exportation

Component X must be able to specify the information it is willing to share with other components. Such a facility should allow the component to specify the export schema, the export database, or any application that the component would like to be sharable. Furthermore, X should be able to specify the access privileges of each remote component on each of its exported information units.

A mobile federation is comparatively more dynamic than a database federation, connecting and disconnecting from the wireless network frequently. A mobile component also enters and leaves a cell frequently. It is difficult for a server component to keep track of which mobile components are currently residing within the cell under its management. Furthermore, a cell can potentially have many components visiting at any moment. Therefore, it is not possible for a server component to indicate the access privileges of each mobile component. An access control mechanism that is scalable with respect to the number of mobile components is necessary. Due to the dynamic nature of a mobile component, it is not always possible to incorporate information from a mobile component.

Information Discovery

Before component X can access or use any remote information, X must be aware of the existence and availability of the information in which it is interested. A facility must be provided to allow X to discover any remote information of interest at various granularity or abstraction, including schema, data, or applications.

In general, there are two ways information could be discovered by component X. One possibility is that X can formulate a discovery request for its interested information, in which case a facility must be provided to identify the components containing information units that are relevant to the request. Another possibility is for component X to navigate or explore the exported information space of each remote component and look for the interested information. An explorer must then be provided for such a navigation purpose.

Information Importation

Once interested information units from remote components are discovered, component X can import the information units into its local database. Through importation, component X can reuse the discovered information in the future. In general, three importation capabilities are required: schema importation, data importation, and application importation.

Schema importation. This refers to the process of importing remote export schema into X's local schema. This process is further composed of two activities — heterogeneity resolution and schema integration. Heterogeneity resolution is the process of resolving any conflict that exists between X's local schema and the remote schema.

Since different components might use different database models to specify the data, a facility must be provided to translate the remote schema from the remote database model to the one used in X's local system. Furthermore, since different components might model similar real-world concepts differently, another heterogeneity that must be resolved is to identify the relationship between X's local schema and the remote schema.

Referring back to the ATIS federation in Exhibit 1, two entity types belonging to two different schema might model the same real-world concept, such as the Attractions information of component A and the Places to See information of component B. Alternatively, two entity types might model related information, such as the Transportation information of component A and the Planes information of component B. Finally, two entity types might model different concepts, such as the Attractions information of component A and the Planes information of component B.

Data importation. Similarly, data importation refers to the process of importing remote export database information into X's local database. This process is composed of two activities — instance identification and data integration.

Instance identification refers to the process of identifying the relationship between the remote database and the local database. Two data instances from different databases might model the same, related, or different real-world entities. This process is complicated because, on the one hand, instances from different databases cannot be expected to bear the same key attributes; on the other hand, merely matching non-key attributes may lead to unsatisfactory results because data instances modeling different entities may possess the same attribute values. This process is further complicated by possible update heterogeneity that might exist between the two instances.

Once the relationship between the remote database and X's local database is identified, the remote database can be integrated into the local database. Again, the remote database should be integrated such that its relationship with the local database is reflected.

There are two different paradigms for integrating a remote data instance from a remote component, Y, into X's local database: imported by copy and imported by reference.

When a remote instance is imported by copy, the data instance is copied into the local database. The copied data instance becomes part of the local database. Any access to the imported instance is referred to its local copy.

When a remote instance is imported by reference, a reference to the remote instance is maintained in the local database. Any access to the imported data instance requires a network request to Y for up-to-date data value. When a remote data instance is imported by copy, the local component, X, has complete control on the local copy of the imported instance and is allowed to specify the access privileges of other remote components on the local copy of the imported instance. However, when a remote data instance is imported by reference from component Y, Y still maintains its control over the imported instance. Component X is still free to export the imported instance; however, X cannot modify the access privileges specified by Y on this imported data instance.

Application importation can only be achieved to a very limited extent due to the possible differences in the computer systems of the different components. However, with the advent of Java mobility code, this could soon become a reality.

In a mobile federation, communication between a mobile component and a server database is usually over an unreliable wireless channel. It is more efficient for a mobile federation to import an instance by copying since a component does not need to rely on the network to obtain the data value of the instance. A mobile component, in general, has less storage space than a federated component. A mobile component, therefore, might not be able to import all data instances and will have to maintain only those instances that it accesses most frequently.

Information querying and transaction processing. Component X should be able to operate its imported information in its local system. The operation on the imported information should be transparent in the following manner:

- *Functional transparency.* All existing local tools of component X, such as its query language and DBMS software, should be operational on the imported information units in the same manner as they operate on the local information units.
- *Location transparency.* Users and tools operating on the imported information units should not be aware of their original locations and remote nature.

Very often, there is a conflict between supporting the described functional capabilities in a component and preserving the autonomy of the component. To preserve the autonomy of a component, modifying any component of the DBMS software is not recommended.

TECHNIQUES FOR DATABASE SHARING

To support database sharing functional capabilities, data model heterogeneity must be resolved. This is usually addressed by employing a common canonical model, which provides a communication forum among various components. Schema and instances represented in the local data model are required to convert to the canonical model. Most research prototypes use an object model as the canonical model because of its expressive power. Most corporations, however, use relational models. ODBC from

Microsoft and JDBC from Sun Microsystems are generally considered the industry standards.

Information Exportation

Information exportation can be easily achieved using database view mechanisms. Exhibit 3 illustrates the management of exported information. A sub-hierarchy rooted at class Exported-Classes is created under the root of the class hierarchy (i.e., OBJECTS). To export a class, O, a class name E_O is created as a subclass of Exported-Classes. To export an attribute of O, the same named attribute is created for E_O; this allows a component to specify exported information at the granularity of a single attribute.

Each exported instance is handled by a multiple-membership modeling construct of the object model, relating the original class to which the instance belongs to the E_ counterpart. In effect, classes belonging to the sub-hierarchy rooted at Exported-Classes represent the export schema, and the instances belonging to the sub-hierarchy represent the export database (depicted by the shaded region in Exhibit 3).

In Exhibit 3, only class Places to Stay is exported because only Places to Stay has a corresponding E_Places to Stay class. All attributes of Places to Stay have the corresponding ones defined on E_Places to Stay. Furthermore, two instances of Places to Stay are exported, relating via a multiple membership construct to

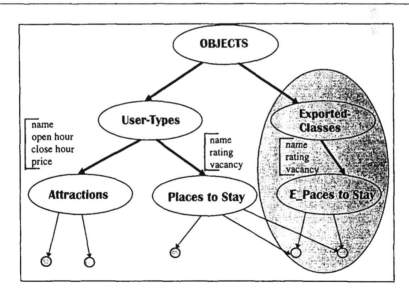

Exhibit 3.   Information exportation via object view.

E_Places to Stay. A component employing a relational data model could use a similar technique to specify its exporting information units since the export schema and database are, in effect, a view of the database.

Access control mechanisms for exported information are limited and especially difficult to achieve in a mobile federation. It is difficult for a server component to keep track of which mobile components are within the cell under its management and specify their individual access privileges. A multilevel access control mechanism is more applicable in this domain.

In a multilevel system, database information units are classified into privilege levels. The privilege levels are arranged in an order such that possessing a privilege level implies possessing all its subordinate levels. For example, a typical multilevel system contains four privilege levels: top secret (TS), secret (S), confidential (C), and unclassified (U). A typical database system could have arbitrary number of privilege levels. To access an information unit, the user needs to obtain a clearance at least equal to the privilege level of the unit. In a mobile federation, a mobile component could join a privilege level that will inherit the database information units that it could access from the server database.

Information Discovery

Information discovery can be achieved by exploring the exported information of a database component. A typical device that explores the content of several databases is depicted in Exhibit 4. This explorer is implemented on the Netscape Navigator, providing a platform-independent browsing capability because of the availability of Netscape in UNIX workstations, Macintosh computers, and PCs.

The explorer in Exhibit 4 allows a component to explore multiple databases at the same time. It employs a relational model as the canonical model. Exported information units are viewed as relations. The explorer has windows to browse four separate databases of remote components and a window to the local database of a component.

An alternate approach to discovering remote information units that are interesting to a particular component is to specify the requirements of the interested information units. Remote information units that are relevant to the discovery specification will be identified. Specification could be initiated in an ad hoc manner. Following are three different types of discovery requests:

- A component can request remote entity types (instances) that model the same real-world concept (entity) as a local entity type (instance).
- A component can request remote entity types (instances) that model a complementary view of a local entity type (instance).

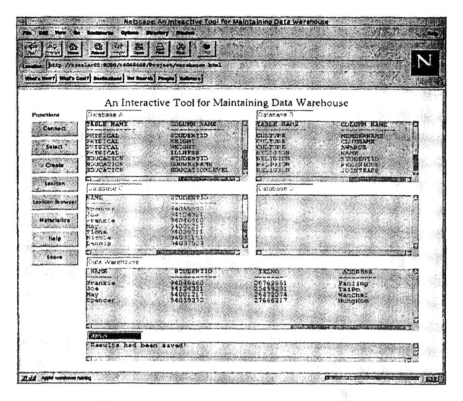

Exhibit 4.   A sample information discovery explorer.

- A component can request remote entity types (instances) that model an overlapping view of a local entity type (instance).

To support these three types of discovery requests, one approach is to use a probability model to determine the extent to which two entity types (instances) from different databases modeled the same real-world concept. The probability model is based on two heuristics derived from the common attributes of the two entity types: intra-concept similarity indicator and inter-concept dissimilarity indicator.

Intuitively, an intra-concept similarity indicator refers to the probability that the common attributes will be modeled in related entity types. Inter-concept dissimilarity indicator refers to the probability that the attributes will be modeled in unrelated entity types. Two entity types from different databases will have a high probability of similarity if their overlapped attributes have a high intra-concept similarity indicator as well as a high inter-concept dissimilarity indicator. The use of these heuristics is based on the observation that different databases might model complementary or even disjointed views of the same concept; on the other hand, different databases might model different concepts similarly.

A more general specification could be achieved using first-order logic like language. Each component will thus require a mediator that understands the specification language and identifies information units relevant to the specification.

In a mobile federation, it is not important if a server database returns all information relevant to a discovery request; rather, it is much more important that the returned information units are indeed relevant because of the typically low bandwidth on a wireless channel. One approach to ensure this is to create a profile capturing the interests of each component.

Information Importation

Schema importation. As mentioned previously, a component, X, can import (partial) remote schema from a remote component, Y, into its local schema by first resolving any heterogeneity between X's local schema and Y's schema.

One common approach to resolve schema heterogeneity between X's local schema and Y's remote schema is through a common knowledge base that contains various real-world concepts. Entity types from different databases are required to match with the concepts in the knowledge base. If both entity types map to the same concept in the knowledge base, they are regarded as modeling the same real-world concept. The knowledge base also provides instructions that define how a remote entity type could be integrated into the schema of a component's local database. The instructions could be specified in the form of rules or in a logic-like syntax. The former is easier to understand, but is less flexible. The latter is more flexible, but is less user-friendly.

In a mobile federation, it is difficult to specify a knowledge base that is applicable to all mobile components because there is a potentially unlimited number of mobile components visiting a wireless cell. It is perhaps more appropriate for a mobile component to provide its own knowledge or its personal profile, containing its own view for integrating remote schema into its own local schema.

Instance importation. To identify the relationship between instances from two databases, one needs to address the data specification heterogeneity and the update heterogeneity problems. Data specification heterogeneity is usually resolved, again, via a knowledge base, indicating how the representation of a remote instance could be converted into the representation of the local database.

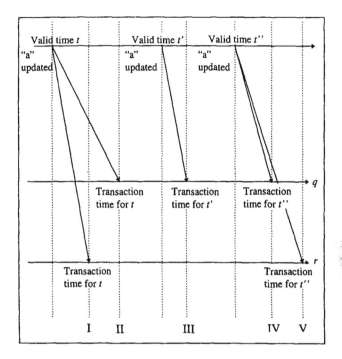

Exhibit 5.   Updated heterogeneity in a database federation.

Exhibit 5 illustrates the importance of update heterogeneity in identifying the relationship between instances from various databases. In Exhibit 5, valid time denotes the time in which a fact was true in reality, while the transaction time denotes the time in which a fact was captured in a database.

One approach to addressing update heterogeneity is to use historical update information on the instances to determine their degree of similarity. The historical update patterns of each instance represent the changes of states of the instance since its creation, inherently capturing its behavioral properties. This allows the instance identification to be performed based on behavioral property in addition to their structural property, as is done traditionally. The historical update information of an instance could be easily obtained through a transaction log.

As mentioned previously, instance integration could be performed via import by copy or import by reference. Using an object model as a canonical model, it is quite easy to support these two integration paradigms within one general framework. Exhibit 5 illustrates the partial conceptual schema of two components, A and B, of the ATIS databases from Exhibit 1.

Instances x and y of component B are imported from class Accommodation of component A. The class Remote-Classes is created in component B to hold the object instance of definitions (OIDS) of the imported instances and the address of components from which the instances are imported (i.e., address of component A in the example). These two types of information are placed in the attributes r_oid and r_host, respectively. A class called R_Accommodation is created in component B as subclass of Remote-Classes to model the imported instances.

In effect, the sub-hierarchy rooted at Remote-Classes represents the import schema and the instances belonging to the sub-hierarchy represent the import database; this is depicted by the shaded region in Exhibit 6. Notice that the import sub-hierarchy has a mirror structure as the export sub-hierarchy mentioned previously.

Attributes of classes belonging to the Remote-Classes sub-hierarchy are user-defined methods. To obtain the attribute value for attribute "a" of an imported instance, x, the method "a" will obtain the "r_oid" of x and initiate a remote request to the remote component, whose address is specified in "r_host" of x, to obtain the attribute value for the instance. This achieves the effect of imported by reference. To support import by copy, the imported instances are added to a local class via multiple-membership construct. The additional inherited attributes could be used as placeholders for the copied attribute values of the imported instance. This is illustrated in Exhibit 6. The obtained value of an attribute of an instance returned from the corresponding method could be stored in the additional attributes inherited.

In a mobile federation, the connection between a mobile component and the server component could be disconnected at any moment, either due to the unreliability of a wireless channel or due to the movement of a mobile component to another cell. It is, thus, more appropriate for a component to import an instance by copy rather than by reference. This also has an effect of caching the instance into the local database of a mobile component. In this respect, one could regard the local database of a mobile component as a data warehouse since the local database is derived from multiple database sources.

Information discovery and importation could be provided within a uniform framework or interface. This allows discovered remote information units to be imported into the local database of a component. The explorer in Exhibit 4 also provides functions for information importation as well. In this particular system, a relational model is employed as a canonical model. The integration of information units from several databases is basically achieved via the "join" operation in this explorer. A component could also create a lexicon containing relationships among attributes of different da-

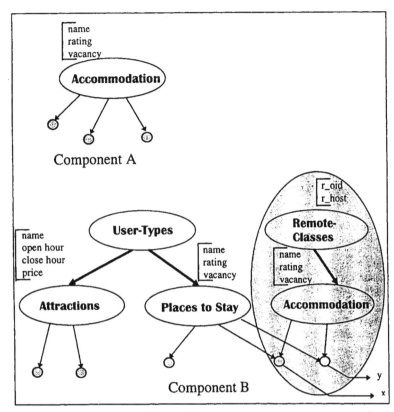

Exhibit 6.   Data integration.

tabases. This resolves the conceptual heterogeneity. This lexicon acts as a localized profile of the component, capturing the perspectives of the component on the relationships among information units from different databases.

Information Querying and Transaction Processing

The notion of transaction is supported weakly in existing database federation prototypes. The reason stems from the fact that it is very difficult to support all the properties of transaction processing in a federated database system without seriously violating the autonomy of individual components and without rewriting the DBMS software of individual components.

Consider a situation in which a component X submits a transaction T to a remote component Y. The transaction T, when executed in component Y, is simply a local transaction of component Y. Component Y is free to abort the transaction without notifying component X. Component X, thus, might obtain inconsistent data.

CONCLUSION

This article has presented a reference architecture and functional requirements for a federated database environment. Techniques for addressing each functional requirement have been presented. Limitations of existing techniques in the domain of a mobile federation have been discussed, and proposed solutions have also been briefly illustrated. Experiences with real applications in a mobile federation are necessary to further pinpoint additional problems that require research.

ACKNOWLEDGMENTS

This work is supported in part by the Hong Kong Polytechnic University Central Research Grant Number 351/217. Part of the materials in this chapter are the results of the Remote-Exchange project at the University of Southern California.

Section IX
Data Replication

DATA REPLICATION COMMONLY SATISFIES SEVERAL REAL-WORLD REQUIRE-
MENTS. These includes data backup, data sharing, and performance improvement. Data warehouses, data marts, and reporting systems also rely
on accessing replicated data stores. This section contains three chapters
that describe tools, techniques, and processes relating to data replication.

Chapter 52, "The Power of Transformational Data Replication," shows
how replication software can be used to simplify the task of moving data
between heterogeneous computer systems and database software, with
extensive programming.

Chapter 53, "Database Replication: Application Design and Deployment
Issues," discusses the benefits of replication, including data availability,
performance, data integration, application integration, and application migration. The chapter also describes other issues related to replication,
such as architectural considerations, heterogeneous replication, managing
replication, and design.

Chapter 54, "Secure Information Through a Replicated Architecture," describes how replication could provide multilevel security. The idea is to
replicate the data based on security levels. Each node stores data at or below the security level designated; that is, a confidential node stores unclassified and confidential data, and a secret node stores unclassified,
confidential, and secret data. This means that unclassified and confidential
data are replicated at both nodes. The chapter then describes a prototype
system based on this approach.

Chapter 52
The Power of Transformational Data Replication

Jason Weir

BUSINESS SOLUTIONS TODAY ARE NOT BUILT BY CONCRETE AND STEEL but rather by data or information. Fast access to data in a format conducive to query and analysis activity by decision-makers and knowledge workers offers companies significant competitive advantages.

Commonly, answers to critical business decisions are hidden away in data collected from various departments or corporate operation centers. For many organizations, accessing and analyzing that data is next to impossible. Production data is often stored in formats not readily interpretable by those who need it. Obscure naming conventions and database codes make extracting the required information a lesson in cryptography.

On top of this, in a business climate where change is the only constant, the proliferation of mixed-system environments is staggering. Rapid corporate mergers and acquisitions often leave IS managers with a variety of computing platforms and database technologies. Further, end users demand better data availability and the freedom to choose from today's variety of powerful front-end access tools, which offer a rich, robust computing experience. To complicate things more, many companies harness the power of distributed computing applications, enterprise resource planning systems (ERP), and continue to tap valuable legacy data housed on mainframe systems.

With the introduction of new operating systems, database software and computing platforms, IS managers face momentous obstacles. Traditionally, solutions would require significant investment of time, resources, and money. Programmers, consultants, new equipment, and support staff would have been necessary to get the job done, not to mention a good deal of time, which many companies hold as a rare commodity.

For businesses facing the challenges outlined by the above scenarios, as well as those looking to implement many of today's distributed data applications such as data warehousing, electronic business, and high systems availability, data replication may be the solution.

WHAT IS TRANSFORMATIONAL DATA REPLICATION?

Historically, sharing corporate data enterprise-wide has involved using one of several options. Companies could copy data to physical storage media, such as tape or disk, and deliver it to remote sites, or rely on batch copy or disk mirroring software. Alternatively, custom applications were built to duplicate local databases and distribute them to other systems.

However, these methods had drawbacks. They were slow, inefficient and, because they all depended on some form of straight data copy, delivered data in the same and, often times, confusing format. With data replication software, businesses can not only move data from where it is, to where it needs to be, but also ensure that it is presented in the required format for decision support, query, and analysis.

Data replication involves selecting and filtering data from production databases, moving it among similar or disparate operating systems, computing platforms, and database technologies, and transforming it so that it is in desired and standardized formats.

Businesses can harness the power of data replication tools for such solutions as data distribution and synchronization, loading and replenishing data marts and data warehouses, high systems availability, and electronic business. Another key use is in integrating enterprise resource planning systems (ERP) like SAP, Baan, and PeopleSoft with relational databases such as Oracle and Sybase.

As with many sectors of the computer software market, the replication space is highly competitive. Several companies focus exclusively on data replication and transformation software and most major database vendors, including Oracle, Sybase, and Microsoft, all offer replication solutions. The various replication solutions built by these vendors vary in approach but outlined below are some basic characteristics every good replication tool should have.

ASYNCHRONOUS REPLICATION

Some replication software packages use asynchronous architecture, meaning that synchronization can occur while other processes continue. This is in contrast with the two-phase commit logic inherent in distributed database management systems (DBMS). Distributed DBMSs involve placing pieces of a database on different systems and accessing data as though it exists on one system.

Two-phase commit architecture guarantees that all database copies are synchronized, regardless of location, but any update failure can cause a transaction to be *rolled back*. This necessitates a complete database refresh, or resynchronization, which can be extremely time consuming. Moreover, as the number of nodes within a DBMS increases, two-phase commit logic becomes unworkable as all subsequent updates are frozen until the commit process is completed for the current transaction. Essentially, system usage comes to a halt each time an update occurs.

Asynchronous replication, on the other hand, provides reliable delivery of data while preventing any possible transaction deadlock between multiple database engines. Asynchronous architecture also allows data recovery in case of communication failure and offers replication on a predetermined schedule to avoid network or resource interruption.

SELECTIVE FILTERING

An effective replication tool should let users distribute database updates based on row and column criteria. Rather than copying an entire database periodically to synchronize remote systems, the software should be able to distribute database changes on a *net-change* basis. That is, the replication tool should send only those records in a database that have changed since the last update rather than sending every record even if it is redundant. It should also let users distribute changes conditionally, based on critical column updates or row selection criteria.

A good example of the benefits gained by the ability to replicate data by row and column selection can be drawn from human resources databases. With sensitive data, such as that stored in human resources systems, many companies want to exclude particular elements or enhance them for easier analysis. For instance, salary figures could be deselected from the replication process or filtered out so that only salaries exceeding a set amount are distributed to data marts or decision support systems. Another example involves replicating location specific data. For example, data could be selected dependent on department or business unit and replicated to specific remote systems for local use. Selective filtering ensures that only relevant data is sent to target systems and avoids decision support systems from becoming unworkable and inefficient.

FLEXIBLE DATA TRANSFORMATION AND ENHANCEMENT

As mentioned, many replication methods simply copy entire databases from one system to another. This may be desirable in some instances, but most companies require the ability to transform and enhance data. This is especially important for businesses with mixed system environments that do not have standardized data formats.

With some replication tools, custom applications have to be developed and extensive programming may be necessary to accommodate the task of data transformation. Robust replication software, on the other hand, has built-in data transformation and enhancement functionality.

A simple example of the power of data transformation involves multilocation businesses or companies that have merged with or acquired other interests. Branch offices within organizations often adopt different database conventions for such elements as inventory databases. Dissimilar codes and abbreviations for product names, sizes, or colors present real problems when synchronizing data throughout the enterprise, especially for those basing critical decisions on this obscure information.

In short, transformation refers to the ability to alter the data being moved between databases. With transformational capabilities, replication software can remedy common discrepancies. For example, if one branch office uses the code "BI" to represent a "backordered item" and the head office uses the code "02" for the same value, transformation can consolidate the difference to represent a meaningful standard. Now, backordered items can be registered as a single, understandable value such as "Back_Order" on the target data warehouse or decision support system.

Another example of data transformation is value translations such as currencies, weights, and measures. This is extremely valuable for international organizations that want to maintain synchronized databases throughout various countries. International weight units can be converted to United States standards or Canadian dollars converted to British Sterling, for example. Another important data transformation involves the Year 2000 date issue. Many databases, especially those housed on legacy systems, have date formats such as 12/27/94 (December 27, 1994). Data replication software that incorporates transformational capabilities can convert two-digit dates to ISO standard, Year 2000 compliant date formats. The above example would be converted to 1994/12/27 at the target system.

HETEROGENEOUS PLATFORM SUPPORT

As discussed, rapid corporate mergers, acquisitions, and takeovers are commonplace. Often times, however, not a great deal of consideration is given to the compatibility of the technology infrastructure of the new entity. Many replication tools assist, to varying degrees, in delivering data across dissimilar computer hardware, databases, and networks.

Good replication software allows for a high level of platform or database independence and is "scalable." That is, not only should the tool be able to replicate data among existing systems and databases, but also be prepared to handle future introductions.

The level of ease with which replication software replicates data throughout mixed-system environments is also an issue. Many database vendors offer proprietary data replication functionality included as part of their software or as an optional component. The capabilities of such tools range from simple import and export functions to full heterogeneous replication.

Companies relying on these built-in database replication utilities would be wise to keep in mind that it is not in the best interest of database vendors to move data off of their own database, but rather to move data into it. This means that, although these types of tools will often readily and easily replicate another vendor's data-type to their own database, replicating data out of that database to another vendor's can be extremely challenging. To provide seamless replication among disparate databases and computing systems, extensive, time consuming and resource intensive programming of *agents* — components that link one application to another — or use of gateways may be necessary.

Comprehensive data replication packages enable seamless integration of multiple databases and hardware platforms. While they pose an initial expense, the savings of high programming costs and the drastic reduction in implementation time can easily justify the purchase.

Furthermore, some database vendor replication offerings require *data staging* — the movement of data into a temporary holding area prior to being transmitted to the target system. This slows the replication process and may necessitate the purchase of additional hardware as some data stages are housed on intermediary systems that sit between the source and target computers. Data replication software moves data directly from source to target, with no stage required. This enables real-time data replication. As transactions or other changes occur on the source database, they are immediately reflected on any target databases.

In short, while database vendor tools provide support for data replication among heterogeneous systems, the feasibility is limited by high custom programming costs, lengthy implementation processes and, in some cases, data staging logic. In contrast, data replication software provides transparent access to data on dissimilar systems and moves it point to point in real-time.

BI-DIRECTIONAL, REAL-TIME REPLICATION

Many companies, especially those with multiple locations, or autonomous business units, require replication for not only distribution of centralized data, but also for data collecting or consolidation from those sites.

DATA REPLICATION

To enable synchronization of databases throughout the enterprise, data replication tools must have bi-directional capabilities. Additionally, in some applications, the ability to move data in real-time, as opposed to replicating data at scheduled times or even staging data, is critical. Real-time data movement allows access to up-to-the-minute information for more accurate reporting and analysis.

However, users should still have the option to choose among a variety of replication *modes.* That is, some applications may not demand real-time data delivery. Users should be able to schedule replication times or replicate data on an *on demand* basis as required. Regardless, the tool should, as mentioned, replicate only those records that have been added, deleted, or changed since the last update. This ensures that the process is carried out as quickly as possible and high communication costs, traditionally associated with refreshing remote databases, are minimized.

In sum, the replication tool should enable replication among a variety of popular databases, including Oracle, Sybase, Microsoft SQL Server, and DB/2, as well as legacy data from mainframe servers, to and from UNIX, Intel-based servers, and IBM AS/400 systems.

REPLICATION ARCHITECTURE

There are several architectures that data replication tools use to deliver functionality. Brief summaries of each are provided below.

Log-Based vs. Trigger-Based Replication

In log-based replication, changes are captured from a journal or system log and then transmitted to the target system. Log-based replication operates asynchronously and, therefore, has the least effect on system performance. Trigger-based replication, on the other hand, relies on database *triggers* — small event-based functions — that are fired with each database change on the main system. Updates are captured directly from the database and then replicated. If many simultaneous updates occur, trigger-based replication has a greater impact on performance than does log-based replication as triggers require system resources to work.

Push vs. Pull Replication

Replication involves either *pushing* or *pulling* data from the production database. With push replication, replication software on the source computer decides what needs to be transmitted and when to send it. Data is then pushed from the source database as it changes (or at specified time intervals) to the target system(s). As a result, users can use push replication to maintain current copies, or snapshots (time-stamped version of data in the database), of source data on as many systems as required.

With pull replication (also known as the gateway method), user queries at target sites pull data directly from the source database via a communication "gateway." Data is never completely current with this method; and that may be adequate in some situations. Instead, updates are pulled based on time intervals specified by the data administrator when setting up the copy requests. E-mail is a basic analogy of both push and pull methodology. Users can ask the server to deliver their mail by logging on and executing a "send and receive" from their mail program. On the other hand, if users are continuously connected to the server, mail can be pushed by the server to the user at specified intervals like every ten minutes or hourly.

Push and pull replication both let users schedule their data transfers at specific intervals or to coincide with off-peak periods. Users can schedule replication to suit end-user update requirements and system availability. For example, with query databases, a daily or twice-daily update schedule may be sufficient; while database changes may need to be available as soon as they occur on the source system. Using log-based or trigger approaches, replication tools recognize when database updates occur and then, using their defined methods, replicate the updates to the target system(s).

Mixed-mode replication, which involves a combination of push and pull methods, is also possible. Mixed-mode replication usually involves periodically pushing data to an intermediate database and then pulling it from that database at predetermined intervals. You may recall the previous discussion of data staging. This intermediate database is also referred to as a data stage. The mixed-mode architecture has some advantages over straight pull methods as it reduces the performance impact on the source system and allows for some data summarization at the intermediate database. Unfortunately, mixed-mode replication does not provide data concurrency because the target system pulls data only periodically. The required intermediate stage database also results in increased processing load and disk storage to work. A data stage does not necessarily require a separate system, but if it resides on the source system, resources could become strained.

Master/Slave vs. Two-Way Replication

Master/slave replication is the least complex of all data replication architectures. Under this model, there is one master data source, typically a production database. Users or batch jobs make production updates to the master database. The master database then replicates updates to the slave database(s), which accepts updates only from the master. Users can then use slave databases for queries, reporting, and any other processing in which data is not updated.

Two-way replication has some beneficial uses. For example, companies could use two-way replication for *workload management* (also referred to as workload balancing). One system could run interactive processes that update and maintain core data and have data replicated to another system which would run batch processes that maintain totals and other summary data. Companies could then use replicated databases for offline batch processing without interrupting online production transaction processing on the main system.

Two-way replication is also a better solution than two-phase commit logic, in which the update process is synchronous. As noted earlier, failures cause update transactions to roll back to the source database. With large-scale distribution of changes through many servers, multi-level rollbacks could cause considerable processing delays.

Cascading Replication

Some form of cascading replication, in which the target computer replicates data to subsequent targets, may be the only way to broadcast data over large client/server installations. Cascading replication reduces the load on the originating machine and creates a multiplier effect that distributes changes quickly to many targets.

APPLICATIONS

With data replication architecture and core functionality outlined, we can now discuss some of the business solutions that it helps enable.

Data Warehousing

Data warehousing as a tool for business intelligence has gained wide acceptance in the last few years. It is estimated that over 90 percent of Fortune 1000 corporations will have data warehouses or data marts (departmental data warehouses) by the end of the current year. The reasons for this trend are many. Undoubtedly, the data warehouse offers businesses a significant competitive advantage with important benefits that allow companies to:

- Monitor sales activity in order to make fast, informed decisions based on up-to-the-minute information.
- Deliver product to market faster using inventory and manufacturing elements of the data warehouse.
- Predict and understand trends to make better business decisions.

An important part of the data warehouse is the software that loads and replenishes the data that is stored there. This component, namely data replication software, involves constructing an information database from production data in a format that is beneficial to knowledge workers and decision-makers. It also includes regularly updating the informational database as changes to production data occur.

Again, most companies implementing data warehouses require the ability to select, filter, transform and enhance raw production data so that only relevant information, stored in appropriate formats for query and analysis, is transmitted to the data marts or warehouse. It is essential to keep these needs in mind when setting up a data warehouse. The right replication software should not require programming to set up the process of delivering data to the warehouse, should be easy to administer, and offer flexible data conversion, enhancement, and transformation capabilities. Additionally, depending on the technology environment, support for cross-platform, cross-database data replication may also be required.

High Systems Availability

With the growing dependence on data as a competitive weapon and, in some cases, the lifeblood of the organization, few companies can afford even a few hours of total system downtime, let alone days or weeks. Without access to production data, business loses momentum or, worse still, stops altogether. Even if companies can avoid the disaster of unplanned downtime, they still have scheduled outages for hardware and software upgrades and routine maintenance. To avoid the loss of data, or the loss of access to that data, companies implement high systems availability solutions.

In most cases, organizations elect to transfer business-critical applications and data to a failsafe system located offsite. The ideal situation is to switch to the failsafe site when needed and have any changes that occur during downtime replicated back to the production machine when it is brought back online. That is, if the main system is down for 2 hours, and no original data is lost, then only the changes that occurred on the failsafe system during the outage should be replicated back — not the entire database. However, if data is lost on the primary system due to corruption or natural disaster, then companies should have the ability to resynchronize it with the failsafe machine.

Solid data replication tools transfer data from primary system to failsafe machine in real-time, as changes occur, or entire databases on a predetermined schedule. This means companies can opt to refresh the failsafe machine nightly or weekly as required, or have replication software move changes to databases in real-time so that the most current data is available in case of planned or unplanned outages.

Ultimately, when the production system comes back online following downtime, the replication software should intelligently resynchronize the database, replicating only the changes to the data that occurred during downtime or, in case of data loss, completely refresh the primary database using the failsafe data.

Data Distribution

Data distribution allows companies to move data from one source system to multiple target systems. With the proper replication software, organizations can distribute entire databases from the source machine to targets or replicate location specific data, such as daily price updates, to branch offices or retail sites. For example, parts of centrally administered files could be replicated to remote locations for local query and analysis purposes. Replication software that allows users to select, filter, and enhance data permits this type of distribution environment. To reemphasize the point, users should be able to select between real-time data replication or scheduled, periodic updates.

Whatever options are selected, only changes to data should be replicated in order to maintain efficient operations and avoid unnecessary redundant data transfer that ties up system resources. Additionally, data distribution across like or heterogeneous environments should be attainable without extensive custom programming. The ability to replicate data using the cascading replication model mentioned previously ensures the highest level of efficiency, especially when distributing data across large area networks or between many sites.

Electronic Business

Electronic business, or *e-business,* is changing the way companies interact with suppliers, alliances, and customers. It is changing business models, streamlining supply chains, increasing efficiency and productivity, and bringing collaborative applications to unprecedented levels. Data replication software, especially if it handles cross-platform, cross-database content delivery, can prove invaluable to companies implementing e-business solutions.

For example, companies may want to share data with suppliers and business partners via a corporate *extranet* — a private Internet site or application accessible by password. To do this, the company could harness the power of replication software to select subsets of data to share beyond the firewall. That is, the company could have the security of knowing that only the data that they choose is accessible and that no threat of intrusion exists. Through e-business, companies can allow customers to check order status, allow suppliers to monitor inventory levels, dealers to access information and run queries on select data for their own reports, and much more.

The ability to move data among disparate systems and databases is critical as many production databases are housed on midrange systems like UNIX and AS/400, while Microsoft Windows NT-based Web servers are rapidly becoming the standard. Being able to replicate corporate data to the

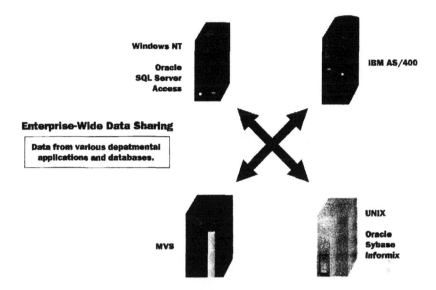

Windows NT

Oracle
SQL Server
Access

IBM AS/400

Enterprise-Wide Data Sharing

Data from various depatmental
applications and databases.

MVS

UNIX

Oracle
Sybase
Informix

Exhibit 1. Illustrates capability of replication tools to share, synchronize, and distribute data across dissimilar computing platforms and databases for business solutions such as data warehousing, application integration, and electronic business.

safety of a Web server kept beyond a firewall is crucial, but many organizations face the obstacle of how to get it there (Exhibit 1). Replication software enables rapid, secure content delivery among heterogeneous systems and databases (Exhibit 2).

Data Transformations

Empl#	Last	First	Hire Date	Status	Salary	Max
1234	Moreiro	Nicole	91/01/05	A	$55,000	$50,000
2345	Ellis-Dixon	Val	91/04/12	A	$40,000	$50,000

Increase Field Size	Concatenation	Add Century Dates	Transform Fields	Create Derived Fields
↓	↓	↓	↓	↓

Empl#	Employee Name	Hire Date	Status	Salary	% of Max
001234	Moreiro, Nicole	1991/01/05	Active	$55,000	110%
002345	Ellis-Dixon, Val	1991/04/12	Active	$40,000	80%

Exhibit 2. Examples of basic data transformations enabled by replication software.

CONCLUSION

Regardless of which data replication architecture or type — either database vendor or third party tools — companies explore, they will soon realize the benefits that the software offers. Data replication software enables a diverse range of applications, while reducing costs and increasing efficiency levels of traditionally expensive, time-consuming projects. By allowing cross-platform data delivery, replication software offers companies unparalleled flexibility. It provides the freedom to choose which software and hardware tools run their business and the comfort of knowing that, as they grow, any introduction of dissimilar computing systems or software can be easily and seamlessly integrated.

Chapter 53

Database Replication: Application Design and Deployment Issues

Jagdish Mirani

REPLICATION IS NO LONGER THE EXCLUSIVE DOMAIN OF INNOVATORS AND EARLY ADOPTERS; it has moved into the mainstream and is perceived to be the obvious solution to a large class of problems. Often, however, the application design considerations and deployment issues are overlooked until the last moment. This chapter describes the benefits of replication, the requirements that must be considered, and application design issues.

As a point of clarification, within this chapter, the term *replication* is used to describe the continuous dissemination of changes to data, as opposed to *copy management*, which is a term that is often used to describe the periodic movement of bulk data.

BENEFITS OF REPLICATION

Data Availability

Replication removes the vulnerability to system and network failures. If a remote system fails, and a replica of the same data is stored locally, then local users can still have access to the data.

In a disaster recovery scenario, the user population connected to the failed system can be rerouted to a remotely located replica. Similarly, network failures are less consequential — if the network fails, local users can access the local replica. Hence, replication provides data availability locally for environments in which the participating systems are mostly accessible, but sometimes inaccessible because of system or network failure.

Mobile Implications. As an extension of this concept, replication can also provide enhanced data availability for mobile users who are only occasionally connected to a central consolidated database. In this case, the mobile users are treated as replicate sites, with their own replica of data residing on laptop computers. These users can access and modify their local copy of data and occasionally connect to the central consolidated database, at which point the remote user is resynchronized with the consolidated database through a process of bidirectional replication of changes.

Performance

Replication can partition a large user population across various replicas of data. Without partitioning, when a large user population tries to access the same copy of data, inevitably there is poor response time. In addition, significant performance gains can be realized by customizing the local replica to the local applications.

A common example is the separation of online transaction processing (OLTP) and decision support system (DSS) processing, and accordingly, optimization of the local schema for either OLTP or DSS. Most performance enhancements are realized by moving some of the performance burden away from runtime. Examples of local customization include removal of extraneous data (through horizontal and vertical partitioning), consolidation and denormalization tables from multiple sources, or schema transformations based on the needs of local applications.

Data consolidation is usually required for decision support applications in which a consolidated view of the business is required before decision support analysis can be performed. Although it might be possible to consolidate these data "on-the-fly" at query runtime, preconsolidating these data by means of replication can shift the performance burden away from runtime.

Data Integration

In special cases involving data consolidation, performance is not the prime motivation, yet "on-the-fly" consolidation is simply not practical, even if the performance penalty is tolerable. In the construction of an operational data store, for example, integration of data from various sources can be exacerbated by semantic differences in the source data models and by "dirty" data. Sophisticated replication schemes can support in-flight transformations of data and transactions to reconcile such discrepancies.

Application Integration

Replication allows multiple applications (or multiple instances of the same application) across multiple systems to share the same data. This capability also encourages the deployment of small and targeted applications rather than large and monolithic applications.

Application integration can occur across disparate environments, such as legacy systems, relational systems, and groupware. Data replication then becomes the "information distribution backplane" through which these applications can be integrated. This integration can even extend to process automation and workflow, in which a new generation of distributed applications can be built by replicating application data and control information.

Application Migration

Replication offers a mechanism through which older applications running on legacy platforms can be gracefully retired, while new or replacement applications can be built on new platforms. Data can be shared between the old and the new platforms through replication, until the old applications have been completely replaced or retired.

ARCHITECTURAL CONSIDERATIONS

Of the numerous design decisions made by vendors of replication products, several have major consequences that affect the performance and applicability of the product. Although these different design points do not completely preclude diversity in the uses of the product, they do optimize the products for a subset of the uses.

Trigger-Based Capture vs. Log-Based Replication

One key difference is in the way in which different products capture information at the source. Some products take advantage of database triggers for capturing information into a staging area from which replication can commence. Although this method is easier for vendors to implement, it involves a substantial performance overhead because the trigger code competes for processing cycles with applications using the database.

External replication schemes take advantage of database logs for capturing changes. These schemes take advantage of normal database processing (logging for recoverability offered by modern relational databases) in order to capture changes. External replication schemes also allow greater architectural extensibility through easier implementation of heterogeneity at the source. In supporting replication from another vendor's database, they simply provide a customized capture component for the database in order to incorporate the foreign source into their replication environments.

In some cases, however, the source may not support logging, or the log structure may not be conducive to log-based replication. In these cases, alternate approaches, like trigger-based capture, need to be adopted. Other schemes might involve actively identifying and selecting (via SQL selects) changed data from the source. However, these schemes are difficult to implement and can require enhancements to the data model and applications at the source.

Push and Pull

Some replication schemes were primarily designed for continuous replication and suboptimally support scheduled (or periodic) replication, whereas other schemes were primarily designed for periodic replication and suboptimally support continuous replication.

Periodic replication schemes often involve an architecture in which a process at the receiving site periodically "pulls" the changes from a staging area. In these implementations, continuous replication can be simulated by constantly polling the staging area and pulling changes frequently. However, this solution produces considerable overhead, especially when the data at the source are not changing frequently and the constant polling and pulling of changes are not necessary. Other architectures are more conducive to continuous replication because they "push" the changes out to all the subscribers as they occur.

On the other hand, so-called pull architectures are more appropriate for supporting occasionally connected mobile users because the mobile computer can pull changes and initiate replication when it is connected. In this instance, a so-called push architecture would incur the overhead of delivering changes to a large population of mobile users, of which only a small subset of users is actually connected.

HETEROGENEOUS REPLICATION

Most large enterprises deploy databases from multiple vendors. Departmental purchasing decisions are made autonomously, with the selection being based on the optimization of departmental requirements. Very rarely are large enterprises able to standardize on a single vendor's database solution. Therefore, large enterprises typically encounter the challenge of implementing replication between multivendor databases.

There are two sides to this challenge:

- Supporting replication *from* multivendor databases
- Supporting replication *to* multivendor databases

Vendor solutions can differ significantly in this respect. Some vendors view replication as an extension of their databases and are therefore focused on enhancing their replication schemes within the domain of their own database products. Other vendors take a broader view of replication and are inclined to promote replication as database-independent middleware.

Support for heterogeneous replication is much more than a checklist of multivendor database sources and targets supported by the vendor. Key questions for customers to ask in the evaluation of a replication solution include:

- Does the architecture easily support the incorporation of heterogeneous replication, or is it case-by-case force fit? Even in cases where a significant amount of heterogeneity is offered, performance, flexibility, and manageability can differ significantly, depending on the specific configuration.
- Can the vendor support bidirectional replication between multivendor databases? Is performance sufficient in this scenario?
- Which of the features in the replication management utility are extensible to heterogeneous environments?
- What are the future directions of the product that will address some of these usability issues in a multivendor environment?
- Are there any automated conflict detection and resolution schemes that support heterogeneous environments?

FLEXIBILITY

Replication is applied as a solution to a broad set of problems. In addition, there is a high degree of variability in the conditions that must be reconciled in a replication environment. This variability precludes any simple turnkey approach to replication, with the implication that an efficient replication scheme must offer enough flexibility for users to customize a solution.

Support for Different Topologies

The replication scheme must support various topologies and usage modes. These topologies range from a one-source-to-one-target topology for disaster recovery, or one-to-many data distribution from a single consolidated site to several subscribers, or many-to-one data consolidation from several distributed sites to a single consolidated site. Alternatively, this could be configured using a bidirectional one-to-many/many-to-one topology, as in a consolidated site servicing several mobile users. One-to-one configurations resembling a workflow topology are also starting to become more common.

In the most general case, replication can be configured in a bidirectional many-to-many data-sharing configuration. An adaptable replication scheme must support any of the topologies that might be required.

Even in a single-vendor environment, replication forces the resolution of differences between databases that participate in replication. Typically, departmental databases are designed and implemented autonomously and end up with differences in the data models and data definitions. Data formats, naming conventions, and schemas often differ between databases. It is important for the replication scheme to support in-flight transformations of transactions so that an efficient replication scheme can be implemented without compromising local autonomy.

More advanced replication schemes offer event notification features, with logic that is automatically invoked in one location, based on an event that was raised at another location. These schemes are beginning to resemble more generalized messaging solutions. Such event notification schemes are of interest to users who are interested primarily in data replication but also want extensions like asynchronous event notification.

REPLICATION MANAGEMENT

Manageability is the Achilles' heel of replication. On the one hand, the management of the various replication components often adds another dimension to an already monumental management challenge; on the other hand, a replication scheme's manageability is important because it can help users mitigate some of the inherently high-touch aspects of replication.

The manageability of a vendor's solution is often overshadowed by elegant product features in search of a problem, yet the lack of manageability can either become a show-stopper to deployment or make a replication solution very expensive when all maintenance costs are factored in. A workable solution must allow administrators to monitor all the components of replication, manage the environment, and troubleshoot when problems occur.

Monitoring

Administrators must be able to monitor components in a way that maps to the specific topology and set of activities being performed via replication. Administrators should be able to monitor objects as groups, defining groups to present a hierarchical view of the components if desired. If replication subscriptions are distributed across several systems, then the administrator should be able to drill-down and view subscriptions at any location. Exception logs must be easily viewable and manipulated if necessary.

Administrators will often need to look for orphaned or skipped transactions in the exception logs. They must then be able to either purge transactions or manually commit them from the log. Much of this work can be automated via custom filters that can extract information or purge transactions from the exception logs. In addition, administrators need to monitor the status of replication queues, including queue size and performance.

Good replication monitoring products allow administrators to automate by providing thresholds that the system uses to raise events when these thresholds are exceeded. Latency events can be raised when a latency threshold is exceeded, or queue events can be raised when a transaction stays in the queue beyond a specified threshold, or the queue size exceeds a specified threshold. In some cases, it is desirable to specify a duration of time a set of conditions can exist before an event is raised.

Management Interfaces

Management interfaces must aid in the task of setting up and initializing the replication environment. In particular, the management interface must allow administrators to create, drop, alter, suspend, activate, or validate subscriptions, database connections, or routes. A drag-and-drop graphical interface can collapse multiple steps into a few visual and intuitive operations.

In large-scale replication environments consisting of many databases, many of these operations need to be carried out on groups of components. For example, if the same change is required to a large number of subscriptions relating to a large number of target databases, it should be possible to carry out this change as a single group operation. For setup and initialization, manipulation of a one-shot default configuration is often a quicker path to the end result, rather than defining the configuration from the ground up.

Administrators need to be able to perform many such operations and perform configuration changes dynamically, especially in mission-critical environments. Schema changes should be possible through the replication management interface so that corresponding replication subscription changes can also be made.

Troubleshooting

The management interface should allow administrators to issue troubleshooting commands that report status and recommend actions if the commands fail. Special commands can help administrators diagnose various components, including replication definitions and subscriptions.

Integrated Management

Finally, administrators usually prefer a replication management facility that integrates well with database, system, and network management. The ideal solution provides all the necessary components within a single open framework so that the components can interoperate and be integrated using shared components and messaging conventions.

APPLICATION DESIGN CONSIDERATIONS

With replication, success is often measured by the amount of time spent up-front in the design phase. Users who are apprised of the various application design considerations can reduce the risk of false starts and overblown expectations.

Data Latency Considerations

The first fact that users must confront is the data latency that is inherent in asynchronous replication. For the data associated with the user's portfolio of applications, the user must determine the degree of latency that is acceptable for each application.

Synchronous vs. Asynchronous Updates. For applications in which no data latency is tolerable (e.g., transactions involving large funds transfers), a two-phase commit protocol for maintaining replicated data may be most appropriate. However, there is a tendency to overestimate the need for data concurrency, and the population of applications that really require perfect concurrency is limited.

On the other extreme, if a data latency period of hours or days is tolerable (e.g., as in many data warehousing applications), bulk data movement or copy management products that are invoked periodically can provide the required degree of concurrency. Asynchronous replication is best suited for the case in between the two extremes — cases in which the data latency must fall within a few seconds.

Application designers should be able to specify thresholds for a tolerable data latency period, and then have the application determine at runtime whether to access the local replicate data or to access the primary instance of the data over the network. The problem, however, is that there usually is no way of determining the age of a particular data item.

In an update scenario, the application designer may want to set a threshold for deciding between a synchronous or an asynchronous update. Distributed application designers must evaluate vendor support for making decisions at application runtime about which version of the data to access and whether to perform updates synchronously or asynchronously.

Peer-to-Peer Replication. In the case of asynchronous replication, users can choose one of two topologies for handling updates to data. Peer-to-peer topologies allow direct updates to local data, which are then replicated to the subscribing sites. Although this approach reduces data latency at the site initiating the update (local updates are immediately available), there are a number of perils associated with peer-to-peer replication (some of which are discussed later in this chapter).

Master-Slave Configurations. Some vendors advocate a master-slave approach in which the database tables or table partitions are assigned ownership, and any update to data elements must first clear through the owner and then be replicated to the subscriber. With this approach it is slightly easier to handle update conflicts; the tradeoff is a small degree of data latency.

However, even in master-slave configurations, there are techniques for minimizing data latency. For example, local updates can be saved in a "pending transaction table" so that they are immediately available to the applications accessing the data. Then, when the owning site performs the update and replicates back to the subscribers, the transaction can be removed from the pending transaction table after the update is performed at the replicate site. This technique, however, requires additional work in designing the application.

Automated Conflict Detection and Resolution

If the distributed application requires bidirectional replication, users must also confront the issue of update conflicts. These perils must be carefully considered in any application that has automated conflict detection and resolution.

Even in master-slave approaches, conflicts can still occur at the owning site, especially in the process of reconciling large volumes of transactions that may have occurred at multiple locations during a network failure. Although a master-slave configuration does not eliminate conflicts, it clearly identifies the owning site as the site at which conflicts can be detected and resolved.

Business Rule Violations. A large class of replication conflicts are manifested as business rule violations, in which the conflict does not pertain to the update of the same table but to interacting tables. In these cases, it may be unclear whether a referential integrity rule (reflecting a business rule) is being violated or a replication conflict has occurred.

Example. For example, there may be an employee table that is related to a department table through a foreign key. As a business rule, the designer may have placed a referential integrity constraint that disallows departments without employees. But what if a department has only one employee and the tables are available at two replicate sites? At one site, the employee is removed form the department — requiring a removal of the department based on the referential integrity rule. At the other site, an employee is added to the department. Each transaction is replicated to the other site.

At the site where there is no department record, a violation is detected (adding employee to a nonexistent department). At the other site, there is an attempt to remove a department with employees — another business rule violation. In effect, each system will end up with an orphaned transaction. If there is a third system receiving updates from the two conflicting systems, the state of the third system will be determined purely by the order in which it receives the updates.

Although there are schemes to detect conflicting updates to the same row, in this case the conflict is manifested through the rejection of two transactions, even though the updates involved two different tables that interact through a parent-child relationship.

Real business applications are replete with such relationships that exacerbate the challenge of conflict detection and resolution. To automate the resolution to this type of conflict, it is necessary to first identify such conflicts (e.g., an integrity rule that is being violated because of a replication conflict) and then take corrective action that maintains the intent of the business rules and corresponding integrity constraints.

"Compensating" Transactions and Business Practices. Even when all conflicting transactions are easily detected, automating the resolution to the conflicts can be challenging. Several schemes are commonly used for automating conflict resolution, such as earliest change wins, last change wins, and designated-site always wins.

These schemes can often leave a database with either inconsistent copies or internal transactional inconsistencies. Any conflict resolution scheme based on time stamps, for instance, can be problematic because each system has its own clock and all the system clocks are not perfectly synchronized.

Conflict resolution based on a message-arrival sequence is also problematic because the asynchronous nature of the system will affect arrival sequences. Different delays in wide area networks will cause transactions to arrive in a different sequence at each location.

Even in a perfect world, in which all conflicts can be successfully detected and resolved, users must confront the fact that committed transactions will be backed out at all the losing sites. This can be disconcerting to application designers who are used to the notion of database integrity resulting from the ACID — atomicity, consistency, isolation, durability — properties. There is now way of avoiding the window of vulnerability from the time at which a transaction is committed to the time at which it is backed out because of a replication conflict.

Inventory examples are often used to illustrate this vulnerability. If the inventory of a particular item is down to one, and the same item is sold to two customers in different locations because the same time is shown as being available in multiple replicate databases, then one of the two customers must be recompensed for a false sale. In the case of airline reservation systems in which the last remaining seat is often sold to multiple customers, the issue is dealt with through policies that provide additional restitution to customers in these situations (e.g., an additional free ticket or frequency-flyer miles for taking a later flight). In fact, the airlines have institutionalized the practice of overbooking through a set of policies that try to restore customer satisfaction in these situations.

Often, a business policy, or adaptation of a business process, can provide the recourse for problems introduced by distributed applications. Thus, all transactions are handled regardless of conflict, and conflicting transactions actually trigger compensating transactions at certain points in the business operations.

In some situations, however, there may be dependencies caused by a ripple effect and a series of transactions may need to back out to truly undo the effects of the conflicting transactions. Obviously, the consequences can be serious if this situation occurs in an environment of financial applications involving large sums of money.

Additional Overhead. In the case of peer-to-peer updates, automated conflict detection and resolution introduce significant performance overhead and complexity. In peer-to-peer configurations, every site must monitor all the incoming traffic looking for conflicts. There is further complexity resulting from the introduction of support tables. These factors can severely limit scalability and manageability.

Conflict resolution in a peer-to-peer configuration also introduces significant disk space utilization overhead. Every site must temporarily save all incoming transactions in order to monitor for conflicts. If one of the replication sites becomes unavailable, the overhead is extreme — for the duration of the failure, every single site must save on disk all incoming transactions to resolve potential conflicts with the unavailable site.

In a peer-to-peer environment, backup and restore operations also become extremely complex. Because there is no official value for each piece of data at any point in time, there is no fast way to restore the entire replication system in case of failure. Data may be floating between writes for hours until conflicts are resolved.

Conflict Avoidance. In many cases, the nature of the application is such that transaction conflicts are not even an issue. In a human resources example, every site can have access to the records relating to every employee in the company. But if the branch office to which the employee reports is the only location that will change the records relating to that employee, then there is no possibility of conflict. In other cases, transaction sequence is inconsequential because the updates are cumulative, in which the end result will be the same regardless of the order in which the transactions are performed (as with some debit/credit transactions, or transactions involving inserts that are unique).

It is also possible to address the concurrency control issues within the application design itself by designing the application to avoid conflicts or by compensating for conflicts when they occur. Conflict avoidance ensures that all transactions are unique — that updates only originate from one site at a time. Schemas can be fragmented in such a manner as to ensure conflict avoidance. In addition, each site can be assigned a slice of time for delivering updates, thereby avoiding conflicts by establishing a business practice.

Special Considerations for Disaster Recovery

One of the most common uses of replication is to replicate transactions to a backup system for the purpose of disaster recovery. However, users are advised to pay close attention to several issues relating to the use of replication for disaster recovery.

In a high-volume transaction environment, many transactions that have occurred at the primary system may be lost in flight and will need to be reentered into the backup system. When the primary fails, how will the lost transactions be identified so that they can be reentered? How will the users be switched over to the backup? The backup system will have a different network address, requiring users to manually log in to the backup and restart their applications.

Is there a documented process for users and administrators to follow in the event of a disaster? Once the primary is recovered, is there a clean mechanism for switching users back to the primary? In the best-case scenario, it should be possible to switch the roles of the systems, making the backup the new primary and making the primary the new backup once it is recovered. This practice eliminates the need to switch all users back to the original configuration.

Special Consideration for Network Failures

Although the availability of data is enhanced through replication because there is a local copy of data, users must understand the implications of extended network failures. Network failures can cause replicate databases to quickly drift apart because local updates are not being propagated. If the application is sensitive to the sequence of transactions originating at various replicate sites, then extended network failures may cause local processing to shut down, nullifying any perceived benefit to data availability through replication.

In addition, once the network is available again, a carefully reconciliation of all the replicate databases must be performed, paying close attention to the sequencing of transactions originating from different systems. This process of reconciliation can encounter many replication conflicts and is subject to all the caveats associated with conflict detection and resolution.

Replication and Triggers at the Target System

Replication can interfere with the normal operation of database triggers used to enforce business rules and integrity constraints. Consider a situation in which a transaction at a primary site causes trigger scripts to be invoked. The direct effect of the transaction is replicated — but so are the effects of the trigger scripts. At the replicate site, if the same trigger scripts exist, they are invoked again as a result of the changes caused by the transaction. Hence, the trigger scripts actually affect the replicate site twice, leading to an unpredictable outcome.

To avoid this integrity issue, the target database must provide a mechanism for suppressing trigger scripts in the case of replicated changes.

SUMMARY

Replication is appropriately used for various problem areas. However, success with replication depends heavily on up-front work done toward resolving department issues and application design considerations. In particular:

- The implications of data latency must be carefully considered.
- Conflict avoidance is the safest way to implement replication, averting numerous perils associated with conflict detection and resolution.

Careful consideration of these factors can lead to the expected levels of payback from the benefits of replication.

Chapter 54

Secure Information Through a Replicated Architecture

Judith N. Froscher

INFORMATION TECHNOLOGY AND AUTOMATION PLAY A MAJOR ROLE in all aspects of an enterprise's business and operations. Computing cycles are cheaper, and computational capability has increased, although the costs of reengineering legacy information processing systems and business processes have delayed the benefits that many enterprises hope to realize.

Nevertheless, investment in the enterprise's information infrastructure and migration to open, distributed access to information have begun. Once these reengineering hurdles are overcome, everyone in the enterprise will have access to consistent information from many heterogeneous data sources, and the enterprise can realize the benefits of its investment and achieve a technological advantage. Modern data management systems play a major role in this endeavor and depend on replication for distributed data access, fault tolerance, availability, and reliability.

Every enterprise has secrets. Global access poses a significant threat to enterprise secrets. For example, aspects of personnel, payroll, finances, planning, marketing, new products, product liability, production problems, research results, test results, and efficiency are sensitive information and need to be protected. Conventional approaches to protecting this information are not effective in environments that are open and seek to provide global access.

This chapter explores these issues of secrecy and how replication can help to provide strong protection against compromise. In particular, the Secure INformation Through the Replicated Architecture (SINTRA) project has demonstrated this approach through various prototypes. Application of SINTRA to an operational application is described, the benefits of the approach examined, and plans for research and development discussed.

CONSEQUENCES OF OPENNESS

An assumption for this discussion is that the information systems supporting an enterprise have migrated to client/server computing environments, and that the enterprise is reengineering its internal processes to make better use of its resources and available information to improve its effectiveness. However, everyone may also have access to critical data needed to achieve the goals of the enterprise, and thus expose the enterprise itself to unnecessary risk.

This migration process is the most difficult part of the enterprise's transition, yet is necessary to take advantage of new technology that can advance the goals of the enterprise. The migration and reengineering problem is not only a technology issue, but also affects what jobs are needed and which personnel can most effectively perform those jobs. Data protection is part of the enterprise reengineering problem as well.

Everyone has access to all the data needed for a given job. However, everyone may also have access to all the critical data needed to achieve the goals of the enterprise and thus places the enterprise at risk. During the reengineering process, an enterprise is especially vulnerable to both insider threats and attacks from competitors, suppliers, and other outsiders.

The Challenge: Protect Data Yet Make It Accessible

The enterprise must protect its secrets. Prior to more open computing environments, these secrets were probably safe because few people accessed the systems containing them and the systems were not connected. Perhaps the data was not even electronically stored.

As a first step, the enterprise must identify secrets and how critical these secrets are. Some secrets will be more important than others and will be sensitive for different reasons. For example, competitors must not be able to access research results that can lead to the development of new products and markets. Employees should not be able to change their own performance data. The requirement to protect data managed by an information processing system is not new; however, the need to protect data and at the same time allow authorized users access to data they need in a distributed computing environment challenges earlier solutions.

Deciding which data is sensitive and to what degree is a difficult task because objective criteria for deciding secrecy are often unavailable. Identification of secrets for each major process of an enterprise can simplify this exercise and is necessary to determine who needs access to which data. However, the major processes identified at the beginning of the reengineering process may change as the enterprise itself changes. Hence, making decisions about data sensitivity and who needs access are continuing aspects

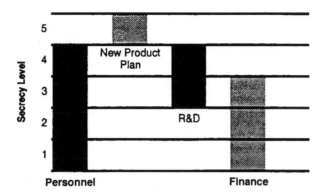

Exhibit 1. Enterprise data organization.

of information technology itself and need to become part of the data management process.

Data Engineering. Data engineering plays a primary role in the migration process. To migrate to client/server computing architectures, the data needed to support major operational or task areas of the enterprise must be identified. Servers are developed that manage and manipulate data to support the enterprise. Data may then become available to other task areas. Task areas themselves may change because of improved data access. Secrecy is another organizing criteria for enterprise data and is orthogonal to the task area organization. Exhibit 1 depicts some example task areas and secrecy levels for an enterprise.

Identifying Authorized Users. Once the data has been organized so that it is accessible and its consistency can be maintained, users authorized for access must be identified. Certainly, users must have access to the data they need to do their jobs. However, the users who need to access more secret data should be minimized and the enterprise should have some confidence that those users will not compromise the more sensitive data. The enterprise needs a means to determine whether an individual employee can be trusted. A person's past employment and personal history is one indicator of character. Background investigations and length of service with the enterprise can be used to establish the trustworthiness of employees.

Creating Computing Enclaves. Enterprise secrets and users authorized for their access can be grouped into a computing enclave. The most secret enclave is physically separate from enclaves containing less sensitive data.

Within enclaves, employees working on closely related tasks can form smaller groups or work domains. Work domains cross secrecy enclaves, and work domains in higher enclaves may need access to work domain data in lower enclaves. High-level users may send requests to lower-level work domain servers to access the data they need. This seemingly innocent communication poses a threat to enterprise secrets, however. A disgruntled employee could pass information protected in the high enclave to the lower work domain server making a request. Worse yet, rogue software could reside in the high enclave and could send information to lower work domain servers, where many more, less trustworthy people have access.

Some enterprises may never connect their information systems outside the enterprise. However, other enterprises must protect their secrets from insider/outsider threats and malicious code, which can encode sensitive information in a query or send information directly to less sensitive information servers as part of a message. All software is vulnerable to these kinds of attack.

Data replication allows users access to information at remote sites and provides fault tolerance in the event that another site becomes inoperable. For quite similar reasons, replication of data in low enclaves to higher enclave servers provides users in high enclaves access to the information they need to do their job without compromise. Because users in different enclaves access only their copy of data at different levels of secrecy, replication thwarts rogue software and attempts by malicious users to leak secrets. Hence, replication used as part of a protection approach enables tolerance of malicious software or users.

Physical separation and replication do not solve all security problems. Each component of an enclave must provide its own authentication and audit mechanisms. To ensure privacy, encryption may be used to pass information through the communication infrastructure. Within enclaves, different work domains may enforce different access policies. If compromise occurs, the effects are confined to the enclave, where everyone is equally trusted. Further attempts to gain unauthorized access can be detected and monitored.

Exhibit 2 illustrates a possible computing environment with three levels of secrecy. Each server represents a different work domain; the upward arrows represent a means by which low data is replicated to more secret enclaves.

MULTILEVEL SECURE (MLS) APPROACH TO DATABASE SECURITY

This discussion of protecting secrecy demonstrates the vulnerability of information systems to rogue software. If a business relies on software to preserve secrecy, then it must be convinced that the reliance is justified.

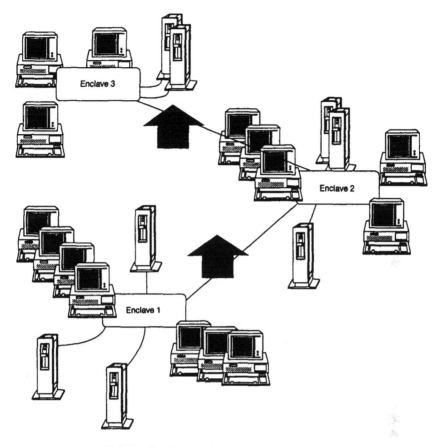

Exhibit 2. Enterprise enclave processing.

Formal methods, rigorous software engineering, testing, peer review, independent adversarial evaluation, and penetration testing contribute to assurance that software is dependable. Once the software is declared dependable, the vigil to protect the software against the introduction of any malicious code begins. However, assurance that software can be trusted and its trustworthiness maintained is quite expensive.

The SINTRA project exploits declining hardware and software costs to avoid the development of costly, high-assurance software and provide a high-assurance, multilevel secure (MLS) database service. Multilevel secure refers to a mechanism that allows users of varying degrees of trust to have access to computerized data and programs for which they are authorized, yet prevents them from gaining access to those for which they are not authorized.

DATA REPLICATION

Replicating Low Data to High Databases

The philosophy of protection for SINTRA is strongly influenced by the need to minimize the amount of software, both trusted and untrusted, that runs on a high-assurance, painstakingly crafted, trusted product while at the same time preserving full database capability without introducing security vulnerabilities. No protection mechanism is more effective than absolute separation; however, the need to provide access to low data for more trustworthy users led to the notion that low data be replicated to high databases.

The strength of the approach lies in the simple observation that if low data enclave users do not have access to the same copies of low data that high data enclave users access, then malicious code cannot be effective in signaling high information to low users. Hence, the replicated architecture can tolerate malicious code attacks.

In the SINTRA approach, a database exists for each hierarchical security level and contains all data at that level and below. Because each database contains only information to which a user has legitimate access, untrusted database management systems can be used. Each database resides on a separate data server. The authentication procedure for each server controls whether the user can access the data stored in that database.

When the low database is modified, the update must be propagated to higher-level databases securely and consistently. The only information flow required by this approach is from low to high — an inherently secure flow. In this way, SINTRA limits opportunities for malicious code in untrusted applications to exploit system vulnerabilities. The technical difficulty with this approach is to ensure the consistency of the replicas without introducing a vulnerability that could be exploited.

Once an update is made in a less secret data server, it cannot be rolled back because a more secret server is unable to make the update. If the rollback were allowed, rogue software could manipulate the completion of these updates to signal more secret information to less secret servers.

This read-at-high, write-at-low channel is a problem for all data separation mechanisms and impacts database schedulers in all approaches to database security. A primary objective of this project has been to discover a transaction management scheme that does not require modification of the commercial data management systems on each server. The approach, how the replica control problem was solved, and the prototype are documented in numerous reports. SINTRA research results suggest that accepting the replica consistency problem in return for a virtually free high-assurance, strong protection mechanism is a choice well made.

Controlled Propagation

Because each data server contains data from less secret servers, update queries have to be propagated to more secret servers to maintain the consistency and currency of the replicated data. If the propagation of update queries is not carefully controlled, inconsistent database states can be created among the distributed servers.

Consider two lower-level update transactions T_i and T_j that are scheduled with serialization order $<T_i, T_j>$ at the less secret data server. Because these two transactions are update transactions, they have to be propagated to the next more secret data server. If these two transactions are scheduled with serialization order $<T_j, T_i>$ at the next more secret data server, an inconsistent database state between these two servers may be created by the execution of conflicting operations at the more secret server.

Even the serialization order of nonconflicting transactions has to be maintained to preserve one-copy serializability. This is a parallel result that has been reported in the context of multidatabase systems. Hence, the serialization order introduced by the local scheduler in the commercial data management system where the update was initiated must be maintained in the more secret servers.

Earlier SINTRA prototypes depended on a trusted replica controller that used either a read-down or write-up capability and a Naval Research Laboratory (NRL) implementation of a global scheduler on a high-assurance trusted product. The spirit of the SINTRA approach is to be able to use commercially available products. When Sybase introduced a replication server that used such a scheduling scheme, it became part of the prototyping effort. However, both forward and backward communication exists between the primary site database and the replicate database with the commercial product. The trusted replica controller also requires a one-way communication device that must satisfy two equally important kinds of requirements:

- Security requirements (e.g., no information flow from high to low)
- Database replication requirements for functional capabilities (e.g., reliability, recoverability, and performance)

A Trusted Replication Component and Buffer. Even though blind write-up and read-down methods may satisfy the security requirements, they do not satisfy the database replication requirements. The NRL Pump is a device that balances these conflicting requirements (Exhibit 3).

The Pump places a nonvolatile buffer (size n) between low and high data enclaves and sends acknowledgement code (ACK) to low data enclaves at probabilistic times, based on a moving average of the past m

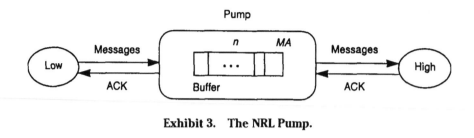

Exhibit 3.   The NRL Pump.

high ACK times. A high ACK time is the time it takes for the buffer to send a message to high and for high to return an ACK. By sending ACKs to low data enclaves at a rate related to high data's historical response rate, the Pump provides flow control and reliable delivery without unduly penalizing performance.

It is important to emphasize that ACKs are not passed through the Pump from high to low data enclaves. In fact, the Pump can acknowledge receipt of messages from low data before high data receives them because of the Pump's buffering capability. Each ACK sent to a low data enclave is generated internally by the Pump only in response to a message from low. The average rate at which these ACKs are sent from the Pump to a low data enclave reflects the average rate at which a high enclave acknowledges messages from the Pump.

The rate of the ACKs from the Pump to low data enclaves represents a downward flow of information. However, the algorithm controlling the rate at which acknowledgements are returned is parameterized to allow the capacity of the timing channel to be made as small as may be required.

Several prototypes of the NRL Pump have been developed to support SINTRA applications, and the basic concept has been expanded to address the complications of fairness and denial of service in a network.

A BUILDING BLOCK FOR SECURE SYSTEMS ENGINEERING

In a cooperative, distributed computing environment, the Pump becomes a building block for secure systems engineering. In effect, security can be integrated without the organization having to worry about whether some feature of the desired system is protection critical, because the protection mechanisms are completely separated from the system's conventional features.

The security engineering and assurance techniques required to develop such a high-assurance building block are affordable in this approach because a Pump can be used with commercial replication products and data management products. The most difficult technical aspect of the SINTRA approach to database security is the development of the interfaces or wrappers needed between the Pump and the commercial products. Wrapper development has become an essential skill for building distributed systems.

A Sample Application

The development of wrappers to permit the use of the SINTRA approach for the Joint Maritime Command Information System (JMCIS) has been the focus of one prototyping activity. JMCIS is an integrated Navy C4I system used for tracking ships and planning missions. Most JMCIS installations have two systems: a less classified (low) JMCIS system and a more secret (high) JMCIS system.

The low and high systems each include its own copy of the Central Database Server (CDBS). Users at each level update their local CDBSs independently, although updates to the low system are provided periodically to the high-level system using tape. The current mode of operation does not permit users of highly secret systems to use less classified CDBS updates promptly or consistently.

The SINTRA approach offers an automated solution for this problem. The conventional solution for this problem is the installation of a bidirectional guard processor between the high and low systems. These guard systems typically require a human reviewer to monitor traffic that is passed, since information moves in both directions. The SINTRA approach does not require any alterations in the basic operation or the computing platforms of the systems. Instead, a small set of untrusted software, the Pump, and the Sybase replication server automatically replicate selected data from low databases to high databases as low updates are made, while preserving the secrecy of the high data.

This application of the SINTRA approach illustrates how strong protection can be obtained without changing the database design, the data servers, or applications. As long as transactions can be defined for any legacy systems, the application of the SINTRA approach results in a secure confederation of legacy system enclaves. Enhanced availability of data can be achieved by assigning labels to a finer granularity of data. For example, secrecy labels can be assigned to each element of a tuple in a relation. This fine-grained labeling is a capability that can be obtained in the SINTRA approach and has been demonstrated in prototypes.

BENEFITS OF THE REPLICATED ARCHITECTURE

SINTRA offers many benefits over conventional approaches to database security.

Resistance to Rogue Software. The architecture is resistant to rogue software attacks because authorized users access only their copy of less secret data. The trusted replication component, the Pump, is analogous to encryption for secure communication: the Pump allows any enterprise to take advantage of readily available information technology while still protecting the secrecy of their information. This is unlike conventional approaches that require the development of a trusted version of the desired technology. Under the best conditions, untrusted mission-critical applications must be modified to satisfy the constraints of the product, and both the trusted product and the application software must be placed under constant vigil to protect against the introduction of rogue software, which can leak protected information. Any software that runs on these platforms can be infected and can pass data through information channels available in every trusted product.

(Relatively) Uncomplicated Database Distribution. SINTRA does not solve all the issues associated with database distribution and heterogeneity. However, it does not make distribution and heterogeneity more complex.

Unlike conventional database security approaches, SINTRA distributed data management can use solutions found for conventional databases primarily because these solutions can be applied level by level. The life-cycle costs of the SINTRA approach to database security are similar to conventional database life-cycle costs. The lifetime vigil to protect against the introduction of malicious software is not required for a SINTRA solution. There are minimal trusted components, and upgrades can be made to the data management technology without disturbing the trustworthiness of the system.

Ability to Meet Security and Operational Requirements. Probably most important, however, the SINTRA approach allows the secure use of current advances in information technology. The use of trusted replica controllers for connecting components securely allows users and developers to concentrate their information technology resources on implementing systems that satisfy operational requirements rather than focusing on security. The approach easily scales to accommodate new data servers and can be inserted without disruption to the operation of an organization.

FUTURE PLANS

The operational need for a high-assurance MLS database management system has resulted in the use of the SINTRA approach in the Global Transportation System, a joint service data management system that tracks all the platforms in the Services. The relative ease with which security can be integrated into an operational solution has prompted several DoD organizations to initiate SINTRA implementations of their operational systems. In particular, DoD's maps and images will become available to users at different security levels through this approach. Several pilot programs that will use a SINTRA implementation for major command and control and tactical combat systems are underway at present.

SUMMARY

Enterprises that rely on distributed computing require software that can be trusted to enforce multilevel security requirements. The SINTRA approach to database security relies on physical separation to provide strong protection and replication to allow users with different security authorizations access to data created at a less restricted security level.

Because this approach exploits distribution and replication to provide a secure data management service, it allows critical information systems to exploit commercial advances in data management technology and to protect sensitive information at the same time. Each node in a SINTRA confederation is a commercially available data management system, but the confederation itself is secure. A simple, strong, reliable store-and-forward device provides the protection-critical component and is reusable with other transactional systems. The SINTRA approach provides an affordable, strong approach to the protection of critical information and allows both government and commercial enterprises to take advantage of the commercial investment in information technology.

Section X
Data and the Internet, Intranet, and the World Wide Web

THE POPULARITY OF THE INTERNET, INTRANET, AND WORLD WIDE WEB has created the need to access databases through these architectures. This section contains five chapters that explore techniques for connecting data stores to the Internet, intranet, and World Wide Web.

Chapter 55, "Building Database-Enabled Web Applications with IDC," provides a substantial example for creating Web pages that are refreshed directly from live databases and database servers. This technique uses basic SQL statements and a minimal amount of HTML coding. Internet Database Connector (IDC) provides the toolset for doing this.

Chapter 56, "Intranets: Notes vs. the Internet," examines notes-based intranets, browser-based intranets, and a hybrid environment in the context of information dissemination.

Chapter 57, "Web-Enabled Data Warehouses," describes data warehouse access through the Web. Some of the unique aspects of Web-enabled data warehouses include special access controls, integrating the architecture with browsers, and infrastructure issues. This chapter describes design and implementation considerations for such warehouses. With the emergence of the Web, there will be a great need for this technology.

Chapter 58, "Publishing Database Information on the World Wide Web," describes how to publish databases on the World Wide Web and the methods by which users can query them.

Chapter 59, "Database Management and the Internet: Developments and Challenges," describes the techniques currently being investigated to ensure data access, quality, and security among databases through the Internet.

Chapter 55
Building Database-Enabled Web Applications With IDC

Ido Gileadi

THE WORLD WIDE WEB (THE WEB) HAS BEEN PRIMARILY CONSTRUCTED FROM STATIC HTML PAGES. These pages generally contain text, graphics, and hyperlinks that give Net users the ability to search and view information easily with the click of a mouse. The static page always displays the same information regardless of individual user selections or personal preferences. Furthermore, the static page displays the entire range of information available to it without consideration of the specific requirements of unique, busy individual users accessing the Web site.

In recent years, there has been a strong movement toward a more dynamic approach for Web page design. Web pages can now be created on the fly, customized to an individual viewer's requirements, and linked with database servers to provide accurate, up-to-the-minute data. There are many techniques for creating dynamic Web pages. Some of the technologies available involve creation of a Web page on the fly, based on selections a viewer makes in previous pages. Active pages and CGI scripting can easily achieve these tasks.

In many cases, creating dynamic Web pages that contain subsets of data based on the viewer's selection of a query is the ideal. A simple example of this type of application is a telephone directory publication on the Web. Such an application requires the ability to select and display one or more entries from the database, based on a selection (query) the user makes on

0-8493-9976-9/99/$0.00+$.50
© 1999 by CRC Press LLC

the screen. Most likely, the selection will involve a last name and/or first name combination.

The traditional way of creating a database-enabled Web application, such as the telephone directory, is to use CGI scripting. The CGI script is a program that is referenced by the selection screen. It is invoked by the submission of the selection criteria (last name and first name) and receives the selections as input parameters. Once invoked, the CGI script works like any other program on the server and can access a database server to retrieve the information that is required. It then builds the dynamic Web page based on the retrieved data and presents it back to the user on the Web page.

This approach is lacking in execution speed and requires programming knowledge in Perl or some other computer language that is used to construct the CGI script. This article describes a database-enabled application using the Internet Database Connector (IDC) technology. Building this application will require no traditional programming skills and relies only on minimal coding statements.

INTERNET DATABASE CONNECTOR (IDC)

IDC is a technology developed by Microsoft to allow the execution of an SQL statement against a database and represents the results in an HTML page format. This technology works only with an Internet Information Server (IIS), which is a Microsoft Web server offering. Any browser can be used to access database information using IDC; the only requirement is that the browser be able to interpret HTML pages. Exhibit 1 depicts the way in which IDC operates.

In this example, a client machine (e.g., a PC) is running a Web browser. The browser requests an IDC page, which happens to be a text-based page. The server intercepts the request and sends the SQL statement included in the IDC file to the ODBC data source defined in the IDC file. The database returns a result set or performs the insert/update operation. The data returned is formatted, using the format specified in the HTX template, into a valid HTML stream that is then sent back to the requesting client to be displayed by the browser.

In the following sections of this article, this functionality will be demonstrated by building a simple telephone directory application.

DEVELOPING THE TELEPHONE DIRECTORY APPLICATION

Requirements

This is a small sample application designed for the sole purpose of demonstrating some principles of database access over the Web. The require-

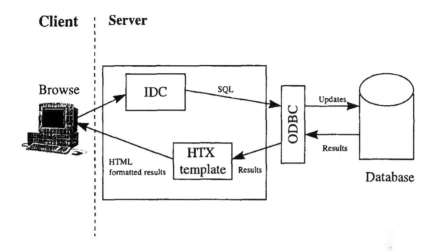

Exhibit 1. IDC operation.

ments are identified in terms of the required functionality and access. The functionality required is as follows:

- Store first name, last name, and telephone number of multiple individuals.
- Allow the user to search for a specific directory entry using a part or the whole of the last name and first name.
- Display a list of all matching entries as the results of a search.
- Allow the users to add a new entry to the directory.
- Allow users to access the telephone directory through a Web browser and their Internet connection.

The preceding requirements are sufficient to begin developing the application. The following sections provide a guide that can be used on a step-by-step basis to develop the application.

The Database

An access database will be used to support this sample application. Any database with an ODBC-compliant driver can be used. A new database that contains only one table will be created to contain the directory entries. The structure of the table is shown in Exhibit 2.

IDC requires an ODBC data source to communicate with the database. Here, an ODBC data source is created for the access database that has just been created using the 32-bit ODBC manager in the control panel.

Exhibit 2.   Example Database Structure

Field Name	Description	Type	Comments
id	The directory entry unique id	Counter	This is an automated counter that will be incremented every time a new record is inserted into the database
LastName	Last name	Text	
FirstName	First name	Text	
tel	Telephone number	Text	

Programming Tip: The datasource must be defined as a system datasource for the Web server to be able to access it.

The datasource will be named Tel_Directory and pointed to the newly created access database. Security will not be added to the database for the purpose of this example. In a real-life application, one will most likely want to create a user ID and a password for the users accessing the database over the network and have them key it in at runtime. Another alternative is to create a user ID and a password with very limited permissions and include the login parameters in the IDC file to avoid the extra step of logging in.

Warning: The IDC file is a plain text file and can be easily viewed by anyone with access to the Web. When storing the login parameters in this file, one must execute great caution to restrict the user access to the very minimum required.

The Application Directory

Any directory that will be accessed by the Web server (IIS) has to be defined in the administration section of the Web server. This allows the Web server to know about the directory and allows the developer to set some parameters for each directory. The parameters of interest in this discussion include the access rights. There are two access parameters:

- **Read** access allows the server to read the files in the directory and send their contents to the requesting browser. This is sufficient for regular HTML files.
- **Execute** access allows the server to execute the program stored in the files in the directory. This is required for CGI scripts as well as IDC files.

For the application here, one directory will be created that contains all the files needed to run the application, with the exception of the database file. Both read and execute permissions will be granted to this directory.

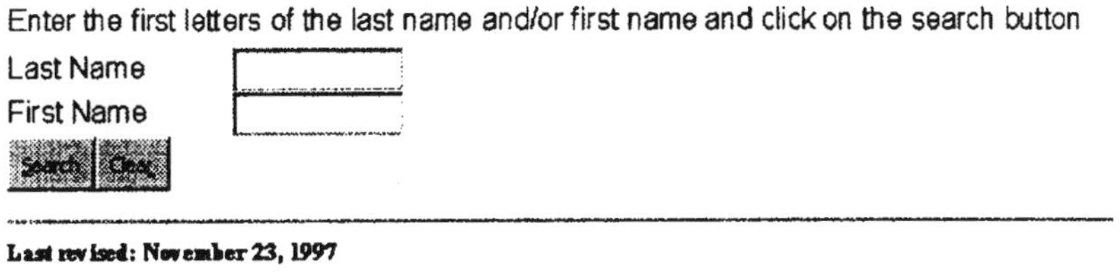

Enter the first letters of the last name and/or first name and click on the search button

Last Name

First Name

Last revised: November 23, 1997

Exhibit 3.   Search screen.

Programming Tip: Create the directory under the Web server's home directory (typically .../wwwroot) and make sure to grant read and execute permissions to the home directory. The home directory is marked in the directory property window of the Web administration section.

The Search Screen

As defined in the requirements, a search is allowed by a combination of first and last name. Defining the search screen as an HTML form will allow for passage of the user's selection as parameters to the IDC script. Exhibit 3 shows the search screen as it will display on the browser.

The HTML code for the screen in Exhibit 3 was created using Microsoft Front Page, and it consists of the following:

```
<!DOCTYPE HTML PUBLIC "-//IETF//DTD HTML//EN">

<html>


<head>

<meta http-equiv="Content-Type"

content="text/html; charset=iso-8859-1">

<meta name="GENERATOR" content="Microsoft FrontPage 2.0">

<title>Search Directory</title>

</head>


<body>


<h1>Search Directory</h1>
```

```
<hr>


<p>Enter the first letters of the last name and/or first name
and click on the search button</p>


<form action="Search.idc" method="POST">
    <table border="0">
        <tr>
            <td>Last Name</td>
            <td><input type="text" size="20"
            maxlength="20"

            name="lname"></td>
        </tr>
        <tr>
            <td>First Name</td>
            <td><input type="text" size="20"
            maxlength="20"

            name="fname"></td>
        </tr>
    </table>
    <p><input type="submit" value="Search"> <input
    type="reset"
    value="Clear"> </p>
</form>


<hr>


<h5>Last revised: November 23, 1997</h5>
</body>
</html>
```

The HTML code is a standard form with fields that are arranged into a table for cosmetic reasons. Highlighted are the names of the input fields that will be passed as parameters to the IDC script.

The Search IDC Script

The general format of an IDC script is as follows:

```
Datasource: <Name of a system ODBC datasource>

Username: <User id for accessing the database>

Password: <Password for the user>

Template: <A URL of the HTML template file *.HTX>

SQLStatement:

+<Lines of the SQL statement>

+<Lines of the SQL statement>
```

There may be more than one SQL statement in the file. This feature will be revisited in the following sections.

The IDC script used with the search screen is as follows:

```
Datasource:Tel_Directory

Username:

Password:

Template:Directory.htx

SQLStatement:

+SELECT id,FirstName,LastName,Tel from Directory

+WHERE LastName like '%lname%%' and FirstName like
'%fname%%'
```

A username or password has not been included for this sample. In a production environment, one would definitely include a user ID and password, or prompt the user for one using a login screen.

The SQL statement containing the SELECT statement will typically return a result set. The result set may be empty or contain one or more rows. The HTML template file will have to handle the display of multiple rows. The field names in the SELECT section reflect the names of the columns in the database, and the parameter names in the WHERE clause reflect the field names on the search HTML form. The parameters coming from the HTML form are enclosed in percent signs (%). In this case, the percent signs (%), are enclosed in single quotes so that the WHERE clause will contain the correct syntax for a text field. In addition, it was desirable to allow the user the flexibility of keying only the first few letters of the name. Also included is an additional percent sign (%) that acts as a wild card character, indicating that any string of characters can replace it. The final SQL statement may look like:

```
SELECT id,FirstName,LastName,Tel from Directory

WHERE LastName like 'Smi%' and FirstName like '%'
```

This will return all the entries where the last name starts with 'Smi,' regardless of the first name.

The Search Result Screen

The search results are displayed using the HTX template. The HTX file is a regular HTML file and can contain any codes included in an HTML file. In addition to the standard HTML codes, it contains the following construct:

```
<%BeginDetail%>

    Any valid HTML code <%FieldName1%><%FieldName2%>

    Any valid HTML code <%FieldName3%><%FieldName4%>

<%EndDetail%>
```

Anything contained between the <%BeginDetail%> and the <%EndDetail%> will be repeated in the constructed HTML file for each row of results coming from the database. The <%FieldName%> parameters are the fieldnames as they appear in the database, and will be substituted with the values returned from the database.

The following is the listing for the search results HTX file. The name of this file is stated in the IDC script; it is 'Directory.htx'. This template was created using Microsoft Front Page. Highlighted in the following example are the important construct elements, including begindetail, id, LastName, FirstName, Tel, enddetail, if CurrentRecord EQ 0, action="AddEntry.idc," and endif:

```
<!DOCTYPE HTML PUBLIC "-//IETF//DTD HTML//EN">

<html>


<head>

<meta http-equiv="Content-Type"

content="text/html; charset=iso-8859-1">

<meta name="GENERATOR" content="Microsoft FrontPage 2.0">

<title>Directory Listing</title>
```

```
</head>

<body bgcolor="#FFFFFF">

<p><font color="#0000FF" size="5"><em><strong>Telephone
Directory
Listing</strong></em></font></p>
<table border="2" cellpadding="2" cellspacing="3">
    <tr>
        <td><font color="#0000FF"><em><strong>Entry
        ID</strong></em></font></td>
        <td><font color="#0000FF"><em><strong>Last
        Name</strong></em></font></td>
        <td><font color="#0000FF"><em><strong>First
        Name</strong></em></font></td>
        <td><font color="#0000FF"><em><strong>Tel
        Mumber</strong></em></font></td>
    </tr>
<%begindetail%>
        <tr>
            <td><%id%></td>
            <td><%LastName%></td>
            <td><%FirstName%></td>
            <td><%Tel%></td>
    </tr>
<%enddetail%></table>

<p> </p>
<%if CurrentRecord EQ 0%>
<table border="0" cellpadding="0" cellspacing="4">
    <tr>
        <td><form action="AddEntry.idc" method="POST">
```

```
            <p><input type="submit" name="B1" value="Add
            Entry"></p>

        </form>

        </td>

    </tr>

  </table>

  <%endif%></body>

  </html>
```

In the preceding listing, there is an additional conditional construct that looks like `<%if CurrentRecord EQ 0%>` any HTML code `<%endif%>`. This conditional construct allows for better control over the creation of the HTML code. In the example, the construct is used to add an AddEntry button that will activate the add entry screen.

Tip: The conditional construct can also contain the element `<%else%>`, which will allow the creation of a completely different HTML code based on the result set.

Warning: The conditional construct will not work if used before the `<%Begin-Detail%>`.

The CurrentRecord is one of the built-in variables that can be used in the template. It indicates the current record being processed. If used after, the `<%BeginDetail%>` `<%EndDetail%>` construct will hold the last record number. The record number relates to the sequential number within the result set.

The Add Entry Screen

The Add Entry button will appear on the search results screen only when there are no records in the result set. Having no records in the result set will indicate that the entry was not found and therefore may be entered into the database. The Add Entry button is a submit button within an HTML form that points to the AddEntry.idc script.

The AddEntry.idc script will fetch the total number of entries in the database and invoke the HTML template named AddEntry.htx. Following is the listing for the AddEntry.idc script:

```
Datasource:Tel_Directory
Username:
Password:
Template:AddEntry.htx
SQLStatement:
```

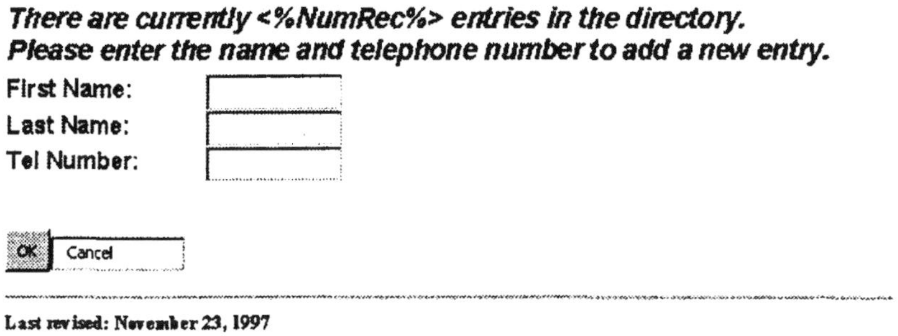

There are currently <%NumRec%> entries in the directory.
Please enter the name and telephone number to add a new entry.

First Name: [   ]

Last Name: [   ]

Tel Number: [   ]

[OK] [Cancel]

Last revised: November 23, 1997

Exhibit 4.   Add entry screen.

+SELECT count(id) as NumRec from Directory

The AddEntry.htx template is different from the search result template previously seen. The user only expects one record to be returned to this screen. That record will contain the total number of records in the database. The rest of the template is an HTML form that will allow the user to enter the details of the new directory entry and submit them to the database. Exhibit 4 shows the add entry screen.

The following example is the AddEntry.htx HTML listing supporting Exhibit 4: Add Directory Entry Screen:

```
<!DOCTYPE HTML PUBLIC "-//IETF//DTD HTML//EN">

<html>

<head>

<meta http-equiv="Content-Type"

content="text/html; charset=iso-8859-1">

<meta name="GENERATOR" content="Microsoft FrontPage 2.0">

<title>Add Entry</title>

</head>


<body>

<h1>Add Directory Entry</h1>


<hr>

<%BeginDetail%>
```

```
<p><font size="4"><em><strong>There are currently

&lt;%NumRec%&gt; entries in the
directory.</strong></em></font></p>

<%EndDetail%>

<p><font size="4"><em><strong>Please enter the name and
telephone

number to add a new entry.</strong></em></font></p>


<form action="Add2DB.idc" method="POST">
    <table border="0">
        <tr>
            <td><strong>First Name:</strong></td>
            <td><input type="text" size="20"
            maxlength="20"

            name="fname"></td>
        </tr>
        <tr>
            <td><strong>Last Name:</strong></td>
            <td><input type="text" size="20"
            maxlength="20"

            name="lname"></td>
        </tr>
        <tr>
            <td><strong>Tel Number:</strong></td>
            <td><input type="text" size="15"
            maxlength="15"

            name="tel"></td>
            </tr>
        </table>
        <blockquote>
            <p> </p>
        </blockquote>
        <p><input type="submit" value="OK"> <input
        type="button"
```

```
        value="Cancel"> </p>

  </form>


  <hr>


  <h5>Last revised: November 23, 1997</h5>

  </body>

  </html>
```

In the preceding listing, note the `<%BeginDetail%>` and `<%EndDetail%>` around the `<%NumRec%>` variable, without which the %NumeRec% variable will not be assigned a value. Also note the form action is referencing yet another IDC script named Add2DB.idc. The Add2DB.idc script contains the SQL INSERT statement that will insert the new record into the database. The listing for the Add2DB.idc script is as follows:

```
Datasource:Tel_Directory
Username:
Password:
Template:Directory.htx
SQLStatement:
+INSERT INTO Directory (FirstName, LastName, Tel)
+VALUES ('%fname%', '%lname%', '%tel%')
SQLStatement:
+SELECT id, FirstName, LastName, Tel FROM Directory
```

Careful examination of this script reveals that it has an SQL INSERT statement that takes as parameters the values that had been entered in the HTML form. The INSERT statement is not the only statement in the script. There is a second SQL statement that selects all the records in the telephone directory. The second select statement will populate the Directory.htx template, which was seen previously. This script performs the insert action and then displays all records in the directory, including the newly inserted record.

Tip: Results returned from the database must match the template.

Each result set returned from the database will correspond with a single `<%BeginDetail%>` `<%EndDetail%>` in the template. There may be more than one `<%BeginDetail%>` `<%EndDetail%>` in the template. If one SQL statement does not return a result set it will be skipped and the next result set will be matched to the `<%BeginDetail%>` `<%EndDetail%>` in the template. In this example, the INSERT statement does not return a result set. The sec-

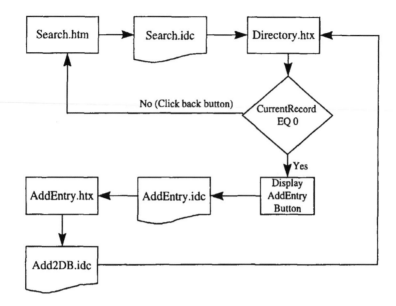

Exhibit 5.   Web telephone directory application.

ond SQL statement does return a result set and will therefore be used by the `<%BeginDetail%>` `<%EndDetail%>` in the template.

Organizing the Application

The application directory was created previously. All the HTML, IDC, and HTX files should now reside in the same directory. They are all built to reference each other in a cyclic fashion. Exhibit 5 depicts the relationships between the various screens and scripts.

CONCLUSION

The sample application created in this article demonstrates the principles of accessing a database through a Web server. The task is accomplished without the need for traditional programming. All the developer needs to know are basic SQL statements and some HTML coding. With this basic knowledge, an application has been created that can be useful and provide value.

The IDC technology is compatible with a Microsoft Internet Information Server. The personal Web server version was used to test this application. Users accessing the telephone directory can do so with any browser that can read and interpret HTML code (e.g., Netscape or Microsoft).

There are many ways to access data through the Web; IDC is the simplest and quickest way of doing so. If the requirements for specific applications can be met with this method, it will be a convenient and low maintenance solution.

Chapter 56
Intranets: Notes vs. the Internet

Brett Molotsky

A BUYER IS LOOKING FOR SOME NEW TRANSPORTATION and a friend recommends a dealer who specializes in many different types of vehicles. The dealer suggests either a car or a tractor, based on the logic that the vehicles are essentially the same; both have engines, drivetrains, steering and braking mechanisms, and both will transport the driver from one location to another.

Although the similarities between the two vehicles may be strong, there are also strong differences. The vehicles are designed and built for different purposes and different environments, and will work differently on different types of terrain. The reasons for choosing one over the other depend entirely on what the driver's transportation needs are and how those needs are affected by the environment in which the vehicle will be operated.

This metaphor can be applied to a current trend in corporate IS strategy. Companies are starting to question how Lotus Notes as a groupware product may fit into a corporate technological infrastructure that seeks to exploit the current rush toward the corporate intranet. Many managers are wondering why they should implement or continue to use Lotus Notes when a World Wide Web browser and a Web server can do the job.

But like the differences between the car and the tractor, there are significant differences between Lotus Notes as a corporate technology and the Web as a corporate technology. They are not the same vehicles, and they each have strengths and weaknesses in different environments.

This chapter points out those differences and raises some of the key issues related to using either or both of these tools in a company's Internet and intranet initiatives.

Some people believe that Web technology will supplant the need for products like Notes in the very near future, and others feel that Notes and products like it offer features that Web technology will never be able to provide on its own. The reality, however, may fall somewhere in between.

THE CONCEPT OF THE INTRANET

The basic premise of the whole Internet is founded on the idea that the computers that are connected to each other need not share the same operating system, platform, or software. All that they need in order to communicate is a common networking protocol, such as Transmission Control Protocol and Internet Protocol (TCP/IP), physical connections, and software capable of displaying and retrieving files in specific formats. By providing each node on the network with the proper tool to access information, the source and/or location of the information becomes secondary.

Managing Distributed Information

As more companies move toward TCP/IP as their standard networking protocol, they have the opportunity to begin exploiting this concept of distributed information within their own organizations. Like the Internet, information will be placed on distributed servers within the company in a standard format (in this case, hypertext markup language [HTML]), and users across the organization will be able to view, print, and give feedback regardless of their hardware/software configuration. As long as they have a Web browser on their workstation, corporate information will be accessible.

Extending this model through a large corporation has tremendous appeal, mainly because browser software is very inexpensive (if not free), and no other client-side tool is required to access data. Coupled with new products emerging for the back-end of the equation, including products that allow HTML publishing of database data, companies see an opportunity to provide client/server computing solutions to all users at a fraction of their originally estimated costs.

The intranet is the collection of servers and workstations connected to each other using the same paradigm as the Internet: the workstations are connected via TCP/IP and browser software to various information stores that may be simple HTML documents or complex database applications using powerful back-end database tools. All of this functionality comes at a low cost per workstation, is generally platform independent, and does not have to disrupt current development projects using standard database development tools.

LOTUS NOTES IN THE ENTERPRISE

Many companies have already found all of this functionality and more by installing Lotus Notes within their organization. Notes, with server and workstation software for all of the major operating systems and platforms, provides exactly the same basic functionality as an intranet: the ability for low-cost client software to access a wide variety of information and database applications using the existing corporate network. Notes also allows users to provide feedback and input into databases, as well as develop sophisticated applications within its own development environment.

Lotus Notes is almost as pure a client/server environment as exists today for the PC platforms. A server task runs on a file server in the network and the Notes client software makes requests for information from that server task. The information is fed to the client, where all the processing is done. Any changes made to the information on the client are submitted back to the server on request.

Companies have implemented Lotus Notes for a variety of reasons. Notes provides a secure, monitored environment for the management of information, has built-in messaging and E-mail features, and allows groups of users to share and exchange information in a controlled environment. Coupled with the development tools built into the product, Notes provides a stable environment for developing and distributing applications in which groups of users need to move, share, or store information.

Costly Implementation

All of these benefits come at a cost, however. There are costs associated with the software, but that is only the beginning. Notes generally requires close administration and management on the server side, and database management on the application side. As the size of the Notes network grows, the administration tasks become more critical to the overall performance of the network.

In the past, Notes has been criticized for the lack of flexibility of its development tools and the overall cost of implementation. Lotus has repositioned Notes with the release of version 4.0. The client software now retails for as little as $70 per workstation (which is not much more than the license for a standard browser tool like Netscape) and $750 per server. Steep discounts exist for volume licensing and members of Lotus' special purchasing programs.

This pricing policy has put Notes right into the mix among companies looking to either leverage their existing Notes infrastructure into a company-wide intranet or extend Notes' influence to build new standards for computing within the organization.

NOTES VS. INTRANETS

There is a pervasive feeling among IS managers that Notes and intranets are somehow mutually exclusive. According to popular opinion, the rise of the intranet means the demise of Lotus Notes as a useful information platform, simply because Web technology coupled with an intranet provides all the functionality of a Notes installation at a fraction of the cost.

For many IS managers, supporters of Notes technology fail to see the bigger picture and the advantages of Web technology that reaches across database platforms and client workstation issues. For managers in organizations using Notes, the reverse is often the case; the benefits they have realized by using Notes cannot be replaced simply by installing a browser on every desk. IS professionals at all levels may wonder why they must make an "either/or" choice with respect to intranetworking and the tools that support it.

If the two approaches are considered opposite technologies as diverse as the car and the tractor, with Web technology at one pole and Notes at the other, the true area of opportunity and possibility lies in the middle. The questions that IS managers should be asking when considering the implementation of an intranet in their organization is not whether Web technology or Notes technology should be used.

Instead, an organization needs to look beyond the technical limits of both technologies into how each might function within the organization. Instead of either/or, the question may become: where are the areas of synergy among these technologies and how can that synergy be used to build the most effective intranet solution for the organization?

Browser-Based Intranets

Netscape, Microsoft, and others already ship or have announced cross-platform versions of their browser tools. Netscape has even stopped calling its tool a browser, preferring instead to call it "an environment." The implication is that the tool used to view HTML content on the network is not just a viewing tool, but with the use of add-in programs, it allows users to execute sophisticated client/server applications from within the tool itself.

The browser, in Netscape's view, becomes the front-end to everything — content on the Internet, content on the corporate network, client/server applications, E-mail, and groupware applications. Because the interface is standard across all platforms and the basic functionality never changes across applications or information types, the focus returns to the information being presented to the user, and not the effort typically required to design and build a comfortable user interface for every application. Because this approach requires only that the user have a compatible browser installed, there is no inherent reason to choose a single browser from a single manufacturer.

Currently, several companies offer low-cost, commercially available browser tools that run on a variety of platforms. The key feature they share is the ability to retrieve and display information from any hypertext transfer protocol (HTTP) server. Minor differences among platforms are accounted for by the browser without the user or the programmer having to deal with them. Font differences, screen resolution differences, even interface object rendering differences (i.e., the way buttons and form fields are drawn by the operating system) are removed from the responsibilities of the programmer.

IS managers may welcome a degree of standardization that is possible by using a browser tool in the context of a corporate client/server computing strategy, especially when coupled with the types of HTTP server software now available. The HTTP server is the backbone of the corporate intranet. Many of the most respected enterprise database software companies have announced products or plans to incorporate HTML document publishing into their database architecture. What this means for the corporate IS strategy depends on which tools are used in the company.

All of the major database vendors have either released or intend to release products that will incorporate the information stored in their databases into Web-compatible content. The features of these new products vary, but most will allow the retrieval and display of information via live queries into the database, as well as allow dynamic updates of information in the relational database via the browser.

Notes-Based Intranets

Notes performs the same basic functions as an intranet installation — the ability to access information in a friendly, comfortable format tied with the ability to generate and store large amounts of data in a database format. The Notes client software is cross-platform in nature, allowing users across the organization to share and update information.

Notes' built-in database development tools set it apart from the browser market; any user with an appropriate license may become an applications developer in Notes simply by invoking the Design menu on the toolbar. The development environment is simple enough for novices to grasp quickly and robust enough for some sophisticated development to take place.

However, it is the inclusion of InterNotes tools, released by Lotus in 1995 and to be upgraded this year for the new release of Notes, that places Notes squarely in the realm of a practical intranet solution. Using Inter-Notes, a standard Notes workstation can become a browser tool.

THE HYBRID ENVIRONMENT

A hybrid environment can be created in which Notes may function for certain users as their primary interface to both workgroup solutions as well as the corporate intranet. For other users who may not need the applications or information currently stored in Notes, a standard browsing tool may be all that is required.

Using InterNotes, users of a standard browser are not kept out of Notes-based information. The InterNotes Web Publisher, a component of the InterNotes tools, allows Notes databases to be published, searched, and updated via Web technology. Regardless of the front-end tool being used, the Notes-based data is just as accessible as other types of information.

Administrative Benefits

Using the standard Notes administration and database development tools, an organization can implement and manage Web-based information. The Web Publisher can publish any Notes database into HTML documents and refresh those documents on a scheduled basis.

This means that users do not have to learn HTML codes in order to generate or update Web information. Much of the cost related to managing Web information comes with maintenance and upkeep of the documents themselves. By using the Notes Web Publisher, that administrative task can be reduced significantly. Because all of the changes are made using Notes, editing and publishing of the HTML information can be greatly simplified.

Drawbacks

The biggest disadvantage to the hybrid approach is that it requires an investment in Lotus Notes. For organizations that have already made this investment for other reasons, there is a logical extension to the Notes environment. Leveraging existing experience with the Notes interface and environment reduces the learning curve and provides seamless integration with corporate information on an intranet. However, the desire to build an intranet or to extend the company's reach to the Internet is not justification for building a Notes infrastructure.

INTRANET IMPLEMENTATION ISSUES

Regardless of the approach a company decides to take — browser-based or Notes-based — there are issues relating to the implementation of the technology that must be addressed.

Fit with Existing Technology

Decisions already made for workstations, servers, and the network play a key role in deciding which directions the organization will take in the future. Platform decisions, standardization of desktop applications, and decisions related to workgroup computing environments all play a part. IS must consider how the new environment will take advantage of the best features of the existing one, and determine which tools will be the most useful when the intranet is in place. IS planners should also determine internal and external workgroup computing needs. As the new infrastructure takes shape, IS may find an opportunity to reshape how the corporate computing environment should be put together.

How Is It Connected?

The current state of the corporate network must be factored into the plans. If an organization is already using TCP/IP, then it already has in place the communication layer necessary to extend an existing Notes network to an intranet or onto the Internet. Otherwise, a network protocol upgrade will need to be planned for the entire corporate network. If the network needs to be upgraded, or if the standard protocol needs to be changed, then the company will have an opportunity to change the fundamental paradigm related to how users interact with the information on the network.

Learning and Training

There is a significant learning curve involved in training someone to develop and manage Internet content. This education extends well beyond the IS staff to the people who will be charged with building individual Web pages. These are the people who, if they are not using a tool like Notes to manage content, are going to have the longest learning curve.

Once the intranet is in place, training will have to be conducted for each end-user on browser techniques, basic Internet protocols, and the use of the intranet itself. With Notes, the standard training on the workgroup computing environment is simply mapped onto the corporate intranet. The tool is already in place from the users' perspective.

Management

If, for example, it is 4:00 p.m. on Friday and a ten-page press release needs to go online immediately, someone must be responsible for putting this content on the company's Web page — be it an IS employee, a Webmaster, or a public relations agent. Once a company Web site is running, there is a daily need to watch and administer the activity. Allowing end-users to manage this content through a standard interface like Notes can reduce production and development time and allow IS to monitor the activity in the site.

SUMMARY

IS staff and managers can use the following questions as general guidelines when setting a corporate strategy for information management and the development of workgroup applications:

- What are the company's strategic information goals?

- Do the goals, in general, include the use of workgroup computing tools such as Notes or Microsoft Exchange?
- Is the organization interested in gaining specific expertise in the management and implementation of the intranet?
- Is the company interested in making the producers of the intranet content experts in HTML and Web technologies, or should those technologies be as hidden and seamless as possible for these users?
- Who is going to administer and manage intranet Web sites?
- Where is the Web site expertise going to come from?

Existing Investments

The following questions can help IS evaluate the existing corporate technology investment:

- Does the company have an existing investment in Notes?
- What are the strategic directions for workgroup computing in the organization?
- Have standards been set for the use of browsing tools or client/server database applications to be used on the corporate intranet?
- Given the direction in the industry toward a more distributed form of information dissemination, how do the company's existing database investments and database systems (i.e., Notes, DB2, Sybase, or Oracle) fit into an overall corporate strategic plan for client/server and workgroup computing?

Long-Term Thinking

IS may want to consider the following questions to plan more efficiently for the future:

- What are the company's long-term plans for integration of all database and non-database content on a corporate network?
- Given the integration of workgroup computing tools into the basic structure of the corporate intranet, are there standards and guidelines in place for the construction, implementation, and maintenance of the enterprise workgroup computing environment?

Chapter 57
Web-Enabled Data Warehouses

Mary Ayala-Bush
John Jordan
Walter Kuketz

DELIVERING DATA WAREHOUSE ACCESS VIA WEB BROWSERS HAS A VARI-ETY OF BENEFITS. Inside a corporate intranet, Web-enabled data warehouses can increase ease of use, decrease some aspects of training time, and potentially cut costs by reducing the number of proprietary clients. Upgrades can also be accelerated given a standard client, and data warehouses can more easily integrate with other applications across a common platform. Extended to corporate trading partners via a so-called extranet (a secure extension of an intranet outside a firewall), the information contained within a data warehouse may be of sufficient value to become a revenue source. While such internal and external benefits may be appealing, they do not come without complicating issues.

In these traditional implementations, data warehouses have been used by a small population of either highly trained or high-ranking employees for decision support. With such a small audience having the warehouse application on their desktop, access control was straightforward: either the end-user could access a given table or not. Once the warehouse begins to be accessed by more people — possibly including some outside of the company — access may need to be restricted based on content. Security concerns also change as the user population increases, with encryption over the public Internet being one likely requirement. Because Web-based access to a data warehouse means expanding the community of people who will access the data, the types of queries will most likely be more varied. Better business intelligence may thereby be derived, but once again not without complications.

In addition to security, performance (and therefore cost) issues become immediately relevant, dictating reconsideration of everything from replication patterns to log-in requirements. This article explores how Web-enabled data warehouses change the strategy, architecture, infrastructure, and implementation of traditional versions of these applications

STRATEGY

Business Relationships

The strategy for a Web-based data warehouse should answer at least two questions:

- Who is being granted access?
- Why are they being granted access via the Web model?

Answering these two questions will supply important information for the cost justification of broader access. Possible justifications might include getting better service from vendors, facilitating better relationships with customers, shortening time of products in the supply chain, and receiving revenues from an internal application. The implications of broader access include having to design an architecture flexible enough to allow for new audiences with needs and requirements that may not be well identified. In addition, going into the information business can distract a company from its core focus: how are pricing levels determined? How does revenue derived from a potentially unexpected external source change payback and ROI models? What are the service level agreements and how are they determined? Who becomes the customer service liaison, especially if the IS organization is already running at full capacity for internal constituencies?

Access Control and Security

Security is a primary consideration when contemplating Web access to sensitive corporate information. Authentication can be required at three separate stages, allowing administrators to fine-tune who sees what when, while encryption (typically through the use of the secure sockets layer, or SSL) protects both queries and responses from being compromised in transit. Initially, the Web server can require either name and password log-in or the presence of a certificate issued by the data warehouse administrator. This grants access to the site and triggers the SSL encryption if it is implemented. Once inside the data warehouse, the user might also be required to authenticate him/herself at the query server, which allows access to the appropriate databases. This might be a dedicated data mart for a vendor, for example, that precludes vendor A from seeing anything pertaining to vendor B, whose information is held in a logically (and possibly physically) separate data mart. Finally, authentication may be required by the database to limit access within a given body of data: a clerk at vendor A can see only a selected portion of the A data mart, while A's president can see that company's entire data mart.

The logistics of security can be extensive. Maintaining certificates requires dedicated resources, while planning for and executing multitiered log-ins is a nontrivial task. At the same time, limiting access can imply limiting the value of the data warehouse, so security must be designed to be flexible and as friendly to legitimate users as possible.

New Components

Broader access to a data warehouse introduces a number of new elements into the traditional application model. What happens to the query engine vendor's pricing model as its proprietary desktop clients are no longer required? Where are the skill sets and hardware to implement Web servers and connect them to the query engine? How much will data be transformed (and by whom) if it is moved out of a central data warehouse into data marts for security, performance, or other reasons?

ARCHITECTURE

If strategy is concerned with goals and objectives, architecture is the unifying conceptual design or structure. It defines a system's component parts and relationships. Good architectures ensure that the component hardware and software pieces will fit together into an integrated whole.

A Web-enabled data warehouse introduces additional components within a system architecture, which must be expanded to include:

- The Web server component.
- The components that connect the Web server to the query engine.
- The component that formats the results such that they are viewable by a Web browser.

The system architecture may also need a component for integrating data marts.

Even given these elements, the architecture must be flexible enough to change rapidly, given both the pace of innovation in the Internet arena and the evolving place of data warehouses in contemporary business. The warehouse components may change due to increasing numbers of people using it, changing aggregations based on security or performance requirements, new access paths required by technological or organizational evolution, etc.

New design considerations are introduced by each of the above components. Web servers introduce new complications, particularly in regard to scalability issues. Secure transactions over a dial-up connection can be painfully slow, but detuning the security at either the firewall or the Web server can expose the corporate network to risk. Middleware between the Web server and the query server can dramatically affect performance, particularly if common gateway interface (CGI) scripts are used in place of APIs. Database publishing to HTML is reasonably well advanced, but even here some of the newest tools introduce Java programming into the mix, which may cause implementation problems unless the skills are readily available. Java also presents the architect with new ways to partition the presentation layer and the application logic, with implications (for the network and desktop machines in particular) that are only beginning to be experienced in enterprise computing.

The system architecture must support competing enterprises accessing the data sources. One challenge is to support competing vendors where access control is data dependent. Both vendors can query the same tables; for example, by product, by region, by week. If a given retail outlet sells both vendors' products, and people from the sales outlet are allowed to query the data warehouse, they will need access to both vendors' history.

A good system architecture must include the facility for access control across the entire Web site, from the Web server through to the database. If a mobile sales force will be given access while they are on the road, the architecture must have a component to address the types of connections that will be used, whether they are 800 dial-up services, local Internet Service Providers (ISPs), or national ISPs such as CompuServe or AOL.

INFRASTRUCTURE

The infrastructure required to support the Web-enabled data warehouse expands to include the Web site hardware and software, the hardware and software required to interface the Web server to the query server, and the software that allows the query server to supply results in HTML. The corporate network may have to be altered to accommodate the additional traffic of the new data warehouse users. This expansion increases the potential complexity of the system, introduces new performance issues, and adds to the costs that must be justified.

The Web-enabled warehouse's supporting infrastructure also introduces new system administration skills. Because the warehouse's DBA should not be responsible for the care and feeding of the Web site, a new role is required — the Web site administrator, often called the Web master. This term can mean different things to different people, so clarity is needed as the position is defined. Depending on the context, corporate Web masters may or may not be responsible for the following:

- Designing the site's content architecture.
- Writing and/or editing the material.

- Designing the site's look and feel.
- Monitoring traffic.
- Configuring and monitoring security.
- Writing scripts from the Web server to back-end application or database servers.
- Project management.
- Extracting content from functional departments.

The amount of work that may have to be done to prepare for Internet or intranet implementation will vary greatly from company to company. For example, if the warehouse is going to be accessible from the public Internet, then a firewall must be put in place. Knowing the current state of Web-based application development is essential: if organizational factors, skills, and infrastructure are not in place and aligned, the data warehouse team may either get pulled from its core technology base into competition for scarce resources or be forced to develop skills largely different from those traditionally associated with database expertise.

Web Site

Web site components include the computer to run the Web server on and the Web server software, which may include not only the Web listener but also a document manager for the reports generated from the warehouse. One of the Web protocols, called the Common Gateway Interface, allows the Web browser to access objects and data that are not on the Web server, thereby allowing the Web server to access the data warehouse. The interface used does not access the warehouse directly but will access the query engine to formulate the queries; the query engine will still access the warehouse. The CGI has been identified as a bottleneck in many Web site implementations. Because the CGI program must incur the overhead of starting up and stopping with every request to it, in high-volume systems this overhead will become pronounced and result in noticeably slow response times. API access tends to be faster, but it depends on the availability of such interfaces from or in support of different vendors.

Application Query Engine

The infrastructure must support the application query engine, which may run on the same computer as the data warehouse or on a separate computer that is networked to the data warehouse computer. This component must be able to translate the query results into HTML for the server to supply to the browser. Some of the query engines will present the results in graphic form as well as tabular form. Traditional warehouses have supported relatively small user communities, so existing query engines will have to be monitored to see how their performance changes when the number of users doubles, triples, or increases by even larger multiplers. In addition, the type and complexity of the queries will also have performance implications that must be addressed based on experience.

Data Warehouse

The infrastructure for the data warehouse is not altered simply because Web browsers are being used; instead, the expanded number of users and new types of queries this may need to be executed will likely force changes to be made. When a data mart architecture is introduced for performance or security reasons, there may be a need to change where the mart will be located: on the same machine as the warehouse, or on a separate machine. The infrastructure will have to support both the method of replication originally specified and new patterns of replication based on DASD cost considerations, performance factors, or security precautions.

Security

Web server access. Access to the Web server can be controlled by: 1) requiring the user to log into the Web site by supplying a user name and password, 2) installing client certificates into the browsers of the clients to whom access is granted, or 3) specifying only the IP addresses that are allowed to access the Web site. The client certificate requires less interaction on the user's part because they will not have to supply a user name and password to access the system. The client's certificate is sent to the Web server, which will validate the certificate and grant the user access to the system. (Part of the process of enabling a secure Web site is to install a server certificate. This must be requested from a third party, called a certificate authority, which allows one to transmit certificates authenticating that someone is who they say they are.) A less secure strategy is to configure the Web server to allow connection from a selected number of computers, with all others being categorically denied access. This scheme will allow anyone from an authorized computer — as opposed to authorized persons — to access the Web site. Because this method is based on IP address, DHCP systems can present difficulties in specifying particular machines as opposed to machines in a particular subnet.

Communication transport security. Both the query and especially the information that is sent back to the browser can be of a sensitive nature. To prevent others along the route back to the browser from viewing it, the data must be encrypted, particularly if it leaves the firewall. Encryption is turned on when the Web server is configured, typically via the Secure Socket Layer (SSL) protocol.

Query server application. To access the query server, the user may be asked to supply a user name and password. The information supplied by the certificate could be carried forward, but not without some custom code. There are various approaches to use to for developing the user names and passwords: one can create a unique user name for each of the third parties that will access the system (allowing the log-in to be performed on any machine), or create a unique user name for each person who will access the warehouse. Each approach has implications for system administration.

Database access. Database access can be controlled by limiting the tables users and user groups can access. A difficulty arises when there are two competing users who must access a subset of the data within the same table. This security difficulty can be solved by introducing data marts for those users, where each data mart will contain only the information that particular user is entitled to see. Data marts introduce an entirely new set of administrative and procedural issues, in particular around the replication scheme to move the data from the warehouse into the data mart. Is data scrubbed, summarized, or otherwise altered in this move, or is replication exact and straightforward? Each approach has advantages and drawbacks.

IMPLEMENTATION

The scope of implementing a Web-enabled data warehouse increases because of the additional users and the increased number of system components. The IS organization must be prepared to confront the implications of both the additional hardware and software and of potentially new kinds of users, some of whom may not even work for the company that owns the data in the warehouse.

Intranet

Training will need to cover the mechanics of how to use the query tool, provide the user with an awareness of the levels (and system implications) of different queries, and show how the results set will expand or contract based on what is being asked. The user community for the intranet will be some subset of the employees of the corporation. The logistics involved with training the users will be largely under the company's control; even with broader access, data warehouses are typically decision-support systems and not within the operational purview of most employees.

Implementing security for the intranet site involves sensitizing users to the basics of information security, issuing and tracking authentication information (whether through certificates, passwords, or a combination of the two), and configuring servers and firewalls to balance performance and security. One part of the process for enabling a secure Web server is to request a server certificate from a certificate authority. Administratively, a corporation must understand the components — for example, proof of the legal right to use the corporate name — required to satisfy the inquiries from certificate authority and put in place the procedures for yearly certificate renewal.

Monitoring a Web-based data warehouse is a high priority because of the number of variables that will need tuning. In addition, broader access will change both the volume and the character of the query base in unpredictable ways.

Intra/Extranet

In addition to the training required for internal users, training is extended to the third parties that will access the warehouse. Coordination of training among the third parties will likely prove to be more difficult: competing third parties will not want to be trained at the same time, and paying customers will have different expectations as compared with captive internal users. In addition, the look and feel within the application may need more thorough user interface testing if it is a public, purchased service.

Security gets more complex in extranet implementations simply because of the public nature of the Internet. It is important to keep in mind the human and cultural factors that affect information security and not only focus on the technologies of firewalls, certificates, and the like. Different organizations embody different attitudes, and these differences can cause significant misunderstandings when sensitive information (and possibly significant expenditures) are involved.

Monitoring and tuning are largely the same as in an intranet implementation, depending on the profiles of remote users, trading partner access patterns, and the type and volume of queries.

In addition, a serious extranet implementation may introduce the need for a help desk. It must be prepared to handle calls for support from the third parties, and combine customer service readiness with strict screening to keep the focus on questions related to the data warehouse. It is not impossible to imagine a scenario in which the third-party employees will call for help on topics other than the warehouse.

CONCLUSION

Because Web browsers have the ability to save whatever appears in the browser, in Web-enabled data warehouses, information that appears in the browser can be saved to the desktop. Protecting information from transmission into the wrong hands involves a balancing act between allowing for flexibility of queries and restricting the information that can potentially move outside corporate control. Legal agreements regarding the use of information may need to be put in place, for example, which tend not to be a specialty of the IS organization. Pricing the information can be another tricky area, along with managing expectations on the part of both internal and third-party users.

By their very nature, however, data warehouses have always been more subject to unintended consequences than their operational siblings. With changing ideas about the place and power of information, new organizational shapes and strategies, and tougher customers demanding more while paying less, the data warehouse's potential for business benefit can be increased by extending its reach while making it easier to use. The consequences of more people using data warehouses for new kinds of queries, while sometimes taxing for IS professionals, may well be breakthroughs in business performance. As with any other emerging technology, the results will bear watching.

Chapter 58
Publishing Database Information on the World Wide Web

James A. Larson
Carol L. Larson

IN TODAY'S BUSINESS ENVIRONMENT, users may be scattered across the globe and still need to access database information at their home enterprise or headquarters. How can users access database information from wherever they happen to be?

Typically, users access database information from a variety of computing platforms, including Windows, Macintosh, and UNIX. It is important that users are able to access database information from their chosen platform in a consistent fashion. This chapter discusses how to publish database information on the World Wide Web and the methods by which users can access it.

THE WORLD WIDE WEB: AN EXPLOSION

The World Wide Web phenomenon has exploded onto the computing scene. In addition to E-mail and file transfer, the World Wide Web (or Web) supports document browsing. Users access a wide range of information available on the Web in the form of documents formatted using the hypertext markup language (HTML).

HTML Documents

HTML documents consist of three components:

- Content (the database information).
- Annotation (the format and layout of the document).
- Links (connections that chain documents together).

0-8493-9976-9/99/$0.00+$.50
© 1999 by CRC Press LLC

Exhibit 1 illustrates a database table and its corresponding HTML document. HTML is used to annotate the document's content with tags (in Exhibit 1, tags are denoted by brackets). The tags specify how to format the content of the document when it is displayed to the user. Any platform can be used to display the document's contents because software on each platform interprets the tags in a manner appropriate for that computer. Thus, HTML provides platform independence.

Once the publisher adds HTML tags to a document, the document can be presented to users. Not only does HTML describe the layout of text, it also integrates images, audio, and small applications (applets) for presentation to the user.

Uniform Resource Locators. A universal resource locator (URL) is a pointer to a document located in an HTML server connected to the Web. Documents may be linked explicitly by embedding a URL within an anchor tag of one document to provide the location on the Web of a related document. In Exhibit 1, URLs are used to link each employee with the home page of the employee's department and browse through sequences of related documents.

Common Gateway Interface Scripts. An HTML document is not limited to content-containing static information; dynamic information also may be included within a document's content. The common gateway interface (CGI) gives programmers a language for specifying how to derive data for presentation to the user.

For example, a CGI script might invoke a hardware thermometer to measure the current temperature and record it in the document's content. CGI scripts also can be used to solicit a database query from the user and insert HTML tags into the query results. Programmers implement CGI scripts using Visual Basic, C, C++, TCL, Perl, or other languages executable on a Web server.

STATIC PUBLISHING: DISPLAYING DATABASE INFORMATION USING THE WEB

Exhibit 2 illustrates how database information is published on a Web server by extracting data and inserting HTML tags into the query results.

First, a database administrator (DBA) extracts the data to be published by submitting an SQL query to the database management system (DBMS). Programmers can insert HTML tags to control the appearance of the final HTML document. The resulting document then is placed on an HTML server that manages and accesses documents much like a DBMS manages database records. The HTML server responds to requests for documents by

A

Name	Amount	Department
Able	400.00	Toy
Baker	350.00	Car
Carson	425.00	Toy

B

```
<TABLE BORDER=1>
     <TH>     <TH>      <TH>      Department
     Name     Amount
<TR> <TD>     <TD>      <TD>  <A href=URL of Toy Department's Homepage> Toy </A> </TH>
     Able     400.00
<TR> <TD>     <TD>      <TD>  <A href=URL of Car Department's Homepage> Car </A> </TR>
     Baker    350.00
<TR> <TD>     <TD>      <TD>  <A href=URL of Toy Department's Homepage> Toy </A> </TR>
     Carson   425.00    <TD>  <A href=URL of Toy Department's Homepage> Toy </A> </TR>
</TABLE>
```

C

<TABLE>, </TABLE>	Begin, End Table
<TH>, </TH>	Begin, End Table Heading
<TR>, </TR>	Begin, End Table Row
<TD>, </TD>	Begin, End Table Data Element
<A>, </A>	Begin, End Anchor

Exhibit 1.   A database table and its HTML description.

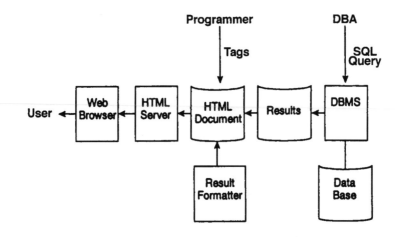

Exhibit 2. Static publishing.

sending them to the requesting client browsers, which could be Netscape Navigator, or Microsoft Internet Explorer.

Alternatively, software automatically can insert HTML tags to generate default layouts. For example, Corel's Web.Data uses a step-by-step process to create a database table to be inserted into an HTML document and guides the DBA through the required steps for formatting. The result is a recipe file, which is a template describing how to process the results of a database query by inserting the appropriate HTML tags into the query's results. Corel's Web.Data can optimize the HTML document for Netscape Navigator or Microsoft Explorer.

BestWeb Pro Version 1.0 is another example of software that inserts HTML tags into ASCII files created by a database query. BestWeb allows the programmer to select specific properties and formatting options for each table field by indicating which fields should be indexed and customizing the HTML document with background images and corporate logos.

Static generation of HTML documents has its pros and cons. The primary advantage is that the process is straightforward because it is subject to automation. The resulting HTML documents are easy for users to browse, and no programming is required. However, the HTML documents are not linked to the source data in real time. The HTML document is not changed automatically when the user changes the source data in the DBMS. Users cannot change the data in the HTML document and may only change the underlying database directly by using traditional DBMS access facilities.

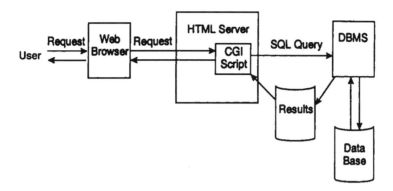

Exhibit 3.   Dynamic publishing with a CGI script.

DYNAMIC PUBLISHING: INTERACTING WITH A DATABASE USING THE WEB

Although static publishing is sufficient for many applications — even desirable from a security point of view because users cannot change the underlying database when they access the corresponding HTML document — many applications require the user to submit a query to retrieve specific data.

Formulating a Query

To formulate a query, the user enters the query parameters into an HTML form consisting of input boxes or other user interface controls. A CGI script, which resides and executes on an HTML server, then takes the parameters and formulates an SQL query to the underlying DBMS, as illustrated in Exhibit 3. After the DBMS processes the query, it returns the extracted data to the CGI script, which reformats the response and inserts HTML tags. Finally, the reformatted response is sent to the user's browser and displayed.

Special controls and CGI scripts not only allow users to specify parameters for a database query, users also may specify a database update. Dynamic publishing enables users to obtain and modify up-to-the-minute database information.

Java Applets

CGI scripts reside and execute on HTML servers. Java applets reside on HTML servers, but are downloaded to and executed on the user's Web browser.

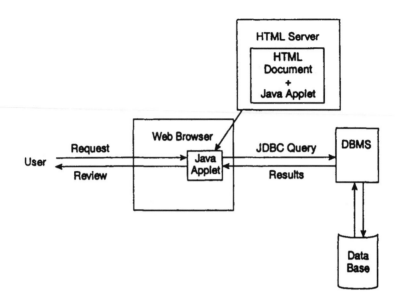

Exhibit 4.   Dynamic publishing with a Java Applet.

Java applets are special types of applications written in the Java programming language. Applets cannot perform actions that may be harmful to the user's environment, such as accessing local disks and printers, accessing the user's identity, or accessing any server other than the one that provided the applet. These limits on what the applet can do ensure, to a degree, that it will not harm the user's computing environment.

Applets can be embedded within an HTML document as shown in Exhibit 4. When executed, a Java applet can produce animation, perform calculations, and dynamically determine the layout and format of information to be presented to the user.

The Java database connectivity (JDBC) standard describes the Java application programming interface (API) for accessing relational databases. Most DBMS vendors support JDBC. Java applets use JDBC to access a DBMS directly to perform database queries and modifications.

User Interface Controls. Java applets can present user interface controls, such as data boxes, pull-down menus, and other user interface widgets, which allow users to enter database queries and update parameters. Applet Window Technology (AWT) is a series of Java classes that provide a collection of user interface controls. AWT is standard on all Java-enabled platforms, including Macintosh, Windows, and UNIX, among others.

Alternatively, programmers also may create or reuse customized user interface controls. CGI scripts execute in the HTML server, whereas Java applets are downloaded from the HTML server and executed within the user's browser. This division of labor minimizes data transmissions between the HTML server and the user's platform.

Limiting Data Transmissions. Generally, database administrators prefer that data element translations and reformatting are done in the HTML server. Thus, a user's request can be satisfied by two data transmissions — one containing the request from the user's computing platform to the server and the second containing the translated, reformatted results from the server to the user's platform. DBAs write CGI scripts to perform the data element translations and data reformatting for execution on the HTML server.

User interface experts may write Java applets to accept data results from the HTML server and generate sophisticated user interfaces, which may involve graphics or animation. For example, Java applets may convert database data to graphs, bar charts, or even animated objects such as fluctuating temperature gauges, nodding heads, or moving clock hands. Java applets execute within the user's browser on the user's computing platform. By executing Java applets at the user's platform, no additional data transmissions are necessary between the user and the HTML server.

SECURITY MECHANISMS

HTML forms provide limited control over database access. Like a relational database view, a form restricts the database elements users may access. For example, the CGI script can provide additional security by requesting that the user supply passwords and by asking questions to authenticate identity. The hypertext transfer protocol (HTTP) also can be used to restrict access to users listed in a file or cause the browser to prompt the user for a password.

Researchers and practitioners have proposed other security mechanisms, such as encryption, watermarks, seals against modification, and certificates of authentication. Many of these advanced security techniques will soon be available, if they are not already.

CONCLUSION

Web publication allows users anywhere in the world with a Web browser to access specific databases subject to specified security constraints. Accessing database information over the Web requires an HTML server to manage documents.

Systems analysts determine whether users need to access static or dynamic data. If users can tolerate static data, software should be used to generate HTML documents automatically. If users require up-to-the-minute data, then programmers must write CGI scripts or Java applets to allow them to request needed information. CGI scripts should be used to perform data transformation and formatting, and Java applets should be used for sophisticated user interfaces.

Chapter 59
Database Management and the Internet: Developments and Challenges

Bhavani Thuraisingham

DURING RECENT MONTHS there has been an increasing demand to access the data stored in different databases through the Internet. The databases may be relational databases, object-oriented databases, or multimedia databases containing unstructured and semistructured data such as text, voice, video, and images. These databases are often heterogeneous in nature. Heterogeneity exists with respect to data structures, data types, semantic meanings, data models, architectures, query-processing strategies, and transaction management techniques.

Many vendors of database management systems (DBMSs) are enhancing their products with capabilities for Internet access. Exhibit 1 illustrates how clients access multiple databases through the Internet. Special Internet protocols are needed for such access. The goal is to provide seamless access to the heterogeneous databases.

Although much progress has been made with respect to Internet database access, there is still room for improvement. For example, database management system (DBMS) functions such as data modeling, query processing, and transaction management are impacted by the Internet. The algorithms for query processing and transactions management may have to be modified to reflect database access through the Internet. For example,

0-8493-9976-9/99/$0.00+$.50
© 1999 by CRC Press LLC

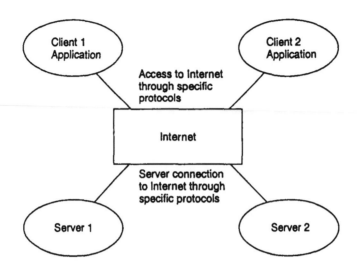

Exhibit 1. Internet-based client/server communication.

the cost models for the query algorithms may have to include the price of accessing servers on the Internet.

Furthermore, distributed object management technologies need to be examined for heterogeneous database integration through the Internet. This chapter discusses the impact of the Internet on various DBMS functions.

DBMS FUNCTIONS

Key DBMS functions include data representation, query management, transaction management, storage management, security management, integrity management, and metadata management. For an Internet database, functions such as browsing and filtering also have to be managed.

Data Representation

Various data representation schemes have been proposed for text databases, including standard generalized markup language (SGML), hypertext markup language (HTML), and office document architecture (ODA). However, a considerable amount of data also will be stored in structured (i.e., relational and object-oriented) databases. Appropriate data models for representing structured as well as unstructured databases include integrated object-oriented, relational, and hypertext-based data models for Internet database management. Currently there are no agreed-on standard data models; appropriate mappings between the standards and the heterogeneous data models used by the databases also must be developed.

Query Management

Query management involves developing language and processing techniques. The query language depends to a great extent on the data model used.

Languages based on structured query language (SQL) are popular for relational as well as nonrelational database systems. For example, object-oriented DBMSs use variations of SQL for database access. An appropriate SQL-based language needs to be developed for accessing structured and unstructured databases. SQL extensions are being examined to handle different data types. Once a standard language has been developed, mappings between the standard language and the languages used by the individual databases must be examined.

For efficient query processing, modifications to current algorithms for distributed and heterogeneous databases should be considered. For example, current cost models focus mainly on the amount of data transferred between the different sites. Database administrators have many issues to consider:

- Are such cost models still valid for Internet databases? Are there other factors that need to be considered in query processing?
- Will the cost of accessing remote database servers over the Internet have an impact on the query algorithms?
- What are the relationships between global and local optimization strategies? What are parameters that are common to both the global and local cost models?

Because of the information explosion caused by the Internet, various technologies, such as agents and mediators, are being considered for locating the data sources, mediating between the different data sources, fusing the data, and giving responses to the user.

Browsing and Filtering

Although many traditional DBMSs do not support browsing, such systems on the Internet need to provide this capability. One of the main uses of the Internet is browsing through and accessing large amounts of information in a short time. Therefore, to access the database efficiently, the DBMS must be augmented by a browser. Numerous browsing tools are available for the Internet; however, they must be integrated with the DBMS.

Closely related to browsing is the filtering technique. With the Internet, the user can become overloaded with information. This means various filters have to be integrated with the browsers and the DBMSs so that unnecessary information is filtered out and users get only the information they want.

Transaction Management

Transaction management, an integral part of DBMSs, involves concurrency control and recovery. New kinds of transactions, such as making a purchase, are taking place on the Internet. In some cases, multiple users may want to purchase the same item and may bid on it. In such a situation, there should be a waiting period before the item is locked. The item then is sold to the highest bidder.

The previous example illustrates the need for flexible transaction models. The ability to perform long-duration transactions and transaction models for workflow management also may be valuable. Serializability conditions may be helpful for concurrency control. Otherwise, it may not be possible to ensure that all the data items accurately reflect the real-world values.

Transaction management also requires consideration of recovery management as well as fine-grained versus coarse-grained locking issues.

Storage Management

For appropriate representation strategies for storing multimedia data, efficient access methods and index strategies are critical. A user should be able to index based on content and context. Research on extensions to various strategies such as B-trees is one possible solution. Internet database management is such a challenge because of the large amount of information and user requirements for quick access. This is why development of methods for integrating database systems with mass storage systems is so critical.

Security Management

Security is vital to Internet database management; however, the policies must be flexible. With the increasing number of databases, negotiations between the different administrators become important. The developers of security for Internet applications are faced with many questions:

- Is there a need for one or more global Internet security administrators? That is, is there a group of one or more individuals responsible for overall database security on the Internet?
- Is it at all possible to designate a group of individuals to be in charge of global security when there may be many different systems on the Internet?
- If there are such global administrators, what are their roles? What are the security features that they enforce?
- What are the relationships between global administrators and local database administrators? That is, should the global and local admin-

istrators negotiate to determine their functions, or is there someone overseeing their actions?

If there is someone overseeing the local and global administrators' actions, then there must be a supergroup that has ultimate authority for security. If there are no global administrators, which may be the case because it would be very difficult to enforce security policies across different systems, then a type of negotiations needs to be established between the systems administrators of the individual systems on the Internet.

Other security issues include enforcing appropriate authorization and access control mechanisms. The implementation of these mechanisms depends on the standard data models and languages used. Extensions to the query language are necessary for enforcement of security constraints, including:

- Mechanisms for identifying and authenticating users.
- Laws on electronic copyright protection.
- Methods for detecting plagiarism.

There are several additional concerns if multilevel security is needed. For example, the trusted computing base must be determined, as well as how much of the Internet software should be trusted.

Integrity Management

Concurrency control and recovery techniques maintain the integrity of the data in the databases. Integrity issues revolve around data quality. With Internet database access, data could come from many different sources. Users need information concerning the accuracy of the source. Appropriate tagging techniques can be enforced and integrity constraint-checking techniques used for Internet database access.

Metadata Management

Metadata describes the data in the database, including schema information. Metadata management is critical to other database functions. Metadata may include not only information about the data in the databases, but also information about the tools, resources, and policies and procedures. Metadata may be used to navigate through the Internet. In addition, information such as transactions history, access patterns, and access control may be part of the metadata. Standards and models are key, in addition to techniques for querying and updating.

Interoperability

The heterogeneous databases on the Internet must be able to interoperate. Distributed object technology can be used for interoperability.

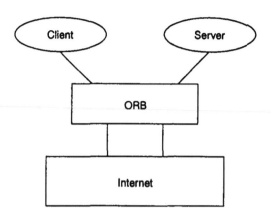

Exhibit 2.   Internet-ORB interoperability.

For example, an object request broker (ORB) based on the Object Management Group's (OMG) specifications can be implemented for interoperation through the Internet (Exhibit 2). The major challenge is to develop appropriate interfaces between the ORB and the Internet. The OMG's Internet Special Interest Group is focusing on these issues. Work also is being done on integrating OMG's common object request broker architecture (CORBA), Internet, and Javasoft's Java technologies.

Java. As a programming language that can be used to develop systems as well as applications for the Internet, Java is showing a lot of promise for Internet database access. One of the major developments for data access is the standard called Java Database Connectivity (JDBC). Simply stated, database calls could be embedded in a Java application program so that databases may be accessed through these calls. JDBC may be built on other standard protocols. Many DBMS vendors are providing support for JDBC.

CONCLUSION

This chapter has examined database management functions and discussed the possible impact of the Internet. There is a need for integrating structured and unstructured databases. Special query optimization techniques also need to be investigated and database management systems have to be integrated with browsers.

Information must be filtered so that users get only the relevant information — for this reason, flexible transaction models are needed for Internet database management. Content and context-based indexing and special access methods for multimedia data should be examined. Integrating database systems with mass storage systems will become important to handling petabyte-size data stores. Support for flexible security policies and techniques for copyright protection and detecting plagiarism are also important.

Data quality issues need further investigation. There are many issues related to metadata. For example, database administrators still are trying to determine exactly what it is, who owns it, and whether it is realistic to have global managers responsible for the metadata that is not specific to any system or server.

Interoperability based on distributed object technology and Java is becoming increasingly popular. However, there is still a lot of work to be done in these areas to provide successful Internet database access. DBMS vendors are moving in the right direction, and the research community also is becoming very active. Once solutions are found to address some of the issues discussed here, users can expect efficient and secure access to the multitude of databases scattered across the various sites around the world.

References

Java White Paper, *Javasoft 1996*. URL: http://java.sun.com:80/doc/language_environment/.

Proceedings of the First IEEE Metadata Conference, Silver Spring, MD, April 1996.

Thuraisingham, B., Database management and the Internet, *Object Management Group's Internet Special Interest Group Meeting Proceedings,* Washington, D.C., June 1996.

Thuraisingham, B., *Data Management Systems Evolution and Interoperation,* CRC Press, Boca Raton, FL, 1997.

Section XI
Data Warehousing, Decision Support, and OLAP

DATA WAREHOUSES SUPPORT ONLINE ANALYTICAL PROCESSING RE-
QUIREMENTS. These include time series analysis, slicing and dicing information, and answering "what if" scenarios. Taken together, these offer
decision support. Data warehousing is growing in size all the time. Where
a 100 MB data warehouse was once considered to be quite large, the new
upper-end data warehouses are in the terrabytes. Data warehouses store
highly summarized data, generally drawn from an OLTP application
through a translation routine that runs on a regular basis and stores data
in a multidimensional data model format. This section contains six chapters.

Chapter 60, "A Framework for Developing an Enterprise Data Warehousing Solution," provides a five-stage framework that is designed to accommodate the common challenges encountered by project teams when
building enterprise data warehousing solutions.

Chapter 61, "Why Dimensional Modeling is Right for Decision Support,"
focuses on the star schema and demonstrates how it can be used to satisfy
the requirements of business managers. This chapter aligns the dimensions of the model with the manner in which real-world questions are
asked. This makes it a powerful communication tool.

Chapter 62, "Comparison of Relational and Multidimensional DBMSs,"
compares and contrasts relational database management systems with the
emerging multidimensional database management systems. It states that
there is a role for both relational and multidimensional databases for data
warehousing. The chapter then describes a layered approach to data warehousing and shows how the various types of DBMSs contribute toward developing a data warehouse.

Chapter 63, "Architecture Overview of OLAP," describes architectural issues for data warehousing. Both the traditional relational database tech-

nology for OLAP, as well as multidimensional and relational OLAP architectures, are described. This chapter also elaborates on the hypercube and multicube approaches to warehousing. Finally, considerations for selecting an architecture for a particular organization are described in this chapter.

Chapter 64, "Creating Value-Added EISs with Soft Information," describes how soft information, such as opinions, predictions, news, and rumors, can be incorporated into executive information systems through E-mail, voice mail, electronic bulletin boards, text annotations, and external databases.

Chapter 60

A Framework for Developing an Enterprise Data Warehousing Solution

Ali H. Murtaza

THE DECISION TO BUILD A DATA WAREHOUSE IS NOT FOR THE FAINT OF HEART — many critical issues must be understood early, or the project will fail. An enterprise data warehousing project is generally a huge, time-consuming investment. In many cases, the benefits are not immediately quantifiable and require a leap of faith to justify. While there are many reasons to build a data warehouse, the two most common reasons are to optimize control of current operations or to gain significant competitive advantage. For instance, a complex, geographically distributed organization may decide that they need to identify their most profitable customer segments for target marketing programs. This is accomplished by extracting customer data from multiple production systems into a single, consolidated data warehouse. On the other hand, a niche company may architect a data mart as the first stage of a large data mining effort — revealing insightful purchasing patterns that could be leveraged for additional revenue. In both cases, the data warehouse defines itself as an integrated, non-volatile catalog of organizational data that is convertible into actionable information for strategic decision-making.

There are numerous advantages to maintaining such a central perspective over the business that allow the end user to monitor both departmental and corporate performance, access all customer account information,

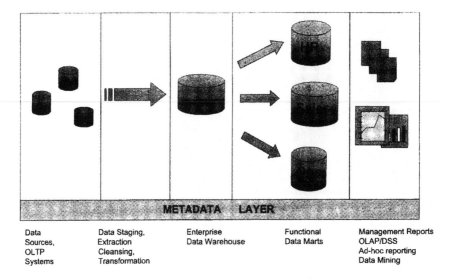

| Data Sources, OLTP Systems | Data Staging, Extraction Cleansing, Transformation | Enterprise Data Warehouse | Functional Data Marts | Management Reports OLAP/DSS Ad-hoc reporting Data Mining |

Exhibit 1.   Enterprise data warehouse model.

increase managerial control, make proactive business decisions, and create sales opportunities. Although an IDC study reported an average data warehousing implementation cost of $3 million, this expensive investment also produces a three-year average return-on-investment (ROI) of 401%. Exhibit 1 shows a standard enterprise data warehouse architecture.

CONSIDERING THE CHALLENGES

An enterprise data warehousing initiative is one the most daunting projects an organization can tackle; a typical effort requires high levels of executive sponsorship, close cooperation between the business and IS communities, cross-functional expertise, and significant time and capital investments. In fact, the high risk of failure prompts experts to depict unsuccessful data warehousing projects as characteristic rites of passage for new project managers; experts state that approximately one out of every five DW projects actually run to completion. This can easily make a project manager's decision to develop a data warehouse a risky move — often the key to success is the simple ability to neutralize the negative elements that could otherwise sabotage the project.

Before embarking on any data warehousing journey, a clearly defined enterprise strategy with specific goals and objectives must be presented to the project sponsors and stakeholders. Also, the project's objectives must align with those of the organization, or the project will fall short; the main driving force of any data warehousing effort is to assist decision making in achieving corporate objectives. Any project that focuses on achieving strategic objectives that differ significantly from the parent organization will be rejected by senior executives, and teach a painful lesson to the project manager.

A data warehousing venture differs from most technology projects in having a high level of executive involvement. There should be no misconceptions about which group is driving a data warehouse project: the business users. Business users define the information requirements, validate the enterprise data model, and access the data for queries and reports. If the business user cannot easily navigate or understand the detailed, summarized, and historical data stored in the warehouse, the benefits are minimized. Frequent communication between the business and IS communities is mission-critical during all project phases to ensure that both groups are aligned and that the development plan meets the original business objectives.

Furthermore, the overall project structure and individual responsibilities must be clearly identified from the start to prevent any confusion among team members. If appropriate technical expertise is not available within the organization to staff the desired roles, the project manager should consider external consultants to fill in the skill gaps. Often, these consultants can provide valuable industry knowledge and vendor relationships important during the data modeling and tool selection stages. Regular meetings should be scheduled at all levels to keep everyone up-to-date and to uncover any potential roadblocks. A mandatory high level of sponsorship ensures political support and reduces resistance from any of the business units. As the project progresses, the project manager must be aware of all organizational or resource issues, and raise them immediately to the project sponsor. Clear communication among the different project teams maintains high morale and strong levels of commitment to project objectives. Many data warehousing projects last over 18 months — albeit in manageable three-to-six month iterations — but their benefits are realized even later, and maintaining the executive commitment and sponsorship becomes a serious challenge. The project manager must be aware of any cultural sensitivities to sharing data among the different functional units. Any political vendettas, power struggles, or personal conflicts should be identified early and handled quickly before they can become destructive. The key to success is constant involvement — business involvement in generating user requirements, creating the logical data models, and choosing the end-user tools, and IS involvement for the hardware/software selection, data extraction, physical implementation, and performance tuning.

A typical driving factor behind data warehousing projects is competition within the industry. As competitors take the lead in implementing their own corporate data warehouses and start to make sizable gains in market share and improvements in their bottom line, many companies naturally follow and expect dramatic results in performance and significant gains in competitive advantage. Consequently, it becomes critical to understand the stability of the organization's industry — potential acquisitions or mergers could leave behind a lot of unfinished work, greater confusion surrounding corporate data, and wasted capital expenditures for both organizations. Today, many vendors are offering vertical solution sets for data-rich industries such as financial, telecommunication, and health care services. These solutions are sought desperately by organizations for common business requirements and data models essential for effective analysis to be done. External consultants are also being leveraged for their vertical expertise and familiarity with vendor tools in addition to their project-related experience.

STAGE 1 — BUSINESS REQUIREMENTS

In the first stage of a data warehousing project, business requirements for enterprise information are gathered from the user community. This process generally consists of a series of interviews between the end users and the information technology teams in order to understand the informational needs and gaps in the organization. The consolidated results of these interviews drive the content of the data models and establish specific objectives for the new data architecture. The selection of business facts, dimensions, aggregations, level of granularity, historical depth, hierarchies, predefined queries, and standardized reports are all driven by the business users. Once the final version of the information requirements is approved by both the business and IS functions, functional data models are created with the granularity, historical detail, and summarization needed to allow end users access to the data while minimizing the performance effects of common table joins and complex queries. Specific vertical knowledge is most valuable here in customizing the data model to handle industry-specific analysis. Every piece of data in the target data model should have some business value attached to it, or it is useless to the business and should be dropped from the model. Lack of trust in the data raises a red flag and severely hinders the success of the project. However, the users must have realistic expectations of the kind of information that will be available to them in the new world. Sample reports or vendor demonstrations can help in this stage to train inexperienced users to visualize the types of querying results and analytical capabilities of the data warehouse front-end tools.

The degree of summarization and size of the data being retained determines whether the data should be stored in a relational or multidimensional database. While the relational DBMS is well-established, commonly understood, and can support very large databases, the multidimensional

DBMS is growing in popularity by offering quicker access to pre-aggregated data and multidimensional analysis capabilities. Multidimensional hypercubes are memory-intensive but reduce the number of physical joins for queries, and take advantage of hierarchical and historical information in the schema to roll-up through dimensions. Many organizations are discovering the need for a hybrid schema; both technologies are used by loading the data first for longer term retention into "near normal" relational models subsequently used to build specific views or dimensional models. All external feeds that are required for additional information must also be mapped into the enterprise model in this phase.

STAGE 2 — DATA SOURCING

Companies with data-intensive businesses typically have great difficulty in accessing their operational data. Somewhere in the depth of the multiple legacy systems, lie valuable nuggets of business information that can never be capitalized upon because of generally poor data quality and integrity. Consequently, this second stage, which involves extracting, cleansing, and transforming the data from the multiple sources to populate the target data warehouse, is vital and often tends to be the most time-consuming part of the project. Further compounding this problem is the possible discovery that the technical resources supporting these legacy systems are no longer employed in the organization, so that cryptic data definitions and programs are left to be deciphered for extraction when they are required. The task of cleaning up enterprisewide data from different functions and departments is often underestimated and can add significant delays to the project timelines. Increased complexity of the data makes the extraction process all the more difficult and laborious. Also, another issue to consider is the capacity of the transactional systems to scale in order to capture larger data volumes or external feeds that might be required in the target warehouse. Tool selection in this data staging layer must be well-researched to integrate well with the proprietary systems and the target warehouse.

STAGE 3 — TARGET ARCHITECTURE

The initial IS task to design a target architecture for the data warehouse can create religious, ideological wars among the architects; debates have raged over the tactical deployment of data marts and operational data stores as compared to the complete vision of an enterprise data warehouse. Some organizations will not take the risk of a failed project that could consume three years of their best resources. The scope of the business vision can also dictate the architecture approach: a short-term vision would require a lower budget, quick ROI implementation with small resource requirements offered by data marts, while more strategic objectives of long-term gain and full organizational control would necessitate the full-blown, enterprise data warehouse architecture. The most popular architecture choices outside the enterprise data warehouse model are the operational data store, virtual data warehouse, DSS data warehouse, and the data mart.

An operational data store is a rudimentary data store that provides a consolidated view of volatile transactional data from multiple operational systems. This architecture often provides real-time operational data that removes the redundancy and resource costs of creating a separate data warehouse. Analysis can be done with basic querying and reporting without impacting the performance of the production systems. This architecture also offers a shared view of the data, with regular updates from the operational systems. It contains current-valued data which is volatile yet very detailed. Unfortunately, operational data is not designed for decision support applications and complex queries may result in long response times and heavy impact on the transactional systems.

A virtual data warehouse is quick to implement and usually less risky than a traditional data warehouse. It involves data access directly from operational data stores without creating a redundant database. This method gives the user universal access to data from any of the multiple sources; however, the extensive process of cleaning up the data to transform it into actionable information cannot be avoided. There are obvious time and cost savings from not having to consolidate the data or introduce infrastructure changes, but the tradeoff exists in the reduced usability of the data from the multiple systems. If there is a lot of data duplication in the various systems, this will easily confuse the end user and remove any confidence they have in the information. Also, if the data distribution across the legacy systems requires cross-functional information between non-SQL compliant data sources, the load, complexity and access time will be impacted on the OLTP systems and network, even if the query can be performed. This architecture also requires more intelligent analysis from the end user to understand the results of multiple queries instead of just one. Distributed query processing software must be in place to decide where and when the queries should be performed in the transactional systems. Once results are obtained, significant data validation may be required to make sense of the business information that was not cleansed or integrated. Also, the end user will not have access to historical snapshots which are one of the most valuable strategic decision-making tools offered by a data warehouse. Finally, the results will not be repeatable as the data is continuously changing.

The decision support data warehouse architecture simply consists of snapshots of corporate information consisting of low-level or highly summarized data. This method has the advantages of minimal infrastructure costs, access to non-volatile data, quick deployment time, and no repetitive data stores. However, the main flaw of this architecture is its inherent lack of flexibility to handle complex decision support analysis expected from a fully architected data warehouse; the data structures are not changed, merely stored periodically as snaphots for comparative analysis. This technique provides good historical information but fails to optimize access to the data. In fact, the snapshots of data are ideal for independent business intelligence and data mining approaches to unearthing customer patterns and trends.

Another potential architecture is the popular data mart or functional data warehouse that captures a subset of the enterprise data for a specific function, business unit, or application. Data marts require less cost and effort to deploy, and provide access to functional or private information to specific organizational units. They are suited for businesses demanding a fast time to market, quick impact on the bottom line, and minimal infrastructure changes. Data marts are essentially mini-data warehouses without the huge cost, long-time investment, high risk of failure, and high level of corporate approval; they are ideal for a rapid, iterative, prototype deployment. Data marts store non-volatile, time-variant, and summarized information used to serve the information needs of the business unit. However, data marts should not be used as a cheaper solution to a data warehouse; they should simply represent an initial step towards an enterprise data warehouse. If data marts are introduced first, they should be designed to integrate with a future enterprise data warehouse, or much rework will have to be done over the long term. As other business units notice the benefits, data marts must not be allowed to propagate freely throughout the organization, or the situation will spell disaster when attempting to integrate them into a single corporate warehouse. When data marts are introduced after the successful implementation of a data warehouse, they can be deployed quickly by replicating required subsets of the corporate database.

STAGE 4 — ACCESS TOOL SELECTION

The level of sophistication of the intended user should be a main driver in the reporting tool selection process. Exhibit 2 illustrates the many levels of query, reporting, and OLAP tools in the marketplace with functions ranging from basic management reporting to complex, drill-down, pass-through analytical processing. It is crucial that the user be comfortable in navigating through the newly consolidated data. Otherwise, this huge capital investment will result in the same scenario the organization started with; namely, lots of data with no perceived method to access it. Sample reports and demonstrations are good aids in assessing the results and the capabilities of the business intelligence tool.

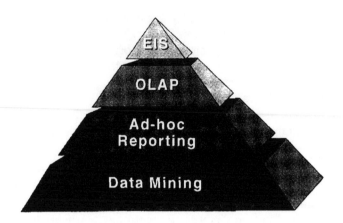

Exhibit 2. User access tools.

In fact, careful training should be provided for the end users to ensure that they understand the various capabilities of the tools. Instead of producing monthly management reports, they should be encouraged to make ad-hoc queries and "slice and dice" through the multiple dimensions and navigate throughout the available information to isolate the specific set of information they require. Once the user taps into the metadata layer (see Exhibit 1) and understands the type of data and relationships that exist in the warehouse, he or she is better equipped to perform meaningful analysis and extract valuable information about the business. Newly evolved data mining technologies promise to bring even greater benefits by performing complex statistical analysis on historical records to uncover business patterns, customer trends, organizational inefficiencies, and even potential fraud.

STAGE 5 — DATA WAREHOUSE ADMINISTRATION

One of the most commonly neglected issues is the administration of the data warehouse after it is built. The appropriate technical resources must be assigned to monitor query load and performance, to handle dynamic changes to the data structures, and to ensure platform scalability with increased user demands. External data may be needed (e.g., stock feeds, Web downloads) and so the architecture must have an open interface to incorporate these new requirements. As users become more sophisticated in their use of the decision support tools, the frequency and complexity of the queries and reports will significantly impact the query performance. A "query from hell" can destroy perceived levels of performance if not identified and managed carefully. Consequently, a dedicated administrator is needed to maintain constant supervision of the query performance and to prevent the data warehouse from grinding to a halt.

Generally, data warehousing projects use the prototype approach to development, and much of the initial success of the prototype will determine the overall success of the project. The data model should be designed against an extensive range of end-user queries and target reports showing enhanced analytical business information, and should be designed to maintain buy-in from the executive sponsors during the pilot demonstration. Most importantly, the information must be accurate, or at least more accurate than the pre-data warehouse data to increase the user's confidence in the information. If the user has unwavering faith in the data, the project has a greater chance to succeed.

CONCLUSION

A common point of debate arises when measuring the overall investment impact of a particular project — the added value of business information is hard to translate into cost savings or generated revenue. The difficulty in quantifying these benefits is one of the most problematic issues facing the project manager in keeping corporate buy-in and team commitment. How can one measure business value? As shown in Exhibit 1, an answer lies in a well-developed metadata repository that allows the business user to easily understand and navigate through the large amounts of corporatewide data contained in the new warehouse. Each piece of data selected for the new data model should be clearly defined in the metadata and perceived as adding business value. If the end user sees no value in it, he or she will not use it and it should be omitted from the new data model. The remarkable change in the business analyst's job is represented by the drastically reduced time needed to gather organizational data — much more time is dedicated to garner meaningful information that will drive the sustained growth and operational efficiency of the corporation.

The designed architecture of the metadata and data warehouse must be scalable enough to support future changes to information needs and analytical requirements (e.g., Web-based delivery). Ongoing management of the data warehouse with minimal adjustments to the data architecture, and business users excited about their data are true indicators of project success. Business value is reflected by the enhanced corporate control, lowered costs, increased revenue, strong market share, and new opportunities that are all direct results of the information delivery architecture called the data warehouse.

References

Bachteal, P., Data warehouses: professional management key to successful implementation, *Can. Man.*, 22: 22, 20-21, Summer 1997.
Barquin, R. C., *An Introduction to Data Warehousing,* Barquin and Associates, The Data Warehousing Institute, 1997.

Benson, B. and Von Hollen, C., *Case Study III: Strategies for a Successful Data Warehouse*, May 28, 1997.
Bischoff, J. and Alexander, T., *Data Warehouse Practical Advice from the Experts,* Prentice-Hall, New York, 1997.
Evans, J., Need for analysis drives data warehouse appeal, *Health Man. Tech.*, 18: 11, 28-31, Oct. 1997.
Foley, J., Data warehousing pitfalls, *Inform. Week,* May 19, 1997.
Hackney, D., *Understanding and Implementing Successful Data Marts*, May 28, 1997.
Stedman, C., Turning to outside warehousing help," *ComputerWorld.*
Waltner, C., Ready-made warehouses," *Inform. Week,* 655, 100-108, Nov. 3, 1997.

Chapter 61

Why Dimensional Modeling is Right for Decision Support

R. Michael Pickering

A DECISION SUPPORT SYSTEM (DSS) IS USED TO STORE AND RETRIEVE INFORMATION needed by a company's managers and executives for use in performance tracking and decision making. Unlike an Online Transaction Processing (OLTP) system, where the primary purpose of the system is usually to store, update, and maintain operational data, the primary purpose of a DSS is to provide answers to business questions. A DSS is used to help manage a business that is run on one or more OLTP systems. The different types of systems are complementary, but designed to serve fundamentally different purposes.

The focus of an OLTP system is usually on getting data into a system. This is often extremely critical to the business because earning revenue may depend, for example, on being able to record orders as they are received. Recording an order requires capturing and storing various related bits of data that make up the order, such as who is making the order, exactly what is being ordered, where and when it is to be sent, and so on. Getting data into OLTP systems quickly is so important that this criterion has been taken up above all others in the generally accepted process for designing them.

NORMALIZATION

There are several variations on the generally accepted process for designing OLTP systems for implementation on relational databases. All the major ones involve the use of normalization, so named because it depends on a series of normal forms defined using the mathematical theory of functional dependencies. Normalization provides a systematic process for ensuring that the size of each record (or bit of data) stored in each table in the system is as small as is reasonably possible. In fact, normalization ensures that each data record is the smallest it can be, while still making sense in the context of the system as a whole. This is the best way to get data into a system quickly. Storing data in small records allows each new record to be processed quickly. In this way, very many small OLTP transactions (updates, inserts, and deletes) can be processed concurrently. However, it also means that the system is made up of very complex and interrelated set of tables.

Because normalization has a sound basis in theoretical mathematics, it has been taken up with great fanfare in academic circles and is taught at the undergraduate level in computer science programs. It has been so successful in designing real OLTP systems that have become a critical part of so many businesses that it is very highly regarded by IT practitioners and business managers alike. It has become almost a religion in that so many people believe in it without question. Normalization has become such a basic part of the design of OLTP systems that people forget it is primarily a tool used to solve the problem of getting data into a system quickly. This just is not a big problem in the design of decision support systems.

DECISION SUPPORT

A decision support system (DSS) is about information. Information is made up of data, but that data must be organized and processed into a form that is appropriate for the situation. In a sense, information can be thought of as data viewed at a higher conceptual level. The data must be organized and processed so that it is meaningful and useful to its intended audience. The intended audience or users of the information provided by a DSS are business analysts and managers. They are concerned primarily with seeing the big picture — trends and variations from expectations (information), rather than all the details (data) of the business. For example, knowing that there were 1000 orders received this month is more meaningful if compared to what was expected. Expectations typically are based on past experiences, so how many orders were received last month or in the same month last year must be known. The fact that 1000 orders were received is data, but knowing that orders are up 10% over last year is information.

Another important thing to remember about a DSS is that users do not care how quickly data gets into it, as long as it gets there. What is important is that they can get the information out when they need it. A DSS must be designed with this essential difference of purpose in mind. It must be built from data, but it must deliver information. The DSS also must be flexible in the way it delivers this information. As has been seen, normalization helps to get data into systems quickly, but this is not particularly important in a DSS. Thus, normalization is not critical to building a DSS. To implement a successful DSS, consider what is important for its audience.

DIMENSIONAL MODELING

A technique called dimensional data modeling has proven very successful in DSS design. Dimensional modeling is based on understanding the nature of information requirements of the DSS.

Dimensional data modeling produces a simple but powerful and flexible database schema, commonly referred to as a star schema. This way of designing the schema for a DSS focuses on the requirements of the target audience. Business managers tend to need to know about certain essential measures that determine the success of the business. They need a way to look at these measures in different ways. For example, it is always important to know how the measures are changing over time. Knowing that sales are high is good, but knowing that sales are high and rising over recent weeks is better. Other breakdowns are typically important to managers also. For example, if the company sells more than one type of product or if the sales of some products are not increasing as quickly as others, the manager may want to know if sales are high for all products. If the business sells to the same customers repeatedly, it may be important to know which customers are increasing vs. which customers are reducing their buying. The business managers need to be able to pick out the contributions to the important measures along whichever axs are important. This often is called *slicing and dicing.*

There are often hierarchical relationships along one or more measurement axis. For example, there may be different classes of products and, within each class, there may be different brands and, within each brand, there may be different colors, and so on. The business manager wants to be able to look at the contribution to the important measures at any level of the hierarchy or by adding in categories from a different measurement axis. This is known as *drilling down.*

In dimensional modeling, unlike the general relational model, there are different types of tables. This is an important logical concept of dimensional modeling intended to help align the data model of the DSS with the business being supported. The different types of tables correspond to the way business people do analysis. This helps the dimensional modeler understand the business the way a DSS user does and helps the DSS user understand the dimensional model. This mutual understanding is crucial toward ensuring that the DSS user gets whatever he or she needs from the warehouse.

The concept of business metrics, also known as key performance indicators (KPIs), is virtually universal across the business world. It is easy to find discussions of business measures in any business textbook or magazine. An obvious example in any business is the bottom line or amount of profit earned or loss incurred by the business for the year. This is a very high-level measure of the success of the business, which is determined by adding up the contributions of all the various operations and processes of the business over the course of the year.

A star schema is a way to capture the important business metrics and store them with all the common business categories and conditions for analysis. The metrics are stored in a fact table, which forms the center of the star, and the categories and conditions (the measurement axes and hierarchies) are stored in dimension tables, which form the points of the star.

The star schema is a very good way to satisfy the requirements of business managers. The model itself clearly shows the important business measures and the dimensions along which they can be analyzed. It corresponds very closely to the way they need to ask questions. This is important not only because it allows the questions to be answered almost directly from the model, but because the model itself can be used as a communications tool. The designer can talk through the model with the users to help them understand what business analysis they will be able to perform using the system. This is a significant difference between a star schema and the much more complex schemas for OLTP systems. A typical OLTP schema is difficult to explain to the users of the system. In fact, many designers refrain from even trying. Due to the inherent simplicity of a star schema, it is much easier for a user to understand.

Most real OLTP schemas are denormalized to some extent — they do not conform to the (theoretically best) highest order normal form. This is the result of a conscious decision on the part of the designer, made typically for performance reasons, or sometimes because the designers did not think that normalization was something that needed to be applied too rigorously. Normalization is a tool that, when used properly, generally produces an OLTP schema to which data can be added and updated quickly. However, normalization is at best a heuristic rather than an algorithm, in that it is not guaranteed to produce a schema that will yield the best possible performance for OLTP systems in all possible cases. The fact is that normalization does not guarantee good performance for OLTP systems and does nothing at all to help produce a correct and complete schema — one that will satisfy the user requirements.

PERFORMANCE CONSIDERATIONS

One of the principle criticisms against star schemas is that they lead to poor database performance. This is largely a fallacy contributed to by practitioners more familiar with OLTP systems. They expect to normalize the data model for performance and think that the two terms are synonymous. In fact, databases designed with star schemas for business analysis can provide excellent performance.

Consider a simple star schema consisting of one fact table and several dimensions. At the logical level, the only difference between the fact table and the dimension table is that the fact table is a dependant entity, although all the dimension tables are independent entities. In some variations on simple stars, the fact table itself may be an independent entity. In addition, at the physical level, fact tables typically contain many more rows of data than dimension tables.

There may be a difference between the fact tables and the dimension tables in a dimensional model at the physical implementation level, depending on the available data structures in the RDBMS on which it is implemented. Typically, the fact table is indexed more heavily than the dimension tables. However, the reason fact tables and dimension tables are thought of differently in dimensional modeling is that they will be used in queries differently. A typical business query set will use certain attribute values of the dimension tables to choose only a small number of rows from the fact table for any given query. Ideally, the RDBMS' query optimizer will be able to benefit from this typical access pattern in choosing a query-processing strategy. Because the fact table contains very many rows, doing a table scan of the fact table would be very time-consuming — this is a very important difference between fact tables and dimension tables. This leads to a reason there is often a difference between fact and dimension tables at the physical level. The indexing scheme needs to be much more sophisticated for a fact table than for a dimension table, due to their very significant size difference. Most dimension tables are easily small enough to fit in memory on most hardware used to store data warehouses, so in many cases, they require only a primary key index to ensure unicity of primary keys. By contrast, fact tables are extremely large, so scanning the entire fact table is usually a disaster. It is important to create any indices that could be used to provide fast access to the target rows in the fact table. Specifically, some kind of index should be created on every foreign key in the fact table, at the very least.

Because the differences between fact tables and dimension tables are confined primarily to the physical design level, one can think of dimensional modeling as a special case of relational modeling. However, to design an appropriate star schema, it is essential to consider fact tables and dimension tables explicitly as part of the design process. In a dimensional design, not all tables are created equal.

Typical business analysis involves very complex queries, which often include aggregations of large numbers of database records, summarized at a high level. For example, a typical query might request the total sales in a region for a year, which could require summing the sales amounts from thousands of sales detail records. To answer this query, the RDBMS query processor also must find a way to retrieve only the records from the requested region. Consider the schema for this query. It is a star schema with at least two dimensions, geography (including regions) and time (including years). There also must be a fact table containing the sales amounts in dollars, along with other significant facts and metrics, plus the foreign key to each dimension table. In forming her query, the analyst browses the time dimension table and chooses the nonempty set of rows that corresponds to the current year. She also selects the nonempty set of rows that represents the region in which she is interested (note that the actual number of rows in each set depends on the form and number of hierarchies in each dimension). She then forms an aggregate query to calculate the total sales for the region for the year. This typically would be done using a query tool with a graphical front end, so that the query could be posed by the user without having to know SQL. The query tool would generate a query that might look something like this:

```
SELECT sum(sales_amount)

FROM sales_facts f NATURAL JOIN time d1 NATURAL JOIN
geography d2

WHERE d1.year = '1998' AND d2.region = 'Great Lakes';
```

Although most real decision support queries would be more complex, this simple example shows the primary characteristics of such queries. It involves an aggregate function computed over a numeric field. It is a join of the fact table with two dimension tables from the star. And it uses the dimension tables to restrict or filter rows from the fact table. (Note that this query is written to the ANSI SQL-92 standard in its use of the natural join operator. Natural join performs an equi-join over common columns of listed tables. This syntax is a good way to separate the table relationships, specified in the FROM clause, from the business criteria, which are specified in the WHERE clause. Not all real query tools or relational databases will support this syntax, but it was used in this example because it is the best way to communicate the meaning of the query.)

As discussed previously, the fact table in a star schema is typically very much larger than the dimension tables, so assume that such is true for this example. This means that the joins of the fact table to the dimension tables would be very time-consuming if the joins were evaluated first, then the restrictions. If possible the restrictions should be evaluated first, and the join done only on the rows of the dimensions that satisfy the restrictions. This should be possible if there are appropriate indices on the foreign keys in the fact table. In this case, because there are restrictions from two different dimensions, it may be necessary to guess which one will give the smallest answer set, create that answer set, and then evaluate the other condition on that intermediate result. This strategy processes queries against the star schema from the outside in.

Many relational database systems are providing combined indices to assist in processing multiple joins in just one step. If they are available, their use generally will improve performance significantly for such queries.

Some relational databases may attempt to process a query from the inside out, starting from the fact table. This usually results in queries that do not return. In these cases, the main tuning strategy is to diagnose the problem and figure out how to get the queries processed from outside in. Tweaking the foreign key indices may help in this process.

During the physical design phase of the project, and particularly during implementation of the data warehouse, it is important to consider the potential for running queries in parallel. Most relational database systems allow spawning multiple processes to run a single query, which is particularly beneficial for complex decision support queries when the host server has multiple processors. To maximize the benefits of parallelism, the physical disk configuration on the host server must be taken into consideration, and database files allocated accordingly. By spreading database files across many physical disks, parallel server processes can access data effectively and concurrently.

The final tuning tool in the data warehouse bag of tricks is to create pre-built aggregates. Typical business analysis usually looks at information at a high level. For example, the user may start by requesting the sales revenue metric for a given year (restricting using the time dimension table), broken down by product category (part of the product dimension). If anomalies are discovered, further queries are constructed to further zero in on the problem area. Most of the queries involve some form of aggregation, either to exclude some dimensions from the star, or to roll up data within a hierarchy in one dimension. By precomputing one or more commonly used aggregates, much of the work to answer this type of query is done up front, so the answer comes back more quickly. This does come at a cost of increased data warehouse maintenance and schema complexity, so appropriate administration and user query tools should be used to help mitigate this.

COMMUNICATIONS GAP

This leads to the normalization communications gap. The designer of an OLTP system must use normalization to ensure that the system will meet performance requirements (it could be argued in some cases, that the actual performance requirements are not so onerous as to warrant the degree of normalization that is done as a matter of course in OLTP system design). This leads to a large and complex schema that is difficult for the prospective users to understand. Although normalization helps in the design of such a schema, it is not much help in explaining such a complex schema to the system's intended users. Explaining normalization and functional dependencies to business people is almost as difficult as explaining the schema itself — and can chew up more time than it is worth. If the prospective users of the system do not understand the schema, it is unlikely that they will be able effectively to draw on their own depth of business knowledge to point out errors or omissions in the design. The designers talk the language of normalization, but the users talk the language of business, and neither group can understand the other effectively.

This is a significant advantage of dimensional modeling for designing decision support systems. The actual schema for the system can be used effectively in the communication and design process. Because getting data quickly into OLTP systems is important, normalization is unavoidable in OLTP design. As has been seen, though, a DSS is not an OLTP system. Although normalization plays an important role in the design of OLTP systems, it has no part in the design of decision support systems.

BRIDGING THE COMMUNICATIONS GAP

Using dimensional modeling in the design of a DSS helps bridge the communications gap. It allows the designer to talk more like a business person and is approachable enough that business people can learn something about how to talk like designers.

The key to this process is to focus on the important business issues that must be dealt with, without getting too deeply into the gritty technical details. The data warehouse designers must succeed at getting the essence of the business needs into the design. Bringing business people into the design process is critical to the success of the project, as they are the only people with the relevant business knowledge. Fortunately, dimensional modeling helps bridge the communications gap between the designers and the business people.

To form the footings of the bridge, try taking the business perspective; the business people have questions they need to be able to answer. Discuss the questions for which they have trouble getting answers and the ones they cannot even ask. It is sometimes surprising how many important questions cannot be answered at all.

What would be the value to the business of providing a better methodology for answering questions? The business value of data warehousing is that it is intended to be just that: a better methodology for answering business questions. It is successful because it is focused on doing just that. That is why, in telling the story of data warehousing to business people, it is necessary to start at the end — with the business questions. Answering business questions is what is important to business people. Business people do not so much care that the data model for the warehouse system is a star schema, but they care very much about what they can do with a star schema. A star schema is particularly well-suited to, for example, slicing and dicing and drilling down. These concepts generally will be understood easily and embraced enthusiastically by business people, because they are naturally effective in business analysis. Therefore, though being able to do this comes only after the design process is complete, it is a good place to start discussions with business people. Describe how slicing and dicing and drilling down work, using terms like categories and metrics, or whatever terms make sense to them. If possible, show them what is meant, and work through examples that are relevant to the business. In this way, ease them into discussions of star schemas by starting them out on solid, comfortable ground.

Chapter 62

Comparison of Relational and Multidimensional DBMSs

Hedy Alban

MULTIDIMENSIONAL DATABASE MANAGEMENT SYSTEMS (MDBMSs) combine the familiar spreadsheet interface with the flexibility of relational database management systems (RDBMSs), combining the best features of spreadsheets and DBMSs. An MDBMS allows the user to reorganize and re-combine data elements with the same flexibility as a relational DBMS, but in a familiar spreadsheet format.

Users are often so delighted with the responsiveness of multidimensional DBMS that they may wonder why MDBMSs do not simply replace RDBMSs altogether. MDBMSs are not appropriate for production applications because they do not have the facilities for data entry, validation, security, performance, and concurrency that are required for online transaction processing (OLTP). They are appropriate, however, for decision support databases that are used for fast queries and decision-making.

A successful information warehouse should be composed of multiple, layered products and databases. Because each layer has different use and performance requirements, there is a place for both RDBMS and MDBMS data structures within the architecture.

This chapter first defines the layers of this data architecture and then discusses the relative strengths and limitations of MDBMS compared with RDBMS.

0-8493-9976-9/99/$0.00+$.50
© 1999 by CRC Press LLC

A DATA ARCHITECTURE FOR THE INFORMATION WAREHOUSE

The classical data warehouse strategy is based on a three-tiered data architecture that enables flexible access among platforms and software products, making each user's workstation a window to the enterprise's information resource. The layers of this three-tiered architecture are commonly called the production, information, and collection layers. Together, these layers encompass the range of intended uses in data, from transaction processing functions to decision support and business analysis functions. (Exhibit 1). The data warehouse is the middle layer in this corporate data architecture.

Production Layer

The production layer stores the highly detailed, transaction-oriented data that reflects the basic daily operations of a company's business, such as customer orders, sales, and accounts payable. Business data are created in their most detailed and raw forms at this level in such applications as data capture/data entry and real-time customer service. The production layer is the source of all the data used by the information layer (i.e., the data warehouse proper) and the collection layer. All business transaction (i.e., update) processing occurs at this level in the model; data in the information and collection layers are derived from the production layer and are rarely updated directly.

Production data are often captured by mature application systems using DBMSs that support online transaction processing. The data may be stored in and managed by relational DBMSs or by prerelational data structures such as IBM's Information Management System (IMS/DB) database, the CA-Datacom database, or some other mature DBMS with existing applications. Alternatively, data may exist in flat files.

More than any other requirement, the storage mechanism used for the production layer must be compatible with existing applications. Frequently, this is the overriding concern, which is why production-level data often reside in prerelational data structures like IMS/DB or Virtual Storage Access Method (VSAM) files. The production layer needs efficient data input facilities, including validation routines, a variety of user access codes, and locks (i.e., read-only versus read/write versus write-only). Features that support continuous operation are highly desirable.

Information Layer

The information layer of the data architecture contains idealized representations of the production data. To create this layer, the data processing organization replicates production data into a new data store, eliminating the redundancies and anomalies that inevitably occur in operational data.

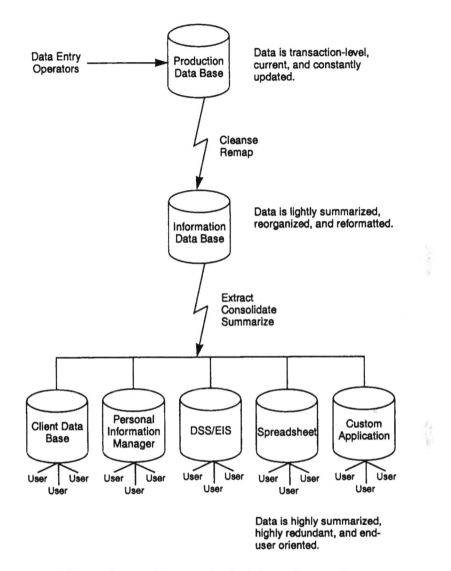

Exhibit 1. Data architecture for the information warehouse.

At the same time, the information is formatted so that it can be retrieved easily by end-user tools and applications.

This level of information still carries a nearly one-to-one level of detail with the operational data, and it captures a stable picture of data as they exist in a moment of time, whereas production data are always changing as new data are entered. The information layer is sometimes called the intermediate level, the snapshot database, or the data warehouse.

The information layer exists so that the data can be accessed by other tools and applications. It performs that data transformation from the production store just once for access by multiple end-user applications.

The storage mechanism for housing the information layer must be able to download data from a variety of data sources and to a variety of user products. In addition, it should efficiently perform joins and other operations that massage, filter, and select data for downloading into a user tool (i.e., the product that holds collection data).

Early adopters of information warehousing have discovered that the data requirements of their projects expand rapidly. For this reason, the storage mechanism for the information layer of the data architecture should be able to handle large volumes of data and many users.

Collection Layer

The collection layer contains synthesized information derived from lower-order and more detailed data sources. The term *collection* refers to any selected or synthesized set of data derived from the underlying information detail. This level of information presents summaries, aggregations from multiple data sources, or selected extracts. The chief tools of synthesis are summarization, aggregation, selection, and point-in-time representation.

Oriented toward the user, the collection layer may present multiple views of the same data to accommodate various end-user interests. Data presentation frequently resembles user-designed reports, queries, or data selection-extract programs.

A query that appears to ask a simple, common-sense question may, in computer terms, access several thousands of transaction-oriented records and require hours of compute time. Thousands of data items may come into play to answer a question that seems fairly straightforward in human terms. There should be a way to anticipate the calculations that are needed most frequently and to precalculate them sometime when the system is not busy, or at least the calculations should be ready for the manager in advance so that the user need not sit for hours awaiting the response.

RDBMS VS. MDBMS: A COMPARISON

In the classically designed data warehouse strategy, RDBMSs are typically used for the information layer and MDBMSs are used for the collection layer. These choices make sense in terms of the strengths and limitations of the product types. Exhibit 2 provides an at-a-glance comparison of some of the capabilities of each technology.

RDBMS products excel in the areas of data retrieval from hosts, data delivery to user tools, performance issues, and ability to handle large volumes of data.

Capability/Function	RDBMS	MDBMS
Data Import Capabilities	Relational and nonrelational data (via gateways and third-party tools)	Relational data only
Data Delivery	Standard SQL interface	Nonstandard interface
Application Development Tools	Many available	Only the facilities that are included with the product
Data Capacity	Terabytes	Gigabytes
Parallel Processing and Parallel I/O	Yes	No
Summarizations and Consolidations	Hand coded	Automated
Analytic Functions	Hand coded	Precoded
Business Dimensions	Hand coded	Automated
Time Intelligence	Hand coded	Automatic
Historical Data	Hand coded	Precoded

Exhibit 2. RDBMS and MDBMS compared.

An MDBMS, on the other hand, delivers a specific kind of application with a minimum amount of professional programming. MDBMS products deliver an excellent user interface for online analytic processing (OLAP). They also provide an excellent framework for defining the business dimensions for an organization, and they automate the creation of aggregations and summations that are defined in terms of the business dimensions.

RDBMS Strengths

A SQL-based RDBMS is typically used for the information layer of the data warehouse. RDBMS products are best suited for access from a variety of user tools, and during the past few years, vendors have been beefing up links to host-based data as well. Usually, a product from one of the leaders in distributed RDBMS — Sybase, Inc. (Emeryville, CA), Oracle Corp. (Redwood Shores, CA), or Informix Software, Inc. (Menlo Park, CA) — is used to house the information layer of the data warehouse. DB2 is also a good choice for IBM shops. These products fulfill the major requirements outlined previously: they provide gateways to mainframe data and have the necessary performance characteristics.

In addition, RDBMSs have powerful systems management capabilities. Probably most important from a practical point of view, they are suitable for production databases as well and may already be installed in the companies that choose to use an RDBMS for data warehousing. More important than all of these reasons, however, is the fact that today's end-user tools — decision support products, data access tools, and OLAP software — are all designed to interact with these relational DBMSs, as are the myriad middleware and APIs that are being marketed.

SQL-based RDBMSs provide superior capabilities in the following areas:

- Retrieving data from host databases
- Delivering data to user tools
- Accommodating application development tools
- Handling large volumes of data

Retrieving Data from Host Databases. A crucial aspect of the information warehouse concept is the data transfer out of production databases and into replication databases. The source database can be anything from flat files to CODASYL-based DBMSs to relational DBMSs. An organization must ensure that its production databases are accessible for replication, no matter what the source. Furthermore, a tool should be robust enough to handle future needs, even if the future need involves dealing with backward technology, as may be the case if a business is involved in a merger or takeover.

The major RDBMS vendors have responded to this market challenge by building gateways to prerelational DBMSs. In addition, independent vendors offer software and services specifically addressing the task of replicating data from production databases to relational databases.

There are also additional tools coming to market, called information catalogs, that are designed to give end-users a "browse" capability, so users can peruse through available data and select what they need, without knowing beforehand the name of the file or report that they are looking for. These tools, as they become available, will be able to handle relational databases from the outset, which is another reason to use RDBMSs.

MDBMSs, on the other hand, are designed to import data from relational DBMSs. Except for a few products, they cannot link directly to other data structures without extensive custom programming.

Delivering Data to End-User Tools. Many tools have entered the market in recent years that allow users to access corporate data for reporting or record-keeping purposes with little intervention from professional data processing personnel. The MDBMS technology covered in this chapter is one of these tools. Others include query tools, reporting tools, and EIS tools.

In addition, PC-based and Windows-based DBMSs and spreadsheets designed for use by single users or small local area networks (LANs) have incorporated database access tools and facilities into their products. All these tools rely on the industrywide consensus to accept SQL and relational DBMS technologies as industry standards. For this reason, RDBMS is the vehicle for delivering information to user tools.

MDBMS products rely for the most part on proprietary data structures. Although most have relational underpinnings at their core, the data are not available to the same range of external software. It is true, however, that some products, such as Essbase from Arbor Software Corp. (Sunnyvale, CA), interface with several popular spreadsheets as well as some EIS products. However, these are proprietary interfaces; they do not provide the broad operability of RDBMS.

Availability of Applications Development Tools. Users may have information requirements that do not fit snugly into one of the packaged applications available today. Alternatively, some organizations have standardized on particular user interfaces that do not conform to these packaged applications. In these instances, professional application developers will step in with development tools such as PowerBuilder that allow custom programs and interfaces to be built rapidly. Like the end-user query tools and MDBMSs, these development tools are equipped with links to the leading RDBMS products, but they are not equipped to interface with MDBMSs.

Handling Large Volumes of Data. Early adopters of information warehousing have found that their initial projects mushroomed to encompass a much larger mass of data than originally planned, with some warehouses exceeding 100G bytes. The data warehouse almost invariably is several times larger than the source operational database. This situation arises for several reasons. Probably the most fundamental reason is that the warehouse stores historical data, which must be available to corporate executives to help them spot trends and to support their decision-making process, but require a lot of storage space.

Second, the information warehouse keeps redundant data. For efficient performance at execution and ease of use, it is often desirable to replicate specific fields of data two or three times in the information and collection layers of the data architecture. In other words, the data may be denormalized in the replicated layers of the information warehouse. As a result, these layers may require storage space several times the size of the original transaction database.

Given the large volume of data that is typical of data warehousing applications, combined with the need for scheduled updates to the replicated data stores, it is prudent to select a storage mechanism that can take advantage of the performance features that are delivered in today's machines. Today's computer hardware relies heavily on parallelism, in the form of multiprocessing and in the form of parallel I/O that is delivered in most redundant array of inexpensive disk (RAID) systems, to achieve high performance levels at a reasonable cost.

Market-leading RDBMSs take advantage of the parallelism available through the hardware architecture, and they can perform such operations as data load, backup, and query processing in parallel. MDBMSs, by contrast, do not take advantage of these hardware features, nor have any vendors declared an intent to do so. MDBMSs are not designed to handle this volume of traffic and must defer to the RDBMS for heavy-duty data movement.

MDBMS Strengths

MDBMS products such as Essbase, Pilot Software, Inc.'s (Cambridge, MA) LightShip Series, and Comshare, Inc.'s (Ann Arbor, MI) Commander are used for the collection layer of the classically designed data warehouse. MDBMS technology arises from older DSS/EIS software. Unlike the older products, the best of today's MDBMS products provide multiuser capabilities and connectivity to relational hosts and spreadsheet clients. These products are typically LAN-based and work best at the departmental or user-group level. For best performance, the amount of data and the number of business dimensions used in any application should be carefully controlled.

The best products deliver the following features:

- A development environment specifically designed for analytic processing
- A user environment specifically designed for OLAP
- Rapid response time to user queries

OLAP-Oriented Development Environment. MDBMS products provide an applications development component specifically designed for creating OLAP applications. They deliver a framework, or a set of tools, for defining business dimensions (e.g., product, sales, or region) and they automatically know how to handle these dimensions.

MDBMS products also have built-in time series intelligence — that is, they can handle such concepts as fiscal year or weekly-versus-monthly reporting. They automatically perform aggregations, summations, and other calculations based on the organization's dimensions and user-specified time series. Furthermore, MDBMS products offer a wide range of built-in functions for business analysis so that personnel from the IS department are not required to program them.

OLAP-Oriented User Environment. MDBMS products typically provide a user environment that automatically contains built-in drill-down, roll-up, and analytic functions. In this way, users can slice their views of the data. This capability is in strong contrast to the older generation of DSS/EIS products, where these capabilities were considered custom requirements of an application and had to be requested specifically for each application.

OLAP user interfaces enable analysts to perform functions such as statistical data analysis, simulation/goal seeking, optimization, and financial calculations. They can calculate and display ratios, comparisons, rankings, consolidations, statistics, and dimensional analysis. Several MDBMS products can access multiple hosts to extract data and similarly can be accessed by different user tools.

Users can choose the style of their user interface. Some MDBMS products provide an automatically generated user interface that can be customized by either a professional programmer or the user. Others are intended to be used in conjunction with an existing spreadsheet product such as Lotus 1-2-3 or Microsoft Excel; these MDBMSs infuse the existing spreadsheet interface with multidimensional capabilities and deliver the data in presummarized and preformatted form so that the user need not key in or import the data from a transaction database.

Rapid Responses to Queries. A query that may appear to ask a simple question may actually need to access several thousands of transaction-oriented records. As a result, the response to the query may take several hours. The user's computer may be unavailable during that period of time, and the entire database system may experience a performance bottleneck. To make matters worse, the results of the transaction may not be saved (unless a program was specifically written to save it), so that reexecution of the query will take as long as the original run.

The most important feature of MDBMSs to the user is the speed at which it can deliver summary information. In contrast to transaction-oriented databases, MDBMS applications anticipate the calculations that are needed most frequently by business analysts, precalculate them during data load, and save them for future use. In this way, summary information is immediately available at execution time, ready for the end-user to view the data on demand and without delay. When the data are refreshed, the results of the current calculations are appended to the existing ones; historical information is preserved in summary form. Furthermore, because the MDBMS stores data that are highly summarized, it does not require the ability to handle the large volumes of data needed by an RDBMS.

ALTERNATIVE DEPLOYMENT STRATEGIES

This chapter has thus far described a classical, three-layered data architecture for the data warehouse. This section explores the feasibility of implementing alternatives to this architecture, including:

- Simplifying the data architecture by eliminating the information layer, which populates the MDBMS directly from transaction databases.
- Simplifying the data environment by standardizing on RDBMS technology.
- Creating additional layers within the basic framework, which is useful in a mature warehousing environment that needs to improve efficiency by synchronizing updates among several data warehousing databases.

Eliminating the Information Layer

The classical data architecture requires a great deal of data movement and replication from one database to another. Some organizations may feel that this degree of layering is unnecessary in all instances and may wish to move data from production databases directly into multidimensional DBMSs, eliminating the intermediate relational database.

This alternative defeats the purpose of the information warehouse, which is to make corporate information available to many users in a format that can be accessed by a wide range of user tools. RDBMSs are ideally suited for this purpose because SQL has become an industry-accepted standard; all makers of user tools build in the ability to access SQL-based relational DBMSs. Among the eight most-popular client development tools, all have an interface to Oracle and most have interfaces to Informix, Sybase, or DB2.

RDBMSs also interface well with MDBMSs, spreadsheets, data access tools, and all the tools that are designed for business analysis as well as other decision support applications. These individual connections are in addition to the open database connectivity (ODBC) interface that is generic to all SQL-based products. No MDBMS can make such a claim for interoperability, and the vendors are not attempting it. MDBMS are designed for a different purpose; they are a specific application that is designed to access data residing on a relational DBMS host.

Eliminating MDBMS Technology

Some organizations may wish to consolidate the number of technologies they use in order to simplify maintenance and training. In this case, it is possible to eliminate MDBMS technology and instead write programs to calculate and store derived data. However, the organization that chooses this route must commit to extensive custom programming, not only of the calculations, but also of the user interface.

Learning to Live with a Multilayered Architecture

The idea of simplifying the data architecture or standardizing on fewer technologies may seem appealing, but the benefits might be short-lived. After observing the experience of early adopters, industry analysts like Ken Orr and Chuck Kelley have discovered that, as time goes on, replicated and multidimensional databases of various sizes tend to proliferate throughout the organization.

These databases are used by various user groups for varying purposes, and there will inevitably be partially overlapping information requirements and duplication of both data and calculations. Furthermore, periodic replication of the production data into these databases is required to stay current. Inevitably, the data must be structured systematically and the timing of updates must be synchronized to keep the system running smoothly. Although IS managers might keep this scenario in mind as they begin to implement data warehousing technology, it would be wise to postpone detailed planning until some warehousing projects have been successfully launched and the need becomes apparent.

SUMMARY

Relational database technology is a cornerstone of the information warehousing strategy that is under consideration by many corporations. Relational technology provides the underpinnings for interoperability among platforms and applications and, at the same time, delivers heavy-duty capabilities for data manipulation and data transfer.

MDBMS technology, on the other hand, is one among several methods for delivering tools for business analysis to users. Today's products are far more powerful than their predecessors, but they are still suited to small work groups and relatively small amounts of data. Nevertheless, corporations that reject the technology have a lot of custom programming ahead of them.

Chapter 63

Architecture Overview of OLAP

Deborah Henderson
Hannan Chervinsky

ONLINE ANALYTICAL PROCESSING (OLAP) APPLICATIONS HAVE HEAVY
COMPUTING DEMANDS that center around performance issues and the
need to support massive or complex retrievals. This chapter enumerates:

- Information systems issues surrounding the selection and implementation of OLAP tools for an "optimal performance" architecture.
- The integration of data, tools and hardware, and the methodologies for development of OLAP applications.

DELIVERY MECHANISMS

Among the issues when choosing an optimal performance OLAP architecture are new delivery mechanisms, the two- and three-tier architecture models, and data storage and retrieval methods for achieving OLAP. There are two options regarding delivery mechanisms.

Option 1: Build an Architecture Using Custom Programs with Relational Databases

This option uses traditional development tools and methods for the delivery of OLAP applications, relying on the database management tools for system performance. This architecture is typically chosen by the organization to address specific business areas and needs and usually has limited analytical functionality.

Option 2: Choose Integrated Programs and a Specialized Data Storage Mechanism Together

This second option has emerged as a robust competitor to traditional relational database programmed solutions. This architectural option comes in two types.

Multidimensional OLAP (MOLAP). This array-based architecture involves proprietary, nonrelational data storage tightly integrated with sophisticated processing and presentation layer mechanisms.

Designed by vendors to optimize OLAP retrieval and considered complementary to traditional RDBMSs, these data storage mechanisms are called multidimensional databases (MDDBs) and provide spreadsheet-like functionality. Instead of accommodating x, y dimensions of a spreadsheet, they go further to support the unlimited dimensions.

Relational OLAP (ROLAP). In this relation-based architecture, relational databases are tightly integrated within an application layer that facilitates OLAP-type functions. There are two basic approaches using relational back ends.

The first approach configures end-user workstations with query and reporting tools with cross-tab, pivoting, drill-down, and other multidimensional analysis features. This is a program-logic interface. The second strategy inserts a multidimensional analysis server between an RDBMS and front-end query tools.

MOLAP and ROLAP: Head-to-Head Competition. The pros and cons of each approach with regard to performance and architectural issues often lead to brawls at database conferences and in online forums and vendor literature. There is no limit on database size for relational databases. Retrievals are optimized for the database, and the relational database may be proprietary owing to such performance-enhancing devices as specialized extensions in SQL or table-driven procedures. Text-based data and multimedia data are easily supported in addition to numerical data. Handling of text-based data is an advantage when OLAP metadata is to be stored. MOLAP-based systems will have add-on relational stores for the handling of this text data.

MOLAP-based multidimensional analysis has some limitations on the size of the database it will support. Thus, MOLAPs may be best suited for use for online analytical processing systems, which support circumscribed subject areas that are often smaller in overall size.

Because relational databases can handle much larger databases and take advantage of more powerful server architectures, this is a distinct advantage for ROLAP. But relational databases have no architectural advantage over MOLAP for exploiting symmetric multiprocessors and massively parallel processors (MPPs); they have just been in use longer.

The use of relational databases as the back-end engine has an associated cost in terms of the overhead and complexity required to join, manipulate, and process relational tables. MOLAPs, on the other hand, provide almost immediate response time because they are based on array architectures, which avoid dynamic joins and logic processing overhead.

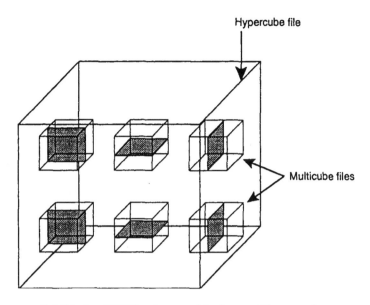

Exhibit 1. MDDB cubes: multicubes and hypercubes.

Clearly, there are a number of facets to this discussion, only a sample of which are noted here. As the MOLAP architecture matures and ROLAP evolves, vendors will want to talk about scalability as the central issue in the debate, proposing whatever technology and techniques will get them the required performance.

MDDB INTERNAL ARCHITECTURES

MDDBs are designed in two basic internal architectures. To the systems designer, the difference is critical in terms of update, maintenance, and performance issues. To the end-user, the differences are transparent. Exhibit 1 is a representation of the hypercube and multicube internal architectures.

Hypercube

The data is stored in one file design and indexed into dimensional designs. Because all data are available, it is possible to also maintain combinations of data that are illogical (e.g., an analysis of sales figures for snowshoes in Florida).

Multicube

In this internal design, the data are stored in multiple cubes. Because the multi-array cubes are individually designed and stored separately, not all dimensions are available to analysis against all others, unless explicitly designed.

Multicubes are not the best choice for distributed database-type applications — drilling from the international corporate summary cube into the detail cube in the northeast business unit, for example. This is because a design principle for multicubes is cube independence. However, multicubes provide control over illogical data combinations and may substantially reduce the sparsity or null values in the matrix.

In addition, multicubes facilitate the analysis of measures against a dimension level that may have more than one logical rollup path. For example, a product could roll up to product classes and lines, but also roll up through a salesperson and sales division.

Storage and Maintenance. The effect of design activities on the file shows the important differences in storage and maintenance between the hypercube and multicube architectures. With a hypercube, the input data design is critical for the availability of the data to the dimensional design; the data relations have to be explicit in the input data layout.

For multicube loading, the input data can be from any number of source tables, and the joins can be performed on the load. This implies that hypercube loading will be faster, although the processing load is simply in different areas. For hypercubes, the processing is in the indexing of the input file; whereas for multicubes, the processing is on the transporting of the data for the load.

Retrieval Issues

Multidimensional retrievals necessitate heavy and very complex processing of millions of rows in a single table. Retrieval is an area of concern for vendors who have developed techniques to address these needs. These techniques include:

- The indexing of every data field against every other data field.
- Hash indexing, which is the indexing of the physical location on the disk for the data.
- Caching, which entails loading optimal-sized chunks of data into memory to increase performance.
- Storing the description of the data item with the data (e.g., grouping of data dimensions in MDDBs, adding attributes to the fact table in an RDBMS). This technique is usually, but not always, limited to the lowest level of a dimension.
- Join indexes, which involve mapping the column values to the indices of more than one table.
- Denormalization of the data storage to optimize I/O in ROLAPs.
- Storing data as objects, so that the context, and perhaps dimensions in which the item participate, are located adjacent to the data themselves.

- Extensions to SQL in order to, for example, correlate queries up and down each dimension.
- Bitmap indexing, which is the coding of values on the bit level.
- Parallel querying (when supported by computer configurations).
- Query optimizers.
- Storing aggregation and calculations of data to avoid query overhead.
- Partitioning of the data (both horizontal and vertical).
- Removal of mirroring, roll-back, and other database overhead that are important in online, updatable databases, but not in read-only databases.

MAKING ARCHITECTURE CHOICES FOR YOUR COMPANY

There are a number of considerations to be addressed that are generic in nature and that apply to a wide range of system selection scenarios. In addition, there are issues and aspects peculiar to the type of OLAP that is to be supported. These issues can be grouped into:

- Systems/products characteristics.
- Business and product considerations.
- Data management requirements.

Together, they must be situated within an overall end-to-end OLAP architecture solution.

Business Considerations

OLAP-based configurations are tailored to the type of audience (e.g., middle manager user, executive user, or power analyst) and nature of the analysis each type of user requires. Consequently, there is a need to identify a mapping between the following business OLAP patterns and your business need for OLAP:

- *Executives.* OLAPs for these users are generally not distributed and not large; volatility of data is low and support for many diverse data formats is mandatory.
- *Line management.* Use of decision support systems by middle management may have very few users, but require constant update of externally sourced data for business or market contextual analysis.
- *Power users.* Data mining OLAPs, and other model-based OLAPs (e.g., forecasts, estimates) may be based on patterns in a sample or based on the analysis of all available data (the larger the sample, the more reliable the model). These applications work on operational-level data and include changes in the data in order to build models on transactional history.
- *End users.* Browsers or end-user query tools support information retrievals. Data may be viewed in an ad hoc manner, allowing the users

to manipulate the data dynamically. Reports that are predefined by information systems staff can be run easily on demand.

Systems/Products Characteristics

Beyond this mapping of business needs to software offerings, there are a number of questions to be raised with regard to software technical architectures:

- Study the internal configuration/architecture associated with the products. Are they ROLAP or MOLAP? The configuration will give a profile on how database growth will be handled and suggest how complex applications and customization, if necessary, can be handled. All these items should yield some performance expectations of the products.
- Study the loading process for the products. Are there extensive administrative tools for the loading of aggregations and calculations from the data warehouse base data? Is distributed or user-profiled data supported, and how easy is the process? All these issues can have an impact on the loading time for new data.
- Benchmark product performance and, if possible, perform the testing in-house.
- Evaluate the performance and customization tuning options that come with the products. Local control may be an important feature as your application will probably grow quickly.
- Consider the connectivity of the product for the purpose of building a custom-developed front end (using API), and for the purpose of exporting data to other products/applications for further analysis or reporting.
- Take time to study timing issues. When and how often do you need the data refreshed, and how is the integration of old and new data accomplished?
- Plan for the future. Examine the growth potential for your system relative to the stated performance limits of the product and explore the possibilities for extracting your information out of the product data store for loading to other stores. Is the migration path limited to product upgrades offered by the vendor?

END-TO-END OLAP DELIVERY ARCHITECTURE

In an end-to-end architecture review, we examine the selection of a full set of products that identifies, documents, models, cleans, transports, and loads data from the transaction systems through the data warehouse layers through to the end-user interface. The selection and implementation of OLAP tools must address and integrate with this larger picture. It is critical for the management and maintenance of the OLAP installation that any issues involved in the movement of data along the architecture are known and brought under control.

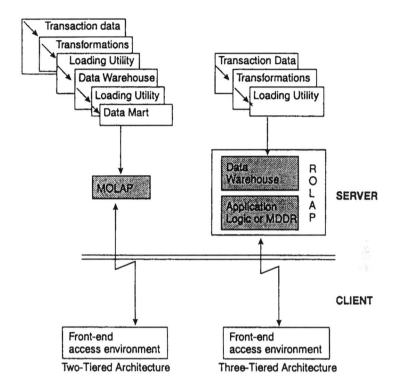

Exhibit 2. A two- and three-tiered end-to-end architecture.

The client/server architecture, in which both MOLAP and ROLAP are delivered, is characterized as two and three tiered in nature. Typically, the analysis functions are performed on the local workstation. The data reside on the server, as does additional optional logic processing. This processing can be database retrieval-focused or OLAP analysis function-focused, or a combination of both.

Exhibit 2 is a sample of some end-to-end architectures that are based on the two- and three-tier models. The exhibit shows where the data warehouse might reside and suggests support software layers. These are two possible scenarios based on MOLAP and ROLAP solutions. It is clear, however, that many other architectures can be imagined based on the considerations mentioned previously.

Data Management Requirements

Data integration may be a driver for some product selections. An end-to-end architecture must support the following data support functions.

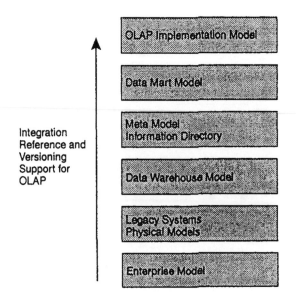

Exhibit 3.   Data model management.

Model Management and Data Transformations. A challenging task is to create and maintain links between the myriad of models necessary to get data from the enterprise overview into the OLAP layer. Exhibit 3 illustrates the problem of multiple models.

Ultimately, the computer-aided software engineering (CASE) modeling tools should support all the linkages and versions of these linkages. In addition, these models should be usable as a set of instructions for the sourcing and loading of all layers in the end-to-end architecture. The modeling toolsets on the market today are lacking in this area, but they are moving toward filling functionality gaps.

Relationship Between Data Marts and Data Warehouse. Does the OLAP layer access the full data warehouse or a data mart subset; or is the data warehouse implemented completely in the OLAP layer? The functional relation between the OLAP data mart and the full data warehouse must be defined. Models for estimates and projections, or other calculations, may create data only available to the OLAP layer. Does this lead to the OLAP layer updating the full warehouse periodically with this unique data?

Data Cleaning. This function should occur upstream of the data warehouse loading. If the OLAP is the implementation of your warehouse, then the data cleaning must be handled upstream of the OLAP load.

There are a number of data cleaning tools on the market. Generally, they supply a list of data values and standard transformations from many forms to one, and identify ranges, once local rules are input to the model. They have no ability to evaluate the data for semantic correctness and are thus limited in their effectiveness.

Metadata. In the management of data models across the architecture, metadata is captured. High-level descriptions plus business and programmer views of data are all necessary to link the strategic picture to the implemented system. Metadata must be available and integrated in the OLAP functions in support of detailed understanding and access of the information examined.

Transport and Scheduled Load. This support function is to automate and minimize the effort associated with the running of end-user query tools to bridge proprietary multidimensional databases and the associated source databases (usually relational). This will minimize the effort associated with the creation and refresh of these multidimensional databases.

SUMMARY

The end-to-end architecture requires many different types of tools. Generally, if you know what you are up against, you can pick from different vendors. If, however, you are concerned about product support, synchronization between vendors, or training of personnel on a number of new products that have to be brought in simultaneously, risk may be controlled by going with a vendor who can supply as many of the pieces for your architecture as possible.

Chapter 64

Creating Value-Added EISs with Soft Information

Hugh J. Watson
Margaret T. O'Hara
Candice G. Harp
Gigi G. Kelly

INFORMATION SYSTEMS TRADITIONALLY HAVE PROVIDED HARD INFORMA-
TION, such as monthly financial statements, sales orders, inventory levels,
and headcounts. This information usually is derived from the organization's transactions processing data base and delivered through schedules,
summary reports, demand reports, and queries. Although it is valuable to
lower-level managers, such information normally has limited usefulness to
executives.

No executive wants to be accused of making decisions that are not
based on hard information. Much of executive decision making, however, is
based on so-called soft information. Predictions, opinions, news, ideas,
and even rumors influence the actions of executives. The importance of
this kind of information is seen in the hours executives spend every day
networking with people inside and outside the organization, reading, at-
tending meetings, making phone calls, and managing by walking around.

The value of soft information to executives makes such information a
logical addition to an organization's executive information system (EIS).
However, providing soft information is very different from providing hard
information.

Soft information is found in different sources (e.g., people, newspapers,
and television) and collected and processed in different ways (i.e., it tends
to be nonmachine-resident and textual). Soft information can be delivered
in a variety of ways (e.g., annotations to screens, electronic bulletin

0-8493-9976-9/99/$0.00+$.50
© 1999 by CRC Press LLC

boards, and E-mail) and through a variety of media (e.g., voice annotations, full-motion video, and personal teleconferencing).

This chapter defines the characteristics of soft information that distinguish it from traditional hard information incorporated into information systems. The current practices in what kinds of soft information are most valuable and how best to capture and deliver it with current technology are derived from actual experiences of 32 EIS developers.

CHARACTERISTICS OF SOFT INFORMATION

Hard information is definite, certain, official, factual, clear, and explicit; in contrast, soft information is fuzzy, unofficial, intuitive, subjective, nebulous, implied, and vague.

Soft information enhances the understanding of past, current, and future events, often by adding value to factual data. Its accuracy and usefulness is assessed by the individual and depends on the timeliness and source of the information and how well the information matches existing understandings. It can be conveyed in multiple forms (i.e., text, graphics, image, and voice) and through multiple channels (i.e., formal and informal, and internal and external to the organization).

Consider this definition in the context of EIS development. To manage effectively, executive decision makers must understand what has happened in the past, what is occurring now, and what might take place in the future, both inside and outside the firm. Often a mix of hard and soft information is needed.

For example, an EIS screen may show that a project is running behind its estimated completion date (this is hard information). A commentary added to the screen may describe what corrective steps are being taken and predict when the project will return to the schedule (soft information). Presented together, the information gives the executive a much clearer understanding of the situation than the hard information alone would have provided.

An EIS expands and enhances the formal and informal and internal and external channels used to gather soft information. For example, the inclusion of E-mail and an electronic bulletin board can facilitate the sharing of soft information. Access to news databases, such as the Dow Jones News Retrieval, helps executives keep in touch with the external environment. An EIS can be viewed as a broadband channel in which carefully prepared information in a rich variety of forms is communicated.

Hard and soft information form a continuum. For example, a financial report generally would be considered at the hard end of the continuum, and a rumor would be placed on the soft end. Although the positioning of a par-

Exhibit 1.   Information Along the Hard/Soft Continuum

Hard						Soft
Financial Statements	News Reports	Schedules	Explanations	Predictions	Opinions	Rumors
Operational Reports	Industry Trends	Formal Plans	Justifications	Speculations	Feelings	Gossip
Historical Information	Survey Data	Assessments	Forecasts	Ideas	Hearsay	
Interpretations	Estimates					

ticular type of information along a hard/soft continuum is subjective, certain characteristics guide its placement. These characteristics relate to the content or source of the soft information. Exhibit 1 groups some of the various types of information executives may receive at points along the hard/soft information continuum.

TYPES AND USES OF SOFT INFORMATION

Rumors, Gossip, and Hearsay

Methods for sharing this information include E-mail and electronic bulletin boards. E-mail messages may be entered into the EIS by the executives or the executives' support staff. In firms where rumors, gossip, and hearsay are communicated through an electronic bulletin board, either the executives or the EIS support staff enter the information.

Predictions, Speculations, Forecasts, and Estimates

This information may be about internal operations or the external environment and is often important for planning purposes. This category of information is included in more EISs than any of the other types, and its importance to executives is well documented.

EIS support staff, executives, and the executives' support staff may enter this information into the system. In some cases (e.g., forecasts), the computer system generates the information automatically based on historical data. Textual information often is provided as an annotation to a screen.

Explanation, Justification, Assessments, and Interpretations

This information helps executives make sense of what is happening inside and outside the firm. It may be entered by executives or by EIS support staff. In some systems, comments are placed on the same screen as the information to which they apply. Other systems place comments on separate screens, which users then access by clicking on the hot spot or button displayed on the screen.

Schedules and Formal Plans

Examples include production schedules, product rollout schedules, and strategic plans. This information is entered both by executives and by EIS support staff. The ability to make textual annotations about deviations from schedules is a key feature in several systems.

Some systems allow users to post electronic notes to a screen. Deviations from schedules may be highlighted by color-coded dates. The traffic light metaphor is used frequently: green indicates ahead of schedule, yellow is slightly off schedule, and red is behind schedule.

News Reports, Industry Trends, and External Survey Data

A majority of EISs provide information about the external environment. The most common approach is to allow users to access electronic news services (i.e., the Dow Jones News Retrieval). The executive can either direct the search online or create a predefined user profile and have stories delivered automatically. Some systems may support TV broadcasts in a window and allow executives to monitor the news on CNN. External survey data, such as competitive information and demographic data about the company's market, as well as external news databases, usually are entered electronically.

CURRENT PRACTICES IN EIS DEVELOPMENT

Soft information has great potential for adding value to EISs, but many of the following observations and practices used by EIS developers are also likely to apply to other computer applications, including group support systems.

The Nature of Executive Work Requires Soft Information

Executives rely heavily on verbal communication. Many of their activities involve gathering and disseminating soft information. One-on-one meetings, private phone conversations, and social activities with colleagues demonstrate several traditional methods for sharing soft information.

Executives who are credited with having good intuition and judgment use (consciously and unconsciously) soft information to influence their actions. Asking executives why they want to pursue an action based on their feelings often yields such statements as, "This fits with the industry projections that I saw in *The Wall Street Journal*."

Soft Information Increases Executives' Awareness of Critical Issues

Many executives rely on personal contacts. When soft information is included in the EIS, executives have faster and easier access to such information. Instead of waiting to contact a person, the executive simply may access the EIS to obtain the information. This can be especially helpful in companies where personal contact is infrequent — for example, in firms that are dispersed geographically.

Executives who actively seek soft information from external sources often find that personal scanning is neither effective nor efficient. External scanning is time-consuming, and executives may miss critical information simply because they cannot scan enough information. This is where an EIS can be especially useful.

Corporate Culture Sets the Pace on Use of Soft Information

A strong organizational culture can control the behavior of individuals within the organization and affect all aspects of the firm. Thus, the inclusion of soft information in an EIS is affected by the corporate culture.

If the culture favors traditional hard data more than less-traditional soft information, the firm's EIS is unlikely to contain much soft information. If providers of what turns out to be incorrect soft information either are embarrassed or have their abilities questioned, the soft information pipeline will evaporate.

As an example, one EIS developer described a new application that illustrates an organization's willingness and desire to solicit and share soft information. In this organization, the EIS has spread to many users in middle- and lower-management positions. The new application allows users to employ the system's E-mail capability to submit questions to the firm's senior executives. The questions and the executives' answers are posted on an electronic bulletin board available to all users. Anonymity is provided by removing the questioner's name, thereby increasing the range of questions that can be asked. For example, one recent question asked why senior executives still were flying first class when the company was trying to cut costs. Only an open corporate culture would support an application such as this one.

Executives who feel that their power will be threatened by sharing soft information they possess are unlikely to share it; thus, soft information will be absent from their company's EIS. Because information is a key currency in an organization, it becomes too valuable to exchange freely. If the reward structure fosters competition rather than cooperation, executives will be less likely to share valuable soft information. When the reward structure encourages the sharing of soft information, the executive information miser no longer will be rewarded for hoarding information.

Sometimes the executive sponsor must mandate (either directly or indirectly) using the EIS as a medium for exchanging soft information. In one company, the CEO told other executives that they were expected to read and respond to his E-mail messages. Over time, E-mail has become an important source of soft information.

Soft Information Enhances the Corporate Grapevine

Including soft information in an EIS helps manage, structure, and enhance the corporate grapevine. Free-flowing rumors can lead to lower productivity and increased employee stress. The EIS can provide a mechanism for addressing rumors by providing more information in a more timely manner to more people. In this way, soft information that is inaccurate is more likely to be detected and corrected. The net effect is to reduce the deficiencies of the corporate grapevine.

The Use of Soft Information Varies by Industry

Although a comprehensive picture of the relationship between industry type and the inclusion of soft information is not available, it appears that for a variety of reasons some industries are more likely to include soft information in their EISs than are others. The type of soft information included in an EIS also varies among industries.

Work with hospitals and vendors of EIS software for hospitals (e.g., Health Quest, Medicus) suggests that hospital EISs tend to contain relatively little soft information. Most hospitals have limited IS staffs, and senior hospital management tends to have small support staffs. As a result, unless the data is already machine-resident — and most soft information is not — or is entered by executives, it is unlikely to be included in the EIS. Vendors and consultants have recognized the difficulty of supporting labor-intensive applications in hospital EISs and have focused on financial applications that draw on summarized transaction data.

In a different example, because government organizations are affected by external events, public opinion, election outcomes, and funding appropriations, their EISs often contain soft information about current and potential developments in these areas. One state government's EIS contains video clips taken from the previous evening's newscasts. A federal agency's EIS contains assessments of which candidates are likely to win upcoming elections and the potential impact on funding levels. An EIS for a state senate contains information about how different voting groups feel about pending legislation.

Soft Information About Competitors Is Highly Valued

The competitive pressures brought by deregulation, foreign competition, and changes in technology have increased in recent years. Firms use a variety of methods to obtain competitive information that helps them deal with these pressures. Firms that include soft information about competitors in the EIS consider this information to be very important.

For many firms, the sales force is the biggest source of competitor information. As sales representatives call on clients, they pick up useful information about competitors that is disseminated by the EIS.

A few firms are very creative in their collection and use of soft information. In one company, an employee is sent out to count the number of cars in a competitor's parking lot. When the number of cars is up, business is good. This information is entered into the EIS and used for competitive bidding. The firm's executives have learned that the competitor is less likely to give a low bid if business is good. The reverse is also true.

Some Soft Information Intentionally May Be Excluded from the EIS

For a variety of reasons, some firms deliberately exclude certain soft information from their EISs. Some firms are concerned about the security of sensitive information. A hospital, for example, may choose to exclude information about mortalities because the potential for lawsuits is too great. Several companies deliberately exclude human resources information because of Equal Employment Opportunity Commission regulations and confidentiality concerns. One company excludes steering committee reports because the information is considered to be too sensitive.

Some government agencies are unlikely to include certain types of soft information. Many states have so-called sunshine laws that make government agencies more subject to public scrutiny than their private sector counterparts. It is not surprising that potentially sensitive information is unlikely to find its way into governmental EISs.

The firm's culture is an additional consideration. In some organizations, soft information such as rumors and gossip is not deemed appropriate for electronic distribution.

The Value of Soft Information Depends on its Timeliness

Yesterday's news is of little value to executives in today's high-velocity environments. The difference between being a leader and being a follower often depends on how a company responds to change. An EIS that quickly delivers valuable information to executives is likely to be perceived as valuable.

The EIS manager at a large oil company provided an example of the importance of timely delivery of soft information. During the Gulf War, the EIS provided access to CNN. The constant monitoring of news through the EIS provided up-to-date information that was used to make critical business decisions. Although access to CNN was available by other methods, the EIS provided the executives with one-stop shopping for their information needs.

Increasing the Quantity and Variety of Soft Information in an EIS Increases Staffing Requirements

The inclusion of soft information in an EIS usually means additional work for EIS support staff. Soft information often is presented as commentaries to screens. Obtaining this information typically involves investigative work, and the soft information then must be entered into the system. Any requirements for external soft information also can increase the staff's workload. In one company, for example, the public relations department scans news stories and prepares summary descriptions that are entered into the system by the EIS support staff. Because collecting and entering soft information is labor-intensive, its inclusion increases EIS staffing requirements.

The Variety and Quantity of Soft Information Increases the Value of an EIS

There seems to be a positive relationship between the amount and variety of soft information and the perceived value of the EIS. Because executives use soft information, it is logical that they would value an EIS that provides such information more than one that does not. When executives have access to soft information in the EIS, they often can reduce their reliance on extensive personal or telephone networking to uncover the latest information or focus their networking on specific issues. Saving executives' valuable time increases the perceived value of the EIS.

Organizations Increase the Variety and Quantity of Soft Information Over Time

The amount and variety of soft information in older EISs is usually greater than in newly established ones. The reasons are clear when the evolution of a typical EIS is considered.

Once executives commit to the development of an EIS, the system needs to be rolled out quickly while executive interest is high. Consequently, the first applications are often extensions of existing reports with a new format or minor enhancements. This early version becomes the foundation for the iterative and adaptive approach that is typical of EIS development. To better satisfy the information requirements of executives, the hard information is supplemented later with soft information. As executives receive the benefits from soft information, they are likely to request additional soft information. Sometimes what starts as simple annotations to graphs blossoms into more sophisticated and detailed explanations.

Identifying the Source Enhances the Value of the Soft Information in an EIS

Anonymity in an EIS is usually inappropriate. Many EIS applications (e.g., E-mail) automatically attach the author's name to the information being entered. Even in instances where input is not tagged, the author is often obvious.

Although hard information usually is taken at face value, soft information may require a source for verification. The identity of this source may be the crux to the perceived accuracy of the information.

TECHNOLOGY FOR DELIVERING SOFT INFORMATION

The inclusion of soft information is affected by currently available EIS technology. For example, some EIS products allow executives to easily add commentaries to screens although others do not. Vendors aggressively are moving forward to include applications and features in their products that facilitate the inclusion of soft information.

Multimedia Support

Multimedia technology may further support the inclusion of soft information in EISs. One firm that deals in resort properties places videotapes of properties being considered for purchase in its EIS. The videos convey information about the properties that numbers cannot. A grocery store chain conducts spot checks of its stores by videotaping the conditions within the stores and making the tapes accessible through their EIS. In addition to helping monitor store conditions, the tapes are used in store manager performance evaluations. More multimedia applications in EISs undoubtedly will follow from the rapid expansion of multimedia products in the marketplace.

Software Agents

A considerable amount of soft information exists in text-based documents such as news stories, E-mail, letters, and reports. With the exception of news stories that can be accessed by many EISs from commercial databases, locating needed information can be very time-consuming and difficult.

Comshare offers a relatively new product — NewsAlert — for use with its Commander EIS product. NewsAlert uses software robots that constantly monitor data sources — both textual and numeric, and internal and external — for changing patterns and trends in both hard and soft information. When the robots detect a significant trend, they send out alerts to the users' desktops. Alerts are displayed in a personalized electronic newspaper, along with background tools needed for analysis.

Groupware

Although EIS and groupware evolved separately, they have had the common objective of sharing information. Vendors have recognized the opportunity to enhance their products and increase sales by providing integrated EIS and group support capabilities. Cyril Brookes and others at the University of New South Wales in Australia have developed grapeVine, a database collection, dissemination, and browsing system for soft information. It combines business intelligence, executive alerting, and information-filtering functions that can be used to augment an EIS.

Pilot Software's Command Center product includes Impact, an application that allows executives to delegate issues requiring action. Project-tracking features monitor what is being done. IRMS and PSR include graphical interfaces to Lotus Notes as part of their OnTrack and TRACK products.

A few firms are going beyond providing an interface to Lotus Notes applications and are making Notes part of the EIS software. One of Notes' attractive features is its text-handling ability. In one firm that is planning to use Notes, the EIS will maintain departmental objectives and commentaries about their status, and departmental personnel will be responsible for keeping the commentaries current. The application will be developed in Notes because of its capabilities for entering, maintaining, and updating textual information. Conversations with the EIS developers revealed considerable interest in the possibility of using Notes in EISs.

Other Enhancements

Another interesting technology-driven EIS enhancement is EIS software that automatically generates certain types of soft information. This is already common with integrated forecasting models that make projections beyond current conditions. One system that automatically generates on-screen explanations for occurrences was built using EXECUCOM's Executive Edge with IFPS. IFPS contains an artificial intelligence-based EXPLAIN capability that provides a textual explanation for changes that have occurred. It is important to recognize, however, that all the explanations are based on the variables and relationships expressed in the underlying IFPS models. The many explanations exogenous to these models must be provided to the system by other means.

ACTION PLAN

The importance of soft information to executives is well-recognized, but until recently, information systems did not include much of it. This is changing rapidly, however, in large part because of improvements in information technology. It well may become the rule rather than the exception for an application to include soft information. The key to success is to

- Give careful thought to what type of soft information should be included.
- Understand how the information should be captured and presented.
- Understand the effect of the information on business decisions.

Section XII
Data Mining

DATA MINING IS THE PROCESS OF EXTRACTING INFORMATION, often previously unknown, from data sources. The data sources may be databases, collections of data, or even warehouses. A warehouse often prepares the data so that it can facilitate mining. Varous technologies, concepts, and algorithms have to be integrated for effective data mining, including database management, statistical analysis, machine learning, and information retrieval. Parallel processing techniques improve the performance of data mining. Furthermore, visualization techniques facilitate data mining by providing a better picture of the contents of a database. This section consists of six chapters devoted to aspects of data mining.

Chapter 65, "Data Mining: Exploring the Corporate Asset," shows how companies, with very large and complex databases, can leverage discovery-based data-mining approaches to realize the complete value of their corporate data.

Chapter 66, "When a Business Abandons a Data Mine: Case Study," examines the corporate expectations, conduct, and reactions towards a data-mining project. This case study takes a unique twist by focusing on the consequences to an organization that abandoned such an effort.

Chapter 67, "Data Mining: Knowledge Discovery in Databases," provides an overview of data mining. In particular, the process of knowledge discovery in databases, the need for data mining, relationships to other areas such as database management, data warehouses, metadata repositories, machine learning, information retrieval, and statistics are described.

Chapter 68, "Multimedia Databases and Data Mining," first provides an overview of multimedia database systems. Data models, query processing, storage issues, and distribution are discussed. The chapter then provides an overview of data mining and shows how it can improve multimedia data retrieval, especially from the World Wide Web.

Chapter 69, "Database Mining Tools," discusses when to use data mining and how to mine the data. Emerging mining tools are described. An overview of various applications for data mining also is given.

Chapter 65

Data Mining: Exploring the Corporate Asset

Jason Weir

COMPANIES TODAY GENERATE AND COLLECT VAST AMOUNTS OF DATA that they use in the ongoing process of doing business. Transaction data such as that produced by inventory, billing, shipping and receiving, and sales systems is stored in operational or departmental data stores. It is understood that data represents a significant competitive advantage, but realizing the full potential of it is not simple. Decision makers must be able to interpret trends, identify factors or utilize information based on clear, timely data in a meaningful format. For instance, a marketing director should be able to identify a group of customers, 18 to 24 years of age, that own notebook computers who need or are likely to purchase an upcoming collaboration software product. After identifying them, the director sends them advance offers, information, or product order forms to increase product presales.

Data mining, as a methodology, is a set of techniques used to uncover previously obscure or unknown patterns and relationships in very large databases. The ultimate goal is to arrive at comprehensible, meaningful results from extensive analysis of information.

HOW IS IT DIFFERENT FROM OTHER ANALYSIS METHODS?

Data mining differs from other methods in several ways. A significant distinction between data mining and other analytical tools is in the approach they use in exploring the data. Many analytical tools available support a verification-based approach in which the user hypothesizes about specific data relationships and then uses the tools to verify or refute those presumptions. This verification-based process stems from the intuition of the user to pose the questions and refine the analysis based on the results of potentially complex queries against a database. The effectiveness of this analysis depends on several factors, not the least of which being the ability of the user to pose appropriate questions, the capability of tools to return results quickly, and the overall reliability and accuracy of the data being analyzed.

Other available analytical tools have been optimized to address some of these issues. Query and reporting tools, such as those used in data mart or warehouse applications, let users develop queries through point-and-click interfaces. Statistical analysis packages, like those used by many insurance or actuarial firms, provide the ability to explore relationships among a few variables and determine statistical significance against demographic sets. Multidimensional online analytical processing (OLAP) tools enable fast response to user inquiries through their ability to compute hierarchies of variables along dimensions such as size, color or location.

Data mining, in contrast to these analytical tools, uses what are called discovery-based approaches in which pattern matching and other algorithms are employed to determine the key relationships in the data. Data-mining algorithms can look at numerous multidimensional data relationships concurrently, highlighting those that are dominant or exceptional. In other words, true data-mining tools uncover trends, patterns and relationships automatically. Earlier in the chapter was mentioned the fact that many other types of analytical methods rely on user intuition or the ability to pose the right kind of question. To sum things up, analytical tools — query tools, statistical tools, and OLAP — and the results they produce, are all user-driven, but data mining is data-driven.

THE NEED FOR DATA MINING

As discussed, traditional methods involve the decision maker hypothesizing the existence of information of interest, converting that hypothesis to a query, posing that query to the analysis tool, and interpreting the returned results with respect to the decision being made. For instance, the marketing director must hypothesize that notebook-owning 18- to 24-year-old customers are likely to purchase the upcoming software release. After posing the query, it is up to the individual to interpret the returned results and determine if the list represents a good group of product prospects. The quality of the extracted information is based on the user's interpretation of the posed query's results.

The intricacies of data interrelationships as well as the sheer size and complexity of modern data stores necessitates more advance analysis capabilities than those provided by verification-based data-mining approaches.

The ability to discover automatically important information hidden in the data and then present it in the appropriate way is a critical complimentary technology to verification-based approaches. Tools, techniques, and systems that perform these automated analysis tasks are referred to as discovery-based. Discovery-based systems applied to the marketing director's data store may identify many groups including, for example: 18- to 24-year-old male college students with laptops, 24- to 30-year-old female software engineers with both desktop and notebook systems, and 18- to 24-year-old customers planning to purchase portable computers within the next 6 months. By recognizing the marketing director's goal, the discovery-based system can identify the software engineers as the key target group by spending pattern or other variable.

In sum, verification-based approaches, although valuable for quick, high-level decision support, such as historical queries about product sales by fiscal quarter, are insufficient. For companies with very large and complex databases, discovery-based data-mining approaches must be implemented to realize the complete value that data offers.

THE PROCESS OF MINING DATA

Selection and Extraction

Constructing an appropriate database to run queries against is a critical step in the data-mining process. A marketing database may contain extensive tables of data from purchasing records and lifestyle data to more advanced demographic information such as census records. Not all of this data is required on a regular basis and should be filtered out of the query table. Additionally, even after selecting the desired database tables, it is not always necessary to mine the contents of the entire table to identify useful information. Under certain conditions and for certain types of data-mining techniques, for example, when creating a classification or prediction model, it may be adequate first to sample the table and then to mine the sample. This is usually a faster and less expensive operation.

Essentially, potential sources of data (e.g,. census data, sales records, mailing lists, demographic databases) should be explored before meaningful analysis can take place. The selected data types may be organized along multiple tables. Developing a sound model involves combining parts of separate tables into a single database for mining purposes.

Data Cleansing and Transformation

Once the selected database tables have been selected and the data to be mined has been identified, it is usually necessary to perform certain transformations and cleansing routines on the data. Data cleansing or transformations are determined by the type of data being mined as well as the data-mining technique being used. Transformations vary from conversions of one type of data to another, such as numeric data to character data, or currency conversions to more advanced transformations such as the application of mathematical or logical functions on certain types of data.

Cleansing, on the other hand, is used to ensure reliability and accuracy of results. Data can be verified, or cleansed, to remove duplicate entries, attach real values to numeric or alphanumeric codes, and omit incomplete records. Dirty or inaccurate data in the mining data store must be avoided if results are to be accurate and useful. Many data-mining tools include a system log or other graphical interface tool to identify erroneous data in queries, but every effort should be made prior to this stage to ensure that it does not arrive at the mining database. If errors are not discovered, lower quality results and, due to this, lesser quality decisions will be the result.

Mining, Analysis, and Interpretation

The clean and transformed data subsequently is mined using one or more techniques to extract the desired type of information. For example, to develop an accurate classification model that predicts whether a customer will upgrade to a new version of a software package, a decision maker first must use clustering to segment the customer database. Next, they will apply rules to create automatically a classification model for each desired cluster. While mining a particular data set, it may be necessary to access additional data from a datamart or warehouse and perform additional transformations of the original data. The terms and methods mentioned previously will be defined and discussed later in this chapter.

The last step in the data-mining process is analyzing and interpreting results. The extracted and transformed data is analyzed with respect to the user's goal, and the best information is identified and presented to the decision maker through the decision support system. The purpose of result interpretation is not only to represent the output of the data mining operation graphically, but also to filter the information that will be presented through the decision support system. For example, if the goal is to develop a classification model, during the result interpretation step the robustness of the extracted model is tested using one of the established methods. If the interpreted results are not satisfactory, it may be necessary to repeat the data-mining step or to repeat other steps. What this really speaks to is the quality of data. The information extracted through data mining must be ultimately comprehensible. For example, it may be necessary, after interpreting the results of a data-mining operation, to go back and add data to the selection process or to perform a different calculation during the transformation step.

TECHNIQUES

Classification

Classification is perhaps the most often employed data-mining technique. It involves a set of instances or predefined examples to develop a model that can classify the population of records at large.

The use of classification algorithms begins with a sample set of preclassified example transactions. For a fraud detection application, this would include complete records of both fraudulent and valid transactions, determined on a record-by-record basis. The classifier-training algorithm uses these preclassified examples to determine the set of parameters required for proper identification. The algorithm then encodes these parameters into a model called a classifier or classification model. The approach affects the decision-making capability of the system. Once an effective classifier is developed, it is used in a predictive mode to classify new records automatically into these same predefined classes.

In the fraud detection case above, the classifier would be able to identify probable fraudulent activities. Another example would involve a financial application where a classifier capable of identifying risky loans could be used to aid in the decision of whether to grant a loan to an individual.

Association

Given a collection of items and a set of transactions, each of which contain some number of items from a given collection, an association is an operation against this set of records that returns affinities that exist among the collection of items. Market basket analysis is a common application that utilizes association techniques. Market basket analysis involves a retailer running an association function over the point of sales transaction log. The goal is to determine affinities among shoppers. For example in an analysis of 100,000 transactions, association techniques could determine that "20% of the time, customers who buy a particular software application, also purchase the complimentary add-on software pack."

In other words, associations are items that occur together in a given event or transaction. Association tools discover rules.

Another example of the use of association discovery could be illustrated in an application that analyzes the claim forms submitted by patients to a medical insurance company. The goal is to discover patterns among the claimants' treatment. Assume that every claim form contains a set of medical procedures that were performed to the given patient during one visit. By defining the set of items to be the collection of all medical procedures that can be performed on a patient and the records to correspond to each claim form, the application can find, using the association technique, relationships among medical procedures that often are performed together.

Sequence-Based

Traditional market basket analysis deals with a collection of items as part of a point-in-time transaction. A variant of this occurs when there is additional information to tie together a sequence of purchases. An account number, a credit card, or a frequent shopper number are all examples of ways to track multiple purchases in a time series.

Rules that capture these relationships can be used, for example, to identify a typical set of precursor purchases that might predict the subsequent purchase of a specific item. In this software case, sequence-based mining could determine the likelihood of a customer purchasing a particular software product to purchase subsequently complimentary software or hardware devices such as a joystick or video card.

Sequence-based mining can be used to detect the set of customers associated with frequent buying patterns. Use of sequence-based mining on the set of insurance claims discussed earlier can lead to the identification of frequently occurring medical procedures performed on patients. This then can be harnessed in a fraud detection application, also discussed earlier, to detect cases of medical insurance fraud.

Clustering

Clustering segments a database into different groups. The goal is to find groups that differ from one another as well as similarities among members. The clustering approach assigns records with a large number of attributes into a relatively small set of groups, or segments. This assignment process is performed automatically by clustering algorithms that identify the distinguishing characteristics of the data set and then partition the space defined by the data set attributes along natural boundaries. There is no need to identify the groupings desired or the attributes that should be used to segment the data set.

Clustering is often one of the first steps in data-mining analysis. It identifies groups of related records that can be used as a starting point for exploring further relationships. This technique supports the development of population segmentation models, such as demographic-based customer segments. Additional analyses using standard analytical and other data-mining techniques can determine the characteristics of these segments with respect to some desired outcome. For example, the buying habits of multiple population segments might be compared to determine which segments to target for a new marketing campaign.

Estimation

Estimation is a variation on the classification technique. Essentially it involves the generation of scores along various dimensions in the data. Rather than employing a binary classifier to determine whether a loan applicant, for instance, is approved or classified as a risk, the estimation approach generates a credit-worthiness score based on a prescored sample set of transactions. That is, sample data (complete records of approved and risk applicants) are used as samples in determining the worthiness of all records in a data set.

APPLICATIONS OF DATA MINING

Data mining now is being applied in a variety of industries ranging from investment management and retail solutions to marketing, manufacturing, and health care applications. It has been pointed out that many organizations, due to the strategic nature of their data-mining operations, will not discuss their projects with outsiders. This is understandable due to the importance and potential that successful solutions offer organizations. However, there are several well-known applications that are proven performers.

In customer profiling, characteristics of good customers are identified with the goals of predicting who will become one and helping marketing departments target new prospects. Data mining can find patterns in a customer database that can be applied to a prospect database so that customer acquisition can be targeted appropriately. For example, by identifying good candidates for mail offers or catalogs, direct-mail marketing managers can reduce expenses and increase their sales generation efforts. Targeting specific promotions to existing and potential customers offers similar benefits.

Market-basket analysis helps retailers understand which products are purchased together or by an individual over time. With data mining, retailers can determine which products to stock in which stores and how to place them within a store. Data mining also can help assess the effectiveness of promotions and coupons.

Lastly, fraud detection is of great benefit to credit card companies, insurance firms, stock exchanges, government agencies, and telecommunications firms. The aggregate total for fraud losses in today's world is enormous, but with data mining, these companies can identify potentially fraudulent transactions and contain damage. Financial companies use data mining to determine market and industry characteristics as well as to predict individual company and stock performance. Another interesting niche application is in the medical field. Data mining can help predict the effectiveness of surgical procedures, diagnostic tests, medication, and other services.

SUMMARY

More and more companies are beginning to realize the potential for data mining within their organization. However, unlike the "plug-and-play," out-of-the-box business solutions that many have become accustomed to, data mining is not a simple application. It involves a good deal of forethought, planning, research, and testing to ensure a sound, reliable, and beneficial

DATA MINING

project. Another thing to remember is that data mining is complimentary to traditional query and analysis tools, data warehousing, and data mart applications. It does not replace these useful and often vital solutions.

Data mining enables organizations to take full advantage of the investments they have made and currently are making in building data stores. By identifying valid, previously unknown information from large databases, decision makers can tap into the unique opportunities that data mining offers.

Chapter 66

When a Business Abandons a Data Mine: Case Study

Ronald A. Wencer

DATA MINING CAN INFLUENCE BUSINESS DIRECTION SIGNIFICANTLY, but inappropriate expectations may arise from a purely operational view of mining: endless strings of railroad cars brimming with ore, fed by machines and by relentless, back-straining labor, everything working together with assembly-line precision. Data mining requires prospecting — the exploration that must constantly guide mining operations. As in any discipline, one must test hard realities against hypotheses, objectivity against preconception. The template that sets directions for data mining must be validated repeatedly by a complementary analysis of what is being discovered.

The object of the study exhibited many characteristics of successful information systems projects, and none of the flaws usually associated with project failure. Yet, its early high-profile success decayed steadily into obscurity, with many perceiving its eventual conclusion as a predictable fate for a project gone awry.

An awareness of the decisions and misunderstandings that shaped the project may prove relevant to future undertakings. Certainly, if the same business culture were to attack the same problem again, a deeper appreciation of data mining concepts could avoid reliance on cultural perceptions, and could instead foster recognition of the true business problems at hand.

CORPORATE BACKGROUND

Building on decades of conservative growth, ABCBank was a widely respected organization. It was meeting challenges from larger, newly aggressive competitors by pursuing a strategic plan, which was to fundamentally change the bank's texture. ABCBank was edging upward; it was solidifying

0-8493-9976-9/99/$0.00+$.50
© 1999 by CRC Press LLC

and enlarging its traditional customer base, yet also gaining footholds in new market niches.

The plan called for a quantitative study of the bank's relationships with its corporate clients, relationships that traditionally had been characterized by networking and informality. Personal knowledge, skills, and judgment played important roles, converging in a negotiation-centered process through which multimillion-dollar transactions were affected.

For many services delivered to commercial clients, bank costs were unknown. Working from uncoordinated bundles of operational data, staff had to rely more on intuition and experience than on information. Despite the bank's track record, executives felt compelled to monitor corporate client services more vigorously.

The information systems environment was an obstacle to the proposed quantitative study, because it focused on client accounts and transactions, ignoring overall relationships. During the years of cultural stability, it had provided a solid foundation, but it now proves brittle. With each application interacting with customers and staff on its own terms, there was little opportunity for synergy. Restructuring the corporate information resource would be critical to ABCBank's future.

BUSINESS FOCUS OF THE STUDY

Centralizing corporate/client dealings at a single bank office had hastened decision making, but it offered no meaningful feedback about the profitability of relationships — doing further business with a given client did not necessarily mean better, or even adequate, return on incremental exposure.

Commercial credit services (ongoing loan commitments, lines of credit, actual borrowings, etc.) were of special concern, because the impact of a single commercial transaction was great. Negotiated pricing bred complex, often unique terms that generally involved hierarchies of potential and actual borrowing agreements. In addition to the obvious, the formulae for each agreement might encompass less expected variables — such as other institutions' lending rates, or client deposits (credit clients sometimes agreed to maintain deposit balances, which fluctuated according to repayments and borrowings).

The bank lacked quantifiable and objective models by which to evaluate such complexity, yet the financial climate demanded objectivity. With commercial loan rates at unprecedented levels, financial institutions and clients alike were reevaluating their positions. Sporadic but large defaults had become a notorious feature of the industry, seriously affecting some of ABCBank's peers. Concerned regulators were monitoring commercial lending more closely. Banks could no longer afford to make uninformed commitments in the credit marketplace.

Moreover, corporate client profiles had become quite intricate. Diversified clients used many unrelated services, traditionally administered by disparate bank units. Subsidiaries and affiliates sometimes dealt independently with different bank offices; sometimes they dealt as a body with a single contact. Interrelated clients might pool their respective credit or deposit accounts. As these factors increasingly muddied ABCBank's view of its biggest clients, loan officers could no longer determine whether deposit obligations were being met.

The bank could not evaluate its loan officers' negotiations with clients. Risk was increasing, but as things stood, achieving the bank's prime strategic objective in this arena — determining whether long-term relationships with given clients were in fact profitable — was not feasible.

INCEPTION OF THE PROJECT

Although it would be rebuilt eventually, the operational system for commercial loans was to remain in place for some time. Expanding business already demanded constant system maintenance. Except for highlighting important but obvious conditions (e.g., defaults), operational data could not directly support any decision to pursue or ignore a given client opportunity.

The lack of adequate aggregated information was clear. Management proposed a decision-support environment, built specifically to permit analysis of corporate/client relationships, to be created and managed by a team with no operational responsibilities. A key deliverable for this team would be a framework for viewing complex customer families.

Assessing client family relationships would enable these primary objectives:

- Leveraging profitable corporate/client relationships.
- Repairing or shedding unprofitable client relationships.
- Identifying extraordinary performance-linked characteristics and trends among client subset.
- Addressing any consistently poor performance by loan officer teams.

Anticipated secondary objectives were as follows:

- Disentangling client family obligations, allowing the bank to identify areas of noncompliance.
- Providing client families more comprehensive information about their banking.
- Promoting the bank's own compliance with regulatory obligations.

If the objectives were met, payback would be certain.

Terms of Reference

With ABCBank's president expressed personal interest, the project was organized swiftly. Sponsorship was delegated to a senior vice-president (two levels below the CEO), and business and technical directors were chosen. The steering committee also included executives from information systems and commercial credit operations.

To free the decision-support environment from operational constraints, the steering body determined that:

- There would be an independent base of replicated data, collected by a quasi-operational application, to be accessed via highly flexible technology.
- The environment would feature new query and analytical modeling tools.
- New processes would replicate selected data from the disparate operational environments; in the new environment, it would be transformed in accord with strategic direction.
- Bank services and clients would be classified, and data aggregated appropriately.
- Association concepts would support the assessment of a client relationship's long-term profitability.
- In response to the periodic feed of operational data, the decision-support environment would return a high-level view of each client's compliance.

The following project constraints were accepted:

- No existing system process or data within the resource-intensive commercial loan environment could be modified. At the most, limited new processing could be injected at noncritical points. Replication and synthesis of the data to be mined would be made as external to the existing environment as possible.
- The mined data would have to be fitted to an effective model, which would feature uniform, readily understood measures by which to appraise phenomena that traditionally had been considered complex.
- Results had to demonstrate high integrity; neither internal management nor clients could question them.
- Because of resource concerns, the priority given to credit arrangements over other services, and expectations of significant benefits based solely on credit service analysis, analyzing non-credit services was deferred to a later project.

PROJECT ORGANIZATION

Three project teams were established:

- Three commercial loan experts, drawing on operational and executive resources as necessary, would develop the initial concepts and direction for the mining effort, including the principles for compiling views of client families. This team was credit from the bank's back-office credit unit.
- Four information systems professionals were to develop the mechanisms by which data was to be collected from the bank's operational environment and partially aggregated. This team was recruited externally; its members had extensive team-oriented experience at various competitors of ABCBank.
- Responsibility for housing the replicated data, and for more fully aggregating it, was outsourced to a vendor that offered appropriate technologies and skills. Vendor personnel were to work closely with the business team to determine classification principles. The vendor would also provide the business team with training and technology for conducting ongoing evaluation and analysis.

All team leaders were to participate as peers, from the onset of detailed project planning through delivery.

CONDUCT OF THE PROJECT

The project plan overlapped business-area and systems activities. It relied on an opening position — a template-like set of assumptions that would drive the initial phase of data selection and transformation. The business experts defined a draft analytical model that quantified profitability while still attempting to respect business complexities and variations. It suggested certain first-cut abstractions that guided the recognition of rudimentary classifications.

Armed with this opening position, the technical team affected a logical mapping of decision-support requirements to operational data structures and timings (Exhibit 1). Analyzing this mapping led to the determination of tactics by which data could be replicated effectively for transformation. Confident that both the logical decision-support view would have a sound foundation of operational data, and that it could evolve through the ongoing exercise of analytical tools, the team began designing bridges to the operational environment.

Simultaneously, the first-cut analytical model was validated through a prototyping exercise. The business and vendor teams mimicked the target environment, populating a bare-bones functional prototype with manually

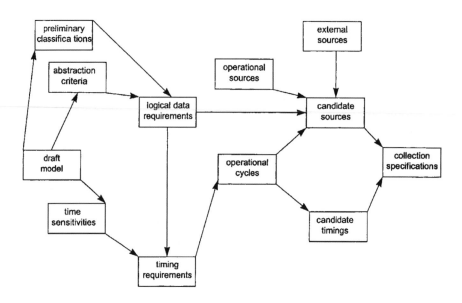

Exhibit 1. Determining sources for data collection.

replicated data. Because this exercise refined, but did not significantly alter, the classification parameters of the draft analytical model, management was convinced that the project was on track, and that its objectives would be met readily.

By this point, the project team knew that the decision-support environment would have to sustain analysis of:

- 25,000 active corporate client accounts.
- 10,000 corporate families (multiclient families averaged about four accounts each, and might include many more).
- On average, two loan arrangements per account.
- As many as seven actual loans per arrangement at any moment.

At the start of data collection, the bank would have as many as 13 months of history for each family. Data would grow daily as new arrangements were made, terms were renegotiated, interest rates changed, and funds were deposited. Projections of these figures were used to validate the proposed architecture and resourcing for collection, aggregation, and evaluation activities.

Thereafter, the activities unfolded in a straightforward fashion, progressing as follows:

1. Using a representative sample chosen by the business team, clients were clustered, thereby refining the initial project scope (i.e., some

clusters were deemed to be not of interest). The project team — and bank management as well — began to articulate the characteristics of corporate client relationships of different sizes.

2. The team elaborated its criteria for considering nominally distinct clients as parts of a single corporate family. Staff then began collecting data in order to identify families (a prerequisite for rendering certain aggregations meaningful).

3. A universal cost model was developed. Management could then envisage a consistent bottom-line comparison of different types of clients and credit services.

4. An expanded set of historical data was replicated from the operational environment. Aggregation was done in accord with the first-cut abstractions that had been posited for the analytical model.

5. The team defined a cyclical framework for managing the ongoing growth of data. It determined the timings for monitoring operational data, for replication and preprocessing, and for the creation of certain "standard" aggregations. These timings were chosen by balancing the need for complete, current data against the risk of overemphasis should spikes occur.

6. An automated process was built to detect potentially relevant changes to operational data. Rules determined whether or not a change was of analytical interest, identified to which client families it applied, and scoped the timeframe for which the change impacted analysis (impacts could be either prospective or retrospective). The replication cycle consolidated the results of this monitoring so that all aggregations remained current.

7. First-cut abstractions were embedded into a rigid automated process to be supplemented by tools that extended hands-on analytical capabilities. This prepackaging of abstractions supported preliminary criteria for the classification of loan officers' performance, for the comparison of clients' deposits against their obligations, and for the much-desired assessment of client relationships.

Thus, upon its first full-scale collection and aggregation of data, the project had achieved these strategic deliverables:

- A framework for analyzing interrelated corporate client accounts (focused on credit services, but intended to accommodate non-credit analysis as data and principles evolved).
- A mapping of all existing corporate credit clients to that framework.
- Complete and accurate aggregated data, which could support exercise and refinement of the first-cut analytical model.
- Operational links for ongoing maintenance of that data.
- Hands-on technology by which business experts could continually explore and refine the analysis of credit-based relationships.
- A high-level view of compliance for corporate client families.

DATA MINING

The project had proceeded per plan, earning a reputation as an exemplary success. Having solidly positioned the bank as intended, the project team now started refocusing on the analysis of non-credit services to corporate clients. Per plan, custodianship for explorative data mining was transitioned to less senior business area resources.

RESULTS

Assessing credit relationships yielded immediate, dramatic results, due primarily to the bank's having (for the first time) comprehensive pictures of its client families. It uncovered numerous unfulfilled deposit obligations, which ABCBank rectified quickly, greatly increasing the bank's average available funds. Smaller gains were realized through financial penalties for clients who consistently failed to meet their obligations, and through the more accurate application of credit-pricing formulae.

Of course, these benefits were essentially one-time corrections of long-outstanding deficiencies, and operational management soon would take them for granted. For the moment, however, the highly visible 8-digit increase in available funds was impressive, and it further enhanced perceptions of the project.

The shining success soon clouded over, as the bank turned its attention to other issues. Foremost among these issues were the daily challenges it encountered in the non-credit arena, which long had been neglected by operations management. Contrary to expectations, the requisite analytical effort was challenging. Furthermore, issues invariably spanned the full operational breadth of the organization; progress was arduous at best. The work persistently outgrew schedules and budgets, and it ultimately threatened realization of the strategic plan, all the while demanding far more executive attention than predicted.

Increasingly diverting critical resources to the non-credit work, senior management began to neglect further exploration of credit relationships. Having already seen one sizeable payback, far in excess of project cost, the custodians did not feel compelled to seek more. Responsibility for analyzing credit relationships was again shifted, now to operational management, who lacked the time and inclination to focus on strategic outlooks. The prospecting elements of data mining ceased abruptly. No one took the time to refine the first-cut analytical models or seek predictive associations. Rather than exploiting the hands-on analytical tools, which did not conform to operational norms, management simply codified the preliminary model's prepackaged analysis, hoping to discover any remaining compliance gaps.

Thus, the first-cut abstractions became enshrined and assumed the role of a fixed application. With this role came the final shift in perception: what had once been a robust data mining effort was now merely another "management information system" adrift in the bank's operational morass. Not a front-line source of bank revenue, it was treated as a frill.

Events continued to outstrip the plan. Resources for collecting new operational data, or for supporting the fixed application, were sometimes unavailable. It no longer mattered. The quasi-application lingered for a time, without visible benefit. Eventually, it was simply ended: the separate-site environment shut down, the replicated data left to wither. No announcement, recognition, or explanation was necessary. Its failure was as silent as its success had been prominent.

REASONS FOR FAILURE

Despite having the tools to rate, compare, and explore corporate credit relationships, ABCBank had not pursued these core project (and strategic) objectives. In large part, this lack of commitment was due to the resistance of key players: the commercial loan officers. Each was responsible for dealing with a given set of clients, and was mandated to maximize both bank business and profit with these clients.

From the start, loan officers had universally objected to the premises of the contemplated analysis, because:

1. Negotiated terms reflected the basic dilemma of a competitive market: higher pricing drove clients to competitors, while lower pricing increased business. The first-cut model had not accommodated this fundamental consideration.
2. Even with the new decision-support capability, the bank still could not accurately measure the profitability of an overall client relationship. A credit-only view of clients was a distorted picture, and (due to the many difficulties of integrating the analysis of non-credit services) the distortion was not to go away in the foreseeable future.
3. In-depth exploration of client relationships, good or bad, seemed irrelevant in the field. It seemed far more valuable to try to understand clients' lines of business, needs, plans, etc., in the context of economies' volatile credit markets. Again, the template had not encompassed such comprehensive factors.
4. Clients were too dissimilar to warrant meaningful comparison. The many complex factors at work within large corporations, and their respective histories of dealings with ABCBank, created unique factors for negotiating with each client.
5. Similarly, it was not meaningful to rank a loan officer's performance, as each dealt with a different client base. No matter how an officer was rated, the officer's response never varied — "I negotiated the best terms that I could at the time."

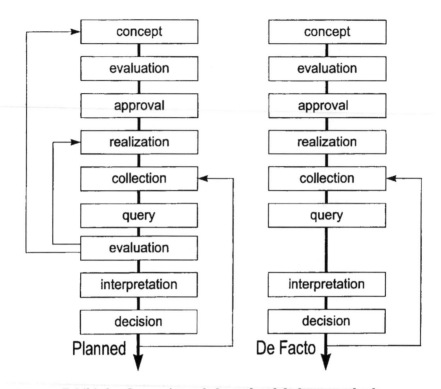

Exhibit 2.   Comparison of planned and de facto standards.

Unprepared to counter these arguments, bank management allowed the project's real analytical objectives to languish. It effectively decided that the first-cut analysis and assumptions, which were based on intuition and some preproject prospecting, were adequate for more than just the moment. The bank was now merely content to excavate the mine's lode, and — as inevitably happens — the lode was finally exhausted.

If a business ceases to explore, it cannot expect to discover further benefits from a data mining exercise. At the end of the day, ABCBank's management viewed its continuing investment as a poor one — it saw an operational system that had already outlived its one-time yield.

Exhibit 2 illustrates the impact of this decision. The opportunities for using feedback to bring forward the vision in which the project had first been conceived, to refine the analytical model or to substitute a more robust one, or even to explore classifications, were negated by eliminating the leftmost arrows on the diagram. Prospecting had been forsaken.

Although the compliance payback far offset project costs, the costs still seemed excessive — a planned throw-away effort with a narrow compliance focus would have been much cheaper. Yet, as costs had been recovered, no one felt compelled to analyze why work on the project ceased. No one thought it wise to comment on the failure to meet objectives, or to assess the consequent impact on ABCBank's strategic direction.

LEGACY: BENEFITS AND DAMAGE

In hindsight, the project did provide both strategic and operational benefits:

- After the initial recognition of widespread deposit noncompliance, wary loan officers and clients quickly learned to avoid ongoing compliance problems — an unforeseen benefit.
- Ultimately, the prolonged follow-up effort for non-credit services ended. Again, ABCBank had deferred data mining to an operational approach, but it nonetheless established a broader base of data about clients, which permitted some rudimentary assessments. This was largely built on the classifications and approaches to aggregation that had been developed earlier in the credit arena.
- Operational management began to appreciate the risks of dealing with large clients on diverse fronts (e.g., bank contact A, seeking to reinforce a client relationship, offers one service at a significant discount; bank contact B similarly discounts another service; C does the same, etc., so that the client relationship becomes uniformly unprofitable).

These benefits were balanced by negative impacts and uncertainties:

- The credit project's demise discouraged the spread of discovery-oriented practices. Non-credit "analysis" mutated into a purely operational system. Its success was attributed to the introduction of a new comprehensive client statement. Ironically, the new statement employed the client family concept to lever operational data to the client's advantage, not the bank's.
- Some key objectives of the strategic plan were never met. Clients and bank performance were not rated, nor was any additional discovery contemplated. In fact, the replicated, proto-warehouse nature of the original credit-services environment had more readily supported data mining than the new environment, which was constrained by production-world technologies.
  - After abruptly introducing more strict deposit compliance and penalizing clients, ABCBank did not contemplate the long-term impacts.
  - Had lax enforcement been an integral part of some client relationships?
  - Had foregoing full deposit compliance encouraged more profitable business with respect to other services?
  - Were relationships less or more profitable once strict enforcement was introduced?

The original data mining environment was poised to explore such questions, but the bank never asked them.

Lessons

Some of the apparent shortcomings of the project were inherent in the culture in which they were spawned:

- Years of success, bolstered by good performance in a changing marketplace, had bred complacency. Decision makers would have accepted anything related to the strategic plan, in which everyone had great faith. New phenomena, such as replicating data into an analytical framework, were accepted without being fully understood.
- The transitions demanded by the plan severely burdened executive visionaries. Sponsorship migrated steadily from exciting vision toward indifferent custodianship. Early project success aggravated this problem, encouraging management to neglect something that appeared to have its own momentum.
- With the bank overtaxed by the restructuring of its entire milieu, there was fierce internal competition for resources. A warehouse-like information environment was seen by many as a frivolous investment, and it became an easy political target.
- Rapid change permeated the organization, fostering the black-and-white mindset that was fatal to the project. Instead of taking the time to understand any effort's potential value, management focused on quick judgments of success or failure. In this case, the compliance payback offered management a political exit — even as they privately judged the project a failure, they could label it a success and quietly end it.

Other shortcomings stemmed from shortsighted project decisions and improperly managed expectations:

- While executives were making sweeping decisions about business direction, the commercial lending experts wanted to make black-and-white judgments about client relationships. Quantifying vague perceptions was a sound notion, but it led to a naive outlook. Executives were sold on the idea of rating clients and loan officers, not on the value of discovery.
- In hindsight, the initial prototype may have been biased in favor of the draft analytical model. Reinforcing that model early in the project served to further obscure the value of future prospecting.
- Deferring consideration of non-credit services seemed pragmatic to a steering body that had been selected for its expertise in the credit arena. People failed to appreciate the implications of not looking beyond their customary boundaries.

- Although sophisticated, the thinking that formed the original model was imperfect. Underlying the model was a substrate of traditional back-office concerns. The first-cut deliverables reflected this situation; instead of seeking a balanced client view across credit and non-credit engagements, operational questions were asked (Are clients complying? Which agreements are relevant?).
- Similarly, front-line questions (At what point will bank profitability drive clients to the competition?) were not addressed, although the collected data might have guided some vital investigations. When later faced with such business realities, the business experts lacked the ability and/or energy to revisit the model, despite being nominally prepared for such an evolution.

Ultimately, the vision that had conceived the project proved too limited to see the job through to the end.

CONCLUSION

Could the bank, or the project itself, have avoided all these shortcomings? Without previously enduring a strategic realignment of such magnitude, it does not seem likely. No one had anticipated all the exigencies that the strategic plan imposed. Management was simply too distracted. If the organization were to repeat the exercise now, it would be better prepared, and it might fare better.

On the other hand, certain problems were not unique to ABCBank, and are of interest to other data mining efforts. The project ought to have resolved or minimized them.

What could the project team have done to promote success?

- *Market exploratory data mining on its own terms.* Whereas business traditionally develops solution definitions for delineated problems, data mining targets unexpected insights that can lead to innovation. Thus, marketing the idea of data mining to potential sponsors may be difficult. The bank's project promised rigid queries that implied predefined paybacks. This approach sold the project, but it undersold data mining. The business bought the queries, rather than the process.
- *Find appropriate sponsors and educate them.* Visibility — the bank president actually participated in the early conceptualizations — proved to be a mixed blessing. The resulting impetus encouraged the unfortunate decision to defer non-credit analysis. A high-level study of this area could have been integrated into the project with little impact on the schedule; such a study probably would have alerted senior management to the problems that lay ahead. Moreover, although visionaries, the senior executives had very strong operational footings — they could see far, but they all tended to stand in the same place. Commit-

ting to a process like data mining, as opposed to an operational solution, was a foreign concept. Under pressure, they relapsed into an operational perspective.

- *Manage expectations of technology.* Mining tools — parallel processing, very large databases, specialized tools for time-series analysis, and related phenomena — quickly acquire promising reputations. Their promise may do them a disservice, however, for it encourages businesses to seek quick remedies for complex situations. The promise may prevent the realization that unknowns make prospecting a continuing phenomenon. ABCBank overlooked this fact.
- *Secure lasting commitments and resources.* Competition for skills and expertise exists in any organization, threatening resource commitments. Because it is inherently open-ended, data mining may be particularly susceptible to such threats. The project team enjoyed conceptualization, construction, and initial discovery, but they disliked prolonged exploration of the same data (perhaps because it might lead to doubts about their preconceptions). They were happy to move on to new problems — as was their management — leaving behind an analytical vacuum.
- *Hear the concerns of all key players.* The business team was expert in the financial principles of commercial lending expertise, but it was blindly biased. There was little consultation with loan officers, and it never did appreciate some of their primary concerns. The team's first-cut model was deficient and did not deserve to be enshrined. Not improving the model precluded its acquiring necessary strategic value.

Perhaps this final point was the project's greatest failing. In retrospect, the very heart of the project — the idea that the back office would evaluate multimillion-dollar front-line decisions, based on incomplete data — was never practical.

Chapter 67
Data Mining: Knowledge Discovery in Databases

Patricia L. Carbone

AN AREA OF RESEARCH THAT HAS SEEN A RECENT SURGE IN COMMERCIAL DEVELOPMENT IS DATA MINING, or knowledge discovery in databases (KDD). Knowledge discovery has been defined as "the nontrivial extraction of implicit, previously unknown, and potentially useful information from data." To do this extraction, data mining combines artificial intelligence, statistical analysis, and database management systems to attempt to pull knowledge from stored data.

MOVING TOWARD TERABYTE AND GREATER DATABASES

One may distinguish between data and knowledge by defining data as corresponding to real-world observations, being dynamic and quite detailed; whereas knowledge is less precise, more static, and deals with generalizations or abstractions of the data. A number of terms have been used in place of data mining, including *information harvesting, data archaeology, knowledge mining,* and *knowledge extraction.* In fact, all the terms imply the process of sifting through potentially vast quantities of raw material (i.e., the data) and extracting the "gems" or useful knowledge that can drive an executive's decision-making.

Data mining continues to receive enormous attention by both commercial and scientific communities for three reasons. First, both the number and size of databases in many organizations are growing at a staggering rate. Terabyte and even petabyte databases, once unthinkable, are now becoming a reality in a variety of domains, including marketing, sales, finance, healthcare, earth science, molecular biology (e.g., the human

0-8493-9976-9/99/$0.00+$.50
© 1999 by CRC Press LLC

genome project), and various government applications. Second, organizations have realized that there is valuable knowledge buried in the data that, if discovered, could provide those organizations with competitive advantage. Third, some of the enabling technologies have only recently become mature enough to make data mining possible on large data sets.

TECHNOLOGIES ENABLING NEW APPLICATIONS

Data mining combines many different technologies to perform the desired analyses. In addition to artificial intelligence, statistics, and database management, technologies include data warehousing and online analytical processing (OLAP), human computer interaction and data visualization, machine learning (especially inductive learning techniques), knowledge representation, pattern recognition, and intelligent agents.

Examples of data mining applications include:

- *Customer segmentation.* Retailers, credit card companies, banks, and other such organizations are very interested in determining if there are groups or clusters of people who exhibit certain similar characteristics. For example, banks and credit card companies use classification for credit scoring to create segments of those customers that are better credit risks than others. Factors that are analyzed include income, current debt, past payment history, and potentially even geographic area and other demographics.
- *Relationship management.* Retailers and advertisers are interested in the buying patterns of customers. Such attributes that are analyzed include items purchased, dates of purchase, and the type of payment. These attributes can perhaps be used in combination with the customer segments described above. Based on certain buying patterns, such as seasonal purchases of camping equipment by upper middle-class people in the northeastern U.S., retailers and advertisers can better target their advertising dollars toward specific media, items, or geographic areas to capture the customers they want to attract. Relationship management is becoming of particular interest in the electronic commerce world.

These types of analyses have typically been performed by human analysts, and the process is time-consuming and tedious at best. Therefore, many organizations are looking to partially automate the process of extracting knowledge from data.

THE PROCESS OF KNOWLEDGE DISCOVERY IN DATABASES (KDD)

Data mining is actually a step in a larger *KDD process*. The KDD process uses data mining methods or algorithms to extract or identify knowledge according to some criteria or measure of "interestingness," but it also includes steps that prepare the data, such as preprocessing, subsampling, and transformations of the database. To follow one particular example, consider the application of credit card fraud, or determining when credit card users are purchasing items with a stolen credit card. (Note that while this example is realistic for the purposes of understanding, it is not based on any actual data.)

Targeting Data

To begin the KDD process, the application or analysis must first have an overall purpose or set of goals. For the credit card fraud example, the purpose of the analysis would be to identify those customers with credit card usage patterns that differ from previously established usage patterns. Databases must be identified that contain the desired data to be analyzed. In this example, incoming credit card transactions must be analyzed to halt fraud immediately. In addition, to identify the fraud trends, historical data should be examined.

The first step in the KDD process is to select data to be analyzed from the set of all available data. In many cases, the data are stored in transaction databases, such as those databases that process all incoming credit card transactions. These databases are quite large and extremely dynamic. In addition, there may be several different transaction databases running simultaneously at various sites. Again, with the credit card example, large credit card companies typically have several processing sites to handle specific geographic areas. Therefore, a subset of data must be selected from those databases, since it is unnecessary in the early stages to attempt to analyze all data.

Target data are then moved to a cache or another database for further preprocessing. Preprocessing is an extremely important step in the KDD process. Often, data have errors introduced during the input process, either from a data entry clerk entering data incorrectly or from a faulty data collection device. If target data are being extracted from several source databases, the databases can often be inconsistent with each other in terms of their data models, the semantics of the attributes, or in the way the data are represented in the database.

As an example of the data models being inconsistent, a credit card company may have two different sites handling transactions. If the two databases were built at different times and following different guidelines, it is entirely possible that they may be two different data models (relational and object-oriented) and two different representations of the entities or objects and their relationships to each other (e.g., a customer-centric view vs. an account-centric view).

As an example of the differences in the way the data may be entered into the database, it is possible for the same customer to be represented in the two databases in different ways. In one database, the name *field* may contain the last name of the customer only. In another database, the name field may contain the first name followed by the last name. The preprocessing step should identify these differences and make the data consistent and clean.

The data can often be transformed for use with different analysis techniques. A number of separate tables can be joined into one table, or vice versa. An attribute that may be represented in two different forms (i.e., date written as 3/15/97 versus 15-3-1997) should be transformed into a common format. If the data are represented as text, but it is intended to use a data mining technique that requires the data to be in numerical form, the data must be transformed accordingly.

At this point, data mining algorithms can be used to discover knowledge (e.g., trends, patterns, characteristics, or anomalies). The appropriate discovery or data mining algorithms should be identified, as they should be pertinent to the purpose of the analysis and to the type of data to be analyzed. In the example, an algorithm could be chosen that would automatically look for clusters of behavior in the data.

This type of algorithm might find, for example, a set of customers that makes relatively low numbers of purchases over time, a set of customers that make large numbers of purchases over time, and a set of customers that make large numbers of purchases in very short periods of time. These behaviors could be examined further to determine whether any of the patterns is representative of credit card fraud behavior. If subsets of data have been established that represent fraud behavior versus normal usage, algorithms can be used that would automatically identify differences between the sets for discrimination purposes. Again, in the example, in looking at two sets of data, the algorithm might characterize fraud behavior as numerous purchases over a short period of time and often in a different geographic area than the user typically shops, as opposed to credit card usage that is relatively consistent for that user over time.

Often, the data mining algorithms work more effectively if they have some amount of domain information available containing information on attributes that have higher priority than others, attributes that are not important at all, or established relationships that are already known. In the credit card fraud example, domain information might include a known relationship between the number of purchases and a period of time. Domain information is often collected in a *knowledge base*, a storage mechanism similar to a database but used to store domain information and other knowledge.

When a pattern is identified, it should be examined to determine whether it is new, relevant, and "correct" by some standard of measure. The interpretation and evaluation step may involve more interaction with a user or with some agent of the user who can make relevancy determinations. When the pattern is deemed relevant and useful, it can be deemed *knowledge*. The knowledge should be placed in the knowledge base for use in subsequent iterations. Note that the entire KDD process is iterative; at many of the steps, there may be a need to go back to a previous step since no patterns may be discovered and new data should be selected for additional analyses, or the patterns that are discovered may not be relevant.

In many steps of the KDD process, it is essential to provide good visualization support to the user. This is important for two reasons. First, without such visualizations, it may be difficult for users to determine the usefulness of discovered knowledge — often a picture *is* worth a thousand words. Second, given good visualization tools, the user can discover things that automated data mining tools may be unable to discover. Working as a team, the user and automated discovery tools provide far more powerful data mining capabilities than either can provide alone.

RELATIONSHIPS TO OTHER RESEARCH AREAS

The area of data mining draws from the technical capabilities of a number of other research areas. This section describes the contributions of database management, statistics, and artificial intelligence to data mining.

Contributions of Database Management

One of the basic differences between machine learning and data mining or knowledge discovery in databases is the fact that analysis or learning (the induction of patterns) is being performed on database systems, rather than on specifically formatted file structures of the data for use with one algorithm. Database management systems (DBMSs) provide a number of essential capabilities to data mining, including persistent storage; a data model (e.g., relational or object-oriented), which permits data to be managed using a *logical* rather than physical view; and a high-level query language (e.g., SQL), which allows users to request *what* data they want without having to write complex programs specifying *how* to access it. In addition, database management systems provide transaction management and constraint enforcement to help preserve the integrity of the data. Database technology also provides efficient access to large quantities of data.

As discussed in the previous section, the KDD process implies that one is performing knowledge discovery against data that resides in one or more large databases. Typical properties of databases that complicate knowledge discovery include:

- *Large volume.* Databases are capable of storing terabytes, and now petabytes, of data, therefore requiring a need to focus or preprocess the data.
- *Noise and uncertainty.* As discussed in the previous section, noise can be introduced by faulty data collection devices. This causes uncertainty as to the consistency of the data.
- *Redundant information.* For a variety of reasons, data can be stored multiple times, causing redundant information. This is especially a problem if there are multiple source databases.
- *Dynamic data.* Transaction databases are specifically set up to process millions of transactions per hour, thus causing difficulty for data mining tools that are oriented to look at static sets of data.
- *Sparse data.* The information in the database is often sparse in terms of the density of actual records over the potential instance space.
- *Multimedia data.* DBMSs are increasingly capable of storing more than just structured data. For example, text documents, images, spatial data, video, and audio can now be stored as objects in databases, and these databases are used to handle World Wide Web sites. It is becoming extremely desirable to mine this data in addition to the traditional structured data.

Recent advances in data warehousing, parallel databases, and online analytical processing tools have greatly increased the efficiency with which databases can support the large numbers of extremely complex queries that are typical of data mining applications. Databases provide a metadata description that can be used to help understand the data to be mined, and can also aid in determining how the database should potentially change (e.g., its schema, indices, the location of data, etc.), based on what has been learned.

Data Warehouses

Data warehousing is a technology that is currently being employed at a growing number of large firms. Data warehouses are extremely large DBMSs designed to hold historical data. The data model for the data warehouse is oriented to support the processing of analyses and potentially complex queries (known as online analytical processing, or OLAP), as opposed to handling large numbers of updates (which is the purpose of traditional online transaction processing, or OLTP, databases). Because the data is stored over time, the data warehouse must support temporal queries.

As an example, a data warehouse was created for a company with transaction processing dispersed to numerous sites. The process for creating and maintaining the warehouse involves selecting the data from the source databases that will be stored in the warehouse. The selection process involves replicating the new data in the transaction databases at some regular interval for further processing. Once selected, the data are passed through applications that scrub the data to ensure the warehouse is clean (error-free) and consistent. The fusion applications draw the data from the separate databases together into one model for storage in the warehouse. Note that the extraction, scrubbing, and fusion parts of the data warehousing process match the selection, preprocessing, and transformation parts of the KDD process.

Once a data warehouse has been created, an organization can create smaller views of the warehouse that are oriented toward a particular function. These more-focused views are called data marts.

It is important to note that data warehouses are increasingly being used to store not only structured data that is collected from transaction databases, but also textual data. Several vendors have constructed large DBMSs that can be used for data warehousing and also to perform data management for an Internet Web site. In addition, online analysis processing tools are being extended to handle not only temporal and spatial queries as part of the complex query and analysis process, but also to perform textual queries.

Metadata Repositories

An important technology associated with data warehousing that could potentially be better utilized in data mining is that of the metadata repository. The metadata repository is essentially a database that contains information about the data models of the transaction databases, the data warehouse, and any data marts. The information can include the meanings of the attributes, agreed-upon conventions for attribute representation, and relationships among attributes, tables, and databases. Metadata can also contain information regarding the rankings of attributes (e.g., attribute "X" from the western U.S. database is often more current than the same attribute "X" from the northcentral American database), or even the validity of the sources of the data.

The goal of the metadata repository is to aid in maintaining consistency among the data warehouse, data marts, source databases, and any analysis applications. Applications performing the selection, scrubbing, and fusion functions rely on input from the metadata repository for criteria on the extent to which the data must be cleaned and transformed.

As discussed earlier, many data mining algorithms can employ domain information when it is available to aid in the analysis of the data. The information in the metadata repository is similar to the domain information and should be used by the data mining algorithms. Some research on data mining techniques includes the use of metadata.

Contributions of Statistics

The area of statistics is an important one to data mining. For many years, statistical methods have been the primary means for analyzing data. Statistical analysis methods are still the standard means of analysis for determining credit scores for loan or credit card companies, for analyzing clinical trials data when determining whether a drug should or should not be approved by the Food and Drug Administration, and for performing other types of market-basket analysis and customer segmentation.

Statistical methods differ from machine learning techniques (discussed in the next section) in that the user must typically have a hypothesis of the attributes that are in relationship to each other, then search the data for the mathematical expression that describes the relationship. In some data mining systems, this is called "top-down" learning.

There are three basic classes of statistical techniques with implementations used in data mining today: linear, nonlinear, and decision trees. Linear models describe samples of data, or the relationship among the attributes or predictors, in terms of a plane so that the model becomes a global consensus of the pattern of the data. Linear modeling techniques include linear regression (for prediction) and linear discriminent analysis (for classification). The linear function discriminates between people committing credit card fraud and normal credit card purchases in terms of two variables, time and number of purchases. Recent advances in this area allow a model to adapt to data that involve multiple attributes (multivariable linear regression) or that are not described easily by only one linear function and may need several functions (e.g., a different function for each time period).

Nonlinear or nonparametric methods characterize data by referring to existing data when a new point is received in order to estimate the response of that point. An example of this is a higher order regression curve. Another example is the nearest-neighbor. In the nearest-neighbor technique, a new point is matched against existing data. Based on proximity to already-characterized data, the new point is classified as being fraudulent usage or normal usage.

A variation on nonlinear techniques is the creation of decision trees. Decision trees describe a set of data in terms of a set of decision points. Based on the response to the decision point, the data are subdivided into regions. In the statistical community, Classification and Regression Tree (CART) algorithms are used to build decision trees.

Very popular commercial tools used for statistical analysis include SAS and SPSS. Other commercial tools include S/S-Plus, MATlab, and DataDesk.

Contributions of Artificial Intelligence. Artificial intelligence (AI) technology provides many capabilities that support the KDD process. Principally, these contributions are in the more specific fields of machine learning and visualization.

Machine Learning

As opposed to statistical techniques, that perform a "top-down" analysis approach, machine learning techniques do not need *a priori* knowledge of possible attribute relationships, thus providing a "bottom-up" analysis approach. Machine learning techniques are automated systems that use artificial intelligence search techniques to look for patterns and relationships in the data. These search techniques should be flexible and employ adaptive or heuristic control strategies to determine what subset of the data to focus on or what hypothesis to test next.

Machine learning techniques are able to perform several types of discoveries. They can generalize, or produce a more generalized set of rules or patterns to describe a specific set of data. A more specialized case of generalization would be to be able to predict. Generalization is typically an inductive process. Deduction occurs when there is a pattern such that if A implies B, and B implies C, then one can deduce that the existence of A will imply the existence of C. However, if C exists, one can only deduce that A exists also. For example, given a set of data that describes a series of events in time, the system deduces that an event at a later time may be correlated to the original pattern. As an example of generalization, a set of data may describe valid credit card usage, and an algorithm could learn that purchases are generally spread over a longer period of time in a regional area near where the customer resides.

The algorithms can also cluster data. Given data that describe specific instances, the system can identify groups of instances that are more similar to each other than to instances in other groups.

Models that are discovered are represented in a knowledge representation language that is sufficient to allow description of the model. These representations include symbolic ones (e.g., rules, decision trees, semantic networks), neural networks, and mathematical models. If the representation language is too limited, then the model will not be accurate enough to describe the data. Finally, the machine learning technique must evaluate how well a discovered pattern actually describes the data. The evaluation can include how accurately the model is able to perform prediction, utility of the model, and understandability.

Systems that employ symbolic representation of the data such as rules or decision trees are quite easy to understand by a user, particularly if the variables being tested have threshold splits (i.e., a threshold split applied to the number of purchases variable). Of course, the larger the number of attributes represented in the rules or trees, or the more complex the split descriptions, then the more complicated the rule or decision tree representation will actually be. Commercial tools that provide a rule-based output include WizSoft's WizWhy, REDUCT and Lobbe Technologies' Datalogic, and Information Discovery's IDIS. Commercial tools that employ the use of decision trees include Isoft S.A.'s AC2, Angoss Software's KnowledgeSeeker, and NASA COSMIC's IND. Commercial tools that cluster data include NASA Ames Research Center's Autoclass III and COSMIC's COB-WEB/3.

Neural Networks. Neural networks are quite popular in the field of credit card fraud detection, as they are easily trainable and quite fast at processing incoming data. Neural networks can be trained to perform classification and other such tasks. The problem in the past, however, has been that one cannot see inside a neural network in the same way as with rules or trees to understand how the algorithm is classifying and where it may fail. Recently, however, neural networks have been expanded to output a rule representation of the learned model. Some popular commercial neural network packages include Right Information System's 4Thought, NeuralWare Inc.'s NeuralWorks Professional II/Plus, and California Scientific Software's Brain-Maker, in addition to neural network components for SPSS and MATLAB.

Multistrategy Learning. Because each type of machine learning technique has positive and negative aspects, depending on the type of data being analyzed and the goal for the learning, it is increasingly desirable to employ more than one technique during a data mining session. *Multistrategy learning* allows a high-level controller to choose two or more machine learning algorithms to be applied to the data, based on characteristics of the data, the available algorithms, and the goals for the learning. Although there is no fully automated tool that will perform multistrategy learning without user intervention, more commercial tools are including multiple techniques in the overall package. Some of these tools include Thinking Machine Corporation's Darwin, Integral Solutions' Clementine, IBM's Intelligent Miner, and Information Discovery Inc.'s Data Mining Suite.

Limitations of Machine Learning. Having pointed out the benefits of machine learning to data mining, it is important to note that these techniques also have limitations. Machine learning can only learn or discover general categories of things for which they are programmed to look. The representation language, as pointed out earlier, can limit the effectiveness or expressiveness of the model of learned behavior. Also, learning algorithms have a learning bias, so they are not always effective on all problems.

Visualization

A picture is worth a thousand words, as the old saying goes. This is particularly true in the area of data mining. Many tools are currently being developed that allow a user to interact with the data and the way that data are portrayed on the screen. One such method employed for a number of years is link analysis. Link analysis portrays relationships among data in terms of links connecting nodes. For example, if an analyst wanted to look at telephone call records using link analysis, the number from which the calls were made would be displayed in the center of the screen with links to all numbers that were called. Depending on the number of times a number was called, the link between the two numbers might be heavier or lighter or color-coded in some manner. This method of portraying the data would allow an analyst to make connections that are not readily visible by simply looking at tables of numbers.

Increasing research is being done to find more effective ways to portray data. Interactive visualization allows a user to change the attributes shown on a screen, or the scale of the attributes. Users can change the scales on the axes of a chart or zoom in on particular portions of the data in order to get a better understanding.

Virtual reality is increasingly being touted as the future way to perform visual analysis of the data. The idea is to allow users to "fly through," touch, and manipulate the data to see relationships that were not previously visible from a 2- or 3-dimensional representation. Virtual reality may be a method that is used in the future to perform data mining against large amounts of textual documents such as those available on the Internet. The visualization technique would group documents according to some criteria, then allow the data to move through those groupings in order to better choose the desired publication — similar to looking through a library in order to select a book.

Commercial tools are becoming more mature in their capability to provide more effective mechanisms for data display. Some of the tools include ALTA Analytics' NetMap, IBM's DX: Visualization Data Explorer, Artificial Intelligence Software's VisualMine, Data Desk, Belmont Research's Cross-Graphs, and Information Technology Institute's WinViz.

PRACTICAL APPLICATIONS OF DATA MINING

Many successful systems have been constructed and are now in daily use in a variety of domains. For example, A. C. Nielson has a system called OpportunityExplorer that analyzes retail point-of-sale information to help formulate marketing strategies. Customers for such systems include retailers, advertisers, and product producers, to name a few. IBM's Intelligent Miner is being used by retail stores to better analyze customer buying trends and product popularity. NCR has also been doing research in this area and has developed tools to aid their retail customers.

Another interesting application is the use of data mining by the Traveler's Insurance Company to determine the cost of hurricane insurance to various coastal locations, based on analyses of historical hurricane tracks and the amount of damage caused to coastal areas.

There has been a great deal of activity in the area of analyzing dynamic financial markets, but little of it has been publicized (because of the huge financial gains that can result from even a slight competitive advantage). The Lockheed Artificial Intelligence Center has a system called Recon that has recently been moved from the research lab to become a commercial product. Recon has been used in a number of applications, including one to select a stock portfolio. Currently, that application analyzes both historical and current, dynamic data on thousands of stocks and makes recommendations for stocks to purchase by predicting stocks that may do well based on certain predictors. Typically, this area has been dominated by the use of statistical analysis, although neural networks and are also being explored for this domain.

In the area of credit cards and loans, there is the application involving credit scoring and credit card fraud detection. In these areas, statistical analysis and neural networks are quite popular. Neural networks have proven quite efficient at being able to distinguish between good and bad credit risks, and between valid and illegal credit card purchases. The neural network is trained based on collected data that characterizes the types of credit risks or the types of credit card purchases. HNC has a popular neural network application being used by credit card companies for both credit scoring and fraud detection that has proven quite accurate and very able to handle the immense numbers of transactions that are being processed.

Many organizations have become extremely interested in the reduction, analysis, and classification of data in large scientific databases. For example, the SKICAT at NASA's Jet Propulsion Laboratory was developed to catalog sky objects from the 2nd Palomar Sky Survey. The input to the system is a digitized photographic plate, and the output is a set of catalog entries for all objects in the image (e.g., stars, galaxies, or other artifacts). SKICAT has been used successfully with a 3-terabyte astronomical data set and has generated catalogs on billions of objects, including 2×10^7 galaxies, 2×10^8 stars, and 10^5 quasars.

In addition to these and other specific applications, there are general-purpose toolkits for building KDD applications. Many of the tools discussed in the previous section are applicable for use in a variety of domains, including financial and banking applications, the petroleum industry, and in marketing analyses, among others. The limiting factor on any use of a data mining tool is to ensure that the appropriate tool is being used with the given data and goals for the analysis.

Information Retrieval and Text Processing

Information retrieval has typically been concerned with finding better techniques to query for and retrieve textual documents based on their content. Data mining is being applied to this area so that the vast amounts of electronic publications currently available may be brought to users' attention in a more efficient manner.

Data mining and information retrieval are being merged to provide a more intelligent "push" of information to a user. Information retrieval techniques have included the use of a user profile to help focus a search for pertinent documents. The addition of data mining techniques to the creation of a profile is currently being researched to improve the documents that are retrieved or brought to the user's attention. For example, if a user's profile shows that a user is interested in reading articles with the topics of "football," "baseball," and "soccer," a data mining algorithm could generalize these specific topics to "organized outdoor team sports." This type of generalization is increasingly necessary when one considers that topics of interest can change over time (i.e., the three above-mentioned sports are typically run during specific seasons), so the data mining can allow the profile to be more proactive.

SUMMARY

Data mining is a "hot topic" in both the research and commercial worlds. It is getting a lot of attention, both because the needs are so great and because technology is just getting mature enough to be able to make a significant difference. This chapter has provided an overview of data mining and how it fits into an overall knowledge discovery in databases (KDD) process, and has included some application examples.

There are a number of resources available to readers who would like to remain current on the latest developments in this fast evolving area. Those with access to the Internet can explore the Knowledge Discovery Mine, a World Wide Web home page maintained by Gregory Piatetsky-Shapiro of GTE Labs. This page has a great deal of information on both research projects and commercial products, and it has links to many other Internet resources related to data mining: `http://info.gte.com/~kdd`. There are also additional books on data mining and knowledge discovery that are quite readable and highly recommended.

ACKNOWLEDGMENTS

The author thanks David Duff and Eric Bloedorn for their helpful comments. Of course, any remaining shortcomings are the responsibility of the author. The author also thanks Len Seligman for work on the previous version of this chapter.

Chapter 68

Multimedia Databases and Data Mining

Venkat N. Gudivada
Yongjian Fu

THE TERM UNIVERSAL SERVER IS FAST BECOMING ACCEPTED as a generic description of user-customizable multimedia add-ons to the RDBMS model. The use of data extensions to manage unstructured data is being implemented by the major DBMS vendors. This chapter explains the characteristics of multimedia data types and other approaches to database management that further expand on this universal technology strategy. A special area with very relevant application of the multimedia database approach is also discussed: data mining.

MULTIMEDIA CONTENT-BASED RETRIEVAL

Faster processor speeds, enormous increases in the capacity of secondary storage devices, and the emergence of CD-ROM and optical disks are contributing to the rise in the production of multimedia, which includes text, graphics, audio, and video, among other data types. More multimedia information sources are being made available for online access through the World Wide Web; with the proliferation of multimedia on the desktop, multimedia data will soon be as common to computers as text data.

Multimedia database systems are expected to coherently handle these disparate data types and provide content-based access to the data. Content-based multimedia information retrieval (CBMIR) means that the system retrieves information according to the textual, visual, auditory, and semantic contents of the media. This content is interpreted at suitable levels of abstraction, but transparently to the user. Relevance of retrieved data may be judged differently by different users, even if an identically formulated query is performed. The notion of relevance is thus subjective and dynamic, and depends on the particular user's retrieval need and context. Semantic correlation across media types is essential to CBMIR.

Tools and techniques for multimedia data organization, search, retrieval, and presentation comprise the enabling technologies of CBMIR. However, they have not kept pace with the insatiable quest for multimedia data generation. The severity of this problem can be seen in the limitations of current tools for searching the Web. Advances in CBMIR are essential to developing multimedia database systems because CBMIR constitutes the primary component of a multimedia database system.

CHARACTERISTICS OF MULTIMEDIA DATA MANAGEMENT SYSTEMS

In contrast to relational and object-oriented systems, multimedia data management systems are defined by the following characteristics:

- *Data model heterogeneity.* Each multimedia data type requires a data model and associated retrieval model that suit its intrinsic nature. However, these disparate data and retrieval models need to be integrated using a layer of abstraction.
- *Temporal nature of data.* Time dimension is intrinsic to image sequences, audio, and video. This has several implications, including the need for intra- and intermedia synchronization for presentation of media on output devices. This affects algorithms and protocols for multimedia servers and communications networks.
- *Feature extraction and semantics capture.* The ability to extract required features and semantics automatically or semiautomatically from multimedia data is necessary for developing large multimedia database systems.
- *Query processing and similarity measures.* Queries are processed and rank-ordered based on some notion of similarity. What features contribute to similarity and the degree of their contribution greatly affect the quality of retrieval.
- *Multimodal query language or specification scheme.* Content-based retrieval is characterized by various generic query operators (e.g., retrieval by color, shape, or spatial relationships). Each operator requires a specification scheme that is intrinsic to its nature. However, these schemes need to be integrated to provide a unified view of querying multimedia data. In contrast with conventional database systems, browsing is commonly used for exploitative querying of multimedia databases. Also, the display of query results is often required in the form of a multimedia presentation, and the query specification scheme is expected to provide this functionality.
- *Indexing structures for efficient query processing.* Not all multimedia data features are suitable for indexing using B-tree or R-tree based methods, especially those that represent spatial and topological rela-

tionships in images and video. Mapping methods are required to transform complex multimedia features into ordered domains so that B-tree or R-tree–based indexing methods can be used.

- *User subjectivity in multimedia data interpretation.* A user's interpretation of multimedia data may differ from its stored interpretation. For example, in an image database of police mugshots, a feature named *nose length* may have one value — "long" — recorded in the database, whereas a system user may interpret this value as "normal." User queries tend to be subjective, imprecise, and uncertain.
- *Distribution issues.* Multidatabase solutions are a possibility for distributed multimedia data management. However, multimedia collections on the Web are not managed by database management systems, which is usually the case in multiple databases.
- *Tertiary storage management.* Because of the voluminous nature of multimedia data, it is not practical or economical to store all the data on secondary storage devices. For example, 30 minutes of high-quality uncompressed video requires about 50G bytes of disk storage. Data migration strategies between tertiary-secondary-primary memory assume paramount importance to meet temporal media synchronization and performance requirements. Compression algorithms are also vital to keep the storage requirements affordable for multimedia applications.

THREE VIEWS OF MULTIMEDIA DATA

Multimedia data management can be broadly categorized into approaches: 1) image processing and pattern recognition, 2) database, and 3) information retrieval. To better explain the distinctive characteristics of these approaches, they are considered in the context of the three views of multimedia data:

- *Structured data.* Structured data are usually managed by a relational data management system. These include character strings and numeric data types. Internal representations for and operations on these data types are well understood.
- *Semistructured data.* Semistructured data fall somewhere in between and includes, for example, E-mail messages, Usenet newsgroup postings, and tagged or markup text such as hypertext markup language (HTML) or virtual reality markup language (VRML). The tags or markup in the semistructured data are primarily intended to provide one specific function. For example, HTML is intended for authoring documents that can be rendered on a variety of output devices of heterogeneous computers dispersed in a global communications network. However, some of these tags can also be used for extracting terms that represent the content of an HTML document (e.g., title and heading tags).

- *Unstructured data.* Unstructured data is simply a bit stream. Examples include pixel-level representations for images, video, and audio, and character-level representation for text. Substantial processing and interpretation are required to extract semantics from unstructured data.

The Image Processing and Pattern Recognition Approach

The image processing and pattern recognition approach to multimedia data management views multimedia data as unstructured. This approach relies on various image processing and pattern recognition techniques to automatically extract features from unstructured data. In other words, the approach transforms unstructured data to semistructured data and uses it to process user queries. The features that can be extracted automatically are usually primitive and geometry based.

The Database Approach

The database approach views multimedia data as structured. Features are usually extracted manually or semiautomatically. The features, referred to as attributes, entail a high level of abstraction on unstructured data. The higher the level of abstraction in the features, the lower the scope for ad hoc queries.

The Information Retrieval Approach

The information retrieval approach views multimedia data as semistructured, which is primarily in the form of keywords, specially crafted captions, or free-form text. This semistructured data may naturally be associated with multimedia data or can be derived manually.

User queries are processed using information retrieval models that range from the simple Boolean search to sophisticated vector processing. Natural language processing techniques are often used to assign content descriptors to the text associated with multimedia data. Although visual and auditory information is reduced to textual form, this approach is widely used because it benefits from the extensive research on text retrieval. Also, this approach has special appeal — image, audio, and video data co-occurs with text, which is the predominant data type in many applications.

Vendor Strategies

Almost all major commercial database vendors are making claims that their products can manage multimedia data and support content-based queries. However, the reality is that most vendors have more work to do to fully support multimedia.

Many database vendors and their products — including CA-Ingres, DB2/6000 C/S, Informix/Illustra, ODB II, Odapter, Omniscience, Oracle

Corp., UniSQL, and Versant — do indeed provide functionality for integrated storage of multimedia data with conventional string and numeric data. Some systems have advanced to support content-based queries.

Datablades and Data Cartidges. Informix/Illustra packages a collection of user-defined data types, functions, and the access methods associated with them as *datablades*. Datablades encapsulate application-specific functionality transparently to the database users and application programs.

The notion of datablades is more general than the concept of an abstract data type (ADT). Datablades are an integral part of the database engine and are not opaque to the query optimizer. The query optimizer can use the user-defined access methods associated with the datablades in deciding an optimal plan for the execution of a query.

Furthermore, datablades and the database engine share the same type system and possibly execute in the same address space. In contrast, ADTs and the DBMS engine have separate type systems and execute in different address spaces. Though the ADT approach reduces the security risk, performance suffers.

Incorporating base type extensions into a relational or object-oriented DBMS is neither a simple nor straightforward task. The biggest challenge lies in making the query optimizer treat the base type extensions as native to the DBMS. Multimedia representations and associated operations for content-based retrieval vary widely across applications. Therefore, it is conceivable that a DBMS is required to support a large number of base type extensions. To provide the ability to add a new base type or an operation associated with the base type to the DBMS (without the need for system shutdown), as well as to contain the size of the DBMS, the DBMS should be capable of dynamically linking the user-defined base type extensions.

Incorporating base type extensions entails choices in the client/server architecture and has implications for system security. For example, where do the functions associated with base type extensions execute? There are two possibilities: client-side activation and server-side activation. Client-side activation is desirable when the function is computationally intensive, does not make frequent calls to the DBMS, and the bandwidth required to transfer data from the server to the client is insignificant. The security concern for client-side activation is not as serious as that associated with the server-side activation.

There are two options for server-side activation. First, the function can be activated in the same address space as the DBMS. The function call is then essentially a local procedure call with little overhead. However, this option has the potential for creating a grave security loophole since the function may accidentally or intentionally erase or modify the data in the database. Second, the function can be run in a different address space or on a different machine. Then a remote procedure call (RPC) must be used and the performance degradation of the DBMS depends on the overhead associated with the RPC.

DBMSs from the major vendors differ in their approach to content-based querying of multimedia data. The Informix Universal Server seems to be ahead of others (in fact, the term *universal server,* coined by Informix to label its new product line, is becoming widely accepted as a generic description of similar multimedia add-ons). Informix offers text, image, spatial (2D or 3D), visual information retrieval, and Web datablades; many more are being developed by independent software vendors. Similar functionality has been announced by Oracle, which refers to its offerings as *data cartridges.*

The real challenge to truly harnessing multimedia information lies in establishing cross-correlation among various data types (i.e., heterogeneous information integration). The current vendor approaches provide a piecemeal solution (based on the data type) to the multimedia data management. The development of datablades and data cartridges is only a beginning. It will be some time before all the defining characteristics described earlier in this chapter are featured in a multimedia DBMS.

DATA MINING

Data mining, a primary component of a larger process referred to as knowledge discovery in databases (KDD), is the effort to understand, analyze, and eventually make use of the huge volumes of the data that reside in databases.

There is a rapidly growing interest in data mining from both the academic and industrial communities. KDD is the process of identifying valid, novel, potentially useful, and ultimately understandable patterns in data. Steps in a KDD process include data selection, preprocessing, transformation, data mining, and interpretation/evaluation of the results, as shown in Exhibit 1. Because data mining is the central part of the KDD process, it is often used as a synonym for knowledge discovery from databases.

A data mining system includes a user interface, a search engine, and a data management component. The architecture of a typical data mining system is shown in Exhibit 2. A data mining session is usually an interactive process of data mining query submission, task analysis, data collection, interesting pattern search, and findings presentation.

Data Mining Tasks

Data mining tasks can be classified based on the kind of knowledge a user is looking for. The most common types of data mining tasks are:

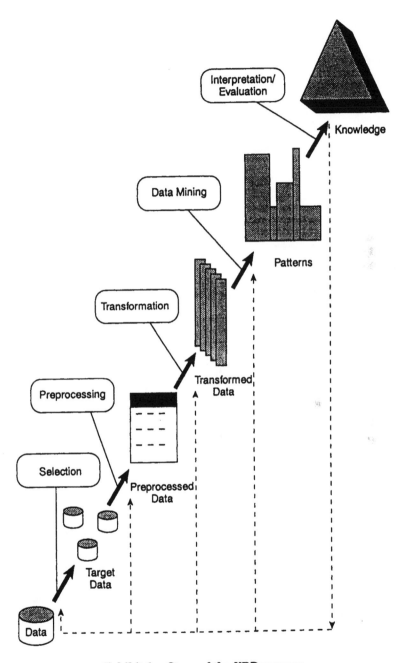

Exhibit 1. Steps of the KDD process.

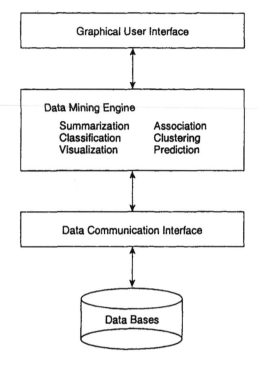

Exhibit 2. A typical data mining system.

- *Summarization.* A set of task-relevant data is summarized and abstracted, resulting in a smaller set providing a general overview of the data with aggregation information. A summarization table can be generalized to different abstraction levels and viewed from different angles. For example, the sales of a company can be summarized by product, region, or year and viewed at various abstraction levels in any combination of them.
- *Classification.* A set of training data (i.e., a set of objects whose class label is known) is given and analyzed. A classification model is then constructed based on the features of the training data. The model can be used to classify future data and develop a better understanding of each class in the database. For example, a classification model can be built for diseases based on symptoms as features that can be used to diagnose new patients.
- *Association rule mining.* An association rule reveals associative relationships among objects, especially in a transactional database. For example, an association rule, "call waiting® call display," says if a customer subscribes to the call waiting service, he or she very likely also has "call display" service. Databases are searched to identify strong

associations among objects and data. As another example, a retail store may discover that a set of commodities is often bought together with another set of commodities. This discovery can then be used to design sales strategies.

- *Clustering.* Clustering is the process of identification of classes (i.e., clusters) for a set of unclassified objects based on their attributes. The objects are clustered so that the intraclass similarities are maximized and the interclass similarities are minimized based on certain criteria. Once the clusters are decided, the objects are labeled with their corresponding clusters, and common features of the objects in a cluster are summarized to form the class description. For example, a company may cluster its customers into several categories based on the similarities of their age, income, or address, and the common characteristics of the customers in a category can be used to describe that group of customers.

- *Trend analysis.* Patterns and regularities in data-changing behaviors are discovered in time-related data (i.e., data that has the attribute *time*). Data is analyzed along the time dimension, and the data-changing tracks are compared and matched. Trends, such as increasing streaks or decreasing streaks, that happen frequently are reported. For example, a company's sales can be analyzed for every year, quarter, or month to discover the sales patterns and analyze the reasons behind them.

Data Mining Techniques

The three most prevalent data mining techniques are: 1) mathematical and statistical, 2) machine learning, or 3) database oriented.

- *Mathematical and statistical methods.* Usually, mathematical or statistical models are built from a set of training data. An optimal model, based on a predefined measure, is searched for, and rules, patterns, and regularities are then drawn from it. The most commonly used tools include Bayesian network, rough set, linear or nonlinear regression, and X^2.

- *Machine learning methods.* Cognitive models are used by most machine learning methods to resemble the human learning process. Like mathematical and statistical methods, machine learning methods search for a best model that matches the testing data. The most common machine learning methods used include decision tree induction, conceptual clustering, and inductive concept formation.

- *Database-oriented methods.* Database-oriented methods do not search for a best model, as is the case with the previous two methods. Instead, data model, or database-specific heuristics are used to discover the characteristics of the data. For example, transactional databases are scanned iteratively to discover patterns in customer shopping practices. Iterative, frequent pattern searching and attribute-oriented induction are two representatives of the database-oriented methods.

There are many other methods for data mining, such as visual exploration, neural networks, knowledge representation, and integrated methods. Most data mining systems use multiple methods to deal with different data mining tasks, kinds of data, and application areas.

Data Mining Applications

Successful data mining case studies can be found in many business application areas, as well as many scientific areas such as astronomy, molecular biology, and medicine. Following are descriptions of databases specific to different commercial industries:

- *Marketing databases*. Database marketing is the most successful and popular application of data mining. By mining historical customer databases, patterns and trends are extracted and customer profiles are built that can be used for more effective marketing.
- *Retail databases*. Retail databases consist of transactions that are lists of bar codes. Data mining can reveal customer shopping patterns that can be used, for example, in sales campaigns.
- *Stock market databases*. By searching stock market data for trends and patterns, stocks that have performed well can be identified. Better investment decisions can be made by selecting stocks that have a potentially high return.
- *Customer claim databases*. Customer claims can be analyzed to detect fraud in insurance claims, health care expenses, and tax returns.
- *Credit application databases*. Applications for credit and loans can be decided based on the applicant's information and the decision support model; the latter is constructed based on existing data.

DATA MINING FOR IMPROVED MULTIMEDIA RETRIEVAL

Multimedia is becoming increasingly available on the World Wide Web, which can be viewed as a large, distributed, multimedia database. However, the data is unstructured and heterogeneous.

Although SQL-3 allows constructs for querying multimedia data, the underlying assumption is that the data are structured abstract data types that are application-specific and can be constructed to transform semistructured data into structured data. As browsing becomes the predominant mode for exploratory querying of multimedia data on the Web, data mining techniques can be applied to research the traversal paths of users accessing data, so frequent paths can be determined and data can be reorganized to reduce the time it takes to access it. Data mining techniques can also be used to learn about user behavior and subsequently develop user models to improve the retrieval effectiveness of a system.

Another area where data mining techniques (especially classification) can prove valuable is in extracting features from new image instances. Feature values for images in the training set are extracted manually to train the classifier. Then the classifier can be used to derive features from new image instances automatically. Although this has long been a topic of interest in the pattern recognition area, the number of classes are relatively few compared to the number of classes that arise in the data mining context.

Because of inherent difficulties in feature quantification and subjective interpretation of multimedia data by users, it is not possible to precisely characterize database contents as well as user queries. This often leads to poor retrieval effectiveness. Only a small fraction of retrieved objects are relevant to a user's query.

Relevance feedback techniques — used successfully in the text retrieval area — can be used to improve retrieval effectiveness in multimedia databases as well. The user specifies relevance judgements on a subset of the retrieved data by labeling them as relevant, somewhat relevant, or not relevant, for example. Inductive learning techniques can be used on this data to improve precision in the user query and to resolve subjectivity.

SUMMARY

The data mining discipline simply draws on well-established techniques in machine learning, probability and statistics, pattern recognition, visualization, and databases; however, synergistically employing these techniques is not an easy task. Data mining addresses the most important aspect of these techniques — scalability. Because multimedia databases are usually enormous, the potential impact of data mining techniques for multimedia data management deserves attention.

Chapter 69
Database Mining Tools

Fritz H. Grupe
M. Mehdi Owrang

BUSINESSES AND GOVERNMENT ASSEMBLE LARGE DATABASES containing as much as 15 terabytes of data that are essential for an organization's operation. Although corporate databases grow by a gigabyte or more of data each day, the expansion often results from the accumulation of data of limited scope. A credit card company, for example, captures transactional data that ensure the accuracy of payments, credit requests, and mailing lists and that provide a basis for approving new cardholders. Management information systems must then summarize this type of data in management reports that executives can use in their decision-making.

One example of findings forwarded by database mining tools originated with supermarket databases. A supermarket chain found that slow-moving, expensive cheeses were purchased by people who were likely to spend more than $250 in a single visit to the store. Such findings have significant implications for advertising campaigns and for the products stores will stock.

To a large extent, transaction-oriented databases lie fallow, even though buried within them is information that is useful for generating facts and relationships that are valuable in creating new business. The question is how to mine this raw data for information that can provide a company with significant competitive benefits available only to that company as sole owner of the data.

THE GOALS OF DATABASE MINING

Database mining aims to use existing data to invent new facts and to uncover new relationships previously unknown even to experts thoroughly familiar with the raw data. Humans are especially adept at these tasks, but the brain makes such advances slowly and sporadically. Computer databases pose additional, unique problems. For example:

- Database structures are highly complex and distributed. They contain numerous tables connected through abstract linkages that the mind finds difficult to trace.
- Digitized databases are hidden from sight, so the details in the records are unseen and unanalyzed.
- The size and distributed nature of databases make it impossible to detect hidden patterns and ill-formed relationships.

The term *database mining* has a variety of meanings. It includes, for example, the derivation of useful information from a database through the use of creative queries such as, "Which airline passengers flew to Germany last year and might be asked to respond to special pricing on tickets for this year?" Database mining also includes the identification of relationships that would have gone undetected without the application of specialized approaches.

For example, one application determined that certain bank customers with occasional overdrafts and characteristic deposit histories were especially good candidates for home equity loan advertising. Another, a fraud detection system, identified a fraudulent mortgage unit that changed names frequently and defrauded many different banks, duplicating in minutes the finding of a team of investigators who worked with the same data for 2 years.

WHAT INFORMATION DOES DATABASE MINING UNCOVER?

There are a variety of database mining tools on the market. Corporations often use several different tools to identify as much new information as possible. Because the tools use different algorithms for discovering knowledge, they report uniquely different types of results. The following queries can be addressed by database mining software:

- Which entities share the same characteristics?
- What subsets of entities look different?
- What events are related to one another?
- What order of events leads up to a given outcome?
- What outcomes are predictable?
- What events or phenomena depend on other events or phenomena?

Underlying Technologies

The improvement in the value of a database's holdings is in large measure the result of rapid progress in hardware and software technologies, including:

- *Faster processors.* Significantly greater computational power is brought to bear on procedures that involve extensive database processing and pattern-recognition processing.

- *Parallel processing systems and concurrent processing languages.* These systems introduce the potential for analyzing data in ways previously beyond realistic computer capabilities.
- *New software technologies.* Products emerging from artificial intelligence, as well as innovative mental constructs about how to carry out intelligent database mining, present new opportunities to reduce processing time and efficiently narrow search paths.
- *Reduced data storage costs and larger secondary devices.* With decreased processing times, data can be made available online in amounts that were previously impossible.

DATA WAREHOUSES

The usefulness of database mining software is being extended by companies that are developing data warehouses. Data warehouses assemble massive amounts of data for a single organization in logically, and sometimes physically, separate processing systems that facilitate access to current and historical data through easy-to-use data query and reporting software.

However, simply storing data does not make it useful. Knowledge is needed to extract payoff information. The data assembled for a data warehouse is useful for database mining because it has already been cleaned and formatted for the report writing and query software in much the same manner as is needed by database mining tools. Missing fields have been added. Fields and records across files have been reconstructed to be identical. Data integrity and consistency have been accounted for.

In contrast, however, database mining software identifies relationships and patterns that the user may not have thought to ask. The same technology used in data warehouses is being used at the departmental and divisional level to create data marts. Data marts provide the basis for database mining tools as well.

Another important asset of the data warehouse is metadata — data about data. A file may have a field with the numeric values 1 through 6. Metadata connect fields like this to tables that contain meaningful correlated information such as credit ratings or affirmative action categories. Metadata also know where data reside and which fields in multiple files and databases are comparable. It provides the information for making these fields comparable in length and format. Database mining tools that are adapted to the data warehouse environment can make effective use of the information stored therein by accessing the metadata as well as the raw data.

QUALIFYING A PROBLEM: KNOWING WHEN TO MINE

As is true of all computer applications, selecting the correct tool for a problem greatly affects how quickly a solution is found. Database mining is appropriate when the following problem scenarios exist:

69-3

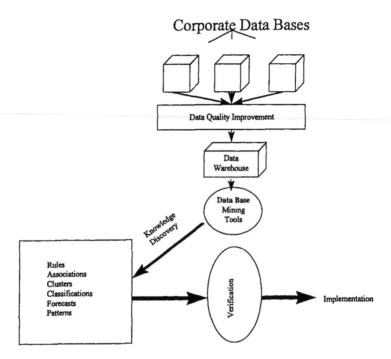

Corporate Data Bases

Data Quality Improvement

Data Warehouse

Data Base Mining Tools

Knowledge Discovery

Rules
Associations
Clusters
Classifications
Forecasts
Patterns

Verification

Implementation

Exhibit 1.   The database mining process.

- Large databases prevent efficient examination of records to detect relationships and select important facts.
- Database structures are complex and involve substantial numbers of variables that may or may not be related to one another.
- Existing querying techniques, decision models, and statistical techniques are insufficient for discovering new knowledge, or an organization lacks expertise in these areas.
- Better predictive models are needed.

Exhibit 1 depicts some of the elements that are part of a database mining and knowledge discovery environment. The key steps in beginning a database mining project include:

- *Identifying sources of data that are to be analyzed.* These sources may include corporate databases, flat files, personal computer databases and spreadsheets, and ASCII files.
- *Cleaning the data.* This step includes eliminating data anomalies, enforcing data integrity, repairing missing or inconsistent data, and cataloging data fields and records for development of metadata.

- *Storing the data in a data warehouse.* The data may be stored in a computer dedicated to the data warehouse or might be stored in the operational computer system.

At this point, the data mining tools will:

- *Analyze the database.* No one tool will do all of the analyses that may be necessary to extract all of the knowledge that is potentially discoverable, however.
- *Recommend knowledge.* Knowledge is recommended in the form of rules, associations, clusters, classifications, forecasts, and patterns.

After the completion of these steps, one or more experts from the corporation will examine the discovered knowledge to determine whether these findings are real and useful, or to discard the discoveries as trivial, previously known, incorrect, or subject to further study. Knowledge that is useful is implemented in the form of expert systems or as improved practices in the marketing, analysis, and financial departments.

SOFTWARE CHOICES

The costs of database mining vary, depending on the size and type of database as well as the computer platform. Specialized workstations can run upward of $40,000, and massively parallel computers can cost more than $1 million. More sophisticated projects may involve staff for more than a year in data formatting and in training. Many other projects, however, are less expensive and simpler.

Several approaches are available for extracting knowledge from existing databases. Because the approaches address specific problems, direct comparisons and rankings among products can be misleading. Among the approaches are:

- Purchased software
- Neural networks
- Expert systems
- Case-based reasoning systems
- Database software extensions
- Data visualization tools

Database Mining Software

Database mining tools differ substantially in the types of problems they are designed to address and in the ways in which they work.

DataLogic/R (Reduct Systems). DataLogic/R is a PC-based package that uses rough sets, an offshoot of fuzzy logic, to help users ferret out rules that characterize the data in the database. It then suggests how to make decisions on categorizing the data for optimum analysis. Users discover the new knowledge in the form of rules through DataLogic/R's pattern-recognition, modeling, and data analysis techniques. In general, the software is able to deal with uncertainty in data, analyze hidden facts in data, represent new knowledge in a rule format, and create models for prediction and classification. DataLogic/R has been successfully used in applications such as consumer survey analysis, process control measurement, substance toxicity identification, insurance analysis, and fault detection.

IDIS:2 (IntelligenceWare). IDIS:2 also examines databases with the intent of hypothesizing possible rules for explaining the relationships among variables. It can uncover information based on questions no one thought to ask by positing a hypothesis and then testing it for accuracy and relevancy. It concludes with a list of rules in two- and three-dimensional hypermedia graphs.

IDIS uses induction, guided by the user, to assign weights to attributes used in the rules. It finds suspicious entries and unusual patterns automatically, including data items that violate correlations, extreme boundary items, and items that exceed normal standard deviations. IDIS has been used to discover knowledge in areas as diverse as financial analysis, marketing, scientific and medical research, quality control, and manufacturing.

IBM Intelligent Miner. Intelligent Miner consists of a set of tools for analyzing, extracting, and validating data stored in data warehouses. It works with both flat files and with scalar and parallel versions of the database DB2. Several algorithms are used for deviation detection, classification, predictive modeling, association discovery, sequential pattern discovery, and database segmentation. The software has three specially designed tool kits: a customer segmentation tool kit for analyzing marketing databases, an item set analysis tool kit for "market-basket" analysis, and a fraud detection tool kit to identify fraudulent transactions.

Pilot Discovery Server (Pilot Software). The Pilot Software offers a sales and marketing analysis library that performs detailed business reporting modules for 80/20 Pareto analysis, time-based ranking, BCG quadrant analysis, trend line, and statistical forecasting. These functions are extended with the Pilot Discovery Server for data mining that uses customer metrics such as lifetime value or new product return on investment to drive a focused market segmentation and a proactive analysis of customer behavior to evaluate the profitability of potential marketing efforts.

KnowledgeSeeker (Angoss). KnowledgeSeeker permits a user to select an entity's attribute and to determine the degree to which other attributes affect that attribute's value. Built-in statistical routines automatically generate the analyses in easy-to-understand decision trees. The software also produces rules that can be used by experts and expert systems.

Neural Networks

Database mining can also be performed with neural networks — systems that attempt to replicate the interaction of neurons in the brain. Neural networks can create knowledge in ways that humans may not be able to articulate.

A neural network parallels a human's learn-through-repetition technique. Given a series of examples, the neural network is expected to learn in a manner that is analogous to memorization. Without being told how to do so, the neural network attempts to induce patterns that distinguish examples from one another. Then, given a new example, the neural network uses its past learning to categorize the current situation.

Use of a neural network follows a top-down development process in which the analyst posits the effect of a group of variables might have on an outcome or outcomes, and then runs the network to determine whether a relationship can be unearthed. For example, an analyst can provide a neural network with accounting ratio information for a variety of companies, along with the knowledge of which companies failed and which succeeded. The neural network examines and reexamines this data hundreds, perhaps thousands of times, attempting to organize underlying patterns. Eventually, it learns the pattern, and when given comparable ratios for a new set of companies, it can predict with a high level of accuracy which companies will succeed and which will fail.

Neural networks have been used to forecast electronic network and component failures, identify loan applicants who are likely to default, carry out image recognition, spot health problems, and perceive stock and bond market fluctuations. Surprisingly accurate predictions and identifications have been made by neural networks in areas in which human experts have had difficulty defining and programming traditional systems to do these tasks.

Neural network software packages are readily available for personal computers and mainframes at commodity prices.

Expert Systems

Expert systems are a recognized and accepted form of artificial intelligence. Generally, expert systems employ fairly specific rules, such as "If SAT-score is greater than 1200 then honors-English is true." Whereas many expert systems applications are limited to diagnostic and prescriptive tasks, some can be used to locate relationships and examples of relationships that may be suspected but unverified.

For example, suppose that one had a database of persons who had contracted a variety of diseases, and another database that contained genealogical relationships among people whose disease histories are found in the other database. Some pattern-matching expert systems are capable of determining which diseases might be genetic because they exhibit characteristics found predominantly in males or commonly found both in parents and in children.

In business, these pattern-matching systems can be used to identify airline passengers who travel particular routes or potentially fraudulent credit requests that differ from an individual's normal buying habits, and to scan electronic network statistics for patterns that usually precede component failures and shutdowns.

Another class of expert systems induces new knowledge from cases. A spreadsheet-like screen is used to represent the cases so that most of the columns contain the variable information available about the cases and a final column contains the outcome or the decision made by an expert who handled the cases. Each row represents the complete information about one case. The software induces an optimized set of rules to handle the cases and to create a dialog and analysis system.

Case-Based Reasoning Systems

Some organizations have created large numbers of cases that store information about the solutions to a variety of situations. Case-based reasoning systems model the behavior of experts who reach conclusions by drawing on good and bad experiences they have encountered through the years. Experts see a problem, recognize it as being similar to one they have seen before, answer a few questions that seem important to confirming its applicability or need for adaptation, and reach a conclusion. They assess the effect of their decision and file the case away in the back of their minds. Later, when a new problem occurs, experts recall from memory the cases most similar to those now at hand and adapt the previous solution to the current problem as necessary. When the revised solution is tried, the new, completed case is remembered for future use.

Problems arise because even experts can forget their experiences. If these people leave a company, their experience is also lost as a corporate resource. Case-based reasoning software is somewhat like database management software. It facilitates the recording of information about cases, a problem description, pertinent questions used to focus the problem, a proposed solution, and the consequences. The software provides a robust means of indexing and retrieving known cases that suggest solutions to the current problem. The content of the cases may consist of only loosely organized text. Case-based reasoning has no particular mining strategy; one simply stores cases on the assumption that is more efficient to store all of them than to attempt to decide which ones will be most useful in the future.

Case-based reasoning software has been used to support help desk operations, provide sales support, catalog and locate in-house expertise, conduct situation analyses, and locate appropriate documentation.

Database Software Extensions

The integration of expert systems and databases is becoming increasingly important to a large class of users. Combining the technologies of data mining-capable, rule-based expert systems with relational database systems enables users to build smarter, more powerful applications. A tight coupling of the two is most favored by integrating rules with Structured Query Language (SQL). Intelligent SQL extensions can take advantage of object-oriented features as well as of predicates for querying and retrieving multimedia objects. This feature is appearing in newer products with intelligent database capabilities, including:

- Comprehensive integrity constraints expressed easily in pattern matching rules.
- Support for flexible query systems for handling inexact, imprecise queries.
- Support for intelligent, less esoteric, more forgiving (i.e., more flexible) user interfaces and for associative structuring information with hypertext.

These types of capabilities are already found in Ingres Corp.'s RDBMS v6.3 and AI Corp.'s Knowledge Base Management System (KBMS).

Data Visualization Tools

Simply reviewing rows and columns of numbers is insufficient for spotting trends and exceptions in data. There is simply too much data to scan. Some software has been developed to display data in such a way that the viewer is more readily able to recognize and spot these trends and exceptions. MindSet, a product of Silicon Graphics, uses visual displays to assist the user in identifying patterns and connections. By displaying data in three-dimensional charts, scattergrams, scaled tree visualizers, and maps, users can scan the data for comparisons that are impossible to spot with other tools. Suggestions for associations and conclusions appear in high profile.

DATABASE MINING IN ACTION: USING DISCOVERED KNOWLEDGE

The knowledge gleaned from database mining can be used in many ways. For example, the Army and Air Force Exchange Services (AAFES), the primary retailer for military installations around the world, has information on 2.5 million customers in 17,000 businesses. A database mining tool was used to assist AAFES in determining the expected purchasing behavior for many classes of individuals and for predicting their future buying behavior. The data were used for inventory control and product distribution. Such data can also be used in the form of if-then rules, which can be studied by:

- Experts to make better decisions.
- Knowledge engineers to create an expert system or knowledge base, and to expand, modify, and improve existing expert systems and knowledge bases.
- Database system managers to tune existing databases by improving the logical database design. New knowledge about attributes and their relationships may suggest the absence of attributes and entities or their misrepresentation in the database.

Other database mining applications that have realized a high return for their users include the following examples:

- A cruise line filled empty berths on expensive tours by identifying high-potential sales to customers.
- A credit bureau increased control over losses in its loan portfolio by selecting out likely defaulters.
- An insurance company searched its data for patterns indicating fraud.
- A medical supplies company increased its return on advertising by targeting doctors who were most likely to make second purchases.
- A collection agency improved its ability to determine which delinquent accounts were most likely to be collectable.
- A bank initiated an auto loan campaign by predicting which customers were likely to be buying a new car.
- A telephone company began predicting which of its newest customers were likely to turn over in a short period of time, limited its advertising to them, and increased its evaluation of their payment patterns.
- A health insurance company discovered that understaffed medical units were sending patients for tests as a means of warehousing them until staff could deal with them.
- A life insurance company discovered the patterns that led to early cancellation of insurance policies.
- A researcher discovered the conditions under which it was most likely that companies would take corporate write-downs.

LIMITATIONS OF DATABASE MINING

Database mining technologies vary greatly, and potential users should be aware of their limitations.

Limited Explanation Mechanisms. A tool may indicate that it has discovered some new knowledge in the form of relationships, rules, and concepts, but the rationale behind the discovery may be hidden from the user. The better the mechanism provided by a tool for explaining its discovery, the better able the user is to assess the finding and to distinguish between real knowledge and an anomaly of little significance.

Limited Data Formats for Input. Not all tools are able to handle different methods of representing data. Although all can handle numeric data, they are not equally able to conduct mining operations with text, graphs, mathematical formulas, or graphic images. Even unformatted data files present a problem, so most database files must be properly formatted.

Limited Validation Techniques. When a tool presents discovered knowledge, it does so through the application of a specific form of analysis and logic, such as abduction, induction, and deduction. It may not have the ability to cross-validate the discovered knowledge.

Another problem is that some of the data provided to the tool may be incorrect. A tool must be robust enough to decide that a conclusion is applicable with some degree of certainty even though exceptions exist. Similarly, the tool should be able to determine why some exceptional cases do not conform to an otherwise more broadly applicable rule.

Computational Expense. Undirected searches for knowledge are expensive. Tools that are asked to determine whether variables A through Z have some bearing on outcomes can generally do so efficiently. When a blind search is being made of a database, many possible input patterns must be compared with many potential outcome patterns. An exhaustive search is time-consuming and, potentially, very expensive.

Limited Support. Not all platforms, database file formats, or database file sizes are supported. Some products are PC-based, some are mainframe-oriented, and some can function in client/server, cross-platform environments. There may be limits on the number of fields or records a database being analyzed can contain. Data files may be required to be of fixed sizes and formatted for specific database management systems. Reformatting data for a platform other than the one on which it is housed may be expensive. Although neural networks can handle image files, most database mining tools cannot.

Data Quality. Not all data is appropriate for knowledge discovery. Database mining tools are designed to establish relationships between entities and events. They cannot infer conclusions from summary or abstracted data. For example, if a clothing store's database stored only the total amount of purchase by each customer, the only relationships that could be identified would be shallow knowledge, such as: "Do credit card customers buy more than cash customers?" This could be answered with a database query. To find that people who purchase red shoes are also likely to purchase jewelry, the tool must have access to a database that contains specific information on purchases by each individual on each visit to the store.

SUMMARY

Database mining applications are enabling IS and business managers to discover new knowledge that was previously locked in their databases. This knowledge takes the form of new relationships induced by the database mining system, the confirmation or rejection of relationships assumed by the users and tested by the system, and new facts added to the knowledge base.

The rapid accumulation of data mandates that companies take full advantage of the knowledge contained in their database systems. Data mining is a process by which the data can be analyzed so as to generate new knowledge in a form that answers questions that managers may not even have thought to ask. Companies that capitalize on their databases can become the sole proprietors of a substantive, unique competitive advantage.

Section XIII
Document Management

DOCUMENT MANAGEMENT OFFERS A STRONG ALTERNATIVE to other methods of data management. Document management solutions are suited to situations where rich text documents require storage under a small set of access conditions. However, the text within a document cannot be searched as readily as those in a relational database. However, traditional relational databases are not well-suited for manipulating the same type of information that is stored in document management systems. As a general rule, document management systems can store more information in a problem domain, but with limited lines of accessibility than other storage mechanisms. A whole suite of tools, including Lotus Notes and intranets, are available to support document management systems. This section contains three chapters that focus on different aspects of document management.

Chapter 70, "Terms of Reference: The Foundation for Implementing Document Management Systems," provides the instructions for properly constructing a Terms of Reference document for an Enterprise Document Management System (EDMS) for increased project success.

Chapter 71, "Integrating EDMSs and DBMSs," describes how to combine the strengths of a database management system and an electronic document management system to support rich and diverse information sources and datatypes, while supporting the quick access and search capabilities offered by relational databases.

Chapter 72, "Using Lotus Notes in Executive Information Systems," examines ways of using Lotus Notes as part of an EIS solution in a variety of architectural formats. The chapter also builds a case for using Lotus Notes in this capacity as well.

Chapter 70

Terms of Reference: The Foundation for Implementing Document Management Systems

Michael J.D. Sutton
Pierre J. Lemay

WITH PURPOSE AND GUIDANCE, MANY MANAGERS HAVE NAVIGATED through numerous projects, project teams, successes, and failures in the area of Enterprise Document Management. During those initiatives, the project manager continually refers back to project terms of reference (TOR). Why? Because the terms of reference is the manifesto — the mission statement. Without it, an electronic document management system (EDMS) manager can experience significant pain. A set of guidelines on the satisfactory ingredients to the TOR is presented for the sake of those project managers and project leaders coming on new and ever-increasing EDMS initiatives. The Terms of Reference is one of the most important communication documents in your leadership toolkit.

BASIC CONCEPTS

Definitions

Terms of Reference. The sustainable agreement (manifesto) for a complex project containing the mission statement, governance outline, and project control structure for accountability, responsibility, and authority.

EDMS. A system of overseeing an enterprise's official business transactions, decision-making records, and transitory documents of importance. The repository for an EDMS contains representations of an object loosely termed a "document." (The medium of the business transaction [electronic, photographic, audio, or paper] is irrelevant.)

Need for Terms of Reference

The Terms of Reference is the manifesto. Why does one need a manifesto? One needs a manifesto because the EDMS initiative about to be embarked on is nothing like anything previously experienced. The territory is not well defined or clearly mapped. The initiative is generally 1 to 2 years in length, has an average team size of 7 to 10 for an enterprise of 1,000 client users, and is primarily comprised of individuals from groups such as information management, information technology, security, training, records and archives management, and the actual business units. The tools used within an EDMS project are the same as a generic information management project: collaborative, project management, E-mail, scheduling, presentation graphics, and office automation software. The same sources of information that were used for traditional project management are applicable for updating an EDMS project schedule.

Individuals in the information management profession have worked for almost 30 years to automate less than 15% of the enterprise's information assets and intellectual capital. Many authorities have pointed out that these individuals have not exactly been stellar performers. Today's project managers have the opportunity to cut their teeth on a project associated with documents. The project bears very little relationship to the data and databases with which they are familiar. In fact, it is significantly more than just data.

Project managers are now responsible for one of the largest and highest impact projects for the enterprise. It will deal with the most critical information asset of the organization — documents. The manifesto is the public declaration of intention and objectives. It just makes good "business sense" and complements traditional, good, project management approaches and methodologies. The manifesto will frame the motives and opinions about the boundaries, constraints, and assumptions of the project. By the end of the project, management or customers will have to "take it out of the manager's cold, dying hands" before he or she will give it up.

Nonetheless, before one can write about something, one must be able to understand, describe, and reconstruct the concepts and principles of that particular something. In this case, the project manager will want to speak intelligently about a "terms of reference." Historically, a "terms of reference" was a sustainable agreement between management and the leader of a project. This did not always include the client or customer in the organization, just a representative of the management.

The project was planned as a set of steps that would change, improve, or somehow alter the "status quo" of an organization. The agreement was reached as the discussion before a decision became formalized into the implementation plan that followed the decision. The sustainable agreement for a complex project became crystallized into a formal document called a Terms of Reference. The Terms of Reference was imbued with accountability, responsibility, and authority. It was now in writing, and it was supposed to have "teeth"!

TERMS OF REFERENCE COMPONENTS

There is no such thing as a "standard" project. The starting point, resources, and approach can differ for every project initiated. However, it is useful to have a standard set of stages or components to describe the Terms of Reference. The standard components of a Terms of Reference generally include:

1. Scope and context
2. Goal
3. Objectives
4. Assumptions and constraints,
5. Critical success factors
6. Suggested approach in implementation
7. Transition strategies

In this way, the project manager can make informed choices about what to include, exclude, and defer.

Scope and Context

The project scope and context answer the simple questions of:

- WHO?
- WHAT?
- WHEN?
- WHERE?
- WHY?
- HOW?
- HOW MUCH?

This scope and context should contain several simple paragraphs that describe in a conversational style the "playing field" within the organization or client area where the project manager will maneuver.

The scope statement should outline specific areas that are included, excluded, and deferred. The first section specifies: WHO will be involved (business units), WHO will do the work (project team business unit participants), WHO will make the decision that the implementation has been a success (the project authority), WHO may put up obstacles, and, finally, WHO will gain from the initiative. Keep it succinct — there is no need to name everyone by title and telephone number.

The second section indicates: WHAT is needed to manage and deliver the project, WHAT resources (in terms of tools, information, people, and facilities) will be required, and WHAT will the cumulative key deliverables looks like to the client. The third section describes: WHEN the project begins and ends, WHEN the major milestones will be complete, and WHEN the significant resources will be available for the project.

The fourth section outlines: WHERE the EDMS application will be delivered, WHERE the training and conversion will take place, and WHERE the technological tools will be maintained. The fifth section stipulates: WHY the problem exists, WHY the project is important to solve, and WHY the enterprise is investing in this project.

The sixth section states: HOW the project should be organized, HOW the project will be measured as completed or successful, HOW the project team will communicate with the project authority and the remainder of the organization, and HOW often the total project committee/team will meet. The seventh and final section qualifies: HOW MUCH the project is estimated to cost, WHERE the financial resources will come from to pay for this project, and WHAT the cost-benefit, ROI, or payback is estimated to be.

Thus, the scope and context consists of four to five paragraphs that concisely define the scope of the project and the management and execution context.

Goal of an EDMS

Following the scope and context statement is a very clear specification of the goal of the EDMS initiative. This is very difficult to express, so do not be fooled into thinking that this step will only take a few minutes. First, what is a goal? A goal is the statement of the business intent toward which the project is being directed. The goal must be measurable by means of a qualitative assessment criteria. The project authority must be able to unambiguously state that the goal has been achieved. The initiative should have only one project goal, but it may encompass a number of objectives.

Some sample goals to choose from might be:

- Enable the client business unit staff and managers to quickly and effectively "file and find" their working documents, official documents, and the shared documents of others stored in the EDMS repository.

- Prove that the storage of important official records can be more efficiently administered within the protection and control of an EDMS Repository.
- Eliminate the need for shared network drives or individual workstation drives of managers, staff, and officers.

Note that quickly and effectively are subjective but measurable indicators mentioned in these goals. The team or project leader should take a baseline measurement before the initiative is underway. The measurement will make it possible for the project authority to assess whether the documents are now stored and retrieved "quicker or more effectively."

Objectives of an EDMS

Once the overall goal has been identified, the project manager then selects measurable objectives. The objectives are statements of business intent that can be measured quantitatively. Targets can be set and specific measurements can be taken at a milestone to see if the objective has been achieved.

Sample objectives to choose from might include:

- Increase the speed for authoring, publishing, and disseminating documents within the individual's scope of control by 15%.
- Decrease duplication of documents by 25% in the repository by making the author of a document accountable for its addition to the repository.
- Increase the volume of documents that can be reused and recycled from less than 10% to over 50% by optimally storing documents in a centrally accessible repository instead of on shared network directories.
- Increase speed and precision of retrieval from 5 days to less than 1 hour through consistent use of a records management classification system when indexing documents for retrieval.

Additional objectives to choose from might comprise:

- Decrease continued reliance on legacy paper documents by quickly scanning and making retrievable paper documents when they are initially requested.
- Increase access control restrictions by appropriately securing documents to the relevant ownership group.
- Preserve a decision and accountability trail for documents by creating an audit trail of all users who accessed a document or series of documents.
- Decrease the backlog volume of paper and electronic documents that are scheduled for review and disposal by bringing forward this information to record administrators faster when they have reached their retention review stage.

Please note that any of these objectives should be easily and unambiguously measurable because of the quantification inherent in their narration.

Assumptions and Constraints

An assumption is a fact or statement "taken as true." As a project begins, there are numerous assumptions. On the other hand, a constraint is an inhibiting factor that restricts the possible success of the project, its resources, deadlines, milestones, volume of deliverables, etc.

Sample assumptions a project manager can choose from may include:

- Forecast of the estimated volume of users and document objects over a particular time period.
- Special situations for mobile/remote users.
- Any use or special circumstances for APIs.
- The applicable conversion subset of the current legacy documents.
- Certain document types that will not initially be accommodated.
- Shared and personal hard drives will no longer be used by clients.
- The access control and security restrictions matrix for users and groups.
- Assigned responsibility for the first tier of support.
- The estimated number of trips required to remote sites.
- Expected interaction and behavior with other, unrelated but integrated software products.
- The expected metadata that will or will not be captured.

Sample constraints a project manager can choose from may include:

- Specific configurations of all office automation software, network, and hardware.
- The status of the current File Classification Scheme.
- Acceptability of initial loss of time by a business unit.
- The EDMS team's development, test, and systems integration environment.
- New or revised policies and procedures that will be required.
- The client language for GUI implementation and documentation (i.e., Spanish, French, English, etc.).
- The method used for storing E-mail and its attachments in the repository.

All assumptions and constraints must be explicitly cataloged for later protection as the project progresses. Most executives and sponsors will remember the project manager's promises, but they seldom remember the assumptions and constraints that went into the calculation of the commitments to promise the goal and objectives.

Note that many constraints are actually assumptions that will inhibit the project; for example, "workstation configurations will remain as 80486-based processors with 8 MB of RAM storage." Other constraints may be more obvious, such as the adaptability to change within the organization, or the planned vacation schedule. Thus, assumptions and constraints are somewhat interchangeable, depending on the inhibition factor.

Critical Success Factors

Critical Success Factors (CSFs) are any factors, events, or circumstances that are regarded as critical to the success or failure of the project. A CSF must refer to those factors that, if not present, will make the project fail. There are numerous CSFs in an EDMS project.

Sample CSFs to choose from may include:

- The executive sponsor and champions must be identified and committed.
- The executive sponsor must be able to commit adequate resources and funding.
- The champions must actively participate and help celebrate the successes.
- The champions must effectively resolve business policy issues as they arise.
- The champions must decide and articulate the accountability, responsibility, and authority issues.
- The managers and staff must recognize the value of document management and accept the organizational changes in their processes.

Other useful CSFs may include:

- A useful and continuous marketing and communications strategy must be put in place.
- An EDMS project team information technology and management infrastructure must be immediately available and sustainable.
- A continuous training strategy must be implemented.
- The scalability and complexity of the application and its applicability to an EDMS must be evaluated.
- The network must accommodate sufficient bandwidth for the document traffic.
- The application, hardware, and network platform configurations must remain stable throughout the prototype and pilot periods.
- The EDMS project manager must be permitted to build a relationship based upon peer respect with other managerial and executive participants.

For example, there are very few successful EDMS projects without a committed and involved executive sponsor. Starting a project without an executive sponsor is a guarantee of failure, because so much change takes place during the project. Without a senior individual backing the requirements for change and aligning these to the business objectives of the enterprise, the project will be shelved or sabotaged by others who see it eroding their power.

Suggested Approach in Implementation

Specify what approach will be used to roll out the EDMS. Also, specifically define each stage in the approach. For example, will the system be rolled out and implemented as a turnkey application (the "clobber them while they're asleep approach") in all business units overnight, or will the application be rolled out on a business-unit-by-business unit basis? Explain which business units should go first, and why. If staging the application instead of "clobbering the client users," then some unambiguous sample definitions for this approach can be suggested:

1. Prototype: a mock-up of the proposed system interface, with very little functionality implemented (like a cardboard cut-out of an airplane).
2. Pilot: incorporates feedback about the prototype into a basic, functional system that can be used by a limited number of people (like an operational plane, with a motor and instrumentation but limited visibility and petrol).
3. Operational system: evolves from feedback about shortcomings, deficiencies, and benefits of a pilot (like the roll out of a new airplane, complete with operating, training, and technical support manuals).

Start with a prototype, refine it, and then reimplement it in a few business units as a pilot application. Then, refine it again based on feedback from the client user community, and finally implement it on a business-unit-by-business unit basis. Regardless of whether the product is off the shelf or customized, this staged approach has saved many project managers from disaster. The project manager must have a chance to test and recover before everyone has a chance to see the weaknesses (and with hope, the strengths) of a particular software product.

Transition Strategies

The transition strategies are just that — strategies. There are generally six strategies worth mentioning in the Terms of Reference:

- Communications strategy
- Data and document take-on strategy
- Training strategy
- Delivery and acceptance strategy
- Installation and support strategy
- Post-pilot follow-up strategy

Do not try to develop the entire project plan within the strategies. Describe the strategies in terms of what "should be" taking place. Nonetheless, the identification of these strategies guarantees that someone must address them in the project plan.

Communications Strategy

The communications strategy is very important because the project is ever changing. As one moves through a period of implementation, there will be:

- New people
- New constraints and assumptions
- New applications
- New technologies
- New methods and designs
- New data models
- New concerns and issues
- New ways of doing business

All of these "new" things must be communicated to both the project team and client community. The project manager will need to establish briefing sessions and ways of broadcasting the project status. The evolving roles of team members must be described to both the team and the client groups.

A familiar situation is one in which the project team entered a new business unit that had been selected for installation and training 6 months previous. Once they arrive, they find out that no one kept them informed and they were not ready to begin. In fact, the business unit thought the project had been canceled because they had heard nothing about it since it was initiated. The executive sponsor and management champion had claimed that all business unit managers were being kept informed. Alas, the channels of communication had remained closed because people were too busy to communicate.

Data and Document Take-On Strategy

The activities here can include loading the File Classification System, identifying the different metadata tables and the required table validation, and most importantly, identifying the specific legacy documents (paper and electronic) that must either be scanned or moved from shared network directories to the EDMS repository.

Training Strategy

Many organizations omit a training strategy. Executives often feel that an EDMS should be so easy to use that zero investment in training is required. This never works. Staff and managers have a difficult enough time with learning the interface and concepts of a new application that demands discipline. The staff must get help to "jump start" into the EDMS environment.

Activities that should be identified include responsibility for instructors, course design and delivery, training location and equipment, training tutorials, training accounts, course duration, and dummy document bases.

Delivery and Acceptance Strategy

This is often omitted in a TOR because the project manager has a challenging time trying to identify and get the commitment of any project authority. The executive sponsor may not yet have committed to their level of involvement. A client project manager may not have been selected, and client champions may not have stepped forward yet to take responsibility for their business units. So, the EDMS project manager is faced with trying to find out who will confirm the completion of the project. Only when the User Requirements have been matched in some manner to the delivered application, will the project authority sign off its delivery.

Installation and Support Strategy

The installation and support strategy ensures the day-to-day operation of the application as it moves from prototype to pilot, and then from pilot to operation system. Without a strategy, there is an ad hoc response to problems as they arise, a very difficult approach to manage successfully.

Activities included here are training support (how and when are new staff trained when they arrive in the business unit after the initial training has been given?); help desk support (are coaches or superusers trained in each business unit to solve the immediate problems before they are referred to the help desk? How do problems get escalated from the internal help desk to the external product vendor if they are not immediately solvable?); backup and recovery actions during pilot (do staff automatically lose what they were doing when the system goes down, or can a rollback be put into place, and over what time period — 1 hour or 1 day?); and finally, technical configuration and upgrades (how does the project manager address the implementation of the new version of the word processor in the middle of the implementation?). The technical support strategies ensure the routine operation of the application.

Post-Pilot Follow-Up Strategy

Finally, the strategies must reflect an evaluation period after the application has been in use for approximately 6 months. First, the project manager needs to schedule an impact assessment on Policies and Procedures of the business. There is a requirement to collect data about volumetric and performance testing, as well as integrity testing of the metadata databases and the document base. Several other activities include a review of the GUI, monitoring of any subsystems and APIs, a security audit, the potential re-design of staff and management roles and responsibilities, the impact on operational support and the network, and an assessment of the adequacy of hardware, application software, and network client/server operating systems.

The follow-up strategy will prove the success or failure of a project manager and project team.

CONCLUSION

Descriptions of the components of a TOR and suggestions for a number of issues that must be addressed in each component have been discussed. The components were:

1. Scope and context
2. Goal
3. Objectives
4. Assumptions and constraints
5. Critical success factors
6. Suggested approach in implementation
7. Transition strategies

With a fully articulated TOR, the project manager stands a chance of defending and maintaining control over the project. This is the best the project manager can expect, other than thanks from the champion or sponsor. The project manager can now carry this TOR as his or her manifesto. Hopefully, the following Latin words will help the project manager reflect on the situation he or she is now at: *animus opibusque parati* — "(you are) prepared in minds and resources."

Chapter 71
Integrating EDMSs and DBMSs

Charles Banyay

DATABASE MANAGEMENT SYSTEMS (DBMS) HAVE BEEN AN INTEGRAL PART OF INFORMATION TECHNOLOGY (IT) and the systems development life cycle since the 1960s. The database, especially the relational database, has received ever-increasing visibility during the past decade due to the mass availability of very cost-effective PC-based DBMSs. As a result, the relational database has become ingrained as the natural metaphor for an information repository with most organizations who utilize IT.

With the advent of the electronic document or, to be more precise, the electronic document management system (EDMS), as a significant new metaphor for an information repository, it is useful to juxtapose the two approaches and to explore their relative advantages. First, it is necessary to discuss the traditional process of using a DBMS in managing data. Second, it is necessary to evaluate the unique properties of documents as opposed to structured data and the challenges associated with managing information using this metaphor. Having considered these two, it is possible to discuss how the DBMS can be used cooperatively with the new metaphor for information repositories — the electronic document or EDMS.

THE DATABASE MANAGEMENT SYSTEM

The majority of IT professionals would not consider developing even the most simple of applications without employing some kind of DBMS to manage the data. The traditional approach to utilizing database technology, regardless of the application, involves some form of data analysis. Data analysis generally consists of four stages called by different names, by the various methodologies, but they all involve some form of

- Data collection and normalization
- Entity-relationship mapping

- Transaction analysis
- Data modeling

At the end of this process, once the type of database management system to be utilized is determined, one has enough information with which to begin a physical and logical database design. The data analysis activities should provide enough information to enable a design which will have a high degree of predictability in terms of data access performance and data storage size.

Data collection and normalization within any organization begins with the analysis of the data as it exists currently. Various methodologies emphasize different approaches to this analysis. Some emphasize beginning with the analysis of source documents, while others advocate analyzing the data as it is presented to the users. For this discussion it is irrelevant where one starts a project, what is important is that a "functional decomposition" process is followed in all instances. Functional decomposition attempts to distill the relevant data from some source (e.g., data collection documents or presentation documents). As recently as 1 year ago, one could have safely assumed that the documents would have been on paper; however, today that may not necessarily be so. For the purposes of this discussion, however, the medium is irrelevant.

Once this distillation process or functional decomposition is finished, one proceeds with a truly data-driven approach to analysis. The next step involves grouping the data into logical groups called entities. Using a process called normalization, one then proceeds to remove as much data redundancy as possible from these entities, sometimes producing more entities in the process. There are many good references on data normalization techniques, and for the purposes of this article there is no requirement to go into any more depth than this.

Once the entities are in third normal form one generally proceeds to associate each entity with the other entities using some entity-relationship mapping technique. Entity-relationship mapping is, in general, an attempt to reconstitute the data back into something that is meaningful to the business where the data originated. A thorough understanding of the business functions and processes that use the data is crucial for creating meaningful entity-relationship maps. During this mapping process some form of quantification of the entities also occurs.

The next step in data analysis is the transaction analysis. Transaction analysis involves listing all of the business events that could trigger access to the information within the as yet undesigned database and mapping the flow of the transaction through the entities as it satisfies its requirement for information. The transaction flow is dependent on the entity relationships. Once all the transactions are mapped in this way and the quantity of each transaction is determined, one has a good idea of how the data should be ordered and indexed.

The final step in the data analysis activity is to construct the data model. Constructing the data model involves quantitative analysis. Using the structure from the relational map and the number of accesses identified in the transactional analysis, one derives a new structure for the model. This new structure may result in new entities that may reduce the number of entities that need to be accessed for certain high-usage transactions. The first data model generally proves to be inadequate. Data analysis is therefore an iterative process. As one proceeds through the iterations, one learns more about the data. The new information may indicate that decisions made earlier in the process may not have been optimal and may need to be revisited.

The ultimate database design will not only depend on the results of the data analysis activity but also on the choice of DBMS. Good design does not just depend on knowledge of the specific data requirements of a particular application or the general information requirements of an organization. These are critical elements of the design, but almost as important is a good understanding of the particular DBMS, its architecture, and its design constraints.

The critical aspect to understand about data analysis for the purposes of this discussion is the process of functional decomposition. Functional decomposition is a process that is extremely important to data analysis. It is the process by which reality or a body of knowledge is decomposed, summarized, or reduced into its most fundamental, elementary components. This decomposition is generally from the one perspective that is important to the particular application being considered. These elementary components are the data items that then ultimately make up the database, such as those shown in Exhibit 1.

An important consideration in Exhibit 1 is that any process of reduction or distillation results in a tremendous amount of other "stuff" that does not make it into the final version. This stuff is lost. Consequently, one advantage offered by functional decomposition is that the process reduces reality or a body of information to its elementary components that represent one or at least a very limited perspective on this body of information. This enables the construction of a database. The "bad" aspect of functional decomposition also relates to its strength, namely, that the process reduces reality or a body of information to its elementary components that represent one or at least a very limited perspective on this body of information. Much of the original body of information can be lost in the process.

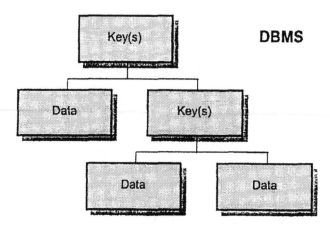

Exhibit 1. Elementary components.

THE ELECTRONIC DOCUMENT

Before comparing the DBMS with the electronic document management system as an information repository, it is useful to build a common understanding of the definition of a "document" in the context of this discussion.

The first thing that most people think of in any discussion of a document is paper. This is due to the fact that most of today's generations have grown up with paper as the most common medium on which documents have resided. A piece of paper or a collection of pieces of paper is usually referred to as a document, especially if it has a collective purpose. Paper, however, is very limiting and is just one method of representing a document. It is certainly not the only way. Even if one disregards the electronic medium for the moment, there is a myriad of ways that documents have existed and do exist. There are stone tablets, scrolls, hieroglyphics, paintings, carvings, and more recently film, just to mention a few. Even the scented letter is a document that is more than just scribbled words on a piece of paper. The scent can convey more information than the words.

If one includes the electronic medium, then a document can be much more than is allowed in the limited paper medium or in anything that has been described above. A document can contain voice-annotated video, with graphics, still images, and drawings with backup text. One can imagine the vast information content of a document of this nature.

The second feature that people think of when discussing documents is the concept of a page. This is also due, in all probability, to the association of documents with paper. People, in general, have an optimum quantum of information on which they can focus at any one moment. This is an aspect of what psychologists call bounded rationality. A page is probably an optimum quantum of information. Represented on paper, information could appear in the format that is most familiar; however, in some other form it could be quite different. The concept of a page is useful and will probably evolve as the understanding of documents evolves and as this understanding moves beyond paper as the common representation of a document. It will suffice for the purposes of this discussion to think of a page as a component of information and of a document as containing one or more pages or one or more quantums of information.

So, in summary, what is a document? The word *document* is both a verb and a noun. To document is to record (e.g., to record an event or to tell a story). It follows that anything that records an event or tells a story can be called a document. A document can and generally does contain many different types of entities. Generally there is either text or an image, but if people expand their horizon beyond paper, a document can contain voice, video, or, in the world of virtual reality, any combination of tactile stimuli. In the most general definition, a document is a representation of reality that can be reproduced and sensed by any combination of the five senses.

The preceding discussion may stretch human creative capabilities somewhat, so for the purposes of this discussion the definition of a document can be limited to a collection of images and textual information types. The information can be coded or uncoded. The essence of the definition of the document, as a representation of reality that can be reproduced and sensed, is really the crucial aspect of the definition that is most germane to this discussion. The representation of reality implies that a document captures information at a quantum level or quantum levels higher than simple data.

The best illustration of this is the well-known "A picture is worth a thousand words." A picture in one entity can represent a thousand data elements or more. An illustration may convey this idea better. Suppose one is creating a document describing an automobile accident report for a property and casualty insurance company. The document would begin with a notice of loss, which could be an electronic form, that is created initially by an agent within a call center. The agent would record all relevant information about the accident, including the name and policy number of the policyholder, the date and time of the accident, the date and time of the call, and all particulars of the loss, such as damages to the car, etc.

The agent then sends a compressed version of the document to the adjuster with some comments and instructions. The information to this point is in coded data format and could be through any traditional data system. The new capabilities of a document-based system allow the adjuster, when the document is received, to attach a few still photo shots of the automobile along with further comments and the detailed cost estimates supplied by the body shop. In addition, the adjuster can scan in the police report of the accident and attach it to the document. The claims document now contains a much more complete description of the entire event. This more complete description could produce a very different result by the end of the claims process. This more complete description is not possible through just simple coded data or traditional relational DBMS systems.

It is not necessary to describe the insurance claims process any further. What it illustrates is the wealth of information contained in a document-based approach to information processing. One needs to contrast this to an approach enabled by an application system containing only coded data in a relational format.

FUNCTIONAL DECOMPOSITION AND DATA DISTILLATION

The primary reason that traditional application systems oriented around a DBMS have sometimes failed to meet the expectations of the business community, and the reason that much of the business information today still resides on paper, is the failure of these applications to capture the entirety of the multifaceted information pertaining to an event. That is a real mouthful, but what it says is that if in capturing information electronically a business user only manages to capture the bare essentials focused on a certain perspective, and loses most of the other peripheral information which may be central to other perspectives, then the business user will, in general, not be completely satisfied. The business user is forced to keep other, nonelectrical repositories of information and continue to work with information in nonelectrical media. This generally adds up to a lot of paper and a lot of traditional, inefficient, and ineffective business processes.

As discussed at the end of the data analysis activity, in any process of reduction or distillation there is a tremendous amount of other peripheral information that does not make it through the process. Reality is reduced to a very limited perspective based on what is retained. This process may leave out information of interest to other perspectives. The result is a very narrow perspective on the information, general dissatisfaction, and alternative repositories of information within the organization.

THE DBMS AND THE EDMS

So why not just discard DBMSs and why not rely totally on documents as the new metaphor for an information repository. The above discussion seems to imply that database systems are bad and documents are good — far from the truth. Documents, despite having a tremendous capability of holding a great deal of multifaceted information, have their own weaknesses. Years ago one would have begun the list of these weaknesses with the fact that documents tend to take up vast amounts of storage space, require a great deal of bandwidth for transmission, and generally require expensive equipment for good presentation, such as large, high-resolution monitors and multimedia processors. Today, these weaknesses seem to be fading in importance, although not as quickly as one had hoped and would like. Bandwidth is increasing, storage costs are plummeting, and high-resolution monitors are dropping in cost.

The real weakness of documents, and this has little to do with storage or display technology, is that they are difficult to search. Because most of the information content of a document is uncoded and because there is very little in the way of search engines for uncoded data, documents are difficult to search. Once stored, they are difficult to find unless they have been indexed with exactly the criteria for which one is searching. Unfortunately, information is of little use if it cannot be found readily when needed.

It seems, then, that there is an impasse. On the one hand, a DBMS is a tool that has tremendous capabilities to search and reproduce information to which it has access, in the combinations that users generally require. The weakness of the DBMS, however, is that it generally has access to only a limited perspective on a small body of information. On the other hand, an EDMS is a tool that can house vast amounts of content about a body of information, from a multitude of perspectives. The primary weakness of an EDMS, however, is that once the information is stored it is difficult to find.

Neither one of the tools on its own seems capable of meeting the expectations for comprehensive information management. They do however have complementary strengths. With the DBMS, information is relatively easy to find, and, with the EDMS, information content is vast and rich. If one could successfully combine these strengths, then one would have a tool that might meet the expectations of the business community better. The combination might not meet all of the expectations, but would certainly be superior to either tool in stand-alone mode. The whole promises to be greater than the sum of the parts in this case.

The logical question arises, "Why use a DBMS to store data?" Why not use the EDMS to store the information, and use the DBMS to store the data about the EDMS or metadata? This would enable one to search the DBMS for the combination of information that one requires contained in the EDMS. This is exactly the approach that many leading vendors of document management applications, such as FileNet and Documentum, have taken. Both vendors use a relational database, such as Oracle or Sybase, to store the metadata that points to various data stores, such as magnetic or optical disk, that house the documents.

The DBMS in many of these document management systems has evolved beyond simple metadata which just houses pointers to content documents. These second-generation document management systems have developed the concept of the virtual document. The virtual document illustrated in Exhibit 2 is more than a collection of pointers to content

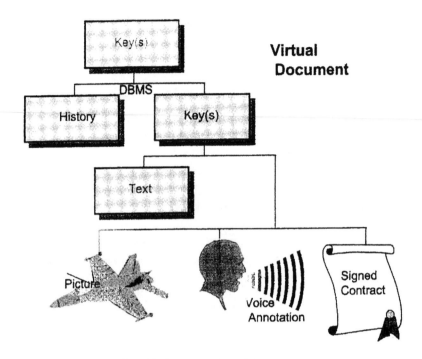

Exhibit 2.   The virtual document.

documents. The metadata in second-generation document management applications also contains far richer information, such as a comprehensive history of the virtual document. The history may contain work-in-process information or information about each member document, such as the time each was added to the document collection, who entered it, and from which application.

CONCLUSION

The combination of DBMS and EDMS certainly offers advantages over either in stand-alone mode; however, the degree of the advantage can be deceptive. The metadata in the database is just that, data about the document and not about all of the information within the document. Here is the crux of the matter. What is metadata but distillation? If the only way to find a wealth of information is through the limited perspective of its metadata, then the information is not nearly as valuable as if one could find it from the multitude of perspectives contained within the information itself.

The challenge facing most document management application vendors today is how to minimize even this more expanded data distillation. The development of new search engines may be part of the answer. Development of such technologies as pattern-recognition applications, which can scan the uncoded components of documents, may be another part.

Whatever the solution to reducing the effects of data distillation, it is not something that will be totally eliminated within the near future. Combining the strengths of a DBMS and an EDMS, however, definitely provides better access to a larger volume of information than if either one is used alone. The combination is by no means a panacea, but it is a step or a number of steps in the right direction toward solving the information-processing problems that knowledge workers face every day.

As the marriage between the DBMS and the EDMS evolves further, there may be a new dawn for IT. This new dawn will be true electronic information processing rather than electronic data processing. The real payoff in this evolution and in developments of this nature is that it may eventually solve the seeming paradox of information processing in the office environment. This paradox is that, even though there has been a tremendous investment in information technology in the office, office productivity has not risen as dramatically as expected during the past 20 to 30 years.

Chapter 72
Using Lotus Notes in Executive Information Systems

Barbara J. Haley
Hugh J. Watson

THE PRIMARY PURPOSE OF AN EXECUTIVE INFORMATION SYSTEM (EIS) is to provide executives with the internal and external information required to effectively perform their jobs. Executives have always had systems to supply needed information. Traditionally, executives have relied on printed reports, subordinates, meetings, networks of people inside and outside the organization, telephone calls, newspapers, and industry newsletters as information sources. Contemporary EISs use computer and communications technology to deliver much the same kind of information as before, but in a better, more timely, accurate, and relevant manner. EISs have unique characteristics. For example, they:

- Are custom tailored to individual executives
- Extract, filter, compress, and track critical data
- Provide status information, trend analysis, and exception reports
- Access and integrate a broad range of internal and external data
- Are user-friendly and require little or no training
- Are used directly by executives without intermediaries
- Present graphical, tabular, and textual information
- Provide support for electronic communications
- Provide data analysis capabilities
- Provide organizing tools

EIS EVOLUTION

The first EISs were implemented in the late 1970s using custom-built software. Although there were a few notable successes, there were more failures. These specially tailored systems were often too difficult to build, maintain, and use. In the mid-1980s, Comshare and Pilot Software introduced their Commander EIS and Command Center products, respectively. These mainframe-based offerings provided a set of tools that greatly facilitated EIS development and use.

The emergence of appropriate software, combined with executives' demand for information, fueled a rapid growth in the number of EISs throughout the decade. The EIS software market has changed seriously, however, as firms have been moving from mainframe to client/server-based applications. Consequently, the EIS software vendors have moved away from their more expensive mainframe offerings to less expensive client/server products.

EIS products were evolving concurrently with general-purpose software. In many ways, general-purpose software began to be more like EIS software in terms of the capabilities they provided. For example, most database and spreadsheet software evolved to include a graphical user interface. Many companies began to question what they should pay for EIS software when they could get nearly the same capabilities in Microsoft Excel, Powersoft's PowerBuilder, or Visual Basic, and at a lower cost. Although these general-purpose alternatives still do not match the functionality provided by specialized EIS software, the gap is narrowing.

The nature of EISs has also changed. Originally developed for a handful of senior executives, they evolved to support the top management team, and now in many organizations have spread to serve hundreds or even thousands of users. For this reason, EIS now informally stands for everybody's information system.

LOTUS NOTES

Lotus Notes entered the EIS software scene in 1988. Notes first appeared in the marketplace targeting groupware and workflow applications. It has been widely recognized as the first popular commercial product to serve this market. Today, Notes is used in more than 2000 companies and on the desks of more than 1 million employees.

Notes serves a variety of purposes, ranging from basic E-mail to complex workflow applications that are closely interwoven with critical business processes. Many companies have capitalized on the product's excellent data storage and sharing mechanisms. Others have been overwhelmed with Notes' extremely diverse capabilities and lack direction or an overarching strategy in their internal Notes development projects. Companies that learn how to harness the power of Notes to create well-planned, business-driven applications are much more satisfied with the results. The benefits from Notes surface when all of Notes capabilities are integrated to create robust solutions.

What Notes Can Do

E-Mail. An effective communications product, Notes provides the foundation for electronic mail exchange. Users can send and receive messages using standard mail forms that can be adapted to corporate standards or individual needs. Messages can include simple text or data that is saved in a variety of formats such as a Microsoft Excel spreadsheet or Lotus Ami Pro word-processed report. E-mail allows a company to reach beyond organizational boundaries through communications with customers and vendors.

Standard Templates. Notes also provides an applications development environment. Users can create applications from scratch or through templates. Notes users can select from several boilerplate applications for sales tracking or internal discussions. Developers can enhance or change these template applications to meet specialized needs. The result is an attractive, personalized form in which users can input data and, with proper access rights, later change or view the information.

Replication. After entering information into a repository through forms, workers are able to share the information that is spread over a variety of departments or locations. Notes' unique replicating ability facilitates information sharing among the most distributed of corporate structures. In a Notes network structure, distributed databases periodically synchronize their information to create mirror images of data located throughout the company. Users can then access information locally, regardless of the location of the original data source. A Notes administrator determines how often data needs to be refreshed and how to best meet user needs.

Searching and Viewing. A powerful full-text index search engine allows executives to filter out pertinent information once it has been distributed to users. In addition, flexible views can be created and manipulated to display the information.

Notes Applications

Broadcast. These applications often resemble electronic bulletin boards that display timely information that managers can check regularly for updates and posted messages. They also are popular repositories for news. Packages such as Newsedge and Hoover compile the day's news from numerous sources and store it in Notes databases. The news can be filtered with user-defined criteria, such as a client name or a particular industry. The information is delivered to executives as conveniently as the morning paper, only the Notes solution supplies articles from news sources all over the world.

Reference. These applications are similar to broadcast applications and serve as libraries for robust, mostly static data. Meeting minutes, management reports, and policy manuals can be stored and categorized for users to access later. This application usually saves companies in the cost of duplication and dissemination of documents that are best stored and updated centrally and accessed on an as-needed basis.

Tracking. These applications contain information that is valuable to a number of employees. Users can record an event and its current status. This event is then monitored, passed along to another user for action, or stored for future access. This dynamic manipulation of documents provides great benefits for processes that need to be automated.

Discussion. These applications provide forums for users to pose questions and dialog through hierarchical replies. These saved discussions serve as an important part of organizational memory because they illustrate the thread of a decision-making process that can later be accessed when similar problems or situations arise.

THE 10-COMPANY STUDY

A study was conducted to learn about the potential role of Notes in EISs. The study was exploratory in nature because of the relatively limited experience firms have, to date, had with the product.

First, firms using Notes for EIS purposes were identified. This information was compiled from a list of companies in the University of Georgia's EIS database and references from vendors of EIS software. Ten firms agreed to participate in telephone interviews. The industries represented include gas distribution, natural gas, banking, consumer products, insurance, pharmaceuticals, consulting, and manufacturing. The companies are located throughout the U.S. and Canada.

In each company, the most knowledgeable person about the use of Notes for EISs was interviewed. The interviews were scheduled in advance and took between 20 and 30 minutes to complete. The focus was on current and planned uses of Notes in the organization, specifically with regard to EISs. The interviews also explored the strengths and weaknesses of the use of Notes for EIS.

Why Use Notes for EIS?

Interviewees were first asked how Notes was chosen for EIS use. Answers revealed that the origins were either opportunistic or strategic. In the majority of cases, Notes was brought into the company for non-EIS applications. Its EIS potential was recognized quickly, however, as developers saw the opportunity to enhance their systems by using Notes. A few firms made the strategic decision to acquire Notes specifically for use with the EIS.

Already having Notes in-house increases the likelihood that it will be used with an EIS, especially if the licensing agreement covers the EIS user base. If not, the incremental cost of obtaining Notes may be prohibitive.

How Notes Is Used

The interviews revealed three different ways that Notes is being used for EIS: as part of the EIS software; as a separate, complementary EIS; or as the primary EIS software.

Using Notes as Part of EIS Software. Notes is often used in combination with other EIS software because users appreciate its capabilities for entering, maintaining, updating, and retrieving textual information. One of the banks profiled in the ten-company study is considering using Notes this way. Its EIS was originally developed using Lightship and Lightship Server from Pilot Software. This software provided an effective solution for handling numerical data but was inadequate for textual information.

Notes, however, provides a management topics application that allows users to initiate topics for discussion and to enter and review comments made by others. All the information is textual and is used as a kind of electronic bulletin board for sharing soft information. The bank's EIS is designed to allow data suppliers and users to add textual commentaries to screens. For example, a comment entered by a data supplier might explain why performance as measured by a key service indicator has dropped. A user might add, for example, that certain actions should be taken to improve performance.

Using Notes as a Separate EIS. Lotus can also serve as a stand-alone system used to complement another EIS. The Notes-based system handles the kinds of applications for which it is inherently well suited. For example, one manufacturing firm in the study operates an EIS based on Commander EIS, but uses Notes for document management applications. The EIS manager would like to integrate the two systems, but has encountered compatibility problems. Both systems operate separately to serve the firms' executives.

Notes as the Primary EIS Software. Notes can also be used as the primary EIS software. This is the case at one company where a Notes-based EIS has replaced a system using more conventional EIS software. Several factors drove the decision to rebuild using Notes. First, there were bugs in the commercial EIS software, and the system's response time was too slow. In addition, the company recently decided on Lotus SmartSuite as an organizationwide desktop strategy, and Notes was compatible with this strategy. Finally, the company's EIS focuses on the display of information rather than

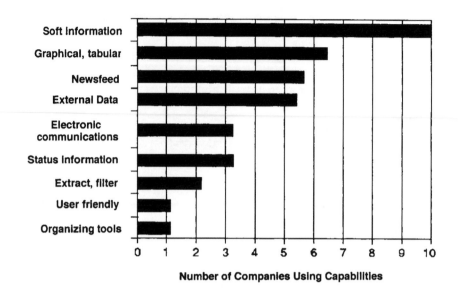

Exhibit 1.   How businesses use notes.

on data analysis; this need could be well served by Notes. The company's new EIS was developed in 6 weeks using Notes, and the reactions of users have been positive.

EIS CAPABILITIES PROVIDED BY NOTES

Notes provides many capabilities that are associated with EISs. Exhibit 1 shows the number of companies from the study that use Notes for these capabilities.

Support for Soft Information

Successful EISs often include soft information such as predictions, opinions, news, ideas, and even rumors. Most senior managers recognize that hard data is not always sufficient for decision-making.

In the document management system for a consumer-products manufacturer, executives are able to add comments to forms that track standard reports at a corporate consolidated level. These comments provide a valuable exchange of reactions, explanations, and issues among the many executives who regularly use the application. This function, in fact, has become so popular that the company has added the ability for commentary as a standard for all of its internal Notes forms.

As shown in Exhibit 1, every company in this study uses Notes to exchange soft information. In addition, each person interviewed noted the ease of incorporating soft information into Notes applications.

Presentation of Graphical, Tabular, and Textual Information

Executives often examine documents that contain graphics, tables, and formatted text. A rich presentation supports analysis and decision-making. Notes manipulates robust documents much better than standard EIS packages. Graphics and tables created in Excel and PowerPoint can be embedded easily into Notes documents. Tools such as Lotus F/X can be used to link the graphics dynamically with their data sources, so that data changes are reflected in the graphical presentation.

For example, at BC Gas Utility Ltd., graphs and analyses are prepared by various functional area groups and deposited in Notes databases. Executives can examine these graphs and tables instead of summary reports that are often more difficult to interpret. Furthermore, the company has used this process to implement management report standards. Users who once constructed numerous paper reports in various graphics packages now deposit reports into Notes documents that have a uniform look.

Support for Electronic Communications

Notes provides the primary E-mail system in some companies. Arthur Andersen & Co. first brought in Notes as a replacement for its Wang E-mail system. Notes E-mail unites its 35,000 consultants worldwide, offering companywide E-mail standards and customized forms. Other businesses integrate Notes E-mail capabilities with existing systems. For example, a consumer-products manufacturer uses Notes E-mail in parallel with MS Exchange, PROFS, and CompuServe's E-mail. Many companies, however, have invested in an E-mail infrastructure other than Notes and do not want to reinvest in an additional E-mail technology.

Presentation of Status and Trend Information

Many executives need to closely monitor events or processes to identify status, trends, or exceptions. Notes displays categorized documents so that users can easily identify the status of a process or event. At Toronto Dominion Bank, a Notes tracking system monitors and maintains relationships of customers for managers and executives. These relationships are vital to the bank's success, and their development is tracked carefully. A bank vice-president can access statistics on how many meetings have been conducted and by whom, presentations that have been given, and the number of prospects each person currently has.

Extracting, Filtering, Compressing, and Tracking Critical Data

Most EIS data resides on mainframe systems or in non-Notes applications, so companies need to download this data directly into EIS applications for their executives to access. Third-party products for Notes, such as InfoPump, offer developers the tools to set up links between various data stores so that data that was not created in Notes can still be used in Notes applications.

Arthur Andersen & Co., for example, is developing a system that can extract data about its consulting engagements from a mainframe using a medium-dependent interface (MDI) gateway. The mainframe collects detailed information about client billing and employee time reporting. Periodically, this mainframe data will be summarized and exported into the Notes engagement information system where the data is categorized and reformatted. Executives can then view this information along with documents such as action items and status reports that are created within the Notes applications themselves.

COLLABORATIVE WORK SUPPORT AND OTHER BENEFITS

Notes provides a few capabilities not typically associated with EIS software. Especially noteworthy is support for workflow applications where the work task requires collaborative efforts.

For example, Toronto Dominion Bank plans to use Notes in its EIS for processing commercial loan applications. A loan officer performs the initial processing on a loan application and enters the information on a Notes form. This information is reviewed by higher-level officers, who add comments and conditions for the loan. The entire history of the loan application can thus be maintained in Notes.

In another example, an international bank has an EIS that provides considerable support for the personnel function. The bank plans to use Notes for processing employee requests for exceptions to personnel policies and procedures. A personnel manager can enter the request on a Notes form. Higher-level managers can review the request and enter comments as the request works its way through the approval chain. A powerful feature of the Notes-enhanced system is the ability to retrieve information about similar requests and the decisions that were made.

In both cases, multiple users are involved in the work and have the need to share information — an important benefit in a corporate environment.

Notes is a relatively inexpensive product to use with an EIS. If Notes has already been licensed for use within a firm, there may be no costs involved in integrating it with EIS software. Even if Notes requires additional expense, its per-user cost is typically less than that of traditional EIS software. Recently, Lotus released an inexpensive runtime version of Notes for use on computers that do not need to access development tools.

IS departments tend to choose generic rather than specialized software because of concerns about compatibility and technical support responsibilities. For this reason, Notes may be preferred over more specialized EIS software.

LIMITATIONS OF NOTES

Notes offers so many functions that it is difficult for some companies to find direction as to how to best leverage its capabilities. In addition, many of the Notes tools and third-party products are just now starting to mature. Although it is possible, it still is not simple to access mainframe-resident data or build applications that run on multiple platforms. The embedded data analysis and display capabilities are not as advanced as in traditional EIS software.

As for the user interface, users access documents through a nontraditional navigational system. They do not maneuver through a hierarchical menu structure, but must learn how to manipulate views and forms to find the appropriate document or piece of information. All reporting must be created through views as well. In addition, building a graphical presentation of data is not inherent to Notes and must be created offline in other packages. The graphics are then pasted into Notes.

THE FUTURE OF NOTES FOR EIS

Future product upgrades and more enhanced toolsets are easing current limitations, and further improvements should make Notes more suitable for EISs. For example, a more robust user interface is expected in the new release of Notes. In the past, developers have been restricted to objects that follow the rules of Notes forms and views. Menus and complex macros required complicated workarounds. The increasing popularity of packages such as VIP and PowerBuilder Library for Notes hint at the growth of more powerful user interface development resources.

Integration between Notes and other databases exists, but capabilities are expanding for companies that want to take advantage of data located in existing applications in a variety of formats. Toronto Dominion Bank is investigating how to integrate its credit processes in Notes with related mainframe information. Once the mainframe systems download customer information into Notes, and the credit is approved, the information will flow back into the financial systems. DataLens for Windows, for example, is a set of drivers that can connect Notes with leading relational database management systems.

DOCUMENT MANAGEMENT

Overall, the consensus among the companies participating in this study is that there is an enormous amount of potential in using Notes with executive information systems in ways that reflect both traditional and non-traditional EIS characteristics. As more companies become familiar with Notes and realize its potential, its use for EISs should grow.

Section XIV
Industry-Specific and Package Solutions

RECENT TRENDS TOWARD SPECIALIZATION AND RAPID DEVELOPMENT lend themselves towards industry-specific solutions. The big question these days is the "build" vs. "buy" debate. The buy includes package solutions like SAP, PeopleSoft, and Baan. Business components and class libraries also offer buy solutions. This section contains four chapters that describe different types of reusable data solutions in different industries.

Chapter 73, "Data Management Challenges of Healthcare Delivery," looks at improving the process of healthcare delivery by capturing data at source and making it available at the point-of-care through innovative new technologies such as Smart Health Cards, Master Patient Index, Interface Engine, and a Clinical Data Repository.

Chapter 74, "Improving Supply Chain Management for the Mining and Metals Industry," uses research data and surveys to describe the supply chain and key concepts associated with new advances in technology and tools. These allow substantial improvements in customer service, speed of response, and cost. Foremost among these is the growing popularity of off-the-shelf package solutions, instead of custom builds from scratch. This chapter shows how to build a business case and what information to include when considering new investments in these technologies.

Chapter 75, "Pharmaceutical Industry Information Issues and Architectures," examines how pharmaceutical companies can leverage technology architectures and information systems to support strategic information management. The chapter also examines how organizational infrastructures are being redesigned to support the new developments in information management in this industry.

Chapter 76, "Integrating Package Processes Over Multiple Application Platforms," discusses business process integration over multiple application platforms, such as Baan, Peoplesoft, and SAP. This chapter shows how to utilize an additional layer, in the *n*-tier client/server model, to store common data between such package applications. This leads into a relatively new category of middleware, called ProcessWare.

Chapter 73
Data Management Challenges of Healthcare Delivery

Winston J. Sullivan

HEALTHCARE IS AN INTENSIVE INFORMATION-PROCESSING INDUSTRY. The delivery of services, the quality of health, and the life of a patient can depend on the quality of the data available at the point of care. The industry manages data in paper media for the most part. It has tremendous resources assigned to the management of paper information to provide appropriate quality of healthcarehealthcare. Based on future demands it will need more paper in more locations and greater paper management efforts to record, copy, duplicate, file, store, retrieve, and secure data.

Massive external change is demanding significant realignment in the delivery of healthcare services to provide more service with reduced funding, to integrate the delivery of service, to promote health, and to accommodate an aging population with longer life expectancy. A more informed consumer and global technologies are creating greater consumer expectations for service.

The healthcare industry must look to electronic information management as both a resource and an enabler to revitalize the care delivery processes, to provide accountability within the healthcare system, and to transform the health system from a focus on disease management to health promotion.

Today there is a lot of paper, some information, and little quality data. The term quality data refers to electronic data that can be accessed, shared, secured, and integrated easily to enable the analysis of financial and clinical outcomes to promote best practice in healthcare.

The medical model of observation, assessment, diagnosis, care plans, and treatment will be used to describe the problems, challenges, and outcomes for the effective utilization of data management.

0-8493-9976-9/99/$0.00+$.50
© 1999 by CRC Press LLC

First, identify the desired performance outcomes:

- Maintain quality of care
- Improve service levels
- Provide more appropriate access
- Promote health management
- Contain costs
- Maximize revenue

There is a gold mine of opportunities and some significant challenges ahead in this industry.

THE SITUATION: OBSERVATION

Paper was a necessary byproduct of healthcare processes in the past. Electronic data was elusive or nonexistent, and the quality of decisions made based on the data that was available was questionable.

The healthcare industry provided quality patient care to the exclusion of the considerations for customer service, the financial costs, and the health outcomes. Care was delivered based on the concept of disease management. The consequence is a healthcare delivery model focused around hospitals and their resources with little consideration of primary care physicians, community clinics, the patient and families, and the consumer. Until recently the belief was that the traditional model worked well … and what worked did not need to be improved upon. There was no impetus to question the medical protocols, the care processes, or the delivery models.

Data management was not considered to be an integral part of the healthcare process. The rooms full of paper charts, X-ray images, and thousands of paper forms were a means to an end in providing care. The historical barriers of distance, time, and location continued to dedicate how healthcare is provided. The concept of keeping data as a valued resource to provide the analysis for accountability, better care assessment, planning, treatment, and cost containment was not feasible due to the massive human effort it would take to manage. Managing the current paper work incurred a heavy administrative load which took the caregiver away from providing patient care.

The absence of appropriate electronic systems to manage data and information contributed to poor service, high costs, and sometimes longer length of patient stay in hospitals. The accessibility to information was resource-intensive and time-consuming and contributed to the feelings of frustration, stress, and anxiety felt by the administration and the patients.

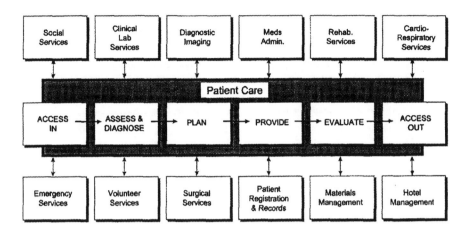

Exhibit 1. Patient care delivery and support processes.

Healthcare Delivery

The following is an overview of the current healthcare delivery process-es, how they currently are managed, and their impact on the delivery of service at a traditionally managed hospital. Refer to Exhibit 1 for the patient care delivery and support processes.

Patient Identification (Name, sex, age, demographics, medical alerts, and insurer). The data was maintained at the point of hospital registration. The same information was collected in other manual or electronic systems in each of the hospital's patient service departments either because electronic data were not accessible to everyone who needed it or it was not integrated with departmental computer systems.

If the person's health status changed from inpatient to outpatient, the same type of data was requested again and new files were setup. Hospital systems for inpatients and outpatients were not integrated for information sharing. The duplication costs of managing the paper files, the question-able accuracy of the information over many locations, and the patient and caregiver time to obtain, confirm, and update the information contributed to the inefficiencies in the process. The redundancies contributed to patient and family frustration, and often caused delays in assessment, diagnosis, and treatment. If the person went to another hospital or clinic, the spiral of duplication of information and effort continued.

Patient Management (admitting, discharge, and transfer of patients). Patient management never was focused on the patient in terms of convenience, accessibility, and preplanning. Discharge planning really did not exist. The patient was often left to learn the healthcare system and to find the alternate healthcare resources after discharge. The family physician was often left out of the loop when a patient went to the Emergency Room because the hospital did not have the systems to communicate effectively, on a timely basis, with a physician. If the physician wanted information on a hospital patient he or she often had to travel to the healthcare facility, taking time away from office patients. The telephone option involved phone tag, buck passing, and taking the caregiver away from patient care. Consequently, the higher costs of an acute care facility were incurred, incoming patients had to wait longer for an available bed, and the patient and family continued to feel frustrated at not knowing what was going to happen.

Patient Scheduling (booking appointments for assessments, tests, and treatment). As clients of the healthcare system, everyone has had to deal with the frustration of having to wait long periods of time for service. Why? Because services were geared around the provider's resources. What existed were stand-alone departmental scheduling systems that could not access or share patient or service information. The negative impacts were higher administrative costs to healthcare providers to locate information, porter patients to service areas, and pay overtime to provide the promised service. To the consumer it led to frustration, anger, and a feeling of having no say.

Patient Care Plans (a bill of materials concept for the care and treatment of patients). Often standard care plans for specific diagnoses do not exist. The patient was treated according to the treatment plan of an individual physician. If the hospital had paper care plans the information was not integrated with a scheduling system and required considerable manual effort to coordinate. The system was open to errors in the service delivery, requests for tests, and the follow-up on results in a timely manner. This resulted in increasing the length of stay (LOS) for patients with increased medical and operating costs.

Patient Order Communications (the placement and reporting of tests or services). The process was manual and in most situations remains so today. The lack of computer systems often increased a patient's LOS and the hospital's operation costs because the caregiver had to wait for paper reports to determine the discharge. The manual systems also contributed to higher medical costs because there were no alert mechanisms to warn of duplicate orders or adverse drug interactions. If a caregiver wanted to see the patient's current medical status he or she had to go to the location of the paper reports, the medical records, and the X-ray library.

Medical Chart (a patient's file kept in Medical Records Department and a second medical record of images stored in Diagnostic Imaging Department). The information existed in one place at one time for one caregiver. This access problem contributed to the lack of timely information to the caregiver and their ability to provide appropriate service and make timely decisions for treatment. Two manual medical chart systems required a significant investment in a staff infrastructure and costs to file, access, update, deliver, and retrieve these medical charts. There was also the risk of loss, confidentiality, privacy, and security of the information when all of the information was available in one file to a caregiver anywhere within the facility. The regulatory record retention policies required hospitals to setup large medical record areas and to invest in transferring paper information to various electronic imaging technologies to reduce the storage space and costs. Most facilities still required off-site storage.

THE PROBLEM: ASSESSMENT

Data quality is a major problem and service is poor. The patient identification and management systems are a mixture of electronic and manual systems that often are duplicated and not integrated. The electronic patient scheduling systems are rare and often support only a department. The care plans systems are often manual and do not integrate with patient scheduling and order communications. The order communications systems are manual in the majority of organizations. The medical chart is paper-based or electronic images of paper in some cases. Most of these systems do not have data networks to provide electronic communication to the point of care. An electronic data delivery infrastructure does not exist.

The situation exists because of the following factors:

- Data were not perceived to be a valuable resource of healthcare delivery.
- Computer technology was viewed as a cost as opposed to an investment.
- Information services could not compete with medical investments.
- There was no alignment of data management with service delivery.
- Lack of corporate data management and technology standards existed.

There was no strategic information services plan aligned to the business strategy. The consequences of this were

- The quality of service was poor.
- Cost of service was high.
- Customer expectation was low.
- The physicians and caregivers were frustrated in their attempts to overcome the shortcomings of a delivery mechanism, which took them away from patient care.

- Healthcare abdicated its responsibility of data management to its vendors who had been proprietary. Vendors locked healthcare into poor and rigid technical solutions.

THE CHALLENGE: DIAGNOSIS

The cost of achieving service quality necessitates that the health funder and the providers make significant capital investments in information systems and technology. The need to do more with fewer resources means outsourcing, sharing, and integrating data management functions.

The change agents forcing the healthcare industry to reconsider how service will be delivered are reduced healthcare funding:

- Case costing to identify best financial practices.
- Care plans to identify the most appropriate protocols of care.
- Need to reduce length of stay in hospitals to contain costs.
- More points of care to provide greater accessibility and enhance the quality of care.
- Health promotion to reduce health costs and improve quality of health.
- Changing demographics (a more mobile population, more diverse cultures, an aging population with longer life expectancy, and more working families).
- Greater expectations and demands for better access and more timely information.
- Competition for market share, dollars, patients, and services.
- Significant technology initiatives now enable the redesign and implementation of a new healthcare delivery system.
- The global Internet overcomes the barriers of building private networks.
- The virtual private networks are providing a wired world for communications without the barriers of distance, time, and location.
- Healthcare utilizes the knowledge, expertise, and infrastructures of the communication and financial industries in terms of networks, data access, security, confidentiality, and electronic commerce.
- Canada recognizes the legality of electronic signatures. The European Union will enact its Data Privacy Standard by October 1998, and the U.S. congress is to issue its confidentiality standards by August 1999.
- The Confidentiality Standards will be the impetus to the development of a Person Identification System for healthcare and a Smart Card similar to a Visa Card.
- The confidentiality standards will drive the need for mandatory electronic validation of Health Card prior to service delivery.

THE OPPORTUNITY: THE CARE PLAN

The healthcare delivery system must have a focus and priority in the design and development of a new system. To be successful, the new model concurrently must address the funder, the provider, and the consumer. The funder can be the government, a large corporation, health management organization (HMO), or an individual.

Funder Focus

The funder must provide the basic communication infrastructures to link the provider and consumer and the delivery of products and services. The funder components are the health identifier, the health network, and the health database.

Most of these technology infrastructures should be outsourced. The standards of each of these components would be regulated by the national/world health organizations similar to the Interact body. The key areas for standardization are health nomenclature and the minimum data set for health, clinical, medical, and financial information. Collaboration is the significant factor of this part of the care plan.

Provider Focus

The providers of health services must shift to the concepts of capturing data at the source to reduce data redundancy, implement electronic workflow to enable service at the point of care, use electronic signatures to authenticate, authorize, and secure access, and install an electronic health record to provide data over the continuum of care. The hospital will be the hub for community partnerships to share the cost, knowledge, and expertise of information technology. Hospitals will be the community custodians of health information and will provide the communication linkages to regional network. Each site will provide the checkpoints for security, confidentiality, and access to the appropriate information based on the consumer's approval. The technology operations and management should be outsourced. Data collaboration, information sharing, and partnership investment are the keys to success in this part of the care plan.

Consumer Focus

With computer technology becoming a household commodity, consumers will use the Internet as a virtual private network for self-service, self-learning, information sharing, and self-help. The key to the feasibility of doing this is the electronic signature to authenticate, authorize, and secure access and information. The information focus of the consumer will be access to the directories of health providers to find the available caregivers best-suited to the requester's profile for service and convenience, electronic mail to their care providers, an "Ask a Nurse" feature to help determine action in possible emergencies, electronic mail to pharmacies to renew prescriptions, and appointment scheduling. Collaboration with primary caregivers and agencies is the key to success in this part of the care plan.

THE PLAN: THE TREATMENT

Success will be achieved through collaboration of the healthcare funder and healthcare providers to identify priorities and synergies in the development of timely solutions. The following is an implementation plan for successful data management of a new integrated delivery system for health.

Funder Priorities

Stage #1: Health Data Network. Implement virtual private networks between primary agencies and care centers. Provide Internet dial-up access to caregivers and consumers to validate and share information. This should be outsourced to enable the funder to deal with more direct involvement with caregivers in developing the nomenclature and minimum data sets for medical and clinical information.

Stage #2: Smart Health Card. The card is used for consumer authorization for services and consumer update of the Health Card Database. The card would have a consumer's PIN #. This also would allow for electronic signature via the health network for remote services and information sharing. This should be outsourced to third parties.

Stage #3: Smart Health Database. The consumer's demographics, primary physician, and health alerts information would be maintained on the Health Card of the consumer. When the card is updated at the point of care, the funder's Smart Health Database also is updated. This information could be updated by the consumer to the Smart Health Database via the health network. The primary caregiver could update the caregiver health alerts and primary caregiver information in collaboration with the consumer. Both would use their Health Card and PIN # to valide, authenticate, and authorize the relationship.

Stage #4: Health Encounter Database. All encountered data must be authorized by the consumer's Health Card and PIN # and collaborated with the provider's Health Card and Pin #. The last encounter data is on the Health Card. All encounters are on the Smart Health Database for payment to providers.

Stage #5: Health Encounter Billing Database. The encounter, funder, provider, and consumer information already have been identified in the Encounter Database. At this stage the service would be identified for billing and the electronic payment transferred or credited. The provider billing systems would be eliminated.

Provider Priorities

Stage #1: Consumer Health Help Center. Implement regional intranets to provide consumer health information and an interactive media for electronic mail and possibly Groupware. Provide consumer search for care provider. Provide appointment request, confirmation, cancellation, browse features.

Stage #2: Master Patient Index (MPI). The MPI is used to unite, across the local healthcare enterprise, the personal identification and management information. The MPI also would provide an electronic link to the consumer's Health Card for access to the health record, and the funder's health Card Database to validate the Health Card information. It will enable the future move to an electronic medical record.

Stage #3: Interface Engine. This technology will provide electronic routing and integration of transactional information between applications, systems, and technologies to overcome the barriers of incompatible legacy systems and to avoid the costs of point-to-point programming of interfaces. The technology will overcome the barriers where standards do not exist or are incompatible. It also will enhance the use of industry standards. The implementations and operations management should be outsourced because of the critical nature of the application and the need for continuous availability.

Stage #4: Electronic Health Record. What goes into the electronic health record, how it is organized, the data structures for access, and the nomenclature are currently under considerable discussion by several standardization bodies. The electronic health record will overcome the immediate barriers of distance, time, and location to provide current access to patient health and medical information. The health identification card, master patient index, and the health data network will enable the creation of a virtual health record.

Stage #5: Electronic Person Identification. This is used to enable the identification, validation, authorization, verification, and authentication of the electronic signature. It is to be used to identify consumers and caregivers with an electronic signature and authorizations for order communications, results viewing, and care delivery with the appropriate confidentiality and security mechanisms in place. The technology will enhance the activity-based case costing process to provide data on financial outcomes.

Stage #6: Electronic Order Communications. The implementation should be phased to get the earlier benefits of access to electronic results.

Step #1: Online Results Reporting. Instead of printing reports, use electronic digital archiving and the intranet to provide the same information to the appropriate caregiver. The digital archive information can be loaded into other decision support tools as well as the electronic health record (when it is installed).

Step #2: Results Management. This is real-time results reporting with information mining, GUI interface, and exception highlighting. The information is sourced from the electronic health record.

Step #3: Order Entry. This is the online real-time entry of orders with decision support and clinical alerts, electronic signatures, and automated routing and notification. This is the most significant change. It will mean the replacement of paper-based methods and procedures and the introduction of physician order entry. The byproduct of the system will be to provide the billing information and case-costing information to the financial systems.

Stage #7: Patient Scheduling. A phased implementation delivers more rapid benefits than the alternatives.

Step #1: Appointment Request. Provide intranet access to community physicians and consumers to request appointments. The booking would be centralized with the confirmation via voice- or e-mail.

Step #2: Online Scheduling. The implementation of enterprise-wide scheduling will take significant effort to re-engineer, automate, and test the business and clinical rules. The system, as a byproduct, will be used to measure service performance in booking, scheduling, and delivering services.

Step #3: Remote Scheduling. Provide physicians remote access to schedule patients, check bookings, and update information from their offices.

Step #4: Appointment Schedule. Provide the consumer with the ability to self-schedule appointments.

Stage #8: Electronic Workflow. The automation of forms and their business processes will have a profound impact on the accessibility of information and the cycle time of decision making.

Step #1: Electronic Forms. Replace all single and two-part forms that go into a health record. With an electronic network there is no need to have this paper. With electronic person identification there are the necessary electronic signatures. Digital archiving and ad hoc workflow will provide a document database of the information that can be accessed and shared across the LAN and intranet. The archive information at a later time can be integrated or loaded into the health record.

Step #2: Smart Electronic Forms and Workflow. With electronic forms and structured workflow, technologies develop the automated systems that will incorporate production database access. The significant advantage is that the business rules will be automated for the conditional flow of information. Policy and procedures are automated. This will reduce staff training time dramatically and ensure compliance.

Stage #9: Electronic Care Plans.

Step #1: Online Care Planning. Implement an automated care plan system with point of care data capture and viewing. The electronic person identification systems will provide for bar code identification of procedures, patient, and caregiver. The information also will provide the data to the financial systems for case costing.

Step #2: Schedule Integration. Integrate the care plan with the scheduling system. When the caregiver diagnoses the problem and selects the appropriate Care Plan, the scheduling system automatically will schedule the requests for service. At this stage, orders entered by a human would be by exception. A byproduct of the integration will be able to provide financial, medical, and clinical data on service delivery performance.

THE FUTURE: THE OUTCOMES

The data management challenges of the current healthcare systems have been identified with a plan to maximize the change opportunities to achieve the performance outcomes of the following:

- Maintain the quality of care
- Improve service levels
- Provide more appropriate access
- Promote health management
- Contain costs
- Maximize revenue

Healthcare now is facing the new challenges associated with new partnerships, mergers, alliances, and new funding formulas. These changes broaden the scope of data management beyond a single enterprise to embrace a group health enterprise.

Funder Mandate

The healthcare funder has taken action to close healthcare facilities and mandate that others merge to provide more appropriate service to the consumer at reduced cost. How can the data and technologies of the new enterprises be co-ordinated, integrated, and managed?

Provider Mandate

Hospitals and community clinics have entered into merger, acquisition, and alliances to overcome the problems of reduced funding and the need for large capital investments to revamp their care delivery processes. How can third parties be incorporated in the outsourcing services and still retain an integrated delivery service and the data management asset for performance measurement?

Service Mandate

The concept of an Integrated Delivery Service (IDS) will drive the providers into more aggressive competition for increased market share and funding. Survival will depend on building partnerships, alliances, and integrating the priorities of corporate data management with regional healthcare enterprises. IDS is based on the concepts of rostering and capitation.

Rostering

To bring all the community providers of health services into a partnership that will provide the complete health services for its regional group on a 7/24 basis in a seamless manner, the consumer would choose and register with a primary physician within a regional health group and sign a contract indicating that the members of the health network will share access to patient health information, as appropriate, to deliver the full services of healthcare. The viability of the regional health group will depend on their success in attracting consumers and providing the timely services.

Capitation

The funding will be based on a fixed sum per capita. The healthcare funder will provide the regional health group (RHG) the global funding based on their patient roster. The RHG will self-determine the allocation of the funds to provide the required services to their consumers. The promotion of health will be critical to longer-term success. Disease prevention will lower the costs and provide funding for the unique needs of the population. It is to everyone's benefit to streamline, reduce redundancy, and stay healthy.

Data Management Mandate

To support IDS there is a greater need to progress beyond application systems management to knowledge management. The systems and technology acquisitions will be shared by the partners within the regional health group. The information support staff will need to be aligned to support the regional priorities. Information and technology standards will be key to successful data management. The true value to be derived from an applications architecture will be from electronic workflow, decision support systems, and information management (data marts and data warehouses).

Data Marts and Data Warehouses

The future direction of data management will be the development of data marts and data warehouses for the regional health groups and members. The data mart is a collection of structured data focused on a particular subject. The data elements reflect the various dimensions of the subject (e.g., distance, time, location, and dollars.). The user would use the data mart in decision support to create views of information, manage variances, and identify trends.

The data warehouse is a replication of the health enterprises' data repositories (key production databases: human resources, financial, clinical, medical, encounter) with a lexicon. The data are not structured, but are warehoused. All data elements are indexed to allow data extract to create data marts. The data warehouse is used in research and development to identify patterns, perform what-if analysis, and identify inferences to create new knowledge.

Exhibit 2 highlights the major components of the patient care delivery and support services and identifies the key subjects for inclusion in data marts and data warehouses.

The Change Barriers

With the gold mine of data management opportunities in the new healthcare delivery model, there are technology integration barriers to be overcome but the real challenge will be the need for collaboration and standardization.

The critical success factors are

- Standardization of medical nomenclature
- Minimum data sets for financial, clinical, and medical models
- Content of the health record
- Health access privileges
- Standardization protocols of care
- Standardization of performance benchmarks

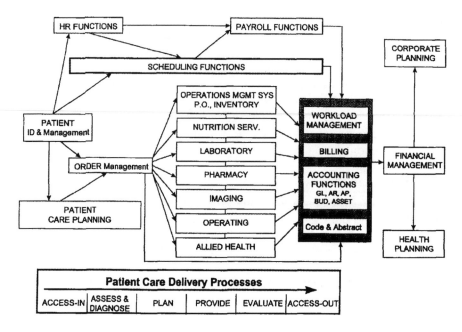

Exhibit 2.   Conceptual application architecture.

CONCLUSION

With the vision of capturing data at its source and providing information at the appropriate point of care and with the collaboration and commitment to a strategic data management plan, the fear, doubt, and uncertainty of change can be managed to deliver innovative new solutions to revitalize healthcare delivery.

Chapter 74

Improving Supply Chain Management for the Mining and Metals Industry

Karl Kelton

THE MINING AND METALS SECTOR is among the last significant industrial area to begin to move forward aggressively with the use of integrated computer systems to renew and improve all areas of the enterprise. These areas include financial management, materials management, maintenance, processing/production, and the supply chain. Momentum is beginning to build now in the mid-1990s, to embrace the information technologies available off-the-shelf to significantly renew these and other business processes across the value chain that, in many cases, have remained unchanged for decades. The impetus for this movement is rooted in the belief, on the part of early adopters, that there is a solid business case for change, a business case which helps to significantly address executives' long-term business concerns about maximally leveraging corporate assets and stakeholder/shareholder value.

In prior years, the business case for change enabled by integrated systems was questionable. Today, each company and sector situation is different, and unique economic or operational complexities greatly can influence whether major investments in information technology (IT) truly make sense given investment constraints. The very recent advent of powerful, flexible and more cost-effective integrated system platforms from reputable vendors has changed the dynamic and created a new window of opportunity that merits a business, not technology-driven, analysis.

It is important to start by examining three key issues facing mining and metallurgy companies today.

0-8493-9976-9/99/$0.00+$.50
© 1999 by CRC Press LLC

- Volatility of commodity prices. Predictability of the factors affecting the balance between supply and demand is becoming increasingly complex. Witness the impacts of recent events such as the Asian flu, major banks selling off massive amounts of their gold reserves, and copper prices over the last year.
- Operating efficiencies and cost control. In today's competitive global economy, base metals producers continue to be price takers. Pressure will continue to build on producers' abilities to provide superior customer service, with the necessary speed and agility, at the lowest possible cost structures.
- Management information systems and technology. The past 5 years have produced an explosion in the power and availability of tools to provide strategic, tactical, and operational decision support to companies.

Our surveys also provide some insights. For example in the contexts of operating efficiency, process changes and decision support, 66% of CIOs surveyed expect an increase in business process reengineering (BPR) activity, including supply chains. Today, of all the drivers of organizational change, one of the largest is supply chain reengineering. And almost invariably, the results of that process mean significant pressures on IT. Remarkably though, a surprising number of BPR projects still take place without IT involvement, approximately one in four, either because IT is out of touch with the business or simply is excluded.

Still the question remains: how can a company achieve its business objectives without IT involvement? Or similarly: how can IT deliver value when it inherits other people's systems or decisions?

Analysis of the survey shows that in the context of IT expenditures, companies have four areas they must evaluate if they are to improve their supply chain operations.

1. Control the duplication of technology. Simplicity is better. Conversely, complexity is expensive.
2. Manage build vs. buy decisions for technology solutions. With the availability of new and powerful packaged solutions, companies need a compelling reason to justify building their own systems.
3. Deploy technology strategically. Before buying, first build a clear business case. The alternative is a technological Tower of Babel; more to support, more confusion, more to go wrong.
4. Manage the human resources aspect of technology. Poor IT supply chain decisions manifest as unfavorable human symptoms: increased training needs, stress on the job, recruiting problems, unchecked outsourcing, and so on.

Supply chain management encompasses a number of key business processes. These include managing the flow of materials, funds, and information from suppliers through manufacturing, transportation, and distribution to customers. It also supports the revenue-generating activities of the company.

Our survey highlights a major challenge in supply chain management today: leveraging advances in technology and systems to manage the flow of information within the supply chain. Managing this complex network requires timely access to information to facilitate rapid decision making.

Production must be optimized to realize maximum efficiency, responsiveness, and throughput. Inventories need to be reduced to the minimum levels necessary to support customer service objectives. Distribution must be planned carefully to ensure product is delivered at the right place, on time. The supply chain manager must be able to see everything, change anything, and to consider all aspects of the supply chain when making major decisions.

This year almost 200 North American manufacturers representing a broad spectrum of industry segments participated in our annual survey, which focused on supply chain systems and technologies. Insights provided include:

- Senior management's perspectives on the overall business environment for North American companies.
- Development of supply chain management in North America, including current industry dynamics, and their impacts on the supply chain.
- Current and planned use of supply chain systems and supporting technologies to improve supply chain operations.
- Increasing focus on formal partnerships with customers and suppliers
- Challenges of information sharing among all supply chain entities through the Internet or other means.

The supply chain is a key area of executive management focus. Ninety-seven percent of respondents rated efficient supply chain management as critical to the long-term success of their business. However, only 33% believe that their supply chain capabilities are above average for the industry. Accordingly, 80% of respondents have supply chain improvement initiatives either planned, or currently underway. Additionally, 80% of respondents plan to increase their supply chain technology budget significantly to support these initiatives and to attain competitive advantage.

To enable a company to make quick and confident decisions, a supply chain management system must be built on the following fundamental principles:

- Constraint management. Businesses require feasible solutions. Plans that fail to consider real-world constraints are of limited use. Effective management means recognizing and minimizing the impact of constraints such as materials, capacity, manpower, transportation, warehousing, suppliers, management policies, customer and channel allocations, and others.

- Concurrent vs. serial planning. Traditional planning is done sequentially, with separate plans for manufacturing, procurement, transportation, sourcing, allocation, and distribution, which results in unsynchronized plans. Intelligent systems are capable of concurrent planning across the supply chain, resulting in faster plan generation and a synchronized, responsive supply chain.

- Global insight. With constraint management and concurrent planning, mining and petroleum companies can grasp the global impact of local changes on all aspects of the supply chain and, thus, can make globally good decisions.

- Advanced warning. When a local change occurs, whether it is a material shortage, unscheduled equipment downtime, or a supplier failure to meet expectations, intelligent systems instantly rely on advanced warning to all stakeholders. This warning defines the change in terms of its effects on sales, inventory and work-in-progress (WIP) levels, lead times, due dates, and other key business drivers.

- Built-in business optimization. Because business scenarios change constantly, intelligent systems must recommend new operational solutions rapidly that maximize quantifiable business objectives such as return on assets (ROA), profit contribution, and cash flow. The decision support logic available with many tools today accommodates different business optimization criteria.

The goal of intelligent supply chain management is to achieve maximum customer responsiveness at the least possible cost.

Many processes now can be integrated across inter- and intracompany supply chains using new, powerful tools:

- Forecasting. Off-the-shelf packages work with forecasts at various levels of abstraction in aggregate, plant-by-plant, or process and perform accurate variance calculations for finished goods, work-in-progress, and raw materials. Impacts of forecast changes on distribution plans and procurement can be calculated instantly.

- Available to promise. Concurrent planning and constraint management functionality makes accurate available-to-promise and real-time order quotation possible. Tools now can conside, simultaneously, materials, capacity, transportation, customer allocations, supplier allocations, and related business constraints.

- Distribution planning. Technology now can support "what if" and " can do" analysis associated with both upstream and downstream impacts of demand. Traditional distribution requirements planning tools only have been able to communicate demand to upstream operations. Tools now provide for simultaneous planning for transportation, plant and warehouse sourcing, refining and purchasing, although recommending optimal solutions for lead times, replenishments, consolidation routines, and synchronization of deliveries.

- Sourcing. Available technology now can integrate efficiently both outside and inside suppliers within the demand/fulfillment formula. User-defined algorithms determine the optimal supplier, whether it is another plant, custom-feed operation, third-party vendor, or a warehouse in another country and automatically computes transportation and processing costs, materials and capacity availability, and service performance.

- Allocations. Decisions can be supported quickly now regarding whether raw materials and finished goods available in one country can be allocated to warehouses and facilities in another.

- Inventory planning. Effective management also means modeling different inventory policies at different nodes in the supply chain. Tools now can accommodate varying reorder triggers, days of supply levels, and service levels — individually and in aggregate.

- Plant operations: planning and scheduling. Traditional MRPII systems are transactional tools that calculate requirements based on local demand. Historically, MRPII has been used to compute a "best guess" master production schedule that translates that data into a materials requirements plan, which in turn creates a capacity requirements plan. Such sequential planning typically requires hours or days to complete and, when generated, is often out of date and ignores constraints on capacity. Tools are now available that generate plans for all requirements and resources, looking both upstream and downstream to refining and distribution processes — in real time.

- Procurement. Tools now available can model supplier capacities and provide information required for mining and metallurgical companies to make more prudent outsourcing and procurement decisions.

- Electronic commerce. With the advent of the Internet, EDI, intranet, and extranets, suppliers, manufacturers, and customers now can be linked by a single electronic system. Nodes in the supply chain can plan their business based on the delivery constraints of their key suppliers. Customers can be appraised of critical supply status and lead times before issuing an order.

Collectively, these are the functions that give an organization the ability to respond swiftly to change and to optimize assets across the supply chain. However, as anyone who has fought for a budget knows, there is nothing more sensitive or contentious than spending, which leads to the final and probably most important point of this discussion.

Information technology (IT) is or should be a strategic resource. This means in turn that IT professionals, along with their other business colleagues, must think and act the part, move beyond the day-to-day and the bewitchments of technology, and ultimately link information concerning the company's supply chain performance to its business objectives.

Developing a business case is critical for the project not only to secure initial funding, but also to help manage change throughout the project and to ensure that business benefits are achieved. To match integrated computer solutions to supply chain needs, a company first must identify the primary areas of the supply chain, which need improvement by asking questions such as the following:

- Is it important to improve manufacturing operations?
- Would the greatest benefit be gained by focusing on logistics?
- Is it more important to focus on the entire supply chain from a strategic perspective?

These questions do not always have obvious answers. A common mistake made by companies implementing packages is to attack the most visible supply chain problem first, without conducting a diagnostic study to identify where the largest potential benefit truly lies. For example, if a company has massive, visible amounts of raw materials, it may determine that an advanced materials requirements planning application will offer the greatest benefits. However, a well-executed diagnostic study might reveal that raw material storage costs are minimal when compared to transportation and distribution costs for work-in-process and finished goods. In this case, the company might benefit most by focusing initial implementation efforts on the strategic and tactical aspects of distribution planning.

Because many software packages offer a wide variety of applications to support different areas of the supply chain, it is important that companies identify where they expect to see benefits, prior to beginning implementation, and what the criteria for success will be. The business case should rely heavily on the supply chain diagnostic to tie expected benefits to areas of the supply chain in which the greatest gains are expected.

When assessing software package requirements, companies must specify what they want the tool to perform, what functionality is required, what type of reporting is needed, how the package needs to work with other applications currently in use at the company, if the package works within the hardware/network constraints of the company, and how customizable the application is. If certain key features are critical to a company, it should define clearly what these are and make every attempt to identify a software vendor that supports them. All these considerations should be built into the business case.

Implementation costs for companies installing either enterprise-wide solutions, such as SAP, Oracle, BaaN, and People Soft, or tailored solutions, such as I2, Manugistics, Numertrix, Indus, Maximo, and others, vary widely. Key factors that ultimately determine the cost are

- Degree of external resources used.
- Investment required for technical infrastructure.
- Scope and scale of the business benefits targeted.
- Overall strategy for implementing the software, including the costs of training and users.

Again, these factors need to be built into the business case.

Just as different packages and applications offer different features, different software vendors work with their clients in different ways. Before deciding whom to work with, a company should agree on specific requirements it has for the software company itself. What type of consulting is needed? What guarantees are required? What experience in specific industries or planning functions are desired? A company planning to implement enterprise requirements planning (ERP), advanced planning and scheduling (APS) packages, or other logistics software should conduct an analysis of vendor capabilities similar to the software requirements process described earlier. By identifying which issues are most important, a company can approach software selection with a clear understanding of what to look for and build these considerations into the business case. Other business case considerations should include vendor demonstrations of a product, site visits where the software has been implemented successfully, and reference checks.

The package selection decision will affect the entire implementation effort. Consequently, provisions should be made in the business case for the use of outside assistance to foster more effective decision making and help assure that the best application is chosen. Qualified third-party system integrators can offer extensive experience in implementing multiple packages, experience in selecting among multiple packages, and knowledge of the types of features offered by the different applications. They also provide significant industry and planning process expertise to help gauge the applicability of a software application to a company's planning environment. This can speed the selection process and help ensure that the company makes its selection decision with as much information as possible.

Finally, does the business case reinforce the following requirements for a successful implementation?

- Active, visible and strong top management involvement.
- A serious appreciation for the change management requirements.
- Rigorous project and partner management.
- Accelerated decision-making processes.
- Creative project team incentives.
- Plenty of training, education, support, and communication.
- Focused alignment of the organization, team, scope.
- Reengineering in the correct doses at the correct times.

- Strategic and tangible benefits and a program to measure progress toward stated goals.

The business case is a critical tool that helps to manage change throughout the project, to keep people focused, aligned, and moving in the right direction, and to make sure that the expected benefits are achieved.

A question often asked is whether or not it is possible to attribute benefits to the software or to improvements in supply chain processes and whether it might not be possible to achieve the benefits simply with improvements to logistics. The answer to both is yes, in some cases; in most cases, however, the two are linked tightly, and it is not only difficult but also unproductive to try to separate the benefits of each. One company executive explained it this way, "We might have been able to make the process improvements, but we never would have been able to sustain them without enabling software."

In closing, the following points summarize the key concepts of this chapter:

- Supply chain management and the need to enable improvements through technology is "top of mind" with executive management.
- Integrated and bolt-on solutions with extensive functionality are available off-the-shelf, eliminating the need in many cases for customized solutions that are costly, take a lot of time to develop and implement, lack the necessary support for end users, and fail to cover the supply chain spectrum.
- Executive management continues to be concerned about the levels of spending on technology and the returns for every dollar invested.
- Objective business cases that support the strategic, tactical, and operational goals associated with technology-enabled supply chain initiatives are critical.

Chapter 75

Pharmaceutical Industry Information Issues and Architectures

Sandra Shuffler
Carmine Cutone

THE HEALTHCARE ENVIRONMENT CONTINUES TO UNDERGO DRAMATIC CHANGE in response to debt control measures and changing demographics and technology. This has resulted in new demands on healthcare suppliers like the pharmaceutical industry. Suppliers have responded by developing new approaches to marketing, repositioning their strategies and reengineering their internal functions. In the first half of the 1990s, Canadian pharmaceutical companies consolidated and reduced headcount in reaction to the converging pressures of restricted formularies, thinning product lines, the trend towards generic substitution, and globalization pressures from corporate headquarters.

In addition, pharmaceutical companies are beginning to shift their focus toward long-term growth opportunities and strategic positioning.[1]

Deloitte and Touche Consulting Group surveyed pharmaceutical executives about this shift. Specifically, executives were asked to identify the most significant growth opportunities and to rank the challenges that their companies will need to consider when trying to achieve this growth. Large North American pharmaceutical companies (revenues greater than $500 million) responded by ranking information technology and corporate culture as the two most significant challenges to developing internally and maintaining a competitive edge in their core competencies.[1] The respondents also indicated that the importance of information technology and data management will increase significantly over the next 5 years. This reflects a burgeoning demand for health economics, disease management, and the development of private formularies.

THE NEED FOR INFORMATION MANAGEMENT

An organization's information capability is critical to the achievement of its goals. But although information technology (IT) was once the sole province of the IT department, today's distributed technology means everyone within an organization forms a part of the information capability. Fully integrated business systems are spanning departmental and hierarchical boundaries to provide information linkages throughout organizations. However, information access alone is insufficient. Information needs to be accessed by the appropriate persons, processed in a meaningful way, and used effectively to support the company strategies and objectives. IT can facilitate this process, but information management is important to ensure information is transferred into knowledge, actions, and outcomes.

Pharmaceutical firms are selling information just as much as they are selling a drug product. Health outcomes analyses, accurate cost reporting, and contract data management are demanded from government formularies, physicians, pharmacists, and patients. The 1996 Pharmaceutical Industry Survey found that managed care and disease management were significant issues for IT customers. However, few organizations had developed a technology strategy to map out a plan for applications to support the needed data management. To meet customer needs successfully, firms must leverage information and technology for a competitive advantage.

The 1996 Canadian Pharmaceutical Industry survey[2] (Exhibit 1) also indicated that pharmaceutical CIOs and their internal IT customers agree that the most important IT activity is supporting the daily operations of the pharmaceutical organization. However, their opinions differ when asked about the importance of IT in meeting the business objectives of the organization and providing a source of competitive advantage through information technology. This difference in perspective may be explained by information and technology. Some players place more emphasis on information although others place it on technology.

This difference in perspective persists when asked about present and future opportunities regarding IT. Clients see significant IT opportunity in areas of disease management, managed care, changing customer and buying patterns, and the need for joint ventures and alliances. This is consistent with industry views toward therapeutic alignment and in developing partnerships with strategic healthcare businesses. However, CIOs perceive that the change in customers and their buying patterns represented the most significant IT organizational issue/opportunity perhaps due to the inflexibility of present systems to accommodate the market changes. Whatever the reason, there is a gap between CIOs' and senior managers' percep-

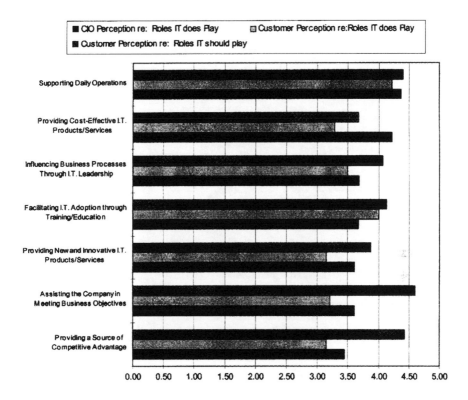

Exhibit 1. Level of importance of IT activities.

tions in the role and in the opportunities that exist in today's marketplace with respect to information and technology. It is important for CIOs to develop a coordinated multiyear information and technology plan to ensure that information technology is matching the needs of internal customers and to plan how information will be used to gain a competitive advantage.

Pharmaceutical Information Issues

Although managed care is not as well-established in Canada as in the U.S., aspects of disease management are influencing the industry. Private insurers and pharmacy benefits managers and other emerging purchasing groups are developing private formularies and using evidence-based information to define first-, second-, and sometimes third-line therapy for specific medical conditions. Information is a key priority for pharmaceutical firms as they position themselves as a premier player in a particular disease category. Some companies are using information technology to assist in tracking data by using disease management software in hospitals and hospital clinics across Canada to track patient outcomes and costs to the

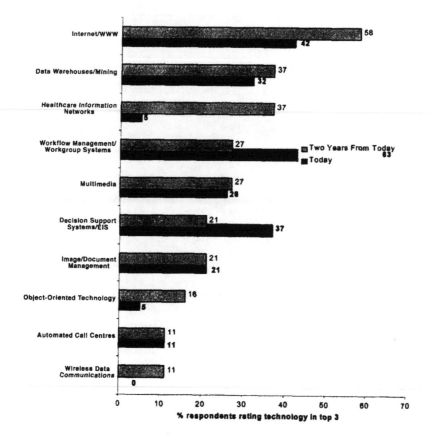

Exhibit 2.   Important information technology tools.

healthcare system. Background data, tracking of health outcomes, competitor costs, and patient compliance have not been tracked consistently and often data comes from different sources. The development of complete systems and system interfaces will be important to disseminate and utilize information stored in both internal and external systems. Additionally systems will help to reduce data acquisition costs and improve market decisions for product positioning.

Different technologies can support this information management and its transformation into knowledge and ultimately outcomes. When CIOs were asked about the most important information technology tools used today in their pharmaceutical organization (Exhibit 2), their response was workflow management tools, Internet/Intranet, and decision support tools. By 1999, the most important information technology tools would be Internet/Intranet, Healthcare Information Systems, and data warehouse/mining tools. These information technology tools will assist pharmaceutical firms in managing data and exchanging information around sales, competitive product costs, total costs of patient treatments, and patient outcomes and statistics.

Promoting the product positioning to formulary groups and purchasing parties will expand beyond generating economic outcomes data to effectively communicating results and demonstrating value in the context of the purchaser. Value-based models use economic outcomes studies as a means of developing software tools for the sales force. These tools use customer data to prove cost effectiveness and deliver a customized educational tool to purchasers. An excellent example of this type of value-added service is the case of a large surgical instruments manufacturer. The high cost of the client's surgical instruments and the lack of knowledge of the economic benefits of laparoscopic surgery were slowing down the adoption of this new technology. An international study of the value-in-use of the client's products was conducted to determine its economic impact on hospitals and healthcare systems. Results of this study were communicated through a variety of mediums including an interactive software tool, which allowed the sales force to input customer data and present customized yet consistent presentations on product value.

Sales forces are undergoing major restructuring as they equip themselves with the skills and tools necessary to deal with revised purchasing criteria. Sales force automation has become an important tool to enable better contract management, enhance customer service, and improve marketing and sales decisions. Traditional sales force automation includes tracking transactions and maintaining account profiles. As these data management tools are evolving they are storing sales contract information and profitability in common databases. Sales associates can connect by modem for price updates, client information, and best practices. In some cases contract information that is downloaded is incorporated directly into the SAP business system. One of the authors' clients, a large pharmaceutical manufacturer wanted to automate its sales force as part of a major restructuring effort. The project aimed to provide the sales force with appropriate portable computer technology to gain a competitive advantage in targeting the marketplace and the authors provided project management, business, and technical expertise. Sales representative were given notebook computers, contact management software, electronic mail, and other remote communications software. By dialing into the company's network, they receive updates on sales force initiatives and strategies as well as the activities and results of their colleagues.[3]

1996

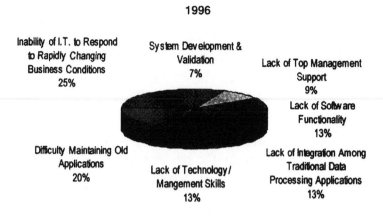

Inability of I.T. to Respond to Rapidly Changing Business Conditions
25%

System Development & Validation
7%

Lack of Top Management Support
9%

Lack of Software Functionality
13%

Difficulty Maintaining Old Applications
20%

Lack of Technology / Mangement Skills
13%

Lack of Integration Among Traditional Data Processing Applications
13%

Exhibit 3.   Most significant challenges facing CIOs.

TECHNOLOGY AND ARCHITECTURES FOR INFORMATION MANAGEMENT

Pharmaceutical companies are finding increasingly their IT capabilities are inhibiting rather than facilitating their desired growth. A high portion of their business processes still are supported by legacy systems. In fact (Exhibit 3), the two most significant challenges perceived by CIOs is the inability of present systems to adjust to the rapidly changing business conditions and the difficulty they are having in maintaining old applications. Companies are restricting their capability to manage their businesses effectively and efficiently by maintaining outmoded legacy systems and architectures and status quo skills and organizations that support them. However, changing integrated systems is a capital and time-intensive project making it difficult to make a quick transition to a rapidly changing market.

Transforming this capability requires the realignment of systems, architecture, and people with strategic objectives and market needs. Many companies have attempted to deal with this escalating problem by tackling only one or two of these elements and have failed. A transformation cannot be a piecemeal process but must be approached with an all-embracing, holistic vision. As the pharmaceutical industry evolves, and as demands for information increase, there is a movement toward using more integrated business systems. Integrated business systems combine all business systems, such as Human Resources, Finance, Production Planning, and Sales Distribution, into a comprehensive linked business system. The move toward fully integrated data and information systems is very clear. When pharmaceutical executives were asked what business systems they expected to operate in 2 years, they found that the key players are changing.

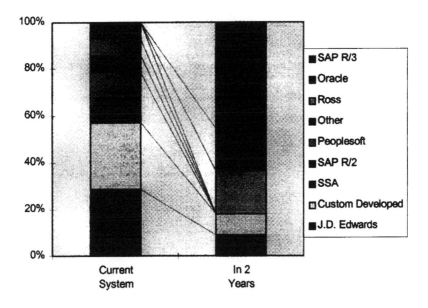

Exhibit 4. Integration business systems.

The architectures of choice will be fully integrated systems (Exhibit 4) offered by SAP R/3, Oracle Applications, and Ross by 1999.

INFORMATION INFRASTRUCTURES

Information management demands change throughout the organization, in culture, processes, and roles. As a result, IT functions are frequently participants and even leaders of reengineering efforts to ensure that the information technology is well-aligned with the information needs of the firm. The return on investment for organizations who implemented IT systems in the past 2 or 3 years frequently was sited as increasing professional productivity, enhanced access to information, and better and more accurate planning (Exhibit 5).

The past 2 years have been significant in the strategic development and positioning of IT as a function within Canadian pharmaceutical firms. Firms are putting positions and structures in place to enable IT to have a greater impact on all business areas. These changes include the development of new CIO positions, the move to a direct CIO/CEO reporting structure, a relatively high business area involvement in a more centralized IT function, and the significant role of IT in reengineering activities. This strategic positioning will allow information technology and information management to proceed in an integrated fashion for the firm as a whole.

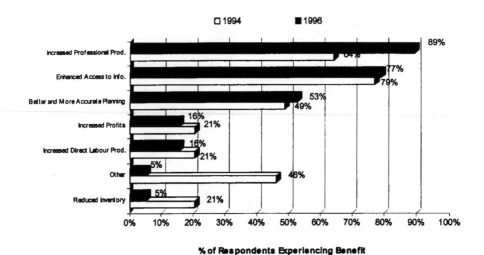

□ 1994　■ 1996

% of Respondents Experiencing Benefit

Exhibit 5.　Benefit from implementing IT systems over the past 2 or 3 years.

CONCLUSION

The use and importance of information technology is growing across most industry groups. To leverage information to gain a competitive advantage, pharmaceutical suppliers first must develop a strategy for technology development. Information technology is capital-intensive, and it is important for CIO divisions to prioritize and align their IT development with overall corporate strategies.

Pharmaceutical companies in Canada are moving in the right direction. They are focusing more on information and knowledge management rather than on process management technologies. The success of pharmaceutical companies lies not only within their product lines, but in how they can utilize information to add direct value to their product and to their customer relationships within the Canadian healthcare environment. Defining information and, more importantly, knowledge needs are essential to determine the best technology to support this. Clear business objectives facilitated by information technology often may provide a competitive advantage. This match of information needs and technology only can occur when CIOs understand clearly their customer's needs and have the ability to react relatively quickly to them.

References

1. *Marketplace 2000,* 1996 Pharmaceutical Industry Survey, Deloitte and Touche Consulting Group, Toronto, Canada, 1, 1996.

2. *CIO Survey,* 1996 Canadian Pharmaceutical Industry, Deloitte and Touche Consulting Group, Toronto, Canada, 1996.
3. Deloitte and Touche in the Pharmaceutical Industry, New Solutions for the New Environment, Deloitte and Touche, Toronto, Canada, 13, 1996.

Chapter 76

Integrating Package Processes over Multiple Application Platforms

Ido Gileadi

COMPANIES AND PEOPLE ARE RELYING MORE THAN EVER ON COMPUTER-IZED SYSTEMS to run their businesses. Traditional computing tasks such as finance, human resources, and contact management now are extended to include additional areas where the business is seeking to gain a competitive advantage. Computerized systems are viewed by management as the primary tool for gaining advantage over the competition.

The introduction of multiple applications at all levels of the organization and the executive attention that these applications are receiving is highlighting a well-known problem. All applications must work in tandem, communicate with each other, and, most importantly, pass meaningful data that then can be rolled up for management reporting.

IT organizations have been integrating packages for many years. The integration programs of the past were created like bridges connecting disparate islands. Point-to-point connections transferred subsets of data, typically in ASCII file format, on a predefined schedule. This type of point-to-point integration required detailed knowledge of each application data and did not provide a satisfactory solution when real-time access to data and functionality was required.

With the introduction of ERP (Enterprise Resource Planning) systems came the promise of support for integrated business processes. The idea was that the ERP systems would cover most aspects of computerization in an organization. ERP, being one integrated package, will allow for a complete start-to-end business process integration. The reality is that ERP

0-8493-9976-9/99/$0.00+$.50
© 1999 by CRC Press LLC

Order Taking Process

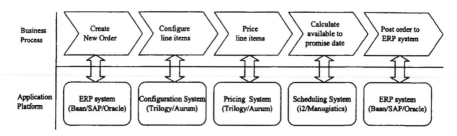

Exhibit 1.   Order-taking process.

packages cannot address all of an organization's business requirements in a satisfactory manner. A combination of packaged software as well as legacy and custom-made software residing along side each other, therefore can be see each providing a solution to a portion of the business process.

Once again IT organizations are faced with the challenge of integrating multiple application platforms into one coherent business process.

THE CHARGE

An organization undergoing a major package implementation such as SAP, Baan, Oracle or PeopleSoft typically will start with identifying the scope of the project. The scope of the project may include a complete BPR (business process reengineering) that will result in new and improved business processes. The project may take the approach of implementing existing processes; this approach may minimize the benefits of implementing a new packaged software because a great deal of benefit is in the reengineering and tuning of existing processes.

The project's business team will be charged with redefining the business processes. The IT team will be charged with identifying the best application platforms to support the business processes and the integration of these various applications into one end-to-end seamless process.

An example of an integrated business process and the multiple application platforms that may support it is depicted in Exhibit 1.

Exhibit 1 describes a simplified order-taking process. Order header information first is created in the ERP system. Line-by-line information then is entered. As the lines are entered, the line items must be configured and priced. These tasks are accomplished by a configuration and pricing application. For each line and for the overall order, an available to promise (first date when this order can be manufactured completely) is calculated by the scheduling application. All of the data collected from the various applications is used to complete the order and submit all the order lines into the ERP system.

It is evident in Exhibit 1 that this is a process that is supported by multiple application platforms and that there is a need to integrate the applications in real time to support the process.

THE PERFECT WORLD

In a perfect world all applications would be on the same hardware and software platforms. The applications all would have well-defined APIs that provide all the functionality required for the business process. The applications all will be communicating using the same communication standards and using the same object models.

THE REAL WORLD

The real world is more complex than the imaginary perfect view. Applications can differ in the following areas:

- Hardware platform — the actual type of computer and processor that is used to run the application (e.g. Intel, RISK, MF);
- Software platform — the operating systems that the application is running on (e.g. HPUX, NT, MVS, Solaris);
- Communication method — the way with which the application communicates with external applications (e.g. RPC, messaging, distributed objects);
- Object model — the definition of the common objects that all applications will adhere to for the purpose of communicating with each other (e.g. CORBA, COM/DCOM);
- Database — the database that the application uses to store the data (e.g. Oracle, Sybase, Informix); and
- Network protocol — the network protocol used on systems where the application is residing (e.g. TCP/IP, IPX).

Looking back at the example in Exhibit 1 we can now concentrate on the differences between the application environments. Exhibit 2 depicts these differences.

Exhibit 2 describes the different platforms used to support the applications that are required for the order-taking process. It is clear that the task of integrating all these applications is quite complex.

SELECTING AN APPROACH AND ARCHITECTURE

Once one has a clear picture of the applications to be integrated and the business process that should be integrated across the multiple application

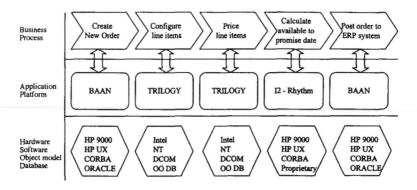

Exhibit 2. Application differences.

platforms, he or she is ready to select an approach and architecture for integration. The following should be considered when selecting an approach and architecture:

- Platform information
  - Hardware platforms
  - Operating systems
  - Object models
  - Communication methods
- Real-time vs. batch processes
- Future software upgrades
- Future addition of new applications
- Ongoing management of integration code
- Error handling and transactions monitoring
- New skills requirements

The above considerations will help one to make a decision on the architecture and the integration objectives. This in turn will drive the selection of middleware software that will facilitate the integration between the applications.

The traditional approach of point-to-point integration will not deliver the required functionality for this process. An order entry clerk cannot wait for batch processes to kick in and perform file transfers while keying in an order. A real-time, processware approach is required. In an approach where the process is defined within a middleware/processware product and the applications act as servers, serving the required functionality is more appropriate.

Examining two approaches to processware implementation, the first approach is based on object definitions and a process definition that acts on

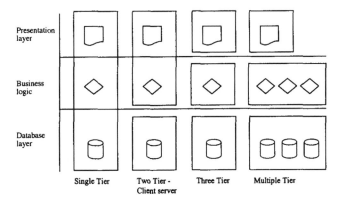

Presentation layer				
Business logic				
Database layer				
	Single Tier	Two Tier - Client server	Three Tier	Multiple Tier

Exhibit 3. Applications distribution.

these objects, and the second approach is based on event definitions and rules agents that trigger the events in a sequence related to the business process.

Stepping back, examine the various operating models of typical applications. A typical application can be divided into three layers:

- Presentation layer — the screens that the user interacts with to view and enter data
- Business logic layer — the processing logic that is triggered by user actions
- Database layer — storage and retrieval of persistent data over time

Most applications consist of all three layers. The primary difference between applications within the scope of this chapter is the degree of distribution of these layers. Exhibit 3 demonstrates the various options that are available for distributing the layers.

Exhibit 3 describes the most common models for application distribution. The single-tier model has all three layers residing on the same machine. The application can be accessed directly on the single machine or through multiple terminals. The two-tier (client/server) model has the database layer separate on a server designed and configured to run a database engine. The business logic and the presentation layers still are lumped together into what is known as a fat or thick client. The three-tier model separates each layer. The presentation layer can run on a Windows-based client or a browser; the business logic can run on an application server; and the database can run on a database server. The database server and the application server can be configured differently to accommodate the special requirements for running logic and database activities.

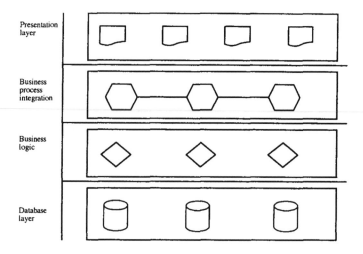

Exhibit 4.   Processware integration.

The multi-tier model accommodates further distribution of the database and the application logic on multiple servers. Distribution of the computing layers allow for better load balancing.

The goal of business process integration over multiple application platforms is to create an additional business logic layer that contains common data structures that all applications can access and populate through a set of agreed-upon calls. The business logic layer can be implemented using distributed object models such as DCOM and CORBA or an event-based system where the common data can be implemented. Examine both approaches in Exhibit 4.

In Exhibit 4, observe that in addition to the familiar multi-tier architecture, there is a new layer for business process integration. This layer defines objects or events that contain common data structures. The business logic layer or the presentation layer can activate methods for these objects as well as access data contained in the objects. The objects data structures contain the data required to support the integrated business process. This layer may be implemented using events that can be published or subscribed to. Any application business logic or presentation layer may publish an event and populate all or part of the data structure for that event. Once an event is published, all the applications that subscribe to the event are notified and processing is triggered.

The preceding architecture supports the creation of an additional process logic layer. The key for successful business process integration over multiple applications platforms is to utilize this new layer for storing the common data between applications and implementing the business process using logic in the layer. Having achieved such an architecture, the business process and data from the applications have been managed, thereby making the integration easy to manage and monitor. It also will become easier to modify specific pieces of the integration; replacing applications or updating them to new versions becomes a much simpler task.

CONCLUSION

A new concept of processware has been introduced. Processware is middleware software that facilitates the creation of an additional computing layer called the business process integration logic. This layer can be implemented using distributed objects or events to encapsulate the common data structures and the business process. Among the benefits of this approach and architecture are

- Isolation of integration business logic from the applications
- Creation of common data structures to communicate information between applications
- Easy migration of integration code upon upgrade or replacement of any of the applications involved
- Ability to manage and monitor the integration of the various applications
- A set of tools that facilitates the creation of the integrated business process and takes care of the communication and networking layer, allowing the users to focus on coding the business logic

There are several products in the market that are in various stages of development that are suited to support processware. In some cases, portions of the products already have been released. Each of these products takes a somewhat different approach to implementation. Time will tell which of these products will thrive and become a major player in this new emerging market.

Section XV
Emerging Practices and Directions

THE INFORMATION TECHNOLOGY (IT) PROFESSION is defined by constant change and unpredictability. This section contains three chapters that focus on some current trends.

Chapter 77, "Helping Network Managers to Cope with Enterprise Transformation and Data Demands," examines designing networks to satisfy data transfer needs across the enterprise. This chapter provides an approach for increasing the accuracy of the design estimates without resorting to expensive prototypes and test environments. This chapter also offers a structured process and a few techniques that can be used throughout the design process to reduce the time required to build the models and to obtain the desired results.

Chapter 78, "The World of Electronic Commerce," provides a definition of electronic commerce, a historical background, electronic commerce standards, and architectures.

Chapter 79, "Content-Based Retrieval and Indexing in Multimedia Databases," addresses indexing techniques for retrieving data from multimedia databases by specifying its contents. Such indeing schemes facilitate the query process and ease the burden placed on the user in extracting information from multimedia databases.

Chapter 77
Helping Network Managers Cope with Enterprise Transformation and Data Demands

Miles Au Yeung

CHANGES IN ENTERPRISES ARE NOT UNUSUAL. What is unique about the changes in the last 10 years is the prominent roles played by information technology in these changes. More and more, corporations take advantage of information technology to create new competitive advantages and to conduct business in the way that was impossible before. Whether these change efforts are to improve efficiency or to improve revenue, information technology is one of the indispensable ingredients to make this happen.

Enterprise transformations can be classified into three categories. The most common one and the one that is familiar is enterprise resource planning (ERP), which focuses on the back-end and support functions of an organization. Examples of these functions include order processing, material management, production planning, warehousing, distributions, and human resources.

Unlike enterprise resource planning, which promises competitive advantages by enhancing efficiency in back-end processes, alternative workplace centers on improving employee productivity and retention by allowing employees to work in places other than at a fixed desk location in an office. These alternative workplaces can be shared offices, mobile offices, and home offices.

0-8493-9976-9/99/$0.00+$.50
© 1999 by CRC Press LLC

Exhibit 1. Common Application Solutions

Enterprise resource planning	Enterprise resource planning applications
	Bolt-on applications that enhance the user interfaces
Alternative workplace	Document management
	Workflow, collaboration, and electronic mail
Sales and customer services	Data warehousing
	Online analysis processing (OLAP) applications
	Automated call distribution
	Computer telephony integration
	Customer relationship management

Another form of enterprise transformation includes sales and customer services. This topic addresses the important questions: How can I improve my sales effectiveness, i.e., lead-to-close ratio? How can I improve the revenue per customer? How can I reduce my customer churn?

All of these different forms of enterprise transformation require overhauling the following three organizational elements, at a minimum:

- Business processes
- Performance metrics, skill requirements
- Information technology

On the information technology front, Exhibit 1 lists some of the most common application solutions deployed in these enterprise transformations.

Any information technology manager with some exposure to the above applications can tell that these applications have large implications on telecommunications and data networks, if a corporation is not using these applications. Even if a corporation is using these applications, changes in how and where these applications are used also will have large implications on the networks. The implications on networks include network capacity, network coverage, mobile and remote network access, voice and data network integration, and network reliability.

To assess the implications on networks, to adjust the network capacities, and to alter the network designs, network managers will conduct detailed analysis of the application traffic profiles and the application service level requirements. Based on these understandings, calculations/estimations of network capacity and alternative network designs are developed. Finally, costs and business cases are put together to determine and justify the courses of action. But how good are these calculations, how viable are these alternative network designs, and will this new network satisfy the response time requirements?

This chapter presents a network design process to help network managers to validate their calculations and designs. This process uses network-modeling techniques and network simulation applications to test the network designs, variables, and assumptions. The output from the process allows the network managers to move forward to implementations with a high degree of confidence and with data to manage expectations. This chapter is organized into five sections that mirror the network design process:

1. Defining the questions.
2. Gathering data and developing assumptions.
3. Building and running simulation models.
4. Mapping results to actual network.
5. Asking new questions.

The first step in the process is defining the questions. It is the most important step as it sets the course and focus for the whole process. The questions determine the necessary data, assumptions, and the design of the network models. Depending on the questions, available data, and the complexity of the network to be modeled, the network should be generalized as much as possible to reduce the complexity, size, and costs of the models. The generalized network then is modeled with multiple models with results that build upon each other, instead of one giant model. This is done to shorten the model development cycle and make the process more manageable. The simulation results should be mapped back to the actual network to incorporate exceptions in the real network and to incorporate additional data into the final analysis. At the end, new questions may be developed because of the newly gained knowledge or new changes in the environment. This is an iterative process that can be repeated, when changes in the business environment are believed to have material impact on network requirements and design.

An SAP implementation in a fictional corporation, Jupiter Investment, with 300 locations and 20,000 employees will be used in the examples in the following sections.

DEFINING THE QUESTIONS

Objectives should be defined before the network design process is set in motion. In the case of Jupiter Investment, the objective is to determine the requirement of the network to support the present applications, SAP applications, and known future applications.

However, objectives are usually too broad and generic to be used to define the network models. Specific and quantitative questions must be derived from the objectives because network simulation applications are essentially number crunching software. Objectives need to be translated into a set of questions to be answered by numbers generated from the simulation models. These questions ensure that a clear focus and scope are defined for the simulation models. With the clearly defined questions, data to be collected and design of the models can be determined in the next steps.

Example: The objective of the network design process for Jupiter Investment is to define the network requirement to support the present applications, SAP applications, and other known future applications. To provide more guidance to the network simulation models, two specific questions are derived: what bandwidth is required at each site and what is the expected SAP dialog step response time at each site?

GATHERING DATA AND DEVELOPING ASSUMPTIONS

Driven from the questions defined, data, and assumptions around network topology and network traffic profile can be gathered and developed.

Network Topology

A network topology is necessary for understanding how and what parts of the network can be represented in models and evaluating how the network can be broken into components for efficient modeling. When developing an understanding of network topology, it is important to keep both the present and future network in mind. Whether the present network or the future network is to be modeled in simulations, an understanding of both is necessary to analyze the impact derived from the simulation results.

A network topology defines the paths that data will be traveling and is the first step in the modeling exercise. The scope of the network topology and network to be modeled are determined by the questions defined. The level of understanding and documentation of the network topology can vary from an overview level where architecture and principles are defined to a detailed representation of the actual sites, as shown in Exhibit 2.

The present network topology can be obtained from existing network diagrams, existing network documentation, network management tools, and interviews with network managers. To decide upon a future design, it is important to interact with business users, application managers, and network managers, as well as to examine the telecommunication service availability (e.g. frame relay, VSAT) data. Approval for the basic design principles should be obtained prior to moving forward with modeling, as the topology has a significant impact on the ultimate results of the modeling.

Example: The following avenues were used to collect network topology in Jupiter Investment:

1. Present network topology — derived from the network topology diagram available at Jupiter Investment and discussions with network managers from multiple divisions.

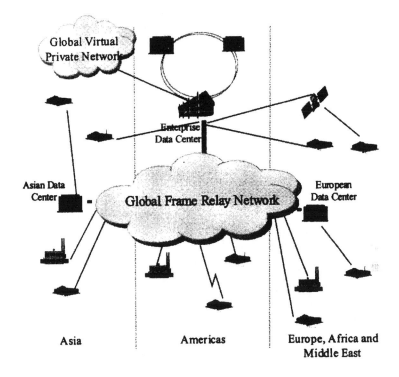

Exhibit 2. Sample of network topology.

2. Future network topology — a work-session involving the network managers and application managers of the different divisions of Jupiter Investment.
3. Network to be modeled — the future network.
4. Telecommunication service availability — data published by local and long distance carriers.

Once an understanding of the network (both present and future) is established, alternative representation of the network in the simulation models should be explored. One important consideration is reducing the complexity and size of the models to increase their efficiency. This can be done in various ways, such as focusing the simulation models on a subset of the network, generalizing the network, representing multiple sites with a single node, and so on. All nine of these alternatives and choices will depend on the defined questions and network topology.

Example: In Jupiter Investment, the network was reduced by developing generic site types. Sites were classified into four types based on their primary business functions. These site types then were refined further based on the number of employees. Therefore, instead of modeling more than 400 actual sites, less than 15 sites were required to be modeled.

The network models now can be built in the network simulation application. Network models must be created before any traffic can be included within the models.

NETWORK TRAFFIC PROFILE

The network traffic profile is necessary for understanding the behaviors of applications and provides the information to evaluate which applications need to be modeled as foreground traffic, which need to be modeled as background, and how their characteristics should be applied to the models.

Applications with response time, load, throughput, or other information that is to be studied will be modeled explicitly as separate streams of foreground traffic. Applications that do not require measurement by individual applications are grouped together and modeled as one single stream of background traffic.

The dimensions of a traffic profile can range from the very broad (for background traffic) to the very specific (for foreground traffic). The following list provides examples of data items that can be used to build a traffic profile:

1. Application architecture (e.g., n-tier client/server architecture, server locations).
2. User locations and counts.
3. Transaction sizes.
4. Transaction arrival rates.
5. Transaction service rates.
6. Traffic load (e.g., minimum, maximum, average).
7. Projected growth.

The amount and specificity of data to be collected will be more for foreground traffic and less for background traffic. The choice of which applications in the foreground thus has an impact of time and effort in gathering and preparing the data for simulation.

There are a variety of methods that can be used to collect the necessary data. The appropriate selection depends on a variety of factors:

1. Available data.
2. Available tools.
3. Available human resources.
4. Available time.

Exhibit 3 suggests different techniques to be used for developing the traffic profiles for foreground traffic and background traffic.

Exhibit 3.   Techniques/Sources for Developing Traffic Profile

Technique	Pros	Cons	Suitable for
Packet capturing using network analyzers	Accurate Detailed Application specific	Time-consuming to write filters and collect the data Limited to locations that can be reached to attach network analyzers	Foreground traffic
Benchmark data	Detailed platform and applications information No testing or operating installation necessary	Gaps between benchmark and actual installation Limited benchmark results	Foreground traffic
Circuit utilization reports from carriers	Accurate total traffic volume Information on peak and average	Not applications-specific Limited to certain telecom services Time-consuming if many different carriers Quality varies with carriers	Background traffic
Router statistics	Accurate total traffic volume Remote access to multiple locations	Not application-specific Databased on 24-hour periods	Background traffic
Application manager interviews	Nonmeasurable factors Growth projection	Not detailed Time-consuming	Foreground and background traffic

Examples: The following techniques were deployed to develop the traffic profile for various applications.

Existing Applications — Background Traffic

- Monthly frame relay utilization reports by port and PVC from the local telephone company.
- Router interface statistics.
- Interview with application managers.

Future Applications — Background Traffic

- Interviews with application managers to estimate user distribution, transaction volume, and transaction sizes.

SAP Online Users — Foreground Traffic

SAP Certified Benchmark #1997040 are for SD (comparable hardware with Jupiter implementation) for transaction sizes, transaction arrival rates, transaction processing rates.

- Assume average employee to SAP user ratio = 10:1.
- Adjust employee to SAP user ratio for different types of sites.

BUILDING NETWORK MODELS AND RUNNING SIMULATIONS

Network Simulation Tools Selection

Consider the following criteria when selecting a network simulation tool or determining if the existing one in the organization is adequate:

1. Do the built-in models included in the suite match the network devices, network links, network protocols and applications that need to be modeled? In the case of Jupiter Investment, does it provide models that emulate the SAP three-tier architecture and transaction processing?
2. Can the simulation application handle large-scale networks by breaking them into smaller models?
3. Does the application utilize symmetric multiprocessors to spread computation to reduce the simulation run time?
4. Does the simulation application provide features to reduce development time and simulation run time? An example of such a feature is loading a data link to a certain utilization level without actually going through the steps of creating network devices to generate the traffic.
5. What hardware and operating system does it run on? Are those platforms robust (do not reboot the system after the simulation has run for 18 hours)? Does the company have the support resources for those platforms?
6. Does it have utilities to reduce the pain of setting parameters for every device in the model? Does it have any interfacing capability to third-party software to reduce data input time? Such interfaces include importing trace files from network analyzers, importing network topology maps from network monitoring applications, importing tables from spreadsheets to populate network models, and exporting results to charting or spreadsheet applications.
7. Does the vendor provide the level of support needed? Are they willing to help build and debug models? Are they responsive to problems?

As a model grows in size, the time taken to run a simulation increases accordingly. The resource requirement is likely to require the use of server-class computers. In addition, the server allows for batch processing of large simulations and significantly quicker response time for GUI transactions.

MODEL DESIGN

Using a technique of building blocks, accurate models should be built by first starting with a small network of one server, one client, two routers, and the appropriate links. By providing predictable values to the application and server settings, it is much easier to predict the outcome of such a small network than by building the entire network at the beginning. After these numbers have been checked carefully, the larger network can be built. The advantages of breaking up of the network into multiple models include

1. Reduced sizes of models.
2. Ease of result validation.
3. Ease of debugging.
4. Short run time.
5. Short development cycle (build → run → validate → debug).

The number of models to be built is dependent upon the questions to be answered and the network topology. Modeling will be more efficient if only a single new untested variable is introduced to the model at a time. In this manner one can troubleshoot errors quickly, as the source of the error should be something related to the newly introduced variable.

Examples: Twenty models were used in a building-block fashion. First 11 models were built to represent the SAP clients and the background traffic client in different site type and size. These models were run to confirm the proper construction. A data center model was built to represent the SAP servers and background traffic servers. Then another eight models were built by cut and paste from these 12 models to build end-to-end models to obtain the results needed to answer the questions.

VALIDATION

Another critical component of modeling is the validation of results. The results produced from the models should be cross-checked to make sure they are coherent and that the models are set up correctly. One common technique is to compare the traffic offered to a link at one end and the throughput measured at the other end. If the throughput is less than the offered load, then the link is not sized properly and traffic was dropped.

The best method for validating results begins before there are any actual results. It is incumbent upon the modeler to attempt to calculate the results that can be expected in the model. Then the expected results are compared to the simulation results. If the simulation results do not resem-

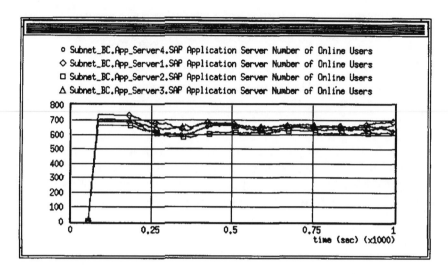

Exhibit 4.   Number of online users per SAP application server.

ble the expected results, then both the calculated results and the simulation models should be re-evaluated and modified.

Example 1: Four SAP application servers were defined in the simulation models. To determine if transactions were distributed evenly across the servers, as they should be in a real installation, the number of online sessions on each servers was examined. The chart in Exhibit 4 shows that the application servers were experiencing almost the same load at any given time.

Example 2: A mathematical calculation of SAP dialog response time was done prior to obtaining the response time from the simulation models. This helped to establish the expected result and was used to verify the simulation result. Because the mathematical calculation was not to get the precise result, a simple formula ignoring queuing delay was used:

Dialog response time = 2 * (transmission time + network latency) + server time

where

  transmission time = bits in a dialog packet(s)/line speed

                    = 12,000 bits/64 kbps

                    = 0.1875 s

  network latency = 0.028 s (the number used in the model)

    server time = 0.83 s (results from one of the building block models)

Hence,

$$\text{Dialog response time} = 2 * (0.1875 + 0.028) + 0.83$$

$$= 1.261 \text{ s}$$

Therefore, 1.261 seconds was the expected dialog response time when a 64 kbps line was used without any contention caused by other traffic on the line. This number can be used to compare with the average response time reported by the simulation.

MAPPING RESULTS TO ACTUAL NETWORK

As described in the previous sections, it is desirable in many situations to reduce the size and complexity of simulation models by using techniques such as subset of network or generic site types. To assess the implication of the results from the modularized/generalized simulation models and to translate these results into action items/recommendations, the simulation results should be applied to the original network with other supplementary data to address the questions defined at the beginning.

This mapping process is a very powerful step. One can derive additional information from this process to develop a more comprehensive and complete understanding of the impact of the subject of the questions. The information that can be derived varies from case to case, depending on the initial questions and available supplementary data.

Example: In the case of this Jupiter Investment, the information generated from this mapping process falls under the following categories:

1. Bandwidth requirement for each site.
2. WAN facility for each site.
3. Expected SAP dialogue step response time for each site.
4. Telecommunications costs for each site.

The following three sections will describe the major steps in the mapping process:

1. Applying simulation results to actual network.
2. Adjusting mapped results.
3. Adding supplementary data.

Applying Simulation Results

At the end of the simulation stage, results produced for the reduced network are obtained. These simulation results need to be matched up with the actual network. The way to do this is to apply the same logic used in developing the reduced network to the results.

Example: An office in Calgary was classified as a medium operation when generic site types were developed. From the simulation model, it was found that a medium operation site generates 145 kbits per second and a 256 kbps line was required to produce 1.6 second SAP dialogue step response time. When this result was applied to the actual network, the Calgary office would officer 145 kbits of traffic per second and it would need a 256 kbps line if 1.6 second SAP dialog step response time would be required.

Adjusting Mapped Results

The previous step of applying simulation results is a rule-based exercise. It takes the rules used in the creation of the generalized network and maps the results back to the actual network. However, there are exceptions to the rules. In this step, a pass of the mapped results is taken and exceptional cases are identified.

Example: Calgary was determined to generate 145 kbps traffic and require a 256 kbps line from the previous step. However, employees in the Calgary office were known to be heavy users and a validation of the router statistics confirmed that. The offered traffic was revised to 299 kbps.

Adding Supplementary Data

To develop a complete understanding of the network in question, data that cannot be or need not be generated from simulation models will be added to the mapped results.

Example: Some of the locations have installed voice over frame relay devices to carry the voice traffic between major offices. The Calgary office also had one and used two voice ports on the device. It was known from the manufacturer's specification that one voice port generated 8 kbps of traffic using its proprietary compression technology. Therefore, another 16 kbps traffic were added to the 299 kbps and totaled 315 kbps. Comparing this offered load with site types with load in this range, it was determined that Calgary office would require 512 kbps to obtain 1.6 second SAP dialogue step response time.

ASKING NEW QUESTIONS

At the end of the design process, answers to the original questions usually lead to a better understanding of the environment, which may lead to a new set of questions. This is a natural part of the process and can be explained for a number of reasons:

1. The objectives set out could be very broad and the questions/answers only may satisfy the objectives partially. New questions need to be developed and solved.
2. The answers evolve into a new understanding of the situation and raise more questions.

3. New requirements emerge or the original requirements have changed since the process began.
4. Data used in the modeling have changed.
5. New data becomes available to replace or update assumptions used in the models.

Regardless of the reason to repeat the process, it always should begin with a concise understanding of the questions that need to be answered to ensure useful results.

Example: At the end, new questions arise around the impact of the potential growth of other applications on the future network requirements. These applications include Lotus Notes and Internet. To address this question, the process described in this chapter will be repeated.

CONCLUSION

The network design process using network simulation is a powerful and useful process to derive answers to establish expectations and validate assumptions. However, the process can become a drawn-out process if not carefully managed. Here are some suggestions to ensure the process will reach the goals within schedule:

1. Define clear questions that are broken down into smaller questions. Determine what parts of the questions will require modeling and which parts can be derived from the simulation results. Minimize the amount of data to be generated from the simulation models.
2. Allocate overall available time to each step of the process and stick to the allocated time. It always is tempting to improve and expand the input data. There is always uncertainty around assumptions. However, to move forward, the data-gathering activities must stop so that the team can proceed to the modeling step. Exhibit 5 provides a guideline for the amount of time and effort to be allocated to each step of the process.
3. Start building small models as soon as the required data is ready. Do not wait until all required data are collected. The knowledge gained from the small models may change the questions or subsequent model design, and thus the data needed.

Finally, structure and resources should be provided around the process described in this document because the business and network environment are never static. A formal structure and resources ensure that knowledge can be captured, accumulated, and reused in the future. When changes in the environments are believed to have material impact on the network requirements and network design, this process should be invoked to develop quantitative understanding of the impact and the corresponding action plans.

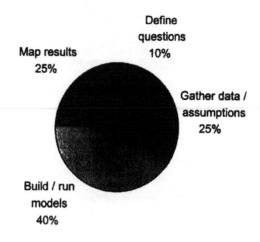

Exhibit 5.   Effort allocation.

Chapter 78
The World of Electronic Commerce

David A. Zimmer

THE WORLD OF BUSINESS IS CHANGING AT A RAPID RATE. Some say that within five to ten years, the way we do business will not resemble our current methods. Electronic data interchange (EDI) and electronic commerce (EC) will prevail, and paper methods of buying and selling goods will be obsolete. In several vertical markets, this prediction has become reality.

The advent of electronic communication throughout all sectors of society and the proliferation of the Internet and World Wide Web would seem to support the move to EC. Understanding the current capabilities of the EC technology, business propositions, and electronic markets is key to evolving our businesses into thriving competitors in the future instead of hulking dinosaurs.

This chapter describes the current landscape and the future horizons of electronic commerce. Understanding how it ties into current electronic communications systems is important. Knowing the evolutionary process from systems today to the future world of commerce will help better position costly networks to support tomorrow's transactions.

A BIT OF HISTORY

EDI dates back to the 1960s, with its greatest growth during the 1980s when several large industries (e.g., trucking and automotive, separately) decided that interconnecting computers for transferring information would provide a cost- and time-savings benefit to business. EDI is used by companies of all sizes, but its greatest use is by companies whose revenues exceed $500 million. With the advent of the World Wide Web and the rapid adoption of PCs into the homes (the network computer will also have an effect), electronic commerce will begin making in-roads into the consumer market.

0-8493-9976-9/99/$0.00+$.50
© 1999 by CRC Press LLC

Paper-Pushing Scenario

Companies wanted to develop a machine-readable data stream format that could be used to replace the multipart paper forms currently in use. Typically, to order supplies from a vendor, a customer would submit a paper order form to the vendor, the vendor would circulate the form to the appropriate internal organizations, the product would be shipped, and the vendor would issue a paper invoice. The customer would circulate the invoice to its internal organizations for the proper approvals and issue a paper check to the vendor. The vendor would deposit the paper check into the bank and get a paper receipt that had to be circulated to the proper organization for crediting. The customer, receiving the canceled check, would have to balance the books.

Although convoluted, paper-based systems worked for a majority of companies. Unfortunately, it inhibited their ability to expand — the time delays causing extra costs in the products and slowing their businesses. In addition, because many had implemented computer-based systems to facilitate tracking, each stop in the paper's journey required reentry of the data. It is estimated that an entry mistake occurred every 300 keystrokes. In the life cycle of one order, many mistakes could occur.

To compound the problem, each company had its own forms and formats. If two large companies needed to conduct business between themselves, they had to agree on whose form to use, knowing that they were not the same format. Having a foreign form floating throughout the corporation could increase the entry error rate.

Moving to Electrons

In the 1970s, no standards existed between trading partners. As a result, each partner had to agree on the format of the transaction data. Because no standards existed, trading with a third partner required a new set of agreements and customized development. After aligning with several trading partners, this ad-hoc approach became expensive.

In 1975, the transportation industry, under the auspices of Transportation Data Coordinating Committee (TDCC), developed and published a standard for transmitting data. In 1979, the American National Standards Institute (ANSI) approved TDCC's standard as ANSI X12 (pronounced X-12, not X-dot-12. If you say X-dot-12, the other person will know you are a neophyte in the discussion).

X12 defines a standard of field-value pairs (a field name defines what the information following is, and the value is the actual data), for example:

PER IC*J. Smith*TE*4125551212*FX*4125551213

IC = Information Contact

TE = Telephone Number

FX = Fax Number

The field-value pairs were separated by a delimiter — in this case, an asterisk (*). Transmission was held to 7 bits, meaning that they could only use less than 127 characters, resulting in an almost human readable format. All the characters are readable, but the format is horrendous for casual reading. The published standard allowed companies to buy third-party EDI products and services.

Unfortunately, each industry has its own terms and needs. X12 has become a large collection of specifications, some specific to an industry while others are used for all industries (e.g., the trucking industry has bills of lading). The automotive industry has it forms. The medical industry has claim forms. They all have purchase orders and invoices.

X12 is not without its problems. The data can vary in length, requiring a delimiter so that software can determine where one data value stops and another begins. X12 does not define a consistent delimiter. Some companies may use "*" while others use ":" for delimiters. Therefore, formatting messages to a trading partner — a company that you trade with electronically — can become a complicated process of negotiation. Whose delimiter is used? Who supports the cost of developing the converter to convert one format to the other format? Who pays for the communication line?

Fortunately, over time, many of these issues have been resolved. Many large companies are trading electronically now. Medium and small companies are getting linked because of the proliferation of powerful PCs and inexpensive (e.g., $800 to $1200) EDI software.

To move the electronic data interchange into the global market, the United Nations defined EDIFACT — a globally accepted electronic representation of business. EDIFACT is used primarily in European businesses; X12 is the predominant standard used in the U.S. Both standards describe only the message format, not the transmission protocol. Therefore, companies can hook to other companies' computers by synchronous or asynchronous connections. X.435 defines EDI over X.400, a messaging standard. And now, there is much discussion about EDI on the Internet/WWW (i.e., EDI over TCP/IP transport).

A CASE STUDY: A BUSINESS TRANSFORMED

Arrow was a company that built custom cabinets for sewing machines. The sewing machine industry has suffered a decline in sales for a long time, resulting in less need for cabinets. Arrow needed to transform its business or risk going out of business. As a result of the company president's friendship with an executive at Sears, Arrow embarked on a new line of business.

Sears wanted to service its customers by shipping vacuum cleaner bags to its customers. Unfortunately, Sears could not handle the low-volume shipments required.

Arrow established EDI links to Sears and some of its suppliers. Arrow stocked the necessary vacuum cleaner bags and received shipment requests from Sears electronically. As the inventory dwindled, Arrow would replenish the stock by electronically ordering replacements. The electronic transactions were extended to cover all aspects of the stocking and shipping systems of a transaction. Invoices, shipment requests, and shipment acknowledgments were all done electronically.

Arrow has expanded its business to include more than just vacuum cleaner bags. Today, they handle many large companies' customer fulfillment needs. Arrow drives all business electronically. To use Arrow's services, large companies must comply with Arrow's electronic systems. (An interesting twist: a small company forcing a large company to do business its way!) Although Arrow has not gone into officially helping other companies implement EDI, it works closely with its customers and suppliers to ensure a smooth operation of EDI transactions.

Arrow ships hundreds of thousands of items, handles tens of thousands of orders, and generates tens of millions of dollars in revenue, all with only 35 employees. Although the employees work very hard, without implementing EDI transactions, Arrow would not be the fulfillment house it is today.

DEFINITION OF ELECTRONIC COMMERCE

What is electronic commerce? Is it simply the electronic exchange of purchase orders and shipment notices, or does it go beyond that? Electronic commerce can be categorized into three areas:

- Business-to-business
- Business-to-consumer
- Consumer-to-consumer

In each category, the needs are different. As a result, the solutions are different. For example, business-to-business has higher-volume traffic, larger transaction values, automatic data entry into various databases, stringent security, and high reliability. Consumer-to-consumer requires simple interfaces, no database input, and smaller transaction amounts.

Each category has different electronic connection needs as well. Business-to-business needs secure networks safe from hackers trying to change transaction values. Consumers can use a simple dial-up connection to place items on bulletin boards or place an order.

Exhibit 1 depicts all three categories, the types of transactions between parties, and the various connection types used by each party. Each section

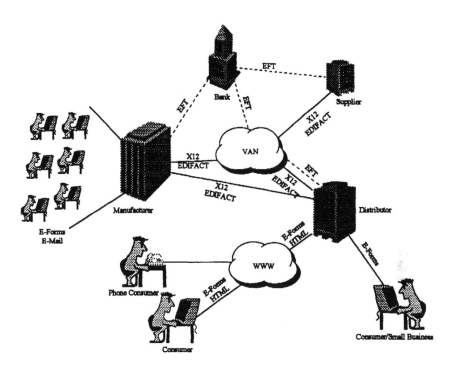

Exhibit 1. The world of electronic commerce.

must be analyzed to understand its perspective. As time evolves, however, parts of this picture will drop out as connections from manufacturer to consumer tighten and intermediate parties are squeezed from the process.

Electronic commerce has several components. Traditional EDI contains the electronic transactions between suppliers' and buyers' computers. EDI is a computer-to-computer data format protocol. Internal software translates the EDI data into internal business applications (e.g., the accounting database, order entry, manufacturing, and shipping and receiving).

Electronic funds transfers (EFT), a computer-to-computer protocol, deals with the transfer of money or payments electronically.

The third component involves electronic forms that generate the transactions. It provides the interface between humans and the automated systems.

Business-to-Business Electronic Commerce

Business-to-business electronic commerce involves translating internal business information into EDI transaction sets. Mapping software extracts data from various business applications and formats the data into the ap-

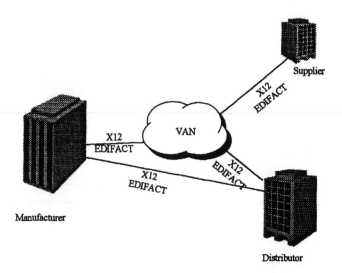

Exhibit 2. Business-to-business electronic commerce.

propriate EDI format for trading with partners. The translation may be specific to a particular trading partner or it may be more general in nature, depending on which connection is used with the trading partner.

Businesses can use two methods of trading transactions: point-to-point connections with trading partners or value-added networks (VANs) (Exhibit 2).

Point-to-point connections require leased telephone lines between the partners. In some large companies, they choose to manage all their communications with their trading partners by providing the leased-line connections. In this case, the large company is considered a hub. Companies they trade with are considered spokes (Exhibit 3). This configuration gives the greatest control over the transactions to the large company. If the company must transact business with a number of other large companies, also acting as hubs, the number of leased lines may become unmanageable. At this point, the company may opt to use a VAN to lower leased-line costs.

Businesses implement EDI for a variety of reasons. The top reason by far is customer-supplier requests. Other reasons usually cited are (in descending order of importance):

- Improving customer service
- Gaining competitive advantage
- Increasing data accuracy
- Cost savings
- Increasing speed of information access/flow

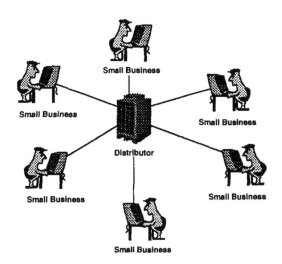

Exhibit 3. Hub and spoke EDI topology.

This interconnection between companies helps to speed the process of acquiring needed materials and supplies, shipping products, and managing the information flow necessary to transact business. The increased speed of the information flow means faster turnaround times for procuring products, manufacturing the final goods, and quicker time to market. Product evolution cycles decrease so that competitive advantages are gained. In addition, manual reentry errors decrease immensely — eliminating waste and lost time.

EFT. Electronic funds transfers provide electronic transmission of funds. The process of electronic ordering, tracking, and delivery receipt would not be complete if the final leg of the process required a paper check to be issued for payment. The EDIBANX standard provides a standardized mechanism for financial EDI. EDIBANX uses X12 formatting so that existing systems require only simple upgrades to support electronic transfers of funds.

The electronic funds transfer supplies several benefits to companies: quicker access to funds, lower processing costs for the funds, and no lost or misdirected paper checks (Exhibit 4). EDIBANX permits companies to tie the money transfer directly into their business applications (e.g., accounts payables or account receivables). For financial transactions to be feasible, networks must provide security and reliability. In some cases, companies have chosen to implement point-to-point connections directly with their banks or they have chosen VANs. For most, the Internet is still too risky for sensitive transactions.

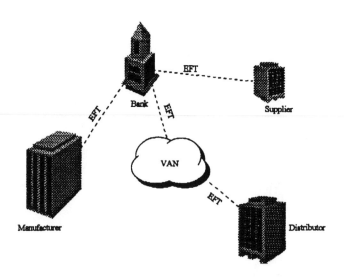

Exhibit 4. Electronic funds transfers.

E-Mail Backbone. Integrating EDI with the electronic mail backbone within large companies is the next logical step. Employees already use E-mail for communication, and workflow for other business processes is commonplace. Integrating EDI translation into the backbone provides employees with a direct link to the EDI process. For example, accountants could put stop-shipment orders on bad accounts, shipping clerks could authorize shipment orders, and employees responsible for ordering parts can do so by filing an electronic form. A workflow could be developed so that a parts order could be validated against an open purchase order or sent on to the authorizing agent for approval.

Using the electronic mail backbone, the process of ordering products can be pushed further into the organization, eliminating the need for middlemen (Exhibit 5). By pushing the task further into the organization, errors and miscommunications are lessened because the person most affected by the order would be responsible for order placement. The rest of the process is automated so other business applications (e.g., accounts payables, receiving, and manufacturing schedules) are notified accordingly. Notices of purchase acknowledgments, shipments, and backlogs are returned electronically. Following the reverse path to the originator, the notice can affect the business applications, as well. For example, back-order parts may affect the manufacturing cycle. The cycle manager could address the effect of the back-order and request that a different supplier be used.

Today, unfortunately, most electronic mail backbones and EDI networks are separate. A few companies (e.g., Control Data Systems and Sterling

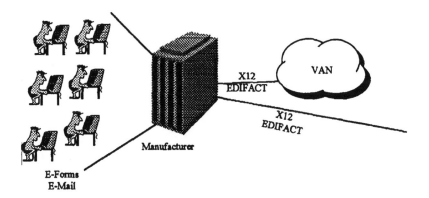

Exhibit 5. Electronic commerce integrated with electronic mail backbone.

Software) provide mapping software that pulls messages from the E-mail store and maps the information into EDI transactions. Incoming EDI transactions are mapped back into E-mail format and forwarded to the originator. A tighter integration between E-mail and EDI must occur for full EDI integration into corporate workflow and everyday communications.

Business-to-Consumer Electronic Commerce

For years, businesses have used telephone mailorder to eliminate the paper chase with consumers. The next step is to develop ordering by PC or MAC using the World Wide Web. The Web browser is a software program that runs on virtually any machine. The company can provide product information to any degree the consumer needs in a very simple and compelling way. Using graphics, sounds, and motion, the company can grab the consumer's attention. Because the Web browser provides easy navigational tools through hot-links (i.e., hypertext links), the company can provide a brief summary of the product with links leading to additional details. Once the customer is ready to purchase, a link will lead them to a secure page where sensitive information can be passed using the secure socket layer (SSL) protocol. The SSL encrypts the data being transmitted for protection.

Several companies have started to use this method for product sales. The volume of sales is still low because of the perceived security risks of sending credit card information over the Internet. Interestingly, the security of the secure links is more secure than the telephone mailorder that generates billions of dollars of sales per year. It is only a matter of time before the misperception is gone and commerce to consumers soars.

Any size business can use the Web to sell its products. The low-entry cost of creating Web pages, retrieving orders, and processing them by way

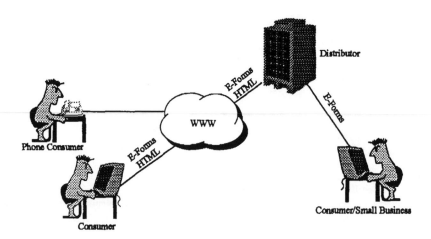

Exhibit 6. Business-to-consumer electronic commerce.

of the Web is enticing to small companies. Unlike traditional channels, small companies have worldwide presence by using the Web. They can easily load search engines to advertise their sites and draw attention to them. Big companies are not excluded from this medium, either. In fact, in this channel, the consumer may never be aware of the company size backing a particular product.

Telephone-based browsers are being developed. Those who do not own a computer to surf the Web can use a browser operated over a conventional telephone. Using interactive voice response (IVR), listeners can listen to a Web page (text only, graphics are hard to describe) and press a button when they want to travel to another page. Using this method, a company can describe a product, and if customers wants more detail, they simply travel to the more detailed pages. Ordering can be done by phone as well (Exhibit 6). Voice recognition is sufficient for credit card input. The products would be shipped to the billing address of the credit card. Of course, this type of information would have to be coordinated with the appropriate credit card company.

E-Forms. Large businesses might make electronic forms available to small businesses for input of orders and fulfillment information. The link might go directly into the larger companies' machines. This type of interface provides a faster, easier method of ordering multiple or large quantities of items with direct feedback access of inventory levels, and part assemblies with a greater sense of security because access would be limited to selected partners. The company could use an intranet to support such interactions so that the interface is a browser supporting forms.

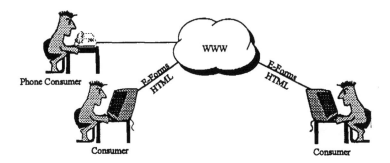

Exhibit 7. Consumer-to-consumer electronic commerce.

Consumer-to-Consumer Electronic Commerce

Consumer-to-consumer electronic commerce will soon begin to emerge (Exhibit 7). Currently, consumers have electronic banking and electronic bill payment. These could be considered the first forms of consumer electronic commerce. As more banks open their electronic capabilities, we will see consumers providing payments for purchases electronically. Consumers can create Web pages to advertise various items for sale (e.g., cars, boats, lawn tractors, and other items commonly found in newspaper want ads). Digital cameras can be used for placing pictures on the pages. Buyers interested in buying the item can contact the seller to make the purchase.

Using some mechanism, the seller and buyer enter into an agreement and the transaction is completed when the buyer transfers money from his or her account to the seller's account. This type of service, although a bit futuristic, may be provided by a third party or by a bank. The transaction is logged and validated by the transacting entity and sealed with the money transfer.

Most likely, consumer-to-consumer commerce transactions will be done over the Web rather than by a specialized service. The ubiquitous nature of the Web, common protocols, easy interface, and rapid acceptance makes the use of private networks obsolete. Using telephone browsers, anyone can take part in the buying network. The same transactions that are completed by PCs can be accomplished by the telephone. Transactions and money transfer authorizations can be completed by telephone interfaces.

THE EVOLVING ELECTRONIC COMMERCE LANDSCAPE

As more companies implement electronic commerce technologies and streamline their business strategies, evolution in supplier-buyer interaction will continue. In his book *Digital Economy*, Don Tapscott's overriding theme was that everything is going electronic. He outlines the following 12 themes of the new economy:

1. *Knowledge.* The new economy is a knowledge economy — things consumers buy will be smart.
2. *Digitization.* All information will be stored digitally.
3. *Virtualization.* As information shifts from analog to digital, physical things can become virtual.
4. *Molecularization.* Old corporations are disaggregated, replaced by clusters of individuals that form the basis of economic activity.
5. *Integration-internetworking.* The economy becomes a network of molecules re-aligning for the creation of wealth.
6. *Disintermediation.* Middleman functions between producers and consumers are being replaced by digital networks.
7. *Convergence.* Computing, communications, and content are becoming one.
8. *Innovation.* Make products obsolete — otherwise, someone else will.
9. *Prosumption.* The gap between consumer and producer blurs.
10. *Immediacy.* The key driver and variable in economic activity and business success.
11. *Globalization.* Customer bases are becoming global because of electronic networks.
12. *Discordance.* Unprecedented social issues are beginning to arise, potentially causing massive trauma and conflict.

Each theme has profound effects on the way people do business. Using electronic commerce, manufacturers will be able to work more closely with the end customer. Knowing their buying habits and consumption rates, manufacturers can more finely tune production runs. This fine-tuning could result in smaller lots of a particular item being made, requiring less inventory and warehouse space before being directly shipped to the consumer's outlet. Wal-Mart has created the model for such activities. Its suppliers work with Wal-Mart to replenish stock only when needed. As a result, Wal-Mart has very little inventory sitting in warehouses costing the company money. Consumers benefit through lower prices and more convenience (one-stop shopping for many items). The manufacturer benefits because they know exactly the buying trends of the consumer.

Manufacturing lines will change. Rather than producing single items, lines will be retooled to produce smaller lots of several items. Orders will be fed directly into the computers that schedule the lines. Workers may produce widgets one day and do-hickies the next. Using the incoming EDI orders and the production line capabilities, computers can schedule the optimal production line to lower inventory and warehousing needs.

Computers will receive data from several sources: consumers buying the finished products, suppliers supplying the required parts, and managing back-orders so that the process can run smoothly. The result of this automation is less people between raw goods and buying consumers. Middlemen will no longer be needed. Consumers and manufacturers will deal directly with each other. Key components the manufacturer needs to track the transactions and consumers are directories. Consumers can find manufacturers of desired products easily through directories.

DIRECTORIES: KEEPING TRACK OF ADDRESSES, TRANSACTIONS, AND INFORMATION

Directories enable users to do business electronically without complicated addressing schemes. The propagation and synchronization of the directory information between companies is a very important success factor. Without accurate addresses, purchase orders and payments will be misdirected.

Synchronizing changes within a single vendor's product environment is simple — the vendor supplies the synchronization tools. Directories used for electronic commerce will not share the single-vendor luxury. Companies implementing directories for use in electronic commerce buy from different vendors. Synchronization becomes complex in this multivendor environment. This complexity has already been experienced within enterprise E-mail networks. Directories open to the public for the purpose of electronic commerce will be even more complex.

A Model Demonstrating Directory Synchronization Complexity

A few years ago, two major West Coast banks announced their merger. Within weeks, an E-mail connection was established between the two banks permitting the exchange of electronic mail between key personnel planning the merger. Directory entries, however, had to be propagated manually by the respective mail system administrators. More than two years passed before an automated process was developed to distribute and synchronize directory updates among the merged bank's 35,000 PROFS, cc:Mail, MS Exchange, and Lotus Notes users.

The lengthy process occurred because no standard existed and each mail system had its own characteristics for naming and addressing. Understanding the differences between naming and addressing became clear in the process. Naming is the tag by which a user is known to other users on the system, while addressing is the tag by which the computer knows the user.

The name contained in a directory is not necessarily a user's name; it may be a server name, an internal organization name, an application, or the name of a mail domain. The corresponding address information is used by the computer for routing purposes. For example, on the Internet, the name of the mail domain known as ameagle.com corresponds to the IP address of the computer that serves as the gateway to that domain. When a user addresses a message to Accounts.Payable@ameagle.com, the messaging system refers to the corresponding IP address to route the message through various computers and gateways until it eventually ends up in the mailbox.

Understanding these concepts is key to developing directories that are useful in the interenterprise realm of electronic commerce. Just as each vendor of directories and E-mail systems has its own ideas on address and name construction, so do the companies that use these products. Each incarnation reflects the personality and culture of the company. This mixture of naming and addressing convention makes it difficult to easily create a network between trading partners.

The State of EC-Related Standards

To facilitate continued growth of electronic commerce, standard protocols must be instituted. Fortunately, the vendor companies have not been idle, but have foreseen the need of such products.

X.500. In 1988, the first version of X.500 was introduced. Products based on the standard have been available for some time. In 1993, a second version of X.500 was introduced. The second version fixed some of the weaknesses of the 1988 version. Products now on the market support the 1993 standard.

It is important to understand that X.500 is best suited for large enterprise networks or inter-enterprise environments. It is not suitable for smaller-scale operations (e.g., desktop or small LAN environments). In fact, proprietary solutions are better fitted for smaller operations if interaction with the directory comes from within the organization.

LDAP. Another protocol becoming popular from the Internet RFC process is the lightweight directory access protocol (LDAP). As the name implies, it is less resource-intensive (lightweight) than the X.500 DAP standard. Therefore, it can run at the desktop level. In addition, LDAP accesses more than just X.500 directories — it can access other directory structures that may exist at all levels of the organizations. LDAP unifies all directory types into a single access method, making it extremely powerful and useful from the end-user perspective.

Rapport Communications, in their report "The Rapport Messaging Review: X.500 Directory Services," predicts that X.500 will not be positioned at the personal address book level and will be slow to emerge at the local server and departmental level. They feel that typically these environments have limited processing power and, given their local nature, will not fully

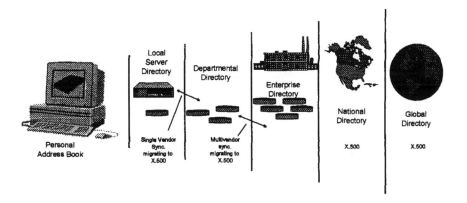

Exhibit 8.   Six levels of directories.

gain from the benefits of the global nature of X.500. X.500 is best suited for complex environments, unlike these localized networks.

In Exhibit 8, each band is a summation of the information of the directory entries in the band to its left, starting with the local server band. Typically, the personal address book contains entries specific to a user that would not be of value to the rest of the organization. Starting with the local server directory, entries describe users located on that server. The departmental directory contains a summation of local server entries within its domain. Synchronization is done within that domain. The enterprise directory is a summation of the department directory entries. The pattern continues all the way to the global directory.

Companies restrict the access to their directories at the enterprise directory level. Because of privacy issues, data security, and other reasons, enterprise directories are closed to outsiders. The enterprise directory may contain entries of people in another organization by an automatic registration process offered by some vendor's products, but access to that entry is only from within the organization. Accordingly, outsider entries are not synchronized with the originating organization. Invariably, the entry becomes stale and is no longer accurate. Inaccuracy in entry values would break routing of information and would impede electronic commerce.

Three Types of Directory Products

In preparing the directory infrastructure for electronic commerce, it is important to understand the different types of directory products: proprietary, standards based (X.500), and X.500-like.

Many of the directory products in use today are proprietary based. Standards and products based on standards did not exist when companies were implementing their enterprise solutions. Vendors (e.g., Soft*Switch — now a part of Lotus Development Corp., IBM Corp., and Digital Equipment Corp.) offered directory products in conjunction with their E-mail systems. As a result, support of the embedded base of products is a must in any transition or implementation of another electronic commerce directory structure.

Standards-based products means they support the X.500 specifications. Hewlett-Packard, Digital, and OSIware offer X.500 directory products. Other vendors offer X.500-like or X.500-architected products. Simply put, the information is organized in a manner similar to X.500, but it does not support the access protocols as specified by the X.500 standard.

A Trio of Concerns: Security, Authentication, and Repudiation

Electronic commerce has three concerns: security, authentication, and repudiation. Transactions must be secure. They must be impervious to outside tampering or misdirection. Values inside purchase orders must be accurate.

For example, a buyer places an order for 10 widgets. During the transmission of the order, the 10 is increased to 20. The seller receives the order with an incorrect value. Unfortunately, the wrong number of widgets will be shipped, requiring a return, extra processing, and expense on both sides of the transaction. Using directories with public key information, buyers can secure their transactions from tampering. The buyer would need to know that the public key information was available and be able to access it. Without using standard protocols for obtaining the information, the transaction between buyer and seller may not have occurred.

Buyer authentication is very important. The seller needs to be sure the persons or organizations placing the order are really who they say they are. With directory entries, the seller can authenticate the buyer through the use of passcodes or other mechanisms (Exhibit 9). The buyer can change those passcodes regularly to avoid impostors obtaining access to their accounts. When the buyer changes the passcode, the process inside the seller's company is not affected. Using the directory, each party is insulated from the inner workings of the other company.

In the case of differing opinions on orders (e.g., buyer placed an order for 10 widgets and seller shipped 20), the directory record can be used to settle disputes. The directory can track confirmation numbers that track back to the order and shipment logs. The directory is used by the automated tracking system to obtain confirmation information and buyer information. Additional information may include credit limits, current balance, and

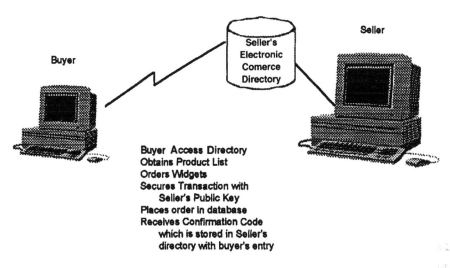

Exhibit 9. Secure orders, tracking with directory, accessible by buyer.

---

last payment received. The directory is a natural repository for this information because all information for a trading partner would be stored in one place and accessible by both parties. Software would check balances and limits so that orders would be placed only if values were within the limits.

VALUE-ADDED NETWORKS VS. INTERNET AND WEB

Currently, many companies are discussing which networks they should use for transporting electronic commerce data. The two main considerations are value-added networks (VANs) or the Internet. VANs charge for transporting data across their networks and provide mailboxes for those customers not requiring full-time connection to the network. The Internet provides a low transport cost option, but lacks in several features critical to data transmission integrity.

DataTransmission Integrity

Companies have five areas of concern regarding data transmission integrity: security, authentication, nonrepudiation, reliability, and customer service.

VANs are universes in which members are required to subscribe to the service prior to the transmission of data. When accessing the service, the members are required to log onto the system identifying themselves. Only certain types of transmissions are permitted (e.g., sending data destined for others and receiving data sent to them). They are not able to surf to another member's mailbox and peruse its contents. The data sent to a recipient is secure from other members. The VANs maintain their service to meet high standards of up-time, data transmission integrity, and data delivery. They track all transmission through their networks, giving customers the ability to determine where a transmission may have gone astray.

VANs satisfy all five concern areas, as well as provide consulting and other value-added services that ensure the security and reliability of transactions over their networks. The Internet has provided increased access to all levels of trading partners, but it is not a single source of service. As luck would have it, a trading partner may use the same Internet service provider (ISP) as another, but most likely that will not be the case. Therefore, the transmission of data may pass through one or several other ISPs before reaching its final destination. Each ISP maintains different levels of service standards. Typically, no tracking of data transmission is done, no single source of customer service exists, authentication of users may be lacking, and other security breaches may exist.

Recently, products have been coming to market to help overcome the Internet inadequacies for electronic commerce. Several ISPs have implemented secure networks within themselves. It is only a matter of time before the technical issues are resolved and electronic commerce over the Internet is reliable. Customer service is the remaining issue to be solved. AT&T WorldNet has advertised that they can provide all five concern areas and are promoting electronic commerce over the Internet. Others (e.g., PSI, MCI, and UUNET) will follow suit shortly.

The Web provides an interesting method of electronic commerce. It provides a cross-platform interface. The plug-ins provide powerful mechanisms to take the data and either translate it into EDI transactions or place it directly into company databases. Within companies, intranets help process orders from manufacturing to shipping to customer delivery. Inventory levels can be monitored and new supplies ordered from suppliers. Agents and Web crawlers can be used to find the best supplier for the need.

The question that remains to be answered for customers is, which system is best — VANs, the Internet, or the Web? The answer remains the same — companies must use the system that best fits their needs and level of quality required. For the foreseeable future, all methods will be used. They will be integrated together so that they work seamlessly and transactions flow reliably from buyer to supplier and back.

SUMMARY

Business is changing rapidly. Product cycles that used to be measured in years are now being measured in quarters. Major corporations have announced that they will update their product lines every 3 to 6 months.

Time is no longer measured in solar months, but in Web weeks. Cutting-edge products are obsolete shortly after they hit the store shelves.

What does all this imply? First, companies must understand the buying habits of the buyers. Second, the time interval from purchase to delivery must be shortened. Third, inventory needs must be calculated accurately. Fourth, companies must ensure that suppliers provide raw materials when they are needed. Fifth, slow, antiquated paper processes must be replaced with automated systems that update various business applications so that better decisions can be made faster. In a nutshell, this whirlwind of faster and faster will continue. Therefore, tools must keep up.

EDI and EC, a technology and a method of doing business, will help companies meet the challenges. Refusing to break the old working methods of today to shape them for tomorrow will cause current thriving businesses to become dinosaurs. The U.S. Government has mandated the use of EDI if a company wants to do business with them. Large manufacturers (e.g., Ford and Chrysler) require that all parts houses use EDI. Other businesses must follow suit.

Electronic commerce, the methodology of using EDI and other technologies to enhance business processes, encompasses the full breadth of the food chain from raw materials to final consumption by consumers. Each intermediary stop must align with the electronic flow of information or else risk planned extinction. It spans business-to-business transactions, business-to-consumer, and eventually, consumer-to-consumer transactions. Beginning with mainframe-to-mainframe transactions, it has spread to the World Wide Web. Anyone with a PC or a telephone can transact commerce with anyone else in the world. A technology born in the 1960s is ready for prime time today and tomorrow.

Chapter 79

Content-Based Retrieval and Indexing in Multimedia Databases

Venkat N. Gudivada

MULTIMEDIA DATABASES OR REPOSITORIES ARE BEING MADE AVAILABLE online using the World Wide Web (WWW) for distributed access. It is difficult to effectively use the information from these repositories unless users know where the repositories are and what pieces of information in the repository are relevant to them. Content-based retrieval helps to alleviate some of these problems.

To facilitate content-based retrieval, content descriptors are first extracted from the data and persistently stored in the database. In addition, access structures (or indexing schemes) to the content descriptors are essential for efficient query processing. In this chapter, several such content descriptors and access structures are described.

MULTIMEDIA SYSTEMS

Multimedia systems coherently handle diverse media types, including structured data, text, graphics, digital ink (allowing users to get files by using their handwritten names, sketch pictures, and compose handwritten E-mail messages), image sequences, audio, and video. The last three types are referred to as *temporal* or *continuous media* because the notion of time is implicit in the media. The other media types are named *nontemporal*.

0-8493-9976-9/99/$0.00+$.50
© 1999 by CRC Press LLC

EMERGING PRACTICES AND DIRECTIONS

Multiple Perspectives on Multimedia

There exist several mutual but complementary perspectives on multimedia systems, including:

- *Systems perspective.* Multimedia systems are characterized by the enabling hardware technologies (e.g., multimedia workstations with high-performance CPU and I/O bus architectures, high-quality audiovisual input/output devices and compression cards, continuous media servers, high-speed networks) and the system software (e.g., file systems for continuous media, real-time schedulers, and communication services for heterogeneous data) required to work with new hardware.
- *Engineering and scientific perspective.* Multimedia enables scientific visualization and virtual reality using multimodal user interfaces.
- *Arts and education perspective.* This view encompasses multimedia authoring and presentation systems, hypermedia browsers, and digital libraries.
- *Teleconferencing and computer-supported collaborative work perspective.* Systems capture multimedia data from multiple sources in real-time, then compress, transmit, and playback the information at multiple destinations simultaneously, in real-time.
- *Entertainment and business services perspective.* Applications include movies-on-demand, interactive television, retailing, and telemedicine.
- *Database and information retrieval.* Multimedia systems assume paramount importance in applications that require persistent storage and retrieval of multimedia data and are referred to as *multimedia database systems*. Multimedia database systems will eventually assume the role of enabling software technology similar to the systems role as the enabling hardware. As multimedia technology becomes mature, even teleconferencing applications will require that a conference session be stored persistently for subsequent retrieval based on the contents/events of the session.

Data Modeling Using Similarity-Based Query Processing

Several issues have yet to be addressed for the development of multimedia database systems. Because the structure and semantic content varies greatly from one image to another, the notion of entity type/entity instance (as in relational data model) or class/class instance (as in object-oriented data model) weakly apply to multimedia data. Furthermore, because the notion of time is inherent to the continuous media types, the data model should accommodate the specification of aspects related to temporal image sequences. Spatial image sequences are similar to temporal image sequences and correspond to, for example, a geographic space in geographic information system (GIS) applications.

The data model should also support spatial image sequences. In contrast to exact match-based query processing in a relational or an object-oriented database management system (DBMS), multimedia database systems employ similarity-based processing. That is, database items are ranked with respect to a query and presented to the user. Furthermore, user queries often tend to be subjective, imprecise, and incomplete. This requires incremental query specification and the user involvement in the form of relevance feedback to reformulate the query.

Because the state-of-the-art in pattern recognition and computer vision is not capable of extracting the media contents and domain semantics automatically, semiautomated tools are essential for developing large multimedia databases economically. Because most of the queries are retrieval only, support for transaction processing is not crucial, at least for the first-generation multimedia database systems.

As in relational and object-oriented DBMSs, indexing plays a critical role in efficient query processing. The remainder of this chapter identifies various issues of indexing in multimedia databases to support content-based retrieval.

GENERIC QUERY CLASSES FOR CONTENT-BASED RETRIEVAL

Content-based retrieval is characterized by the ability of the system to retrieve relevant images to a user query. The relevance is determined by examining the image contents at various levels of abstraction appropriate for the query context and nature. Furthermore, relevance of a group of images retrieved for an identically formulated query by two different users may be judged differently. That is, the notion of relevance is subjective and dynamic, and depends on the retrieval context and user characteristics and requirements.

The content-based retrieval characteristics of several image retrieval applications were studied by the author and a set of generic query classes is proposed. These classes include:

- *Retrieval by browsing.* Employed by users who are not familiar with the structure and contents of multimedia repositories or databases, browsing is also often used for exploratory querying.
- *Objective attributes.* This query is similar to a structured query language (SQL) query in relational database systems and is used in contexts where the query can be specified precisely.
- *Subjective attributes.* In contrast to objective attributes, a subjective attributes query is composed of attributes whose interpretation varies considerably from one user to another. For example, in a mug shot image database, an attribute such as "long nose" is subjective.

- *Sketch queries.* This class retrieves images based on the similarity of edge maps corresponding to the query and database images. An edge map is a depiction of prominent edges in an image.
- *Color and texture queries.* Images that are similar to the color and texture specified in the query image are retrieved.
- *Spatial queries.* These are used to retrieve images that are similar to the query image in terms of directional and topological relationships between the corresponding pairs of objects in the query and database images.
- *Shape and volume queries.* A shape query facilitates retrieving images that have domain objects whose shape is similar to the objects specified in the query. Its 3D counterpart is referred to as volume query class.
- *Sequences.* In some domains such as GIS and microbiology, there is a need to retrieve spatiotemporal image sequences that depict a domain phenomenon that varies in space or time. Such a need is modeled by sequence queries.
- *Keywords.* In some applications, keywords are assigned to images to indicate their semantic content. Keyword query class determines relevant images to a query based on the keywords.
- *Natural language text.* In other applications such as photojournalism, a caption or natural language text typically accompanies images. Relevant images are determined by employing natural language processing and information retrieval techniques.
- *Domain concepts queries.* These are formulated by using the other query classes as fundamental, primitive building blocks. For example, in diagnostic medical imaging, retrieving similar images to a query involves employing spatial and shape queries in a complementary manner.

Images contain domain objects, and the notion of domain object is domain dependent. A domain object is a semantic entity meaningful in the application. For example, in a residential floor plan image, various rooms and functional units are considered as domain objects. To support these generic query classes, requisite information about the image, its domain objects, and relationships (e.g., directional, topological, semantic) among the domain objects is extracted *a priori* or on-the-fly in an automatic or semiautomatic mode.

INDEXING IN MULTIMEDIA DATABASES

Information retrieval is concerned with automatically managing large collections of textual documents. The term *indexing* is used to refer to the process of assigning terms or phrases that represent the information content of a text document. These terms are often referred to as *index terms*.

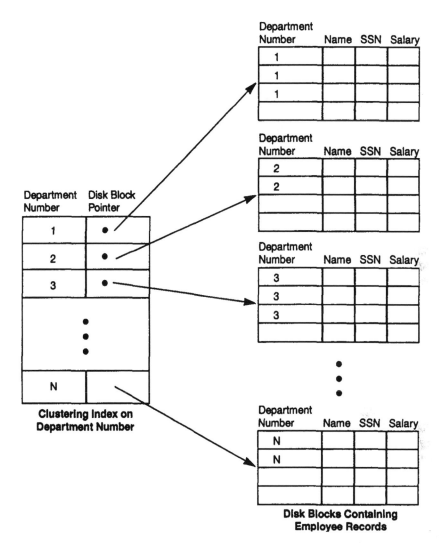

Exhibit 1.   Clustering index on department number attribute of employee file references.

In contrast, the notion of an index in relational and object-oriented DBMSs refers to access structures (e.g., primary, secondary, and clustering indexes) built on a file of records to facilitate efficient query processing. For example, using a clustering index on the department number attribute of an employee file (Exhibit 1), a user can efficiently retrieve all employees that work for a given department. Indexes are always specified on attributes that have ordered domains. That is, a collating sequence must exist for the values of an indexing attribute.

Multimedia indexing is primarily concerned with assigning suitable descriptors to media that indicate the information content of the media. This is not a trivial task because the interpretation of media content is subjective, and it is difficult to determine *a priori* what type of descriptors are needed. The type of descriptors needed depends on the query type. For these difficulties, there has been limited research into developing access structures for facilitating efficient query execution. However, to efficiently process queries in large and practical multimedia databases, access structures based on content descriptors become necessary.

From the multimedia database viewpoint, an index should encompass both the assignment of content descriptors to media and to the access structure associated with the content descriptors. There have been several studies on content descriptors to support the various generic query classes listed previously. (These results will be described in a subsequent section.)

Multidimensional Data Structures

One study on access structures makes use of multidimensional data structures. A multimedia object (say, an image) is represented by an n-dimensional vector and thus constitutes a point in the multidimensional space. For example, the first three components of the n-dimensional vector represent texture, the next represents color, and the next two represent shape, and so on. Finding similar images to a query involves retrieving those images whose corresponding locations in the n-dimensional space are within some measure of proximity to the point corresponding to the query image.

The assumption is that all content descriptors are numeric. However, many content descriptors are nonnumeric and the domains are unordered. This introduces an additional problem of mapping the existing content descriptors onto a numeric domain. However, it may not be possible to find numerical substitutes for all the content descriptors. In short, the complexity of indexing in multimedia database systems stems from the fact that a multiplicity of content descriptors (possibly subjective) is required to characterize the information content of multimedia objects and the nonnumeric nature of these content descriptors.

INDEXING FOR GENERIC QUERY CLASSES

For each generic query class, there are specific indexing issues and methods to discuss. This section groups the query classes listed previously into discussions centered on:

- Content descriptors for characterizing spatial relationships between the domain objects and their shapes.
- Content descriptors for color, texture, and sketch.
- Content descriptors for captions and full-text associated with multimedia objects.

Indexing of Spatial Relationships

There are two major approaches for describing the spatial content of images. (For this discussion, *spatial content* means directional and topological relationships between the domain objects.) In the first approach, a single content descriptor or structure captures the spatial content; in the second approach, several content descriptors collectively capture pairwise spatial relationships between the domain objects.

In both approaches, an algorithm is used to compute spatial similarity between two images. Some algorithms based on the second approach perform logical deduction/reduction before applying a similarity algorithm. Spatial content descriptors based on the first approach include 2D-string and its variants, spatial orientation graph and $\theta\mathfrak{R}$-string. Each of these content descriptors and access structures (if any) are described in the following sections in some detail.

2D-String and Its Variants. 2D-string was introduced as a spatial knowledge representation structure. It is a string consisting of two components — the first is obtained by projecting the domain objects on the x-axis and the other by projection on the y-axis. 2D-string considers domain objects as point objects situated at their mass center. For example, consider the image shown in Exhibit 48-1. Let R = {=,≪,:}, where =,≪,: denote the relations "at the same location as," "left-right or above-below," and "in the same set as," respectively. Projection of the domain objects on the x-axis gives:

Child ≪ Plant ≪ Monument ≪ House ≪ Animal

Similarly, projection on the y-axis gives:

Monument ≪ Animal ≪ Child ≪ House ≪Plant

Therefore, the 2D-string representation is:

(Child ≪ Plant ≪ Monument ≪ House ≪ Animal, Monument ≪ Animal
≪ Child ≪ House ≪ Plant)

Various extensions have been proposed to 2D-string to include the spatial extent of domain objects. A major drawback with 2D-string-based representations and the associated algorithms is that it is difficult to recognize rotational variants of images as similar images.

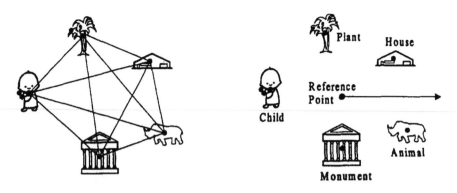

Exhibit 2. Content descriptors for spatial relationships.

Spatial Orientation Graph. A spatial orientation graph (Exhibit 2) also has an associated algorithm for spatial similarity. A spatial orientation graph is a completely connected, weighted graph. Vertices correspond to the centroids of the domain objects and there is an edge connecting every vertex to every other vertex. The weight of an edge is the slope of the line connecting the corresponding vertices. If v_1 and v_2 are the vertices corresponding to domain objects o_1 and o_2 with centroid coordinates (x_1, y_1) and (x_2, y_2), weight of the edge connecting v_1 and v_2 is given by $(y_2 - y_1) / (x_2 - x_1)$.

The algorithm for spatial similarity is robust in that it recognizes translation, scale, rotation variants, and variants obtained by an arbitrary composition of translation, scale, and rotation as similar images.

$\theta\Re$**-String.** $\theta\Re$-string is based on a total ordering of the domain objects induced by a binary relation $\leqslant \theta\Re$. As shown in Exhibit 2, a total order is obtained by sweeping the image plane using a radial sweepline pivoted at a reference point and noting the order in which the domain objects are intersected by the radial sweepline. If more than two objects intersect the sweepline for a given radial position, the Euclidean distance of the domain objects from the reference point is used to break the tie (the object that is closer to the reference point comes first in the total order). The spatial similarity algorithm based on the $\theta\Re$-string representation is also robust.

Spatial Representations Based on Pairwise Relationships Between Domain Objects. The approaches based on pairwise spatial relationships differ as to whether or not all the possible relationships are exhaustively enumerated and persistently stored. Spatial relationships in an image are exhaustively represented by a set of ordered triples of the form (o_i, o_j, γ_{ij}). The domain objects are o_i and o_j, and γ_{ij} is the directional relationship of o_i with respect to o_j. The triple o_i, o_j, γ_{ij} is an ordered triple if $o_i \leqslant o_j$ is true using lexicographic ordering.

The approach requires that all the spatial relationships be approximated with either the eight directional relationships (north, northeast, east, etc.) or the relationship "at the same location as." Furthermore, similarity algorithms based on this approach recognize translation and scale variants but not rotation variants.

To eliminate the exhaustive enumeration and persistent storage of all the pairwise spatial relationships, the notions of logical reduction and deduction are introduced. Left-of, right-of, behind, in-front-of, above, below, inside, outside, and overlaps spatial relations are considered.

For example, domain object A is to the left-of B, if the x-coordinate of every point that constitutes A is less than the x-coordinate of every point that constitutes B. Given a set $\Re$ of spatial relationships and spatial inference rules, the reduction problem is to generate a minimal set of relationships from $\Re$. Only this minimal set is persistently stored in the database. All the original relationships in $\Re$ can be recovered from the minimal set using a deduction algorithm at the query processing time. Efficient query processing is facilitated by an access structure of the form O_1 *op* O_2, where O_1 and O_2 are object types that have a spatial relationship of type *op*; each O_1 *op* O_2 contains a list of triples of the form (*iid, oid1, oid2*), such that *oid1* and *oid2* are of types O_1 and O_2 in image *iid* satisfying the relationship *op*.

Indexing of Shape. Shape representation and matching has been an active research area in image processing and computer vision for quite some time. Most of this work has been carried out from the automatic object recognition point of view. Only recently has there been focus on similarity-based shape matching and retrieval. However, many of these algorithms have high computational complexity that renders them unsuitable for interactive query processing. Furthermore, how well algorithmic shape similarity of existing algorithms captures human perceptual similarity remains to be investigated.

A taxonomy for shape description is shown in Exhibit 3. The description schemes are broadly classified into two categories: boundary and region based. Boundary methods are based on the outline or contour of the shape and completely ignore interior information. Region-based methods consider both the contour and interior of the shape.

Region-based methods are further classified into transform and spatial domain representations. As the name implies, transform-based methods represent a shape in terms of the result of a transformation on the shape. Further distinction is made in spatial domain representation: structural and geometric. Structural representations employ certain primitives and rules for shape description. Geometric schemes are based on interior geometry of the shape and different representations are used according to whether shapes are occluded.

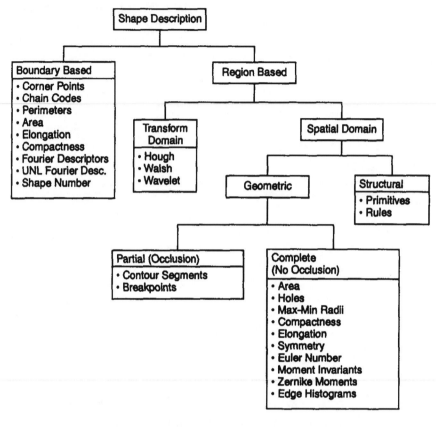

Exhibit 3.   A taxonomy for shape descriptors.

Most of these representations exist in image processing and computer vision literature. However, they are currently being investigated from the shape similarity perspective. Similarity measures are typically based on Euclidean distance between the shape representations. No conclusive evidence exists as to which representations are more effective than the rest. Studies on how algorithmic shape similarity corresponds to human perceptual shape similarity are only beginning.

Indexing of Color. The most widely used representation for color is a histogram. A discrete color space comprised of n colors is first chosen. Then, every pixel color in the image is mapped to a color in the color space. A color histogram is simply a summary of the number of pixels that map to each of the n discrete colors. (Here, n is also referred to as the number of bins in the histogram.)

The color histogram of an image *I* with *n* discrete colors in the color space is designated H_i, and is given by $H_i = (h(j), 1 \le j \le n)$, where $h(j)$ represents the number of pixels that map to bin *j*. The set of histograms corresponding to all the images in a collection forms the histogram space for the collection. An image that has only one color will have only one bin.

Because color histograms do not incorporate spatial adjacency of pixels in the image, two images having visually, distinctly different color distribution or composition can yield identical histograms. To remedy this problem, an image is divided into several regular regions, and histograms are computed and stored for each region.

A suitable metric is defined on the histogram space to measure color similarity between two images. The existing methods for color similarity computation vary on the metric employed (e.g., L_1 norm, L_2 norm) and whether all the bins are used in the computation. Histograms are invariant under translation and rotation (about the view axis) of the image.

Indexing of Texture. Though texture can be characterized by a variety of features, coarseness, contrast, and directionality features have been used in prototype systems.

The coarseness feature characterizes the scale of the texture and helps to distinguish, for example, a texture of pebbles from that of boulders. The contrast features measures the vividness of the texture and is a function of the variance of the gray-level histogram. Whether or not the texture has a favored direction is measured by the directionality feature. Thus, a texture can be represented as a three-dimensional vector. Similarity of two textures is defined in terms of the weighted Euclidean distance between the corresponding texture vectors. For color images, texture features are computed on the luminance band.

Indexing of Sketch. An edge map is a suitable content descriptor to support sketch queries. Color images are first converted into single-band luminance images. A canny edge operator is then applied to derive the binary edge image. All binary edge images are reduced to a size of 64×64 pixels and the image is then thinned. Sketch similarity between two images is the correlation between the corresponding edge maps.

Indexing of Captions and Text. Information content of a caption or text is usually represented by terms or phrases and is referred to as indexing in the information retrieval area. Indexing language defines a term vocabulary and specifies methods for constructing user queries and descriptions of text using the term vocabulary.

Term vocabulary is either controlled (i.e., determined *a priori*) or uncontrolled. Optionally, a weight (usually in the range 0 to 1) can be associated with a term to indicate the degree of relevance of the term to describe the contents of an image. Terms can be automatically extracted and weighted from the text using automatic indexing methods, including statistical methods that take into account the frequency of occurrence of a term in the caption or text and the frequency of occurrence of the term in other captions or texts in the collection.

Natural language processing (NLP) methods are also used to identify content-bearing terms and to discover inter-term dependencies. The same NLP techniques can be used to process the user's natural language requests into effective search queries. Queries are processed using information retrieval models ranging from simple set-theoretic Boolean to advanced algebraic models such as vector space.

Inverted Lists. The most frequently employed access structure is the inverted list. There is an inverted list corresponding to each term. An inverted list of a term is the set of all images whose caption or text contains that term. If the user query involves a conjunction of two terms, the set of potentially relevant images includes those in the intersection of the inverted lists corresponding to the query terms. Query processing algorithms are applied to this set of images to rank the images.

FUTURE DIRECTIONS

Many more multimedia repositories will be made available for distributed access on the Web. However, without an effective system for retrieving relevant information efficiently, the repositories will continue to remain unexploited or underutilized. Many users are discontent with the navigation and retrieval mechanisms on the Web. If this situation continues, the principal purpose of World Wide Web — providing instant, easy, and efficient access to distributed, heterogeneous information — will be defeated.

A multimedia database system with content-based retrieval capability will help to alleviate this problem. A multimedia database system should effectively support various generic query classes (discussed in this chapter) to realize content-based retrieval and to achieve a reasonable degree of domain independence. For this, various content descriptors are required.

Low-level and numeric content descriptors have the advantage in that they can be derived automatically and are amenable to building access structures using existing multidimensional data structures. However, the following factors should be considered in designing suitable content descriptors, though manual or semiautomatic methods may be required to extract them from images:

- *How suitable are the content descriptors for expressing user queries?* If user queries are at a substantially higher level of abstraction relative to the content descriptors, then establishing a mapping from the query to the content descriptors is difficult.

- *How compact are the content descriptors?* Compactness has a direct impact on the amount of storage required for the descriptors. Distributed multimedia applications may choose to store the data at a single site and replicate the content descriptors at multiple sites for better performance.
- *Will two or more distinctly different images map to the same content description?* If so, a greater degree of weak ordering in the ranked output of a query will result.
- *How flexible are the content descriptors for building access structures to facilitate efficient query processing?*
- *How complex is the algorithm for similarity computation? Is it robust, and how well does it correlate to perceptual similarity?*

Though several similarity algorithms do exist, there has been no systematic study of their relative performance to determine under what conditions one is preferred over another, for example. Such a systematic study requires carefully designed testbeds for various query classes. The testbeds should be designed to inquire into the robust behavior of the algorithms and make it possible to quantify the correlation between algorithmic and perceptual similarity. A testbed typically features a repository, a set of queries, and the expected results for each query.

Another area of concern is how the retrieval effectiveness is evaluated. Current approaches are based on the position of a target image in the ranked output of a query. The target image is one that is either identical or closely similar to the query image. These approaches do not incorporate the correlation between algorithmic and perceptual similarity, which should be an important component of the evaluation process.

Although these various generic query classes have been discussed in isolation, in reality, processing user queries often require complementary functionality of two or more query classes. For example, color and shape, shape and spatial, or color and shape and spatial query combinations are very useful. The next step, then, should be to devise algorithms for processing combination queries and to evaluate their effectiveness.

ACKNOWLEDGMENTS

The author wishes to express his appreciation to Kannan Thiruvengadam for his careful scrutiny of the manuscript and helpful suggestions.

About the Consulting Editor

SANJIV PURBA is a Senior Manager with the Deloitte & Touche Consulting Group and leader of the Object-Oriented Practice in Toronto, Canada. He has over 14 years of experience in Information Technology (IT) and extensive financial and retail industry experience as a consultant in the areas of telecommunication, travel and tourism, ticketing and reservation systems, and manufacturing.

Prior to joining the Deloitte & Touche Consulting Group, S. Purba managed his own computer-consulting business, Purba Computer Solutions, Inc. During this time, he also was a consultant for Canadian Tire, Sun Life Assurance Company of Canada, and IBM. His background includes Senior Architect and Consultant for Flynn McNeil Raheb and Associates, ISM, The Workers Compensation Board, Alcatel, and the Ministry of Education.

S. Purba has written four IT-related books and over 50 articles for *ComputerWorld Canada*, *Network World*, *Computing Canada*, *DBMS Magazine*, and the *Hi-Tech Career Journal*. He also is the editor of *ITOntario*, a publication of the Canadian Information Processing Society (CIPS), as well as author of fantasy and sci-fi novels. He is a regular speaker at industry symposiums on technical and management topics and lectures at universities and colleges such as Humber College, the University of Toronto, and Ryerson Polytechnic University.

Index

HANDBOOK OF DATA MANAGEMENT

Printed and bound by CPI Group (UK) Ltd, Croydon, CR0 4YY

28/10/2024

01780011-0001